PART I.

HOMEOPATHIC PRACTICE

OF

SURGERY.

THE

HOMEOPATHIC PRACTICE

OF

SURGERY,

TOGETHER WITH

OPERATIVE SURGERY,

Illustrated by Two Hundred and Forty Engravings.

BY

B. L. HILL, M. D.,

PROFESSOR OF OBSTETRICS AND DISEASES OF FEMALES, AND LATE PROFESSOR OF SURGERY IN THE WESTERN HOMEOPATHIC COLLEGE.

AND

JAS. G. HUNT, M. D.,

PROFESSOR OF SURGERY IN THE WESTERN HOMEOPATHIC COLLEGE.

CLEVELAND, O.

J. B. COBB AND COMPANY.

1855.

HUDSON, OHIO:
Stereotyped and Printed by the Hudson Book Company.

PREFACE.

To those who have been desiring the speedy publication of this work — the *first* on *Homeopathic Surgery* — some explanation of its tardy appearance is due.

The reasons may be summed up as follows: — The desire to make the work as perfect as possible, embracing both that knowledge already written and that evolved in the clinical experience of the Homeopathic profession; the difficulty and time consumed in obtaining and condensing communications from our physicians; the severe labor necessary to prepare the *first Homeopathic Surgery;* and the interruptions from sickness and professional life.

The want of a work giving the Homeopathic treatment of what are called surgical diseases and a description of the various surgical accidents and operations, with the specific treatment, has been long and severely felt by the Homeopathic profession. At the urgent solicitations of numerous Homeopathic physicians of Ohio, Dr. Hill (then Professor of Surgery in the Homeopathic College at Cleveland), was induced to undertake the preparation of such a work. But knowing, somewhat, the magnitude of the undertaking, he secured, as a co-laborer, Doctor Hunt, his former partner in professional practice, since elected to the chair of Surgery in the Western Homeopathic College at Cleveland. And in order to obtain that large amount of material necessary to the perfection of this work, which was contained in the private records of the clinical experience of our practitioners, the following circular was addressed in January, 1852, to all the most learned and experienced Homeopathic physicians of America and a large number in Europe:

WESTERN HOMEOPATHIC COLLEGE,
CLEVELAND, OHIO, January 30, 1852.

DEAR SIR: — I am engaged, with another Homeopathic Physician, in preparing for the Press a systematic work on the practice of SURGERY, adapted to the wants of the Homeopathic profession.

The work is designed as a text book for students, and an aid to practitioners generally.

Inasmuch as practical experience in our Science dates back but a short time in this country, it can not be supposed that any *one* man would have sufficient experience in "Surgical diseases" (a considerable portion of which are of rare occurrence), to enable him *alone* to furnish the proper material for such a work.

We are well aware that in all our attempts at producing books on the Homeopathic practice, we must, at present, depend very much on the able European authors. It is, nevertheless, desirable to incorporate in any *new* work as much of *recent practical experience and new discovery as possible;* that every new book may be one step further towards that state of perfection which we firmly believe our noble science is destined to reach.

For the accomplishment of this purpose, we have determined to ask some favors of our most learned and experienced practitioners, which, we hope, for the sake of the cause, will be granted.

We are aware that it is asking much, but we hope, some time, to be able to render a suitable reward for the favor. We wish you to give us, in as full details as practicable, any *very successful* treatment you may have employed for the following affections:

Traumatic Erysipelas, Burns and Scalds, Frost-Bites, Irritable, Indolent and Varicose Ulcers, Necroses, Scrofulous Swellings and Ulcers, Chronic Rheumatism, Hip Disease (Scrofulous), Lumbar Abscess, White Swelling, Hydrops Articuli, Polypus of the Nose and Uterus, Cancer of the Womb, *Cancer in general,* Osteo-Sarcoma, Fungus Hæmatodes, Scald-Head of children, Fistula Lachrymalis, Fistula in Ano, Maxillary Abscess, Ophthalmia (Purulent, Scrofulous and Gonorrheal in particular), Amaurosis, Nebula and Leucoma, Ulcers of the Cornea and Lids, Cataract, Dropsy of the Eye, Enlarged Tonsils, Goitre, Mammary Abscess, Hernia, Hydrocele, Hæmatocele, Orchitis, Hemorrhoids, Prolapsus Ani, Stricture of the Rectum and Urethra, Spermatorrhea, Gonorrhea, Primary, Secondary and Tertiary Syphilis.

It would be asking too much to expect an article from your pen on each of these complaints, but if you can afford to comply with the request to any extent, please select such cases from your list as you think would be most useful in carrying out the object of the work, preparing what you write for the pages of the book, or furnishing us the material for preparation, as your convenience will allow.

We further ask that you will allow us the privilege of giving you credit *in the book* for what you contribute.

As we wish to incorporate the matter we receive from our friends with our own; as we proceed in our labors of preparing it for the press, it is desirable that we have it at as early a day as possible, and hope to hear from you soon, while we remain,

Very respectfully,

Your co-laborers in the good cause of Homeopathy,

B. L. HILL, M. D.,

PROF. SURGERY, WEST. HOM. COL.

Numerous commendatory letters were immediately received in reply, with the promise of the desired contributions; which from time to time were received. To those who thus responded we tender our sincere thanks, particularly to that veteran in Homeopathy, Doctor C. Neidhard, of Philadelphia, for the number and completeness of his communications. Had each old experienced practitioner done as well, we have no doubt that the profession would have had much valuable matter — now lost to them.

In the preparation of this work, in addition to the above clinical experience, we have freely availed ourselves of any matter contained in the Homeopathic works on practice, or the literature of the profession: where it could be well done, we have used the words of the author, but where the arrangement did not suit his ideas, either in his own language or ours, our aim has not been originality, but condensation of present medical knowledge upon the subjects treated. Some of the surgical treatment, however, either in whole, in part, or combination, is contained in no other works, and is original with the authors.

We have not hesitated to give that treatment which we knew, from a large and successful personal experience, to be the most efficient, even though it might be objected to by some as not agreeing strictly with their ideas of Homeopathy; and we trust the day is not far distant when the superiority of the Homeopathic treatment of surgical diseases and accidents over any other, will be as manifest, as it now is, in common and epidemic diseases. The major portion of Part II. (Operative Surgery), and a considerable part of the description proper of diseases in Part I., are copied from a work of which Doctor Hill is author, published several years ago, while he was Professor in another school (Lectures on American Eclectic Surgery, by Benjamin L. Hill, M. D.), and we cheerfully give credit to that work for the portions above referred to.

Among the physicians who have contributed materials from their experience, of which we have availed ourselves, we would mention, particularly, the names of Drs. C. Neidhard and Prof. Kitchen, of Philadelphia; Dr. Shipman, Chicago, Ills.; Dr. Prowell, Lexington, Ky.; Drs. Tifft and Beckwith, Norwalk; Dr. S. M. Cate, Augusta, Maine; Drs. Babcock and Foote, Galesburg, Ills.; Dr. Rogers, Farmington, Ills.; Dr. Sharpe, England; Dr. Rosa of Painesville, Ohio; Dr. A. Bauer, Dr. W. Owens, Dr. Parks, of Cincinnati.

PART I.

CHAPTER I.

INFLAMMATION IN ITS GENERAL ASPECTS.

Inflammation — Inflammation not *a* disease, nor "*the* reparative principle" — Etymology — Heat and other vital manifestations — Excess of, vascular or nervous? — Simplistic questions and varied researches — Acceleration or Retardation? — Chemical and Microscopical results — Inflammation not indispensable to recovery from local injury — Its stages up to "mortification," and particularly of suppuration.

"INFLAMMATION," says the celebrated surgical philosopher of England, John Hunter, in his great work on the blood (page 205), "is the first principle of Surgery." As it is indeed of primary importance, and has been long customary to begin a book upon Surgery, with a dissertation upon it, we shall not in this respect depart from the old path.

Among the conditions of life is a certain range of temperature, above or below which it cannot be maintained. This range is much wider than might at first be supposed, owing to nature's wonderful provisions of adaptation. The result is, that the human body has the power of keeping up to about its hundred degrees, in all climates and under all ordinary circumstances. Heat, then, is one of the manifestations as well as conditions of vitality. It is one of the most striking manifestations. It is popularly and poetically expressive of life; its reverse of death. "Ere coldness wraps this mortal clay" is the poet's translation of *dying;* the chemist's version would only be verbally different. It would show that the "fire of life" is not a mere metaphor.

The word "inflammation" is derived from the most striking phenomenon of the states, — the unusual development of heat accompanying them. It means that the body is "burning up."

Modern chemistry would accept the definition, with the addition of "too fast." Liebig has a complete "Theory of Disease," founded on and confirming this simple idea. The slow combination with oxygen throughout the body, as well as in the lungs, is made not only to explain the problem of animal heat, but of the common morbid increase of temperature. The degeneration of the diseased parts, and the subsequent decomposition, of the whole, are accounted for on similar principles.

Not only has it been speculatively doubted whether inflammation is not an altogether necessary and beneficial operation, or at least "effort" on the part of nature, of a beneficial tendency; but it often becomes practically requisite to consider it in some such light. We speak of it as a desirable condition, though more often as an evil to be removed or averted. In Carlisle's Notes of Sir Astley Cooper's Lectures we are taught, without qualification, that "Inflammation *is* the process by which local injuries are repaired, and may be considered as *the* restorative principle." Physiological authors often speak in a similar manner, though at other times the state in question is discriminated as "abnormal." It is *then* contrasted with *a* reparative process, one of "growth analogous to the natural one," attended with little or no irritation, or confusion and waste of material, and more complete and permanent in its result. "It is consequently," says one of the most esteemed of these writers, the very mode of repair "which the surgeon should aim to produce; and the means of accomplishing this aim consists *in keeping down the inflammatory process.*" In the other diseased or *more* "abnormal" mode, a new and distinct kind of tissue is formed, a merely provisional growth *not* analogous to the natural and permanent one. And the result of this "granulation structure," as it is called, "is not so perfect as that of the simple or non-inflammatory process."

It is, of course, in some sense true, that the "efforts of nature" must be all directed to good ends. We see, however, that no doubt with the best intentions, "Nature" errs from her presumed end, and works evil instead of good. This may not be a very respectful way of speaking, but it is inevitable when our individual ends and aims are attributed to "Nature" as a whole. In a wider sense, Nature can do no wrong; but this, like the corresponding maxim, "Kings or sovereign bodies can do no wrong" is to common sense untrue, absurd, and practically mischievous. As the political doctrine alluded to, the divine right of kings, led to the servile corollary of "passive obedience," so the divine *infallibility* of nature points consistently to non-interference, and letting nature take her course in all cases. Strange as it may appear, this practical *reductio ad absurdum* has not daunted some reasoners. They have accepted it, and founded on it a system of practice, or no-practice. In fact the views in question cannot be maintained without arriving at the conclusion of such "Medical Reformers" as Dr. Jennings, of Oberlin, who really advocate a simple "faith in nature," discarding all our presumptuous attempts to interfere with her, since she always aims at the best possible results under the existing circumstances.

Besides the practical, common-sense objection, to considering inflammation as a sanatory process, or the reparative principle, recent researches give us additional reason for doubting it even in its most abstract and general sense. Microscopic observation shows us that in the mode of reparation "analogous to the natural growth," in the union of wounds "by the first intention," for instance, under the most favorable circumstances, there is no evidence of what we call inflammation, or any of the changes always accompanying that state. Nature gets through her extra work of repair, with the same ease, precision and uniformity, as her regular business of growth and preservation. And in those lower orders of animals, whose reparative powers are greater than ours, extending to the reproduction, for instance, of a lost limb, the process, as we are informed, always takes place without any appearance of inflammation.

The common, convenient distinction, between "healthy" and "unhealthy inflammation," would seem to imply that the process may, or may *not*, be one of *disease*. The expressions, however, may be better understood as characterizing those modifications whose tendencies are toward health, or toward still *greater* disorder: "healthy inflammation" thus means *health-ward*, and self-limiting, such as takes place, under favorable circumstances, in an *otherwise* healthy constitution. John Hunter, who was one of the first investigators of this subject in a philosophical spirit, and makes great use of this distinction, speaks also in perfect consistency of "too much health," or, "health above par." These expressions would be regarded by most as involving absurdity; and perhaps "healthy inflammation," though it is hardly possible to avoid its use, may come to be considered a contradiction in terms.

Increase of other vital properties, besides that of heat, is so obvious in inflammation, that the fact has for a long time been considered a sufficient definition and explanation. The state has been identified with over or undue excitement. The natural functions of any part stimulated too much, or too long, may, indeed, run into inflammation; but the latter state is clearly a new one, and will continue for a longer or shorter time, after the stimulus causing it has been withdrawn. Although a stimulus produces the diseased state in question, we may reasonably suppose that it never does so except by exhausting the natural and healthful excitability, and substituting morbid irritability, thus depressing, instead of exalting the vital powers of the part. After much controversy on this subject, this seems now to be the general opinion, or tendency of opinion.

Nevertheless, it once seemed to be the only question — to which agencies of the system to refer this increased activity. The blood-vessels appeared plainly most concerned in the business; but when the implication of the nerves became known, the priority of their action was generally recognized.

The ancient definition of its state was wholly independent of any idea as to its nature. The "four signs" it distinguished may still be remembered with advantage. When a part feels "hot and painful," and looks "red and swollen," it is very apt to be in a state of inflammation. These evidences, however, have to confirm or correct each other. One or two may concur, without proving the point; and serious inflammation *may* exist without either being very manifest, and often does run through its course without manifesting all these symptoms. "Redness," of course, can only be observed on the surface of the body, or at the extremities of mucous openings. The sensation of "throbbing" is considered by some as more generally characteristic of the state than "pain." Perhaps *soreness* (or tenderness to pressure and other irritants) would more frequently hold than "pain," if by that be meant spontaneous sense of suffering, without any external cause.

A change of action tending to, if not, also, resulting from a change of structure, may be regarded essential to our modern idea of inflammation. Placing this characteristic tendency first, as more important than the sensible appearances, Druitt suggests the following definition as an amendment of one given in a French Medical Dictionary: "A state in which there is a tendency to morbid secretion and change of structure, accompanied by increased vascularity and sensibility."

According to this, the blood-vessels and nerves must both be concerned in the result. Where there are no nerves of sensation, the organic nerves commonly become such, when the part is inflamed. In a paralyzed part, however, inflammation appears to go through its course independently of "increased sensibility." This, though an exceptional case, might be supposed to prove that the sensitive nervous system is not essentially concerned in the process. "Increased sensibility" to an intolerable degree, as in neuralgia, may exist, without necessarily being or becoming inflammation.

Irritation is often spoken of, especially by the French "physiological" or Broussaian school of theorists, as the first stage, or rather the invariable antecedent, and of course "cause" of inflammation. There is, however, no more necessity for looking to the nerves than the blood-vessels, as the primary source of the evil. *Known* causes or occasions of inflammation may act directly on the nervous or vascular system, or even on solid structures of the body, independently of either. Whatever destroys or depresses vitality to a certain extent, or what only *seems* to excite its ordinary manifestation beyond the regular limit, will equally induce the state in question.

As far, then, as this single question between the nervous and vascular systems is concerned, it is evident that they are both involved in the ordinary phenomena of inflammation, as the usual signs, "redness and pain," plainly indicate. It is clear, moreover, that they act and react on each other, and no question of necessary priority between them can be maintained, unless by affirming that every change in the action of a blood-vessel implies a prior, but almost synchronous change in its innervation, from the ganglionic system of nerves. An active determination of blood to the brain (for instance) may be for a while quite distinct from cerebritis, but is very apt to lead to some form of it. A cupping glass, producing all the external "signs" of inflammation, would actually *cause* that state, if not removed. Over-stimulation of a part by blood, even in its healthy state and flow, *is* itself *irritation*, the very state of the nerves in question; and stagnant arterial blood soon proves itself a source or occasion of a similar state. On the other hand, over stimulation from any cause, however unconnected, originally, with the circulation, has in general a tendency to bring about a preternatural determination of blood, according to the old empirical maxim, *ubi irritatio, ibi affluxus.*

The functions of the nerves and blood-vessels can as little be separated, or studied apart, without implying each other, as their course and structure can be distinctly investigated in anatomy, and demonstrations made of the one without touching or seeing the other.

Inquiring more closely into "the nature" of inflammation, some might, perhaps, be tempted to adopt the favorite philosophical "conclusion in which nothing is concluded," viz., that "we know nothing at all about it."

The obvious increase of some of the vital manifestations in an inflamed part, seems for a long time to have so impressed observers' minds, that they made little or no question that this first view was a full, correct, and sufficient one. Its apparent accordance, in the majority of cases, with successful practice, no doubt greatly strengthened this first impression. Heat, for instance, is an ordinary manifestation of vitality; in inflammation the calorific function is evidently too active; we reduce it, or remove its self-sustaining results, and the case improves. What plainer, therefore, than that heat* is one of the supporting influences of inflammation, as of life, and cold a remedy. The same may be said of other vital stimuli,—air, food, motion, &c. Hence, the once

* So influential was this one consideration, that it has, in connection with an exploded chemical theory of heat, given name to the routine of practical measures: "*anti-phlogistic*" still means "anti-inflammatory."

fashionable, and still too prevalent, confidence in "starvation;" and at one period, not many generations back in the dark ages, patients, with certain fevers or inflammations, were absolutely refused *fresh air!* As to the great *internal* stimulus, the living fluid, or fluid life itself, it is unnecessary to point out to those who have witnessed the abuse of blood-letting, and wish to learn something better, — how destructive has been the consequence of a partial and superficial view of inflammation, as consisting merely in too much blood, or too much activity of the circulatory functions. This simple view has evidently been influential in the popular mind, as well as that of the mass of the profession. If inflammation *were* solely vascular excitement and excess of blood, there would be some excuse for invariably, and as a matter of course, removing the cause or means of the mischief. It is beginning, however, to be acknowledged by all, that venesection is, by no means, a panacea, even for pure inflammation. The lancet is found at last to be no more the best remedy for physical evils, than the sword for moral. Bloodshed is looked upon with somewhat of the same suspicion, when resorted to for the purpose of restoring health, as for "conquering a peace."

Speculative men, even when they did not question the prevalent opinion, had many hypotheses about the *proxima causa* and *causa efficiens.* Many of these guesses were, perhaps, not quite so unworthy of consideration as they have since been considered. Some have been ridiculed, since solidism became the prevalent fashion of thought, as belonging to the humoral pathology, and others as much despised by our exclusive vitalists, as too mechanical. At one time inflammation and all diseases were explained by the help of *strictum* and *laxum;* or relaxation on the one side, and tone or tension on the other. *Spasm* of the extreme vessels once played an important part in these imaginary explanations. When it was necessary to account for obstruction as well as acceleration of the circulation, and "stricture" did not seem sufficient, the less mechanical and more chemical-humoralistic speculation invented a "spissitude," or thickening of the blood. This was the doctrine of the celebrated Boerhaave, and led to a reliance on "attenuants."

Our more experimental or carefully inductive mode of philosophizing, is no doubt much safer than such hypothetical theorizing, yet it is in vain to protest against hypothesis and theory. All men theorize to the extent of their leisure and ability. The only question is between good theorizing and bad, reasoning with facts or without, or with few or many. It is speculation that stimulates observation and directs experiment. Hypothesis anticipates experience, and is only injurious when mistaken for it. Ideas are necessary to animate mere matter of fact knowledge. Thought is the soul of Fact.

Whether Inflammation really consists in an acceleration, rather than in a *retardation* of the local circulation, has been much discussed by more recent investigators; and the microscope as well as experiment has been brought to the aid of observation. But with all these advantages, this question was not so easily settled as might have been supposed. Many recorded experiments seem to contradict each other. As it cannot be supposed that inflammation excited in one frog's foot is different from that in another's, or from inflammation in any animal body from the same cause, it becomes necessary to discriminate as to the *period* of the process when the observation was made, and also the particular *part of* the supposed inflamed part, more especially noticed. With attention to these points the different statements of facts might not appear to contradict each other. The result would seem to be that, according to the means used to excite the inflammation, it may begin either in apparent acceleration or retardation of the local circulation; either, however, soon inducing the other to a greater or less extent. When obstruction is the first state, it becomes a cause of excitement, which again may change, and a future observation find only a feebler circulation. If everything go on most favorably, there is increased action in the absorbents, and "resolution" the result. If the diseased state continue long enough, there may even be impeded or entirely suppressed circulation at one point, and greatly increased activity or force of the vessels in another.

Restricting the enquiry to the purely physiological question, as first put, the answer must no doubt be that of Professor Burns, of Glasgow, in his work on the "Principles of Surgery," — "That neither debility nor increased action sufficiently accounts for inflammation." One satisfactory test of the one-sidedness of such views is suggested by this author — that of availability in practice. Could the morbid state in question be really accounted for on either hypothesis, or any other "simple idea which fancy might fix upon," such state, so easily understood, could be as easily treated. If the question could be settled or arranged as the old kindred one in nosology, between diseases of increased or decreased excitability, the surgeon might "defy nature to set up inflammation," with means almost as simple as the Brunonian physician — armed to encounter all diseases, with the lancet in one hand and the brandy bottle in the other. Unfortunately, the war with death cannot be carried on with such weapons. The watchwords of sthenic and asthenic have been of little avail in the day of battle; nor have pathologists, since they ceased to be nosologists, or mere classifiers of the names of diseases, found them of much use as mere descriptive words. So with the question under consideration, which, as once regarded, was little else than the old "sthenia or asthenia" in its local application.

It is by no means necessary, however, on account of the unsatisfactory nature of this limited question, to conclude with the author above quoted, that of "the peculiar nature of the action (Inflammation) we know but little, and I fear have in the present state of science no prospect of knowing more."

This tone of despondency in regard to truth is anything but philosophical. The history of science contains too many brilliant triumphs of "impossibilities" and "improbabilities," for any ill-omened predictions to have much longer any influence. Fortunately, a different spirit has animated, and always will animate, some minds. On the subject in question much light has been thrown from different, and in some instances unexpected, quarters.

When we find one route of research blocked up, it is only a reason for pursuing another, with the advantage of already knowing at least that the one abandoned was not the right or best. When Nature is cross-examined in our experiments, she often refuses to depose merely "yes or no;" and her answers are not the least significant and worthy of record when they seem to evade the question. They furnish hints for other questions, or the same in other forms, that she will be more disposed to answer directly.

In the investigation as to the nature of inflammation, the advocate of both sides of "*the* question" have found it necessary to vary and modify their enquiry, and make many limitations and discriminations not before thought of.

The subject has not been allowed to remain as a merely curious and limited physiological or pathological question. Comparative Physiology and even Pathology have been brought to bear upon it. The enquiry has not been restricted to what we can see even under the microscope. Chemistry has carried us as much beyond Optics, as the latter beyond the ken of unassisted vision. It is now known that the old humoralists were not wrong in the directions their enquiries took, so much as in the conclusion in which they stopped and *rested.* The changes or *actions* going on in the blood itself, and other fluids, are at least as important as the resulting changes of structure or action in the solids. The contents of the vessels in inflammation, and the discharges from them, require to be studied, no less than their calibre and contraction.

In fully developed inflammation of any extent, the whole organism sympathizes with the affected part, not only sensibly or physiologically, but, so to speak, chemically: there is not only general uneasiness or irritation, and it may be symptomatic fever, but all the absorbent and secreting functions are modified, and consequently the constituents of the blood changed, both by what it receives and what it ceases to give off.

The change called the buffy coat has been long since empirically known, and it may be empirically acted on. The same *appearance* may be produced by circumstances so trifling as the shape of the vessel in which the blood is poured. A deeper stratum of the blood, or a greater slowness of coagulation, gives opportunity for the red globules to subside and leave the lighter colored film at the surface to form this buffy coat. Even the size of the orifice through which the blood runs may have an influence on the buffy appearance; and it has been well ascertained that the buffy coat may frequently be absent in cases of severe inflammation. Yet there are physicians who still bleed to get this evidence of "bad blood," and bleed again because they find it!—this buffy coat, so much talked about when bleeding was more in fashion, appears really to be the result, not perhaps of inflammatory blood, but of a modification of the blood accompanying inflammation. There is found, on actual analysis, to be nearly as much as one per cent, more fibrin in the circulating fluid in some cases of inflammation than in health, and less than the average proportion in certain typhoid or non-inflammatory diseases. Fibrin appears to be the material of nutrition and of the *reparative process*. Its corpuscles indeed exhibit the transition of organizable matter into living atoms, or germs ready to take their place in any part of the organism. The corpuscles differ from the proper blood globules, in being white or colorless.

According to the chemists "there is a direct connection between the quantity of oxygen introduced through the lungs and the amount of fibrin in the blood." The coagulation of blood, when out of the body, or precipitation of fibrin, seems analogous to its solidification or assimilation when *forming part* of the living organism: just as the brightening of venous into arterial blood may be effected by the presence of oxygen anywhere else as well as in the lungs. The red globules or blood discs, according to chemists, are the parts concerned in oxygenation, and have nothing to do with nutrition. The different degrees of oxydation of their iron (an element not found in the solid structure of any part) constitute the principal difference of venous and arterial blood, and principal source of animal temperature. Hence, perhaps, a reason for thinking redness and increased heat no necessary concomitants of the merely reparative process; and this view accords with the aim and result of treatment. The practical object always is to keep down the temperature of the inflamed part. Observation confirms this opinion: when divided parts unite most favorably "by the first intention," or when a breach of continuity is filled up with "healthy granulations," no preternatural heat is noticed.

At the *beginning* of the true inflammatory *process*, and afterward in the *middle* of the inflamed part, as a nucleus of disorder, there is a greater or less cessation of the ordinary vital functions. This much seems to be generally if not universally acknowledged. "The extraordinary tendency to the production of fibrin," previously noticed as the most important character of inflammation, is said by Carpenter to be "*always* conjoined with a *depressed vitality* of the tissues of some part of the body, which indisposes them to the performance of their regular nutritive operations; and this part may undergo a variety of changes, according to the degree in which it is affected." This "depressed vitality" is shown to involve a languor in the movement of the blood, with which the capillaries are distended. There is nevertheless a determination of blood toward the part, with a special attraction to it of the "white corpuscles," that is, of the fibrin, which is necessarily in excess from the check to the nutritive process throughout the system. The "effort of nature" in inflammation, or the final cause of the process with which it is connected, is evidently good. Some degree of, or tendency toward, this state is indispensable to the *reparation* of injuries, and still more plainly though less directly to *preservation*, by limiting the progress of disorganization.

Slight irritation in a part may pass off without much affecting its vascular functions; and engorgement of vessels, as after cupping, may be gradually removed, and the *eddy* carried on again into the general current of the circulation. In these cases, we do not say there has been any inflammation.

Even where the cause has operated long enough to develop all the recognized "signs" or symptoms of disease, the reaction of the "depressed vitality," or that of the surrounding parts, proves sufficient to overcome all obstruction. The disorder of the part "resolves itself" into the normal state; and this *resolution* of inflammation only differs perhaps from the disappearance of irritation or stagnation last mentioned, in having been preceded by more or less *transudation*, for the relief of the distended vessels. The fine gelatinous fluid long known as "coagulable lymph" is thrown out, first distending the parts, and then ministering to its repair. This "coagulable or organizable" fluid, may be familiarly defined as "white blood," or blood *minus* its red globules, with, at this time, an additional amount of colorless ones. These when naturally coagulated, or, so to speak, vitally precipitated and crystalized, become integral parts of the living *solid* body. According to common observation and language, the effused lymph (or fibrin) "becomes organized." According to the recent microscopic, or what may be called, from analogy to chemistry, *atomic* anatomy, the colorless corpuscle or molecule of fibrin, becomes a "primordial cell" or cytoblast. "Corpuscles" seems a correct name for these organic atoms, for they appear to have their own independent vitality, even anterior to being organized, or *assimilated* to already formed structures. The serous part of the blood or lymph is the first nutriment of these cell-germs, and hence called the "cytoblastema."

"The shooting out" of new *vessels*, or prolongations of branches, into the newly deposited fibrinous matter, has long been investigated, as an interesting process. We are now informed by microscopists that the cells arrange themselves in rows, the cavities of which connect into canals, by obliteration of the transverse surfaces of the cells themselves. Thus all animal, as well as vegetable structures, are originally cellular. In the proper fibrous formations (including muscles) the cells themselves undergo a change of form, become fusiform instead of spherical: the single cells become fibres or fibrillæ. Drawings of this transformation are shown expressly from "plastic exudations."

The red blood, or the proper coloring portion of it, seems to have nothing to do with the nutritive, nor consequently with the reparative process. The globules or discs containing iron and carbon, play a part only in the respiratory or calorific function, with its necessary consequence of transformation of tissues throughout the system. As far then as increased "heat and redness" are developed in inflammation, they may be regarded as injurious. The development of heat, so far from being proof of stronger vitality, may be the means of *destroying* life, and continue *after death*, as recent researches have shown. It is altogether too common and explicable a result of chemical change, to be regarded as otherwise than incidentally connected with life.

When there is besides or instead of a mere transudation of serum as lymph, holding the fibrin in solution, an effusion of complete blood, the process of reparation and restoration will be more complex and difficult. This is the case, not only in injuries which open or divide the blood vessels, but, whenever the obstruction and increased action in the vessels are so great as to cause their rupture. It is as much from this extravasation or ecchymosis as from structural injury to the solids, that "contused wounds" are so troublesome. In "lacerated wounds," the careful surgeon always removes clots of blood, and sponges out all he can that is yet fluid, as if still living, it must, in that situation, soon die and become a source of irritation.

When the direct injury causing the inflammation has been greater, when the "depression of vitality" amounted more nearly to extinction, or when the inflammatory process has proceeded unfavorably, so as to result in at least the death of the fluids, there must be SUPPURATION. Pus is dead blood, or fibrin. The globules still found in it are larger and apparently partially decomposed, certainly so far changed that they can take no farther part in the chemistry of life, or be of any possible use, except in some situations to act as a temporary cuticle and protect the surface of a wound from the air. Suppuration is spoken of as a "secretion" when it takes place from a mucous surface. It is usually accompanied with sensible relief to the distended vessels and neighboring parts, which then, if not before, throw out good coagulable lymph, by which the tissues of those parts are consolidated, so as to prevent the spreading of the pus. When from "too low a grade of inflammation," constitutional weakness, peculiarity of structure in the part, or any cause, this isolation of the suppurating part and product does not take place, we have the very serious result of "diffused inflammation." In this case the infiltrated matter not only acts as an irritant, which has long since been well enough understood, but the decomposition going on in the pus appears to be of the self-continuing or self-communicating kind, recently investigated with so much interest by the chemists. The deleterious agency of pus is rather active than passive, of a *ferment** rather than that of a foreign or "effete" substance. Hence, under the most favorable circumstances, ab-

* Notwithstanding the ridicule attached by modern purists to the use of such words, which they consider antiquated, we prefer to retain this word *ferment*, which is sanctioned by chemical science. See Cooper's Surgical Dictionary, Theory of Suppuration, Vol. II, page 313 — where, because the old ideas of the fermentation of *solids* into pus are shown not to be the whole truth of the case, the use of such terms as "acrid or corroding pus" is condemned unqualifiedly as unworthy of educated medical men.

scesses, though limited by the *effused* and organizing fibrin, become *ulcers*, the pus "eating" its way out.

If the original injury or the subsequent *inflammation* itself be so great as to cause the disorganization of a sensible amount of the *solid* structures, we have what is called *sloughing*. The difference between this result and that of mere suppuration being that the solid matter is not so easily converted into pus as the devitalized fluids. In this case the local "depression of vitality" amounts to a *sup-pression* or destruction. Hence positive inflammation may seem more necessary than in simple division or excision of a part. The question remains, however, whether fibrin might not be effused for both reparation and protection, as in the case of mere suppuration, without sensible inflammation, — that is, without its phenomena. In actual *Mortification*, — which, in the view here taken, only differs in the *extent*, not the intensity of the evil, from the preceding degrees of injury, — there is death throughout a considerable part, both of the solids and fluids. Here the *sloughing* is on a large scale, and inflammation with suppuration, &c., can only take place in the connected parts, where the depression has not amounted to a suppression of vitality. This is one of the cases where the apparently beneficial effect of the inflammatory process is the most striking. Gangrene, or the *dying* process, like the simple suppuration, has a tendency to spread; and is limited by the effusion of fibrin, which also prevents hemorrhage from the partially destroyed vessels, and sets up the well marked "line of demarcation" between life and death, — on the one side of which all vital action has ceased, while on the other it is manifested to the inflammatory degree.

The tendency of inflammation to diffuse itself is particularly manifest in *ulceration*, which is hence sometimes called "*destructive* inflammation." In this case, a peculiar layer of cells have been noticed, "which appear to possess the power of drawing into themselves the materials of the solid tissues on which they lie, and thus causing their destruction; and this destructive action may take place to an unlimited degree, if no measures be taken to check it." The author quoted goes on to explain the efficacy of the "most successful mode of treatment in these cases," that of caustics, by the fact of their destroying these peculiar cells and the adjacent matter partially affected by them; and thus to draw another argument for the necessity for inflammation. He speaks of the inflammatory action beneath the surface killed by the caustic, as the only possible mode by which "fibrin can be effused and preparation made for filling up the breach of substance." The treatment he appeals to, is undoubtedly the best in many cases, to which it is not commonly applied. The burn is more manageable than a phagadenic ulcer. The sloughing process, limited by the contiguous inflammatory effusion, is less destructive than the parasitic cells of which he speaks. But, after all, does this amount to more than saying that one kind of inflammation is preferable to another, as the lesser of two evils? That the excitement of inflammatory effusion is, in all cases, the only way of arresting the destructive progress of such ulceration, is contrary to the experience of all who have used appropriate remedial means or *milder caustics*, such as the sesquicarbonate of potash, an intermediate between the common pearlash and saleratus. This article is often better than a substitute for escharotics, destroying morbid growth and arresting morbid action, without exciting inflammation or acting in any way *unfavorably* upon sound parts. In many cases it very evidently allays both irritability *and inflammation.*

According to the view here taken, Inflammation, — though perhaps to be regarded as originating in the healthful function of reparation, is still an excess of that necessary action, and, therefore, a disease, — a condition which, if carried to a certain degree, defeats the very object for which it is said to be constituted. If continued too long, it will more or less transform, or wholly destroy the part; and if extended too far, must certainly be fatal. That this morbid and dangerous state appears sometimes to be a relative advantage, like every other general provision of nature, is no reason for calling physical evil, good. If nature ever cures, or partially saves by means of inflammation, when she could not by any other means, this is only saying that nature, like other intelligent agents, sacrifices a lesser to a greater object, and like *other* practitioners of the healing art, sometimes inflicts transient pain and inconvenience for the sake of permanent benefit.

The slight exaltation of vital action that seems necessary to the *recuperative process*, is but that process in operation, the performance of overwork and the making up of lost time, in the more active resumption of functions that have been impeded. When the amount of the injury, or the want of steady health-preservative power in the constitution, is such that this resumption of increased business on the part of nature cannot be got through without evident hurry and alarm, and more or less confusion and damage done to the agents and material concerned, there is, of course, *disorder*, *disease* and danger, — what we call from one of its obvious symptoms and dangers, the "burning state," or inflammation. If the danger is obviated, the obstructions removed, and the orderly performance of the functions of the part resumed, there is a resolution of the inflammation. In this case the depression of vitality was but temporary as well as local: the *part* was in a state of "suspended animation," occasioning the subsequent and surrounding "reaction" of excitement. When the original mechanical injury, or subsequent *chemical* or chemico-vital one of inflammation, excited in the *imperfect* effort to repair the former, has gone to the extent of so altering any of the living "atoms" of the organism, that *their* vitality must cease or become latent, they are *discharged* from further service, and thrown out as "dead matter." The "secretion" of pus, which has been the professional doctrine, since the rejection of early and superficial chemical views of putrefaction, is more properly an *excretion*. None will contend that it is the elaboration of anything *positively* useful, and therefore the main object of the process must be to get rid of something which is the reverse. Suppuration may be regarded as a slower and modified process of decomposition, if we must not say "fermentation," modified, "controlled" if you please, for wise ends, by the "vital *principle*."

If thus a mode of local or partial dissolution, it may still be the most favorable mode. It often prevents "mortification," or the quicker and more complete death of a larger amount of the living mass, already solidified. In suppuration nature expends, if possible, only her superfluous resources, to save what is more identified with the permanence of organism, just as nations, to preserve *their* vitality or independence, send against an invading foe the portion of society that can best be spared, to preserve the rest from destruction. Here, too, the analogy with inflammation holds strictly. The preservative process or means often turn out destructive to friends, more than to foes. The arming of society is often found an "inflammatory" and disorganizing business,—a *fatal* necessity.

CHAPTER II.

INFLAMMATION CONTINUED UNDER ITS MOST PRACTICAL ASPECTS.

"The four Signs"—Constitutional Symptoms—Changes of Function and Structure—Divisions—Common, Specific, "Healthy," &c., Acute and Chronic—"Terminations," Modifications from circumstances and in different tissues—Causes—Effects—Adhesion, Suppuration, Ulceration, Cicatrization, &c.

GOING more technically and practically into the subject of Inflammation, we will revert again to the so-called *signs*, pain, swelling, increased heat and redness.

The PAIN cannot be wholly attributed to distension and "stretching" of the nerves by the engorged blood-vessels, for it is not proportionate to the vascular distension, and may precede, being often the first symptom. The tenderness or soreness, which is often a diagnostic symptom between inflammatory and merely nervous affections, shows that the *sensibility* of the nerves is itself altered or heightened. This is further manifest from the *sensation* of heat, which is out of all proportion to the actual elevation of temperature. Bones, moreover, and other internal parts not naturally sensitive, become intensely so when inflamed.

The pain is always *lessened* by discharges from the engorged vessels; and while it lasts, more severe in structures that are hard and unyielding. Adhesions also lessen pain, or prevent it altogether. It is generally less in chronic than acute cases, and in what are called specific inflammations, as scrofulas, than in the ordinary forms.

The pain may exist in or be referred to parts *distant* from the seat of the inflammation. In the hip disease the first complaint of the patient is often "pain in the *knee*."

The *character* of the pain, as well as the amount, differs in the different structures and tissues. Throbbing is the characteristic of proper phlegmon or circumscribed inflammation in the cellular structure: and a dull heavy sensation that of the substance of most of the internal organs. When the external covering of the body is affected, the pain is generally described as "stinging or smarting;" when the internal or mucous surface, as a sensation of "burning and soreness."

The SWELLING may be, in the beginning, from mere increased flow of blood to the part, though if the "increased vascularity" meant activity of the veins as well as arteries, the more rapid current would not account for the rise of the stream, much less the *overflow*, without an obstruction at some point. There is always, perhaps, more or less transudation, often effusion of the blood entire. When the "coagulable lymph" is thrown out, and its fibrin deposited, the thin serum permeates the neighboring cellular tissue. These are the chief causes of proper inflammatory tumefaction, which may be surprisingly great and rapid. It is to be distinguished, however, from the sudden swelling of a part from internal hemorrhage, as well as the gradual development of a tumor. If the vessels are not sufficiently relieved, fibrin of an inferior quality is thrown out, often mixed with blood from the rupture of the vessels. In a more advanced case, the accumulation of pus may be the principal cause of the swelling.

The swelling, in as far as it results from effusion, is a relief to the distended vessels, and appears to enable them to resume or continue their proper functions. As observed before, the less opportunity for swelling, the greater the pain. The swelling or effusion may, however, be the very cause of suffering; as beneath the periosteum, or between the cartilages. It may even become a source of danger, by pressure on vital parts. Next to loose, cellular textures, glands are the parts apt to swell most largely.

INCREASED HEAT, though so prominent a symptom, has been much questioned and debated. After the thermometer was resorted to, it was a matter of surprise that so little if any change of temperature was discoverable. Hunter *sometimes* failed, after exciting artificial inflammation in animals, to ascertain any definite increase of heat. It has been generally allowed, however, that in the lower extremities, and other parts distant from the center of circulation, the inflammatory state raised the temperature a few degrees, — up to that of the heart or lungs; and this slight change was attributed wholly to the increased quantity, and more rapid flow of the blood. "Heat," then, as a symptom, is referred rather to the morbid susceptibility of the nerves, than to an abnormal physical or chemical condition of the parts. A difference, however, of seven or eight degrees, which is allowed to be not unfrequent, is certainly considerable. That the part is cut off, as it were, from the general level of temperature, and has lost any power of regulating its own, is sufficiently important. The relief from abstracting heat, and *after* effusion and suppuration, the appearance of the pus globules, and other more manifest results of molecular action, all seem to favor the idea that "inflammation," after all, may be essentially nothing else than what the word imports, a "burning up" of the part, — in the chemical dialect, a too rapid combination with oxygen. In the theory of Liebig, before alluded to, it is a too rapid "transformation of the tissues," not only destructive of itself, but developing *other* destructive and superfluous "force," as well as that of heat. The fact that not only does an inflamed part rise six or seven degrees, but that some parts of the human body rise as many degrees more after life has ceased (or up to 113 degrees*) clearly shows that chemical considerations cannot be dispensed with, in the explanation of morbid phenomena.

The REDNESS is not only owing to more blood being in the part, but to that blood itself being richer in the coloring matter, or red corpuscles, in proportion as the serum with the fibrin or white corpuscles has been thrown out. There may be also transudation or effusion of the blood, red particles and all. Redness of surface proves the distension of the vessels, not as was once supposed by the red globules taking the place of the supposed smaller lymph-corpuscles, but by their being visible only in mass,

* An important fact long overlooked, and but very recently settled, by the experiments of Dr. Dowler, of New Orleans, and Davy, and others, in England.

and not in "single file." As the inflammation advances new vessels may also be formed, thus adding to the *degree* of redness. This varies with the structure of the part, the kind of inflammation, its amount, stage, &c. It is greater, for instance, on mucous membranes than on the skin. There is said to be "uniform redness" in Erysipelas, "capilliform" when only *some* of the capillaries are rendered visible, as in conjunctivitis. There may be only red *points* or larger *spots* called maculæ, — the latter from sanguineous effusion. The effusion in most specific or asthenic inflammations becomes of a dusky or even coppery hue. In chronic cases generally the "redness" is but that of venous blood. The more acute and sthenic the action, the more it has of the bright scarlet hue, or that of the freshly oxygenated blood.

The CONSTITUTIONAL SYMPTOMS of inflammation ought not to be overlooked. When the disease is at all severe, or in an important part, the whole system is affected with what is hence called "sympathetic or symptomatic fever." This is usually of the active grade — distinguished as "inflammatory" even when not dependent on any known disease of a particular part. Its development is usually preceded by chilliness and weakness, with a diminution of the secretions. It may become a source of greater danger than the local affection itself, and greatly retard the favorable progress of the latter. The nervous system may sympathize, without the circulation reacting to the febrile extent, constituting general irritability; or be depressed, with a feeble excitement of the heart, and derangement of the secretions generally, thus changing from the inflammatory to the typhoid character. Lastly, from extensive ulceration or absorption of pus, *hectic* fever may set in, with exhausting efforts at reaction.

The ALTERATION of function and structure, in the part affected, is a more important consideration than mere external symptoms. The "increased sensibility," like the "increased vascularity," may be but temporary as well as partial, even in respect of the whole part seemingly affected. It is *around* the injured part that inflammation most displays itself. At the central point there is probably *less* irritability as well as less activity of the vessels. The change of structure, *consequent* on the diseased action, may again reduce both the nervous and vascular system below their average of functional power. The secretion proper to the part is always modified or checked at the commencement of inflammation, but subsequently it is often greatly increased and mingled with the products of diseased action. *Structural* change becomes chiefly manifest in chronic inflammation, the acute ending in complete destruction or more or less *incomplete* restoration. Increase of weight is often a marked symptom or sensation of the patient, as when a limb is the part affected. Most parts, however, are softer in the acute form or stage. Hardness is the characteristic of chronic inflammation, and may consist with increase or diminution of bulk and density.

After death redness and swelling may disappear, but often remain as *prima facie* evidence of recent inflammation. It requires, however, to be corroborated by the presence of pus or lymph, as well as serum, and *softening* of the part. After mere congestion, the larger *veins* will be found distended rather than the capillaries. Both serous and sanguineous infiltrations may occur in the corpse from many other causes than inflammation.

There are many DIVISIONS of inflammation, some of them not very concurrent or consistent with others. Some of the least satisfactory, in a philosophic point of view, are among the most practically convenient. Such is that into "healthy and unhealthy inflammation." The first division that requires attention may depend either on the exciting cause or modifying circumstances, giving rise to the distinction of

Common and *Specific* Inflammation. The *former* is such as arises from mechanical injury, or slight physiological derangement in an otherwise healthy constitution. Its most favorable form is seen in what is called "adhesive inflammation," the healing of a cut finger. It is always to be understood when the *specific* is not expressly in question. This term is almost synonymous with "unhealthy," though common inflammation may lose its natural tendency to recovery, and would then be called unhealthy rather than specific. The latter word implies some particular known cause for the inflammation being peculiar and generally unhealthy in its character. This cause may be a contagion, affecting the part directly, or the constitution. Gonorrhea is an example of the former, Syphilis of the latter. Or it may be the result of a dyscrasia, predisposing the individual to inflammation, or to an unfavorable modification of it, when produced from ordinary causes. Thus, scrofulous swellings or other inflammations in scrofulous patients, are easily excited, but difficult to reduce. Their progress is tedious; and a thin fluid, with curdy matter, takes the place of serum and healthy fibrin, or of consistent "healthy pus." After these explanations, it is hardly necessary to define, very formally,

"*Healthy and Unhealthy* Inflammation." The former is "Common Inflammation" in its best or least unfavorable form, and under favorable influences. Though a morbid action, it may be under the circumstances of the case inevitable, or even desirable, as where it limits a still worse form of inflammation or actual "mortification." Its tendency is self-limiting and restorative.

The simplest form of *unhealthy* Inflammation is that which tends to self-diffusion, from lack of good fibrinous deposits. Its products may be deficient or excessive in quantity, as compared with those of "healthy inflammation," and always differ in quality, if not in sensible appearance. It is, therefore, an essentially destructive and dangerous state, requiring the interference of art, in cases where healthy common inflammation would do well enough of itself. The differences between them will be noticed when speaking of particular instances, as well as the general subjects of abscesses and ulcers.

An important practical distinction is into

Acute and Chronic, which may be plainly translated the quick and slow, or "active and passive." The limits between the two cannot be defined by time alone, and the kind or degree of action is often a better criterion. Generally, however, the higher the inflammatory action and more obvious the symptoms, the speedier its termination, whether in restoration or destruction. Hence the necessity for some word to mark a certain degree of activity, and amount of immediate danger. That the distinction in question is not absolute, is shown by the necessity that often arises for such additional epithets as "sub-acute;" and still more clearly by the chronic forms being often a result or continuation of the acute. The effects of the two modes of action are, however, often sufficiently distinct. Hence the kind, as well as degree of danger, is different in the two cases.

Such expressions as "Adhesive Inflammation, Suppurative, Ulcerative or Gangrenous Inflammation," must be understood as descriptive, as denoting degrees, stages or accidental tendencies of the same action, rather than distinct kinds of diseased action.

All these peculiarities may depend on the state of the patient's constitution, the part affected, and a variety of other circumstances. They are, therefore, sometimes found enumerated among the, so-called

TERMINATIONS of Inflammation. Almost every result enumerated under this head by one author, is criticised and objected to by others. Generally speaking there are but two "terminations" of the disease in question, as of all others, — convalescence or death. These, regarded as local, are technically called *Resolution* and *Mortification*. The latter, however, as well as Transformation or permanent Degeneration of the part, may be classed as only a modification or result. It seems absurd to speak of inflammation *ending* in suppuration, and then of the suppurative process being still an inflammatory one. So of other "terminations." Still there is a tendency to one or other of the following results, and the sensible relief accompanying most of them, accounts for this expression continuing in use. These, then, are the results or effects of inflammatory action: —

Resolution, when the increased action of the larger vessels is supposed to overcome the obstruction or debility in the smaller, and perfect circulation through the part is restored; — increased or modified *Secretion*, from naturally secreting surfaces, as serum within the cavities and mucus in the outlets of the body; — *Effusion*, which may be of three kinds, merely serous, sanguineous or of "coagulable lymph," — serum containing plastic fibrin, and necessary to *Adhesion;* — the discharge of devitalized fluid in the characteristic form of "pus," the "secretion" or transformation being called *Suppuration;* — and finally *Gangrene* or rather *its* termination, local death or *mortification.*

Among the *circumstances* that will render one or other of these tendencies more probable, the most important is the state of the patient's constitution. Health might be measured by the vigor and freedom from aberration of "the restorative principle," *i. e.*, by recovery from local injury without, or with little, inflammation. It is a familiar observation, that "some people's flesh will not heal like others." Some are in danger of bleeding to death from the smallest wound, and are hence said to be of a hemorrhagic diathesis. Others, it might be also said, have a suppurative or gangrenous or at least inflammatory diathesis. "A full habit of body," however, is not to be mistaken for the best possible health. Plethoric persons are in danger from too high inflammatory action, as are debilitated and emaciated ones from too low. Habitual beer drinkers are obliged to submit to amputation, for injuries that could easily be cured in others, not saturated with such a blood-making beverage. Inflammation is of a higher grade, and more rapid in its course in the young than in the old, and in parts nearer the source of circulation than in the extremities.

The structure affected exerts a marked influence.

Inflammation in the *cellular tissue* is favorably situated for effusion, after which absorption and consequent resolution can often be effected. When it is not, suppuration follows, constituting an "abscess." When the disease is not properly circumscribed as the true "phlegmon," and the pus, then sure to be unhealthy, is infiltrated through the cellular structure, a form of inflammation more or less resembling erysipelas ensues. When near the surface, the healthy abscess is the common boil. This, though the very type of "healthy inflammation," may degenerate, some even believing it, in constitutions at the same time weak and irritable, to become the carbuncle. (For a different view, see Lecture on Carbuncle, &c.) Cellular inflammation, when it becomes chronic, may produce various tumors, and even schirrus, or the malignant induration that precedes cancer.

Inflamed Glands resemble the cellular structure in tendency to swell; but they are more apt to suppurate, and in chronic cases to harden.

In the *skin*, inflammation tends to spread, and by its effusion separates the cuticle, producing what is called vesication. The effusion is usually merely serous, but in some cases contains fibrin, occasioning a thickening. After removal of the cuticle, the exposed cutis is liable to suffer from cold air; from which, however, it is protected, if not artificially, by a thickening of the matter effused into what is called a scab. Small and distinct elevations of the cuticle are called "vesicles." If they contain pus instead of serum, they are distinguished as "pustules," and the process of their formation "pustulation." Pimples, rashes, &c., might perhaps be mentioned as peculiar results of cutaneous inflammation. The skin is more disposed to ulceration and gangrene than many other tissues.

The *mucous membranes* have a strong tendency, when inflamed, to relieve themselves by suppuration; this process appearing to be substituted for the ordinary secretion of mucus. When the inflammatory action is very violent, however, the "coagulable lymph," which is the common product in other parts, may be thrown out, as in croup, when it organizes into an additional or "false membrane." Were adhesive matter as frequent or as capable of organizing itself in the mucous outlets, as in other parts, the result would be frequently fatal. The suppurative "secretion" is often only partial, and the discharge spoken of as "muco-purulent." What is called passive hemorrhage is another not unfrequent result of mucous inflammation. As structural results, contraction, thickening, and softening, may be named.

In the SEROUS CAVITIES, where the danger is reversed, so is the relative order of suppuration and adhesion. The natural tendency is for the inflamed membrane to coalesce with its opposite fold. The consequence of this "termination" is often of no *appreciable* disadvantage. Chronic inflammation of these investing membranes, however, is liable to relieve itself, though unfortunately *not* as a termination of the diseased action, in serous effusion or exhalation, constituting dropsy of the part, as hydrocele, hydrothorax, &c. The effusion may be bloody, but is commonly of a whey-like color and consistency. The membrane itself may exhibit ecchymosed spots. Neither ulceration nor thickening, except by adhesion, as before mentioned, is frequent in these parts.

In the FIBROUS STRUCTURES, the characteristic effusion is gelatinous, within which bony matter may be afterward deposited. Independently of this, their substance is liable to be thickened and indurated. Their liability to ulceration and gangrene has been disputed.

Tendons and *Ligaments* are both described by Sir Astley Cooper as "not very susceptible of inflammation," at least in healthy persons. The pain, however, produced by injuries of the former, particularly punctures, is more than a set-off for this exemption, oftener producing tetanus than in any other part. The *synovial membranes* connected with the ligaments, are very liable to take on inflammation and advance to the suppurative stage. When they do not, the substance of the ligaments thickens, and the joint is greatly enlarged. When matter is formed *under* tendons, it burrows far and produces violent irritative fever. The same may be observed of fasciæ, inflammation *in* which has also a great tendency to become diffuse.

Within the substance of the *muscles*, inflammation is characterized by "twitchings," particularly noticeable after comminuted fractures.

The substance of the *vessels* or *nerves* may be itself the seat of the inflammation. Phlebitis is more common than inflammation of the arteries, both as a spontaneous disease, and after mechanical injuries. In the latter case the termination is often in adhesion. This takes place most frequently at the valves, "gluing the sides of the vein together and preventing further mischief." The affected vessel may be traced as a thick hard cord, and is very sensitive to pressure. When not thus limited, "phlebitis" is distinguished as "diffuse," and is then a very serious disease. The great danger is from discharge of pus into the current of the circulation, giving rise to extreme depression, restlessness, hectic fever, &c., with secondary inflammations in other parts. The arteries are seldom separately inflamed, except from wounds. Inflammation from the application of a ligature may extend to the heart itself. "This," says Cooper, "I have frequently observed in patients who have died from constitutional irritation, after an operation where a ligature has been made on an artery." Gangrene of the affected vessel is an occasional result. Inflammation in the nerves, "though very painful at first, is followed by little irritation."

Inflammation in *cartilage* tends to ulceration, and destruction of the joint or bone with which it is connected. All the usual phenomena of inflammation take place in the BONES; their gangrene and mortification, however, are usually spoken of under distinct names, as "*caries* and *necrosis*." The result of their suppuration is often diagnostic, "bone-pus" being so rarely healthy, that it is synonymous with ichor, generally fœtid, and often quite dark.

CAUSES. — Of the "proximate cause" of Inflammation enough was said, when speaking of its disputed "nature." "Exciting causes" have been divided, like the disease, into "common and specific," the former affecting more or less all persons, — as exposure to heat and cold; the latter requiring a peculiar susceptibility, as well as producing peculiar results, like the various contagions. An obvious division is into those which act *directly* on the part, producing structural injury in the first place, and only affecting the functions or exciting inflammation secondarily, — such as mechanical violence and chemical corrosion, — and those which induce visible structural change, if at all, only through the functional disorder (it may be the proper stimulus of the part or organ, as volition in the case of excessive exertion). Thus the structural effect is not only *indirect*, but often on a different part from that to which the cause was applied, as a current of cold air. Cold and heat, however, as well as other agencies, may belong to the direct or indirect class, according to their intensity.

ADHESION, — or "Adhesive Inflammation," as it is called, in consequence of generally occurring in connection with inflammation, — is properly the uniting of divided or contiguous parts, and may occur without any such degree of incited action as amounts to inflammation. This is the case, under the most favorable circumstances, in what is technically called "union by the first intention," when an incised wound or cut heals without new formation or leaving a cicatrix. More commonly, however, the term is applied to the process of union between divided and other surfaces already *inflamed*, and also to the coalescence of tissues by fibrinous matter, as around an abscess, and to new growths on the surface of membranes, as in croup. It limits cellular inflammation, and is often a result of the state in serous membranes, appearing to divert the excessive activity or "force" then generated. This is one reason why it is often spoken of as a termination. The *pain* attending this process is "thrilling," while in

SUPPURATION it is dull and throbbing, with a peculiar sensation of uneasiness in the part. When the suppurating tumor is near the surface, the formation of matter is preceded by flush on the skin above, and followed by the tumor rising and becoming softer at some point, where a *liquidity* or "fluctuation" will be felt on pressure. The abscess is then said to have "pointed." The extension of matter will be attended with constitutional irritation, rigors and subsequent febrile reaction. The time usually requisite for inflamed parts to relieve themselves, by this process, is from one to two weeks.

What is called "healthy" or "laudable" pus, is a thick bland homogeneous fluid, nearly white, and of the consistence of thin cream, with a peculiar smell while warm, and it is said a sickening taste. It differs from the natural secretion of mucous membranes, in containing swollen and decomposing globules, and in sinking in water, and being rendered gelatinous and ropy by the action of potash, while mucus swims and is readily dissolved by the alkali. Pus is considered unhealthy whenever mixed with blood, in which state, usually called sanious, it will often irritate the parts with which it comes in contact. The more common variation from the healthy standard, is by its being too thin and serous, when it is called ichor or ichorous. *Fœtor* is another symptom of unhealthy suppuration. Healthy pus answers many secondary purposes, besides relieving the system of dead or dying blood. It is nature's own "healing salve," protecting parts from the air, and promoting granulation. It is very slow in putrefying or undergoing further chemical transformation, perhaps from the very fact of having already undergone a certain degree of decomposition. When improperly constituted or elaborated, however, it may possess every variety of bad quality, from the slightly irritating to the specific poisoning properties of contagia. Even the healthiest pus seems to communicate the suppurative quality to any other parts than those discharging it, unless when they are protected from it, as by cuticle or epithelium. Its injurious effects when taken back into the blood, and thrown by it on internal parts, are well known.

Abscess, as a result of suppuration, has been before explained. The pus is confined by the inflammatory effusion itself. The abscesses produced by *acute* inflammation generally run their course, including the necessary ulceration for the discharge of matter, in less than three weeks. The situation of the matter has, however, much to do with the period, as well as the amount of danger, and will often of itself make the case necessarily chronic.

ULCERATAON has usually been described as an exaggeration or excess of the ordinary absorbent process, as adhesion or fibrinous formation is of the ordinary nutritive function. Mere pressure is well known to stimulate the absorbents. An unusual flow of blood has the same effect. In inflamed parts both these causes concur, the ulceration usually following the effusion or suppuration. When necessary for the discharge of matter, the ulcerative action tends toward the surface of the body, — a beneficial provision of nature, "explained," however, by the greater irritability conjoined with less tenacity of life, in the more superficial textures. For the same reason, newly-formed parts, the result of recent "adhesive" organization, and parts at the greatest distance from the center of circulation, are more liable to ulcerate than others. Textures, however, that have little vascularity, are proportionably indisposed to ulceration, and more liable to mortify, as the tendons. Though the swelling, &c., of ordinary inflammation may be considered a cause of ulcerative absorption, the latter may go on, when once instituted, where there is no longer effusion or tumefaction. Certain forms of the ulcerative process are found to depend on a peculiar order of cells, and to continue until these are destroyed. (See former chapters.)

The ulcerating part appears and *feels* worm-eaten, — "as if insects were about it," The constitutional symptoms are moderate, the fever rather hectic than inflammatory.

Particular parts in a state of ulceration, or "ulcers," will be more particularly considered hereafter in connection with their treatment.

GRANULATION is the name given to the process by which lost parts are reproduced, and to each little fleshy pimple or particle of the new structure. These are red in color, and generally protected by a covering of pus. They rise in successive layers, as the fibrin is thrown out, and the vessels from the parts beneath elongate and branch through them. After the cavity is completely filled up, and closed over with skin, "the granulative structure is absorbed and a contracted cicatrix is left." When divided parts, or the walls of emptied abscesses are not brought together, healing commonly takes place by means of the granulative structure. Granulations, however, readily unite with each other, and the requisite contact can be effected after the process of filling up has commenced. It is by the union or inosculation of granulations, spoken of, that new skin or

CICATRIZATION is effected, cuticular granulations proceeding, with their necessary vessels, from the surrounding sound skin, and uniting with each other as they advance toward the center, as well as with the granulations beneath. A fresh cicatrix is redder and more vascular than the original skin, but afterward becomes less so, the vessels contracting, and that part of the surface having ever after less vitality.

CHAPTER III.

TREATMENT OF INFLAMMATION.

Blood-letting — Objections to Venesection, theoretical and practical — Local Bleeding — Leeches and Scarifying — Dry Cupping.

THE first thing that occurs to the mind of old-school practitioners, if it is not actually put in practice in all serious cases, — the first measure directed in all their books, is

BLOOD-LETTING.

It is true there is a great difference in regard to this measure in the practice of different individuals, and generally speaking, much less blood is taken now than formerly. With some of the class of physicians in question, bleeding is now the exception in cases where it was once the rule. Its direction by the authors is accompanied with so many conditions and qualifications, that a cautious beginner can never be sure when he is warranted in resorting to this once never-failing expedient. Still it is *the* remedy of the books, and sufficiently relied on for other better means to be habitually neglected, even when that also is omitted. A living authority, who for more than a quarter of a century has been a teacher in one of the first schools in America, in attending to the uncertainty of the signs for omitting or *repeating* venesection, concludes that, "perhaps the most certain indication of the presence of inflammation is the continuance of *pain*," and further assures us that "so long as *this* remains severe, *we can scarcely go wrong in the detraction of blood*."* The insidious relief of pain has long been the tempting motive for bleeding, and often the measure of the amount taken; if its existence were indeed made the criterion for the measure, — as seems to be the design of the celebrated professor alluded to, — what a sanguinary business would medicine become!

Local suffering, however, even in connection with other more decisive evidence of dangerous inflammation, cannot safely be made our only consideration, when we come to treat a case, or lay down general rules of treatment. General disorder is the necessary accompaniment of the local difficulty. The over distension and over action of the part are necessarily at the expense of the rest of the body. If there is "increased vascularity and sensibility" in and about the inflamed part, there is a decrease of *both* throughout the rest of the system. This inequilibrium of circulation and sensibility is generally obvious. A deficiency of blood in the extremities and throughout the general surface (unless the inflammation be located in the skin), is manifest in almost all cases. "Dryness of the skin and decreased secretion generally" are laid down among the diagnostic symptoms.

The correction of this inequilibrium is well known to be one of the surest means of relief, and signs of the local disease having ceased. If you can bring it effectually about, you have

* Gibson's Surgery, Vol. I, p. 28.

secured "resolution;" if not, suppuration or sloughing must generally ensue.

Now blood-letting, by merely lessening the general amount of the circulating fluid, can certainly have no direct tendency to bring about this desirable result. The amount removed is drawn in at least equal proportion from all other parts, which then have an inadequate instead of a superabundant supply. The inequilibrium must therefore be increased instead of lessened. The whole system must be thus debilitated, and rendered less capable of resisting the morbid influence, or of sustaining the effort necessary to repair the damage already done. The heart is less capable of propelling the blood through the extreme vessels, and through the deranged part; and while that part is weakened in its recuperative resources, it is not proportionately relieved of oppression. It is not the more energetic flow of blood to the part, but its obstruction there, that *adds* to the disease and constitutes its danger. All experience proves that general vascular excitement is not necessarily of itself a dangerous condition. Still to lessen the force, or rather the *rapidity* of the circulation for a time, is very desirable when accomplished without weakening the system.

That the loss of blood is debilitating, no one pretends to deny. It is the most directly debilitating of all measures used in medicine, and its weakening effect is generally proportionate to the amount of blood taken. It is only in cases of "oppression," that is, of *apparent* weakness, that the pulse rises and the patient's vigor revives after a bleeding. The patient is nevertheless debilitated in reality from the loss of blood, though apparently stronger than when the vital powers were oppressed. The removal of the oppression may more certainly be accomplished by other means without any risk of debility.

Nor can it be urged that venesection has any tendency to reestablish the cutaneous function. When, indeed, it is carried so far that the debility approximates prostration, *ad deliquium animi*, as the books say, then there is perspiration enough, or rather *deliquium* enough of the blood as well as of the senses; for it is not a real perspiration from the proper stimulation of the secreting organ, but a mere exudation from its collapse, just as the fainting also results from a similar deficiency of stimulus on the brain. It is a cold, clammy death-sweat. In the natural action of this function, the whole surface of the body is in the active condition, warm and red, and the pulse full and soft.

Experience confirms physiology in showing that blood-letting cannot effect the object for which it is practiced. It is now, indeed, sometimes said that the bleeding is rather a preventive than a curative measure; that it is chiefly useful as a means of gaining time or facilitating the cure. In other words, it is found that this measure does not facilitate the cure of inflammation, without the aid of others, — which other measures, we contend, would have accomplished the object in a far better and safer manner. Even if the desired results *were* as unquestionably attained as might be supposed, from the long prevalence of the practice, still the risk of other results is sufficient to make it doubtful whether it ought in any case, or ever, to be resorted to. It could be easily shown, that no one can bleed in any given case without a violation of some or other of the rules laid down for the use, or rather the disuse of the measure.* The exceptions to bleeding

* "Of all the therapeutical appliances," candidly remarks Professor Flint, of Louisville, in a note to Druitt (where he seems to regard bleeding, at least in case of internal inflammation, rather as a *preventive* than *curative* means, — a distinction he tells us to be *always* borne in mind by the surgical practitioner, in order to determine the extent to which he may *safely* carry the means of depletion and depression; concluding that of all measures this of direct "depletion and depression," is the most dangerous and presumptuous: or in his own words, which I began to quote) — "Of all therapeutical appliances, there is none in which *art ventures* on such extreme *liberties with nature* as in this of blood-letting; and unfortunately there are few in regard to which the *principles* that are to regulate its *administration* are so *unsettled* and *contradictory*." Among the principles or rules "most approved" of by "the authorities," he refers us to the text (Modern Surgery, page 49 et seq.), where, among other things, we find the following: —

"As a general rule, the blood should be permitted to flow" ("as quickly as possible," "from a large orifice," &c.) "till paleness of the lips, lividity about the eyes, sighing, nausea, fluttering pulse, and relief of the pain indicate the *approach* of syncope." Diseases in which bleeding "is most *injurious* and worst borne are putrid fevers and *diseases of debility*." (Page 50.)

"But the junior practitioner must bear in mind that he may occasionally meet with some *thin bloodless* patients, whom it would be very injurious to bleed. but who nevertheless, from some peculiarity of constitution, do *not faint*, even though *bled to excess*." Yet we were told on the previous page that, "it is often *absolutely necessary* to bleed persons in acute disease, who are *extremely debilitated*."

Not only is the bleeding of certain *thin* persons doubly dangerous, as we have

for inflammation are now so many, that they will no doubt become the rule, even among Allopaths. It is well known that Homeopathists have always proscribed blood-letting.

TOPICAL BLEEDING

is a very different measure from venesection, but this is liable to many of the same objections. The same quantity of blood, taken

just seen, from their systems not knowing when to give the fainting sign of "hold, enough!" but the *fat* and some of the *fleshy* are also expressly exempted — "it will be *borne worse* when the muscles are large and flabby, and the pulse habitually open, soft and full." "Fat people generally bear bleeding worse, and contain in fact less blood, proportionally to their bulk, than those of a spare lean habit and rigid fibre." "It will be borne *worst of all*, when the complexion is sickly and pale, — the pulse quick, small and feeble, — the lips, conjunctiva and tongue pale."

"If there should happen to be a state of passive dilatation and weakness of the heart, *syncope* would most likely be *instantly fatal;* and if there should be *any organic* disease which impedes the *formation of blood,* its loss is liable to be followed by *irrecoverable sinking* and *exhaustion.*" (Pages 50 and 51.)

Yet with all these dangers and exceptions, "the first and most important measure" in inflammation is still "general blood-letting; which, if *carried far enough,* induces a state of insensibility and suspended circulation, to which the name syncope or fainting is given." (Pages 48 and 49.)

It is true, we are afterwards told to stop short of this desirable state, and the "*approach* to syncope" is made "the general rule;" "because, *after* the depressing effects of *bleeding* there naturally ensues a degree of *reaction; the pulse rising* in frequency and the local *pain returning:* and this reaction will be the greater if the venesection has been carried to the extent of producing full syncope." *If* this reaction (with "rising pulse and returning pain!") exhibit "well-marked inflammatory symptoms, the *bleeding* must be *repeated* till the disease is vanquished *provided that the strength permit.*"

"The propriety of the second bleeding *must* in a great measure *be determined by the effect* which the first has had on the pulse; for if that be more frequent and quick, or more sharp and jerking, instead of slower and softer, it would seem that the bleeding had *diminished* the *strength more than* it had reduced the *disease.*"

Not only is the degree of this "*tolerance*" of bleeding, as it is technically called (varying, as it has been *experimentally* discovered, it does, with the different diseases as well as classes of patients for which it is nevertheless said to be indicated), made the criterion for a repetition of the measure, but for other measures also, and even an "aid to" or *test* of *diagnosis* itself! "If faintness occurs from the loss of a very small quantity of blood, it will be certain that it is *not* an *inflammatory* but nervous" disease, "or that if inflammatory, it *must be treated by other measures than blood-letting.*" So that even in inflammation, syncope, with all its confessed evil of aggravated reaction, *may* ensue on but slight loss of blood.

The danger is still greater of *not fainting* when the operation is not conducted exactly *secundum artem* (as well as sometimes when it is, "owing to some peculi-

slowly and gradually from the small vessels of the part, will not produce the same immediately dangerous effects. There is no shock produced upon the general system, the vessels having time to contract so as to reduce their calibre to the amount of fluid contained. Still, if much blood be taken, even in this way, evil consequences must ensue.

But the great objection to local bleeding is, that the necessary applications cannot be made directly to the part affected; and any partial attempt near it is likely to draw the blood in that direction, and add to the congestion already existing. Unless the vessels of inflamed parts can be "entirely drained," and the sur-

arity of constitution"), "the bleeding may be continued almost to death, without the occurrence of syncope." (Page 49.)

"Tolerance" is generally represented as greater, and the necessity for bleeding more urgent, the more vitally important the organ affected. But this again depends on the time when it is resorted to, our author's American annotator assuring us that, "after violent reaction," in other words, when there is actual inflammation, "the utmost discretion is necessary, in the use of this potent means." With respect to the disease or injury, "bleeding is not well borne," continues Druitt, when there is *great depression* of the vitality, whether from the peculiar nature of the morbid cause, or the inflammation excited, "nor in the case of an injury requiring *great constitutional efforts* for its restoration, as a compound fracture; nor if the disease be advanced toward *suppuration* or gangrene."

To vary these quotations with one from a writer of a very different character, supported, however, too strongly, by less popular and more professional authority. After showing that the diseases of the poor in Europe arise in a majority of cases from defective food and impure air, creating a deficiency of blood; "yet," continues Dr. Dickson, "enter the crowded hospitals of England, and see how mercilessly the lancet, the leech and cupping-glass are employed, in the diseases of the poor. What a contrast to the eager pupils and attendants thronging around their beds, — those attendants with bandage and basin, ready at a moment's notice to take from the poor creatures whatever quantity of life-blood solemn pedantry may prescribe, as the infallible means of relieving their sufferings."

How well does this "rhetoric" agree with the confessed *results*. "*Patients* who have been apparently *cured* by large bleedings," which according to Dr. Rutherford, of Edinburg, "have conquered pain in the first instance, *remain* eventually longer *in the hospitals* than those who have not been so speedily relieved (other more efficient means not having been resorted to): moreover, you will find them *return* again, with dropsy and chronic affections."

"One objection to venesection," says one of Great Britain's most distinguished surgeons, "is that, after frequent and copious venous hemorrhage, the internal vessels become gorged with blood, and *a disposition* to *apoplexy is induced.*" (Liston, page 26.

rounding ones nearly exhausted also, it is confessed that little or no good can be done.

LEECHES are, in some countries, and by some practitioners in this country, the most approved means of local depletion. But of these agencies in surgery it may be said, as of blood-letting in general, that the cautions necessary to be observed in their use, nearly amount to a prohibition.* Besides, they must not be applied directly to the part inflamed; and their sucking off blood from any other part can have little influence, except as it lessens the general circulation, or acts as a "derivative or counter-irritant." In the latter case, their poisonous effects are often more to be dreaded than the original disease. Fatal hemorrhage frequently results from applying leeches to children, and adults do not always escape injury. It is impossible to know beforehand what bad effects will follow their use; and, inasmuch as all cases to which they are applied, can be cured by other means, we would never recommend a resort to them.

Scarifying is only less objectionable than leeching. Scarification of the inflamed part, in acute disease, aggravates the disease, and renders it more troublesome to heal. We do not mean to say that scarifying is never beneficial; but that the benefit in addition to that of the cupping used at the same time, is due to the additional local counter-irritation, and not to the amount of blood taken away. The revulsion and counter-irritation are, perhaps, more complete and permanent after the scarifying; but according to our observation, the amount of good done is never in direct proportion to the quantity of blood drawn, but rather in the inverse proportion.

* "LEECHES," we are told in a recent work, "should not be applied in *females* where the cicatrix would be unsightly. In *children* large superficial *veins* should be avoided. Nor should they be placed on the *eye-lids*, since in this situation they are apt to cause ædema and ecchymosis in the part; nor where *cutaneous nerves* abound, as erysipelas is apt to follow. They should *not* be applied directly to *the inflamed part*, for the reason that the stimulus of their bites adds to the existing inflammation; nor should they be applied near an acute *ulcer*, for their bites are apt to degenerate in this case into ulcers: if the ulcer be of a specific character, the bites become inoculated, and thus extend, instead of decreasing the ulcerated surface. Neither should they be placed where *bandages* are of paramount importance, as in fractures, for in such cases *the bites are apt to inflame and ulcerate*, and thus cause the removal of the apparatus at a critical period." (Hasting's Practice of Surgery, page 42.)

Dismissing the subject of abstracting blood, together with cathartics, &c., as measures not only unnecessary, but highly injurious, since healthy organs are attacked in order to relieve diseased, the vital force is impaired, and the means employed have no special adaptation to the end proposed, — we will speak briefly of the

SPECIFIC OR HOMEOPATHIC TREATMENT.

Its simplicity, its harmlessness, is in as strong contrast to other modes, as it is superior in efficacy. It could never yield such wonderful results were it not in accordance with a divine law. The charge is sometimes made against Homeopaths, that they neglect the *causa occasionalis* of disease ; but if we observe the difference between them and others, in the treatment of inflammation arising from different causes, it will be seen at once that the charge is not only false, as against us, but is true against those who make it. Instance a person who has received a severe injury upon the head, and inflammation of the brain is present, apart from attention to the wound, in what respect would the Allopath treat this case differently from one of cerebral inflammation from another cause, — venesection, or if not in favor of that, active cathartics, &c. Would the fact that the difficulty was the result of a mechanical injury determine, or have any influence in the selection of the medicaments to be given ? not at all !

But with the Homeopath, that fact would be most significant, and direct his mind to a remedy, which he would not have thought of employing in inflammation of the brain from other causes. The great remedy with which the Homeopathic Surgeon has to combat inflammations, the result of external violence, is

Arnica Montana, the specific for diseases from mechanical injuries. Its timely administration, and local application, upon the occurrence of an accident, would, in a large majority of cases, prevent the rise of inflammation, which under different medication would be attended with great danger. *Calendula offic.*, *Rhus. Tox.* and *Ruta* are equally valuable in special cases, but clinical experience has not assigned to either of them so large a sphere of curative action. When the inflammation is very high, *Aconitum Napellus*, that general "anti-phlogistic" of the Homeopath, so superior to the *depleting* means usually employed, will be needed, and in some cases, *Belladonna*, *Bryonia*, *Cantharis*, *Merc*, &c., are useful. (For the particular indications for each remedy, see WOUNDS, ABSCESS, DISLOCATIONS and FRACTURES.)

The local applications will be spoken of in connection with the different classes of injuries, but we would state here the general rule for their use. Immediately upon the occurrence of an injury, and until considerable inflammation is present, and in chronic inflammations, cold or cool applications should be applied. Cloths kept constantly wet with cold water are usually employed; but by means of *arnicated water*, or *aqua calendulæ*, we not only obtain all the advantages derived from the cold water dressings, but, in addition, we have all the benefits that flow from the direct applications to the injured part, of a remedy that is specifically adapted to the prevention of inflammation: we would, therefore, recommend that the Tincture of Arnica, or the appropriate medicament, be added to the water, cold, cool or warm, as may be proper, in all cases of injury, and that where poultices are applied, they should be mixed with a dilution of the remedy; but in all high grades of inflammation, hot applications should be employed. Carpenter speaks in the highest terms of the efficacy of hot steam in removing local inflammation. Had not empirical experience long since proved their superiority, their homeopathicity would have suggested their use. (For Hæmastasis in subduing inflammations, see note to CONCUSSION AND COMPRESSION OF THE BRAIN.)

CHAPTER V.

THE DIFFERENT KINDS OF WOUNDS, ERYSIPELAS, TETANUS, AND HYDROPHOBIA.

DEFINITIONS — Simple, &c. — Cuts, Bruises, &c. — their respective importance, pain, bleeding and danger — TREATMENT — Incised Wounds and Hemorrhage — Compression, Styptics and Ligatures — Punctured and Penetrating Wounds — Suppuration — Lacerated and Contused — Irritation, Gangrene, &c. — Gunshot Wounds — their varieties and peculiarities — Probing, &c. — Calendula — Poisoned Wounds — Wasps, Snakes, &c. — Remedies, general and topical — TETANUS — successful and "experimental treatment" — list of "hopeless measures" — ERYSIPELAS — HYDROPHOBIA, preventive and *curative* measures.

WHAT may be termed artificial maladies, — derangements, chiefly local, produced directly by external agents, — constitute the special and characteristic province of the surgeon. Men's more frequent indulgence, in former times, of their "organ of destructiveness" on each others' bodies, gave rise to a separate art of surgery. The German name for its practitioner is still "wound-doctor" — *wundartz*. The reaction, however, of the organism against injurious influences of all kinds, is of more importance than the peculiar nature of those influences, — the study of *cure*, than that of cause. Hence, Surgery has become a branch of medicine ; and while there are general diseases called surgical, the local derangements that are external and make a breach in the bodily substance, have been spoken of by some surgical writers as *wounds*, though not *occasioned* directly by outward mechanical force. In this sense an ulcer will be a species of wound!

A WOUND is defined as a recent solution of the continuity of the animal structure, always *accompanied* with more or less violence done to the vitality of the parts.

Still the formal classification of wounds now to be considered, depends on the nature of their external causes.

The most general DIVISION is into simple and complicated.

A *simple wound* is a mere division of a particular part under the necessary conditions for healthy restoration. Any departure from this definition, either as to extent of injury or amount of vital reaction, constitutes a *complicated wound*.

Five or six *classes* of wounds require separate consideration:

— the incised; the punctured and penetrating (distinguished by their depth); the contused and lacerated (often connected); those occasioned in any way by explosion of gun-powder, and called for convenience "gun-shot wounds;" and lastly, those that, besides the mechanical injury, are the means of introducing into the body some poisonous substance.

1. An *Incised* Wound is, in plainer English, "a cut," — more precisely defined as a "solution of continuity by a sharp-cutting instrument." "A *simple* incised wound" is further distinguished as made "by a *clean*, sharp-cutting instrument," and in a *healthy* individual. A scrofulous or syphilitic taint makes it *complicated*, no less than a bruising in addition to the cutting. A simple incised wound is always one that heals, or might heal, by the first intention: whatever prevents it, is a complication.

2. A *Punctured* or *Penetrating* Wound is one made by a sharp-pointed instrument, thrust to a greater or less extent below the surface. A needle "punctures," a bayonet "penetrates," — perhaps into the great cavities, on which circumstance the distinction is, by some, made to depend. These wounds are not apt to heal by the first intention; hence more or less suppuration.

3. A *contused* wound is inflicted by some *blunt* instrument, that injures the parts underneath, without any breach of the surface.

4. A *Lacerated* Wound, on the other hand, is generally occasioned by a rough as well as blunt instrument, *tearing* the integuments.

5. *Gun-shot* Wounds require no definition, except to repeat that they are made to include all injuries occasioned by the explosive *force* of gun-powder. Scorching by powder belongs, of course, to the subject of "burns." Stones and other substances thrown by explosion, often strike with the force of balls; and balls often kill when it is very difficult to know whether they have struck or not. The cases called by the old surgeons "wind-contusions," are no longer spoken of, under that name; and most modern writers seem disposed to question the whole subject of "windage," — without, however, bringing forward any hypothesis more tenable. There is not any sufficient reason for doubting that the violent concussion of the atmosphere, by the passage of

a ball, may inflict severe injury. The stratum of air impelled before the ball, or contained between the ball and the skin, is doubtless sufficiently condensed to impart a decided impulse to the surface that is grazed.

The subject of *cannon* balls will be found more curious than practically important, except to surgeons in the navy or army.

The *rifle* or *pistol* balls, with which the surgeon is more likely to be concerned, generally make at once a punctured and a lacerated wound; and require particular attentions, which we shall point out when speaking of treatment.

6. *Poisoned* Wounds are inflicted by some instrument that inserts a virus into the wound it makes. The bite of a rabid dog, some kinds of serpents or other reptiles, and the stings of various insects are familiar examples. Commonly the wound itself is trifling: the poisoning of it makes all its importance.

The first striking circumstance attending most wounds is the *flow* of BLOOD. This, when not externally visible, is called simply "extravasation;" and is then often more dangerous than "the bleeding," so alarming to patient and friends. The amount of hemorrhage is no criterion of the importance of the wound, unless it is so great as to endanger life by its mere loss. It depends not only on the size and situation of the wound, but on its nature or mode of infliction, and sometimes on the constitution of the patient. A liability to profuse bleeding on slight injuries, constitutes the "hemorrhagic diathesis."* Gun-shot wounds often bleed but little; and the severest *contusions*, if merely such, none at all.

The PAIN is another circumstance that frequently deceives. It bears, in many cases, no relation to the danger, unless that of *inverse* proportion. It is only in the extreme degree, threatening tetanus, that it becomes itself a consideration of vital importance. Nature generally ceases her *alarm* of pain, where the injury is already irretrievable. The general rule is, that parts well supplied with nerves, are the most susceptible to painful irritation. The skin is a vast net-work of nerves, while many vital parts are nearly insensible in their normal condition. In amputation, it is

* See remarkable case under Ligating Carotid Artery, Part II.

the superficial cutting that hurts most. The back is much less sensitive than the front of the body, the feet than the hands. Wounds in the knee occasion little suffering in proportion to their danger.

The DANGER of wounds depends on many circumstances, besides the obvious ones of depth, direction, &c.; among which, those of the patient's constitution and habits are especially important. With the same kind of wound, in the same part, you must be careful not to give, as a matter of course, the same prognosis. Some persons have an irritable temperament, and their slightest injuries require great caution and attention.

AGE, also, makes a difference. *Young* persons suffer more, when wounded, from the first shock and reaction, than the *old;* but their danger is much less, and they recover more quickly.

TREATMENT OF WOUNDS

It is especially in connection with the first class of wounds, *the incised*, that the subject of *hemorrhage* requires our consideration. The first thing that arrests the surgeon's attention, and excites the alarm of the patient and spectators, is *the bleeding.* This should be stopped as soon as possible. We effect this object by the application of cold, — tourniquet, — compression, styptics, and the ligature. *Arnica, Diadema* and *Phosphorus*, internally and externally, have been strongly recommended.

If no large arteries or veins have been cut, a lint compress and bandage will be sufficient. If not, the *continued* application of cold *arnicated* water, or exposure to cold air, will arrest the hemorrhage, except when large arteries are injured. Should these means fail, styptics may be used, such as pulverized galls, lint steeped in the tincture of the same article, or in a solution of alum, or strong decoction of white oak bark, or (what is better than either of these articles) we would recommend to scrape off and use the fleshy side of a piece of spongy, oak-tanned sole-leather. This presents a very soft, unirritating surface, while it is strongly astringent, and may be strengthened in that respect, by wetting in any styptic liquid. It may be pressed firmly into the wound, so as to give the additional advantage of compression. If these means fail, or are not considered sufficient, recourse must be had to the ligature. Its use should, however, if possible, be avoided.

When an artery has to be tied, it should be done at the wound, if it can be reached by the forceps. When the end of the vessel has too far contracted, the arterial needle may be used, and a portion of the surrounding parts included in the ligature. If this measure does not answer the purpose, the wound will have to be dilated, or an incision must be made at some other point. Dilatation should, if possible, be avoided. It is frequently attended with serious consequences; and is altogether unnecessary in a simple incised wound. If a large artery is even *wounded*, it must be tied, otherwise there is danger of aneurism, and the surgeon must be careful not to mistake a wounded artery for a vein, and thus not employ the ligature.*

Dangerous hemorrhage from any large arteries must be first guarded against by the tourniquet, or some other mode of applying pressure. If the bleeding is from the lower extremity, compress the femoral artery, just below Poupart's ligament; if from the upper, restrain the brachial artery in like manner, somewhere above the middle of the arm, if the wound be below this point.

* It would seem entirely superfluous to give this caution against the commission of *so gross a mistake*, but an important case that fell into our hands, while practicing together in Cincinnati, would show it is not.

A boy, aged about 14, son of Mr. J. D——, Flour Merchant, while cutting a stick with a long-bladed knife, wounded the inside of the thigh, puncturing the femoral artery. The blood was of a *bright red color*, and came from the wound *in spirts*, and not in a *continuous stream* (*generally* regarded as pretty sure indications of an artery being wounded), and yet two prominent Allopathic physicians of the city (one of whom made considerable pretensions as a *surgeon*, and the other has since been made a *professor* in one of the colleges), *diagnosed* a wounded vein, bound it up, and notwithstanding it afterwards bled, upon three different occasions, the last one being five days after the accident, they persisted in the simple bandage. The result was an *aneurismal* tumor. This they endeavored to cure by compression, assisted in council by the most distinguished surgeon in the west; — result, for the *surgeons*, a most glorious exhibition of ignorance; for the boy, "a dozen deaths"— mortification of the foot, and "amputation at the thigh, with one chance out of ten, or death inevitable." We were called, and the boy is now (without amputation), attending the college at Delaware, Ohio. Had a ligature been applied at the time of the injury, the boy would have been saved over a *year* of severe suffering, and had an uninjured limb.

There is some *choice in ligatures.* The best is made of animal membrane. Whatever substance is used, it should not be so thin as to cut through the coats of the arteries, on being tightened. If silk or linen is used, one end should be left hanging out of the wound, the other cut off close to the knot. Learn to tie the "surgeon's knot" — one that won't slip. When ligatures of animal fibre are used, both ends may be cut off close, and the wound allowed to heal by the first intention; the ligature being absorbed after having done its office.

In *taking up arteries*, great care must be observed, never to tie up a *nerve* with them. Important nerves frequently accompany arteries, and are attached to the same sheath. In such cases they must be carefully separated. Neuritis, neuralgia or fatal tetanus, may be the consequence of neglecting this precaution.

After having suppressed hemorrhage, bring the parietes of the wound *together*, and secure them as nearly as possible in their original position, by adhesive strips, collodion,* or sutures. The edges of the wound, and the neighboring surface, should be made perfectly dry, or the adhesive plaster or collodion will not adhere. An excellent mode, when you wish to effect exact apposition, is that recommended by Mr. Skey: — "two narrow strips of adhesive plaster should be cut, and warmed, if necessary; each should be applied by one-half of its length to the opposite surfaces of the wound: when thoroughly adherent, the other ends of each strip should be drawn simultaneously but slowly across the fissure, and as soon as the edges are brought into perfect contact, and *even drawn closely and pressed together*, the plaster should be fixed on the skin beyond." Avoid sutures if possible. When they must be used, have very few, — two or three may often suffice in the largest wounds — relying on the other means in the intermediate spaces; though in some cases a larger number will be required.

After these things have been attended to, nothing more locally is necessary than simple dressings, such as will shield the wound from the action of the atmosphere. Cloths kept *constantly* wet with cold weak *arnicated* water (one teaspoonful of the Tincture

* See *Arnicated Collodion*, Appendix.

to a pint of water), are excellent. A dose of *Arnica*, 3*d*, should be given internally, and repeated once in five or six hours, if there are any indications of sympathetic fever. Should this rise high, *Aconite* should be alternated with the *Arnica* once in two or three hours.

If the patient has lost much blood, *China* should be alternated with the *Arnica* from the first.

If severe syncope, with deadly paleness of the face, is present, or the countenance assumes a livid appearance, and there is subsultus tendinum, *China* is indispensable. If the patient does not speedily rally, use a stimulant until reanimation takes place. The *China* should be continued until the patient has recovered from the effects consequent upon the hemorrhage.

Staphysagria has been recommended as a remedy for severe incised wounds.

Momordica Balsamina will, we think, be found valuable in incised as well as lacerated wounds.

Calendula Offic. is recommended by Dr. Thorer, of Gorblitz, as preferable to *Arnica*, in incised wounds. (See his remarks, after gun-shot wounds.) We have succeeded so well with *Arnica* in this class of wounds, that we have found it unnecessary to resort to any other agent.

Direct an unstimulating nourishing diet; food highly spiced or seasoned to be, of course, avoided under all circumstances.

PUNCTURED WOUNDS, when slight, do not commonly give the patient much inconvenience. This depends very much, however, on their situation and the constitution of the patient. The prick of a needle may bring on tetanus. Any puncture through tendons, nerves or fasciæ may produce excessive pain and distress. Matter may infiltrate into the cellular tissue, and occasion extensive inflammation. Swelling of the lymphatics is a frequent consequence of punctured wounds. When the injury is in the foot, for instance, we may have buboes; or swelling of the sub-maxillary glands, from a punctured finger. In such cases a red line may nearly always be traced from the point of injury along the course of the lymphatics to the glands.

A variety of punctured wounds has been distinguished, as the *penetrating*, the generic term being restricted to shallow punctures.

Penetrating wounds, then, are such as enter the great cavities, Their diagnosis and prognosis are very doubtful (as will be seen when we come to treat of particular wounds). A large instrument may pierce the cavities of the vital organs, and the patient recover: a very slight entrance in another direction may cause death. The result depends not only on the extent and position of the wound, but on the constitution and habits of the individual.

In treating these wounds, as all others, the bleeding, if any, must be first attended to. Next, the extraction of any foreign matter that may have been thrust and left in. When any is suspected, you must ascertain by probing. The finger is the best instrument, when the wound is large enough, and not too deep. If there be any poisonous substance introduced by the instrument or otherwise, such fluids should be injected as will, if possible, neutralize it, and cleanse out the wound. If you can apply pressure, so that the sides of the wound can be brought in apposition throughout its entire length, do so, and dress with *Calendula.* But if you cannot be certain of doing this, the *lips* of these wounds should be kept *apart*, as there is always a liability to their uniting, while suppuration is going on actively within. If the matter is not allowed a free exit, it will spread and aggravate the injury. There is always considerable danger of inflammation from this source. Hence a tent should be kept in the external orifice, and often removed; and the wound should be kept covered with cloths *constantly* wet with cool *Aqua Calendulæ.* If, however, much inflammation should rise, an emollient poultice, made of the *ulmus fulva* flour, wet with the *Aqua Calendulæ*, will be the best dressing for the wound.

As the *pus* that accumulates should be allowed to escape as quickly as possible, it is proper to renew your dressings two or three times a day, pressing gently on the part, but not so as to give pain. Never allow the outside to heal before the interior. Internally, give *Calendula* once in from three to six hours. We prefer drop doses. (For an interesting case of *penetrating* wounds treated with *Calendula*, see Wounds of the Abdomen.)

When the abdomen is penetrated, give *Aconite* immediately.

For punctured wounds caused by splinters, *Aconite*, *Cicuta*, *Nitric Acid*, *Silicea* or *Hepar* are recommended.

From credibly reported cures of punctured wounds by the first intention, with the application of the freshly-bruised root of the common table beet, we should suspect that beets possessed some specific virtues in the treatment of this class of wounds, and that they were worthy of experimentation.

LACERATED WOUNDS differ from incised, in being generally unaccompanied with hemorrhage. Large arteries may be ruptured without bleeding. The only danger in this respect is that of "secondary hemorrhage."

The *constitutional effects* are often very great. Chills, spasms, and tetanus frequently occur. There is great liability, also, to erysipelatous inflammation.

Diagnosis is not difficult, the condition of the injury being generally very apparent.

Prognosis is more questionable, depending much on the habits and constitution of the patient. On this account the practitioner should be guarded in his opinion.

There is often great injury done to parts not directly involved in the laceration, and much foreign matter adhering to the wound. If the parts are so lacerated as to produce any insensibility, or a partial loss of vitality, it may be necessary to use stimulants, such as brandy and warm water, for a short time.

Supposing, then, that there is no hemorrhage, the first thing to be attended to, is the removal of all foreign substances. But be very careful about too much handling. After *clearing* and *cleansing*, bring the torn parts as nearly together as possible, and *fix* them, either by adhesive straps or bandages, that the wound may heal by the first intention. As these wounds, under the ordinary treatment, heal by granulation, the surgeon is frequently careless about bringing the torn parts into entire apposition. Bransby Cooper says of contused and lacerated wounds: "they are not to be treated in the same manner as incised ones, for there are no hopes of union by adhesion, until the injured parts have been removed, either by slough or disintegration." We would, therefore, caution the Homeopath particularly on this point, as many badly lacerated wounds would heal by the first intention, even under the cold water dressings, if the parts were brought and confined in complete juxta-position, and kept at rest;

much more when dressed with *Aqua Calendulæ.* The dressing of these wounds, as well as all others, should be done as *expeditiously* as will admit of being *thorough.* They should be frequently changed, and this should be done with great *carefulness*, lest you tear the imperfect adhesion that may have formed, and prevent healing by the first intention. The violent manner in which some surgeons remove "dressings," would indicate either a want of sympathy for the feelings and disregard for the speedy recovery of the patient, or ignorance of the injury that such violence may do, and cannot be too strongly reprobated. Sometimes sutures are needed. It is better, however, to let the wound gape considerably, than to cause much irritation by them.

After arranging the wound, one of the best local applications for this class of wounds, in all cases where the surgeon is called immediately upon the occurrence of the accident, is cloths or lint kept constantly wet with *aqua Calendulæ.** If there is, however, a great deal of *irritability* present, before it is dressed, apply an emollient poultice of the flour of the *ulmus ful.* and *Aqua Calendulæ.*

In treating lacerated wounds, it is certainly more desirable to heal them by the first intention, if possible; if not, to so control the morbid action, that healthy granulations shall form, and cicatrization take place, with but slight suppuration. No one will question the importance of accomplishing these results; although those only who have witnessed the frightful sloughs, excessive exhaustion, and almost entire extinction of the vital powers, that sometimes result, under the ordinary treatment, from these and contused wounds, even in healthy subjects, can fully realize it, or the blessing that would be conferred upon mankind by those who should give the surgeon the knowledge of a remedy exerting a

* The preparation of *Calendula* we have used is prepared differently from that of Dr. Thorer; about one-third alcohol, two-thirds rain water, poured over the flowers, and permitted to stand till medicated; diluted with water, when used, in an inverse proportion to the extent of the injury. This dilution we have called *aqua calendulæ;* whether it is equal to the *aqua calendulæ.* of Dr. Thorer, as a dressing to wounds, we leave others to determine. Internally, we have generally given drop doses of the above preparation, or put a few drops in water, and given in teaspoonful doses.

specific action in their accomplishment. No school but our own propose any such remedial agent — the language of a distinguished Allopathic surgeon has been already quoted — the Eclectic Surgery says, "these wounds must heal by granulation."

Calendula Offic., both by its provings and clinical use, is clearly shown to exert a preventative and controlling influence over the suppurative process, and should consequently be given *internally*, as well as applied locally, in all lacerated wounds. Dr. Thorer employed it only locally. (For cases, see his remarks, after gun-shot wounds.)

The *Momordica Balsamina*, Balsam Apple, employed as a dilute tincture, for lacerated wounds, may yet rival the *Calendula.* Mr. J. J——, bricklayer, had one of his fingers crushed, and the nail torn entirely off; he immediately replaced it, and bound it up with Balsam of Fir. It soon became painful, with signs of incipient suppuration; he removed the dressings, applied a bandage, and kept it wet constantly with a diluted tincture of the *Momordica Bal.* Inflammation left, and the nail firmly united, without suppuration.

Should there be much contusion with the laceration, *Arnica Mon.* should be alternated with the *Calendula*, and if considerable irritative fever should arise, an occasional dose of *Aconite* should be exhibited.

When tendons or ligaments are injured, *Rhus. Tox.* should be alternated with *Calendula*, except where the tarsal or carpal joints are involved, when *Ruta* should be preferred. (For those cases where there is copious suppuration or gangrene, see CONTUSED WOUNDS. For tetanic symptoms, see TETANUS.)

Lacerated wounds, occurring in compound fractures or compound dislocations, are very frequently connected with *incised* ones, by our Allopathic friends. Their ignorance of specific means to control the disastrous inflammation, so likely to arise, if at all excusable, is an excuse for their too frequent resort to amputation. As Homeopaths are better informed (at least upon this point), we hope they will have a higher opinion of the integrity of the human form — a firmer reliance on the curative resources of nature, especially when aided by specific medication, and be chary of the use of the knife. We are heartily glad to hear one of the latest Allopathic writers on the other side of the great water, teach upon this point a course so opposed to the bloody path of some of his distinguished brethren out our way. We hope his teachings may soon reach their ears, and himself not only trust more to nature, but aid it by *specific* medication.

After reducing the dislocation, or adjusting the fracture, and applying the splints and bandages, so that the wound may be dressed, treat as in other lacerated wounds. Those occurring in compound dislocation require especially *Rhus. Tox.*, as the ligaments are ruptured, and it has a specific relation to their injury.

Amputation is only indispensable in lacerated wounds upon healthy subjects, when, after attending to the limb, its temperature continues to become lower, and the sensibility to lessen, showing that circulation and innervation are both cut off, and that there is no hope of restoration. (See AMPUTATION.)

If, however, the patient's arm or leg is of no consequence, amputation may be resorted to in other cases. An incised wound heals more quickly, and the treatment requires less skill than a lacerated one. (For an interesting case, see FRACTURE OF THE HUMERUS.)

A VERY IMPORTANT POINT, not to be lost sight of in the treatment of lacerated, as also contused wounds, is the necessity of guarding against *secondary hemorrhage.* Although the wound may be at considerable distance from any large arteries, and there may have been very little bleeding in the first instance, yet we never know to what extent the injury may have gone. Deep-seated arteries may inflame, sloughs take place, and dangerous hemorrhage set in, weeks after the original injury.

CONTUSED WOUNDS. — These wounds are more tedious than any other. In many cases there is great suffering, though but little injury. There may, on the other hand, be no pain at all when the case is serious : in fact, the more extensive and severe the contusion, the less the pain ; when the vitality of the part is completely destroyed it must slough.

If there be extensive *extravasation* of blood, forming a tumor, it may be let out by *puncture.* This, however, if done at all, should either be done early, or after the subsidence of inflammation. If neglected till severe inflammation has set in, your new punctured wound will do more harm than the blood. It will occasion the occurrence of gangrene; or it may itself be the cause of tetanus.

The danger is of extensive inflammation, with mortification, sloughing, hectic fever, &c.

The great aim in treatment is to prevent these results. The usual means, in the old school, in milder cases, are to apply cold, to prevent inflammation, but in all severe ones, warmth, as emollient poultices, to facilitate suppuration or sloughing. In some cases local depletion is recommended, and, if need be, the usual antiphlogistics.

While we can realize all, and even more advantage from local treatment, we are not under the necessity of endeavoring to remove the effects of contusion by indirect means: deranging still more the action of organs already impaired by the shock to the nervous system. We have remedies, *Arnica Montana* in particular, that we can apply locally as well as give internally, that act directly in removing the effects of the shock, prevent, in a great measure, the sympathy of the general system with the local irritation: restore tone to the injured tissues and vessels, capacitating them for the discharge of their former duties: excite the absorbents to the removal of any extravasated fluid, thus preventing inflammation, suppuration, and all the injurious consequences of contusions. We do not claim that they will reanimate parts where vitality is destroyed, or prevent the injurious effects that follow contusions in persons of cachectic habits; but that they have a *specific* effect in removing and preventing the consequences resulting from contusions, as is shown by the provings upon their healthy and extensive clinical use, and that they will yield superior results, in all cases, to the usual or any other remedial means, prescribed upon a different principle. In all cases of contused wounds, therefore, as soon as possible give *Arnica Montana* internally, and repeat, according to circumstances, in from three to six hours, until all danger is obviated. *Locally*, apply cloths, or rather a moderately tight bandage, and keep it *constantly* wet with *Arnicated water*;* the temperature of this is to be determined by

* When there is much extravasation of blood, except in persons of an irritable habit, or who have very irritable skins, and are liable to be affected with erysipe-

the severity of the injury; if not very severe, it should be cool, but if the vitality of the part is much impaired, it should be tepid.

The difference between *Arnica Mon.* and *Calendulæ* is that the former is adapted to wounds *without* laceration — the latter to open wounds.

Hypericum perforatum (St. John's Wort) has been used (though not yet thoroughly proven), by some eminent practitioners as a substitute for *Arnica*, with excellent effect.

Cynoglossum Officinale (Hound's Tongue, not regularly proven) appears to resemble Arnica in its efficacy in removing the effects of contusions.

Rhus. Tox. is particularly beneficial when the joints, synovial membranes, or tendons are injured by contusion.

Silicea, given daily, or at intervals of four to eight days, in susceptible habits, is a most important and eminently successful remedy, when, from contusion, any of the *bursæ mucosæ* is inflamed, causing swelling, with considerable pain, and inflexibility of the joint (as in house-maid's knee, bunion, &c).

Ruta is serviceable when the periosteum or tarsal and carpal joints are injured.

Arnica is the best remedy for recent contusions of glandular organs, but when induration has taken place, Conium is more efficacious.

Aconite is required, should much symptomatic fever be present or arise, as also in wounds of the eye, for which it is the specific. We prefer to alternate it with the Arnica.

When we are called too late, or are unable to prevent suppuration, and an abscess is about to form, our aim should be to cause it to point as soon as possible. (See SUPPURATION, p. 29.) Warm emollient poultices should then be applied, as they assist in forwarding the suppurative process; we prefer one made of the fine flour of the Ulmus Fulva, with a small portion of ground flaxseed. This forms a complete soothing shield from the action of the atmosphere, and retains its warmth and moisture for some

las, more of the *Arnica Tr.* should be put in the water. *Arnicated* water should be discontinued whenever it causes a decided aggravation of the pains, redness, and inflammation in the injured part, and a lotion of another medicament be employed, such as *Hypericum*, *Cynoglossum*, *Heleanthus*, *&c.*

considerable time. Bread and milk, frequently recommended, soon dries, and crumbles, and the crumbs become an irritant to any inflamed surface, especially to an open wound. As a good poultice is a very important thing, when needed, we will give directions for making what we think a good one: Take of the Ulmus Fulva flour three-fourths, of ground flaxseed one-fourth, knead into a moderately stiff poultice, with hot milk and water; let the vessel in which it is mixed stand in hot water for half an hour — this will prevent any lumps — spread this upon a cloth, about half an inch thick; then keep adding a small portion of water at a time, to the face of the poultice, and working it in, until the surface is quite soft. (A little sweet, or *Arnica* oil may, at pleasure, be spread over the face of the poultice.) This furnishes a soft, soothing application, in contact with the inflamed surface, while the outer portion, being firm, prevents the poultice from slipping down to the most dependent part, as it will do, if it is all made thin, often leaving the most important part exposed, or else so thinly covered that it soon becomes dry. It also remains of a more uniform thickness, and thus we have a more even temperature and moisture and a complete shield from the action of the air — important considerations.

Some might object, that it would be too heavy. A proper position and support to the affected part will obviate any difficulty upon that point. We prefer to apply them *directly* to the inflamed surface, except we have a fine piece of open lace to spread over them. No difficulty need be apprehended about getting them off, if they are not left on too long. The gentlest way to remove poultices or adhesive plasters, is to loosen one edge, then evert it, and draw carefully backwards, instead of raising it perpendicularly. These are small matters, but the patient will *feel* their importance. When it is not necessary to remove these poultices, on account of suppuration, they may be kept fresh for some time, by occasionally pouring a little fluid under one edge, so that it can permeate between them and the inflamed surface.

We do not, however, depend upon the local means, to forward the suppurative process. Again, the *specific* method comes to our aid with remedial agents; having a direct influence in hastening the formation and expulsion of healthy pus. As soon as it is evident that an abscess is about to form, after employing *Aconite*, *Chamomile*, *Belladonna*, *Bryonia*, or *Ledum*, if necessary, for the removal of severe constitutional disturbance, give, to facilitate the *pointing of the abscess*, *Hepar. Sul.*, in repeated doses, in alternation with *Silicea;* when, however, a considerable portion of the skin has been much distended, by the large accumulation of pus, and is of deep red or bluish appearance, *Lachesis* is to be preferred; when there is induration, *Mercurius*, *Carbo. Ac.*, or *Baryta*, is useful — *Baryta*, when there is considerable surrounding swelling, as well as induration, even after the opening of the abscess. If there are violent *burning pains*, or chills, fever, clammy sweats, *restlessness*, and *great prostration*, *Arsenicum* is the proper remedy; it will often so ameliorate the symptoms, and sustain the patient, as to render severe cases comparatively mild.

After the opening of the abscess, if the matter is unhealthy and offensive, *Arsenicum* will generally remove these symptoms, even when gangrene is strongly threatened.

Asafœtida is indicated, when the matter is *thin* and *discolored*, and the parts affected *highly irritable.*

Belladonna, when the pains are burning, pressing, and tearing, with a discharge of *curdled*, *flaky* matter.

Calcarea, when the pain and swelling have much diminished, and the pus becomes thicker and whiter than at first.

Calendula, when the suppuration has a tendency to become too profuse, and the granulations are slow in forming.

China, for the *exhaustion* consequent upon a copious discharge of pus; this may be advantageously alternated with *Calendula* or *Arsenicum.*

Mezereum, in cases affecting fibrous and tendinous structures, or in those laboring under mercurial poison, and when there are stinging and throbbing pains in the ulcer and its border.

Pulsatilla, when the abscess *bleeds easily*, or with severe *itching* and stinging pains, particularly when the *veins are varicose.*

Rhus. Tox. is most useful in suppuration of the glands, particularly the axillary and *parotid*, with a discharge of *ichorous matter*. (See also ULCERS, TUMORS, SCROFULA, HIP DISEASE, PSOAS ABSCESS.)

Generally, after the opening of an abscess, if a few doses of *Mercurius* be given, and followed by *Hepar. Sul.* and *Silicea*, or *Calc.* and *Phosphorus*, or *Calendula*, healthy granulations will form, and the abscess heal.

An important point, especially in the treatment of acute abscesses, is to prevent the air from entering their cavities. Therefore, shield them with the Elm poultice; and if healthy granulations are slow in forming, syringe them out once or twice a day, with *aqua Calendulæ*, or a dilution of such other remedy, as the totality of the symptoms may indicate, as a constitutional remedy.

As to the *opening of acute abscesses*, Homeopathic writers have recommended to abstain *entirely* from the use of the lancet, and to rely upon the evacuation of the matter by appropriate medicines, "except when the pus, by its extensive diffusion or pressure (especially when seated under ligamentous or tendinous expansions), is liable to injure important parts: or when, from its situation, there is reason to apprehend its discharge into any of the cavities of the body." The reason assigned is, that "the subsequent treatment is generally more easily conducted, and the healing of the cavity more speedily effected, when the matter has been evacuated by the aid of appropriate medicine, instead of the lancet." This we regard as an assertion only partially true; while the direction is incomplete, and fallacious, and liable to do injury. It is an extreme, begotten by the formerly too prevalent practice of plunging a lancet into everything which simulated the appearance of an abscess.

There is a period when the suppurative process is being set up — a period when that is fully completed, and then follows the ulcerative (not the suppurative) stage, when the cellular tissue is being destroyed, for the evacuation of the pus. That any advantage can be derived from the presence of pus, a moment after the completion of the suppurative process, we cannot imagine, and that this process is never complete until the completion of the ulcerative stage, we think none will contend. Once set up, suppuration continues, and when the opening is effected slowly, more or less pus is absorbed, and this tends to produce constitutional irritation. It also, by its pressure upon the surrounding parts, as well as the cutaneous surface, tends to cause absorption of the granulations, and thus to cause the abscess to degenerate into an ulcer. Its evil effects are more evident upon the cachectic or debilitated.

That our remedies exert a most salutary influence in maturing the suppurative process, and completing the absorption necessary for the exit of the pus at about the same time, as well as warding off constitutional irritation, we are happy to admit; but not that they consummate the two at the same moment. We would therefore recommend, as soon as it is *evident* the suppurative process is matured, *i. e.*, the abscess has pointed, or there is the least symptom of constitutional disturbance from the absorption of pus (especially in the debilitated), that the abscess should be opened with the lancet, so as to allow a free exit to the pus. In the case of the healthy, where no unpleasant symptoms have made their appearance, we can if we choose, with safety, permit the abscess to open of itself. After opening, apply, as before directed, the Ulmus poultice, to prevent the entrance of air and to absorb the pus as fast as it is discharged. If the aperture seems disposed to close, keep a small tent in it to prevent this from taking place. The incision should, if possible, be made at the most dependent portion of the abscess.

The diet should be regulated by the degree of inflammation present, and the constitutional vigor of the patient. In inflammation from plethora, it should be abstemious and antiphlogistic; but in the inflammation of debility, as also during the suppurative stage, it should be nutritious.

We cannot, however, in lacerated or contused wounds, always have so favorable a termination even as suppuration.

Mortification will sometimes occur, notwithstanding the efforts of the best surgeons. Sometimes the vitality of the part is entirely destroyed by the extent of the injury; at other times, in consequence of constitutional debility, the inflammation cannot be controlled. Whatever the remote cause of mortification may be, the immediate one is interruption of the circulation. Thus, in the aged, we frequently have *gangræna senilis* (dry gangrene), from an abnormal deposition of the phosphate of lime in the coats of the larger arteries. *Gangrene*, as has been before stated, is the *dying*, or state of the part preceding the actual death, *mortification*. The latter condition is also designated by the term *sphacelus*.

If symptoms of gangrene arise, and we cannot remove them, mortification is the result, of which the only favorable termination is *limitation;* which is known by the formation of what is called the *line of demarcation*. This is a white line, constituting the structures between the dead and the living portions; on the outside of it, coagulable lymph is thrown out by the parts in a state of vitality, and granulations are being formed; while on the inside there is naught but death and desolation; the parts have lost their natural temperature and sensibility, serum transudes, and the blood is extravasated. It is in an intermediate state, between life and death, and, within its limits, all the tissues ulcerate, except the bones and blood-vessels; the latter usually fill with coagulated blood, as high up as where the first branch is given off; this excites an inflammatory action, coagulable lymph is thrown out, the vessel closed, and hemorrhage is prevented. Should the artery be not thus closed, hemorrhage will occur on its division.

This is always an unfavorable indication. The character of the granulations will materially aid us in forming our prognosis, by interpreting the constitutional symptoms.

Formerly it was thought expedient to amputate before this line of demarcation was formed; but as the stump generally became gangrenous, in those patients whose constitutional powers were unable to limit the gangrene, the best surgeons now recommend to *always* wait until it is formed. What necessity is there, then, of amputation? Might not the additional shock and irritation to the nervous system, consequent on amputation, or the depressing influence of the anæsthetic agents, if they are used, and the loss of blood, so impair the vital powers as to cause, in some instances, the stump to become gangrenous and the case to terminate fatally, that would have recovered if nature's restorative process had been aided, and not interfered with?

The approach of *gangrene* is indicated by an increase of the sensibility and pain in the inflamed part; the latter is sometimes of a pungent, burning character; the inflammatory tint becomes of a darker color. (If it is a suppurating wound, the pus changes to a sanious or ichorous character, and the granulations begin to look darker, and finally to ulcerate.) The skin is dry, with thirst, but inability to take large draughts of water; pulse quick and irregular; small vesicles filled with serum and red particles of blood, make their appearance, frequently at some distance from the wound. Soon, however, the blood ceases to circulate and coagulates; the color of the inflamed part consequently becomes of deep purple or livid hue; the temperature and sensibility, which was before augmented, rapidly diminishes; the pain is no longer located in the affected part, but in the surrounding tissues—the parts are in a state of *gangrene.*

If not arrested at this stage the result is mortification or sphacelus. The affected part becomes of a dirty brown or black color, sometimes grey or greenish; the vesicles become larger and more numerous; the portion begins to decompose, and we have that peculiarly offensive, cadaverous odor, pathognomic of mortification. If not *limited,* the pulse becomes more feeble, and finally sinks; the skin, at first hot and dry, is frequently cold, and covered with a clammy sweat; the tongue and teeth become coated with sordes; the breath frequently fetid; the countenance cadaverous; the feces sometimes involuntary. Hiccough, low delirium, coma, and death, close the scene.

Cinchona should be given, as soon as any symptoms of gangrene are noticed in wounded parts, before the skin has begun to turn black; but if not followed by a speedy improvement, it should be alternated with *Arsenicum.* If these have the desired effect in arresting the gangrene, the circulation will become more active around the circumference of the diseased part; the coagulated blood gradually separates and passes into the circulation; the effused fluids are removed, more or less rapidly, by absorption, and the natural temperature and sensibility are restored. But if not, and the skin begins to assume a dark, livid appearance, *Lachesis* should be alternated with *Arsenicum,* once in two or four hours, which will generally cause a favorable termination. Should these fail, resort may be had to *Carbo. Veg., Crotalus, Ophiotox, Secale Cor., Viper. Redi.,* or *Vipera Torva.* We would recommend, also, *Sulphureted Hydrogen.* It is well known that the bites of some serpents are peculiarly liable to become gangrenous, and also, that the *Sulphureted Hydrogen* evolved in the decomposition of a slough seems to be absorbed, enter into the circulation, and frequently, in itself, to produce *gangrene*. *Secale Cor.* is particularly beneficial in dry gangrene (*Gangræna Senilis*), and will, we well know, cause it.

Besides the administrations of the appropriate medicines, it is very important to sustain the constitutional powers; to keep the limb of a uniform, natural temperature until the line of demarcation has formed. Then, to facilitate the separation of the slough, correct the fetor, and prevent the absorption of the putrid fluids.

The diet should, therefore, in the incipient as well as the advanced stages, be *nutritious* (not stimulating); roast beef, egg-nog, &c. When the digestive organs have been disposed to receive but little solid food, we have derived great benefit from the white of eggs beat up until they are light, but not frothy, mixed with cold water, and sweetened with loaf sugar, to suit the taste of the patient. This may be used as a common drink, is universally acceptable, and will not soon cloy the appetite.

The natural temperature, also, may be best maintained, by wrapping the entire limb in "carded wool," as soon as any symptoms of gangrene are noticed. This casing should be continued until the gangrenous symptoms have been removed, or a well-defined line of demarcation is formed. In contused wounds, no other application may be necessary to the injured part; though sometimes benefit may be derived from a poultice made of the green root of the *Altheæ Officinalis*, bruised, and boiled in milk, which has acquired considerable reputation as a preventative of gangrene.

In suppurating wounds, lint, saturated with a dilute preparation of the appropriate medicament, should be applied to the wound, or such as are mildly stimulating in their character. The pus should be carefully removed. (See Ulcers.)

When, however, mortification has taken place, and the line of demarcation has formed, the local applications should be such as to facilitate the separation of the slough, and correct the fetor. The putrid fluids of mortified parts should be carefully removed, as fast as formed, otherwise, their absorption will produce very deleterious effects. Poultices of the Ulmus Fulva, frequently changed, will best accomplish the latter object, particularly where there is much fluid. Pulverized Carbo. may sometimes be incorporated with them, and will at least, absorb a large portion of the Sulphureted Hydrogen that is evolved.

Where *Arsenicum* is indicated, by the totality of the symptoms, a saturated solution of the same should be frequently applied. (See cases under CARBUNCLE, and CANCER OF THE LIP.)

We have also applied in some cases, with advantage, the *Sesqui-Carbonate of Potash*, and the *Sulphate of Zinc*, in solution or powder, and pyroligneous acid diluted. The *Sesqui-Carbonate* has the peculiar power of dissolving dead portions of tissue or bone, while it simply stimulates to healthy action the living portions. The *Sulphate of Zinc* will dissolve the slough, and correct the fetor, but will also destroy the healthy tissue. Prof. Newton (in vol. i. of the Eclectic Medical Journal), speaks highly of it, as efficacious, prompt, and unattended with any danger to the patient. The pyroligneous acid is excellent to correct the fetor.

GUN-SHOT WOUNDS.—The orifice of these wounds is no guide to the *course* of the *ball*. For example; a bullet may strike the middle of the forehead, and emerge from the occiput, just as if it had passed through the center of the brain, yet the patient be almost uninjured, the ball having simply whirled round the skull under the integuments. One of the authors witnessed a still more remarkable case, where the ball seemed to enter the thorax near the sternum and fifth rib, and passed out behind at the junction of the spine and the rib, along which it had slid, doing no material damage. The direction of the shot does not even require bone to change it: cartilage, intermuscular ligament, and even fasciæ, have been found sufficient.

The orifice which the ball makes in entering, is always much smaller than that of its emergence. The latter has ragged, everted edges; and the parts contiguous to its course are always more or less contused or lacerated. When bones are broken, the fractures are generally comminuted. Injury done to nerves is apt to occasion tetanus, sometimes even after the wound has healed. Primary hemorrhage is rare; the secondary more dangerous. *Diagnosis* and *prognosis* must therefore be regarded as difficult. An individual in Erie county, of this State, had a rifle ball pass directly through the belly, from side to side, yet scarcely endured a minute's suffering, and in three weeks was perfectly well. The ball entering just below the false ribs, must have passed along in front of the colon, so as to avoid both the intestines and any considerable blood-vessel. In other cases, a small squirrel shot, entering the abdomen, has caused speedy death.

The *treatment* depends much, of course, on the site and direction of the wound. The union, it should be noticed, must always take place by *granulation*. In your examination, use your finger as far as possible. It is the best of probes, causing less pain and injury than any other, and giving the most reliable information. Remove the ball, shot, clothes, or any other substance it may have introduced. If, however, the ball be so situated as to be got hold of with difficulty, and do not interfere with recovery, let it alone. Many persons carry shot in their flesh without any inconvenience. If it is near the surface, and cannot be removed, *via* the wound, it is better to cut through to it, than to dilate the original wound. After cleansing, proceed as with a punctured wound. We may here mention an accident that occurs occasionally in this class of wounds. A nerve of considerable size may be inclosed in the cicatrix, and give rise to neuralgic or tetanic affections. In such an event the cicatrix must be excised, and a new one allowed to form.

Dr. Thorer, of Görlitz, strongly recommends *Calendula Officinalis*, in preference to *Arnica*, in wounds of every description, but especially incised, punctured, or lacerated wounds, and those with considerable loss of substance. The sphere of the latter, as a traumatic remedy, he confines to contusions, sprains, bruises without abrasion of the surface, or lacerations of the soft parts. Dr. Thorer speaks, moreover, in favorable terms, of the effect which Calendula appears to exercise over the process of granulation and cicatrization. Very frequently, even after amputations, the cure, under the employment of this remedy, was effected by the first intention, and in almost every instance where it was impossible to avoid suppuration, the extent to which it occurred was comparatively insignificant. He employed two different preparations of this remedy as lotions; the one to which he gave the name of *Aqua Calendulæ Officinalis*, he prepared as follows: "I filled one-third of a clean bottle with the petals or leaves of the flowers, the remaining two-thirds with pure spring water, corked it well and exposed it for two or three days to the warm rays of the sun. The water was by this process, rendered aromatic, and having been poured off from the leaves, it was put into a bottle well sealed up like wine bottles; then immediately placed in the low temperature of the cellar. Whilst the bottle, with the mixture of the leaves and water, is exposed to the higher temperature of the sun, it should be narrowly watched, and the moment that any signs of incipient fermentation make their appearance, measures must be taken to arrest it. The second preparation was a *Spiritus Calendulæ*, for which I employed the same quantity of leaves of the flowers, as in the preceding instance, and pure rectified spirits of wine in place of the water. I employed the latter preparation only on one occasion, very much diluted, in order that the spirit of wine might not exercise a detrimental influence on the injured parts. Its effect was equally beneficial." We give the following cases, as instances in which Dr. Thorer applied *Calendula* as a lotio vulneraria Homeopathica, with success:

1. R. K—— had the under lip much bruised and *lacerated* from the kick of a horse. The lips of the wound were brought together, and retained there by means of a strip of adhesive plaster; in addition to this the patient was furnished with a phial containing *Aqua Calendulæ*, and desired to keep the wound covered with a compress saturated with the lotion. Already, after an interval of three days, healthy cicatrization began to set in, without suppuration. The process of healing went on quickly and uninterruptedly, per primam intentionem, and the scar of the divided lip is now scarcely perceptible.

2. M. A—— had the misfortune to fall down a flight of stairs, and in addition to several contusions on the chest, two extensive wounds were inflicted, one on the forehead and the other along the ridge and at the point of the nose, producing great disfiguration. In this case also, the healing process proceeded most

rapidly and favorably, without suppuration and without leaving any disfigurement, such as a wound of so severe a character might reasonably have led me to anticipate.

3. This case was of infinitely greater importance than the above. Flöder, a boy 16 years of age, while engaged at his occupation in a cloth manufactory, had the misfortune to become entangled in the machinery, in consequence of which the following injuries were sustained: 1, compound fracture of the left arm, the sharp extremities of the broken bone protruding through the integuments; 2, a deep wound at the bend of the elbow; 3, the bones of the left forearm completely stripped of their muscles, and laid bare to the extent of six inches; 4, the hand torn off, being only kept adhering to the stump by a slip of skin; 5, the skin, and portions of the muscles of the exterior surface of the right leg were torn off, leaving a large and deep wound extending down to the bone; 6, face and chest severely contused and exhibiting many small flesh wounds. The unfortunate patient was reduced to a state of extreme exhaustion by loss of blood and excessive suffering; amputation of the left upper arm was, nevertheless, rendered imperative, and was accordingly performed. Compresses, saturated with *Aqua Calendulæ*, were applied to the exposed lacerated muscles of the right leg, up to the period of recovery of the patient, and it was striking to observe how dry, and without suppuration, incarnation proceeded in the parts to which the *Calendula* was applied, in comparison with the extensive suppuration, and slow curative process, which took place in the stump of the amputated arm, treated according to the ordinary surgical rules. I was not at this time aware of the peculiar properties of *Calendula;* but, in consequence of the striking beneficial effects which it produced on the injured lower extremity of the patient, I subsequently applied it to the wound of the stump, and was gratified by the peculiarly favorable granulations which soon ensued there likewise. All the wounds henceforward filled up and healed in so satisfactory a manner, that it was scarcely possible to conceive that they could have been of so serious a character, and attended with so much loss of substance, as they in reality were. The patient was restored to perfect health, and I have no hesitation in attributing his recovery to the very favorable process

of granulation and cicatrization which took place under the employment of the *Aqua Calendulæ*.

4. C. in G. lost his footing, when in his mill, and had the third phalanx of the left index-finger, the second and third phalanx of the ring-finger, and the flesh of the middle finger torn off. A small portion of the bone of the second phalanx of the ring-finger remained, but was entirely bared and exposed; the patient was desirous that this remnant of bone should be removed. I refrained from doing so, however, in the hope that it might become covered by means of favorable granulation. And so the result proved. After the hemorrhage had been arrested, by the application of cold water dressings, *Aqua Calendulæ* was employed, two days from the occurrence of the accident; the wounds thereupon assumed a drier aspect, incarnation went on uninterruptedly, and a perfect cure was rapidly accomplished. On the ring-finger alone, a very minute exfoliation came off from the exposed bone. Mr. Surgeon Schulze, to whom I had recommended the *Calendula* as a remedy in wounds, and who had employed it extensively, with much satisfaction to himself, for the past two years, recently favored me with the following cases, amongst others, in which he had used it with success:

5. A laborer received a comminuted fracture of the right index-finger, while engaged in lifting a heavy stone. The splintered and more or less loose pieces of bone were removed, and the *Aqua Calendulæ* applied as a lotion. The cure followed rapidly, and without any particular suppuration.

6. A miller's apprentice had two of his fingers so completely crushed, that, as in the foregoing case, it was necessary to remove the shattered particles of bone; the Calendula effected an equally rapid cure, with a very trivial degree of suppuration.

7. In a case of complicated fracture of the leg, with a wound nine inches in length, from which the tibia was laid bare, Arnica, largely diluted, was employed for a few days, in consequence of the accompanying extensive suggillation. The *Calendula* was then brought into requisition, and produced a speedy cure, without extensive suppuration.

I could quote a multitude of other cases, in which the *Calendula* alone was employed, and with singularly successful and satisfactory results; but I shall content myself with adding, that in all instances where there is extensive loss of substance, and where it is found impracticable to bring, and retain the lips of the wound together by means of adhesive plaster, &c., I consider the *Calendula* to be the best aqua vulneria. It has long been occasionally employed by the lower orders, in form of an ointment, made of fresh butter mixed up with the ground or powdered leaves of the flower, and sometimes, though rarely, in the form of infusion, and taken internally. Its *homeopathicity* in wounds, as well as several other affections, has, moreover, been demonstrated and confirmed by the provings of Dr. Franz."

POISONED WOUNDS.

Of these the most familiar are the bites and stings of insects and reptiles.

The sting of a *wasp* or *bee*, though very painful, is generally attended with no serious consequence. Yet in some individuals it occasionally produces alarming, and even fatal results. We have for some years past been in the habit of making one and only one prescription. If this prove as successful in other hands as it has in ours, no one need ever suffer more than a few minutes. Cut in two a *raw onion*, and apply a section to the part affected. It has in every case relieved the pain, and in most, prevented or reduced the inflammation. Dr. Hill applied this simple remedy, in one case, where the nose had been stung three days before. The countenance was completely disfigured by the swelling; eyes closed, and lips and tongue so much envolved, that the individual could not articulate. There was violent sympathetic fever, with pain in the head, amounting almost to delirium. All these severe symptoms subsided in a few hours, and the tumefaction went down in the course of twenty-four. In fact, the pain was relieved in a few moments. The onion is to be changed every fifteen or twenty minutes.

Inasmuch as this convenient application has proved a specific in so many cases, we have not found it necessary to try other means. Is not the *onion* the antidote to *Apis Mellifica?* Dr. Pulte recommends to cover the injured part immediately with damp earth, and keep it wet with arnicated water. Internally,

Arnica and Camphor every three or four hours. Irritation from the bite of gnats, musquitoes, &c., we have relieved by directing the patient to chew the common plaintain leaf, and rub the spittle on the bite.

We will mention the poison of the *scorpion*, on account of the very simple *isopathic remedy* which, we are informed, both prevents and cures. The common people in Italy, who are much exposed, rely with perfect confidence on the application of a little olive oil, from a bottle they carry about with them, and in which a scorpion is kept. On the coast of Barbary, where many persons go nearly naked, and sleep in the open air on the sand, they are in the habit of anointing the whole body with such a preparation of *scorpio;* after which the live ones run over them without stinging. Of the immunity enjoyed through this article, we are assured by eye-witnesses.

The only dangerously poisonous reptiles we have in this country, are the moccasin, copperhead, and rattle *snakes*. The effects of their bite are so much alike as not to require separate notice.

The person bitten is seldom at a loss about the cause of his sufferings. He feels a smarting pain at the wound, extending up the limb, which swells, and in the case of the rattlesnake, turns spotted. Nausea soon comes on, with dizziness. The swelling continues, extending to the other limbs, and sometimes over the whole body. One of the authors saw a case where the tension was so great, that the skin burst open in several places. The patient often becomes delirious, &c.

A course of *treatment* which has proved successful where we have known it to be tried, is to make the patient drink freely of a strong decoction, in milk, of common plantain and horehound, and apply a poultice of the same articles to the wound. Speedy and permanent relief follows. It is best, however, to continue the prescription, in smaller quantities, for several days, when a complete cure may be relied on. An old practitioner, Dr. Baldridge, states that he has succeeded by this means, in a great number of cases, with brute as well as human patients. We have other testimony to the same effect. The plantain, we think, is the remedial agent, and will be found to possess specific properties in antidoting the poison of serpents. The *Uvularia grandiflora,* prepared in the same way, is said to be equally efficacious. The successful administration of sweet oil and scorpion was mentioned when speaking of the scorpion. Would not Crotalus be equally beneficial? An unfortunately more accessible and popular remedy in many parts of this western country is *whisky*, *rum*, or *brandy*, applied externally and internally, *ad libitum*, or in quantities unlimited, and almost incredible. Of the success attending this course we have been assured by many professional as well as non-medical persons. The quantities stated to have been given to those who had been bitten, without producing intoxication, or leaving any bad effects, are almost incredible. Of course this cerebral insensibility to the article is an indispensable *condition* for its prescription; and people need not be made dead drunk for *fear* of being poisoned.

In India, where the poisonous Cobra de Capella abounds, the most successful treatment reported, is the immediate application of a tight ligature above the bitten part; the extraction of the poison by a cupping-glass, or by the patient himself, or some one else sucking the poison from the wound; the administration of large doses of Ammonia internally, and the thorough washing of the wound with a solution of the same.

In conclusion, with our present information, we would say, that we think the best and most successful treatment would be, immediate application of a tight ligature above the bite; excision of the wound, and the radiating heat — afterwards a poultice of plantain to the wound. Internally, a free use of the plaintain decoction or the spirits, whichever is the more convenient. After difficulties to be prescribed for by the totality of the symptoms. (See ULCERS.)

Dr. C. Hering, the best Homeopathic authority on this point, speaks as follows:

"*Envenomed Wounds.* — The best domestic remedy against the bites of *venomous serpents*, *mad dogs*, &c., is *radiating heat.* This should be done by the readiest means at hand, — a red-hot iron, or live coal, or even a lighted cigar, for instance, must be placed as near the wound as possible, without, however, burning the skin, or causing too sharp pain; but care must be taken to have another instrument ready in the fire, so as never to allow the heat to lose its intensity. It is essential also that the heat should not exercise its influence over too large a surface, but only on the wound, and the parts adjacent. If oil or grease can be easily procured, it may be applied round the wound, and this operation should be repeated as often as the skin becomes dry; *soap*, or even saliva may be employed when oil or grease cannot be obtained. Whatever is discharged in any way from the wound ought to be carefully removed. The application of burning heat should be continued in this manner, till the patient begins to shiver, and to stretch himself; if this takes place at the end of a few minutes, it will be better to keep up the action of the heat upon the wound for an hour, or until the affections produced by the venom are observed to diminish. Internal medicines must be judiciously administered at the same time. In the case of a BITE FROM A SERPENT, it will be advisable to take, from time to time, a gulp of *salt and water*, or a pinch of kitchen salt, or of *gunpowder*, or else some pieces of *garlic*.

"If, notwithstanding this, bad effects shew themselves, a spoonful of *brandy* or *wine*, administered every two or three minutes, will be the most suitable remedy, and this should be continued till the sufferings are relieved, and repeated as often as they are renewed. If the shooting pains are aggravated, and proceed from the wound toward the heart, and if the wound becomes bluish, marbled, or swollen, with vomiting, vertigo, and fainting, the best medicine is *Arsenicum*. It should be administered in a dose of three or four globules in a tablespoonful of water, and if the sufferings still continue, the dose should be repeated at the end of half an hour, but if, on the contrary, the state remains the same, it should not be repeated till the end of two or three hours. If there is an amelioration, a new aggravation must be waited for, and the dose ought not to be repeated before its appearance.

"In cases in which *Ars.* exercises no influence, though repeated several times, recourse must be had to *Bell. Sen.* also frequently proves efficacious.

"Against chronic affections, arising from the bite of a serpent, *Phos. Ac.*, and *Merc.* will generally be most beneficial. (For the bite of a mad dog, see HYDROPHOBIA.)

"For wounds that are envenomed by the introduction of animal substances in a state of putrefaction, or of pus from the ulcer of a diseased man, or animal, *Ars.* is generally the best medicine.

"Lastly, as a *preventative* against bad effects, when obliged to touch morbid animal substances, envenomed wounds, or ulcers of men and animals, under the influence of contagious diseases, the best method that can be pursued is the application of *dry burning heat at a distance.* To effect this purpose, it will be sufficient to expose the hands for five or ten minutes to the greatest heat that can be borne, and after this it will be proper to wash them with soap. The use of of Chlorine and Muriatic Acid in similar cases is well known."

Of the efficacy of *radiating heat* we cannot speak from our experience, never having used it but in one case, of the bite of a *mad dog.* Dr. Hering's recommendation, however, is a sufficient guarantee.

HYDROPHOBIA.

The *bite of the rabid dog* is by far the most serious species of poisoned wounds, on account of the inoculation of the hydrophobic virus into the bitten part. The treatment should be applied early, and be such as is calculated to remove, destroy, or antidote the virus, and thus prevent the development of hydrophobia, although the major part of those bitten would never exhibit any symptoms of the disease. Such is Dr. Hering's confidence in the absolute efficacy of distant heat as an antidote to this, and all other animal poisons, that he simply recommends "to apply distant or radiating heat to the recent wound, as described under *envenomed wounds;* or until shudderings appear, and continue this practice three or four times a day, until the wound is healed without leaving a colored cicatrix.

"At the same time the patient should take, every five or seven days, or as often as the aggravation of the wound requires it, one dose of *Bell.*, or *Lach.*, or of *Hydrophobin*, till the cure is completed."

We should however prefer, immediately after the bite, to cord the limb above the wound, so as completely to cut off the returning circulation; to excise the bitten part, and then apply the *distant heat*, &c.*

If any small vesicles should make their appearance *under the tongue*, between the seventh and fourteenth days, puncture them, and rinse out the mouth with salt and water. This course will generally, if not invariably, prevent the development of HYDROPHOBIA.

Symptoms of Hydrophobia. — The first symptoms generally manifest themselves between the seventh and fortieth day after the bite; there are said to be cases, however, where the poison remains latent in the system for years. The precursory stage frequently lasts from two to twelve days. The wound heals very shortly, as every other slight wound. If the wound should not be completely healed while the precursory symptoms are developing themselves, it assumes a livid and spongy appearance, and secretes an ichorous humor. If the wound has closed, it inflames again, and breaks open; the patient complains of itching pains, striking from the wound or cicatrix along the nerve to the neck and trunk; the bitten limb frequently feels numb, or as if it had gone to sleep, or it becomes rigid, or is convulsively moved. *General Symptoms:* anxiety; melancholy; tendency to start; excessive apprehension about his condition and future; he wants to be alone; his sleep is restless, interrupted by dreams (about dogs), and starting as if in affright, or he is completely sleepless. The patient complains of languor, drawing pain in the nape of the neck and back, burning sensation in the fauces and stomach, sensitiveness to cold and draughts of air, alternative heat and chilliness. Frequently we observe vertigo, ringing in the ears, obscuration of sight, nausea, vomiting of green bile. The face is frequently distorted, pale; the eyes faint; the voice hollow and trembling; breathing oppressed; pulse small; urine pale. Many patients manifest an uncommon desire for an embrace, and a constant urging to urinate, the urine being discharged drop by drop. *Symptoms of the disease when fully developed.* — We term this the convulsive, hydrophobic or furibund stage.

The patient shows the most frightful aversion to liquids, in

* For some interesting remarks on this subject, see Dr. Hering on Psoricum, in N. A. Homo. Jour., Nov. 1852.

spite of his violent thirst; he cannot swallow, nor see, nor hear the noise of any thing fluid; whenever he attempts to swallow a few drops of water, his throat and chest become constricted, and the most violent suffocative convulsions of the facial, cervical, thoracic, and abdominal muscles take place; they are excited even by merely swallowing saliva, or by thinking of drink. The patient experiences a most violent sensation of oppression of the chest, and has to sigh frequently. In some cases the convulsions are excited by the least draught of air, the motion of the curtain in contact with the body; the eye dreads the light; shining objects, looking-glass, a burning candle, are painful to the patient, and excites his spasms; every kind of noise is unpleasant to him; hence it is that frequently, without any apparent cause, periodical paroxysms of spasmodic oppression, constriction of the fauces and larynx, set in. At first there is a constant secretion of a thick tenacious, frothy saliva; hence slavering and spitting, for fear the saliva should have to be swallowed. At last, rage breaks out, and tetanic or epileptic convulsions take place; periodically the patient is attacked with furibund delirium, during which his muscular strength increases to an enormous extent, and he can scarcely be controlled; at the same time he spits about, bites, endeavors to escape from his attendants, tears clothes and beds, howls, barks like a dog, and endeavors to destroy himself; his blood-shot eyes roll wildly in their sockets, and fright is depicted in the features of the patient. He is frequently attacked with epileptic convulsions, or tetanus. The attacks last a quarter or half an hour. During the intervals the patient is entirely exhausted.

He is generally conscious of himself; warns his attendants of the danger to which his rage might expose them, and prays them to terminate his frightful sufferings. Sometimes vomiting takes place; and men are attacked with priaprism and seminal emissions, and women with *furor uterinus.* The pulse is up to 130 or 150 beats, small and irregular. As the disease increases, the paroxysms become more frequent and violent, until death ensues after twenty-four hours, two or three, and less frequently five to eight days: generally by exhaustion (apoplexia nervosa); towards the end the patient sometimes becomes quiet, is even able to drink, and dies quite composedly in a state of sopor, or in a violent paroxysm of convulsions, suffocated. Modifications occur in this disease as in any other; but the symptoms are the same, except more or less intense. For instance, in some cases the patient is able to swallow; in others he is able to swallow coffee, beer, or solids, but no water; or the hydrophobic symptoms only occur during the paroxysms; or the patient is able to swallow water, provided he does not see it, and his nose is kept closed. There are cases where the disease did not break out, but the cerebral affection was confined to anguish and sensitiveness; this is probably the case when the patient, after being bitten by a dog, is tormented by the fear that he will be attacked by the disease; this might be termed an imaginary hydrophobia. *Anatomical changes.* — The bodies of hydrophobic subjects generally decay very rapidly; the blood is dark, fluid, and is rapidly imbibed by the tissues; the veins are engorged. Air is frequently found in the larger vessels, and emphysema develops itself rapidly. The whole surface of the body is blue-red; the epidermis very dry; all the muscles are dark red, and, like the tendons, they are rigid and tight. *Causes.* — This disease develops itself spontaneously among the canine and feline races. Spontaneous rage has been observed among every species of those races, wolves, foxes, jackalls and cats. The virus can be transferred to men and to all sorts of warm-blooded animals, horses, cattle, sheep, swine, goats; but animals that live on vegetables do not seem to reproduce the virus. The same remark applies to man, and all the observations which have been gathered on that subject go to show that the bite of a man is not dangerous. The primary cause of this disease is not known. It is supposed that it can be excited by excessive heat or cold, unsatisfied sexual instinct, decayed food, deprivation of fresh meat, want of water in very hot weather. The rage of dogs is either raving or silent. Formerly it was supposed that a mad dog dreaded the water; that he had foamed at the mouth; that he took his tail between his hind-feet, and went straight on his course. All this is either false, or only partially true. We now know that dogs, even in the last stage of the disease, do not always dread the water; on the contrary, real hydrophobia only attacks man. Foaming at the mouth and slavering occur only among dogs attacked with silent rage, &c. Other and more important symptoms of hydrophobia among dogs are; alteration in their conduct, restlessness, constant roving about, escape from their masters, loss of appetite, devouring of things which are not natural food for them, such as wood, straw, dirt, &c.; constipation, vomiting, a peculiar rough, hoarse, howling bark, disposition to attack and bite people, hasty snapping at inanimate objects, altered, lean, shaggy, sleepy appearance, redness of the conjunctiva, photophobia; in dogs attacked with silent rage, the lower jaw is moreover depressed, as if paralyzed; they slaver, the tip of the tongue is protruded between the teeth, and finally the hind-legs are paralyzed. Dogs attacked with rage die after six or eight days, and sometimes even before that time, in an apoplectic fit. The following anatomical alterations have been discovered in the bodies of mad animals: dark, tarry blood; inflammation of the pharynx, tonsils, epiglottis, larynx, and mucous membrane of the stomach; pieces of undigested food in the stomach. Sometimes the duodenum and jejunum were found inflamed; the trachea and bronchi were filled with a tenacious, bloody foam; congestion of the brain and spinal marrow. The hydrophobic virus is transmitted by the saliva or slaver being applied to a sore or a part covered with a very delicate epidermis. Contact is necessary to establish the infection. The flesh, spleen, or the substance of the nerves do not contain any virus. It has no poisonous effect when received into the stomach. A peculiar predisposition on the part of the poisoned subject is likewise necessary to create hydrophobia. Not every bite of a mad animal is contagious, if the necessary susceptibility be wanting. Hunter relates that four men and twelve dogs were bitten by a mad animal: all the dogs died, but the men remained uninjured. In another case, twenty individuals were bitten by the same dog, but only one was poisoned. It is probable that the virus loses its intensity, whenseveral animals or men are bitten in succession, and that those only who were bitten first are poisoned. Age, sex, or constitution do not modify the action of the virus. The hydrophobic virus retains its infectious power for a long time; it attaches itself to straw, wood, clothes, and other substances, covered with the slaver of the mad animal; in this way the disease may be communicated a long time after a mad beast had been seen on the spot. Physiologists differ as to the period how long the virus can remain latent in the organism, before manifesting its destructive agency. This rarely takes place before the tenth day; according to some it has remained latent for months and years. This, however, may be an illusion, for hydrophobic symptoms may supervene while some other disease exists, and may thus lead to the belief of hydrophobia having set in. Spasms of the pharynx, and dread of swallowing liquids, are observed in hysteric patients, individuals afflicted with typhoid and other fevers, local disease of the pharynx, esophagus, nervus vagus. The development of hydrophobia in man can be hastened by excesses, emotions, and passions: anger, fear, fright, sexual intercourse (*Canstatt*).

Prognosis:* Tolerably favorable.

Treatment. — Hahnemann says in his preface to Belladonna: "A small dose of Belladonna every three or four days is the best preventive of hydrophobia; one or two doses of Belladonna will cure it." Belladonna, however, not being the only remedy for this disease, it may break out, even though Bellad. should have been taken as a preventive; but it will probably be very much modified in intensity, and will then be easily combated.

The preventative treatment has been before mentioned. Should a cicatrix have formed, and the hydrophobic symptoms not speedily yield to internal remedies, we should advise to get up a free discharge from the original wound. The internal treatment must be conducted in accordance with the state of the patient. If the patient had already been treated with the plaster of Cantharides, or had been salivated, the homeopathic remedies have to be chosen with reference to the results of that treatment. It should be observed that under homeopathic treatment, the patients experience no pain from the treatment, whereas the allopathic treatment inflicts upon them untold tortures.

The principal remedies for hydrophobia are: *Belladonna, Hyoscyamus, Stramonium, Cantharides, Hydrophobin, Lachesis. Belladonna* is principally indicated by the following symptoms:

* "Hydrophobia may still be considered an incurable disease." — *Gibson's Institutes of Surgery.*

ineffectual attempts at sleep, anxious breathing, frequent desire to drink, though the patient rejects every drink which is offered; burning sensation in the throat, with great dryness, red, bloated face, and glistening eyes; excessive thirst, with suffocative constriction of the throat on attempting to swallow liquids (this constrictive sensation in the throat does not exist continually, but only at the commencement of every new attempt to swallow a liquid); inability to swallow, fear, alternating with a desire to snap and spit at those present, or to escape from the attendants; constant restlessness of the whole body, and jactation of single muscles, particularly the muscles of the face.

Though *Belladonna* is not counter-indicated by convulsions of the extremities, yet *Hyoscyamus* is preferable when the convulsions are more permanent, when the spasmodic constriction of the throat is less violent, and there is not so much a desire to snap and spit at the attendants as to injure them in some other way. *Hyoscyamus* is particularly adapted to the following symptoms:

The patient complains of great dryness and burning heat in the throat, with stinging in the throat, and a suffocative constriction of the throat when swallowing; he has a dread of drinks, because he is unable to swallow them, and if he does succeed in swallowing a liquid, he is attacked soon after with spitting, and with convulsions that deprive him of his senses. He is constantly delirious, even when there is no paroxysm; or he is taciturn, and exceedingly fearful, or he has paroxysms of rage, during which he endeavors to injure others, and is so strong that he can scarcely be controlled; frequently excessive anguish alternates with startings, as if in affright, trembling convulsions; he shows a peculiar fear of being bit by animals; at times the upper and lower extremities are only slightly convulsed, at others the extremities are spasmodically curved, and the body is tossed off the bed; during such attacks the patient is often drenched with sweat. His face is red and bloated. There is some sleep, but it is disturbed by starting, and by anxious visions and dreams. In this respect, *Hyoscyamus* is distinguished from *Belladonna*, which has ineffectual attempts to go to sleep.

Stramonium is indicated by the following symptoms: restlessness, violent convulsions (of a rather tonic nature), during which the patient becomes so frantic that he has to be tied; he has no sleep, and tosses about his bed, uttering hoarse screams; he is delirious, without memory or consciousness; his pupils are very much dilated; violent desire to bite and to tear every thing with his teeth; excessive dryness of the inner mouth and fauces; the sight of a candle, of a mirror, or of water, throws him into frightful convulsions, with irresistible aversion to water, constriction and convulsions of the pharynx, slaver at the mouth, and frequent spitting; loquacious mania, with gesticulations, dancing, singing, laughing." *Lachesis* may be advantageously alternated with Belladonna or Hydrophobin, in the raging state. *Hydrophobin*, however, from the experiments of *Dr. Hering*, we should regard as the best *prophylactic*, and most valuable remedy for every stage of Hydrophobia.

Drs. Hartlaub and Trinks recommend Cantharides as a preventive of hydrophobia. Dr. Hartmann thinks it should be recommended for the following symptoms: alternate paroxysms of rage and convulsions; the convulsions can be excited by touching the larynx, which is painful in the region of the thyroid cartilage; by making pressure on the abdomen, and by the sight of water; the eyes look fiery and flashing, and roll about in their sockets in the wildest manner. The patient is scarcely able to swallow, especially liquids, on account of a burning and dryness of the mouth and pharynx. There is an excessive desire for sexual intercourse, with constant painful erections, or constant itching and burning in the internal sexual parts. The oppression of breathing and anguish are less striking than in cases for which Bellad. and Hyoscyam. are indicated; the covulsions, however, are sometimes frightful. In general, Cantharides seems to be more indicated when the inflammatory symptoms are more prominent, and when the impeded deglutition does not proceed from spasmodic constriction of the fauces, but the spasm proceeds from the inflammation of those parts, or from the pains caused by the swallowing.

It is said that a strong decoction made of the bark of the roots of the white ash (Fraxinus accuminata), drank freely, will cure hydrophobia. It is also stated as a fact, which we omitted to mention when speaking of snake bites, that rattlesnakes can be made more easily to crawl over live coals than white ash leaves, and that they are never found in forests where the white ash grows. We will conclude this subject (treatment of real Hydrophobia), with the interesting case of *M. Buisson*, as reported by himself to the Paris Academy of Sciences, as it suggests to the Homeopathic Surgeon a valuable auxillary means, which he may employ at the same time that he is administering his internal remedies. "He had been called to visit a woman, who for three days was said to have been suffering under this disease. She had the usual symptoms: constriction of the throat, inability to swallow, abundant secretion of the saliva, and foaming at the mouth. Her neighbors said that she had been bitten by a mad dog about forty days before. At her own urgent entreaties, she was bled, and died a few hours after, as was expected. M. Buisson, who had his hands covered with blood, incautiously cleansed them with a towel which had been used to wipe the mouth of the patient. He had then an ulceration upon one of his fingers, yet thought it sufficient to wash off the saliva that adhered with a little water. The ninth day after, being in his cabriolet, he was suddenly seized with a pain in his throat, and one still greater in his eyes. The saliva was continually pouring into his mouth, the impression of a current of air, the sight of brilliant bodies, gave him a painful sensation; his body appeared to him so light that he felt as if he could leap to a prodigious height; he experienced, he said, a wish to run and bite, not men, but animals and inanimate bodies. Finally he drank with difficulty, and the sight of water was still more distressing to him than the pain in his throat. These symptoms recurred every five minutes, and it appeared to him as though the pain commenced in the affected finger, and extended thence to the shoulder. From the whole of the symptoms he judged himself affected with hydrophobia, and resolved to terminate his life by stifling himself in a vapor bath. Having entered one for this purpose, he caused the heat to be raised to 42° (107° 36′ Fah.), when he was equally surprised and delighted to find himself free from all complaint. He left the bathing room well, dined heartily, and drank more than usual. Since that time he says he has treated more than eighty persons bitten, in four of whom the symptoms had declared themselves, and in no case has he failed, except in that of one child, seven years old, who died in the bath."

Symptomatic hydrophobia is much less dangerous than the real disease; it is not contagious, and is not always attended with violent symptoms; the frightful anguish is likewise wanting, nor is there any slavering. It is not caused by virus; frequently by fright or anger, or it is a symptom of some inflammatory, nervous, or hysteric disease, or attending a very acute eruption, or some other spasmodic or malignant disease. Fear and imagination, after an innocent bite, may, in very sensitive persons, cause the disease. The allopathic preventive treatment, with large doses of Belladonna, Cantharides, and Mercurius, may likewise lead to a medicinal hydrophobia, which ignorant physicians might mistake for symptomatic hydrophobia.

To cure this disease, it is of the utmost importance to find out its cause. If it was caused by the continued use of large doses of Belladonna, large quantities of black coffee should be administered by the mouth and rectum, to be followed by one, two, three, or four doses of Hyoscyamus. Repeated doses of Camphor may likewise be required, particularly if the disease was occasioned by the abuse of Cantharides. If there should be symptoms of poisoning by Mercury, Camphor, Opium, Belladonna, Electricity, or some other of the above-mentioned remedies will have to be given, according as indicated.

If, however, the symptoms should point to the existence of a more general and more deep-seated disease than symptomatic hydrophobia, in this case the physician will have to select one of the remedies mentioned in the preceding paragraphs; and this will be so much easier, as the hydrophobic symptoms constitute the more prominent symptoms of the patient's illness.

TRAUMATIC TETANUS.

It will be proper in this connection to speak of tetanus as connected with wounds. When the jaws only are affected, it is called trismus.

It arises in consequence of the violent pain, or nervous irritation, immediately after a wound, when it is fatal in a short time; or in the first few days after the wound, during its inflammatory stage; or eight or ten days afterwards, while the wound is in the best process of healing and suppuration, without any inflammation and pain. Here the wound is apparently the predisposing cause, increasing the sensibility of the nervous system.

In some cases the attack occurs suddenly with great violence, but generally it comes on gradually.

The first *symptom* is a sensation of soreness and stiffness in the muscles of the neck and face. This rapidly increases; the forehead wrinkles; and the countenance assumes a ghastly appearance. Swallowing becomes difficult, and soon impossible. The jaws are locked fast, and the whole body is rigid. There is often a cold and clammy perspiration, accompanied in general with costiveness. The pain is extreme, but somewhat remittent. Though every muscle in his body seems in painful contraction, the patient still retains his consciousness. The pulse is at first strong and full, then small and rather feeble. Death results from suffocation or apoplexy.

The most dangerous cases are those arising from wounds in tendinous and aponeurotic parts, as in the palm of the hand, or sole of the foot. Exciting causes are the presence of foreign bodies in the wound, mental affections, taking cold, impure air, or tension and *distraction* of single fibers in the wound from suppuration.

A sad summary and just estimate of a common practice may be seen in the following extract, from a quite recent work. Under the head of "*Treatment*," in Hasting's Practice of Surgery,* we are informed that "this" (the treatment) "has been, as yet, but *experimental* — no form is settled on as rational and *hopeful practice* — remedial means, as comprehended in the present day, seem to hold forth but a slender chance of success — therefore nothing more can be done than to give a *catalogue* of remedies that have been employed" (with little or no success!). "The following means have been *constantly* tried, and it is said of each, *occasionally* with success; amputation, division of the nerves, cupping the part, the incision being deep enough to cut off *all nervous communication* (!) — the actual cautery — cold bath — hot

* Published in Philadelphia, in 1850.

bath — *general bleeding* — active purgation — enormous doses of opium — tobacco enemata — large and repeated draughts of brandy — counter-irritation over the spine, with the *endermoid* (endermic?) use of morphia, aconite, belladonna, &c., — the external application of cold, stimuli being given internally at the same time, and *salivation by mercury*" (*!!*)

The prognosis under our treatment is far more favorable. The treatment must be both internal and external. If the disease arises from a puncture, the wound should be enlarged, either with a knife or caustic (the latter is frequently preferable, allaying irritability, by the destruction of all sensibility), and a warm emollient poultice applied, to promote suppuration as soon as possible. If the wound is lacerated, cleanse it, and remove all irritating substances, and then apply the warm poultice. Ligatures around the thighs or arms may be of service, if the injury is upon the extremities. (See different classes of wounds.)

Arnica is doubtless the most important remedy in traumatic tetanus. It should be given internally, and at the same time applied to the wound in dilution. It is better to keep the poultice constantly moistened with the *Arnica* lotion. If after the use of *Arnica* for several hours, the patient does not improve, and is afflicted with frequent *shiverings* and *faïntness*, use Lobelia in the same manner, both internally and externally. This, in large doses, under the Eclectic practice, used to be our great reliance. Calendula, applied to lacerated wounds in the early stage, before the tetanic symptoms are fully developed, will often prevent any further progress, and restore a healthy action in the wound. Whether it will prove as valuable after their development in that class of wounds, is yet to be seen. Should the disease prove still unyielding, *Angustura*, and *Cocculus*, or *Opium* and *Hyoscyamus* will prove serviceable.

Belladonna, though particularly beneficial in idiopathic tetanus, has been useful in the traumatic variety, when there is a sensation of *constriction* in the throat, *spasmodic clinching of the jaws*, foaming and distortion of the mouth, the paroxysms being excited or made more severe by attempting to drink. It is frequently advantageously alternated with *Lachesis*.

Nux Vomica is also a valuable remedy in idiopathic, and will often be found useful in traumatic tetanus, especially in cases of drunkards.

Where a nerve has been injured, *Hypericum* will be useful.

Rhus. is valuable when the disease arises from contusion of the joints, synovial membranes, or tendons.

Stramonium is also indicated in the latter stages, when the other remedies have not relieved the symptoms, and there is delirium. If, however, the delirium occur in the early stage, *Opium* is the most important remedy. Other remedies, as Acon., Ign., Bry., Cicuta, Camphor, Merc., Mosch., Sulphur, or Verat., may sometimes be indicated. When it is impossible to introduce the medicine into the mouth, moisten the lips and nostrils with it, dissolved or diluted in water, and administer the same as an enema.

TRAUMATIC ERYSIPELAS.

This is a species of inflammation with eruptions, which sometimes occurs on the margins, and around wounds which themselves have degenerated into an unhealthy, and more or less irritable condition. It is an evidence that the vital powers are much impaired. The surface affected has a dark purple appearance, with vesicular eruptions around, and is very irritable and painful. The pain is often of a severe itching and burning character. A sanious fluid exudes from it. The remedies are, *Bel.*, *Arren.*, *Rhus. Tox.*, *Lach.*, *Caust.*, *Carb. Veg.*, and *Phytolac. Dec.*

Bel. and *Rhus.* will be found very valuable when there is severe local inflammation, partaking of the erysipelatous character.

If the pain is burning, with chilliness and thirst, *Arsenicum* or *Lachesis* is the proper remedy.

Carbo. Veg. is to be used when the wound bleeds easily, discharges sanious and corrosive matter, with burning pain.

Rhus. Tox., if the pain is more of the itching character, but if the *itching* and *burning* both be severe, *Causticum.*

The surface of the affected part should be cleansed often. The pus will, if allowed to remain, act as a contagious, corrosive poison. A solution of the same remedy that is given internally should be applied externally to the affected surface by means of lint. We have sometimes applied, with very great advantage, as a detergent and mild local stimulant, a solution of the sesqui-carbonate of potash, before spoken of. It did not, as we could perceive, interfere with the action of the specific remedy. It should be applied once or twice a day, and will cause, for a few moments, a slight smarting. But should any case remain obstinate, and resist treatment, we should not hesitate to cautiously touch each vesicle with the pure caustic potash, so as to disorganize them, following this with an Elm poultice, to promote suppuration. We have relieved some cases by the simple application of the Tr. of Phytolacca Decandria. (See ULCERS.)

CHAPTER VI.

OF WOUNDS AND INJURIES LOCALLY CONSIDERED.

Scalp — Peculiar Dangers and Precautions — Face and Eyes — Concussion and Compression — Hæmastasis — Treatment for, and Cases — Throat-cutting — Wounds of the Chest and Venesection — Of the Abdomen and Intestines — Peculiarities of Treatment — Of the Joints, Anchylosis, &c.

WOUNDS OF THE HEAD.

THE scalp is much exposed to cuts and contusions, and the more liable to be seriously injured by them, inasmuch as it is abundantly supplied with nerves and vessels, some of which communicate directly with those of the membranes investing the brain within the cranial cavity. Erysipelatous inflammation may be easily excited in this part, and extend over the whole head and face. A trifling blow may occasion effusion of blood between the scalp and bone, which may form a tumor and remain stationary for a long period. This tumor will take on inflammation from a very slight additional injury, and this inflammation may extend within the cranium, producing meningitis; or the pressure on the bone, without any violent action, may occasion caries. Such tumors sometimes appear on the heads of new-born infants, being occasioned by pressure against the parieties of the pelvis.

Months, and in rare instances even years, after the scalp has been injured, troublesome *nervous symptoms* may ensue — twitchings of the muscles of the face — sometimes paralysis of the limbs, or convulsions resembling epilepsy, occur.

Gun-shot wounds of this part are more dangerous than other kinds; though recovery is not impossible, even when the skull has been fractured and the brain itself injured. Both tables of the skull may, however, be fractured, without affecting the brain. A ball will often take a circuitous course for a considerable distance between scalp and skull.

Wounds of the face are no more to be dreaded than those of other parts, except in as far as the organs of sense are involved, or permanent disfigurement becomes a consideration. Another peculiarity that may be noticed, is closure of the salivary ducts, giving rise to fistulous openings. (See Second Part.)

The sight is generally more or less injured by any wound *near the eye*, — though a ball has been known to enter the socket, and lodge between the eye and orbital plate, without obstructing vision. The destruction of one eye may cause paralysis of the other. When the eye-ball has been so injured that it must evidently be destroyed, it will save the sufferer much pain to puncture it and let the humors out. This, however, should not be done merely because the sight is irretrievably lost. Save the eye to look at, if not to look through. The external ear may be lost altogether, without any loss of hearing.

In treating wounds of the *hairy scalp*, the first thing you have to do is to turn barber. *Shave* off the hair for a considerable distance around the wound. Neglect of this, by preventing proper examination as to the extent of the injury, may lead to the death of your patient. Remove any foreign substance or coagulation of blood. Then ascertain, with scrupulous care, whether or not the bone has been injured. The mere fact of fracture does not authorize trephining. (The symptoms requiring it will be noticed when speaking of that operation — see Second Part.) Carefully adjust any portions of the scalp that may have been torn loose. Fix them by adhesive straps and bandages, if possible, — if not, the interrupted suture may be used. Then treat as other incised or lacerated wounds. Symptoms of concussion may be present. (See CONCUSSION).

The *diet* should be light, unirritating, and unstimulating. Regard must be had to this rule for several weeks.

If the head has been simply *bruised*, without laceration of the integuments, but with sensible effusion below the surface, it is customary to open the tumors and let out the extravasated blood. This should never be done, unless in the three following cases: — immediately on the receipt of the injury, before any soreness or sensible inflammation comes on; or after it has entirely passed off, and a large tumor continues stationary for a long time; or, finally, when a large blood-vessel is ruptured, and requires to be tied. In ordinary cases, any extravasated blood is soon absorbed under the use of *Arnica*. (See CONTUSED WOUNDS.)

The scalp, *after healing*, under the common treatment, will in some instances remain *tender* for a long period; the *Arnica* will prevent, and generally cure this. If necessary, however, resort may be had to *Ars.*, *Bovis.*, *Carb. An.*, *Phytolac. Dec.*, *Silic.* or *Sul.*

Should *erysipelatous* inflammation at any time supervene, resort must be had to *Rhus.*, *Bel.*, *Phytolac. Dec.*, &c.

CONCUSSION AND COMPRESSION OF THE BRAIN.

A sudden and violent blow on the head, whether organic injury be occasioned or not, generally *stuns* the person. That common word expresses a degree of *concussion*. In severer cases, the patient is found in a state of entire insensibility; the face is pale, the hands and feet cold, and the pulse weak and fluttering: *even the function of respiration being for a while suspended.* This returns, and with it a gradual restoration of the senses. The mind, however, is still for some time wandering. At this stage the pulse is nearly natural, but if you attempt to rouse the patient his breathing is disturbed, and the action of the heart quickened. He may try to get on his feet, but falls again, like a drunken man. This inability to move will sometimes continue after the person has become conscious of all that is going on around him. Nausea and vomiting are frequently concomitant symptoms.

Concussion, as observed, is a "stunning," — a *shock* to the very center of the nervous system, occasioning a slight temporary or entire suspension of consciousness, and has no necessary connection with *compression*, contusions or extravasation.

In some instances this shock is so severe that the patient dies very soon after the injury. The brains of those who have thus died show, on dissection, no organic lesion; though Mr. Collins, of Dublin, thought that those he examined were diminished in size, and did not completely fill the cranium.

It is usually divided into three stages: *depression* or insensibility, already described — *reaction*, or the return to the normal action, and lastly, *inflammation*, or excessive reaction.

Compression, frequently an attendant or sequence of concussion after injuries to the head, may arise from direct pressure of the bone upon the brain — from extravasation of blood, effusion of serum, or the formation of matter.

In compression there is a loss of all consciousness, sensation, and volition. The pupils are dilated, and do not contract under the stimulus of light. This is, however, not invariable, as there is sometimes contraction of both pupils, or contraction of one and dilatation of the other. The respiration is laborious and stertorous. The pulse is small, hard and laboring: usually irregular, and occasionally intermitting. Paralysis, generally on the side opposite to the one injured, is sometimes present.

When compression is the result of depression of the bone, it comes on *immediately* after the accident; but if from extravasation of blood, effusion of serum, or formation of matter, the symptoms come on gradually. In the case of extravasation of blood, or effusion of serum, should the ruptured vessel be small, or the inflammation not very violent, several hours or even days may pass before the symptoms are fully developed; the time may be extended even to weeks when it is the result of the formation of matter. In the latter case the symptoms frequently come on insidiously, though they are usually preceded by pains, rigors, &c., such as result from the formation of matter in other parts.

When the skull is fractured, and one edge is depressed, the inequality may easily be detected by pressing the finger for a few moments *firmly* upon the edges of the fracture; sometimes, however, the internal plate is fractured and depressed, while the outer one is uninjured; and occasionally the fracture occurs upon the side opposite to the injury. The last two cases would render the diagnosis difficult; but in either of these, as also when it is the result of the formation of matter, the scalp will become puffy; if raised, the periosteum will be easily separated from the bone, and the skull itself be dry and of an ashy color. When there is an external wound the edges become glossy, and the matter thin and ichorous, when matter forms under the cranium.

The *prognosis*, except in those cases of concussion where the patient dies in a few hours after the accident, is favorable under our treatment. Formerly it was the plan to bleed people back to life in these cases of suspended animation; but it was as mischievous as absurd. The brain is not inactive from too much blood, but too little, as the pallid face plainly shows; the loss of an ounce or two of blood in such a state of the system may be the loss of life; indeed all modern authorities are against bleeding until reaction is established. Sir A. Cooper, seeing that reaction was frequently preceded by vomiting, was in the habit of ordering an emetic to excite it; although it was successful in his hands, surgeons generally have been fearful of causing effusion by the rush of blood to the brain in the act of vomiting. The common practice now is to resort to stimuli (more or less active, according to the views of the surgeon) till reaction is excited, then to bleed; or if not in favor of venesection, to catharticize to control it. The danger of subsequent inflammation resulting from the use of stimulants, has made the most judicious surgeons favor the let-alone treatment.

The Homeopathic treatment is, however, unattended with the hazard of the stimulant or the let-alone, or the debilitating effects of bleeding or purgation. The remedies used to excite, also control the reaction; they not only arouse but sustain the constitutional powers; and should inflammation arise, we have remedies specifically adapted to control it.

Treatment.—In all severe cases of concussion, place the patient in a horizontal position in a dark room; keep the body warm, and do not let him be disturbed by questions, conversation, or any noise, as perfect quietude is the most favorable state for the brain to recover its normal action; and for some time after all unpleasant symptoms have subsided the patient should be kept free from all excitement, and the diet should be very light and simple.

At the same time *Arnica Mon.*, dissolved in water, should be given once in two hours, until reaction is beginning to be established; then not so often. Should the patient have been frightened very much at the time of the accident, a dose of *Opium* should precede the *Arnica.* If no symptom of reaction appear soon after the administration of the *Arnica*, wet the nostrils occasionally with a dilution of the *Arnica Tr.* The beauty of the *Arnica* is that it has a specific power in removing the effects of the shock upon the nervous system, restoring it to its normal condition, thus preventing violent reaction, arresting hemorrhage, and exciting the absorbents to the removal of any extravasated fluids. It is thus admirably adapted to the treatment of concussion and compression.

One or two doses of *Aconite* should be alternated with the *Arnica* as often as once in three hours, when the reaction threatens to terminate in inflammation. The patient's hands and feet should be immersed in water as hot as he will bear, for twenty-five or thirty minutes; the temperature being kept up by constant additions of hot water, and the head kept cool by cloths frequently wet with cold water. If the inflammation should not yield, recourse must be had to *Belladonna*, almost a *specific* for inflammation of the brain and its membranes, which is especially indicated when the *head is hot*, the face red and bloated, with *violent pulsations of the carotids*, increase of suffering from the *slightest* noise, and intolerance of *light*, *eyes red and bloodshot*, with a wild expression, pupils contracted or dilated, *violent* and *furious* delirium, loss of consciousness; sometimes low mutterings, convulsions and vomiting. If necessary, *Hyos.*, *Bry.*, *Merc.*, *Op.*, *Stram.*, *Cupr. Acet.*, &c., may be used. The particular symptoms indicating each remedy may be learned from any Homeopathic work on Theory and Practice. As this work will probably fall into the hands of some who are inexperienced in the use of Homeopathic remedies, and who have been accustomed to frequent doses, we would here caution them especially against the repetition of *Belladonna* in these cases. It should never be used lower than the third dilution, nor repeated oftener than once in three or four hours, generally not under six, and as soon as an amelioration of the symptoms takes place, it should be discontinued until there are some indications of a return.

Much benefit may also be derived from the use of *Hæmastasis*. This is no more nor less than mechanically confining the blood in one or more of the extremities. By applying ligatures around the arms and thighs sufficiently tight to check the venous but admit the arterial blood, we can in a few minutes remove from the trunk from one-third to one-half of its usual supply of blood, and thus break up severe congestions, by keeping the blood away from inflamed parts. If the patient is feeble, the application of the ligatures will cause him to faint in a few moments, when they should be loosened. The simple ligature is *always at hand*, and usually all that is necessary to avail ourselves of the advantages of *Hæmastasis*; but as Dr. Junod some fifty years ago invented an ingenious instrument acting upon this principle, which was highly prized and made use of by Hahnemann, we give, from the British Journal of Homeopathy, a description of it, as well as the report of an interesting cure: "The object sought to be accomplished by the ingenious inventor, is to determine a large portion of the blood of the system into a limb, and thus abstract it from congested or inflamed internal parts. This design he accomplishes by means of a tin boot into which the leg of the patient is inserted, and from which the atmospheric air is gradually withdrawn by means of a small air-pump, the top of the boot being kept in air-tight apposition to the leg by means of a broad belt of vulcanized india-rubber. The effect of thus exhausting the air is to cause a rush of blood into the limb contained in the apparatus; it resembles dry cupping on a large scale, a whole limb in place of a few square inches of skin being subjected to the action of the instrument. No pain, but only a slight uneasiness is experienced in the limb inclosed in the boot, which is found on being withdrawn to be much increased in size, and the blood does not entirely return into the circulation and the leg resume its original size at first for twenty-four hours; but the oftener the operation is repeated the more transient is its effect. The effect of the operation in the cases for which it is applicable is almost instantaneous —congested states of internal organs, all the symptoms of acute local inflammations vanish as if by magic, the pain of many forms of neuralgia is at once subdued, hemorrhages from the lungs, uterus, &c., cease. In many of these cases the effect is, as may be imagined, transient, and the diseased states recur as soon as the blood is restored to the circulation, though the effect may be often rendered permanent by repeated applications of the boot; still, even supposing the effect to be transient and palliative, it is for us a matter of great importance in many cases to procure a suspension of the dangerous symptoms, in order to gain time for the action of our specific remedies. Thus, in threatened apoplexy, in hemoptysis, in violent metrorrhagia, and many other conceivable cases, the palliation of the paramount and dangerous symptom is of the utmost importance, and if this can be done by such a simple appliance as that of Mr. Junod, we should be very wrong to despise it. In cases of congestion, hemorrhage, &c., we seek to attain the same object by placing the patient in certain positions, by the application of cold water, ice, hot foot-baths, &c.; but M. Junod here presents us with a much more powerful and certain mode of effecting our purpose. By means of one boot he can draw into the limb four pounds of blood, and the effect of this, when rapidly performed on a robust individual in the erect position, is so powerful as to produce perfect pallor of the countenance and syncope. Dr. Junod attended in Paris several cases, in conjunction with Hahnemann, who had a high opinion of the utility of the hemostasic apparatus. One case which he attended along with the founder of Homeopathy deserves to be detailed, as it illustrates forcibly the value of the treatment pursued. The case was that of a young lady, the daughter of a late noble earl, formerly English ambassador at one of the European courts. This lady had long been afflicted with a most curious and sad disease; she had entirely lost the use of her limbs, and lay constantly on a couch, her head generally supported by an attendant's arm. She seemed to be entirely destitute of any power of volition, never spoke except when roused, lay constantly in a half-comatose state, the face being very much flushed, and the head very hot; evidently she labored under severe congestion of the brain. She was under Hahnemann's treatment; he went to see her very frequently, in fact was in almost constant attendance upon her, but was unable to produce any favorable result, and after nearly a year of ineffectual Homeopathic treatment, Hahnemann called in Dr. Junod to his assistance. When they met together beside the patient, Hahnemann said, 'Now, Dr. Junod, you shall operate on the legs, and I on the stomach.' After the first application of the boot the patient roused up, addressed those around her, and chatted familiarly and quite sensibly with her friends: her face assumed a natural color, and to the surprise of all, she was able to walk about the room, a thing which she had not done for a very long time. After ten applications of the boot, on ten successive days, the patient was perfectly cured, and was able to travel into the country, where she remained perfectly free from all symptoms of her former complaint, and was able to take a considerable amount of walking exercise. It is possible that the Homeopathic remedies administered by Hahnemann at the same time, were the cause of the permanent character of the result obtained in this case, though as long as the congested state of the brain existed, it was evident that the medicines were of no avail. Dr. Junod's apparatus has been introduced into all the hospitals in Paris, and is frequently employed by the Parisian medical men in their treatment of many diseases that were formerly supposed to require blood-letting; it has also been adopted by almost all the London hopitals, and letters from London hospital physicians and surgeons of eminence, testify their satisfaction with the performances of the instrument."

When symptoms of compression are present, if the skull is shattered, any depressed portions may be removed or elevated with forceps, Hey's saw, or perhaps, in some instances, an air-pump. The trephine should not be used until after our remedial means have been thoroughly tried without success. The brain, it is generally conceded, possesses the power of accommodating itself to considerable pressure, and the *Arnica*, every Homeopath well knows, has a good deal of efficiency in increasing that power, and is unequaled in removing extravasated fluids.

When the internal plate only is fractured, or the side opposite to that upon which the injury was received, we should rely upon remedial measures, and if these are insufficient, and the scalp becomes puffy, and being incised and raised, the periosteum is found loosened and the skull of ashy color, we can then be pretty certain of the exact seat of the injury, and are justified in the use of the trephine. Miss B. had fallen and struck the left temporal bone upon the corner of a bench: inflammation followed. Dr. Hill, at that time Professor of Surgery in the Eclectic Med. Institute, being in attendance, called in consultation his partner, Dr. Hunt, who was in favor of relying solely upon Homeopathy. The Doctor, although partly converted, had not sufficient confidence. He accordingly subjected her to a thorough antiphlogistic course, without perceptible benefit. *Arnica* being then exhibited once in six hours, cured the patient, and converted the Doctor and the family to Homeopathy.

A distinguished old-school surgeon says: "If we examine the history of injuries to the head, we shall find by far the greater number of successful cases have been those in which there has been the least surgical interference." We give below two cases, illustrative of this and of diagnosis.

One of the authors was cognizant of a case where a falling limb produced a comminuted fracture,—a literal smashing of the parietal bone. The patient lay several hours in a comatose condition. Three physicians agreed that nothing could be done for him. His widowed mother, a poor woman, but not so ignorant as many a wealthy lady, believing in the good old maxim, "while there is life there is hope," observed, as reaction advanced, that his head was too warm, while his feet were too cold. On her own responsibility, therefore, and the suggestion of her common sense, she immersed his feet in hot water, and kept pouring a cold stream on the wounded part. She also administered a strong stimulating injection. By these "*unprofessional*" means, he revived and escaped the danger of inflammation. As the cranium was *fortunately*, under the circumstances, completely *fractured* and not merely *compressed* (which might have required more surgical skill than it was worth while giving a *poor* boy), the elasticity of the brain *set* its own bone—more accurately, perhaps, than art could have done it, and the boy recovered perfectly. In an adjoining neighborhood, and about the same time, a rich man's son met with a similar accident. In his case the trephine was used by one of the medical gentlemen, whose prognosis was mentioned above, though not till after the patient had been allowed to lie fourteen hours — nothing done for him, of course, *secundum artem*, till "the doctor" could be brought from a distance of sixteen miles; this patient died.

WOUNDS OF THE NECK

are principally important from the liability to fatal hemorrhage. Death may quickly ensue from this cause alone, if any of the larger vessels are wounded.

Suppression of hemorrhage is, therefore, the first point of TREATMENT, for which purpose it is often necessary to apply the ligature to veins as well as arteries. It is always best, however, to check the hemorrhage from veins by compression, rather than the ligature, to avoid the danger of phlebitis. When the hemorrhage has been checked, bring the lips of the wound together, and fasten them by sutures, using precaution to prevent your dressings from being thrown off. Most cases of serious wounds in the throat occur in persons attempting suicide, and may require the hands to be tied, as well as the head to be secured in one position, leaning over toward the wound. This last precaution is proper in all cases. The patient should not even be allowed to talk. Eating and drinking have often to be restricted, or altogether interdicted for awhile. These wounds heal very rapidly, and require but little attention after the first proper dressing, except from good nurses.

WOUNDS OF THE CHEST.

When the cavity of the thorax is entered, the lungs are, of course, almost always injured. When this is the case, air will pass out through the wound, causing a bubbling of the blood as it flows. The respiration will be short, and the expectoration bloody. The patient will often complain of a sensation like a *stitch*, at every breath.

The external passage of air must be stopped as soon as possible. Apply a wet bandage firmly around the chest, to prevent motion of the ribs, leaving an aperture to admit dressing the wound (for which see the different classes of wounds), and place the patient in such a position that the wound may be the most dependent part. Frequently change the dressing, to give exit to the blood and matter, using, however, *no compression.*

Venesection is recommended in the books, "to divert," as they say, "the blood from the lungs." But surely it is as well to bleed to death through a wound in the chest as through one in the arm! We are told that the bleeding "can hardly be carried too far, for if the patient be not relieved by this measure, *no other can possibly save him.*" *—(Gibson, vol. i., p. 19.) The reason given for bleeding in such cases, is as absurd as the process itself. We are told by the same author to "*draw blood copiously* from the arm, which will have the effect of *diverting it from the lungs,* and thereby save the patient, perhaps, from suffocation." Now, it is an anatomical absurdity to speak of diverting the blood from the lungs by drawing it from the arm, as if the lungs and arm were merely supplied by different branches from the same arteries. The blood going to the arm comes through the aorta from the left side of the heart. The blood going to the lungs proceeds from the right ventricle; hence it is obvious that by taking blood from the arm, we act upon the systemic instead of the pulmonary circulation, and cannot possibly influence the determination to the lungs, or produce any diversion. The only effect that we can produce is to diminish the amount of venous blood returning to the right side of the heart, which object could be accomplished by a loss of venous blood from any portion of the body, and which can be accomplished with far greater facility and efficiency by the application of ligatures, without any loss of blood.

As the only object which the surgeon can hope to attain by bleeding, if he understands anatomy, is not the diverson of blood from the lungs, but a diminution of the total amount of blood in the body, common sense would suggest the query, Why should we make such efforts merely to diminish the total amount of blood, when this loss of blood is the very evil and danger which is threatening the life of the patient?

It is desirable, however, that less blood be thrown upon the lungs. Any means, therefore, that will retain a larger quantity

* Such expressions are frequently used by old-school writers, who seem to think that when they have reached the limits of their knowledge, they have exhausted all the resources of science.

in the extreme vessels, or prevent its return to the heart and lungs without permanent loss of it, ought to be resorted to without hesitation. Such a means we have in *hæmastasis:** cording the arms and legs so as to partially arrest the returning circulation, without impeding the arterial flow, or using Dr. Junod's Hæmostasic Apparatus.

Should severe inflammation arise, notwithstanding the use of *Aconite*, *Arnica*, *Calendula*, &c., resort must be had to *Bryonia*, *Phosphorus*, and such other remedies as are appropriate in the treatment of inflammation of the lungs (for which see some Homeopathic work on practice).

A gentleman lived eleven years after having the chest transfixed by a gig-shaft. Both lungs were transfixed. The anterior portion of the thorax of this patient is preserved as a specimen in the Hunterian Museum.

WOUNDS OF THE ABDOMEN

are no less dangerous than those of the thorax. The amount of danger will depend, of course, on the part and organ injured, but any penetration of the peritoneum is likely, from its great vascularity and sensibility, to bring on serious inflammation.

When the *intestines* are wounded, nausea and vomiting generally occur, the matter thrown up, as well as the stools, being bloody. Fæcal matter and fetid wind pass out of the wound. A portion of the bowel may also protrude. There is often griping pain about the precordia. Cold clammy sweats are among the fatal symptoms.

Wounds of the *small intestines* present more dangerous symptoms than those of the large. Any part, however, of the intestinal canal may be injured, and recovery take place.

If an intestine has protruded, it will be too late to return it two days after the injury. The only chance then is to leave it open as an artificial anus.

The *adhesive* process goes on very rapidly in the intestines. If there be no protrusion and no division of the bowel, no sewing up is required. If it is cut for a considerable distance lengthwise, and also protruded, one stitch for three or four inches is sufficient.

* See CONCUSSION.

If it is quite severed, only two sutures are required, one opposite the other. The smallest thread and needle should be used, with as little handling as possible. And you need not be very nice about bringing the edges together exactly in their natural coaptation. They will unite in any part; and your turning and handling will do more harm than some degree of displacement.

Keep the wound open and in a dependent position, dressing it with lint wet with *Aqua Calendulæ*, to protect it from the air. The patient must remain quiet for the first twenty-four hours at least. At each dressing, press upon the wound a little, to force out the matter. After the second day the external wound may be allowed to heal. For the first day let the patient eat nothing, and as little as possible for some days after. Let his *diet* then be cooling and unirritating. Every thing he takes should be of easy digestion; solids had better be avoided altogether. Stimulants of all kinds of course must be proscribed. Constipation should be avoided by small injections of cold water.

After healing, the intestine may contract so as considerably to diminish its caliber. This may give rise to colic-like pains in the passage of its contents. In such a case great strictness of diet must be observed. All indigestible things, such as raisin-seeds, fruit-rind, had better be avoided, and the appropriate internal remedies employed.

In July, 1851, a boy, son of Mr. L., of Berlin, Erie co., *aet.* 13, while riding a horse, raking hay with a horse-rake, the horse ran away with him and threw him upon the rake; a tooth, one and a quarter inches in diameter, entered his abdomen about midway between the umbilicus and left anterior superior process of the illium, passed through the colon, making a hole two and a half inches long in it, tore off the peritoneal coat some distance further, and emerged at the right ischiatic notch, passing through the pelvic cavity, penetrating through the rectum, and severely lacerating the sacral plexus. The wound was dressed and treated by Dr. G. S. Hill; — B. L. Hill, consulting surgeon. The parts were washed with a dilution of *Tr. Calendula* — half an ounce to a pint of tepid water — this was made to run through the whole course of the wound; the parts brought in contact and kept there by straps, compresses, and bandages, and kept constantly wet with the same fluid. *Arnica* was given internally every four or six hours for two days; then *Calendula* was given internally.

At first there was considerable depression in the circulation, but reaction came on, and the pulse rose but little, if any, above the natural standard, and the case went on; healing took place by the first intention in all the parts except the opening at the ischiatic notch. Through this the fæces continued to pass, as well as through the rectum, as in health. In a few weeks he was able to walk about; still he suffered much from the soreness and chafing of the wound, by the passing of fecal matter, as well as a neuralgic affection of the limb, in consequence of injury of the sciatic nerve. After the healing of the upper wound, no further medicine had been given for several weeks, during which time no progress towards a complete cure seemed to have been made, but the pain and soreness grew rather worse, and his general health had failed very much; he was evidently fast running down. *Calendula Tr.* in drop doses, once a day, was given, and no local application made. He began to improve from the first day, and in about two weeks the wound had healed, and all symptoms of disease soon disappeared, since which he has enjoyed perfect health (Oct. 1853). The *Calendula* was continued daily for about ten days.

WOUNDS OF THE JOINTS.

Injuries of the larger joints are almost as dangerous as any in surgical practice. The danger consists as usual in inflammation — which it is much safer preventing than trusting to cure.

The limb should be placed in the *easiest position* that will bring the lips of the wound together, and be kept there perfectly still, so as to avoid the necessity for suture. Adhesive straps will be sufficient, if this point be attended to; but the patient must positively learn what we mean by "rest:" must not be allowed for several days to move the affected parts at all.

If the KNEE joint is concerned, you should keep the limb *extended*, that your patient, in the event of *anchylosis*, may still be able to walk, though with a stiff leg. The arm, on the contrary, when it is the elbow that is affected, had better be secured in a *half-flexed* position. The danger in question results mainly from adhesion between the synovial membranes, on losing their contained fluid. The joint should not be kept too long motionless. As the wound improves, it should be gently exercised.

For other treatment see the different classes of wounds, and consult the pathogenesis of *Arn.*, *Alum*, *Chin*, *Calen.*, *Led.*, *Nat. M.*, *Nux Vom.*, *Petr.*, *Puls.*, *Rhus.*, *Ruta.*, *Sep.*, *Silic.*, *Sulph.*

The practice of scarifying, blistering and leeching, about the wound, cannot be too strongly reprobated.

If *inflammation* should have progressed so far before you are called that suppuration is unavoidable, it will be proper to make such local applications as will induce or promote it. Retaining the limb in an elevated position is an important auxiliary in restraining or preventing inflammation.

In cases of this kind, a most excellent local application to the joint, for the prevention or moderation of the inflammation, and one which has been eminently successful *alone*, in our hands, is simply pure yellow clay kept moist with water, or dilute *Arnica*, *Calendula or Rhus. Tr.*, at the option of the surgeon.

Inflammation alone does not authorize *amputation*. A stiff joint is preferable to an amputated limb. Should the bones and cartilage be extensively shattered, leaving little or no hope of restoration, while danger of tetanus is imminent, immediate recourse to the knife and saw is justifiable, without waiting for inflammation. When we *must* operate, the sooner the better.

CHAPTER VII.

BURNS AND SCALDS

Distinction — Four degrees of Burning — Their respective symptoms and dangers — Heat — Spirits — Rum and Molasses — Carbonate of Lead — Flour — Soap — *Ulmus Ful.* — *Vertica Urens* — Internal Remedies — Prevention of Deformity.

UNDER this head are usually included all local injuries caused by the application of heat. Scalds are distinguished from burns by the mechanical state of the heated and heating substance; the popular meaning of the words may be considered as the technical one. All cases, then, caused by hot liquids are "scalds," while "burns" proper are those produced by solids at a high temperature. Greater injury may be done by oils and some other fluids, as they can be heated above 212°, the maximum of temperature for water under ordinary circumstances. On this account some writers would restrict the "scalding" to injuries done by hot or boiling water. They are all, however, degrees of "burning;" and the specific difference is better marked by the distinction of solid and liquid, than by that of the chemical character or temperature of the substance inflicting the injury. The effect of a hot liquid, or

Scalding, is likely to be more superficial, and is chiefly dangerous from the extent of surface affected.

Burns (including scalds) or the local effects of great heat, are *divided* into several kinds or degrees. Some distinguish four, some five or six.

The first degree of burning is when there is only a slight irritation produced, with redness of the surface and the stinging or peculiar pain, but without vesication, or with only small vesicles, the fluid in which is readily absorbed. The inflammation, if any is excited, terminates in spontaneous resolution. At worst, only a superficial dry scab is produced, involving little more than the cuticle. There may, indeed, be considerable tumefaction, produced by serous effusion in the cellular substance; but the effusion is absorbed, the swelling goes down, and the part returns to its natural state and appearance, leaving no trace of the injury.

In the second degree, there is more redness of the surface in the first instance, and this is succeeded by diffused vesication. The serous fluid is not absorbed; and when the vesicle or vesicles are broken, a purulent secretion from the surface takes its place. Still there is no real ulceration, or destruction of parts, further than the cuticle, and no necessity occasioned for granulation. The skin is merely converted into a secreting surface, and may continue to discharge pus for a considerable time. If exposed to the air, a crust or scab will form, protecting the parts beneath, and allowing a new cuticle to form there, as appears when the scab falls off, and presents the surface restored, without a scar, as in the former case.

In this form or stage of the burn, if care be taken not to puncture the distended cuticle until purulent matter begins to be formed beneath, the pain will be but slight, and the cure facilitated: but if by any accident or officious ignorance, the cuticle is ruptured, and the raw surface exposed to the action of the atmosphere, the pain is often intense, and the danger from irritation and inflammation may become very great.

In cases, otherwise of this character, where gunpowder or other coloring matter is forced through, under the surface, it will remain for a long time, as no sloughing occurs to carry it off.

The third degree is when the heat is so intense as, if not directly to disorganize the surface, to so far lessen its vitality as to render destructive inflammation inevitable. If, however, the extent of the injury be small, and the patient's constitution good, the ulcerative process will very generally terminate of itself, granulations form, and the surface heal up, leaving only an ugly cicatrix. But if the burn be large, much constitutional irritation will generally attend it, and the granulations, instead of healthy, will be of a fungoid character. The discharge also will be often excessive, and accompanied with an offensive smell. All these bad symptoms will be worse, if there is much constitutional derangement. Indeed, serious ulceration may follow the simple vesication, when the general health is very bad, but such a result is rare.

In all cases of ulceration from burns, the cicatrix remains red and glossy for a long time after, or of a higher color than the surrounding surface, with a puckered appearance, which is permanent.

When the heat is so great as of itself to destroy the skin (which some make a fourth variety), the pain is very great during the whole progress of the case, and even continues after the cicatrix has formed. The patient will be unable to use the part, or the muscles and tendons passing near it, in consequence of the preternatural susceptibility, especially if it were a part of a limb that was burnt, and that be in a dependent position. The tendons often contract, if near a joint, and when, in addition to this, adhesions have been allowed to occur, the use of the part or limb may be lost forever. These contractions and adhesions may not occur, in some cases, till after cicatrization, the irritation still continuing and producing a deposit of coagulable lymph.

The fourth and last degree (in our scale) is the true or complete burning up of the part; vitality being at once destroyed and disorganization effected. The cause of this is usually the application of some highly-heated *solid* substance, as white-hot iron. The part itself being involved in flame or other burning substance, will of course have the same effect. If this complete burning be also extensive, it will be most certainly fatal.

The patient in this case experiences no pain for a time; at least none after the first *touch*. The part is so effectually killed as at once to annihilate sensibility. The burnt part is "burnt to a crisp," leaving only an eschar. If there is sufficient power in the system to react, sloughing takes place, the eschar is thrown off, and a deep ulcer is formed.

The ulcer, in this case as in the last, is liable to suppurate and excite, also, an unhealthy condition of the surrounding parts. Not unfrequently abscesses will form there, with sinuses. The adjacent bones or joints soon become affected. The inflammation excited is sometimes immediately followed by extensive mortification.

If the patient does not *die* before reaction comes on, the constitutional irritation produces *hectic*, and he soon sinks from *exhaustion*.

The *danger* depends much upon the constitutional vigor of the patient, and upon the locality of the burn, as well as its extent. Children are not so likely to recover from the effects of a scald as adults, owing to the greater susceptibility of their nervous system. Very small children are apt to be thrown into spasms, when the effect upon the brain frequently proves speedily fatal. Very old persons suffer much less than any others; but erysipelas occasionally follows, which is very difficult to control. Erysipelatous inflammation is particularly to be apprehended, when the head is the part affected. When it is the abdomen, the inflammation is liable to extend to the vital organs beneath. A burn or scald on either of these locations is always to be regarded as dangerous, and proportionally more dangerous as the patient is younger. A slight injury of this kind upon the scalp is to be looked upon with suspicion; and you should take care to heal as soon as possible when upon the abdomen. Burns upon the genital organs are very hard to cure, and give rise to strong constitutional symptoms, in consequence of their peculiar susceptibility and great sympathy with all the vital functions. Upon the course of the *tendons*, these wounds tend more than any others to produce contraction, and when *nerves* are also involved in the eschar, or contraction, there will be danger, for a long time after, of tetanus or neuralgia.

Violent *constitutional symptoms* follow an extensive burn, let it be in what part it may. There will, at first, be rigors, disturbed and oppressed respiration, and general depression, with a pulse for a time low and feeble; but if there is sufficient vigor in the system for reaction, the subsequent inflammatory fever is often very violent.

Scalds, — unless when caused by hotter liquids than boiling water, or unless the part should remain in the hot water long enough to be itself boiled or cooked, — belong to the second degree in which nothing worse than vesication is the necessary result. Generally, therefore, their only danger is from the extent of surface involved. How large an amount of the cutaneous tissue may thus have its function stopped or changed, without *thereby* causing death, is not known. Some author has stated that life could not be supported after one-seventh of the surface was vesicated; but we are sure we have had cases in which a much larger fraction was not only blistered, but "flayed" away with the clothes.

The most important point of

TREATMENT

without doubt, in all kinds and grades of burns, is the *keeping* of the *surface entirely shielded from the atmosphere.*

Numerous *applications* "for burns and scalds" are in repute with the profession or the public, some of them are as "specifics." Many of them are really valuable, and we will mention a few, selecting those whose good effects we have had opportunity of testing, or those which, if not intrinsically superior to others, are oftener to be relied on, because universally accessible. Not the best possible, but the best practicable — the best under the circumstances of the case — is the rule for the medical man as well as the moralist.

In slight cases when the skin is not destroyed, it is best to expose the part for a short time to a moderate, dry heat, or apply water as hot as the patient will bear. When practicable, this can best be done by immersing the part in hot water. In either case the heat should be constant. Warm spirits have been recommended, but will be much more beneficial with molasses.* Prof. Gross of Louisville (in his notes to the American reprint of Liston's Surgery), strongly recommends the application of carbonate of lead and linseed oil, mixed as in common white paint; but this should *never* be used, since fatal consequences *have*, and are likely to result from the absorption of the lead. Lime water, sweet oil and soap, have been used with good results (see remarks on soap). But the applications most beneficial and easiest applied, are flour, soap (castile) or *ulmus fulva.* Of these the flour is most convenient, and from the testimony in its favor *at least* as beneficial. As soon, therefore, as possible, after the accident, oil the injured surface with sweet, or linseed oil (if the burn or scald is severe, the linseed oil will be rather too severe), and then sprinkle, or dredge with a common dredging-box flour over it until every part is *completely and thickly* covered. The fluids discharged, are absorbed by the flour and form it literally into a "crust," beneath which a new cuticle is *concocted,* and resolution readily effected, if the case admits of so favorable a termination.

* *Rum and Orleans Molasses* is a southern specific, which has been much extolled by several physicians. One of them assured one of the authors that he had seen it used, with the happiest results, in the most severe cases, both of scalds and burns. It frequently prevents vesication, and even discusses the inflammation where extensive vesication has previously been caused. In a few instances, Dr. Hill made this prescription for the grocery instead of the drug-store; and he says the result of its use has fully answered to its reputation. The spirits and molasses should be intimately mixed, and applied cool, either by wetting an elm poultice with the mixture, or saturating raw cotton or Canton flannel with it, and then applying a covering wet with some article impervious to air, such as a solution of gum arabic.

We are informed by one of the oldest and ablest Homeopaths in Ohio (Dr. Blair of Newark), that he has been in the habit of prescribing pure molasses for a long time, as a specific for all forms of burns, with the happiest results. He applies it so as completely to cover the affected surface, and keep it constantly covered by rewetting the dressings with the molasses until all inflammatory action has ceased.

Should the flour fall off, or any part become exposed, repeat the application.

In the use of the *soap*, Dr. Tifft, of Norwalk, O., in a communication to the authors, states one peculiarity which is worthy of especial notice. He makes a stiff lather with shaving soap, which he applies with a brush again and again, till he forms a thick coat, a complete covering, to all of the injured part; over this he places linen cloths, spread with a thick layer of soap. This plan he has found far more successful than any other; it is best to cut the linen in small strips, as it can thus be applied more accurately to an uneven surface. The same course should be pursued at every subsequent dressing. By means of the brush and lather, we can bring the soap in contact with every part of the surface, no matter how uneven, which sometimes cannot be done when it is spread on cloths. The application of the soap at first rather increases the pain, but soon mitigates it; it also generally prevents suppuration and those hideous scars. The frequency of the removal of the dressings should generally be governed by the state of the patient. If there should be an exacerbation of the pain after being relieved, apply another coat of lather. The *ulmus fulva* forms an excellent soothing shield from the atmosphere for the injured surface, is adapted to any stage, and has, in many cases, in our practice produced admirable results. The best way is to make it into a poultice with the warm dilute tincture of *Urtica Urens* (or the *dioicæ* seems to have the same effect), and apply over the burnt or scalded surface. From time to time, a little of the liquid may be poured on so as to permeate between the surface and the cataplasm. This is particularly beneficial where there is extensive suppuration or sloughing. It allays the pain and irritation, protects the surface from the action of the atmosphere, promotes the formation of healthy granulations, and is the best vehicle for the application of the specific *Urtica Urens*. After acute symptoms have subsided, simple dressings, such as simple cerate, are all that is necessary for the ulceration. If high febrile excitement comes on, give *Aconite*; also when the system has received a severe shock from fright at the time of the accident; in this *last* case *Opium* is of service. But if the patient sinks into a low state with feeble reaction, use *Carbo Veg.* and *Arsenicum.*

If his nervous system is much affected, fever being present, give *Belladonna*, or *Hyoscyamus*. *Cham.* has proved beneficial in convulsions from burns. *Tr.* of *Urtica Urens*, regarded by some as a specific, at a low dilution, we have found useful in very bad cases; we always use it internally when we apply it externally. When the suppuration is so extensive as to debilitate the patient, it should be used in alternation with *China*. If the ulcer becomes fungoid, use *Silicia*, *Arsenicum*, *Antimonium*, *Causticum*, *Sulphur*, or *Petroleum*. The latter article may be applied with excellent effect, undiluted to the surface of the sore. It will generally dissipate the fungous growths in a short time. When the fungus remains obstinate, apply the Sesqui Carbonate of Potash in powder two or three times at intervals of a day or two, until the sore assumes a healthy appearance.

An important *caution* for those who are not accustomed to these cases, is to keep fingers, toes and other contiguous parts, from coming in contact at the abraded surface. Another cause of *deformity* to be guarded against, is the contraction of muscles and tendons. For this danger you must study the anatomy of the parts, and resist the tendency with suitable splints or other modes of applying force, flexing or extending as the case may require. When this precaution has been neglected, the case is not quite irremediable. The contracted tendons can be divided when necessary, though we have hitherto only found it necessary in any cases that have fallen into our hands for repair, to dissect away the *adhesions*.

Superficial deformity, by irregular formation of the new integument, is best obviated by proper dressing and attention during the healing process. This becomes an important consideration, when exposed parts of the body, as face, hand or neck, is in question, — particularly in the case of females. A bad cicatrix may sometimes be divided or reopened by blistering, with a fair chance of improvement.

CHAPTER VIII.

EFFECTS OF COLD.

Frost-Bites and Freezing to Death — Recovery from suspended animation — Progress, symptoms and results of Frost-Bites — Liability of particular parts and persons — Precautions in restoring frozen parts — Efficacy of Snow — Chilblains — Variety — Liability — Relapse and chronic cases.

Too low a temperature is equally inimical to life with too high; and indeed the ultimate effect of a "frost-bite" is very similar to that of "a burn." Some parts of the body will suffer from exposure to cold much sooner than others. The peculiar stinging pain of intense cold ceases after a while, and the part becomes so entirely insensible that the individual knows not that he is partially *dead.* Complete freezing to death comes on in a similar way. After the first ineffectual effort of the system to bear up under the continual abstraction of heat, an irresistible sensation of drowsiness comes on, and the sufferer feels only inclined to rest and sleep. The sleepiness, however, is death in its most attractive and insidious form of approach. If the exposed person be aware of his danger, he may bear up a long time by force of will and muscular motion. Snow being a bad conductor of heat, and the surface of the body already reduced to its temperature, vitality may be preserved longer by wrapping up in that natural blanket than by *resting* in any other cold environment. Loss of voluntary power and of consciousness is soon followed by a cessation of the organic functions: the lethargy becomes the sleep of death. This sort of death, however, may be only temporary; from even this complete and dreamless sleep, the sleeper may be awakened, by a gradual restoration of the vital stimuli.

The essential difference between this sort of death and the more common is, that it results rather from a cessation of the functions than a change necessitated by a greater or less disorganization. It is a stagnation rather than an evaporation of life, so to speak. When an individual is found in this state of

SUSPENDED ANIMATION

from cold, he should be carefully removed to a *cold* room, where he will be protected from the *slightest* draught of air. If the limbs have become stiffened, cover him over with snow, to the depth of several inches, leaving only the mouth and nostrils free. As the snow melts and runs off, it should be replaced with fresh. Should there be no snow, the body of the patient may instead, be immersed in an iced salt-water bath for a few minutes. As soon as all parts have lost their rigidity, carefully remove the clothing, and rub the whole surface briskly with the snow or iced water with the bare hands, until the skin becomes red. The patient should then be well rubbed with dry flannels, wrapped up in a dry blanket, and laid in a cool bed in a cool room. If he does not soon begin to revive, small injections of tepid water containing a small portion of camphor may be given, and if necessary, repeated every fifteen minutes, until symptoms of restoration, when an infusion of browned coffee may be used instead of the former. As soon as the patient can swallow, which he will often do instinctively, before perfect consciousness has returned, a little of the coffee infusion may be given, a teaspoonful at a time. A persevering application of the above course has been rewarded by restoration, even when animation has been suspended for several days. A person thus resuscitated, should avoid exposing himself to much heat for a *considerable* time, as disease of the bones may be thus induced.

Carbo Vegetabilis should be given in repeated doses for the severe pains which generally follow a return of animation, and if not sufficient followed by *Arsenicum; Aconite* will be of service, if heat or stinging pains are felt in the head.

When a part of the body only has become insensible, and had its organic functions suspended, or been, as it is said,

FROST-BITTEN,

the same *principle* of treatment is to be observed. If much heat be too suddenly applied to the part, violent inflammation, if not speedy gangrene, is almost sure to occur. The spontaneous restoration of vital warmth, on entering a warmer medium, is of itself painful and dangerous enough, and to be made as gradual as possible.

The parts most liable to suffer first from cold, are those at the greatest distance from the source of circulation, as the fingers and toes; or most isolated from the general current, as the nose, ears, &c. The trunk of the body is not only protected by clothes, but by its mass and the easy communication of heat from part to part, in addition to the fact that the heat is conducted or radiated from a much less proportionate amount of surface. The importance of this distinction is very sensibly felt in the superiority of mittens over gloves, for the mere purpose of warmth. Hence one reason for the instinctive drawing up of the body when suffering, or, as it is said with mechanical correctness, shrinking from cold.

The *first* visible *symptom* of a part having been unduly exposed to cold is not paleness, nor the *florid* redness of over action or inflammation, but a sort of livid or dull red, indicated by the expression, "looks blue." This is accounted for by the stagnation of venous blood, and the diminished quantity of arterial blood attracted to the part. Certain depressing emotions, or states of mind, seem to be indicated as having a tendency to produce the same effect upon the cutaneous capillaries. Shame reddens, but chagrin or disappointment "looks blue." The depressing or *negative* feelings are, as it were, internal cold. Real physical cold, however to a mortal degree, is the only thing that produces the complete blue or "black looks."

If the exposure to cold, or abstraction of heat, still continue, even the venous blood disappears, all the blood is thrown upon the internal or less exposed parts, and the surface in question becomes white, considerably contracted or "shrunk up," and quite insensible and motionless. The part is in fact killed for the time, as much as if it had "mortified,"—only the process by which the latter state is brought about is usually the very reverse, and necessarily irremediable. The deadening of a frost-bite is temporary, because it is merely functional, instead of structural. Its danger, after withdrawal of the cause, is, that structural disease, inflammation, and common mortification, will ensue on a too sudden or on only partial restoration of vital temperature and activity.

This accident may happen much more readily to some persons than others. It is generally supposed that the degree of cold must be below the zero of our common thermometer (or 32° below the ordinary freezing point of water), in order to freeze a part of a living body. But the length of time the person or part has been exposed, must be taken into account, as well as the state of system at the time, in regard to food or fasting, clothing and exercise or the reverse, the general plethoric or active habit, and in short, so many other circumstances, that no general rule can be laid down. One individual may have a limb or member of the body frost-bitten, while those about him, exposed to the same amount of cold and for as long a time, will scarcely suffer at all. Indeed, the person who is said to "suffer the accident," does not feel it after it has occurred, or always know what has happened until he is told of it by others. If, however, it is a foot or hand that has been frozen, he will discover the fact from the loss of voluntary motion, as when the nerves are paralyzed. If heat is not restored to the part, it may be regarded as already in a state of sphacelus; and a sudden restoration, either of external or internal warmth, is very likely to bring on gangrenous inflammation around the part.

Habit, as well as original vigor of constitution, has much to do with a person's power of resisting cold. All know that individuals accustomed to wear gloves will suffer, from exposure without that protection, much sooner than those who habitually go about with their hands bare. Individuals, living on the shores of our northern lakes, are accustomed to wear boots without stockings, all the year round, and to work out in the open air through the winter, handling their ordinary implements of labor, or stones and metals, when necessary, without any covering on their hands.

Notwithstanding the present suspension of vitality, and future danger in the restoration of a frozen part, it is well known that not only small parts or members of the body may be restored to life and health but that whole limbs which have become white and quite brittle, may recover under a judicious course of treatment.

Though *haste*, in these cases, is more dangerous than *delay*, no time need be lost, after the discovery of the accident. The direct effect of the cold, and the indirect influence of partial death, should not be allowed to continue and extend. Wherever the patient may be, the first and most indispensable measure for his relief can be adopted. The accident never happens but where there is ice, if not snow, within reach. First, then, the rule given by all authorities, and sanctioned by the greatest of authorities, — *universal experience*, — is *Homeopathic:*

Rub the frozen part well with *snow* (where it is not to be met with, smooth ice may do for a while). After a while, the snow may be laid aside, and the part put into cold water, and there rubbed first with flannel and then with the hand. All this while the patient should be kept out of any room in which there has recently been a fire, and in an atmosphere not much, if any, above the freezing point. These precautions must be observed, and the means spoken of continue to be used, until the parts become sensible, or feel natural again, which may require several hours of constant rubbing. The patient will generally be thirsty, and it will be well to have him drink frequently small quantities of cold water. By so doing we have frequently seen persons, who were just before suffering extremely from cold, break out into a warm perspiration, with a genial glow of the whole surface.

By this management, the patient may experience no bad effects from the freezing, further, perhaps, than a slight swelling of the part, or desquamation of the cuticle as from a trifling scald. In such a case the part should be treated by some soothing application. If the part concerned be a limb, it will generally be found, though there is little sensible disease or suffering, to be much weaker for a long time after.

CHILBLAIN OR PERNIO.

This troublesome affection is a peculiar *atonic* kind of *inflammation* of the skin, induced by partial freezing, or rather by too sudden a change of its temperature, such as warming the feet or hands at a fire when very cold.

Children and very *old* persons are the most liable to this species or degree of "frost-bite," though it depends more on the degree of constitutional vigor than on mere time of life. Scrofulous individuals generally suffer most from these affections, in consequence probably of their tender susceptibility to cold.

At first the skin is red or *purple*, in round spots of an inch or two in size, and somewhat *swollen*, with a severe *itching* sensation, very much aggravated in moist or damp weather. In some instances vesications occur in the center, the skin around continuing to wear the same purple or bluish aspect; at other times the inflammation proceeds to the extent of sloughing. A serous fluid is generally discharged, or the mere swelling may become indolent, when it is very difficult to cure.

But by far the most troublesome cases are those in which *no ulceration* takes place. This is most frequently the case where the surface is protected by thick or horny cuticle, as on the ball of the great toe, and the sides of the bottom of the foot. When these parts become once affected, the patient is apt to suffer an intolerable itching and burning, not only during the cold season of the year, but still more in the fall or spring, when there is much moisture on the ground, and whenever the feet get damp.

Although the patient's sufferings may often be palliated by soaking the feet in hot salt water, and then rubbing them with palm oil, and holding them for some time to the fire, any relief obtained by this or other domestic means is only temporary; the predisposition to the recurrence of the disease must be removed by appropriate constitutional means.

The remedies most useful are *Agar.*, *Ars.*, *Arn.*, *Carb. Veg.*, *Cham.*, *Kali Carb.*, *Lyc*, *Nit. Ac.*, *Nux Vom.*, *Petr. Phos. Puls.*, *Rhus. Sulph.*

When the inflammation is slight, with bright red swelling, cracking and bleeding easily, and a burning itching when warm, *Nux Vom.* will relieve. *Cycl.* will also often be of service.

If the inflammation be caused by bruising or pressing upon the affected parts, or the swelling be hard and *shining*, *Arnica* should be used. In more severe cases, with *severe itching*, *burning* and *redness*, *Agaricus* will be effectual. When the parts are swollen and blue with itching and throbbing pain, aggravated in the evening or towards midnight, and the patient of a mild or phlegmatic disposition, *Pulsatilla* is indicated.

When the inflammation is *considerable*, not so dark as that of *Pulsatilla*, more of a bluish red, with a creeping tingling sensation, temperament melancholic, at times vehement, *Belladonna* is to be preferred. For these blue-red chilblains, with severe itching, *Kali Carb.* is also a valuable remedy. *Sulphur* is only suitable when the violent itching occurs during warmth.

Nit. Ac., *Petrol*, and *Phos.*, will also be found efficient in very painful chilblains; the first two, especially, if the inflammation sets in with very cold weather.

Rhus. when with the burning and itching there is a severe stinging in the chilblains, obliging to scratch, after which pustules arise. When the pains are very violent, with severe burning, or if blisters should show themselves on the inflamed parts, with a tendency to gangrene, *Arsenicum* alone, or in alternation with *Carb. Veg.*, should be used.

Should the inflammation degenerate into an ulcer, see *Ulcers*.

A lotion of the remedy given internally may be advantageously applied to the affected parts.

CHAPTER IX.

ULCERS — THEIR VARIETIES AND TREATMENT.

Definition and division — Boil or healthy Ulcer — Irritable and indolent Ulcers contrasted — Varicose Ulcers — "Specific Ulcers."

An "ulcer" has been defined a *chronic purulent* solution of the continuity of the animal texture.

Writers have generally divided them into a variety of classes, according to their appearance, progress and effects. The division here adopted will be sufficient for all practical purposes, though not so minute as may be found in some of the books.

We would distinguish then these five *kinds* of *ulcers:* 1st, the healthy; 2nd, the irritable; 3rd, the indolent; 4th, the varicose; and 5th, the specific.

This last class includes a great variety, which will be considered separately, as we come to speak of the diseases or causes which produce them. As examples, we may here mention the scrofulous, the syphilitic, the schirrous and the sinuous (or fistulous) ulcers.

1. As to the HEALTHY ULCER, it may be defined *Hibernice*, by saying it is no ulcer at all. It is a suppurative, but not an ulcerating, *i. e.*, destructive process. The pus discharged by it is a normal secretion.

Its *surface* has a florid appearance, without any offensive smell. The *pus* is consistent and easily removed. The granulations are small, and of a uniform size. It *heals* spontaneously and regularly, leaving little or no trace of having existed. Patches of granulations may be *early* noticed, over the top of which is thrown a delicate membrane or cuticle, which finally thickens and becomes true skin.

An example of the "healthy ulcer" is the common *boil*, — which, if not an evidence of perfect health, is regarded, and no doubt correctly, as the next thing to it, — a successful effort of nature to throw off some slight obstruction or impurity. It may appear on any part of the body, and occasions no difficulty further than the local pain and temporary inconvenience.

Treatment, as every one knows in the case of the boil, is little more than the "let well enough alone" practice: a little *salve* to protect it from the atmosphere, is all-sufficient. The only true "healing salve" is that which nature prepares for herself, — *healthy pus*.

II. THE IRRITABLE ULCER

is very sore to the touch, and easily made to bleed. It generally wears a dark purplish appearance, discharging but little matter, and that of a thin, ichorous or sanious appearance, and sometimes very fœtid and corroding. Its imperfect granulations are spongy, of a dark red hue, or having a whitish vesicular look, appearing at different points, or leaving vacant spaces between them, and often disappearing again by absorption. It is bounded by a sharp undermined (or shelving) edge, sometimes ragged, nearly what would be called in Botany, "serrated." The parts around the ulcer are swollen and reddened, — sometimes edematous.

The *constitutional effects* of this kind of ulcer are often very great, and manifested by thirst, chills, and great nervous prostration, as well as irritability. The pain at the part affected, which is often great, is of a smarting or burning character.

The worst result is, when the irritable ulcer becomes gangrenous.

THE INDOLENT ULCER

is in almost every particular the opposite of the *irritable*. Each can be best studied in contrast with the other. Reverse the definition of the one, and you have that of the other. The *edges* of the sore, for instance, are now *everted*, instead of being inverted, as in the former case; being, moreover, rounded and thick, somewhat glossy and quite regular. The *granulations*, instead of being red and sensitive, are insensible and of a dull pale aspect, with round flat heads, and generally located on the bottom of the excavation: they have, in short, a fungoid character. The pus, instead of being ichorous, is thick, of a dark yellow color, and so firmly adherent to the base of the ulcer that it cannot be removed without considerable force, and causing a good deal of pain (which, of course, should not be done).

This kind of ulcer is the more important, inasmuch as it is the most common form of "sore" which you will be called upon to treat professionally; while it deserves your attention still more, from the fact that it is an affection as rarely cured by the profession generally, as any that can be named, not in its nature incurable. *You* must not think of turning off these "hard cases," though you will meet with many persons who have worn their old ulcers for ten or twenty years, and exhausted in "doctoring" all their funds, faith and patience, without the least benefit. If there is in the whole catalogue of human sufferings, any disease in which the superiority of one form of practice over another is plain and palpable, it is this: our success in this class of cases, both before and since embracing Homeopathy, has been truly gratifying.

Indolent ulcers most frequently occur on the lower extremities, and much oftener in males than females (the latter seldom being troubled with them, unless in connection with a varicose condition of the limb, of which we shall speak further on).

VARICOSE ULCERS

are so named, because always connected with a swollen or varicose condition of the neighboring veins. In other respects, they may present the characteristics of either of the other two contrasted classes — may be either indolent or irritable. They are, however, almost always extremely tender to the touch, and often very painful when the part is exercised. The pain indeed is occasionally excessive, and the nervous system may become involved, even to the extent of delirium.

Varicose ulcers seldom occur any where but on the lower extremities, and then only *below the knee.* Nearly all the smaller veins, adjacent to the ulcer, are involved. The reddish brown color of the sore extends to some distance around. The ulcer itself may be superficial, or deep and burrowing.

SPECIFIC ULCERS,

meaning those that result from some specific inflammation or disease, as scrofula or syphilis, will be considered in connection with the disease producing them.

Wounds upon the lower extremities often degenerate into ulcers, and ulcers are often rendered intractable, not from any particular dyscrasia, but from the limb not being kept in the horizontal position until perfectly healed. The weight of the column of blood retards the circulation, the capillaries thus become congested, and are hindered in the reparative process; such wounds and ulcers, although before intractable, have changed to a healthy character immediately upon a change of position.

Ulcers are sometimes also rendered irritable by the depending position. The minute nervous filaments that are so numerously distributed upon and connected with the capillaries are put upon the stretch, and irritated by the congested state of the blood vessels; a few days' maintenance of the horizontal position will remove this, and the use of an appropriate bandage will entirely prevent its return. Hence the bandage, although usually contra-indicated in irritable ulcers, is sometimes useful.

Another fact to be borne in mind, is that the continuity of the skin is broken, and that it does not exert its accustomed pressure upon the superficial veins. The value of this pressure may be suspected from ulcers which have before shown no disposition to heal, being completely and effectually cured by an artificial cutis, *i. e.*, drawing the edges together by means of successive strips of adhesive plaster: hence one of the advantages of the bandage. The *local treatment* of ulcers upon the extremities, consists mainly in removing these mechanical obstacles to the cure. Whenever, therefore, ulcers are situated upon the limbs, they should be kept, as far as circumstances will admit, in a horizontal or even slightly elevated position. This is particularly important in the irritable, while they are such. In the majority of chronic ulcers, as it is impossible for the patient to do this much of the time, a substitute is provided in the strapping or bandage (for which, see next chapter).

In all forms of ulcers, it is best to use, as a topical application to the ulcer, a solution or dilution of the same remedy given internally. This is best applied by means of patent lint, or a soft sponge. The sponge is best in indolent ulcers, as by it we may obtain a slight elastic pressure upon the granulations, which will tend to stimulate them to a healthy action. It will sometimes, however, be necessary to apply soothing applications to the *irritable*, exposing the limb twice each day for half an hour to the vapor, from a weak infusion of hops, or an effusion of tepid water, and in the interval dressing with an emollient poultice, ulmus fulva, linseed or the common carrot. The latter, grated and wet with scalding water, makes an excellent one. When the irritability arises from the distention of the capillaries, gentle compression, by means of a bandage wet with tepid, occasionally cold water, will be very beneficial. (See also *Capsicum.*)

Indolent ulcers, when very foul, should be cleansed with a few applications of a weak solution of the Chloride of lime, or the sesqui-carbonate of potash, before applying the remedy used internally. At each dressing, the edges of the ulcer should be drawn together by means of straps spread upon the ends with adhesive plaster, and over this should be the bandage.

In *varicose* ulcers, the engorged and enfeebled state of the veins constitutes the most serious difficulty. To overcome this, the bandage or strapping (see next chapter) is indispensable; sometimes the principal veins around the ulcer have to be obliterated. For this, three plans are recommended: tying the veins, destruction by caustic, and coagulating the blood by means of electro-galvano puncture. The *obliteration* of the *veins* by ligature is much recommended, among other authorities, by Mr. Phillips, Surgeon to the Marylebone Infirmary (London), but is condemned by Bransby Cooper, Mr. Skey, and others. It is undoubtedly attended with much more danger than the caustic. We have applied the potassa fusa to each vein, from one to two inches from the ulcer. In the cicatrix which is formed, the vein is effectually obliterated. No fears need be entertained about the healing of the *caustic ulcer* (as there must be in that of the ligature). Such a stimulus is given to the part that it will only require simple emollient dressings. Mr. Skey, however, recommends three parts lime, and two of good fresh caustic potash (Vienna paste), made into a paste by the addition of spirits of wine, at the time of its application. His manner of applying this is to take three or four layers of good adhesive plaster, and make holes in them of about the size of a pea, the number to be regulated by the extent and complication of the disease; fix these firmly over the veins. Then fill the apertures with the paste, and over each of them place a piece of adhesive plaster. After twenty or thirty minutes, the whole may be removed.

Any number of eschars, he says, may be made on diseased veins, — that he has had as many as nine on one leg at a time, — but that they should be all made at one operation. This treatment he regards, after several years' trial, as both efficient and safe. He acknowledges, however, that occasionally the ulcers heal very torpidly, and that in one or two cases the disease of the veins partially returned at the expiration of three years. *Galvano-puncture* is certainly superior to the caustic, if the cures effected by it prove as permanent. No artificial ulcers are produced, and the cure is less painful and more rapid. The operation is performed by inserting into the vein two fine needles, which are connected with the positive and negative poles of a moderate-sized galvanic battery. This causes the vein to fill with a firm coagula of blood, without injuring its coats. The needles are best made of gold or silver, and should always be insulated by being covered, except at the points, with a varnish of shellac.

The magneto-electric instruments should never be used, as the interrupted currents produce severe pain. Dr. Restelli prefers a pile of many pairs of small plates, since less caloric is evolved, while the coagulating power is increased.

He also thinks that, by inserting the needle in connection with the negative pole, in direct opposition to the current of the blood, its flow will thus be checked, and coagulation accelerated. Cases will be given with those of ulcers in the next chapter.

Dr. Roth says that the tourniquet, applied for a few minutes every day, will cure varices.

We come now to the most important part, the internal treatment. The totality of the symptoms present, of each remedy, must all be carefully considered in connection with the previous medication and history of each case and the pathogenesis of the medicament. We can only give a few general indications.

The remedies found most generally useful are *Asaf.*, *Ars.*, *Carb. V.*, *Lach.*, *Lyc.*, *Merc.*, *Puls.*, *Sep.*, *Silic.*, and *Sulph.*

For *irritable*, particularly *Asaf.*, *Ars.*, *Bel.*, *Caps.*, *Lach*, *Lyc.*, *Hepar.*, *Graph.*, *Merc.*, *Mez.*, *Acid M.*, *Nit. Ac.*, *Phos.*, *Puls.*, *Silic.*, *Sulph.*

Indolent—Acid Phos., *Carb. V.*, *Euphorb.*, *Sang.*, *Sep.*, *Lach.*, *Lyc.*, *Ars.*, *Silic.*, and *Sulph.*

Varicose—Arn., *Puls.*, *Fluoric Acid*, *Kreos*, *Lach*, *Silic.*, and *Sulph*; also, *Ars.*, and *Phos. Ac.*

When proud flesh forms in ulcers—*Sang.*, *Sep.*, *Ars.*, *Petr.*, *Silic.*, and *Sulph.*

Asafœtida. Ulcers with elevated bluish edges, discharging a thin, ichorous, and fetid pus; painful upon pressure, particularly those affecting the bones and venereal-mercurial ulcers.

Arsenicum, when the ulcer bleeds easily, is very painful, with a *severe burning*, which sometimes changes to a tearing, when the parts become cold; the edges hard, irregular, and everted; the discharge is rather scanty, thin, offensive, and bloody, or blackish, copious, very fetid and ichorous: also old ulcers, with red shining areola, and a basis, which is either black, blue, or has the appearance of lard, and those with *proud flesh* and *fetid ichor.*

Belladonna, when the areola around the ulcer is inflamed and painful; there is a *burning* in the ulcer, upon its being touched, or at night, with lameness of the affected part; discharge bloody and ichorous. (See Scrofulous Ulcers.)

Carbo Vegetabilis is indicated by symptoms similar to those of *Arsenicum*, except that the ulcer, instead of being inflammatory in its character, is *torpid*, and *entirely destitute of organic reaction*. It is sometimes useful in alternation with *Arsenicum*, when the ulcer is disposed to be gangrenous, the discharge very fetid, and there is much exacerbation of the burning pains towards evening, or at night.

Capsicum we have frequently used internally and externally for those obstinate cases, when nothing else affords relief; such as will be met with in ulcers on the legs of females who have been affected with *phlegmasia dolens*. The pain being of the severest character and nearly continuous, *smarting* and *burning* as *though the part were enveloped in fire;* the nervous system much affected; chills and great prostration, with loss of appetite and great thirst, being accompaniments. For the external application, dilute the tincture, leaving it strong enough to produce severe smarting, and wash the ulcer freely with it. Though it first aggravates the suffering of the patient, it will soon allay the burning and smarting. It may be reapplied upon a return of the pain, and will soon change it to a healthy ulcer.

Graphites is beneficial when the pain is of the itching and smarting kind, with a feeling of pressure and sticking, the pain being very violent, with a sensation as though the bone would be broken when the limb is moved.

Fluoric Acid, in repeated doses, reduced to one-half their former size, numerous varicose veins, of twenty years' standing, on the left leg of an old man.

Kreosotum. Scrofulous and varicose ulcers, particularly on the feet of old people, secreting an acrid fetid ichor, bleeding easily, the edges irregular and raised, looking as if corroded by insects. (See GANGRENOUS ULCERS.)

Hepar Sulphuris. Ulcers with itching, corrosive, gnawing pain; burning and throbbing at night; *bleeds even when slightly wiped;* pus having a *sour smell*, as old cheese. If on a limb, the pain is so aggravated by the depending position, that it is insupportable. Sometimes follows Arsenicum, with advantage.

Lachesis. Foul, flat ulcers, of various sizes, scattered over the body with ichorous discharge: old, very painful ulcers, deep, foul, uneven at the bottom; edges raised, pad-shaped; a spongy appearance; cannot bear to be touched or moved; burning pain at night, palliated by bathing with cold water; tightness of the skin around the ulcer, as if too short. The leg sometimes of a livid, dark brownish mottled appearance, enlarged, with numerous small ulcerating pustules around the ulcer.

Lycopodium. — Phagedenic ulcers; edges callous or everted, with very great itching tearing pain, especially at night in bed, and pus of a yellowish citron color.

Mercurius. — Deep ulcers, disposed to spread rapidly, bleed easily, very sensitive, least touch causing severe pain; base uneven, of a dirty reddish or lard-like appearance; edges raised, irregular, serrated, varying in appearance, some parts red, shining, others livid; pus thin and offensive; pains are generally burning with stitches, sometimes shooting. Should there be also present an unequal quick pulse, restlessness, profuse night sweats, great nervousness and impatience from the slightest causes, it will be more strongly indicated.

Muriatic Acid. — Ulcers covered with scurf, on persons whose vital powers are much impaired, and disposed to become dropsical; very painful, with burning, more around than in the ulcer; exercise causes a sort of throbbing in the ulcer; fetid, ichorous pus.

Pulsatilla. — Flat, putrid, carious, *varicose* and easily bleeding ulcers, surrounded by a hard, shining red areola, which is affected with severe itching, pain in the ulcer of a stinging, biting-burning character, which is somewhat relieved by the pressure of the bandage.

Sanguinaria. — Old, indolent, ill-conditioned ulcers with callous borders and ichorous discharge, and those disposed to the formation of proud flesh.

Silicia. — Old, unclean ulcers on persons who have become debilitated and cachetic, whether from abuse of mercury or drunkenness. It is often, in obstinate cases, advantageously alternated with *Sulphur* or *Sepia*, and *Nitric Ac.* It is useful when granulation takes place slowly and imperfectly, or proud flesh is disposed to shoot up. In ulcers with rough callous edges, the parts around the ulcer, if on the legs, enlarged, bluish red, and hard, sometimes like bone; pain stitching and burning around the margin, but aching in the ulcer; pus either thick and discolored, or thin, bloody, ichorous and offensive.

Sulphur, — in most all old ulcers, Scrofulous, Fistulous, Psoric, Mercurial, &c., when there is a very strong tendency to the production of proud flesh, and there is no distinct appearance of granulations. In the irritable, easily bleeding with raised, swollen and sensitive edges, discharging a thin, fetid, ichorous or sanious fluid, as well as those almost destitute of sensibility, surrounded with a dark bluish areola, the base covered with pale-red, spongy, insensible proud flesh, with a smooth shining surface, and discharging a thick yellow pus. The *Tincture* of *Sulphur*, first attenuation, one dose night and morning, is highly recommended by Hartman for phagedenic and varicose ulcers. He says it will remove the itching and burning, and the inflammation around the ulcer in a few days, though it generally takes a number of weeks to cure the ulcers.

CHAPTER X.

CHRONIC ULCERS — "OLD SORE LEGS" — "FEVER OR BRANDY SORES."

Chronic Ulcers — Their frequency and supposed incurability — Description — "Ought old sores to be cured?" — Old School treatment — Bandaging and strapping — Therapeutic indications from Dr. Boenninghausen — Report of Cases.

THAT the subject of ulcers may be as complete as possible, we shall in this chapter call attention to another species or compound of the ulcer genus, give the peculiarity of topical treatment, and in addition to the remedies and their indications given in the preceding chapter, quote from that valuable work of Dr. Böenninghausen (Therapeutic Pocket Book, translated by Dr. Hempel), his remarks upon ulcers, and in conclusion give the report of a few cases.

This species we have designated by the truly descriptive, if not very classical name of

OLD SORE LEGS!

That it is of more importance than any of the others, must be evident, if for no other reason than for this, that it *includes all* the others, — the same limb often producing specimens of the indolent ulcer, the irritable, the varicose, and perhaps, too, at the same time, one or two in a tolerably healthy condition.

These cases will often be brought under your notice as "*fever sores;*" and as they not unfrequently afflict those who are, or have been, hard drinkers, they are also called, in many parts of the country, "*whisky*" or "brandy *sores.*" Though intemperance, as this name implies, may have been the principal cause, "signing the pledge," or even the keeping of it, will not always be sufficient to obtain a remission of the penalty. Physiological sins are not pardoned on simple repentance. Medicinal means of grace have been provided.

But, unfortunately, the sinners, or sufferers, lack *faith* in the Old School ministry, and little wonder! They have often gone the rounds of the profession, consulted every doctor within their reach, been treated or maltreated in hospitals and in private hands; and if their general health, which is often tolerably good, escapes *this* great additional danger, the only result is, that they get resigned to their original affliction as well as the disappointment, and can hardly be brought to believe there is for them any "balm in Gilead," — any hope from surgery. Few cases come into our hands that are not of long standing. We have had them ten, twenty, and even thirty years old.*

Although the patient is apparently well, and will tell you that his general health is perfect, he is often more or less lamed (the ulcers being deep), and suffers much, particularly at night. The chief suffering is from the heated state of the parts, which is so great that cold water affords no sensible relief, and you will often find that, even in the coldest nights, he lies with the limb entirely uncovered. But grown accustomed to the evil, and faithless as to any remedy, the sufferer makes no complaints and calls for no aid.

* In one case of *thirty-five* years' standing, where thousands had been spent for medical treatment, a complete cure was effected in a little over twelve months.

His cure, however, is not hopeless, though he is past hoping for it. Of however bad a character and long standing may be the case — and though all the "eminent" surgeons and doctors in the country may have failed, — the Homeopathic surgeon need not fail, and will not, if he carefully selects his internal remedies, and faithfully applies the topical treatment as recommended in this and the preceding chapter.

One peculiarity of these ulcers was alluded to: they are often from an inch to an inch and a half deep. They often appear deeper than they really are, from the edges being raised, and hardened by a deposit in the cellular tissue. Sometimes *sinuses* are present, and retard the cure. The patient may suffer much more, however, from the swelling, where there is no open ulcer at all.

Aside from the character of the ulcers themselves — the *condition* of the *limb* is remarkable. This is hardened as well as swollen, and in some instances not to be distinguished by the touch from bone. Not unfrequently the patient will say that Dr. somebody or other has pronounced it an incurable "enlargement of the bone," and thrown out a pleasant hint about amputation in prospect! Around the ulcers, and at other points where ulcers have formerly existed,— sometimes the limb all over, from ankle to knee,— it is as *dark* as a negro's leg: where the cuticle scales off, as often happens, it leaves a shining, bluish or livid surface, which becomes *white* on *pressure* with the finger.

It is a popular opinion or prejudice, that if these old sores could, they *should not be cured!* This notable idea is often encouraged too, by professional men!! Is it to conceal their own want of skill, or because they really have seen bad effects follow the "cure" of such cases *under their practice?* Certainly no *physician* will consider the *mere external closure of a chronic ulcer as a cure*, while the diseased state of the system which occasioned it, and which perhaps required it, remains uncorrected. Physiology does not enumerate among the natural emunctories, an artificial anus in the leg. The human mechanism was surely constructed to be kept in order without such a safety-valve as *that!* Restore the *general health* by proper constitutional means, giving due attention to *all* the functions, secretory and excretory, and there will be *no danger whatever.*

Nature will be able to preserve the general system without the sacrifice of any particular part. Nor *need* there ever be any necessity for reopening the unfortunate ulcer, or setting up of a substitute in the shape of an artificial issue in some other part of the body, as is the practice of some surgeons. The drainage and sewerage of the system are better provided for than they can be by our art. Where, however, constitutional treatment is resorted to by the *old Alleopathic school* of practitioners, it is often worse than useless. They are informed, indeed, by one of their greatest American lights, that "constitutional means often (!) exert great influence (! !) over indolent ulcers." And what do you suppose is indicated as the very best of all "constitutional means?" "In the words of the Philadelphia Hospital," continues the professor quoted,* "I have succeeded in numerous instances by the use of *blue pills*, and other preparations of *mercury*, after *most other means* had been tried for months ineffectually."

How much, or rather how *little* is implied by this expression, "most other means," we may perhaps guess from what follows: "where the patient's constitution has been prostrated by intemperance and other similar causes, the internal use of carbonate of ammonia, wine, brandy, opium, &c., will prove of immense service; indeed, in most instances, chronic ulcers cannot be healed without the use of such remedies." These eight or ten lines include all the constitutional treatment recognized as necessary by a distinguished teacher in one of the first Old School colleges in the world! The blue pill and other preparations of mercury, with wine, brandy and opium!! When such a guide as that is blindly followed by thousands, can we wonder at the consequences to the tens of thousands whose lives and health are at stake? *Opium* and *Mercury*! The former of these *never-failing* resources is also recommended by Druitt, the author of a much esteemed practical compend of English Surgery. He tells us (p. 85) "to begin with half-grain doses night and morning, and gradually increase to keep up the impression,"—as of course we must to a Chinese or Turkish extent, and probably never be able to leave it off again, while it *leaves life*. Besides this often fatal *inconve-*

* Gibson's Surgery, vol. 2, p. 163.

nience, the use of the *article as recommended* is clearly contra-indicated by the very state of the system assigned as a reason or *excuse* for giving it. We are encouraged to rely on this tempting palliative, because forsooth "it acts on the surface!" as if its certain *secondary* effects on the surface in those large doses, when long continued, as in this case it must be, were not *visibly* the reverse of those designed! Who knows not the sear and dried-up skin of the opium eater?

It is these partial and superficial views of disease, and the action of remedies, that occasion such frequent failures, and even fatal errors. Not only has the *general surface* been for years in a diseased condition, but the system at large is as plainly out of order. Yet opium and mercury are to be prescribed! the former being certain in the end to lessen the healthy action of the skin and other excreting surfaces, and the latter having a direct tendency, when used as recommended, to derange the liver and stomach, and through its constitutional influence aggravate the local difficulties already present. What ulcers are so ill-conditioned and intractable as *mercurial ones?*

Not in a single instance is any application recommended for the skin, — that most important and most neglected of the health-preserving, and health-restoring organs, — no, not even soap and water! Is it then surprising, that in these chronic diseases, under the old Alleopathic practice, the *rule* should be the failure, and *cure* the exception? and that, in a large proportion of cases, such doctoring should prove worse than unavailing — positively and grossly mischievous?

Homeopathy keeps us from any such empirical practice, by teaching us to carefully consider the *totality* of the symptoms present in each case, and the selection of that remedy whose symptoms correspond most fully.

The peculiarity of topical treatment, consists in making use of such mechanical appliances as will remove the mechanical obstacles to the cure. The weight of the superincumbent column of blood, retarding the circulation, tends to produce congestion of the capillaries, and consequent tension of the filaments of nerves distributed over them. These difficulties are increased by the division of nature's bandage — the skin. They are overcome by the artificial bandage. It is true that they may also be obviated by confining the limb in a horizontal position. This is, however, impossible in the majority of instances, during the length of time necessary for the cure of these long standing cases, either from the circumstances or unwillingness of the patient. But if it were possible, it would be impolitic; depriving a patient of the advantages of exercise in the open air, might injure his health. Besides, experience has shown that a cicatrix formed while the limb was kept in the horizontal position, is not as firm as one formed where the limb was exercised. Some Homeopathic writers have said that "the treatment of chronic indolent ulcers ought to be solely internal at the *commencement.*" If the internal remedies are sufficient to overcome the mechanical obstacles, as well as remove the dyscrasia at the *commencement*, and convert the ulcer into one of a healthy character, why not let them complete the cure? Why is it more improper to remove the mechanical obstacles to the cure at the commencement than at a later period of the treatment?

The bandage, for some time after commencing the treatment, should be applied once or twice a day by the surgeon himself, so that he may know that it *presses equally upon every part.* Any part left constantly uncompressed by unskillful bandaging, will soon become sore, and probably break out in an ill-conditioned ulcer. The pressure should be gentle at first, and gradually increased according to the feeling of the patient. If it acts favorably, the swelling will decrease, and the pus become thicker, and more cream-like.

Fig. 1.

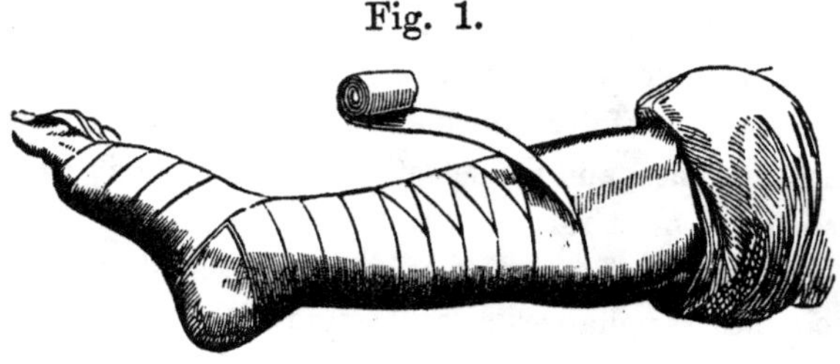

To *apply the bandage*, which should be about two and a half inches wide, begin with it at the extremity of the great toe, so as to compress it equally all round. At the next turn include the second toe, and so on with the others, one at a time. Then go on smoothly and firmly all over the foot, first placing compresses in the hollows round the ankle, so as to have equal pressure at every point. Continue to the knee, or should the state of the limb require it, include even the thigh also. Let each layer of the roller overlap the preceding for at least two-thirds of its width. Where the limb is tapering (as just above the malleoli), it will not lie smooth unless it is folded over itself and slightly changed in its direction at almost every turn. When it reaches the knee, or as high as you wish to go, bring it, in the same manner, down to the foot again, taking care to bind it no tighter than before.

The limb may now be kept wet with cold or warm water, and covered with flannel or oil silk to prevent evaporation (see preceding chapter). When there is a hard, callous welt around the edge of the ulcer, a compress of thin sheet lead over it, will hasten its absorption. When there are sinuses, they should be daily injected with a dilution of the internal remedy, after which, lint, wet with the same, should be pushed into them until they are quite filled. Where they connect, lay them open with a ligature.

With the appropriate internal and this topical treatment, the *ulcers* will soon heal, but the *cure* is not complete so long as there is any hardness or discoloration of the limb.

The limb should be daily bathed in cold water, and the *bandage* continued for some time after all traces of the difficulty have disappeared.

The diet in these cases, needs generally to be *nutritious*, not stimulating. And besides the sponge-bath, which should be universally used, if only for the purpose of cleanliness, a great advantage may be derived from the wet-sheet pack, and other invigorating appliances of Hydropathy. The bandage has been sufficient in our hands, yet as there are cases in which we think Mr. Scott's plan of

Strapping may be advantageous, we quote the directions for it as given by Dr. Critchett in the London Lancet, vol. ix. He says: "You must seat your patient opposite to you, and support his foot upon a small stool about a foot and a half in height, and so constructed as to receive the point of the heel, and leave the rest of the foot free. You should be provided with strips of plaster, about two inches in width, and varying in length from twelve to eighteen inches, according to the size of the limb. The best material for this purpose is the simple *emp. plumbi*, of the Pharmacopoeia, spread upon soft, unglazed calico, and free from resin, which is often introduced to increase its adhesiveness, but which is very liable to irritate the skin. If the plaster be well made, and of the best materials, it will adhere perfectly. I have often found it unmoved for many weeks and even months. It is convenient to provide yourself with a metallic warmer, made with a flat top, upon which you can lay three or four pieces, heated either by hot water or by small lamps, which are better, if you require it for any length of time. This form of warmer is far preferable to the circular one, ordinarily in use, saving both time and trouble. But to proceed. You then take the center of the first piece, and apply it low down to the back of the heel, and then with the flat part of both hands, press the plaster along both sides of the foot. This plan is preferable to taking hold of the ends, and endeavoring to apply them, as it insures a perfectly smooth adaptation of the plaster to the part, and also because it enables you to regulate the amount of tightness, which is a very important point. As you proceed with the remainder, you must always remember the principle is to make one portion hold on another; you must, therefore, alternate them round the foot and ankle. Your second piece should be placed in a similar manner underneath the heel, then carried upwards, at a right-angle to the last, so as to cover a portion of each malleolus. The third piece should be again applied to the back of the heel, overlapping the first by about one-third. The fourth piece under the foot and carried upward, each piece being pushed along so as to allow it to take its own course; this must be continued until the foot and ankle are enveloped. The strips must then be carried in a similar manner up the leg, increasing in length as the calf increases, and extending as far as the knee, and in some few cases even above this. A calico bandage, about three inches in width, and eight yards in length, varying, however, according to the size of the limb, must now be applied, to keep the plaster in its place, and the limb is supported in the most complete and efficient manner that human ingenuity has yet devised." In small ulcers, situated in the hollow, between the malleolus and os calcis, he directs, previous to the support just described, to apply some pieces of strapping, about six inches in length, and two inches in width, in a crucial manner, over the wound, so as to extend a few inches above and below it.

For the selecting of internal remedies, see the remedies spoken of in the preceding chapter, and carefully consult the following indications as given by Dr. Böenninghausen.

"**Ulcers in general.**

Acon. alum. ambr. amm. anac. ang. *ant-crud.* ant-tart. arg. *arn.* ARS. ASAF. *aur. bar.* BELL. bor. bov. BRY. CALC. camph. canth. *carb-an.* CARB-VEG. *caust. cham. chel. chin.* cic. cina. *clem.* cocc. coff. colch. CON. *creos.* croc. cupr. cycl. dig. dros. dulc. euphorb. *graph.* guaj. HEP. hyosc. ignat. jod. ipec. kali. LACH. led. LYC. mgs. m-arct. m-austr. mang. MERC. *mezer. mur-ac. natr.* natr-mur. NITR-AC. n-mosch. n-vom. par. *petr.* PHOSPH. PHAC. plumb. PULS. *ran-bulb.* ran-scel. RHUS. *ruta. sabin.* samb. sassap. scill. *sec-corn.* selen. seneg. SEP. SIL. spong. STAPH. stram. stront. SULPH. sulph-ac. tar. *thuj.* veratr. vit. zinc.

—— **bruised, with pain as if.**

Ang. ARS. cham. *chin. cocc.* CON. HEP. hyosc. natr-mur. *n-vom.* rhus. *ruta.* SULPH.

—— **biting** (smarting).

Ars. bell. *bry. calc.* carb-an. *caust.* cham. chin. *colch.* dig. EUPHORB. *graph.* LACH. LED. LYC. mang. *merc. mezer.* natr. petr. ph-ac. PULS. ran-bulb. rhus. ruta. selen. *sil.* staph. SULPH. sulph-ac. thuj.

—— **black, turning.**

Ant-tart. ARS. ASAF. bell. *carb-veg.* con. *euphorb.* ipec. *lach. mur-ac.* PLUMB. sas. *rhus.* scill. SEC-CORN. SIL. *sulph.* sulph-ac.

—— —— **on the bottom,**

ARS. *ipec.* plumb. *sil.* sulph.

—— —— **on the edges.**

ARS. lach. *sil.* sulph.

—— **bleeding.**

Ant-tart. arg. *arn.* ARS. ASAF. bell. CARB-VEG. caust. con. creos. croc. dros. HEP. *hyosc.* jod. KALI. LACH. LYC. *mgs.* MERC. mezer. natr-mur. NITR-AC. PHOSPH. *ph-ac.* PULS. rhus. ruta. sabin. *sec-corn.* sep. SIL. SULPH. sulph-ac. thuj. zinc.

Ulcers, bleeding on the edges.

ARS. *asaf.* caust. *hep.* *lach.* LYC. MERC. phosph. ph-ac. puls. sep. SIL. sulph. thuj.

—— with blisters around.

ARS. bel. *caust.* *hep.* LACH. mgs. merc. natr. petr. phosph. *rhus.* *sep.*

—— bluish.

Arn. *ars.* *asaf.* *aur.* bell. bry. calc. carb-veg. CON. HEP. LACH. mang. *merc.* ph-ac. sec-corn. seneg. *sil.* staph. *veratr.*

—— boring.

Arg. aur. *bell.* calc. caust. chin. *hep.* kali. natr. natr-mur. *puls.* *ran-scel.* sep. SIL. SULPH. thuj.

—— burning.

Ambr. ARS. *asaf.* aur. bar. *bell.* bov. *bry.* calc. *carb-an.* CARB-VEG. CAUST. cham. chin. *clem.* CON. *creos.* dros. graph. HEP. ignat. kali. *lach.* LYC. mang. MERC. MEZER. mur-ac. *natr.* natr-mur. nitr-ac. *n-vom.* petr. phosph. ph-ac. plumb. PULS. *ran-bulb.* RHUS. sassap. scill. sec-corn. selen. sep. SIL. *staph.* stront. SULPH. *thuj.* zinc.

—— —— in the edges.

ARS. *asaf.* *carb-an.* CAUST. clem. HEP. *lach.* LYC. MERC. *mur-ac.* petr. phosph. ph-ac. *puls.* ran-bulb. sep. SIL. staph. *sulph.* thuj.

—— —— in the circumference.

ARS. ASAF. bell. CAUST. cham. *hep.* LACH. LYC. MERC. *mezer.* mur-ac. natr. n-vom. petr. phosph. PULS. RHUS. sep. SIL. staph.

—— as if burnt.

Alum. *ant-crud.* ARS. *bar.* bell. bry. calc. CARB-VEG. *caust.* *creos.* CYCL. hyosc. *ignat.* lach. *n-vom.* *puls.* *sabad.* *sec-corn.* *sep.* stram.

—— cancerous.

Ambr. ant-crud. ARS. aur. *bell.* calc. *carb-an.* *carb-veg.* caust. chel. clem. *con.* *creos.* dulc. HEP. LACH. MERC. *nitr-ac.* phosph. *rhus.* sassap. scill. SEP. SIL. spong. *staph.* SULPH. *thuj.*

—— cold, with a sensation of.

Ang. ARS. BRY. *merc.* petr. plumb. *rhus.* SIL. thuj.

—— —— with corroding (gnawing) pains.

Bar. bell. calc. *cham.* cycl. *dros.* hyosc. *kali.* led. *lyc.* mang.

merc. mezer. natr. *phosph. ph-ac.* PLAT. PULS. RAN-SCEL. rhus. *ruta.* STAPH. *sulph.* thuj. VIT.

Ulcers, crusty (scabby).

Ars. bar. BELL. bov. *bry.* CALC. carb-an. cic. clem. CON. GRAPH. *hep.* led. LYC. MERC. mur-ac. *puls.* ran-bulb. RHUS. sas-sap. SEP. SIL. staph. SULPH. viol-tr.

—— **cutting.**

BELL. CALC. *dros.* graph. ignat. *lyc.* mur-ac. NATR. ph-ac. rhus. sep. *sil.* sulph-ac.

—— **deep.**

Ant-crud. ars. *asaf. aur.* BELL. CALC. *carb-veg.* caust. chel. clem. CON. creos. *hep. lach.* led. LYC. mgs. *merc. mur-ac.* natr. natr-mur. NITR-AC. *petr.* phosph. *ph-ac.* PULS. *rhus. ruta.* sabin. selen. *sep.* SIL. staph. stram. SULPH. *thuj.*

—— **digging.**

ASAF. bell. bry. calc. *chin.* natr. phosph. **ruta.** *sep.* stront. sulph.

—— **drawing.** (See Tearing).

—— **dry.** (See Pus too little).

—— **even** (flat).

Amm. ang. *ant-crud.* ant-tart. ARS. ASAF. *bell.* carb-an. carb-veg. *chin.* LACH. LYC. MERC. natr. *nitr-ac. petr.* phosph. PH-AC. *puls. ran-bulb.* SELEN. SEP. SIL. *sulph.* thuj.

—— **feeling, destitute of.**

Anac. ARS. CALC. *camph. carb-an.* CARB-VEG. CON. dulc. *euphorb.* graph. *jod.* ipec. kali. *lach.* LAUR. LYC. mgs. mur-ac. *nitr-ac. oleand.* OP. phosph. PH-AC. *plumb.* rhus. sec-corn. *sep.* SIL. stram. SULPH. vit. zinc.

—— **fistulous.**

Ant-crud. ars. ASAF. *aur.* BELL. bry. CALC. CARB-VEG. *caust.* chel. clem. CON. creos. *hep. lach.* led. LYC. merc. **natr.** natr-mur. NITR-AC. *petr.* phosph. ph-ac. PULS. rhus. ***ruta.*** sabin. selen. *sep.* SIL. staph. stram. SULPH. *thuj.*

—— **flat.** (See Even).

—— **gangrenous.**

Ant-tart. ARS. ASAF. *bell.* carb-veg. con. EUPHORB. LACH. merc. PLUMB. ran-bulb. SCILL. SEC-CORN. SIL. *sulph. sulph-ac.*

Ulcers, with gnawing pains. (See Corroding).

—— hard.

Arn. ARS. ASAF. aur. bar. BELL. BRY. CALC. carb-an. *carb-veg.* caust. cham. chel. CHIN. cic. cina. CLEM CON. cupr. cycl. dulc. *graph.* HEP. hyosc. jod. LACH. led. LYC. MERC. mezer. natr. n-vom. *phosph. plumb.* PULS. ran-bulb. ran-scel. selen. *sep.* SIL. *staph.* SULPH. thuj. veratr. *vit.*

—— —— on the edges.

ARS. ASAF. *bry.* carb-an. caust. cic. cina. *clem.* HEP LACH. LYC. MERC. petr. phosph. ph-ac. PULS. ran-bulb. sep. SIL. staph. *sulph.* thuj.

—— —— in the circumference.

Arn. ARS. ASAF, BELL. caust. cham. cina. *hep.* LACH. LYC. *merc.* mezer. natr. n-vom. petr. phosph. PULS. sep *sil.* staph. sulph.

—— with high, hard edges.

ARS. ASAF. *bry.* carb-an. *caust.* cic. cina. clem. hep. lach. LYC. MERC. mur.ac. *petr.* phosph. ph-ac. PULS. ran-bulb. *sep.* SIL. staph. *sulph. thuj.*

—— difficult to heal.

Alum. amm. *bar.* CALC. *carb-veg.* caust. CHAM. chel. *clem.* CON. croc. GRAPH. hell. HEP. kali. LACH. LYC. magn. mang. MERC. mur-ac. *natr.* NITR-AC. n-vom. PETR. *phosph. ph-ac.* plumb. RHUS. *scill.* SEP. SIL. STAPH. SULPH.

—— hot. (See Burning and Inflamed).

—— jerking.

Arn. ASAF. aur. *bell.* bry. CALC. CAUST. *cham. chin.* clem. *cupr.* graph. *lyc. merc.* natr. NATR-MUR. *nitr-ac. n-vom.* petr. PULS. RHUS. *sep.* SIL. *staph. sulph.*

—— inflamed.

ACON. ant-crud. *arn.* ARS. *asaf.* bar. BELL. bor. bov. BRY. *calc.* caust. *cham.* cina. cocc. *colch.* con. creos. croc. cupr. dig. HEP. hyosc. ignat. led. LYC. m-arct. mang. MERC. *mezer. natr. nitr-ac.* n-vom. petr. *phosph.* plumb. PULS. ran-bulb. RHUS. *ruta.* sassap. sep. SIL. STAPH. *sulph.* thuj. veratr. vit. zinc.

—— itching.

Alum. ambr. amm. anac. *ant-crud. ant-tart.* arn. ARS. bar. *bell. bov.* bry. *calc. canth.* carb-veg. CAUST. *cham.* chel. CHIN. *clem.*

con. creos. dros. GRAPH. HEP. ipec. *lach.* led. LYC. *merc.* mezer. natr. natr-mur. nitr. *nitr-ac.* n-vom. petr. *phosph.* PH-AC. PULS. *ran-bulb.* RHUS. ruta. sabad. sassap. scill. selen. SEP. SIL. STAPH. SULPH. *thuj.* veratr. viol-tr. zinc.

Ulcers, itching round about.

Ant-tart. ars. bell. caust. clem. HEP. LACH. LYC. merc. mezer. natr. n-vom. petr. phosph. *ph-ac.* PULS. *rhus.* sabin. *sep.* SIL. *staph. sulph. vit.*

—— looking like lard.

Ant-crud. ART. *creos.* cupr. HEP. MERC. NITR-AC. *sabin.* sulph. thuj.

—— —— on the bottom.

Ars. *hep.* MERC. *nitr-ac.*

—— with maggots.

Ars. calc. merc. SABAD. SIL. *sulph.*

—— old, opening again. (See Cicatrices).

—— painful. (See Sensitive).

—— painless.

Ambr. anac. ant-tart. arn. ARS. aur. bar. BELL. bov. *bry.* camph. carb-an. cham. *chel.* chin. cic. COCC. CON. croc. graph. *hell.* HYOSC. *ignat.* ipec. *laur.* led. LYC. *mgs. merc.* n-mosch. n-vom. OLEAND. OP. PHOSPH. PH-AC. plat. PULS. *rhus. sec-corn.* staph. STRAM. *sulph.* veratr. zinc.

—— with pressure.

Camph. *carb-veg. chin.* GRAPH. par. SIL.

—— pricking.

Acon. alum. ant-crud. arn. ARS. ASAF. *bar.* BELL. bov. BRY. *calc.* camph. canth. *carb-veg.* cham. *chin. clem.* cocc. *con. cycl. graph.* HEP. *led.* LYC. m-arct. magn. mang. MERC. *mezer.* mur-ac. *natr.* natr-mur. nitr. NITR-AC. *n-vom.* PETR. *phosph.* PULS. *ran-bulb.* RHUS. sabad. *sabin.* sassap. scill. selen. SEP. SIL. spong. STAPH. SULPH. thuj.

—— —— in the edges.

ARS. ASAF. *bry.* clem. HEP. LYC. MERC. mur-ac. *petr.* phosph. PULS. ran-bulb. *sep.* SIL. *staph.* SULPH. thuj.

—— —— in the circumference.

Acon. ARS. ASAF. *bell.* cham. cocc. *hep. lyc.* MERC. mezer.

mur-ac. natr. n-vom. *petr.* phosph. PULS. *rhus.* sabin. *sep.* SIL. *staph.* SULPH.

Ulcers, with tingling.

Acon. ant-tart. ARN. *bell.* caust. *cham.* CLEM. *colch.* CON. croc. graph. *hep.* kali. *lach.* *merc.* natr. natr-mur. *n-vom.* *ph-ac.* plumb. *puls.* ran-bulb. RHUS. sabin. *sec-corn.* SEP. spong. *staph.* *sulph.* sulph-ac. thuj.

—— with flesh in the ulcer.

Alum. ant-crud. ARS. bell. *carb-an.* carb-veg. caust. CHAM. *clem.* creos. *graph.* LACH. merc. PETR. *phosph.* sabin. SEP. SIL. *staph.* SULPH. *thuj.*

—— pulsating.

Acon. arn. *ars.* ASAF. bar. bell. bov. bry. CALC. *caust.* cham. chin. *clem.* con. *hep.* hyosc. ignat. KALI. LYC. *mgs.* MERC. mezer. *mur-ac.* *natr.* natr-mur. *nitr-ac.* petr. *phosph.* ph-ac. *puls.* rhus. *ruta.* *sabad.* sassap. *sep.* SIL. staph. SULPH. *thuj.*

—— pus of the ulcers. (See Suppurating.)

—— with pustules around

Acon. ARS. bell. CAUST. cham. hep. LACH. *lyc.* mgs. merc. mezer. mur-ac. natr. petr. phosph. PULS. *rhus.* SEP. *sil.* staph. sulph.

—— putrid.

Amm. *ars.* *asaf.* aur. bell. bov. *bry.* CALC. carb-veg. caust. chel. CHIN. cic. con. *creos.* cycl. *graph.* HEP. *lyc.* mang. *merc.* mezer. MUR-AC. natr. *nitr-ac.* n-mosch. n-vom. phosph. PH-AC. plumb. *puls.* RHUS. ruta. sabin. sec-corn. *sep.* SIL. staph. SULPH. sulph-ac. thuj.

—— with redness around.

ACON. ant-crud. arn. ARS. ASAF. bar. *bell.* bor. bry. *calc.* CHAM cocc. creos. cupr. HEP. hyosc. ignat. LACH. led. LYC. MERC. mezer. natr. *nitr-ac.* n-vom. *petr.* *phosph.* ph-ac. plumb. PULS. ran-bulb. RHUS. sassap. *sep.* SIL. STAPH. *sulph.* thuj. veratr. zinc.

—— salt-rheum.

AMBR. ARS. *calc.* chin. GRAPH. LYC. merc. natr. *petr.* *phosph.* PULS. SEP. *sil.* *staph.* sulph. zinc.

—— scabby. (See Crusty.)

—— sensitive (painful).

Alum. amm. anac. ang. ARN. ARS. ASAF. aur. BELL. carb-an. CAUST. *cham. chin.* cic. CLEM. *cocc.* coff. con. *creos.* croc. *cupr.* dig. *dulc.* GRAPH. HEP. hyosc. jod. LACH. led. LYC. MERC. mezer. *mur-ac.* natr. natr-mur. nitr-ac. *n-vom. petr. phosph.* PH-AC. PULS. ran-bulb. ran-scel. rhus. sabin. scill. selen. SEP. SIL. sulph. thuj. *veratr.*

Ulcers, sensitive on the edges.

ARS. ASAF. *caust. clem.* HEP. LACH. LYC. MERC. mur-ac. petr. phosph. *ph-ac. puls.* ran-bulb. *sep.* SIL. sulph. thuj.

—— —— in the circumference.

ARS. ASAF. *bell. caust.* cocc. HEP. LACH. *lyc. merc.* mezer. mur-ac. natr. n-vom. petr. phosph. PULS. rhus. *sep. sil.*

—— suppurating.

Acon. ambr. *amm.* anac. ang. ant-crud. ant-tart. arg. arn. ARS. ASAF. *aur.* bar. BELL. bov. bry. *calc.* CANTH. caps. carb-an. CARB-VEG. CAUST. cham. chel. *chin.* cic. *clem.* cocc. *con. creos.* croc. dros. *dulc. graph.* hell. HEP. hyosc. ignat. jod. ipec. kali. *lach.* led. LYC. mgs. mang. MERC. *mezer. mur-ac.* natr. natr-mur. nitr. NITR-AC. *n-vom.* petr. *phosph.* ph-ac. plumb. PULS. *ran-bulb. ran-scel.* RHUS. *ruta.* sabad. *sabin.* sassap. *scill.* sec-corn. selen. SEP. SIL. spig. spong. STAPH. SULPH. sulph-ac. thuj. viol-tr. zinc.

—— scrofulous, of the glands.

Cistus canadensis.

—— with shocks in them.

Ang. ARN. cic. CLEM. mezer. *mur-ac.* plat RUTA. *sulph-ac.*

—— with pain as of soreness.

Alum. ambr. ant-crud. arn. *ars.* bell. *bry. calc.* caust. cic. GRAPH. HEP. hyosc. *ignat.* kali. *lyc.* mgs. m-austr. MERC. *mezer.* natr-mur. *n-vom. phosph.* PH-AC. PULS. *rhus.* SEP. *sil. staph.* SULPH. sulph-ac. thuj. *zinc.*

—— spongy.

Alum. *ant-crud.* ant-tart. ARS. *bell.* calc. CARB-AN. *carb-veg.* caust. *cham.* CLEM. con. *creos.* graph. jod. LACH. lyc. *merc.* nitr-ac. n-vom. *petr.* PHOSPH. ph-ac. rhus. sabin. SEP. SIL. STAPH. SULPH. THUJ.

—— —— on the edges.

ARS. CARB-AN. caust. *clem.* LACH. lyc. *merc.* petr. *phosph.* ph-ac. *sep.* SIL. *staph. sulph. thuj.*

Ulcers, with white spots.
ARS. *con.* LACH. phosph. *sep.* SIL. sulph.

—— **speckled.**
Arn. ars. CON. ipec. LACH. sulph-ac.

Ulcers, suppurating:

The pus being blackening.
Bry. *chin.* lyc. SULPH.

—— —— **bloody.**
Ant-tart. arg. arn. ARS. ASAF. *bell.* CARB-VEG. CAUST. con. creos. croc. dros. HEP. hyosc. jod. *kali. lach.* LYC. mgs. MERC. mezer. natr-mur. NITR-AC. *phosph.* ph-ac. PULS. *rhus.* ruta. sabin. sec-corn. *sep.* SIL. *sulph.* sulph-ac. thuj. zinc.

—— —— **brownish.**
Anac. *ars.* BRY. calc. *carb-veg.* con. puls. rhus. SIL.

—— —— **cheesy.**
Merc.

—— —— **too copious.**
Acon. *arg.* ARS. ASAF. bry. CALC. *canth. chin.* cic. creos. graph. jod. kali. *lyc.* mang. MERC. mezer. natr. PHOSPH. *ph-ac.* PULS. RHUS. ruta. sabin. *scill.* SEP. SIL. *staph.* sulph. thuj.

—— —— **corroding** (acrid).
Amm. anac. ARS. bell. calc. CARB-veg. CAUST. cham. chel. *clem.* con. *creos.* cupr. *graph.* HEP. ignat. jod. lach. LYC. MERC. mezer. *natr.* natr-mur. NITR-AC. *n-vom.* phosph. plumb. *puls.* RAN-BULB. RAN-SCEL. RHUS. ruta. SCILL. *sep.* SIL. spig. *staph. sulph. sulph-ac.* zinc.

—— —— **fetid.** (See Stinking).

—— —— **gelatinous.**
Arg. arn. bar. cham. ferr. *merc. sep.* SIL.

—— —— **greenish.**
Ars. ASAF. *aur.* carb-veg. CAUST. *clem.* creos. *merc.* natr. *n-vom.* phosph. PULS. *rhus. sep.* SIL. staph.

—— —— **gray.**
Ambr. ars. carb-an. CAUST. chin. *lyc. merc.* sep. SIL. thuj.

—— —— **ichorous.**
Amm. ant-tart. ARS. ASAF. aur. bov. *calc.* CARB-VEG. CAUST. CHIN. cic. clem. *con.* creos. dros. *graph. hep.* kali. *lyc.* mang. MERC. mur-ac. NITR-AC. n-vom. phosph. ph-ac. plumb.

ran-bulb. RAN-SCEL. RHUS. scill. sec-corn. *sep.* SIL. STAPH. *sulph.*

The pus being lingering. (See Too Little).

—— —— **too little** (tarrying, lingering, wanting).

Acon. ars. *bar.* BELL. *bov.* bry. CALC. *carb-veg.* caust. chin. cina. *clem.* coff. creos. CUPR. dros. DULC. *graph.* HEP. hyosc. ignat. ipec. LACH. *led.* lyc. *magn.* MERC. n-vom. *petr.* *phosph.* PLAT. plumb. puls. rhus. *sassap.* SEP. SIL. spong. *staph.* sulph. VERATR.

—— —— **with maggots.**

Ars. calc. merc. SABAD. SIL. *sulph.*

—— —— **too much.** (See Copious).

—— —— **putrid.** (See Stinking).

—— —— **salty.** (See Salt-rheum).

—— —— **smelling like old (rotten) cheese.** (See Stinking).

—— —— —— **like herring brine.** (See Stinking).

—— —— **of a putrid smell.** (See Stinking).

—— —— **of a sour smell.**

Calc. graph. HEP. MERC. natr. *sep.* SULPH.

—— —— **stinking.**

Amm- ARS. ASAF. *aur.* bell. bov. bry. CALC. *carb-veg.* caust. chel. CHIN. cic. *con.* *creos.* cycl. GRAPH. HEP. LYC. mang. MERC. mezer. *mur-ac.* *natr.* *nitr-ac.* n-mosch. n-vom. phosph. PH-AC. plumb. puls. *rhus.* ruta. sabin. *sec-corn.* SEP. SIL. *staph.* SULPH. sulph-ac. thuj.

—— —— **stinking, like herring brine.**

Graph.

—— —— —— **like old (rotten) cheese.**

HEP. *sulph.*

—— —— **like tallow.**

Merc.

—— —— **thin.**

Ant-tart. ASAF. carb-veg. CAUST. dros. jod. kali. lyc. MERC. *nitr-ac.* plumb. puls. *ran-bulb.* *ran-scel.* *rhus.* *ruta.* SIL. staph. SULPH. thuj.

—— —— **tenacious.**

Ars. *asaf.* BOV. cham. CON. MERC. mezer. *phosph.* ph-ac. *sep.* sil. staph. *viol-tr.*

The pus wanting. (See Too little).

—— —— watery.

Ant-tart. ARS. ASAF. calc. *carb-veg.* CAUST. *clem.* con. dros. *graph.* jod. kali. *lyc.* MERC. *nitr-ac.* n-vom. plumb. puls. RAN-BULB. RAN-SCEL. RHUS. *ruta. scill.* SIL. *staph. sulph.* thuj.

—— —— whitish (like milk).

Amm. ars. CALC. carb-veg. hell. LYC. PULS. *sep. sil. sulph.*

—— —— yellow.

Acon. ambr. amm. anac. ang. arg. *ars. aur.* bov. *bry.* CALC. caps. CARB-VEG. CAUST. *cic.* CLEM. con. *creos.* croc. *dulc.* graph. hep. jod. *lyc.* mang. MERC. *natr.* natr-mur. *nitr.* nitr-ac. n-vom. PHOSPH. PULS. *rhus.* ruta. sec-corn. selen. SEP. SIL. spig. STAPH. sulph. sulph-ac. *thuj.* viol-tr.

Ulcers, swollen.

Acon. arn. *ars.* aur. bar. BELL. BRY. *calc.* carb-an. *carb-veg. caust.* cham. cic. cocc. *con.* dulc. graph. HEP. jod. KALI. led. *lyc.* mang. MERC. natr. *natr-mur. nitr-ac.* n-vom. petr. *phosph.* ph-ac. plumb. PULS. RHUS. sabin. samb. SEP. SIL. staph. SULPH. vit.

—— —— round about.

Acon. *ars.* BELL. caust. cham. HEP. *lyc.* MERC. natr. n-vom. petr. phosph. PULS. *rhus.* SEP. *sil.* staph.

—— —— on the edges.

ARS. *bry.* carb-an. caust. cic. HEP. *lyc.* MERC. petr. phosph. ph-ac. PULS. SEP. SIL. SULPH.

—— tearing (drawing).

ARS. bell. *bry.* CALC. *canth.* carb-veg. caust. *clem.* cocc. CYCL. *graph.* kali. LYC. mgs. MERC. mezer. natr. nitr-ac. n-vom. phosph. *puls. rhus.* SEP. SIL. *staph.* SULPH. zinc.

—— tensive.

Arn. ASAF. aur. BAR. *bell. bry. calc. carb-an. carb-veg.* CAUST. cham. chin. *clem. cocc.* CON. creos. *hep.* jod. *kali.* LACH. *lyc.* MERC. *mezer.* mur-ac. natr. nitr-ac. *n-vom.* petr. PHOSPH. ph-ac. PULS. RHUS. *sabin. sep. sil.* SPONG. *staph.* STRONT. SULPH. *thuj.* zinc.

—— tensive, in the circumference.

ASAF. bell. *caust.* cham. cocc. hep. LACH. lyc. *merc.* mezer.

mur-ac. natr. n-vom. petr. *phosph.* ph-ac. PULS. *rhus.* sabin. sep. sil. staph. STRONT. SULPH.

Ulcers, with indented edges.

Hep. lach. MERC. PH-AC. sil. *staph.* sulph. THUJ.

—— with pain as of subcutaneous ulceration.

Amm. anac. *arn.* ars. ASAF. aur. *bar.* BRY. CALC. CARB-VEG. chin. colch. CON. creos. *cycl.* dros. euphorb. GRAPH. *hep.* hyosc. jod. *kali.* *led.* *natr-mur.* nitr-ac. n-vom. par. *petr.* PHOSPH. PULS. RAN-BULB. RHUS. ruta. sassap. *sec-corn.* SIL. *staph.* SULPH. *valer.* veratr. *zinc.*

Varices.

AMBR. ANT-TART. ARN. ARS. *calc.* CARB-VEG. CAUST. coloc. CREOS. FERR. GRAPH. LACH. LYC. M-AUSTR. magn. NATR-MUR. *n-vom.* PULS. *sil.* SPIG. SULPH. *sulph-ac.* *thuj.* ZINC.

—— suppurating.

Ant-tart. ARS. creos. LACH. LYC. PULS. SIL. *sulph.*

—— inflamed.

ARN. ARS. *calc.* *creos.* LYC. n-vom. PULS. *sil.* *spig.* SULPH. thuj. *zinc.*"

REPORT OF CASES MOSTLY FROM THE BRITISH JOURNAL OF HOMEOPATHY, AND RUCKERT'S THERAPEUTICS.

Arsenic cured the two following cases as reported by Dr. Miller (Hygea xi., 108):

"The wife of a rope-maker, aged sixty-five, had been affected with an ulcer of the foot for *eighteen years.* A great many physicians and quacks had treated her in vain. I had treated her myself in 1830, according to the principles of the old school. The disease began in the left foot, near the ankle, by the formation of small, pustular elevations, which burst, and discharged a clear, acrid fluid, and formed an ulcerated surface, which gradually encroached on the neighboring healthy skin, till it reached the size of two hand's breadths. It grew gradually more foul and fetid, and the pains, which were at first more tearing and drawing, became at length sharp and burning. The patient had been confined to bed for the last two years; the foot was edematous, and the swelling increased almost daily; and also the foot swelled often. The patient was becoming visibly thinner, her appetite declined, and she had a cachetic appearance. I treated her for nine weeks with Arsenic 8, a dose every other day; upon this she gained strength daily, and the ulcerated surface gradually diminished in extent and dried up, the burning pain subsided, so that in the fifth week she was able to be up half the day, and at the end of thirteen weeks was able to resume her usual occupations."

"I treated in the same way a man aged twenty-three, affected with a psoric ulcer on the foot, arising from suppressed itch. He had been treated for two years with outward and inward remedies, but the disease had at last gained such a height that amputation was proposed. At first the ulcer had been covered with a scab, from under which oozed an acrid fluid, and the edges were thick and surrounded by scabious pustules; but latterly it displayed a foul blackish surface, almost insensible, discharging a fetid ichor, and was in fact sloughing. By the use of *Arsenic*, used as above, the patient was quite cured in seven weeks."—*B. J. Hom.*, vol. iv., p. 356.

"*Arsenicum* 30, 2 pellets, removed black-blue ulcers, surrounded with a shining red border, one being situated on the front part of the thigh, one in the bend of the knee. The swelling hindered walking. The ulcer in the bend of the knee required two more doses of *Arsenic* to complete the cure. —*A. H. Z.* vii., p. 327.

Arsenicum 30, one dose, was effectual where the following symptoms were present:

The whole body, except the face, was covered with small, ichorous ulcers, painful and burning when becoming cold; the pain is somewhat relieved by warmth. Emaciation; great exhaustion; every kind of food causes a pressure in the esophagus, as if it had been arrested there. Restless sleep; fever every day; first chilliness, afterwards heat, and lastly sweat; mind full of uneasiness and despair. — *Arch.* p. 156.

Graphites 30, commenced the cure of an ulcer on the foot of a female, which was completed by *Lycopodium.*

Symptoms: a flat herpetic ulcer of the skin, in the region of the ankle, on the whole anterior surface of the tarsal joint; it secretes a good deal of ichor, and is bordered with small, irritable ulcers, penetrating deep into the skin, and looking like pustules when making their first appearance. Violent itching and smarting; pains in the whole ulcer, accompanied with chilliness and extending up to the knee. The ulcer suppurates a good deal at the time of the menses. Frequent alternation of costiveness and diarrhea.

Graphites 30, and after a long interval *Sepia* 30. *Symptoms:* Ulcer on the dorsum of the foot, covered with impure, ichorous pus, having a fetid smell; red granulations on the base of the ulcer; callous edges, very painful to the touch. Constant lancinating pains in the ulcer, especially in the night and forenoon. The foot is swollen, blue-red around the ankles and hot, accompanied with a chilly feeling in the foot.

Lachesis, valuable in old ulcers of the foot: one or two doses of *Lachesis* 30, brought on a rapid cicatrization of several ulcers on the leg, having a dirty appearance.—*Arch.* xiii. 2, p. 102.

Lachesis 12, three times a day, followed in a week by *Arsenicum* 12, repeated in the same way, produced a rapid healing of a varicose ulcer of twelve month's standing, after lower attenuations were ineffectual.

The ulcer was over the right ankle joint; the pain accompanying it was intense and burning, preventing sleep at night.—*Brit. J. Hom.* vol. x., p. 667.

Lycopodium 27, one-fourth of a drop removed an ulcer on the leg which came on after a knock in the region of the inner ankle; became deeper and deeper; had callous edges; secreting a fetid, impure ichor; finally occupied the whole of the tarsal joint, and caused violent burning pains, especially at night.—*Ann.* iii., p. 196.

Lycopodium has been beneficial in malignant, inveterate ulcers of the foot, phagedenic ulcers generally occupying the legs. In one case repeated doses of the 15th attenuation were given at the commencement; afterwards one drop of the 30th. *Symptoms:* The left leg was covered with a multitude of ulcers; they are all of them flat, and do not penetrate through the skin; edges red, hard, shining, raised. The base has a dirty-yellow appearance, greenish, bluish, pale red. Pus copious, watery, ichorus, fetid, diminishing when at rest, and yellowish. The ulcers are surrounded with a blue-red, hard, hot, painful border; the leg and foot are thick and swollen, hard shining, red, inflamed. The pains are partly tearing, partly lancinating; sometimes there was a continued aching, which was almost insupportable in the night and in bad weather. Likewise ulcers on the right leg and forearm.—*A. H. Z.* v., p. 195.

Merc. Sol., one-twelfth of a grain, cured an ulcer upon the tongue in sixteen days. *Symptoms:* On the edge of the tongue there is an ulcer of the size of a bean; along the adjoining parts of the tongue, in the substance thereof, there are several hard nodosities, and a deepening resembling an incision. The base of the ulcer looks gray, reddish, uneven, secreting a fetid matter; the edges are hard, elevated, of a blue appearance; burning in the ulcer. The tongue is swollen, coated white, speech unintelligible. Ptyalism; fetid odor from the mouth. The edges of the gums are bright red, inflamed, standing off from the teeth, swollen in several places, bleeding frequently, tearing toothache at night. The vermillion border of the lower lip is covered with small painful pimples having brownish crusts. Hot water was used to rinse the mouth.—*A. h. Z.* v., p. 231.

Psoricum 6, has cured ulcers of the lower limbs, with intolerable itching over the whole body.—*A. h. Z.* ii., p. 192.

Psoricum 30, and *Anthracin* in alternation, cured ulcers on the leg and tibia of an old man.—*A. h. Z.* v., p. 64.

Rhus 30, four pellets, followed in six days with three pellets, cured a patient with the following *symptoms:* Gradually the whole body except the head, chest and back, became covered with large and small vesicles, containing a clear, yellow fluid, and itching considerably. The opened vesicles had become gangrened ulcers, secreting an acrid, fetid ichor, which was likewise secreted from the inner surface of the toes. Continual and violent fever; pulse small and quick. The whole head, especially the face, was bloated and red, with edema of the lower eyelids and the penis. The throat was somewhat swollen, making deglutition difficult. Stool delaying, but every day. Urine suppressed, scanty, turbid and brown. Little appetite; much thirst, disposition impatient; out of humor.—*Pr. Com.* i., p. 172.

Silicea 18, smelling, repeated in three weeks, ulcer of the foot, the original cause of which was congelation. *Symptoms:* Deep ulcer on the dorsum of the foot, with an impure base; the wound, which secreted a quantity of thick jelly-like mucus, being covered with a quantity of spongy and readily bleeding flesh.—*Arch.* vii. 2, p. 46.

Silicea 30, one dose, cured an ulcer of the tibia, which was brought on by a previous violent inflammation; the ulcer secreted a quantity of fetid ichor. The periosteum appeared injured and the bone to be affected.—*Arch.* viii. 1, p. 23.

Silicea 30, two pellets, and in six weeks *Sulphur*—Ulcers of the leg brought on by vesicular erysipelas. *Symptoms:* Swelling of the legs up to the knees; seven ulcers, partly open, partly bordered with indented crusts, having a bad appearance and secreting a cadaverous ichor; burning pains, especially in the night; intolerable itching round the ulcers, obliging one to scratch, which is followed by burning as of hot coal, and bleeding of the scratched parts.—*Arch.* viii. 3, p. 57.

Silicea 3, one grain—Ulcer on the leg, brought on by a blow. *Symptoms:* Round ulcer below the patella, over the upper extremity of the tibia; the ulcer had penetrated down to the bone. The base of the ulcer was dirty bluish-red. Copious secretion of a sanguineous, thin fluid; stitching pains in the ulcer, especially at night; the margin and the surrounding parts of the ulcer were sometimes itching and somewhat burning.

Silicea in repeated doses has proved curative in the following cases: *Symptoms:* Unimportant external injuries bring on wide-spreading, erysipelatous, or deeply-penetrating asthenic inflammations, followed by a troublesome suppuration; a fetid, sanguinolent, badly colored, yellowish ichor is secreted from fistulous openings; slow separation of dead fetid pieces of cellular tissue, muscles and tendons, of a dirty color, partly penetrated by tenacious yellow pus. There remain open ulcers penetrating down to the bone, and surrounded by shaggy callous borders; the ulcers refusing to heal, with vanishing of strength; the adjoining soft parts are swollen, hard bluish-red.—*A. H. Z.* v., p. 326.

Sulphur, three doses, cured ulcers on the ankle of an old man, situated at a place which had formerly been occupied by varices, with stitching pains, especially at night.

Sulphur 30, one dose, cured three psoric ulcers on the tibia in three persons.—*Arch.* xi. 2, p. 115.

Sulphur 30, three doses, in a fortnight; ulcer on the foot. *Symptoms*: Inflammation in the region of the tibia after a bruise; this results by the formation of a flat ulcer, with raised edges and secretion of a quantity of benign pus. The ulcer is surrounded by small itching pimples. There is a similar, but smaller ulcer in the region of the left tarsal joint.—*J. d. h. H.* i., p. 155.

Sulphur, three doses, removed in five weeks an old, fetid, deep ulcer, on the inner ankle, secreting a thin ichor, and surrounded by some swelling. — *A. h. Z.* iv., p. 15.

Galvano-puncture. — "A miller in good health was received into the hospital at Varese, with considerable enlargement of the trunk of the vena saphena above the knee, and ten knotty dilatations, varying in bulk from the size of a bean to that of a nut, below the knee. The pain and weakness of the limb were so great, that he had been obliged to give up his occupation.

"August 3d, 1846. M. Milani, having bandaged the leg above and below the spot chosen for the operation, inserted two steel needles into one of the dilated knots, and brought them into communication by means of copper wires, silvered, with the two poles of a voltaic battery of twenty-six pairs of plates, two and a half inches in diameter. At first the patient suffered a slight shock; afterwards, merely a sensation of burning. The needles were left in the vein for twelve minutes, when a hard clot had formed around that in communication with the zinc or negative pole, cold water and vinegar were applied to the part.

"August 4th. Needles were introduced into the saphena above the knee, and into the varicose enlargements below. A battery of twenty-six pair of plates was connected with the upper needles (Dr. Milani tried one of thirty-one plates, but the patient could not bear it;) another of twenty-four plates, with the needles inserted below the knee. Hard clots were produced in the veins of the leg and in the saphena, blocking up the latter for two or three inches. Subsequent operations upon the remaining varices proved equally successful.

"In ten days all the varicose dilatations had disappeared. Although the points of the two needles were never in contact, and they were covered with a varnish of gum lac, which left only their points bare, a slight areola of cauterization had taken place round each puncture, the extent of which was greater around the negative pole.

"In a second patient, still under treatment at the time of the report, a tumor as large as a goose's egg, near the internal malleolus of the left leg, filled with coagula under two applications, and diminished two-thirds in volume." — *Chapman on Ulcers*, pp. 149–150.

CHAPTER XI.

DISEASE OF BONES.

Inflammation and Ulceration of Bone — "Caries and Necrosis" — Causes, Constitutional and Exciting — Symptoms — Stages — Diagnosis — "Bone-pus" — Probing — Prognosis — Treatment.

Bones in their healthy state are hard, smooth, and destitute of sensibility. But, like soft parts, they are liable to become inflamed, and be far more painful and distressing than ordinary inflammation — the pain is deep-seated, worse at night — attended with swelling, heat, and often redness of the parts. This nightly exacerbation is specially prominent, if the inflammation arises from syphilis or abuse of mercury.

The inflammation of bones may be developed in an acute or chronic form, and, if not resolved, may proceed to adhesion, suppuration, ulceration and mortification. It may be located in the periosteum, or in the substance of the bone. If the periosteum is the part inflamed, the progress of the disease is much more rapid than if the bone alone is affected. The swelling and pain also comes on then, very rapidly. The latter being caused principally from the periosteum being put on the stretch by the effusion which takes place between this membrane and the bone. An incision into it will remove the tension, and afford great relief.

In chronic inflammation, generally arising from mercurial poisoning or scrofula, the progress of the disease is slower. The pain, at first, is dull, heavy and deep-seated, worse at night or upon pressure; as soon as matter is formed the pain becomes throbbing, and rigors are felt. The skin over the abscess becomes discolored when deep-seated, as suppuration takes place and enlarges the cavity of the abscess, there is a deposit of bony matter on the outside, so that the bone continues to enlarge until an opening is made for the exit of pus, either by ulceration or mechanical means.

The condition called *Caries*, is the same as ulceration in soft parts; while by necrosis and exfoliation are both meant the death of bone. The former being internal and more complete, usually arising from inflammation of the medullary membrane; the latter external but partial, the consequence of inflammation of the periosteum. Caries may take place in any of the bones or at any period of life, but most frequently occurs in young subjects. The tarsus, carpus, sternum, vertebræ and extremities of the long bones, are usually the ones involved.

The general *causes* to be noticed in our day, are the syphilitic, mercurial, and scrofulous affections. Thousands have died from the two former being confounded. The pathogenetic power of mercury has been proved on a tremendous scale.

The admissions of so distinguished a surgeon as Bransby Cooper on this point, are worthy of careful consideration. He says, p. 179, "Syphilis is supposed to be a frequent cause of caries, *but it is a matter of question whether the caries so often concomitant with syphilis, does not in fact result from the action of the mercury given to cure the specific disease.*"

Again, p. 180, "I have used the term 'syphilitic taint' again and again, but I am not sure that I have done so advisedly, *for it is doubtful if this caries in bone does not result from the use of mercury, and not from syphilis.* Whoever heard of a person having diseased bones in syphilis, unless mercury had been given? Sailors have often been known to become infected immediately before embarkation, to have made a long voyage, and not to have taken any medicine, what is their condition? Extensive ulceration of soft parts, propagated perhaps by inoculation on the thighs and scrotum, but no disease of the bones. Why then do we recommend mercury when caries has commenced? The answer is, I admit, difficult, I can only say, that *this is one of the few instances somewhat corroborative of the truth of the homeopathic hypothesis.*" [The italicising is ours.]

Necrosis, or mortification of bone, may involve only a limited portion of bone, or it may extend to the whole shaft. It generally affects the tibia, femur, clavicle, humerus, inferior maxilla, radius, and ulna. It is seldom met with earlier than ten or later than thirty years of age, except when it attacks the inferior maxilla. Violent inflammation of the periosteum or anything which affects the substance of the bone or the medulla, so as to prevent the proper nourishment of the bone, may cause necrosis. A simple fall on the feet is said to have caused it.

When a portion of bone becomes necrosed, the surrounding parts throw out lymph, this is changed to cartilage, and the cartilage to *provisional* bone, by deposition in it of ossific matter. As in mortification of soft parts, a line of demarcation is formed separating the dead from the living tissue. The living bone throws out granulations while the necrosed bone or *Sequestrum* is gradually dissolved and absorbed, or discharged in the form of pus, through the openings which nature generally leaves in the provisional bone.

Pus, from diseased bone, may be easily *distinguished* by one who has had any sensible experience of it; its very offensive odor is quite characteristic. *Touch* is, however, a better test of diseased bone than smell. Apply the finger whenever possible, or probe. If the surface of the bone be felt rough or uneven, with loose pieces, or can be seen to be either much whiter or darker than natural, the case is clear. If the suspected part of the bone can not be reached, by subjecting the pus to a chemical examination for *phosphate of lime*, it will be easily determined whether the pus is from diseased bone or not. In healthy pus there is scarcely a trace of this phosphate, but in that from bone an appreciable quantity will be found in an ounce or more of pus. The quantity found will in part enable us to judge of the extent of the disease. The *prognosis* of ostitis, caries and necrosis, under our treatment, is usually favorable; almost all cases, even in their advanced stages, being curable without amputation. Diseases of bones, of the upper extremities, are more favorable than the lower.

In treatment assist nature and avoid all unnecessary interference. Here, as everywhere, remove causes and obstructions, and let nature proceed with her remedial work; when she is doing well, "let well enough alone." The patient should be kept quiet, the limb in a horizontal position, and his diet regulated according as the constitutional powers are vigorous or enfeebled. General bathing should be practised daily. If called at an early stage, we should by all means endeavor to discuss the inflammation. Much benefit may then be derived from local applications as recommended for wounds and fractures. Though for a poultice in this and other scrofulous affections, we have employed, with the happiest effects, one made of the common white bean pulverized, and wet with hot water. But when it is evident that an abscess has formed, and there is severe constitutional disturbance, make an opening for the evacuation of pus. This may be done by cutting down to the bone with a scalpel and using the trephine, or with the potassa fusa.

When there is dead bone or a sequestrum, as it is called, it is desirable to remove it as soon as it is *entirely* loose, provided it can be done without much violence. On this point there have been two extremes. One, trusting *entirely* to the absorbing powers of nature; the other, to cutting, boring, or chiseling, wherever dead bone was suspected. The disintegration of the sequestrum may be facilitated, and the necessity of an operation for its removal avoided in all cases where it is not too large, and does not cause too much constitutional disturbance, by daily injections of a solution of the sesqui-carbonate of potash.*

Bransby Cooper speaks highly of the use of phosphoric acid diluted with an equal weight of water. (*See wounds — abscess —*

* This article is one not generally known in surgical treatment. The mild caustic, sesqui-carbonate of potash, has the peculiar property of dissolving dead bone and destroying morbid growths, without injury, or preventing new granulation.

mortification.) If, however, the sequestrum causes great constitutional irritation, which threatens to destroy the patient and is *entirely* loose, it should by all means be removed. Then lay bare the provisional bone over one of its openings, and if this is not sufficiently large, enlarge it with a saw or trephine so as to admit a pair of forceps. Sometimes it will be best to divide the dead bone into small pieces with a pair of cutting-bone nippers, before extraction.

When a patient has become much exhausted by suppuration and long continued suffering, and the necrosis has extended so as to involve a joint, amputation of the limb had better be performed. The chances of saving the limb will not justify the risk of losing the life of the patient.

The limbs of necrotic patients should be protected, by the proper splints, from curvature by the action of the muscles. And the patient should be cautioned against bearing much weight upon the limb until perfect consolidation of the bone has taken place.

Internal Treatment.—Except where the result of some mechanical injury, inflammation of bone is generally dependent upon some constitutional taint, which must be removed in order to effect a resolution of the inflammation. The careful examination of a patient recommended by Hahnemann, is especially important in this disease, otherwise we shall overlook the cause, from a very erroneous estimate of the true nature of the case; and probably be unsuccessful in the treatment.

When ostitis is the result of external violence, particularly if the periosteum has been much injured, *Ruta*, internally and externally, as recommended in the treatment of wounds, is a valuable remedy. *Arnica* and *Calendula* will also deserve consideration. *Aconite* will only be necessary in a few cases of severe inflammation. *Bryon.* and *Puls.* will be found serviceable when the inflammation is not far advanced, the skin being red, with slight swelling of the bone and extreme sensibility to the touch. The first for persons of dry, meager habit and of a nervous temperament; the latter for those of phlegmatic temperament, with lymphatic constitutions.

If the inflammation is of an erysipelatous character, *Bell.* will be beneficial. *Mangan. Acet.* is particularly valuable in periostitis and inflammation of the joints with excruciating pains. Hartmann also recommends *Asa.* and *Ac. ph.* for periostitis. Where the disease is not the result of mercurial poisoning, and occurs in constitutions impaired or enfeebled by scanty or innutritious food, living in damp, dark, or badly ventilated apartments, or otherwise, or in persons of the lymphatic temperament, with severe nightly exacerbations of pain, *Mercurius* will prove an invaluable remedy.

But where it is the result of that poisoning, *Hepar s.* and *Nitric ac.* are the two most important remedies. *Aurum*, *Ac. ph.*, *Asa.*, *Mez.*, *Merc.* and *Silic.*, are also excellent. For ostitis from syphilis or the combined effects of syphilis and mercury, the most valuable remedies are: *Daphne*, *Mez.*, *Asa.*, *Staph.*, *Aur.*, *Man. Acet.*, *Ac. ph.*, *Phos.*, *Sulph.*, *Sil.*, *Calc. c.*, *Lyco.*, *Nit. ac.*, *Sep.*, *Bary.*, and we would suggest *Stillingia Sylvatica.* If from a scorbutic taint, *Carb. v.*, *Merc.*, *Staph.*, *Dulc.*, *Ac. Nit.*, are the most appropriate.

If the disease is located on the shin or superficial bones, *Asa.* and *Mez.* deserve the preference; but if in the facial bones, *Aur.*, *Phos.*, *Merc.* and *Staph.* The two latter are also useful in inflammation of the iliac bones.

In the earlier stages of caries and necrosis the remedies as recommended for ostitis will be found serviceable. In the more advanced there are but few symptoms present. Hence the cause of the difficulty; the general condition of the patient, and clinic experience, must determine the appropriate remedy. In some cases it has been found best to alternate two or more of the prominent remedies, as *Sulph. and Calc.; Sulph., Calc. and Silic;* or *Silic.* and *Phos; Aurum* has been found very valuable in affections of the bones, particularly if from *Merc.*, or from a complication of *Merc.* and *Syphilis.* It has a special relation to diseases of the nasal and palate bones.

Ac. Nitricum is useful in caries of the assa nasi as well as the skull bones of children; and to counteract the effects of the mercurial poisoning, *Ac. Fluoricum* has been employed with excellent results in some cases of caries, and will probably prove a valuable remedy in diseases of the bones in general.

Asafetida is very beneficial in diseases of the bones from scrofula or a complication of syphilis and mercury, the bone being more than ordinarily sensitive to touch. *Calcarea*, although used with advantage in alternation with other remedies, does not seem to exert so beneficial an influence over the ulcer as over the constitutional depravity. It acts most favorably after the previous use of sulphur.

Lycopodium is recommended for diseases of the bones from scrofula, syphilis and mercury, particularly if the discharge is thick and lemon colored.

Phosphorus has caused necrosis where persons have been much exposed to its vapor. It will be beneficial when it has not given rise to the disease. It is also very important in disease of the bones in persons with impoverished vitality. The experiments of *Noote* on dogs show that it exerts a particular influence over fibrin.

Silicea is perhaps more frequently useful in diseases of the bones than any other remedy. It seems to exert a specific influence both over the separation of the sequestrum from the living bone and the state that follows, when it is loose and there is a very copious discharge of pus and ichor from the fistulous opening, as well as controls the attendant nervous excitement preventing sleep.

Sulphur is needed in diseases of the bone in scrofulous persons, or in those of a lymphatic or bilious temperament.*

CHAPTER XII.

SCROFULA — ULCERATION.

The SCROFULOUS Diathesis, Tumors, Abscesses and Ulcers — Treatment.

FAMILIAR as we are with this word "scrofula," what is meant by it is by no means a simple thing. It is a generalization. Va-

* The following cases are reported by Laurie and Ruckert:

Three cases of caries cured by *Hepar s.* and *Silic.* in alternation. Another by the above with the addition of *Mezereum* and *Rhus*. A fifth complicated with mer-

rious morbid conditions, having a certain general resemblance, are thus regarded and referred to as one disease. This similarity, it should be remembered, is not sameness; the things brought together are one rather in our minds than in nature. In cases that we identify as "scrofulous," we have not the advantage of a casual unity, as in syphilis and other contagious diseases. It is, then, a

curial disease by *Sulphur* and *Acid nitr.* (*Perussel.*) Caries of the elbow joint, with fistulous ulcers of the bone; *Calc. c.*, (*Rhus.*,) *Silic.*, *Lycop.* and *Sulph.* Caries of the thigh bone of a scrofulous boy; *Sep.* 10 and *Ac. nit.*, a fungous caries of the hand; *Rhus* and *Arsenic.* Caries of the facial bones; *Calc.*, *Carb.* and *Silic.* Caries of the foot with hectic fever; *Arn.*, *Lycop.* and *Silic.* Caries of the radius with bluish red swelling of the forearm and hectic fever; *Puls.*, *Mez.*, *Sab.*, *Silic.*, *Cal. c.* and *Lycop.* Caries of the tibia and the left forearm, with several fistulous passages, debilitating diarrhea and utter prostration of strength; *Sulph.*, *Asafet.*, *Ac. nitr.* and *Ac. phos.*, accomplished the cure. Numerous cases of syphilitic caries of the palate and nasal bones; *Aurum.* Chronic caries in scrofulous children *Silic.* 30, some, however, required lower potencies. Two cases of caries of the mastoid process, *Silic.* 30. Recent caries of the tibia, *Silic.* 10.

Acid Fluoric. — "A boy became affected, after scarlet fever, with caries of the temporal bone, which, during a period of five or six years, periodically broke out afresh, discharged an offensive pus, and then healed again. The entire left side of the cranium was arrested in its growth and consequently rendered much smaller than the other side, the left eye also appeared strikingly smaller than the right one. The intellect of the boy was not at all impaired. Several remedies improved but failed in curing the caries. After the employment of *Fluoric acid*, the periodical attack came on earlier and in more aggravated form than usual, but never returned. From that time onward, the left half of the cranium commenced to grow, and the previous inequality of size between the two sides of the head became gradually less, and finally imperceptible."

"The first and second phalanx of the left index finger, particularly the former, were swollen to four times their natural size, so that the finger presented the shape and appearance of a pear. On the dorsum of the finger an opening sometimes made its appearance, from which pus and ichor oozed out. The entire tumor was very hard to the touch; the skin otherwise unaltered. The cause of the affection was not ascertainable; the pains were intermittent. With the exception of some degree of dyspepsia, the health of the patient was good. Of *Silic.* 10, two doses were prescribed. Twelve days afterwards, the patient returned and said that she thought the finger better, but there were no outward signs of improvement. *Ac. fluor.* 10, in two doses, was next prescribed. The patient did not come back again until about twelve weeks after her preceding visit. The affected finger was so much restored, that it differed little or none in appearance from that of the other hand. She had merely returned because her digestion, after having been rendered much stronger, had threatened to become somewhat disordered again." Caries of the leg, *Asa.*, one dose of one drop. Caries and necrosis, *Asa.* and *Phos. ac.*, in larger doses.

certain modification of the general system, with peculiar morbid tendencies, that is now meant by scrofula. This *general state*, usually referred to as the "scrofulous diathesis," requires to be studied, even more than the *special* "scrofulous *diseases*," — which, for the most part, are obvious enough, presenting no difficulty of diagnosis.

The SCROFULOUS constitution, or *diathesis*, is characterized by a fair and florid complexion, with thin and delicate skin, and generally fine, light hair; a large head (with precocious development of intellect) but a small chest, defective in depth from the shoulders to the diaphragm, with feebleness of the whole muscular system, which is of a relaxed texture and usually of a puny development. The neck is thin, the eye and other features large, but regular and well formed. The upper lip especially is very prominent and rosy, the coloring of the eyes generally light. The emotions are vivid, "the social sentiments" generally strong, but the more heroic passions, which impart force of character, are less developed. The intellectual organs are large and the reflective apt to predominate. There is generally a remarkable deficiency in those portions of the brain which have been demonstrated, by Prof. Buchanan, to be the source of muscular power and force of character, and to be well developed in constitutions of much vital energy — viz., the basis of the occiput, the region of Firmness, and the occipital organs generally. Hence, the basis of the cranium being often narrow and shallow, the neck is necessarily slender.

The most characteristic peculiarity, perhaps, is the predominance of the lymphatic glandular system. The salivary and lymphatic glands in particular swell from the slightest cold, to which moreover the individual is very susceptible.

Scrofulous TUMORS are, however, not confined to the lymphatic and salivary glands. They may present themselves with the same general character in any part of the body. They are most common during childhood. There is at first a simple

Swelling of the part, without much if any pain or increased heat. This may go back, or go on enlarging, until the patient complains both of the preternatural *warmth and compression*, feeling as if something were pressed on the tumor. In this stage it may continue for a long time, and then disappear. More commonly it at length takes on active *inflammation* and terminates in suppuration — the *scrofulous abscess* or running sore. Occasionally it runs through all these stages in a few weeks.

Before the ABSCESS breaks, and in some instances for a long time previous, the *skin* over it becomes of a *purple* or *leaden* hue, which color it will often retain long after healing.

The *matter* discharged in true scrofulous suppuration is of a *thin* unhealthy appearance, sometimes quite "gleety" and containing occasionally small *solid pieces* of something like cheese. This discharge may continue for a considerable time, without occasioning much inconvenience or undergoing much change, for the better or worse. In other cases, the whole tumor will rapidly be involved in a process of destructive inflammation, being, in fact, converted into a malignant ulcer, wearing a peculiar appearance, which will be described further on.

When the scrofulous *abscess* is near the lymphatic gland, it not unfrequently happens that the *gland* itself is *unaffected*, except by distension. This may be ascertained by the probe, or by the fact that the tumor does not *soften* or *diminish* in size as the purulent discharge becomes free. The matter thus forming all round it sometimes completely dissects it out; and the gland is then discharged entire.

The large abscesses about the neck, so long well known as the "*King's Evil*," very generally involve several glands at the same time.

The scrofulous ULCER is never very painful unless when irritated by rough handling or some loose portion of carious bone. Its edges are usually overhanging, thin and smooth, and of a pale red hue. Loose granulations may sometimes be seen at the bottom, of a glossy and somewhat rosy tint. The pus discharged is thin, as in the case of the abscess, but soon becomes offensive. The whole sore, however, when irritably inflamed becomes fiery red, with a rough ragged appearance, fungous granulations sprouting up rapidly, with a greatly increased discharge of watery matter.

The CAUSE of scrofula is a very obscure question. As in other diseases, there is a concurrence of many causes. In this case it is perhaps impossible to fix on any one as the principal. As improper nutrition is obvious, bad living has generally been regarded as the principal source of the evil. The prevalence of the disease in this country, however, proves that it is not always brought about by poor living, in the usual sense of the word, — by insufficient or innutritious food. Even in Europe it is not confined to the ill-conditioned classes. Aristocratic and even some royal families are not exempt. Although it is undoubtedly to be classed among *hereditary* diseases, it is the tendency only that is inherited. The actual development of scrofula is never inevitable. Hence the utility of preventive medication. The inborn predisposition may, moreover, be very slight or altogether wanting, and the morbid diathesis be *acquired.* We often have to treat scrofulous children whose parents both possess sound constitutions, and whose ancestry, as far as we can learn, have been always free from the disease.

Among the *causes*, a prominent place should be given to *bad doctoring* as well as bad diet. Mercurialism may be in a large portion of cases the whole hereditary cause. If this be so, and it is a conclusion from numerous facts falling under our observation, we need be at no loss to account for the perpetuation or rather perpetual reproduction of the malady in *this country.* How frequently have the otherwise healthy mothers of scrofulous children, been mercurialized while pregnant or nursing, and thus the infant had to suffer the effects of a poison blighting the very germ of vitality! — See *Hamilton on Mercury — Allopathic Authority.*

Another source of scrofula in towns and cities, among the poor, is living in *dark* rooms, and especially crowded, *damp*, and dark apartments. Men may vegetate as vegetables grow in the dark, but like such, they will be feeble and unhealthy. If we would have our children and our race the most vigorous and capable of resisting disease producing influences, they must have plenty of pure air and sunlight

THE TREATMENT must have special reference to, 1st: The removal of the constitutional taint; 2d, the inflammatory condition or tendency of any part; 3d, the abscesses; and, 4th, the ulcerated or, perhaps, scirrhus complication.

Homeopathy furnishes the only means of preventing the development of scrofulous ulcers, disease, and of removing entirely the hereditary or constitutional tendency. The physician, if called upon to prescribe with a view to such prophylactic results while the patient is in apparent good health may, doubtless, ward off impending disease, and thus prevent the necessity for any aid from the *surgeon*.

Besides the medicines, the proper regulation of the diet, exercises and bathing, are matters indispensable to successful prophylactic treatment.

The patient should have constant, but not over-fatiguing exercise in the open air, *in day time*, but be free from exposure at night. Bathing the whole body daily, should be enjoined, but the temperature of the bath should be so regulated as not to make too strong a draft upon the vital heat of the system, while they should not be so warm as to produce relaxation and a sense of debility. The diet should be always nutritious, but unstimulating. Meats being too stimulating, should be prohibited. The natural tendency in such persons is to a too rapid growth and too early maturity; hence, all diet calculated to over stimulate the tissues should be avoided; all stimulating condiments and alcoholic drinks must be forbidden, as they are directly inimical to the animal economy.

Pure sweet milk should enter largely into the diet of scrofulous children, and unless the tone of the digestive organs has become so impaired as that milk will be too indigestible; it is also useful for adults.

The most reliable medicines, before any painful or inflammatory symptoms appear, are *Sulphur*, *Calcaria*, *Conium* and *Dulcamara*.

Sulphur, to be used early, before any enlarged glands are noticed, administered in high dilution at long intervals.

Calcaria, to follow *Sulph.*, where there is a feebleness and a deficiency in the development of the bones. It should be given at intervals of two or three weeks at a high attenuation.

Conium, to be used when the lymphatic glands are simply enlarged in young children, administered at a high dilution, and applied to the surface over the enlarged glands, at a low dilution, or the Tr.

Dulcamara, for persons further advanced in life, after or near the age of puberty, where the enlargement of lymphatic glands continue, or is excited by taking cold, without becoming inflamed, tender, or painful.

SCROFULOUS SWELLINGS AND ULCERS.

Sulphur is to be used in the early stage of scrofulous swellings. It is also one of the best remedies in any stage, where the patient is affected with eruptions, tetters, swelling and soreness of lymphatic glands, with a weak sickly appearance and a great susceptibility to cold.

Arsenicum, for atrophy, hard distended abdomen of children, glands of the neck swollen, puffy, pale countenance, pains of *a burning* character, with dry skin.

Baryta Mur., is an important remedy for scrofulous persons, especially children, when the glands of the neck are enlarged and painful or tender to the touch, the appetite poor, bowels costive, emaciation, abdomen distended. This remedy is especially useful for scrofulous children affected with rachitis, the spine and limbs being distended. It restores the patient to health, and by promoting healthy growth corrects the deformity — it has been successful where the deformity existed in connection with extensive disease and ulceration of the lymphatic glands.

Phosphorus, dissolved in olive oil, (1 gr. to the oz.) may be applied with benefit to indurated glands about the head and neck.

Belladonna, for hard, engorged and ulcerated glands, with frequent bleedings at the nose, occasional incontinence of urine. This remedy is best suited for persons with blue eyes and light hair.

Nitric Acid is to be used where the scrofulous patient is suffering from mercurial affection, has weak lungs, acidity of the stomach, stinging pains in the affected part, dry skin, pains change with changes of the weather, great emaciation.

Mezereum, where the pains are aggravated by a slight touch; the ulcer is easily inflamed. This remedy is especially serviceable in inflammation and induration, and even suppuration or ulceration of the auxiliary glands.

Sepia, for delicate young *females*, weak, debilitated persons, the nails deformed with scirrhus indurations.

The Oleum Jecoris Asselli, is recommended by Hartmann as a valuable remedy in scrofula; but from our own experience, and the utter impossibility of getting a reliable article, we have no confidence in it.

Hepas Sulphuris, is best adapted to the tumors when in a state of suppuration.

Lycopodium, for lymphatic persons where the bones are affected, especially those of the nose, palate, or face.

We have used in numerous instances the *Arum Triphyllum* (Indian turnip,) as a local remedy for the *discussing* of inflamed scrofulous tumors, which is frequently an important object, and never have failed of success where it was not clear that pus had formed before the application was made.

It is best applied in form of a poultice, made by bruising the green root and wetting it with warm water. The finely pulverized dry root will answer the purpose, but is not quite as efficient. It should be given internally at the same time, either in dilute Tr., or weak infusion.

The *Stillingia Sylvatica*, has beyond a doubt great specific powers in scrofula.

Dr. Hill formerly made much use of the *Scrophularia Marylandica* in infusions, and in many cases it proved a specific, even in ulcers of a scirrhus character. His attention was particularly attracted to its homeopathic effect in this disease, some years ago, by a physician in Pennsylvania, who stated that he was in the habit of prescribing an infusion of it to be taken freely until the symptoms were much aggravated, and the patient begun evidently to sink under its effects, when he discontinued all medicines, and in a few days the patient would begin to improve and a rapid recovery to health would be the result. This physician also applied it to the sores as a poultice. The last two articles deserve a *thorough "proving."*

If the tumor assumes a hardened, scirrhus condition, *Arnica, Conium, Lachesis, Baryta c., Mercurius, Staphysagria, Carbo v., Hep. Sul., Calc. Sil., Jodium, Lycopod., Bovista, Belladonna, Dulcamara, Sulphur*, or *Sepia* should be used according to the symptoms. The *Conium* may be applied with good effect to the tumor. *Phytolacca decandria* (the root), in form of a poultice, may be applied with success in many cases, while a dilute Tr. of the same is used internally. It has relieved some of the most inveterate cases. But if the induration does not yield to any of these remedies, and it should be very important to remove the tumor, apply *caustic potash* and completely destroy it if practicable. After the caustic, use emolient poultices until the eschar has sloughed out, then cleanse the ulcer, thus formed, daily with a solution of the *Sesqui-carbonate of potash*, and continue the poultice until it heals.

The *Scrophularia* may be used internally during this treatment; or you can use any of the specific remedies for such symptoms as may arise.

In concluding our remarks on the treatment of ulcers, and especially *scrofulous* ulcers, we deem it our duty to record the results of our experience in the use of the same remedies locally (to the ulcer) that are given internally. We use a wash, generally of a lower dilution, of the article that we are giving internally, and when the internal remedy is changed for another, the same is done with the external. From a comparison of our success in the treatment of ulcers with that of those who used the remedies internally only, we are bold to assert that double the success attends this mode, both in respect to the number of perfect cures and in the time of accomplishing them.

But we derive a still further advantage by the use of remedies entirely neglected or discarded by a large portion of the profession, (at least until lately) — we refer to the local and general application of *water*—either cold, warm or hot. We are fully warranted by experience in saying, that all cases of ulcers, and especially the scrofulous kind, will be cured in a much shorter time with the combined use of water, properly and scientifically applied, and other homeopathic remedies, than by any other mode of medication now known, while it will, we are quite confident, cure some cases not amenable to any other plan of treatment whatever that has yet been presented to the profession.

The application of water in the various modes does not, in the least, antidote or interfere with the action of the specific drugs prescribed, but rather *facilitates* their action by rendering the system in many cases more susceptible. It should be applied in the form of general baths to the surface daily, or oftener as the surgeon may deem proper, either with the hand alone or by means of a sponge, accompanied with frictions and sufficient exercise to keep up the activity of the circulation. Occasional *packing* with the wet sheet is very useful, and wet compresses to the part affected, either cold or warm, are highly beneficial. There is too much ignorance in the profession on the subject of water applications in surgical practice, and this ignorance has been perpetuated by a few journalists who were themselves entirely ignorant of its value; never having used it or bestowed any time to the investigation of its use by others, and who are too conservative and narrow-minded to venture upon any new field of investigation, however much inducement it may offer, or however unsuccessful may be their present practice. It is an easy matter for journalists to decry any particular mode of practice and to call it quackery or mongrelism, while the attempt to *prove it such* is too serious a task for them to undertake. It is sufficient for the *practitioner* to know, that, while he violates no known law of cure in the use of a particular remedy, though he may use that which is discarded by others, he is far exceeding them in point of success.

It is a strange hallucination that causes these journalists to persist in their opposition to the employment of means so valuable as hydropathy offers, in the face of the admissions and recommendations of the ablest homeopaths. Numerous cures are on record showing the successful results of the *water treatment alone*, in cases which had resisted the efforts of the ablest homeopaths.—*See Hempel, in note on p.* 197, *Jahrs' Pocket Manual.*

We fully endorse the following sentiments expressed by *Dr. Hartmann:*—"After all, it matters little whether we adhere to this or that name or system provided we *cure the patient* in the safest, shortest, and cheapest manner." This is the physician's duty, and he who fulfills that duty well is the *really great* practitioner.—*See Hartmann, Chron. dis.*, vol. iii, p. 183.

CHRONIC RHEUMATISM.

This disease, under homeopathic treatment, does not require the services of the surgeon proper, and we had concluded to leave it out, though under the allopathic practice it so often requires the cups and scarifier, the blisters and the scalpel of the surgeon. But having received from *Prof. C. Neidhard* of Philadelphia, a brief article on this subject, so valuable and so directly in point, we insert it in full:

"Inasmuch as this general affection often *locates* itself, producing states of particular parts that require surgical interference, it is necessary for us to have regard to the general cause as well as special results.

"The *remote cause*, as the name implies, is generally an acute attack — rheumatic fever or inflammation. The acute affection may, however, be so slight as to be altogether overlooked and forgotten. There may be long continued inflammatory rheumatism located in a particular tissue or organ.

"The *knee* is a joint very frequently affected. In slight cases there is stiffness and pain only when exercise is attempted. At other times the joint swells enormously, and there is a constant though dull pain. The bone itself seems to grow out, often to a monstrous size. This, however, is seldom more than a semi-cartilaginous deposit, and, indeed, the bony appearance is commonly owing only to condensed coagulable lymph, or to the thickened and hardened condition of the synovial membrane and capsular ligaments. This affection of the knee is often confounded with scrofulous or true 'white swelling.' It is most common in the colder regions, particularly in the vicinity of our lakes.

"When the disease locates itself in the *hip* joint, it is a variety of 'coxalgia,' and similarly confounded with the more formidable scrofulous affection of the same part.

"Confined to the *lumbar* vertebræ it often goes under the name of 'lumbago.' When the *cervical* vertebræ are its seat, it occasions 'stiff neck.'

"Rheumatic inflammation of the joints often terminates in a serous effusion, giving rise to true hydrops articuli."

If the rheumatism be complicated with syphilis as is sometimes the case —

Phytolacca Decandria is a remedy of great value. It is also a specific for this complaint, whether connected with syphilis or not, when the pains are all of a neuralgic character; especially if the stomach is affected with rheumatic or gouty symptoms. We have used this article externally to the affected part, as well as giving it internally.

"The external application is best made by cloths wet with the

Tr., applied as warm as the patient can bear it. The applications may be made at night, and discontinued during the day.

Prof. Neidhard thus speaks of *Chronic Rheumatism, &c.:*

"In nine out of ten cases *Rhus* will be found to deserve the preference in rheumatic affections, as they are so common in our climate. It will be particularly applicable in the most inveterate chronic cases. Characteristic symptoms are the following: rigidity; paralytic weakness of the joints, with stinging pain along the tendons and muscles; swelling and redness on or near the joints. Rheumatism of hip-joint and wrist seem to be most effectually controlled by its action. The greatest *rigidity and pain is experienced on first moving the joints and waking up in the morning.* After the joints have been moved for awhile the pain is lessened. I have numerous cases on record in corroberation of the above experience — these cases would amount at least to sixty. The first ten cases, consisting of three women and seven men, had rigidity and pain as above described with the same conditions; the others had more or less the same symptoms with the difference, that, in some cases, the joints of the upper and in others those of the lower extremities were more affected.

"Many cases assumed the form of paralytic rheumatism; in a few, that were cured, there was complete hemiplegia. The pricking, stinging sensation was seldom wanting."

"LUMBAGO RHEUMATICA."—"The seat of this disease is the muscles of the lumbar vertebræ as far as the crista ilii; the pain is rending, drawing, and moves from one place to another, coming on periodically; the least motion excessively painful, on which account the patient keeps his back very stiff; there is very little fever.

"The cases which fell under my notice in this disease I treated chiefly by *Nux .Vom.*, and a new remedy, the *Lobelia Syphilitica* or *Cerulia*, (as it has been also sometimes called.) *Nux* is indicated when the pain comes on periodically, with sudden jerking stitches, which extend to the shoulders, and also down to the genital organs, producing stiffness and lameness of the lower extremities. In the cases where I used *Lobelia Cerulia*, the characteristic symptoms were: shooting pain in the right side of the back, and in the right sacro-iliac symphysis in attempting to rise; the greatest pain is felt on turning in bed."

Chronic Rheumatism of the extremities frequently depends upon disease of the spine, where there is no curvature or pain to attract the attention of the patient. An examination should be made, in all cases, by pressing firmly along the spinal column, and if any tenderness is found give *Arnica*, a dose every two days. Apply a wet compress, covered with dry flannel, over night to the tender portions.

The proper use of water is of great service in this affection. The patients whole surface should be cleansed daily with pure water at the proper temperature, and wet bandages, at night, around the affected part will be serviceable.

The cold douche is to be used where the joint is stiffened, enlarged, but not painful, except from pressure.

The diet of the patient should be simple, unstimulating, and rather spare — he should be restricted to less at all times than his appetite craves. The affected joints should be regularly exercised, care being taken not to subject them to any sudden or violent action, so as to give severe pain and excite inflammation.

CHAPTER XIII.

WHITE SWELLING — HYDROPS ARTICULI — AND ANCHYLOSIS.

Scrofulous or True White Swelling, a Suppurating Joint — Symptoms and Progress — Rheumatic White Swelling, or Dropsy of a Joint — Anchylosis, or Stiff Joint — Treatment, mechanical or medicinal? — Extension — Exercise.

WHITE SWELLING.

This formidable and well-known disease is one of the opprobia of the profession. In the country, indeed, the people seldom think of calling in a physician with any hope of cure.

Cases known as "white swellings," are divided by some writers into *rheumatic* and *scrofulous*, — the latter being such as occur in scrofulous subjects, and all persons being liable to the former on exposure to the exciting causes. The propriety of such a distinction, for the sake of popular designation, has been doubted; and as chronic inflammation of the synovial membranes and capsular ligaments will be spoken of under the head of "Hydrops Articuli," attention will be first called to the proper —

Scrofulous or *true* white swelling, which never occurs in any but scrofulous persons. It is scrofula in a joint. For a long time after the disease has located itself there, the pain may be very slight. Gradually the patient's sufferings increase, and become at last very intense, particularly at night. The central part of the joint seems the point most affected. The *swelling* also is very slow in its progress. Even then, there is *no discoloration* of the skin, or, rather, it appears whiter than natural, (whence the popular name.) It becomes very tense, with a smooth, shining aspect, and marked with varicose veins. The patient constantly experiences a *sensation* of increased *heat* in the part. In this condition the joint may remain for months, or even years, without any material change. Gradually, however,

The *tumefaction increases*, till the thickening of the soft parts becomes so hard as to present the appearance of enlarged bone. In very bad cases, involving the cartilages of the knee, (for as that is the joint most commonly affected, we may as well study the disease as there manifested,) the tibia is thrown *backward*, the condyles of the femur projecting forward. The limb, both above and below the knee, emaciates; and as a flexed position is easiest for the sufferer, *anchylosis* takes place, with the limb permanently bent. Finally,

Matter collects in the joint, either from ulceration of the cartilage or bone, or both, and *sinuses* form for its discharge. Extensive *caries* may ensue, producing

Severe *constitutional irritation*, under which the patient gradually sinks.

Treatment.—Where the disease has been produced, originally, by a strain or bruise, as is often the case, and the acute inflammation still exists, suppuration not having come on, we have succeeded in affecting resolution of the inflammation by the internal and external use of *Arnica*. If, however, the patient does not soon improve under the *Arnica*, *Rhus.* should be alternated with it.

Calcarea is useful at a later stage, after *Arnica* has subdued the acute symptoms but some traces of the disease remain, or in the first instance, the pain in the joint being pressing as if dislocated, shooting, acute pains coming on at intervals, the patient weak and sickly. More particularly useful when the disease is in the knee. If, however, there is dull, heavy pain in the center of the joint when at rest, changed to severe pain upon moving or pressing the part, with occasional paroxysms of fever, or after suppuration, the pus becomes yellow and ichorous, *Iodine* is a valuable remedy.

Colocynth., for stiffness of the joints, with only dull aching pain, the pains increased by mental excitement, especially anger.

Kali Hydriodicum, is a remedy of great value in this disease, especially of the knee joint. It is indicated by all the pains being *tearing* and twitching, with twitching of muscles of the leg, the pains worse at night or when at rest, palliated by motion.

Phosphoric Acid, for heaviness of the joint with great weakness, pains worse when at rest, especially at night.

Hepar Sulphuris, for shooting pain in the joints with a bruised feeling. The ulcers smell some like putrid cheese and bleed easily. Useful when the disease is complicated with mercurial cachexia.

Rhodendron, is a remedy upon which great reliance may often be placed in this disease. It is especially indicated by coldness of the swollen knee, with severe pains extending to the leg, a drawing sensation in the popliteal space. It seems to bear a particular relation to the *right* knee. It should be used when the swelling extends to the leg or thigh, pains appearing in stormy weather and going off when the weather is fine, pain confined to a small spot, most violent at night and during rest.

Mercurius, for white swelling in persons affected with syphilitic taint, night sweats, pains worse in damp weather, fungous ulcer, especially where the bone is affected.

Silicea, also useful where the synovial membranes are affected; or when emaciation has taken place, in alternation with *Arsenic* and afterwards with *Iodine*.

Lachesis, is indicated by great emaciation with tearing and contracting pains in the joint, great *dread of exercise*, deeply penetrating suppurations. This may be alternated with *Silicea* and *Sulphur* with advantage.

The *Cornus circinati* has yielded excellent results in this disease. So also the *Phytolacca Decandria.*

The *Scrofularia* exerts a marked beneficial influence in scrofulous white swellings. It is one of the best remedies. The physician heretofore referred to gave patients affected with "white swelling," the infusion of *Scrofularia* freely several times a day and washed the ulcer with the same, keeping in covered with a warm poultice of leaves of the plant, when the patients began to get worse under the effects of the drenching, he discontinued it and gave no medicine, a rapid recovery in many cases was the result.

The *Stillingia Sylvatica* may also be used with advantage. Much advantage will be gained, during any stage of the treatment, by washing it freely and cleansing all the ulcers thoroughly two or three times a day, with cold or cool Castile soap-suds, by injecting the fluid freely into the sinuses, if any are formed. The strength should vary in proportion to the sensibility of the ulcers. The bandage should be used in all cases. The application of water to the general surface frequently, is of great importance and should never be neglected. The diet of the patient should consist mainly of milk, eggs and unleavened wheat bread. Meat, especially fat meat, should not be allowed.

It was observed before, that these are almost always tedious, as well as troublesome cases. It is important that we forewarn the patient and his friends of the necessity of persevering in the treatment a sufficient length of time. In some cases, a cure can not be anticipated in less than half a year; and even a whole year may be required, though, in others, half that time may be sufficient. In the most favorable cases, a six weeks', instead of six months' treatment will effect the object.

HYDROPS ARTICULI,

Is the result of rheumatic disease, that often passes under the popular name of "White Swelling," and should, if so called at all, be distinguished as

Rheumatic White Swelling. In this case the synovial membrane and capsular ligament are enormously distended, by serous effusion. It renders the limb stiff, though the pain is slight, unless when aggravated by exercise. The dropsical effusion extends along the tendons of the muscles. The whole limb even may be distended with it.

The *symptoms* are frequently very obscure, as the patient suffers, oftentimes little or no pain and in other respects is in tolerably good health.

Sulphur is, without doubt, a useful remedy to begin with, and though there may be no very marked symptoms of any particular remedy, after the use of *Sulphur* for a few weeks together with a proper use of water, either the disease will yield entirely and the cure be complete, or some symptoms will be developed indicating the specific remedy.

The symptoms indicating the use of *Sulphur* are, however, often presented. They are: unusual muscular weakness, the patient sweats easily, the pains are worse at night, the sensation of fatigue is relieved by exercise, though the pain is aggravated, trembling of the affected limb — it feels numb.

Silicea is generally useful in this disease. For enlargement and lameness of the joints from pressing upon them, bruising or straining, as by kneeling, dancing, &c., *Silicea* is *particularly* applicable. The patilla is pressed out by the increased secretion of the synovial fluid, the whole joint being enlarged.

Iodine: Patient much emaciated; very nervous, weak and trembling, twitching of the tendons occasionally, tearing sensations in the joint; night sweats.

Sabina: Rheumatic pains continue more or less severe after the effusion has taken place, sense of paralysis after exertion, dull drawing pains in the limbs. Exercise in the open air relieves the uneasiness.

Conium is suited to persons who have a lack of vital heat, and lack physical or mental energy.

Digitalis, for a sense of painful tightness in the affected part, great dejection of spirits, he is "weak and nervous," sweats too easily, feels remarkably weak after meals.

Lycopodium, for persons who take cold easily, the affected joint most painful during repose, glandular swellings, general dryness of the surface, ill humor, sad, anxious, dullness of ideas.

Arsenicum: pain worse at night, of a burning character, great weakness, emaciation of the affected limb, dread of exercise, countenance pale and appetite poor.

Antimonium: Great sensibility to cold, sense of weight in the limb, contraction of the tendons.

Bryonia: the affected part sweats a great deal, pain of a tensive character.

The affected part should be exposed for from half an hour to an hour daily to the vapor of hot water, followed immediately with a cold douche, then rubbed off briskly and tightly bandaged. The roller should commence at the toes and continue above the knee. General bathing should be constantly enjoined. Passive motion of the joint should be daily practiced, but over fatigue by walking should be avoided, though gentle exercise by walking, when it gives not too much pain, is advisable.

ANCHYLOSIS, OR STIFF JOINT.

This may be complete or incomplete. It is the result of disease or injury to the joint.

In *incomplete* Anchylosis the ligaments, tendons and surrounding cellular tissue only are involved. The joint admits of slight motion. In *complete* Anchylosis the extremities of the bones are firmly united.

In TREATMENT, if there be any inflammation or soreness of the joint, remove it.

If, after having removed the soreness, the joint admits of any motion, hopes may be entertained from further treatment; but if, on the contrary, it be stiff and immovable, any attempt to disturb it by motion will do harm. It should be let alone.

If the joint admits of motion, *machinery* which will gradually extend the limb, such as Dr. Chase's apparatus, (of Philadelphia) will answer for this purpose. While the machinery, whatever it be, is applied to make the extension, absolute rest on the part of the patient should be enjoined. He must not be allowed to attempt any use of the limb or any other exercise. He should be kept perfectly free from all mental excitement or anxiety, and as much retired from company as possible. As soon as the limb has become straight, or as straight as is thought practicable, all further use of the extending *force* must be discontinued; but the limb should be *kept* in that position until free from all tenderness, if any should have been induced by the treatment.

If any tenderness of the affected joint is present when we are first called to the case, it must be removed by such remedies as the history of the case or the symptoms present indicate. If it arise from any injury, *Arnica* is the proper remedy. If from rheumatism, *Rhus* will probably be sufficient; if from syphilis, *Mercurius;* from mercury, *Nit. ac.* or *Aurum.*

During the time the extending force is being applied, the joint should be exposed to hot vapor of water twice a day, if practicable, then lubricated with the oil of the Rattle-snake (Crotalus Horridus). At the same time a dose of the *Crotalus* should be given every two weeks.

For any soreness of the joint that may be excited by the forcible extension, *Arnica* is the proper remedy.

CHAPTER XIV.

THE HIP DISEASE.

Description and Progress — Diagnosis and Prognosis — Treatment in different stages — Rest or Exercise? — Carved and Gummed Splints? — Direction for making and applying Gum Shellac supports — Diet.

This disease, though mostly occurring in weak and scrofulous children, may occur in persons of any age and constitutional character.

The symptoms sometimes come on so gradually as scarcely to excite attention. Months may elapse before assistance is called for. The first thing complained of is very generally a slight *pain* in the *knee*, no doubt from some implication of the nerves leading to that part. On examination, it is found that the limb is slightly disfigured: it may be increased in length, which occasions the knee to be habitually bent. The elongation itself is usually referred to a partial protrusion of the head of the femur out of the acetabulum. May it not rather be apparently increased on account of a relaxation of the muscles, and an inclination of the pelvis towards the affected side? At this period the pain is referred to the groin, or, perhaps to the posterior surface in the region of the trochanter. This pain will, in some cases, be very severe from the commencement, and continue so until relieved by suppuration, although many patients do not complain for a considerable time.

The *pus* does not make its appearance till the disease has committed great ravages. Sometimes the head of the femur is entirely destroyed, a large abscess occupying its place, without any tendency to approach the surface at any particular point. It may finally open and discharge at different points about the hips; more commonly it directs itself to the groin.

The *ulceration* almost invariably injures the joint, destroying the cartilages, if not the articulating surfaces of the ilium and femur. Sometimes the matter may make its way out of the acetabulum without destroying or forcing out the head of the thigh bone, in which case, though there is no dislocation, we may expect anchylosis. More frequently the head is thrown out, and dislocated backwards on the dorsum of the ilium, where it may form a new joint, producing in effect a short deformed limb, though there has been no actual destruction of bone. When the head of the bone has been entirely destroyed, the constant contraction of the muscles will draw the limb up several inches. It is only in *rare* instances that *recovery* occurs spontaneously, the ulcers healing up and the use of the limb being restored, without deformity.

Though a short leg is the frequent result of the disease, it should be borne in mind that its first effect is, generally, as was remarked, to lengthen the limb and turn inward the foot and knee — a sign by which the mischief may be often detected in its incipient stage.

The patient's constitution suffers severely during the progress of the malady. Chills and hectic set in, with occasional night sweats — no doubt from the absorption of pus.

As to *prognosis*, Professor Gibson gives us the following encouragement: — "Some patients die dropsical before any important change has taken place in the joint — others perish from hectic in a few months — a still greater number live for a much longer time, [!] — a few have been known to survive nine or ten years. [! !] * * Upon the whole, there are few more difficult or *incurable complaints.*" [! ! !]

And Laurie remarks, that it is only in the incipient period of the disease that a favorable prognosis can be given. Such has not been our experience.

The *diagnosis* requires notice. When the pointing occurs in the groin it has been mistaken for *psoas abscess!* If the appearance of the matter is not sufficient, a critical examination should enable the practitioner to determine the difference. In the hip disease, the character of bone pus will be noticed, and some portions of carious bone, or phosphate of lime, will generally be observed in it. Probing will often be decisive. Placing the thumb upon the trochanter, and pressing it firmly into the acetabulum, will often excite pain in a very early stage of the disease, before its existence is suspected.

The errors of diagnosis in this disease, even among men who stand high in the profession as surgeons, are most remarkable. We might instance numerous cases which have fallen under our notice within a few years past. One case, that of a lady in Cincinnati, whose disease had been pronounced and treated for several months as Psoas Abscess, after regular consultation with the Professor of Surgery in the Medical College of Ohio, is reported by the late Dr. Morrow, in the Medical Reformer. It was treated *by him* for hip disease, and cured. A son of Col. F., of Pickaway county, in this State, was brought to consult the same distinguished Professor, who agreed with the country physicians who had been long treating the case as a rheumatic affection *of the knee*, and decided that amputation of the thigh was the only remedy. On seeing the patient, Professor Morrow at once inquired of the father what had been done for the hip, and learned that any disease there had never been suspected. A touch of the finger upon the trochanter, pressing toward the acetabulum, produced excruciating pain, and more extended examination displayed all the well marked symptoms of the Hip Disease — which was, no doubt, the original cause of the trouble in the knee, and would certainly have been little benefited by amputation. We make these statements for no invidious purpose, nor by any means as *singular* occurrences, but as warnings, seeing that men of such standing and long experience, are liable to oversights so serious. We have had two cases of *club-foot* produced by coxalgia, and removed by curing the *hip*.

If the history of each case can be carefully traced back it will generally be found that some mechanical violence has been done to the capsular ligaments of the hip joint. A fall, or perhaps, a strain by a false step or slip of the foot, the recollection of which has passed entirely from the mind of the patient, is the exciting cause. It is true that a depraved constitution is often the ulterior cause.

Arnica and Rhus, internally and externally, alternated once in three or four hours will, therefore, generally arrest the progress of the disease and prevent it passing into the more advanced stages. If not, resort may be had to *Mercurius*, which is often a specific in the early stages of this disease in scrofulous patients, with pale bloated countenance, suffering little or no pain in the hips, except a sense of stiffness and lameness.

Belladonna is more particularly needed when there is considerable pain and inflammation present.

Sulphur, is required for chronic and scrofulous cases, affected with eruptive disease, scorbutic or hepatic affections, or caused by the recession of eruptions; great exhaustion, profuse sweats and great sensitiveness to the open air.

These means are sufficient to counteract the disease, and restore health, if the suppurative process has not already advanced too far; but if *matter* has *formed*, and not yet made its way to the surface, make use of *poultices* and *fomentations* over the whole hip, till there appears a tendency to point at some particular place. At this place open a caustic *issue*, to facilitate the exit of matter as soon as possible. So far from apprehending any evil consequences from the freest escape of matter, we regard it as an essential condition of any successful treatment. No one, certainly, can point out any good result from the retention of a large amount of pus in the system. Its *absorption*, if we could insure it, might occasion as much mischief to the constitution of the patient as its presence is now doing to the part. But to bring about absorption would be a very difficult matter, inasmuch as the absorbents, in common with the rest of the system, are by this time much debilitated.

If, however, the matter seems to be rapidly approaching the surface in a natural way, apply your emollients, and wait patiently for a spontaneous opening. As soon as this occurs, or if there is, when you are first called—

A *free discharge*, encourage it with poultices. Also, wash out the abscess freely, once or twice a day, with injections of weak Castile soap-suds, and then follow with an injection of *Calendula offic.*, giving it also internally. Although not mentioned by any of our authors, we esteem it an important remedy in the suppurative stage, having used it with decided benefit in several cases. Sometimes, owing to the great irritability of the patient, you may not be able to use an injection oftener than once in two or three days. Repeat the operation, however, as often as the patient can bear it. Should there be several

Fistulous openings, each is to be treated in the same manner; and, if they are connected, introduce a ligature, and if practicable, bring them gradually together. Should the patient not improve, or if caries is present, or if there are fistulous pipes, use *Silicea* internally, and as an injection in the form of solution. Where there is much emaciation, it may be advantageously alternated with *Arsenicum*, *Iodine*, or *Calc. phos.; China* is needed in all cases where copious discharges of pus are exhausting the vital powers of the patient.

In some cases *Calc.*, *Hepar s.*, *Ac. phos.*, *Phos.* and *Lach.*, may be advantageously employed. (*See Ulcers*, *Wounds*, *Caries*, *and Necrosis.*)

If after the use of the solution of Silic. for a fortnight, as directed above, there is no improvement visible in the character of the pus, employ a solution of the sesqui-carbonate of potash, instead of it, as recommended in *necrosis*. This will soon destroy and bring away all carious bone, and stimulate a healthy restorative action in the part.

Attention should be paid to the condition of the skin in all diseases; but especially in this and similar ones where there is a chronic formation of pus. It then not only has to throw off the ordinary transpirable matter, but a great deal of poisonous material taken up by the absorbents.

Judicious hydropathic treatment is an invaluable aid. Let the *diet* be of the most *nutritious* but unstimulating kind — milk, farinaceous food, soft boiled eggs. And, in very debilitated patients, the white of eggs beat till light, but not frothy; then sweetened according to taste, and diluted largely with cold water, and used as a common beverage.

Rest is an important adjuvant. Let the affected part be moved as little as possible. We are far, however, from sanctioning the routine recommendation, of keeping the patient confined for several months to his bed. The depressing, and even *irritating* effect of such restraint in a young and otherwise lively patient, more than counterbalances all the advantages of inaction to the affected part. On the contrary, we take the responsibility of advising, with proper precautions,

Exercise in the open air. For this purpose, the patient must be supplied with a *crutch* or crutches, the affected limb being so secured as to allow as little mobility of the joint as possible. If no dislocation has yet occurred, a suitable *splint* may answer the purpose. The "carved splint," to fit the patient from chest to foot, so highly prized by Dr. Physic, is still insisted on by many surgeons (some writers taking particular care to require that it be made and exactly fitted by a professed carver). But any wooden splint, however neatly made and fitted, is too heavy and burdensome for a young patient, to say nothing of the fact, which professional *authors* so generally leave out of sight, to the great embarrassment of actual practitioners — that most families have not an inexhaustible purse to draw upon. The expense of the required "carved splint" would be enormous, if changed, as it would need to be, with the progress of the disease, every month or two. Happily, however, at least for all but the wealthiest, for whom alone some medical men seem, *in their works*, to prescribe,

— A far *better splint* can be made with little trouble and comparatively no expense, one that is just as firm, though much lighter than wood, and fitting *exactly* to the limb and body, as no carved work ever can. Get a piece of thick woolen cloth, (old will do as well as new,) and saturate it in a solution of *gum shellac* (one pound to a pint of alcohol.) Expose it to the air, and when the menstruum is evaporated, your cloth will be almost as firm and elastic as steel. Two sheets, however, may be welded together, by covering again one side of each piece with the dissolved gum, by means of a common paint brush, evaporating as before, and then pressing them together with a hot flat iron or tailor's goose. Three or four thicknesses of heavy woolen cloth thus prepared, will be as strong as any splint ever required for any surgical purpose whatever. Have your prepared material nearly of the size required, and then heat it at the fire or by dipping in scalding water until it is as soft and pliable as the original cloth. In this state, or after it is cool enough not to burn, you can, with two or three assistants, apply it to the parts, and fit it exactly by pressing it down closely to the surface, where, in the course of two or three minutes, it will stiffen. It will always retain the shape thus given it. No heat of the body can ever be sufficient to soften or weaken it. It should, however, be lined with canton flannel, or some such material, to prevent its irritating the surface, such lining being fixed by a weaker solution of the same article or common gum Arabic.

This *shellac splint* should extend from above the middle of the thorax to the ankle, reaching half way round the limb, and above nearly to the spine and sternum. It should be attached all the way by rollers or bandages, applied moderately tight. It will bear being pressed on the surface much more tightly than any other material less accurately fitting. Should the thigh or leg be flexed, no force should be at first used to straighten it. The splint must be *adapted* to the limb in its *easiest position*, and re-fitted as often as the position of the limb changes.

With such a splint, so fixed, almost any desired amount of proper exercise can be taken without risk of exciting the affected joint. Holes may be made in the splint to allow us to dress the opening of the abscess or ulcer, so that the apparatus need not be removed. A gutta percha splint may be used instead of the shellac splint.

In adjusting the splint care must be taken not to apply too much pressure about the hip while it is still sore or painful; but when the disease has become more chronic and indolent, slight pressure, equally applied, is decidedly beneficial.

When the head of the femur is protruding but not yet entirely dislocated, *judicious pressure upon the trochanter* may serve to restore the bone to its natural location and the patient have the use of the limb again. But generally when there has been any degree of dislocation and much suppuration, no other result can be anticipated than anchylosis or a locked joint. This is worse for the patient than when the head of the bone is thrown entirely out of the socket, without other injury, as it then forms an artificial joint, allowing a certain use of the limb, though with shortening and deformity.*

CHAPTER XV.

CHRONIC PSOITIS — PSOAS ABSCESS.

ORIGIN and early symptoms — Secondary symptoms and diagnosis — Matter to be all let out — By puncture or caustic — Dressings and injections — General treatment essential, not mere "anti-phlogistics" — Necessary measures — Baths — Preventive means.

THIS most formidable affection of its class (that is to say, of phlegmonous disease not directly affecting vital organs,) especially the chronic form, is another of the opprobria of ordinary practice — the terror of both patient and physician.

Lumbar abscess sometimes shows itself suddenly and runs quickly through its course. Usually, however, it is *slow* and insidious in its *progress*. It is even said occasionally to take years in coming to maturity.

* The late Dr. Morrow, preceptor and partner of the authors,' spoken of in giving the diagnosis, was eminently successful in the treatment of this and other *esteemed incurable* diseases. The main features of his treatment were *appropriate surgical* aid, attention to the skin and secretions, and the use of a large vegetable irritating plaster over the entire hip. The irritating plaster acted not simply as a counter-irritant,but he contended it produced a constitutional influence by the medicines of which it was composed, being taken up by the absorbents as was proven by their presence in the secretions.

The *suppuration* generally commences in the sheath of the psoas muscles, *high* up on the spine near their origin, and runs down along their course *over the pelvis*, at various lower parts of which it finally points, most commonly in the "groin" just below Poupart's ligament, near the insertion of the psoas magnus into the femur. Occasionally it opens into the abdomen, causing death immediately, the rectum, or in the case of females, into the vagina.

The early *symptoms* are, a dull, heavy *aching* in the *lumbar region*, occasionally extending down the outside of the thigh, and, in some instances, to the foot, causing lameness of the limb, — speedy *fatigue*, on taking exercise, and general locomotive dullness. When he lies down, the patient is disposed to *flex* the *thighs* upon the abdomen, to take off all tension from the affected muscles.

A sudden CHANGE takes place after awhile, and very *different symptoms* occur. Those just mentioned may have continued stationary, and the patient grown accustomed to them, or been gradually aggravated, the local *pain* becoming at last more *throbbing* and intense. The appetite fails, the breath becomes foul and fetid, *chilly sensations* are experienced, and, not unfrequently, night sweats occur, with other accompaniments of *hectic*.

The *swelling*, which is caused by accumulation of matter in the cellular tissue, usually appears in the region of Poupart's ligament, may be at first mistaken for hernia. Sometimes the matter passes down by the urinary bladder and makes its appearance in the perineum, or it may affect the bladder and open into it. The character of the swelling may be known by its fluctuating, particularly when the patient lies down. If he continue the recumbent posture, it will recede. When he stands up, it is much more tense and firm. When he coughs, the tumor suddenly enlarges, as if blown up with air. These peculiarities constitute the

Diagnosis from *hernia;* but the hectic fever is perhaps the clearest criterion, that not being necessarily or often present in the latter disease.

When the *vertebræ* are affected, the result may be curvature of the spine, or even loss of the locomotive function. Such cases may be confounded with original spinal disease.

The causes of Psoitis are sometimes mechanical violence, straining, lifting or carrying, a blow, a fall on the back or nates, pelvis, or rheumatism.

In the early stage of the disease, while the pains are but slight, rather dull and pressive, or even when quite severe, though we see no symptomatic fever, or if any, it is rather of a low grade, the patient stoops to relieve the tension of the psoas muscles and has to be careful in moving lest it hurt him severely; give *Bryonia.*

But if the pains resemble the sensation produced by a bruise, and there is rather a sense of *soreness* from *motion*, than *constant* aching or pain of any kind, use *Nux vomica.*

Pulsatilla, is to be used for a similar group of symptoms, occurring in females.

Mercurius, is to be given when these pains are worse at night. But if acute inflammation sets in, threatening the immediate formation of abscess, with high symptomatic fever, acute and constant pain, with loss of appetite, give *Aconite*, and as soon as the acute symptoms have abated, follow by *Belladonna*, or these may be with advantage alternated, if the symptoms of both are present to any considerable extent.

Colocynth is useful after the acute symptoms have somewhat subsided, but there is still a stiffness and constricted feeling on moving the limb of the affected side.

Mercurius should be used where, notwithstanding the use of *Aconite* and *Belladonna*, we have failed to so far subdue the symptoms as to prevent the formation of abscess, and we have reason to apprehend such a result.

Hepar Sulphuris: To be used after abscess has formed, to facilitate the pointing to the surface; to be followed by *Mercurius* as soon as the matter has been discharged. This remedy should be continued until the discharge assumes a healthy appearance and is rapidly diminishing in quantity, unless the symptoms should sooner clearly indicate some other remedy.

As soon as a fluctuating tumor is discovered, if the patient is not in too great danger from the absorption of pus, apply a poultice of equal parts of elm and flax seed pulverized, wet in warm milk and water, until the pus has approached very near the surface, then puncture and let it be discharged. But when there is great constitutional disturbance from absorption of pus and it still lies deep, you may make an issue with caustic potash over the point where it appears to be nearest the surface, or at the most depending point if you can choose, then apply the poultice until the eschar sloughs off and the abscess opens. In puncturing, never make the mistake of puncturing a hernial tumor for an abscess and kill your patient, as did a physician of our acquaintance. Let your artificial issue be large enough to allow the matter, as well as your injections, to flow out freely. A small orifice may give trouble, by closing again too soon.

Should the *pus* lie *deep*, no local means will be safer, and tend more to bring it to the surface, than the caustic issue. It may enable you to gain much valuable time. After applying the caustic, the elm poultice should be constantly used. After having the abscess open, drain off *all* the *pus*, — whether you have punctured, or let it open spontaneously, or aided the efforts of nature by caustic, let the matter pass out freely. Assist it by compression, as far as you can, along the course of the muscles, and by a slippery elm poultice over the opening, the latter being frequently changed, so that it may not become an impediment.

There is *no danger* from the mere escape of matter, as the books will lead you to apprehend. The sooner it is got rid of, the better. The exhaustion of the system is in its production, not its ejection. Lest, however, when the quantity is excessive, the patient suffer from the shock of too great a change, by the sudden relaxation of the parts that have been so long distended by the accumulated matter, you may at first restrain it a little. If, at any time during the flow, he shows symptoms of fainting, stop it for a while, and give him a little wine. Then replace the poultice, so that the matter may flow more slowly. Be sure, however,

In dressing, *not* to let the *air enter* the wound. This constitutes the only danger, as it may produce excessive inflammation. It is no reason, however, for only "having a small and oblique opening with the lancet, to be occasionally opened and then carefully closed!" When covered with the slippery elm poultice, it is "hermetically sealed" against the action of the air. As an additional precaution, however, compresses should be kept upon the part, bearing, as much as possible, from above, downwards.

When the flow of matter has entirely ceased, you may let the opening *close*. If the evidence of continued suppuration again appear, *re-open;* give it exit; and then throw in an infusion of *Calendula*. Your best mode of injecting, in such a case, is by means of a common catheter, pushed up as far as possible into the opening. If the opening be large enough, as those recommended to be made with caustic, the liquids you throw in will soon return. The catheter should be filled with the fluid to be injected, *before* being introduced, so that no air may be forced up in advance of it. Keep the external *orifice open* until the *abscess heal up internally*. Whenever the matter reappears after healing, open again and proceed as before.

These or similar means are *all* the strictly *local* treatment required. But, though it is absolutely essential to drain off the pus and make such applications as will aid the healing process, these measures are, after all, the least portion of a radical cure. We are told by an old school authority that "very few patients recover from this disease under any circumstances, and those that escape remain puny and debilitated." This confession is not surprising, when we find that this same author says not one word about constitutional treatment, after matter has once formed. By proper attention and the administration of suitable remedies, you may generally, we ought perhaps to say, almost always, succeed in curing this much dreaded affection.

There is, perhaps, no chronic affection in which the beneficial results of the proper application of water will be more striking than in this case. General daily ablution, wet compresses over the affected part and a wet girdle around the loins, are not to be neglected. Observing, always, to temper the water to the susceptibilities of the patient.

The *preventive treatment* against the formation of pus, mentioned in allopathic works, is admitted, even by those who recommend it, to have failed. We, however, have remedies that are specifically adapted to any stage of the disease that will arrest any such case, if applied in time and with sufficient skill.

That such measures as "purging, bleeding and low diet," should have altogether failed, is no reason for not having confidence in a better and more rational plan. This antiphlogistic trio is *all* the constitutional treatment mentioned by one very generally received authority.

During the suppurative stage, *China* may be advantageously employed, when there is much exhaustion from *excessive* suppuration. Should the ulceration extend to the bones, *Silicea* or *Phosphorus* should be used. *Phos.* is also useful and may be applied to the surface of the abscess when the patient suffers from diarrhœa and exhausting sweats. Where the pus is large in quantity, fetid and sanious, *Staphysagria* is an important remedy. It is also useful in the incipient stage of suppuration, when the pain is of a beating character.

When the flow of pus is very profuse, healthy in appearance, but there seems to be no disposition to heal, or diminution of the discharges, the use of *Calendula* internally and the infusion applied to the abscess by injecting will soon bring about a favorable change.

CHAPTER XVI.

TUMORS.

Definition and distinctions — Causes — ADIPOSE TUMORS — Nature? — Removal, the knife preferable to cautery or ligature — FIBROUS TUMORS, structure, diagnosis and prognosis — Excision, or incision and dissecting out — Late or early? — Precautions in and after operating — CELLULAR TUMORS — Origin, progress and termination, dangerous transformation — Early treatment, absorption or excision? — Later means and methods — MALIGNANT TUMORS, and particularly the *Vascular* — Description — Precautions — Compression, caustic Circumvallation.

A "TUMOR" may be defined a preternatural enlargement or protuberance of the soft parts of the body, distinguished by its permanence from an ordinary swelling. It is further characterized by a structure, differing more or less in every case from that of the part from which it arises. Every enlargement that merits the name of a tumor, arises from some disease or unnatural action, and is, therefore, a *new formation*.

Tumors that have the strongest resemblance to the natural tissues, the merely fleshy or fatty tumors, contain a considerable amount of lymph, and their bulk is indeed most generally made up of that deposit.

A common *induration*, resulting from phlegmon, possesses a peculiar structure, which, however, is not permanent; but, being gradually absorbed, gives place to the natural conformation of the parts. But in some instances, even of common inflammation, neither resolution nor suppuration takes place. The inflammation ceases, but the swelling remains; the "tumefaction" has become a "tumor." After this the action going on in the part is neither inflammatory nor healthy; it is a peculiar increased or perverted development of the organism. The tumor is as permanent as any other portion of the body; and in the regular progress of physiological action, it is absorbed only to be redeposited.

ADIPOSE TUMORS,

or *fatty* tumors, may be occasioned by a rupture of the vessels of a part from any mechanical cause, or by a change in the nutrition of the part brought on by previous inflammation.

Tumors, however, often appear spontaneously, that is, without any obviously assignable cause. But it is by no means certain that one or other of the above mentioned causes has not been in operation. The injury may not have been so violent, nor the inflammation so high, as to excite attention or be remembered.

It has even been supposed, by some, that all these fatty tumors originated in living vesicles, thus assigning them a separate vitality, as a sort of hydatids. This idea of their *nature*, does not invalidate that of their mechanical or pathological *origin*, just given. This independent parasitic vitality, appears as the result of the original vitality of the part perverted, but not destroyed.

These tumors, then,— possessing a new organism, if not "vital principle," and each existing upon the body as a distinct member, if not as an independent body or whole, — are not easily removed by any constitutional means. The ordinary means for discussing chronic inflammation, and promoting absorption, have little or no effect upon them.

In the stage of *tumefaction*, however, or while the action in the part still continues inflammatory, discussion of the *incipient* tumor may almost always be accomplished.

If the tumor is painful or tender to pressure, give *Arnica* and apply the Tr. with cloths wet in hot water, over its surface, using as strong compression as the patient will bear.

Baryta, is reported as having removed the pain and arrested the growth of a steatomatous tumor of the neck — also of the axilla.

Bovista, has removed painless swellings on the lip, of many years standing.

Causticum, has also removed sarcomatous tumors, causing them to inflame, suppurate and then heal up.

Silicea, has cured lymphatic tumors of large size, on the thighs and head, producing suppuration, followed by healthy granulation.

Dr. *Geyrard*, of Paris, reports a case of two steatomatous tumors cured by *Thuja* 15, once a day. The tumors disappeared in about a month.

If, after a fair trial of the means pointed out, we fail, as we may expect to do in many instances, and the tumor is so situated as to be conveniently operated upon, the *knife* is generally the best means we can resort to.

Tumors, can, however, in some cases, be removed by the *ligature* or *caustic potash*. The latter must be applied so as effectually to destroy every portion of the organized mass, and cause it to slough off. For the former, two needles must be drawn through under the tumor at right angles and touching each other, carrying

Fig. 2.

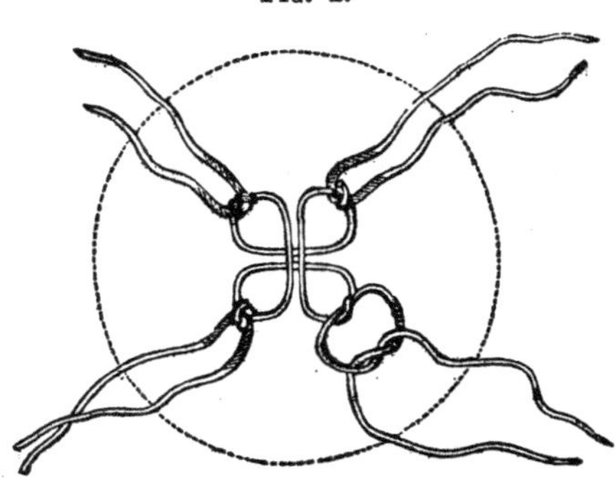

each a double ligature. The loops being cut, leave four ligatures, or the "eight tailed ligature" under the tumor. The ends being tied in four knots, it perfectly strangulates every part of the tumor. [See Plate.]

The knife is far preferable to either of these means, when the patient can be brought to submit to it, as it causes less pain, and there is no danger, *in this character of tumor*, of a return, after it has once been wholly removed.

FIBROUS TUMORS.

These tumors, so called from their peculiar structure, appear, when cut into, to be composed of a uniform yellow or whitish substance, sometimes divided into lobes by septa of condensed cellular membrane. Few vessels penetrate them; and, in some cases, none at all can be discovered. The substances of the fibrous tumor is always contained in a capsule of greater or less density, to which it adheres very loosely, and which seems, in fact, to be the surface from which the substance of the tumor is secreted.

This *substance*, — though the tumor very often has much the appearance of the adipose tumor, — is not found, when *removed*, to melt by heat; nor indeed does it contain proper fatty or sebaceous matter. It is composed apparently, as the name imports, of fibrinous matter.

The *shape* and *surface* are always irregular, but never feel hard and firm like schirrus, but rather of the consistency of *dough;* nor is it painful and slow of growth as that malignant formation. However, if it acquire great *size*, it may become *painful* and irritating from its weight upon the surrounding parts; and may even burst and form an *open sore*, after which an alteration may take place in the character of the tumor itself. In fact the principal annoyance of this sort of tumor to the patient is from its bulk, which also constitutes the principal *danger* from its mechanical effects upon the surrounding parts, rather than any originally malignant character.

The *removal* of fibrous tumors is easy. They are almost always so situated as to be accessible to the knife. It is simply necessary to make an incision through the skin, and divide the capsule so that the tumor can be removed with the fingers or forceps, its adhesion to the capsule being so slight as to offer little or no resistance. If there has been inflammation excited, it may be necessary to *dissect it out.* There may also be adhesions to *vessels* so large as to require them to be taken up and tied. Another precaution to be observed in the cure of these vascular adhesions, if there be also any appearance of present morbid action, is *not* to permit healing by the first intention, but keep it open and excite healthy suppuration, and treat it in other respects as a case of cancer.

But when the surgeon is consulted early, before any adhesions have occurred, or any degeneration in the action of the part, and the patient is willing, these tumors may be *cut out* without any hesitation.

CELLULAR TUMORS.

These are formations of an evidently cellular structure. They may, at first, be divided into laminæ of cellular substance. After a while the laminar structure becomes indistinct, and the layers compacted together. There is always more or less albumen, sometimes fibrin also, in the cells; but the mass of their contents is evidently oily or sebaceous matter.

This kind of tumor may have its original *nisus* in a small gland, in which case it will appear to have a distinct capsule. When it forms in the subcutaneous substance, there is no proper capsule, although the condensation and thickening of the surrounding cellular tissue may bear a strong resemblance to a capsular formation.

These tumors are *smooth* and compact, without the indurated appearance of schirrus. Nor have they any cartilaginous or membranous septa, like cancer and the fibrous tumor. They are *never painful* unless they become inflamed, or from their weight and pressure upon the surrounding parts affect the nerves. The cutaneous veins involved in the tumor sometimes become *varicose,* and the skin over its whole surface may be destroyed. There is, however, no tendency to fungous growths; nor much susceptibility to suppuration or ulceration. When abrasion takes place it is more apt to *slough away.* In this way it is often, when small, *spontaneously* or accidentally *cured.* But when the tumor is large, the slough is a long time in being thrown off, and there is, meanwhile, a very offensive sore. This is accompanied also with great constitutional irritation and injury. It becomes, in fact, as *dangerous* as true cancer. In its original character, however, this tumor has nothing malignant about it: it is as free from danger, as it is easy to manage. Even after inflammation and sloughing, it is much more easily eradicated than any cancerous tumor.

In the TREATMENT of these cases, like the former, you may sometimes succeed in promoting *absorption* by such means as were before recommended. If these means fail, or if the tumor is already very large, recourse had better be had to the knife, caustic or ligature. If called to the case before any inflammation has occurred, and there appears to be no disease in the surrounding parts, *excision* will be the best of all treatment.

But *after sloughing* has commenced, even if the knife be available at all, it should be relied upon alone.

If suppuration or sloughing should take place from the effects of your remedies (*Baryta, Bovista, Silicea, Causticum,*) before mentioned, discontinue the remedy or lengthen the interval, and let it go on until the cure is complete. If, however, the sloughing come on spontaneously, or the patient becomes much prostrated from the discharge of pus, give *China.*

Cleanse the abscess several times a day of all pus, by gentle washing with soap and water, injecting the same into any sinuses that may exist. Keep the tumor covered with an emollient poultice and *warm.* Give the patient nourishing diet and keep him very quiet.

OTHER VARIETIES,

and other DIVISIONS of tumors, are presented in the books, but the division into the three classes mentioned, comprehends all the forms of non-malignant tumor, and appears as good — that is, as practically useful as any.

"Encysted tumors" might be instanced. They are distinguished as consisting of a sac, containing a thin fluid, which is not pus. The definition evidently corresponds to the description of cellular tumors above given. Strictly fatty encysted tumors are sometimes called "steatomous;" those embracing honey-like matter, "melicerous;" and those having a pap-like fluid, different from either of the others, "ætheromatous."

What might seem the most important practical division, is into those which are, and are not,

MALIGNANT TUMORS.

It should be remembered, however, that almost any tumor or sore *may* become malignant. Thus, the fibrous tumor, above spoken of, as well as the cellular, may become a tumor or sore as "dangerous and difficult" to manage, by ordinary means, as any schirrus or open cancer. Those forms known to be malignant, we shall speak of as varieties of cancer. Among these,may be named the *tuberculated* (a congeries of small, hard, rounded tumors), and the *medullary* sarcoma, or fungus hœmatodes. Under this head, however, we may distinguish the

Vascular Tumor. (*Telangiectasia.*)

This is sometimes called *Aneurism by Anastomosis.* It is, in fact, a complete net work of vessels. Some suppose it is caused by arteries opening into the cellular interstices, giving rise to corresponding veins; others, that it is originally a particular structure, formed by fibrous membrane, from the internal surface of which prolongations pass off, crossing each other in various directions, and accompanied by as many arteries and veins, to a "prodigious subdivision." Certain it is, that the tumor, when fully developed, seems to be wholly composed of vessels, a sort of placental formation.

When the vascular tumor forms just beneath the skin, or in the integuments, it can be readily distinguished, by the external appearance. But when it occurs beneath the fasciæ, the external appearance is no guide, and the diagnosis is very obscure for a long time. There will be some degree of tension and swelling, with a sensation of throbbing and pain. It may be noticed, however, that the tumor will vary in size, according to the tension or relaxation of the neighboring muscles, and according to the degree of excitement in the whole vascular system. Whenever we discover a swelling to have these peculiarities, we should be on our guard as to any

Treatment that may be adopted. Wounds, or incisions, into such tumors, are very troublesome, as it is almost impossible to suppress the hemorrhage. No attempt at an operation should be made, unless the tumor be so situated that every portion of the mass can be at once removed. Their most common site is about the eye, or upon the temporal muscle, or other parts of the head and face.

In cases of children they may be removed by specific medication; but in adults the result is much more doubtful. Compression immediately after birth, will facilitate the cure.

Carbo. veg., has succeeded in young children.

Nitric Acid, in persons farther advanced.

Sulphur, has also been successful. It has been used with success in alternation with *Phos.*

Any, or all these remedies, may be used in their turn, for such a period of time as may be deemed necessary to give each a fair trial. Long intervals should intervene between the repetition of doses. As there are generally no marked symptoms to guide us in the selection of remedies in the early stages, we must select with reference to the general condition of the patient.

If all specific remedies fail and the case is one threatening danger, you can resort to

Obliteration of the vessels by exciting adhesive inflammation, which may be accomplished by surrounding the part with an eschar, made by caustic potash, when that is practicable, and then applying the plaster and compression. The vessels supplying the tumor will thus be destroyed, and active absorption at the same time promoted. At this *circumvallation* of the tumor is not always practicable, the caustic may be applied to the surface of the tumor itself, if the proper care be taken, at the time, not to cauterize so deeply as to rupture the vessels before inflammation is set up, and afterwards to keep up sufficient compression. This pressure is important in all cases, in order that the vessels be not allowed to continue their regular action and growth.

CHAPTER XVII.

GANGLION AND EXOSTOSIS

TUMOR on the TENDONS or LIGAMENTS — Character, causes, etc., — Ulceration and Induration — Excision — Treatment, medical or surgical? — Tumors on BONES, or EXOSTOSIS — Description and distinction from Hypertrophy of Bone — Progress — Treatment, general and local — Starvation and Gluttony — Operation.

THIS term GANGLION is used in *surgery* to designate a peculiar encysted tumor which forms in the fasciæ near the tendons and joints, usually on the wrist, hand, and top of the foot. The fluid it contains is like the white of eggs, or sometimes more like milk or cream. It is generally found adherent to the tendons of the muscles, or the ligaments of the joints.

The probable CAUSE is some mechanical injury, which occasions a slight rupture in the sheath of the tendons, or the synovial membrane; in consequence of which the secretion of the bursæ mucosæ, or the synovial fluid itself, escapes, and occasions the formation of the membrane, sac or cyst, in which the fluid is retained, and continues to accumulate. As the fluid accumulates, its new membraneous investment constantly enlarges, producing, first, stiffness in the adjacent joint, then emaciation of the muscles, contraction of the tendons, and sooner or later, a total loss of the use of the joint. Thus, on the back, or even front of the wrist, it may affect several tendons at once, so as to destroy the power of extending or flexing the fingers.

If the ganglion is allowed to follow its own course, an opening is at last formed, from which a sanious fluid exudes, and a very malignant ulcer is sometimes the consequence.

The Homeopathic treatment for wounds and injuries prevents the development of ganglion. Hence its great superiority. It not only removes present symptoms, but prevents evil results of the injury upon the organism in future.

Arnica, Rhus, Silicea and Ruta, are the most important remedies.

In all cases of ganglion arising from mechanical injury (and nearly if not all cases are such), *Arnica* will prove valuable. We have removed ganglion of years standing with it, when the tendons were so involved as almost entirely to destroy the use of the hand, and the tumor had become very painful. Give it internally once a day, at first, and as the case improves, lengthen the interval. At the same time apply the Tr. to the tumor, together with as much compression as it will bear. Subject the tumor to a stream of cold water from a height for several minutes each day—prohibit the use of the affected joint as far as practicable.

Rhus, after *Arnica* has been used for a few weeks, is often advantageously alternated with it.

Ammonia Carb., is beneficial when it becomes very painful.

Phos. Acid, when it ulcerates and is painful; this should also be applied to the ulcer.

If it becomes highly inflamed, *Plumbum* is useful.

Ruta, for ganglion from injury of carpal and tarsal joints, particularly for the painless swelling.

Silicea, is useful both when painless and when ulcerated.

EXOSTOSIS.

All tumors formed upon the bones in a healthy condition, are included under this term. These tumors are of various forms and densities, differing in their structural arrangement. They may be solid, dense and smooth as ivory, cellular and smooth on their external surface also, or rough and jagged, what is called "tuberculous."

Professor Gibson divides them into four classes:

1st. The *circumscribed*, which is the most common kind,—smooth, seldom painful, and rarely becoming very large.

2d. The *lamellated*, consisting of numerous plates laid over each other, and often piled up in irregular masses.

3d. The *tuberculated*, consisting of knobs or irregular excrescences, either closely connected or insulated.

4th. The *spinous*, having slender processes terminating in points or knobs.

These tumors are most frequently found upon the extremities, the humerus and femur being oftener affected than other bones.

Bone tumors grow from the periosteum, or from the external surface of the bone, under cover of the periosteum. In some cases the point of attachment is a small neck, the main portion of the tumor being bulbous. These are apt to be broken off accidentally. Others are attached by a more extensive surface.

When the surface of the tumor is rough or sharp pointed, it is often a source of much *inconvenience*, by impeding the motions of muscles, or pressing upon some important organ. They have no malignant character, being governed by the same laws as other bony formations.

Bones sometimes become *enlarged* throughout their whole extent, and yet appear to be free from disease. This enlargement, though perhaps produced by a similar state of the system, is not properly " exostosis " — it is no tumor.

The *causes* are not well understood. External injuries are said to be the most frequent. Their *progress* is very slow and attended with but little pain or inconvenience. They can be *distinguished* by the peculiar hard bony feeling at points where bone is not usually perceptible. If the tumor projects into a natural cavity, as that of the skull, the diagnosis is difficult or impossible. After having attained a certain size, it generally remains stationary, the surrounding parts becoming accustomed to its presence and accommodated to its size. No inconvenience then attends it. Occasionally, however, the pressure causes suppuration of the surrounding parts and becomes a source of much difficulty, if not danger.

The principal remedies are: *Arnica, Asafetida, Dulcamara, Belladonna, Calcarea, Aurum, Lycopodium, Mezereum, Phosphorus* and *Silicea.*

Arnica, is to be used when the disease was caused by an injury. *Asafetida*, is particularly applicable when it appears on the legs or arms. *Belladonna*, when it appears on the os frontis. *Aurum*, is used in cases caused by the use of mercury. *Calcarea*, for exostosis on the spine. *Dulcamara*, when the affliction arose from suppressed itch. *Lycopodium*, for scrofulous persons. *Mezereum*, particularly for the affection on the *legs* and *arms* of scrofulous or syphilitic persons. *Phosphorus*, is used for *painful* bones, tendons on the head and clavicle. *Silicea*, is most serviceable for this disease in infants.

All stimulating food and drinks should be avoided, and the accustomed quantity of *food* should be gradually *diminished*. This may be done, if carefully managed, without inducing debility.

Most persons eat too much, at all times, and by thus over-taxing the digestive and assimilating organs, the absorbent process is enfeebled; and hence we see sores, of various kinds, appear on the surface to give outlet to noxious fluids, which should have been taken up by the absorbents, and carried off through the natural evacuations; or we have tumors appearing in the soft parts, or on the bones. If then we can institute a course of regimen that will correct this gormandizing habit, we do much toward removing these tumors, by promoting the natural activity of absorption. We once knew a young man in college, who made the experiment upon himself, of limiting and diminishing, from day to day, his allowance of food, until he could live, and feel well, on less than one-fifth the quantity he had formerly taken. His strength was not impaired in the least, either physically or mentally; though he became very much thinner, all the fat of his system seeming to have been gradually absorbed without injury. Care should be exercised in this matter, however, for if debility or nervous irritability is induced by the low diet or starvation, it will result in evil. If these means fail, the tumor may be removed by an operation. The soft parts over the tumor should be laid open and dissected sufficiently to expose its face, and then it may be removed with a saw of the proper dimensions, a trephine, or a chisel. The surface of the bone from which the tumor is removed, should be made smooth by the bone-forceps or file and the soft parts replaced, and adhesion by the first intention promoted.

CHAPTER XVIII.

POLYPUS OF THE NOSE—POLYPUS OF THE WOMB.

POLYPI in general—NASAL POLYPUS—Cause—Various incipient symptoms—Progress and results—"Cancerous polypi"—Treatment—General Remedies and regimen—Relapse to be prevented—Mechanical surgery insufficient.—UTERINE AND VAGINAL POLYPI—Slow Progress—Diagnosis—Application of the ligature—Injections and topical applications—Examples of mistake—Treatment for prolapsus uteri.

POLYPI may be defined as fleshy excrescences, of a vegetative or zoophytic, rather than animal character, varying in size, color and density, and occupying some of the cavities of the body, generally growing on the introverted surface, lined with mucous membrane.

As the nasal or uterine mucous surface is by far the most usual *habitat* of these troublesome growths, all that need be said of them will occur under the two heads of Polypus of the *nose* and *uterus.*

POLYPUS OF THE NOSE.

This is a very common disease, particularly in climates that are both damp and warm. Wherever it occurs the state of the weather has considerable influence over it. A polypus is a living *hygrometer.* Just before a storm and during wet weather, it is much more swollen than at ordinary times, and when a change to dry weather occurs, it perceptibly shrinks in size. Further than this direct subjection to atmospheric vicissitudes, little is known of its character and

— CAUSE. It has been supposed that it always originates in some *mechanical injury.* Another opinion is, that the predisposition to this disease is very generally *hereditary.*

The polypus often *comes on* as a mere swollen and thickened state of the mucous membrane, independent of local causes, with many of the symptoms of a common cold. This swelling frequently appears to *change its seat* from one part to another, or even from one nostril to the other. In other cases its distinct existence may be detected when it is not larger than a pin's head, like a little fungous pimple, generally quite insensible. In other parts it becomes dark-colored, but in the nose it is generally light-colored and sometimes white, having a clear cartilaginous appearance, and being much less vascular or liable to bleed.

The SYMPTOMS are at first those of *catarrh,* with unusual *sneezing,* especially when the patient changes his position. As the disease progresses, various unpleasant sensations are experienced, chiefly attributable to the mere mechanical obstruction. A sense of fullness and dull pain in the head are seldom absent. The *eyes,* one or both, are liable to become suffused with tears: the ductus ad nasum may even be quite closed up, causing "fistula lacrymalis." The sense of *smell* is generally lost. That of *hear-*

ing, too, may be subsequently injured, in consequence of the polypus growing backward into the throat and pressing on the eustachian tube. Even the *teeth* are sometimes crowded out, and the voice assumes what is called the *nasal* sound from the air *not* passing through the nose!

The actual *sensation* of *fullness* is generally first felt at the *side* of the nose, the parasite most commonly taking root in one of the turbinated or spongy bones. After enlarging so as to fill up the whole nasal cavity, it may project externally through the *nostrils*, or backwards into the *throat*, occasioning difficulty of *swallowing* and even of *respiration*. Sleep is thus often disturbed, the patient having to lie with his mouth open. The disfigurement of the face from swelling of the nose may be very great, independently of any secondary diseased action. The ossa nasi may be separated for nearly an inch.

If the disease is allowed to continue it may occasion *ulceration* of the *bone;* after which the patient rapidly sinks. The breath becomes very foul, and hemorrhage from the part now occurs very frequently, as well as from other parts of the body. Hectic soon follows, with coma and death.

Precise distinction is sometimes attempted between *fungous* and *cancerous* polypi. But we are clearly of opinion that the attempt must be ineffectual and often practically injurious. Any polypus may, by neglect or improper treatment, assume a malignant character; and a tumor that is plainly cancerous from its origin is improperly called a polypus. That cancers do result from polypi is to be attributed more to bad management than any natural tendency in the latter to such a transformation. Still, it must be confessed, that a polypus may become, especially in scrofulous individuals, quite as malignant and fatal as any "true cancer."

In TREATING this affection, you have generally time to attempt its removal by internal remedies. The principal remedies for polypus of the nose are *Phosphorus*, *Staphysagria*, *Calcarea*, *Sepia*, *Silicia*, and *Sanguinaria*.

Phosphorus is indicated in the early stage, when the patient sneezes often, and begins to feel a fullness in the nostril, especially in the morning. *Staphysagria* should be used when, in addition to the foregoing, there is a suffused condition of the eyes. *Calcarea*, at a later stage, when there is oppressive fullness and a fetid smell constantly complained of, or where he has lost the sense of smell, but the part emits a fetid odor.

Sepia, when, in addition to the foregoing symptoms, or any of them, there is pain in the head as a constant symptom, especially in damp weather.

Silicia is most useful in scrofulous ulceration of the polypus.

Sanguinaria. Coryza, profuse lachrymation, watery discharge from the nose, redness of the nose, frequent sneezing, heat in the nose.

We have frequently removed polypus of the nares, when not too far advanced, by the simple application, with a camel's-hair pencil, of this remedy finely pulverized.

Dr. Goullon reports a case of polypus of the nose, filling one nostril and crowding upon the other so as to impede respiration through it, cured by *Calcariæ carb.* three doses in fourteen days, when all traces of the polypus disappeared.

A case of nasal polypus, of thirty years standing, in a man of sixty, cured with *Teucrium*, is reported in the *Allg. Zty. Hom.*, vol. i., p. 69. The polypus extended into the posterior nares and the antrum—both nostrils were closed and the sense of smell destroyed. One drop of the 3d dilution was taken every evening, and an inhalation from the mother Tr. every morning. In two months the polypus dwindled away to a small spot, sense of smell returned, with free breathing through the nose.

If we should, however, meet with any case where all of those remedies fail to make an impression, disorganization and sloughing of the tumor may be *safely* caused by an application of the pure sesqui-carbonate of potash. When the remedies are operating properly, the polypus will *turn black*, and *begin* to slough off. This degree of success will indicate the continuance of the same remedy until the whole is removed. Where even the sesqui-carb. is not sufficient to disorganize the tumor, aid it by *mechanical force*. Take hold of the polypus with sharp pointed forceps, and crush it in various directions, even tearing away any parts that can be detached. Be sure to disorganize the main part of it, squeezing and twisting freely with the sharp teeth of the instrument, in order that the subsequent applications may penetrate the center. There is but little sensibility to embarrass the operation; and any hemorrhage that may be occasioned can be checked with *Phos.* After this "operation," reapply sesqui-carb. to the lacerated mass, in the shape of a strong wash, as often as once a day, at least — occasionally applying a little of the dry powder, if it do not give too much pain.

This plan will invariably succeed, the whole product of "perverted nutrition" passing away in the suppurative process. Continue the specific medicines according to the symptoms, with a view to preventing a relapse and removing a disposition to return of the disease.

Pungent articles should never be carelessly used as "errhines," *i. e. snuffed up.* The mere local irritation of them may, through sympathy, excite severe sneezing and coughing, and their actual *inhalation* may occasion inflammation of the lungs.

The *diet* may require to be restricted or regulated, watching the effect of any change on the constitution. As in all cases, be cautious of a too spare as well as too "full habit of body" — avoid sins of omission as well as commission. The patient should be neither starved nor stuffed.

The mere *mechanical treatment* of these affections does not deserve to be called scientific. Little or no good is done by all this violence. The excrescence may be removed for a time, but is sure to return again, if not to assume a worse form. There is an old gentleman now in Cincinnati, who was operated on in Edinburgh every year, for several years in succession, by the celebrated Liston, and subsequently by other surgeons, — once by Professor Barton, in Philadelphia. The polypus is now larger than ever, completely filling both nostrils, separating the ossa nasi and spreading the nose half across the face. It is not only a great disfigurement and local inconvenience to the patient, particularly in wet weather, but seriously affects his general health, though there is still no appearance of malignancy or even ulceration.

POLYPUS OF THE UTERUS OR VAGINA.

This polypus is usually of a pear shape, and attached by its smaller end within the cavity of the womb, or about its neck. It is sometimes found adhering to the os tincæ, at others just within the cervix, or even to the fundus. It has often a small stalk or pedicle, and the great mass of it projects into the vagina.

It may be very *slow* in its growth, and for a long time unnoticed, occasioning no inconvenience except as an obstacle on the occasion of childbirth. It may give trouble in this way long before it is large enough to prevent conception. Dr. Hill examined a case where he was fully satisfied the patient had given birth to three children since the existence of the parasite. The difficulty of parturition increased each time. The polypus grew out from the body of the womb, and finally filled up the cavity and protruded into the vagina.

Polypus in the Vagina may be mistaken by the patient, and by careless or very inexperienced practitioners, for inversion or prolapsus of the womb. In such cases,

Your *diagnosis* will be aided by the history of the case. Of course, there is no question of *inversion* if the patient has never borne children.

An alleged case of "falling of the womb," however, which does not soon right itself by suitable measures and regimen, must be serious enough to demand an *examination*. If, as is very possible, the supposed descent of the uterus turn out a polypus, the latter will be distinguished from it by its greater hardness, and readiness to bleed, by being dark instead of florid, and insensitive instead of very sensitive to the touch.

Polypus of the womb is sometimes, but by *no means necessarily*, connected, as will be pointed out hereafter, with a *scirrhus* condition or tendency in that organ.

The principal remedies are, *Aurum*, *Belladonna*, *Thuja*, *Nux Vomica*, *Sepia*, *Kreosote and Mercurius*. *Cal.* and *Styphy.* are recommended to remove this tendency to the formation of Polypi.

Calcarea, for hysterical women, the menses too early and too profuse.

Aurum is to be used when the patient is tremulous, easily debilitated, is rather melancholy, desires to think and reflect a great deal on her disease, but complains of being easily fatigued by thinking; the mind gets tired. She suffers more or less from pains in the abdomen resembling labor pains.

Belladonna is indicated when she has no disposition to think or reflect; she feels a fullness of the head, is forgetful and rather hypochondrical, or has a kind of monomania about her disease, or, it may perhaps, be some other subject; complains of habitual dullness of ideas and occasional dizziness, is affected with leucorrhœa and colic pains, hemorrhoids.

Nux Vomica is useful when she has great fear of death, is sure she will never recover, is peevish and fault-finding, or she is inclined to "build castles in the air," wants to accomplish some great thing, but fears to undertake it, because she will not live to see it perfected.

Sepia is indicated by great sadness and weeping; she imagines that she has consumption, though she has no symptoms of that disease; she loathes life, is melancholy and peevish; is affected with debilitating leucorrhœa attended by severe itching in the vagina.

Mercurius for polypus with corrosive leucorrhœa, attended by itching, while there is much sympathetic affection of the mammæ. If the patient has a scrofulous or cachetic constitution, give *Mercurius*, unless she is suffering from the effects of mercury; if so, give *Hepar sul.*, or *Sul. acid. Staphysagria* is also useful in this latter case.

The medicines should be given only at long intervals — say from two to three weeks between doses. Jahr says six or eight weeks.

Though by perseverance you may be able to effect the cure, you will often have much difficulty in inducing your patient to wait patiently for the action of your remedies. If you cannot induce her to do so, or you are disappointed in the results, the polypus still remaining unchanged or increasing, you may resort to surgical means for the removal of the tumor, and after that is effected, return to the specific remedies to rid the system of the tendency to a relapse.

The idea sometimes put forth by some of our homeopathic brethren, that the interference of surgery for the removal of parasites is prejudicial to the specific action of remedies in removing the morbid condition on which their growth depended, will not stand the test of practical observation, while every day's experience proves the contrary to be true—that morbid condition will be much more easily corrected after the removal of the tumor, the great obstacle to a speedy cure.

The *removal* of polypus of the womb is generally facilitated by its pedunculated shape and position in the vagina. Having ascertained, by very strict manual examination, or by the speculum, the exact state of the case, introduce your ligature, by means of the *polypus forceps*, or *double canula* (Fig. No. 3,)* and draw

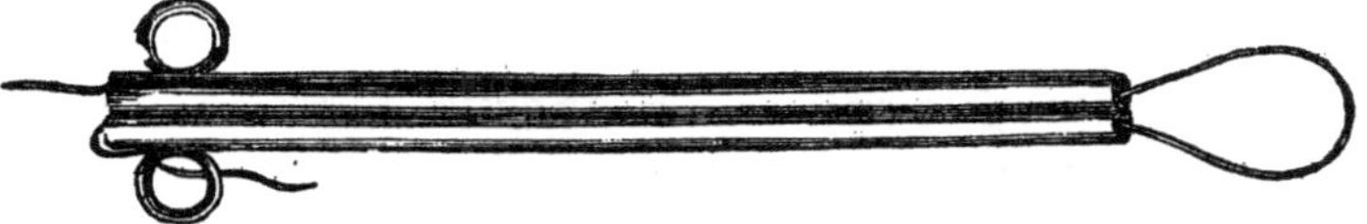

it tight enough round the pedicle to cut off the circulation. In from four to six days the strangulated parasite will slough off. There may be some bleeding at this period: it can easily be stopped with sanguinaria, arnica or calendula. If the body of the polypus does not come away altogether, on the division of its attachment, remove it with the forceps.

It may, however, be difficult or impossible, to get at the neck of the polypus, so as to apply your ligature, from its lying too far up, or being too large to be passed; or from rigidity of the mouth of the womb.

It may be necessary to speak of the errors in *diagnosis* to which uterine polypi may give rise; even experienced men have committed very great blunders. In "women's matters," the young surgeon may be excused some hesitancy of judgment, since he is not always readily permitted the necessary means of information. A very respectable lady, about forty years of age, who once came to consult Dr. Hill, had been *mis*-treated for several years by diff-

* The double canula, represented in Fig. 3, is made of two silver tubes, attached at their sides, with a ring on the lateral surface of each at one end. A ligature of silk cord, cat-gut, or a silver wire, is passed into each tube by its two ends, leaving a loop at the extremity: while one end is fast to one of the rings, the other is loose, and can be pushed forward, or drawn up, as you wish to enlarge or diminish the size of the loop. The loop is passed over the polypus, or tumor, and then the loose end of the ligature is drawn upon as tightly as is required, and fastened to the other ring. The canula is allowed to remain attached until the tumor is strangulated, or sloughs off. The ligature may be tightened, from time to time, if necessary.

erent physicians, on the supposition that the leucorrhea from which she constantly suffered, depended for its cause and continuance on prolapus uteri. At last she determined to try if there was not a better practice. Her physician, however, too much accustomed to seeing such failures to regard the ill success of such treatment as she had been under, as any reason for suspecting false diagnosis, and influenced, perhaps, a little too much by the *fact* of so many doctors *not* differing, continued to treat the case as one of prolapsus. This, of course, could not remove her local difficulties, though she acknowledged to Dr. H. that her general health had been much benefitted by the prescriptions. Her physician informed Dr. H., also, that the prolapsus was very deep, and the uterus so changed in its form as well as place, that the os tincæ could not be found! Upon an examination he found simply a polypus, of the size of a goose-egg, attached at about an inch within the neck of the uterus, and reaching bodily into the vagina, where it would, by acting as a pessary, have effectually prevented any falling of the womb, had there been any tendency that way; and where, by its pressure on the delicate lining of the walls, it kept up the irritation and discharge, which latter it would have been worse than useless, had it been possible, to stop without "removing the cause." The whole mystery of the obstinacy of the disease was explained at once; and the long-sought remedy easily applied.

Another case was that of a young lady, of about twenty, who had suffered much for two years previous from uterine hemorrhage, — so much indeed, that on several occasions her immediate death from exhaustion had been anticipated. Her appearance was such as indicated that the gradual exhaustion by hemorrhage would ere long terminate in death. She was so emaciated that osteology might have been studied upon her figure; and her face was a bloodless white. Her physician spoke of the case as prolapsus, rendered difficult by debility from former hemorrhage, although *he* had made no examination. The patient herself stated that another physician, a man of years and of reputation for science as well as experience, had examined and pronounced the cause of her afflictions to be a "falling of the womb." On examination, two polypi were discovered, one of the goose-egg size wholly in the vagina, though springing from the cervix uteri, the other as large as an ordinary hen's egg, extending some distance up into the cavity of the womb.

What we wish to impress on the mind by relating these cases, is the *necessity*, in all obstinate uterine difficulties, of a thorough and *critical examination*, before venturing an opinion, much more undertaking treatment.

CHAPTER XIX.

CANCER IN GENERAL.

THIS subject is one of very great importance and demands as full an elucidation as is possible within the limits of this work. When we bear in mind the intolerable sufferings of the unfortunate patient, and the results of treatment, and the expressed opinions of distinguished men as to its curability; as true physicians, esteeming it our highest privilege to alleviate and remove the suffering of our fellow men, we may, with solicitude, ask if the beneficent Creator has not given any means to stay the ravages of this terrible destroyer.

Many seem to regard the terms cancerous and incurable as synonomous. Said a distinguished allopathic authority to his class: "Gentlemen, I never cured a cancer, and (consequently) I don't believe any other man ever did!" This class, measuring others' knowledge by their own ignorance and others' abilities by their own impotence, denounce as quacks and impostors those who profess to have succeeded. If they were cured, say they, in reference to cases abandoned by themselves because *cancerous*, and returned cured, they were not cancer; if they were not, they probably were, and failure was the necessary consequence of so hopeless an undertaking. They will rather disbelieve their own eyes, than take another's word; rather impeach their own judgment, than authenticate another's skill; rather give up their own infallibility in all other points, than doubt that they can fix the exact boundary between the possible and impossible. They confess that they do not always know what is cancer, but still insist that they do know that cancer (if it *were* only known) never has been and never will be cured. They are like the dog in the manger. And while their course may do very well for the *routinist*, the follower of "authorities" too lazy to think and investigate for himself, it is not that of the *true* physician or surgeon. If it could be proven that a case of cancer never had been cured, that should be the most urgent reason for elaborating and trying new means and modes of treatment.

The name cancer has been applied by modern pathologists to the morbid structures designated as scirrhus encephaloid and colloid, and is applicable to them in every period of their development, before as well as after softening and ulceration. That these formations should be thus grouped together is evident, since they agree *anatomically*, *chemically*, *physiologically* and *pathologically*. "Anatomically, for they are all composed of a containing and contained part, forming a combination unlike any other in the natural structures; chemically, since they are all distinguished by the very great excess of albumen in their composition; physiologically, for they all possess in themselves the power of growth and of extension by continuity of tissue, that is, of assimilating to their proper substance the most heterogeneous material: an inherent tendency to destruction and the power of local reproduction; pathologically, since they all tend to effect simultaneously or consecutively various organs in the body, and produce that depraved state of the constitution known as the cancerous cachexia. They are not entozootic, since they do not live without vascular connexion with the parent organism, which is the case with entozoon. Yet the heterologous material of all carcinomatous formations is organizable, susceptible of vascular development, and hence of undergoing all the changes of increase and decay consequent on such susceptibility." M. Cruveilhier remarks, that cancerous products are living foreign bodies which possess vital powers of their own, and, like the fœtus in utero, assimilate materials derived from the individual in whom they are developed, to their own peculiar substance.

Scirrhus is either infiltrated into the substance of organs, or is developed in the form of a tumor. A scirrhus tumor is distinguished by its *extreme hardness*, whence the common name *stone cancer*, the resistance to treatment ordinarily sufficient for resolution and the very strong tendency to intractable ulceration. They rarely become larger than a fair sized apple, and are usually rounded or oval and flattened. At first the surface is smooth, but soon becomes irregular and knotty to the touch; and the skin becomes wrinkled or puckered and of a leaden hue, occasionally dark or purplish. Sometimes there is an absence of pain, at other times it is of a burning character, but generally it is at first merely itching, crawling, or twinging, afterward lacinating and gnawing, and very severe. Its growth is often slow, continuing in the condition above described, without any material change for several years; sooner or later, however, the wrinkled skin about it seems to become dry, and finally cracks open in several places; forming deep grooves, from which is discharged a thin, fetid and excoriating fluid. These *fissures* deepen and widen in some instances slowly, in others very rapidly, with extensive ulceration and sloughing. The cavity thus formed constitutes one form of "*open cancer*," which, however, frequently fills up with an irregular fungous growth.

The infiltrated form is most common in the uterus, female mammæ and the lower lip. When it attacks the bones it gradually produces softening.

If a *dissection* be made of a scirrhus tumor, in its early stage, it appears to consist mainly of pale, gray, cartilaginous or fibrous bands, in appearance. In some instances these form spheroidal cells, others a rectilinear disposition predominates, and in others still there appears to be a fibro-cartilaginous nucleus, from which they radiate to the surface of the tumors and sometimes extend to the surrounding cellular tissue. These radiating bands are intersected by others, not so distinct, thus forming a kind of fibrous *net-work*, enclosing the softer parts of the mass, which are of a bluish white color, and always presenting a glossy and peculiar semi-transparent aspect. When, however, the tumor has approached the *ulcerating stage*, its various parts become more blended together. They are, however, still distinct *cysts*, including a pulpy mass of dark greenish color, which has lost its transparency, and is sometimes even black. There are frequently several of these cysts of different colors. Sometimes they are very numerous, presenting a strong resemblance to hydatids.

These *cysts* in a tumor are regarded by some as the most positive, if not indispensable, evidence of the cancerous character. "I am not prepared," says Professor Burns of Glasgow, "to prove that cysts invariably exist in true cancer; but my examinations enable me to say that they are rarely if ever absent."—*Principles of Surgery*, page 339.

By forcibly pressing a slice of scirrhus tumor, a thin albuminous fluid may be made to exude, which is called the scirrhus juice or ichor, and which M. Cruveilhier affirms, forms the only distinction visible to the naked eye, between some scirrhus and fibrous tumors in the bones.

Encephaloid, so called from its resemblance to the brain, is also infiltrated into the tissue of organs, or occurs as a distinct tumor *encysted* or *non-encysted;* found most frequently in the common cellular membrane, the testicle, liver and stomach. Laurie describes the investing cyst as a smooth membrane, about half a line thick, of a silvery white color, imperfectly transparent, and easily removed from the mass.

The *non-encysted* variety is generally globular, but may be flat, oval or irregular in form. Very rarely the surface of encephaloid tumors is perfectly smooth; *usually*, however, convoluted like the brain, whence the name. They grow to a larger size than almost any other morbid growth. Professor Berard saw an encephaloid tumor in the thigh of a female as large as the body of a man, and Abernethy relates the case of a patient who had a tumor of this class in each groin as large as the head of an adult. We have seen them larger than the head of a man. In the diffused or infiltrated form, cancerous matter is deposited in the interstices of a tissue, and if its growth is not arrested, gradually transforms that tissue into its own substance.

Upon cutting into an encephaloid tumor we find a containing part, consisting of firmer septa, which rarely intersect each other, but describe curves circumscribing loculi of various shapes and sizes, and dividing the mass into lobes and lobuli, — a contained part, the cancerous matter, which gives the brain-like appearance to the whole. It has the appearance of homogeneous matter of an opaque milky color, usually dotted with pink-colored spots, varying in their number, size and shape. Its consistency is that of the healthy brain. This class of tumors is abundantly supplied with blood-vessels; hence the great difference between this and other species of cancers in the rapidity of their growth.

"There are two conditions under which the relation of the encephaloid matter to its other contents is productive of appearances, which have led to the application of particular names to the disease. 1. When interstitial hemorrhage leads to sanguineous infiltration of the mass or irregular accumulations of blood, and when, especially after ulceration of the integuments, a rapid development of fungous growths take place from its substances, the disease, in imitation of one of one of its earliest describers, Hey, is termed

Fungus Hæmatodes, or as is called by some, *Rose* cancer. The circumstances under which this name is applicable are, however, merely fortuitous, and do not imply any fundamental distinction in the nature of the growth exhibiting them. If (inasmuch as the changes to which it refers materially affect the local and general pathological influence of the morbid formation) this name be retained for practical purposes, it should be strictly limited to the disease when in the state described; as a general term for the species, it is strongly objectionable; nor, strictly speaking, can fungus hæmatodes be considered a variety. 2. This term has also been applied in cases where an abundant vascular and erectile rete forms a striking constituent of the growth (Dupuytren); but this state is by some designated as hæmatode cancer."

Colloid, so called from the resemblance of the internal or contained part to *glue*, is developed as a distinct tumor, or in numerous small masses scattered throughout the substance of an organ, or in the infiltrated form. It attains considerable size, occurs most frequently in the stomach, and is the form of cancer most frequent in osteo-sarcoma and spina ventosa. A marked characteristic of colloid growths, before ulceration, is, that they are equally transparent, firm and similar in appearance throughout the entire mass. "The section of a colloid growth presents an appearance, which once seen, can scarcely be forgotten. The surface is divided into a vast number of alveoli regularly arranged, of an oval or rounded shape, varying in size from that of a grain of sand to the largest pea."

The septa composing the walls of these loculi possess distinctly fibrous characters; their thickness is pretty uniform throughout; occasionally, however, they are broader in some situations than in others; in this case the thicker septa may generally be found to give off productions forming the walls of secondary loculi, and these again, others, constituting a tertiary order. The loculi sometimes form shut sacks, in other instances communicate with the circumjacent cells. It is not very unusual to observe alveoli, of which the walls seem to have collapsed and coalesced from the removal of the contained matter. In point of consistence a colloid mass, of which the loculi are perfect, usually resembles firm cheese, but may be much harder; the general color of the divided surface is a greenish yellow. The latter is more especially the case with the contained matter, which is, besides, semi-transparent, tenacious and clammy, and resembles in respect of density, as in other physical properties, soft jelly. It is not easily expressible from the containing loculi, but may be picked out with the point of a scalpel, or removed by maceration.

These tumors may continue for some time, even years, slowly, almost imperceptibly increasing in size; giving the patient but little trouble, except occasional lancinating pains; frequently, however, their course is rapid. The character of the tumor and nature of the tissue in which it is developed, will in part decide the rapidity of its growth and its dimensions. Encephaloid is increased most rapidly, colloid next, and scirrhus least. Sooner or later, however, the work of destruction commences. Some part of the carcinomatous tumor begins to soften. The skin over it cracks or ulcerates, and we have the cancerous ulcer or the *open cancer*. The course of the disease is thence forward, usually very rapid. The cancerous matter is then discharged in the form of an ichorous liquid or in masses.

"The appearance of the opening, or *ulcer* is, at first especially, in a great manner accidental. Its edges are sometimes thin, irregular, level with the surrounding surface, or, it may be sunken, undermined, and *inverted;* the latter condition amounting, in some cases, to a kind of reflection of the skin on itself. But this aspect usually changes, and the edges become elevated, and turned upwards and outwards or *everted;* a state which is of sufficiently constant occurrence to have been considered almost characteristic of cancerous ulceration. The surrounding skin acquires a bluish red tint to a variable extent round the sore; and the excavated surface of the latter presents an irregular series of elevations and depressions, smeared with a thin watery matter, mixed with decomposed blood or pulpy detritus, or studded with black patches of concrete hardened blood. The surface of a scirrhus ulcer is, however, sometimes dry, and of reddish, grayish, or brownish color, or in other instances, covered with a stratum of soft and putrid fleshy substances, generally about one or one and a half line in thickness and of the same colors as the surface of the sore; underneath this layer, hard scirrhus is discovered."

The *discharge* or ichorous liquid from these ulcers is thin, acrid, and generally of a dirty green color, with a peculiar and characteristic *fetor.* The color varies from blood or melanotic fluid being mixed with it.

A marked characteristic of these ulcers is their disposition to *hemorrhage.* By some, cancers in their primary stage are considered a purely local disease. The best authorities, however, now generally concede that they have their origin in a cancerous diathesis, whether this is the result of hereditary transmission or an acquired vitiated condition of the system. The fact that mechanical injuries are often the exciting causes is not sufficient to prove the local theory. What proportion of local injuries are followed by the development of cancer? Will any degree of inflammation induce cancer in a healthy constitution? It is a well-ascertained fact, that age, sex, and civilized life act as predisposing causes. Would this be so if the disease was the result of purely local agencies?

The *Diagnostic* characteristics of cancerous ulcers have been mentioned.

Hardened tumors, as well as simple indurations, not preceded by acute or sensible inflammation, seldom present the excessive hardness and lobulated surface of true scirrhus. The tumors themselves, and the surrounding parts, retain much more of their natural character. They are not so isolated as the cancerous tumor, there being generally a serous effusion into the cellular membrane around them.

Tubercles are distinguishable from incipient cancers, in being always more granular and in smaller masses, though frequently causing much more visible *swelling* of the part in which they are formed. The latter is a transformation and sometimes literally *condenses* and diminishes the part.

There are also distinctly *circumscribed* and *fibrous tumors* that may appear in various parts and be at first mistaken for cancerous; but they are more regular and rounded in shape, and unaccompanied by pain. Should the over-excited fears of the physician lead to their extirpation, no great harm will be done.

A softened encephaloid tumor has been mistaken for an abscess, and the introduction of the lancet been followed by immediate and dangerous hemorrhage, induration, and soon death. It may, however, be distinguished by a sort of doughy elastic feeling, with a moderate degree of softness in some of the parts, while others will be hard and firm. Dupuytren says that pressure gives rise in some portions of the growth to a sound like that of crumbling parchment. The history of the case, &c., will also aid. The subject of diagnosis will be further considered in treating of "Cancer, locally considered."

The *prognosis* of cancer will be determined by the predominance of the cancerous diathesis, the exciting cause, the species of cancer, its locality, the rapidity and stage of its development, and the extent of the cachexia, or contamination of the general system by the absorption of its secretions or excretions.

In the *treatment* of cancer, numerous modes and means have been employed and with varying success. For a time, one plan or remedy has been extolled, then with glory it has sunk in oblivion to be again resurrected, glorified, and condemned. Is not the Homeopathic law destined to be the clue that shall guide us out of this labyrinth? the test that shall determine the value of each remedy and furnish the sure criterion for its employment?

The knife, ligature, cauteries, compression, and the application of various remedies have been and are employed in the cure of cancer.

The knife can be used successfully in the earlier stages, and even the more advanced, provided the lymphatic glands are not affected, and there is a *distinctly circumscribed tumor which can be removed entire.*

The general rules contraindicating an operation are well laid down by Walshe: "1. When such adhesions or local extensions of the primary disease exist as would render it impossible to remove the mass completely by excision or by amputation of the limb. 2. When the disease is manifestly spreading or in a state of active growth. 3. When the existence of internal carcinoma is even probable. 4. When the cancerous cachexia is thoroughly established. 5. When the disease has existed for a number of years in an almost stationary condition; gives rise to no serious derangement of health, and is rather an inconvenience than a malady."

While this excellent writer is so particular in warning us against having a particle of diseased matter, that he advises to remove a stratum of healthy tissue along with the morbid growth. He has embraced (what we conceive) the *great error in the use of the knife;* the idea that it is advantageous to *heal the wound by the first intention.* We believe, except in case of amputation or removal of the testicle, just the opposite, and would, on the contrary, advise that the surface be repeatedly washed with a solution of the chloride of zinc, and poultices of elm be applied, and the wound *healed by granulation;* such Homeopathic remedies being given internally as seem to be indicated or are known to exercise a powerful influence over this disease.

The ligature (see Chap. XVI.) has been employed for the removal of cancerous tumors instead of the knife. It is certainly preferable, where there is reason to fear obstinate hemorrhage. Some also think that cancers are less likely to return when thus extirpated.

Cauteries have been used and by some relied upon. They form the main reliance of Dr. Newton (who has been quite successful in the treatment of cancers), though he uses the knife as we have recommended as an adjunct. He holds to the theory formerly promulgated by Dr. Adams, that this disease is dependent on the generation of cancer animalculæ, and that such applications are to be applied as will kill these entozoa. His principal cauteries are oil of vitriol, sulphate of zinc, the lye from the ashes of red oak bark evaporated to a convenient consistency, improperly called extract of red oak bark; the chloride of zinc, and the sesqui-carbonate of potash. The chloride of zinc has been attended with considerable success in the hands of M. Cancoin, A. Ure, and Mr. Lawrence. Cases will be reported under the head of cancer of the mamma and face.

Acid nitrate of mercury is claimed by M. Recamier to possess a marked affinity for the diseased tissue, and to produce healthy granulations, even on a cancerous basis. The chloride of gold is also extolled by him. An interesting case will be reported under the head of cancer of the uterus. We were formerly in the habit of relying upon the free use of the sesqui-carbonate of potash to complete the cure, after the greater part of the diseased mass had been destroyed by a thorough application of the potassa fusa or some other powerful cautery. The principle of successful *escharotic* treatment is, *complete* and *rapid* destruction of the diseased mass, and the *prevention of the absorption* of the depraved fluids. When the battle commences there is no time to parley with the enemy. Other local applications have been relied upon for the cure of cancers, which seem to act by their specific influence. The most prominent among these is

Arsenious Acid; this has formed the principal ingredient of most of the cancer plasters that have attained much celebrity—and although it has been alternately praised and condemned, the testimony in its favor is such that we must ascribe to it much value in the treatment of this disease, provided we can discover some rule for its safe and appropriate employment. The objection to the use of this article and the reason why many of these cancer plasters have fallen into disrepute, after having performed repeated noted cures, is that the arsenic has been sometimes absorbed and produced its poisonous effect.

The *yellow arsenic* (Sulphide, Orpiment) seems to have been more generally useful than the arsenious acid. It is the principal remedy in one or two cancer recipes that have been very successful. We have it, from what we believe reliable authority, that this is *the* important remedy in the preparation of a celebrated cancer Doctor, operating at the present time in New York city.

His preparation we are assured differs but little from that of a friend of ours, in which this is the active agent, and with which he has been almost universally successful. He applied it in the form of paste made with the white of eggs. A specimen of some of his cures is shown in Fig. 4.

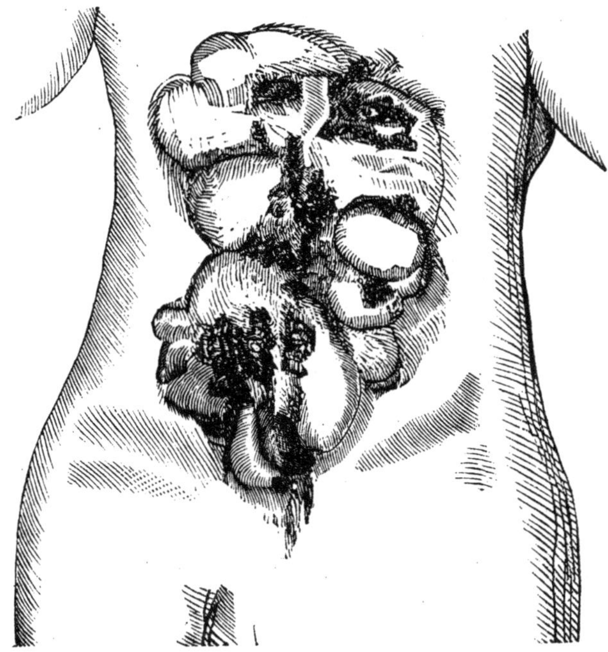

It is from a cast now in the pathological cabinet of the Homeopathic College at Cleveland, which was taken at the commencement of treatment. A lady aged about 40 years had a tumor which had continued to grow slowly for a number of years. An operation for its removal was performed, and the wound healed by the first intention. It soon after began to grow, and in several months attained to the size represented by the drawing. The Doctor gave arsenicum internally, and daily applied his paste to the diseased mass, keeping it constantly covered with wet cloths. The cancer sloughed off in large pieces and finally healed by granulation. The lady recovered her health, and was afterwards delivered of a healthy child, and continued well when last heard from.

Compression has been successfully employed by M. Recamier: "Of one hundred patients, sixteen appeared to be incurable, and underwent only a palliative treatment; thirty were completely cured by compression alone, and twenty-one derived considerable benefit from it; fifteen were radically cured by extirpation alone, or chiefly by extirpation and pressure combined, and six by compression and cauterization: in the twelve remaining cases the disease resisted all the means employed."

The principle of its application is the same as when applied for the cure of aneurism. It should be uniform over the entire surface of the tumor; at first gentle, and gradually increased as the diseased portion becomes habituated to its action. According to M. Recamier, the conditions preventing a successful result are, "Excessive magnitude of the morbid growth; the existence of cavities in its interior; the conversion of the tissue of the diseased organ itself into carcinoma; a state of softening, ulceration, or fungous vegetation; the extension of the disease beyond the reach of direct compression; obstinate local neuralgic pains and great fullness of person."

Ligature of the principal artery leading to the cancer has been attended in a number of cases with excellent effects. An interesting case is reported by Dr. Hosack. A lady, aged fifty-five years, had a scirrhus of the parotid gland, which had continued to grow for three or four years. It was then so large that she was unable to open the mouth further than to admit the smallest-sized teaspoon, "and protruding from behind, through the space posterior to the angle of the jaw occupied by the parotid, extended itself over the masseter muscle, quite up to the zygoma, carrying before it the lobe of the ear, and encroaching so much upon the external meatus as to close it entirely." The doctor took up the common carotid on the affected side. The tumor was sensibly diminished in the course of a month, and finally so entirely removed that a depression was formed, in form like that of the gland in the natural state.

So unsatisfactory have been the result of all proposed allopathic internal medication, that Dr. Walsh states as a fact the following proposition: "Cancer has never been removed by medicinal agents alone." The cases reported in connection with cancerous diseases of the different organs will prove, as far as Homeopathy is concerned, the falsity of this declaration. As the different remedies with their indications will be given when treating of "Cancer, locally considered," we shall here only give a general classification of them, and mention the leading characteristics of a few of the more prominent, together with such general measures as we think important.

Scirrhus in the

OCCULT STAGE; *Arnica, Conium, Bell., Carb., veg. and an., Aurum, Phos., Silic., Staph. and Sul.*

For OPEN CANCER, *Ars., Ars. sulphide, Con., Brom., Sil., Kreos., Carb., Phyto., Lach., Nit. and Mur. ac., Thuj.* [*Calen., Plantago maj., Cornus circin.*]

For FUNGUS HÆMATODES, a form of encephaloid, sometimes called Rose cancer; *Bel., Phos., Thuj. Carb., Nit. ac., Staph.*

Arsenicum album, which has been thought, from the days of the ancients to the present time, by many, to be a specific for cancer, appears to be especially valuable in the *ulcerated* stage. It is our principal remedy in cancer of the nose, lips, face, tongue, and uterus. It is particularly indicated where the vital powers are enfeebled and the destructive tendency very rapid. The ulcers consequently assuming, almost from the first, a malignant appearance; the edges are irregular, everted and thin, or indurated, and bleed easily; the discharge is a scanty sanies, or a copious fetid ichor. The base of the ulcer frequently has a lardaceous appearance. The pain is of a burning character and worse early in the morning, or when the parts become cold—but then it is tearing.

The *Orpiment* (*Sulphide of arsenic*), we think, will prove ultimately of even more value than the arsenious acid.

Belladonna is more particularly indicated when the tumor begins to inflame and become painful, or, having ulcerated, there is discharge of bloody ichor, the ulcer *burning* when touched and at night. It would seem to have considerable power in that form of encephaloid denominated as fungus hæmatodes.

Carbo., veg. and animal, are indicated both in the occult and ulcerative stages. Like *Arsenic* they are suited to cachectic individuals; but they are characterized by an almost entire want of reactive power. The ulcers are, therefore, distinguished by their torpidity instead of manifesting that disposition to extend into surrounding parts, as in the case of *Arsenic.* The base is dark and putrid in appearance.

Conium; another remedy that has at different times attained much celebrity in this disease, appears to be of but little use in the stage of ulceration; its sphere of action being confined mostly to that of the occult, except where the effect of contusions. It is specially indicated in cancer of glandular organs which have resulted from pressure or mechanical injury, both when the indurations are painless and inflamed. Noack and Trinks state, that the principal influence of *Conium* is to fluidify and liquify animal matter, both normal and abnormal.

According to Dr. Boenninghausen, after its employment for some time, it will lose its power of impressing the system, but on giving an intermediate dose of some other remedy, such as *Ars.* or *Bell.*, it will again act favorably.

Thuja, from its power over morbid excresences, we would be led to infer to be valuable in the treatment of those cancerous growth, especially where fungus increases very rapidly and there is much hemorrhage. Clinical experience has verified it. — See case under *Cancer of the Eye.*

Phosphorus, we might suppose, would be useful in cancers from its isomorphous relation to *Arsenic.* Clinical experience has proven it. It is suited to scirrhus formations which begin to inflame and become painful, threatening ulceration and open cancer, with a *great disposition* to bleed. This tendency to hemorrhage always exists where much fungus is formed, consequently we find it very beneficial in fungus hæmatodes, one of the forms of encephaloid. Its specific action upon the lower jaw, the most frequent seat of osteo-sarcoma, would point to it in that disease.

Silicia is suitable for either stage; indurated, that itch a good deal, and those badly ulcerating and abounding in proud flesh. It is said to have been used successfully in fungus hæmatodes.

We prefer to repeat the remedies tolerably frequently, and think it very important that they should be employed *locally* as well as internally. The most convenient way to do this when they are ulcerated, is to have small pieces of patent lint, wet with a dilution of the remedy and apply them piece by piece until every part of the ulcer is covered. Over these wet cloths should be laid, so that the affected part will be shielded from the irritating effects of the atmosphere. In treating of wounds and ulcers we urged the importance of removing the pus as fast as it was formed; it is even more indispensable in cancerous diseases. — See *Ulcers*.

The diet of cancerous patients should be nutritious, but unstimulating; milk, eggs and farinaceous food. They should use water freely, internally and externally, and have plenty of pure air.

CHAPTER XX.

CANCER LOCALLY CONSIDERED

CANCERS of the *Eye* — Encephaloid and scirrhus — Case of Count Radetsky — Of the *Lip* — Their origin in cracked lip — Prospects and Fatality — Early treatment — Of the *Tongue* — Description — Mercurial variety — Of the *Breast* — Frequency — Origin and Progress — Cause by *cross*-lancing — Of the *Rectum*, susceptible of treatment — Of the *Penis* — Description — Medical treatment more convenient than amputation — Of the *Testicle* — Frequency — Excision necessary and effectual.

CANCER OF THE EYE

Is either of the nature of scirrhus or encephaloid. The latter is the most frequent and fatal form of the disease. It may be first detected, according to some of the authorities, by a metallic appearance in the back part of the eye, which continues to advance and enlarge. The pupil is permanently dilated. The progress of the disease is slow while confined to the posterior chamber of the eye; soon, however, the globe becomes enlarged, causing excessive pain, and in a short time the cornea, or the sclerotic coat at its junction with the cornea, bursts, and a fungous growth sprouts up, the eyeball frequently becoming as large as a hen's egg, completely filling up the orbit and projecting out beyond the lids. The fungus in the eye is sometimes dark, sometimes of a light color. Profuse hemorrhage will occur from the slightest touch, or even spontaneously from ulceration. In this stage of the disease the patient rapidly sinks, and, if not cured, dies of exhaustion or from the brain being directly involved in the disease. The scirrhus form begins upon the external surface, involving the cornea, lens, humors and membranes in one mass of disease. The size of the eye is not materially increased.

In most cases the surgeon will not be called before the eye is irretrievably ruined; and any treatment may then be considered successful which even saves the unaffected eye and the life of the patient.

The eye may be removed by the knife, but so unsatisfactory have been the results of *extirpation*, and so promising those of Homeopathic practice, that it is entirely unwarrantable.

After the constitution has suffered much, and there is evidence of the brain having been affected, the chances are against the recovery of the patient under the best treatment that can be adopted. When there is still any considerable amount of constitutional vigor, great hope may be held out, even if the local injury is extensive.

When a cure is effected, the orbit will not always be completely filled up again. An artificial eye is then the only means of avoiding great deformity. In most instances, however, there will be a sufficient amount of fleshy granulations to prevent the ghastliness of mere "holes where eyes should be."

Laurocerasus has proved beneficial in lessening the pains in cancer of the eyes.

Belladonna has been successful in malignant affections of the eyeball, with violent pain in the afflicted part; bright red spot in the posterior chamber, dilated and fixed pupil, indurated condition of the eye, vision destroyed, iris blood-shot and dark colored.

Dr. Z. Stapf reports a case of fungus hæmatodes threatening to destroy the whole eye, checked and circumscribed by *Calc. carb.*, and finally cured by the successive employment of *Lycop.*, *Sep.* and *Silic.*

Phos. has proved successful in fungus hæmatodes in other parts; we should think it valuable here.

Carb. an. or *v.* and *Thuja*, also promise to be powerful additions to our means of combating this dreadful disease.

These remedies effected a complete cure in the celebrated case of the Count Radetsky, within the short space of two months.

This was pronounced by Dr. Flaser, an allopath, Professor of Opthalmic Surgery in Pavia, fungus hæmatodes, and a case that neither allopathy, homeopathy, hydropathy, or any other method of treatment would be of any avail. This opinion was also concurred in by Dr. Jäger, allopath, Professor of Opthalmic Surgery in the Joseph's Academy at Vienna, and staff-physician to the Austrian emperor, who had sent him to Milan to consult with Dr. Hartung, homeopath, having charge of the Count.

Both Dr. Flaser and Dr. Jäger refused even to prescribe for the case — so hopelessly incurable did they consider it.

One tumor was situated at the external canthus of the eye, near the lachrymal gland, extending to the internal canthus. Another under the lower lid, a grayish-blue tumor, extending to the nose.

The whole fungous excrescence was affected with lancinating, burning, tearing and itching pains; it bled readily. The eye was protruded from the socket and motionless. The disease extended over a space of four inches.

After using various remedies without benefit, *Dr. Hartung* exhibited *Carbo an.*, which arrested the progress of the disease. He then determined to rely upon *Thuja* and this; giving first *Thuja* 30, three times daily.

After three days he applied, warm, to the eye every two hours, an embrocation of six drops tr. *Thuja* to four oz. dist. water. The *external* application of *Thuja* was continued for ten days.

Carbo an. 30, was then given evening and morning; and after seven days the tumor was moistened with the 12th dilution of *Carbo. an.* The *Thuja* embrocations were continued.

The *internal* and *external* use of *Thuja* and *Carbo an.*, alternately every eight days, completed the cure.

CANCER OF THE NARES,

Generally of the encephaloid species, is not of common occurrence, unless as the result of maltreated polypus. Sometimes tumors in the nostrils have their origin in the ethmoid bone. Liston gives the following favorable! prognosis of these cases —

"Such growths, when they present in the nostrils, are perfectly irremedial and uncontrollable by any surgical proceeding. If such tumors are ever interfered with, in order to give relief to the patient, by diminishing the obstacles to his breathing or swallowing, there is a risk of considerable loss of blood, and a certainty of very rapid reproduction." Hartmann, on the contrary, says *Arsenicum* is a *sovereign* remedy.

A form of cancer that frequently locates on the side of the nose, though it may occur on any part of the skin, and eventually destroys this important feature, is *Noli-me-tangere*.

Quite a number of surgical writers have confounded this with *Lupus*, using the term as synonomous.

The first appearance of this serious disease is very various, though essentially the same kind of ulcer is the result.

It most usually commences as a *small tumor*, of so little apparent importance, that it does not generally attract the patient's attention until some abrasion of the surface occurs. This may be months or even years after the tumor commenced, and it then looks like a large red bullet.

There may, however, be only a *slight inflammation* of the surface, with little, if any, tumor or tumefaction. This results in a dry "scaly scab" of a darkish color, which is rather easily detached, leaving a red and inflamed surface beneath. After this *scab* has been several times removed and renewed, an *ulcer* takes its place.

At other times it begins as a large and prominent *wart*, which, from its exposed position, is easily bruised, and then becomes very sore and inflamed. If it be entirely removed from the surface, a new one will soon sprout up and attain the original size, if not probably grow a little larger.

Beside the small tumor or the scaly scab, and the warty excrescence, another form is the *tubercle*, a tumor of an oblong shape, somewhat resembling a split bean. This form, however, is not constant, there being often projections out into the adjacent parts. The surface is sometimes smooth and shining, in others, rough and indented. Occasionally it is white, in others, livid or purple, when it is not inaptly called a "blood wart." If the surface of this tubercle become abraded, a scab forms, and ultimately an ulcer, precisely as in the case of the pimples first mentioned.

The first form, or its resulting scab, is most frequently noticed near the inner canthus of the eye, or the side of the nose — the wart is more common upon the cheek — the tuberculous form occurs upon the body, most generally upon the back and shoulders. After ceasing to be protected by a scab or crust, the ulcer generally increases in size and depth very rapidly. Sometimes, however, it will become covered over with little projections, giving it the appearance of a strawberry or mulberry (whence the name Moriform cancer), and may remain comparatively stationary. Hemorrhage is very frequent, especially where large fungous growths sprout up, and there is usually a copious discharge.

It may be distinguished from *Lupus* by commencing as a *single* tubercle or tumor, which, sooner or later, has *lancinating* pains; by the scab coming off *easily;* by affecting the *bones* and *deep-seated parts;* by attacking persons *advanced* in *life;* from being *aggravated* by escharotics, and by affecting the glands. The reverse is true of *Lupus.*

CANCER OF THE LIP.

This very common affection often appears at first as a mere *fissure* or "cracked-lip," which, when the weather is cold, is very troublesome to the patient. It will commonly heal up in summer and re-appear in winter, or on sudden changes of the weather. It may thus continue for years, a mere periodical complaint, the patient having occasionally to wear a patch upon it to shield it from the air. At last it fails to heal again and the *lip* gradually *enlarges*, a tumefaction rising all along the fissure. It is at this stage of the disease that the patient generally thinks it worth while to apply for medical advice.

In other cases, however, the disease appears from the beginning in the form of a small *tumor.* It looks on the red lip like a common squirrel *shot*, both in size and color; it will also roll under the finger when pressed upon.

This little tumor is for a time devoid of *pain;* but if pressed upon or handled it will easily become *irritable.*

As it increases in size, it becomes more and more firmly attached to the surrounding parts. In some cases it is immovable, even from the beginning, being deeply imbedded in the muscles. As it approaches the surface, it ulcerates, giving out a fungous growth, which sometimes increases to a monstrous size, so as to cover the whole mouth and chin. The upper lip is seldom the seat of the disease.

A third form under which it may make its appearance is that of a "scaly scab," or squamous little ulcer — one of the forms described under the head of NOLI-ME-TANGERE.

Any of these forms of lip disease will, if not arrested, extend to other parts of the face, throat and neck, and prove certainly *fatal.* The *glands* about the mouth and throat become early affected, and even the *brain* is not always long secure.

Arsenicum, as was before stated, is pronounced by Hartmann the sovereign remedy for cancer of the nares. It is our most important remedy in Noli-me-tangere and cancer of the lip, except where the latter is the result of injury. It is indicated by tumors in the nose, particularly if accompanied with a severe burning pain and much hemorrhage, or if there is an ulceration high up in the nares, discharging a fetid ichor. Also, cancer of the lower lip, with lardeous base; disposed to spread much; very painful, particularly when touched, or becoming cold; causing swelling of the submaxillary glands. And in the different forms of noli-me-tangere the ulcers of which it will be observed correspond to those of arsenic; *Sulphide of arsenic?*

Antimonium cr. is also useful in noli-me-tangere, particuarly in the tuberculous kind.

Aurum for cancers of the nares and lip, occurring in scrofulous, syphilitic, or syphilitico-mercurial constitutions, and the form of noli-me-tangere that begins as a small, dark, reddish-brown spot, painful to the touch, especially if it commences on the nose, or if it has ulcerated and has involved the nasal bones.

Clematis has proved curative in cancers of the lips, particularly if they have a strong tendency to fungus growths, and occur in persons laboring under the influence of mercury.

Conium — cancer of nose, lip and face, when the effect of contusion — has cured a carcinomatous ulcer of the lower lip caused by irritation from the pressure of a tobacco-pipe. It is indicated for the scirrhus and the occult stage when the edges of the ulcer are black, being corroded by the profuse discharge of sanious ichor. Dr. Stens states that he had employed it with the happiest effect.

Calcarea; where cancer of the nares has originated from polypus or in those of the lip or face, commencing as a slight thickening or scurf, finally proceeding to ulceration, with stinging, itching, tearing pains, relieved by warmth, and aggravated by a draught of cold air.

Nitric ac.; Hartmann exhibited, internally high and externally low, for mulberry cancer of the face. It is also useful where the noli-me-tangere *wart* is first affected with lancinating pain, or when ulcerated, there is a prolific growth of fungous, which stings, and burns, and bleeds easily. According to the observation of Professor Neidhard, this remedy is particularly beneficial in persons of a *dark complexion*, while the *Muriatic acid*, with which it is very closely allied, is preferable in those of a *light color*. This distinction should be borne in mind in prescribing these remedies. Should the disease be complicated with syphilitico-mercurial poisoning, its employment will be the more important.

Phosphorus, *Phytolacca*, *Bromine*, *Lachesis*, *Sepia*, *Silicia*, *Thuja* and *Sulphur* are valuable in some cases.

Dr. Attomyr reports the following case: "Alrysia Lyde, six years old, lost the left half of the upper lip and the soft parts extending upwards to the zygoma, and sideways, a considerable portion round the angle of the mouth, by a cancerous ulcer. *Arsenic* (6th dilution), repeated every eight days, brought about the healing of the ulcer in six weeks. As a detergent application, the decoction of marsh-mallows was used outwardly."

Dr. Ganwerky stated at the *Hom. Con. W. G.*, 1852, that he had cured a case of cancer of the cheek with *Conium*, eighteen years before, in a woman of sixty, who was then alive and well.

A case of fungus hæmatodes on the neck, just above the clavicle, was presented at the Clinique of the Cleveland Hom. College in the winter of 1853. The subject was a young lady. The tumor the size of a goose-egg, dark, soft, and affected with lancinating and burning, gnawing pains; had existed for several months, but grown rapidly of late, and become more painful. Prof. L.

Dodge treated the case with *Plantago maj.*, locally and internally, effecting a speedy and permanent cure.

Sepia cured the following case: *Tubercle* on the lip of a man of about thirty years, increasing to the size of a bean, having sometimes a cartilaginous appearance, sometimes bleeding, and resembling a scirrhus very much, with a broad base."

Dr. Ganwerky mentions a case of *fungus* hæmatodes upon a man, bleeding profusely every day, in which *Phos.* 30 did no good, but *Phos.* 200 effected a most rapid cure. — *Hom. Con. N. G.* 1850.

Phosphorus 30 effected the following brilliant cure of a case of *Fungus Hæmatodes* — *Symp:* "Conical swelling of the size of a fist on the thigh, between the trochanter and the spinous process of the ilium; it is somewhat movable near the root, hard, elastic; was painless before and cool, but is now warmer and painful. The tip has burst open like an abscess; venous blood is continually oozing out, at times coming out in one stream, at times in drops. A similar, but smaller swelling on the left limb, one dose effected a complete cure, being permitted to act a long time. A second fungus hæmatodes on the little finger yielded to the same drug. — *Ruckert's Ther.*

Dr. Bœnninghausen reports a case of *fungus hæmatodes* of the cheek, cured with a single dose of *Staphysagria*, 200th dilution.— *Hom. Con. N. G.* 1850.

Dr. Hunt reports the case of a cancer involving the whole lower lip, scirrhus, ulcerating, with a good deal of fungus and burning pain. It had progressed so far and so rapidly under the internal use of *Arsenicum* 5, and the constant application of lint, kept wet with a weak solution of the same remedy, that a cure was almost certain. During the absence, however, of the Doctor from the city, the patient was taken sick — sent for his former family physician (allopath) — lip became aggravated, and he was persuaded to consent to an operation.

Hartmann removed with *Antimonium cr.* 3, one dose every day, and the local application of a little butter of antimony, a horny excrescence under the lower lip: "the horn fell off every eighth day, after which it grew again; after falling off, the surface of the stump, which kept increasing, looked like raw flesh;

the fleshy papillæ looked like the papilla on the tongue; a viscid humor oozed out of every single papilla. If the scurf to which the thickening of the humor gave rise, remained more than eight days, the humor oozed out between the scurf and the horn which now developed itself in breadth. The horn was painless, except when knocked against, in which case it bled.

With *Ranunculus bulb.* 6, m. and n., first being applied externally, he cured, in a few weeks, similar excrescence on the forehead. "The patient complained frequently of a burning itching in the excrescence; the scurf formed more rapidly than in the former. After falling off, the stump resembled a deep, eating ulcer with sharp edges."

Mr. Laurence states that he had effected two permanent cures of cancerous ulceration of the face, superficial, though of long standing, by the application of chloride of zinc.

CANCER OF THE TONGUE.

This organ is not unfrequently attacked with a species of eating ulcer, which, although it resembles it, cannot properly be called a cancer. True cancer, however, may attack this as well as other parts of the body.

A peculiar species of cancer of the tongue is the *mercurial;* and this is not the least difficult and tedious to manage. It is more apt than all others to reappear when seemingly cured. In some cases the simple ulcer that existed before, seems to become cancerous under the mercurial influence. The whole tongue may become very much enlarged, having small tumors at different points; sometimes of a hard and semi-cartilaginous feel, at others of a spongy structure. But generally there are deep fissures or cracks of an irregular form upon one or both sides of the tongue, rarely in the center. The edges of these fissures are always hard, having a bluish or purplish appearance, and their surface covered with a tough yellowish, or thick gray looking pus.

At other times we have a hard rough tumor with a broad base of a warty appearance, situated about the middle of the tongue or towards the tip, becoming after a time a ragged ill-conditioned sore of a fungous character. It then bleeds very easily and occasions a sharp lancinating pain, extending to the throat and to the base of the skull.

This latter form of the disease, if not arrested in the early stage, is very liable to prove fatal, owing to excessive irritability and hemorrhage.

Ulcers on the tongue frequently assume a malignant appearance from being irritated by the projection or sharp point of a tooth. A removal of the tooth is then indispensable to a cure.

Cancers of the tongue are removed by excision and ligature; the last is now generally preferred as being less liable to be followed by hemorrhage. Bransby Cooper says, "although the hopes held forth by an operation in this complaint are but slight, it offers the only chance of saving the life of the patient." He further states as the result of his experience, "I have on four occasions extirpated the diseased portions of cancerous tongue by ligature applied so as to completely include the affected parts, which were of course ultimately removed by sloughing. None of these cases were, however, successful; the lympathic glands under the jaw sooner or later became involved in the disease, and in no case did the patient survive more than two years after the operation."

Specific medication promises a much more favorable result.

Arsenicum, Hartmann says, is a sovereign remedy for this disease. It is indicated by corrosion and cracks in the edges of the tongue, with burning pain and fetid discharge. (See also *General Treatment, art. Arsen.*)

It may be sometimes advantageously alternated with *Muriatic acid,* which has the following pathogenetic symptoms—tongue feels heavy and elongated, with great dryness in the mouth and fauces; tongue becomes sore and bluish-red, burning vesicle on the tip of the tongue; deep ulcer on the tongue, with black base and inverted edges.

Conium; for scirrhous or ulcerated conditions of the tongue that have been caused by irritation of a tooth.

Lachesis promises to be exceedingly valuable, as would appear from the following case: Dr. Laomis of Syracuse, reported in *Symp., Cod., art. Lach.,* "was called Dec. 5th, 1846, to see a young lady, aged nineteen, who had been ten days in this country. Three days previous to my visit she was attacked with severe pain, of a burning nature, in the right side and near the point of the tongue. Salivation and sloughing soon followed. The disease extended along the side of the tongue for sixteen lines. The surface became black, accompanied with pricking pains, as from needles, in the whole body of the tongue. Under *Lachesis* 400, every four hours, the patient improved for thirty-six hours, when a severe aggravation was experienced, which was checked by *Samb. n.* 12, one dose, when the case went on without a repetition of *Lachesis*, until the tongue was entirely restored.

Mercurius sol., one-twelfth of a grain, cured, in sixteen days, a case with the following symptoms: "On the edge of the tongue there is an ulcer of the size of a bean; along the adjoining parts of the tongue, in the substance thereof, there are several hard nodosities, and a deepening resembling an incision. The base of the ulcer looks gray, reddish, uneven, secreting a fetid matter; the edges are hard, elevated, of a blue appearance; burning in the ulcer."—*Ruck. Ther.*

CANCER OF THE BREAST.

Carcinomatous affections of the female mamma are perhaps more common than of any other portions of the glandular system, or of the body. Women who have nursed a great many children, and such as have arrived at the age when the catamenia cease, without having had children, are the most liable to suffer from this disease, though it may occur at any age. It has occasionally been developed in girls as young as sixteen. Cancer of the breast is generally of the scirrhus species, sometimes of the encephaloid, and occasionally of the colloid.

The first appearance of cancer is usually as a *small tumor* near the nipple, which at first appears to be loose under the skin, and nearly insensible.

This tumor may be *stationary* for years, while, at other times, it *grows* rapidly. In those cases which are considered most malignant, it may acquire a very considerable bulk in a very short period. Commonly, after having grown to a moderate size, the tumor becomes *shriveled* or contracted. The nipples are thrown inward, and buried beneath the surface. The skin becomes of a dark leaden hue, and is closely adherent to the tumor. The whole breast assumes an irregular shape, and feels as if it were filled with knotty, hardened tumors, of an irregular form. The pain becomes lancinating, frequently extending into the axilla, and even through the chest. As the disease advances, other lymphatic glands, besides those of the axilla, become involved, particularly those of the neck.

Eventually, the skin over the tumor yields; a thin sanious matter is thrown out through the *ulcer* that is then established. This assumes, at first, the form of a fissure or crack, and becomes partially filled with fungous growth.

In some cases, the patient sinks, from the cancer affecting vital organs, particularly the lungs, even before the stage of ulceration. In others, life may be protracted ten, twenty, and even thirty years, before the slow but steady progress of the disease cuts it short.

A simple mammary *abscess* may become cancerous by ill-timed and improper *lancing*, especially where the incision is made ACROSS the course of the lactiferous ducts, so as to divide a considerable number of them. Out of some fifteen or twenty cases of mammary cancer, into the history of which we have inquired, there were *only* two that had *not* been thus operated on, and did not have the evidence of the bad surgery in the cross-cut scar!

According to Sir A. Cooper, scirrhus of the breast is from two to three years in growth, and from six months to two years in destroying life after reaching its acme. Velpeau estimates the mean duration of encephaloid, at from six to twelve months. The exciting cause of many of these cases is some contusion or mechanical injury.

Hartmann says of these cases, "a cure is impossible in every case where the knife has been used." "No scirrhus or cancer has ever been cured by an operation, and where such a cure is said to have been effected, the operator mistook a simple glandular swelling for a scirrhus induration." Were such men as Sir A. Cooper, Dr. Warren, M. Velpeau and Dupuytren, always unable to distinguish scirrhus from simple glandular induration? Even when they dissected it after ablation?

M. Velpeau saw patients in perfect health two, four, six, and in one case, ten years after excision of well-marked encephaloid, that worst form of cancer. While we think that the most of these cases can be cured without ablation, we know from our own personal experience and observation, that it will be generally successful if performed in the manner before directed and before the axillary glands are affected. The great *error* has been in healing by *the first intention* and not by *suppuration*. In relying upon the *knife* as a cure, and not as an *adjunct*.

The removal of the morbid mass can not be relied upon to eradicate the cancerous diathesis, although it will sometimes produce such an alterative influence upon the constitution that no manifestation of the disease will be perceived during life.

The remedies appropriate to a removal of this constitutional disease ought, in all cases, to be given internally and applied externally to the wound until after a healthy cicatrix has formed.

Injuries of the mamma if treated homeopathically are not likely to be followed by scirrhus formations, even in persons of the cancerous diathesis. It does not leave indurations, the germ of future disease. Where these are present and are the result of recent injury, *Arnica montana* will usually be sufficient for their removal. It is also indicated for the painful lumps in the breast of girls, traceable to no particular cause, rendered more distressing by the open air.

Conium is, however, more appropriate in old indurations. It is our most valuable remedy in all cases arising from a contusion of the gland. In the occult stage with occasional shooting or darting pains, or when every little cold inflames the scirrhus gland and excites severe stinging and burning pains, so aggravated at night as to arouse the patient from sleep, as well as in the open cancer. Further indications are, oppressed breathing and an aching pain in the sternum. Dr. Boenninghausen recommends to give a dose of *Ars.* or *Bel.* as an intermediate remedy, to renew the susceptible of the system to the action of the *Conium*.

Pulsatilla; if hard tumors appear in the breast of young girls, resembling in form and density true scirrhus, and are insensible. But if sore or painful, with drawing pains, getting worse in the open air or at night, or if they become inflamed and red, give *Chamomile*.

If inflamed, with stinging, burning pains, increased on the least movement or contact, and a flush around the part, *Belladonna;* which is also aplicable for similar symptoms in older persons.

Arsenic, where there is burning and tearing pains in the tumors, lessened by motion, but aggravated by rest and warmth, and so tender to pressure that she can not lay on the affected side. In the open stage, when the ulcers have the *Arsenical* character.

Clematis is particularly indicated when the indurations are only painful when pressed upon, or where the cancer is open, with burning, throbbing in the ulcer and stinging in the edges on contact.

Kreosotum, when the breast is rough, scurfy and bluish, frequently discharging a good deal of thick, dark blood.

Carbo. veg., when the scirrhus indurations of the mammæ are accompanied with burning pain, low spirits, and constant complaining, or great itching of the back.

Lachesis, for those cancers that have an extraordinary disposition to *bleed.* The bottom of the ulcer is bluish, with dark streaks of coagulated blood over it. Dr. Petrasch says, he knows no remedy so efficacious against the pains in cancerous ulcers as *Lachesis.*

Hepar has cured a scirrhus ulcer on the mamma, with a burning, stinging in the edges, the pus having the smell of old cheese.

The empirical use of the *Yellow Arsenic* (Sulphide) we have mentioned before. We would suggest a trial of it in very bad cases.

Bromine promises to be a valuable addition to our means of combating this fearful opponent. (See case of Dr Ganwerky.)

Phosphorus is all powerful in inflammations of the mammæ, has proved invaluable in fungus hæmatodes, and has isomorphous relations with *Arsenic,* whose efficacy has been proven. It may be sometimes advantageously employed.

The indications for *Phytolacca decandria* may be learned from the following article by Dr. Neidhard:

"*Cancer of the mammæ connected with rheumatic affections.* —The effects of *Phytolacca dècandria* in the following case was so striking, and the symptoms so well correspond with those obtained by experiments on the healthy that I can not help adducing my testimony to its power, in order that it may be employed by others in similar affections. This is the more important as the remedy possesses an ancient reputation for the cure of cancer, among the people of this country. Miss S—— had for three years a pain in the left mamma, where, on examination, an indurated tumor was discovered, having all the characteristics of true cancer. She describes the pain as darting through, and even before the tumor appeared, she had, for a long time, a similar pain; the pain comes and disappears like griping, sympathetically affecting the wrist and the shoulder of the right side, she limps about from a pain in the hip also, on the same side—it is worse at night, is constantly shifting from one place to another, without producing any swelling or alteration of the part which it attacks. The nearest she can describe the pain is, that it is of a jerking kind, also highly characteristic of the pains produced by *Phyto. dec.*

"Of the numerous medicines prescribed, *Jayne's Expectorant* gave the only transient relief; the same was the case with the homoeop. *Sulphur* and *Pulsat.* From the *Phytolacca* a more permanent benefit was experienced than from any other medicine.

"In a case of cancer of the left mamma (an old lady), *Conium* always relieved the induration and produced a softening of it; it also relieved the violent sticking pain.

"Next to *Conium, Carbo. an. and veg.*, deserve our consideration, if the above symptoms are present, especially if conjoined with extraordinary itching in the back. These two remedies were also given in the above case.

"In a case of an old lady, Miss G——, *Phos.* and *Carbo. veg.*, given at intervals, retarded, for ten years, the progress of the disease. The *symptoms* were the following:

"Burning in the cancerous tumor of the mamma, which also extends down the side; the sanies which is discharged smells badly, headache over the eyes every morning; tongue full of blisters. The pain in breast is worse in damp weather, and shoots through to the shoulder; there is also burning between the shoulders and over the eyes, the arm is lame, the patient is very weak and feverish. I do not know on which side the tumor was situated, as I forgot to mark it down on the record."

A young lady had a lump of considerable size in one of the mammæ; this and the other breast wasted. She had taken *Iodine* from the allopathic practitioners in large quantities. The nipple of the affected side was retracted; the tumor was very sensitive to the touch and painful. She had a few doses of *Conium* and the cure was completed in about three months with the *Iodide of Arsenic*. (*B. J. H.*, vol. vii., p. 514.)

Dr. Ganwerky reported to the Hom. Con., N. G., 1852, that he was treating a case of cancer of the breast, accompanied by swelling of the axillary glands and burning, lancinating pains in the scirrhus parts, which was first exceedingly improved by *Bromine*, and had advanced so far toward a cure under the subsequent alternate use of *Brom.* and *Con.*, that he had no doubt of a favorable result.

Dr. Burritt stated to one of the authors that he was congnizant of a case, where a lady was given up to die with cancer of the mamma. Upon recommendation she began to use freely, as a drink, a decoction of the *Cornus circinnati*, and to keep the diseased breast covered with cloths wet with the same; she entirely recovered.

CANCER OF THE RECTUM

Is usually situated from two to four inches above the anus, where it is a primary affection. It generally progresses upwards rather than downwards, is of the scirrhus or colloid species, and is either in the form of a tumor or a thickening, by a deposition of cancerous matter, of a part or the whole of the circumference of the rectum, terminating abruptly both above and below. The course of the disease is in other respects similar to that in other parts, ulceration, fungus, &c.

The first symptoms of cancer of the rectum are the same as those present in stricture of this part. Constipation, the taper-like feces, pain in the sacral region, constipation alternating with diarrhea, and finally ulceration.

In this disease hemorrhage is frequent, especially when in examination the finger or other instrument is brought in contact with the diseased part. Touch also excites stinging and burning pains. The reverse is true of permanent stricture. The character of the discharge is different, being bloody and ichorous, while that from ulceration of simple strictures is similar to ordinary pus from mucous surfaces. Examination with the speculum ani will also show a difference in the appearance.

Cancer of the rectum is spoken of as necessarily incurable, because not accessible to the knife, but with specific medication this conclusion does not inevitably follow. It is, however, a very dangerous disease, and the cure rendered exceedingly difficult by the feces constantly irritating the part. Should the disease not be too far advanced, and the cancerous cachexia too deeply seated, we consider it curable.

None of the Homeopathic works, or any journals that we have been able to procure, ever mention this disease. We would not infer, therefore, that cases had been successfully treated by specific remedies.

Dr. Bauer, of Cincinnati, was called to a case pronounced cancer of the rectum by the late Dr. Shotwell (professor of anatomy in the Ohio Medical College), and cured it with internal remedies. He relied principally upon *Arsenicum* and *Carb. veg.*

Dr. Hunt was called to prescribe for a case in the last stages, and succeeded far in relieving the sufferings of the patient and staying the progress of the disease. That he thinks treatment at an earlier stage would have been successful.

Arsen., *Brom.*, *Carb. veg.*, *Con.*, *Kreos.*, *Lach.*, *Phos.*, *Thuja*, will be found of service. (See *Cancer in General.*)

CANCER OF THE PENIS

Is mostly of the scirrhous kind and generally effects the prepuce or glans. The prepuce and the glans are the parts most commonly affected. A small tumor, usually resembling a wart, first appears. Its base is generally broader than its surface, and as it is deep-seated it looks much more like a continuation of the substance of the glans, than any outgrowth. By this circumstance it can be distinguished from a venereal tumor, the latter having an evidently diseased character, and only a small neck, the base always smaller than the apex. The reverse, in all respects, is the case with the scirrhous or cancerous glans, presenting itself only as an irregular tumor, and growing slowly. It finally ulcerates, and throws out fungous growths as in other cases; and the matter discharged becomes fetid and bloody. As the disease progresses, it involves all the surrounding parts. It may extend along the body of the penis up into the abdomen, or still farther down towards the rectum, destroying especially all the inguinal and adjacent glandular structure.

In other cases, cancer of the glans penis assumes more of a chronic character, the glans enlarging very greatly, becoming hardened, and discharging by fistulous openings into the urethra, at the base of the glans, and then out through the meatus urinarius, — the cavity of which becomes very much enlarged, having hardened callous edges, very painful on pressure.

The TREATMENT in these cases should be as for cancer in other parts. We have never seen but two cases. In one of these the glans penis was three or four times as large as the original size, hard, almost of callous firmness. The meatus urinarius was permanently dilated to three times its usual caliber, lined with a cartilaginous wall, an inch and a half in its length, discharging a profuse ichor, pain, burning and lancinating. The cure was completed with sulphate of zinc.

CANCER OF THE TESTICLE.

The cancerous testicle appears externally considerably enlarged, rough and heavy, like a lump of lead. As the disease progresses, the Spermatic Cord and Inguinal Glands become affected, though it may exist for a long time before there will be much suffering. The first symptom is a constant lancinating pain, extending along the cord and through the loins down into the thighs. This tumor does not usually attain a very large size, though in some instances it is an enormous burden and deformity. The scrotum becomes inflamed, and sometimes ulcerated, throwing out the peculiar cancerous fungus which easily bleeds. The distinguishing features of the case are the hard, rough feel and the dull leaden weight.

In this case, ablation had better be performed *at once*, as experience has clearly shown that it is almost invariably successful. [For the Operation of Castration, see Part II.] If, however, the disease has been communicated to the contiguous membranes, or to the cord, the case will have to be treated in the same manner as cancer elsewhere.

In one case operated upon by the late Dr. Morrow, that of Mr.

K——, of Lockland, in Hamilton county, the diseased mass that was removed was found the day after the operation to weigh five pounds and three-quarters. In this case, the cord was involved in the disease, so that to complete the operation, a dissection had to be made through the external up to the internal abdominal ring. This was the largest *scirrhous testis* we ever saw. The parts healed kindly after the operation, and the cure was effectual.

CARCINOMA UTERI.

This is not of as frequent occurrence as is generally supposed. Many of the cases usually called such being nothing more than bad cases of ulceration. The patient sometimes will not complain of much pain until it has proceeded to ulceration. Generally, however, there are occasional darting and twinging pains in the uterus itself, coming on and going off suddenly. The patient complains much of bearing down. There is a sense of weight in the lower part of the abdomen. The pains become very severe, especially at night. There is over the pubic bones and in the small of the back a violent burning and stitching-boring. This extends to the thighs and makes walking difficult, and even sitting painful.

On examination, the neck of the womb will be found hard and rough, and not unfrequently much enlarged. The os tincæ may be entirely closed, or considerably dilated, its lips having become a hard, jagged ring. There is, frequently, large fungous growths. Soon an ulcer forms, which is usually so irregular that it can easily be detected by the touch, which discharges freely a *peculiarly offensive* sanious ichor. When the disease is far advanced, dangerous hemorrhage is frequent, and patients experience great constitutional irritation and emaciation. It is indispensable to an accurate and thorough knowledge of any of these cases to make an examination with the vaginal speculum, as the severity of the symptoms do not, in all cases, bear a strict relation to the extent of the organic lesion.

The remedies should be employed locally through the speculum as well as internally, and this is so much the *more important*, as the disease is malignant; and he who depends alone upon the internal treatment of bad cases, will have the registry of his success upon the tomb-stone. From our experience we should expect more favorable results from exclusive local, than exclusive internal treatment. But from both combined, success where either singly would fail.

The symptoms resulting from induration and ulceration, and the incipient forms of this disease, and their respective boundaries being so difficult to define, we have spoken of the remedies applicable to each.

For induration of the womb without ulceration use, *Carbo. animalis, Aurum, Belladonna, China, Sepia, Staphysagria, Rhus tox., Iodine, Phosphorus and Sabina.* For the ulcerated condition or true cancerous state, *Graphites, Kreosote, Carbo. an., Arsenicum Aurum and Lachesis.* For phagedenic ulceration, *Nitric acid, Thuja, Arsen., Bell., China, Cocculus, Bryonia, Mercurius, Sepia, and Platina.* Consult, also, the remedies and their indications under other forms of cancer.

The symptoms requiring *Belladonna* are, excessive nervousness, pressing pains in the back, sanguinous ichorous discharge, with a sense of fullness in the pelvis.

Platina is to be used for stinging pains in the ulcerated state, with hemorrhage of thick, dark, venous blood, and has cured indurations of the uterus with spasm and stinging.

If the patient is costive, occasionally, in alternation with other remedies, give *Nux vomica*, especially if there are frequent, periodical, long-continuing, acrid and bloody discharges, accompanied with itching and burning.

China should be used when the patient is much debilitated by profuse hemorrhage.

Arsenicum is indicated by burning sensations, phagedenic or corroding ulcer, internal and underneath the pubic bones, worse at night, towards midnight insupportable anguish in the chest, restlessness, burning thirst, induration of corroding ulcer on the neck of the uterus, and an acrid discharge per vaginum.

Aurum, for desponding, melancholy persons, with simple or malignant chronic induration of the womb, particularly if scrofulous or mercurialized.

Cocculus should be given for the spasmodic pains behind the symphysis, with a *serous* discharge.

Bryonia is used for a state of great nervous irritability, pain in forehead and eyes.

Kreosotum is useful in advanced stages, where there are stitching pains in the womb, with burning and swelling of the labia, hard tubercles on the os uteri, with eating, ulcerative pains, where the menses appears a week or more before the proper time and continues for several days too long, with dark, bloody, lumpy and ichorous discharge, with pungent smarting and itching pains, aggravated during the night. Menses intermittent coming, and in three or four days going off, and then reappearing; pains bearing down; the patient in constant low spirits.

Iodine is to be used for induration of the neck and part of the body, or when the neck is destroyed, the patient being much emaciated, occasionally affected with faintings and spasms.

Thuja, for the above symptoms in addition to a cauliflower excresence on the neck, with ulceration and stinging, burning pains, and manifesting the hemorrhagic disposition of fungus hæmatodes.

Graphites, for painful lymphatic swellings in the vagina, the neck of the womb being hard and swollen, with fungoid tubercles that bleed easily and are very painful to the touch; the patient complains of a sense of weight in the abdomen and lancinating pains in the uterus, running down the thighs, darting like electricity. Frequent chills, livid, anxious countenance, and frequent pulse, menses delayed, at which time the sufferings of the patient are aggravated.

Scale, for a putrescent state of the uterus.

Sabina, for labor-like pains, the ostincæ being open.

Carbo. veg., for excessive burning pains, deep in the pelvis, paroxysmal in their character, with regular intermission between the paroxysms; occasional cerebral congestions.

Conium is a very valuable remedy in uterine cancer, especially when the lymphatic glands are diseased. The symptoms indicating *Conium* are, cramping, pinching pains in the uterus, a sense of tightness in the lower portion of the abdomen, with lancinating pains, itching of the external and internal organs, bearing down pains; catamenia premature and small in quantity, pains in the breasts before the appearance of the catamenia, burning and excoriating leucorrhea.

Dr. Neidhard thus remarks of genuine carcinoma uteri: "Having carefully sifted the homeopathic literature without finding any cases on record of carcinoma uteri, I must presume that no cure of a fully developed case has taken place uuder homeopathic treatment, else, if such had been the case, we should have heard of it in the homeopathic journals. I have no doubt, however, that at its commencement it can sometimes be arrested and the painful symptoms always mitigated by *Kreosote*, which has been of great service to me in more than one important case. Next to this come *Conium*, *Phos.*, *Sulph.*, *Ars.*, *Carbo.*, *an. and veg.*, *Phytol. dec. and Orobanche*, which must be selected according to the predominating symptoms and the history of the case."

Dr. Kallenbach mentions a case of carcinoma uteri, where all the symptoms of cancer of the uterus had given place to those of cancer of the stomach, but where, nevertheless, on post-mortem examination, no disease of the stomach was found, *Kreosote* had produced this apparent removal of the symptoms. In his case, as well as those relieved by myself with *Kreosote*, the pain was always diminished in the uterus, and the fetid, brownish, watery discharge removed. In Kallenbach's case the uterus could not be reached by touching.

The *Chloride of Gold* (aqua regia 1 oz., pure chloride of gold 6 grs.) appears to have produced extraordinary effects in the hands of M. Recamier. "A woman affected with fungating cancer of the cervix uteri, which had already destroyed almost the entire of that portion of the organ, underwent seven or eight applications of this caustic; the local and general symptoms yielded completely; the ulceration ceased; the body of the organ, which had been engorged, lost its unnatural size; lancinating pain and hemorrhages were no longer complained of." He afterwards, however, preferred the chloride of platina.

CHAPTER XXI.

ANTHRAX, OSTEO-SARCOMA.

ANTHRAX, a malignant boil? — Boil, "a miniature carbuncle!" — Early symptoms and progress—Persons and parts liable — Prognosis not discouraging — Size and character — "Equivocal" — Treatment.

OSTEO-SARCOMA, bony or bone cancer — Symptoms — Old school prognosis and prescriptions

CARBUNCLE OR ANTHRAX.

ANTHRAX is an unhealthy inflammation of a circumscribed portion of the cellular tissue and integument, attended with more or less mortification and sloughing.

Illustratively, it might be said that a carbuncle is a malignant boil, that is,—still more popularly interpreted,—"the worst kind of a boil," one that "won't get well." Such expressions, however, must be regarded as *but* popular, as rather indicating analogies, than stating facts of identity or direct connection. Such a "definition" will not stand the test. You cannot safely reverse it, and make the two things compared define each other. Yet this is what one surgical writer, in high repute, has actually ventured on — "Boils," says Mr. Druitt, "are miniature carbuncles!" This is the reductio ad absurdum of such comparisons.

Carbuncle and *boil* differ as health and disease, life and death, positive and negative. In the one, nature is doing her best for us; in the other, her worst. A common boil is plainly, if anything is that ever occurs in the organism, a successful effort of the "vis medicatrix;" a carbuncle is something worse than an unsuccessful effort of such a power — to characterize it, you must refer it to a *vis necatrix*. It scarcely differs less in its symptoms than its termination; for —

Anthrax commences as a livid red swelling, exacting attention by its burning, smarting pain, which continues, worse and worse, to an insupportable degree. Its distinction from a common healthy phlegmon becomes more and more marked as it progresses; and it is only in rare instances that it does not show its true character from the beginning. As an abscess, it has no particular source, or central "core," and, as an ulcer, it may be said to commence "fistulous." As soon as the more ordinary symptoms of local inflammation have subsided, — or without their having gone through their regular stages, vesication commences; and when it bursts, instead of a truncated cone with one opening or crater, as in the boil, there is a flat top with several sinuses. From their orifices, instead of healthy consistent pus, an acrid fluid exudes, resembling thin gruel, and excoriating all parts with which it comes in contact. The parts where they originate seem to be in a state bordering on mortification.

Anthrax always implies an unhealthy and debilitated, if not an exhausted condition of the system. It rarely occurs in any but aged persons, and those, too, whose constitutions have suffered other ravages than those of time. Hard study, anxiety of mind, trouble, and consequent depression of spirits, intemperance, etc., are enumerated among predisposing or remote causes.

Severe *constitutional* symptoms generally attend. The digestive function is always more or less deranged, and nausea very commonly complained of. Under great suffering and attending fever, loss of sleep and consequent prostration of strength, the patient rapidly sinks.

It is generally located on some part of the back. The next common seat is the head, where it is still more dangerous, though not "almost surely fatal," as some of the books would have it.

The *prognosis*, indeed, need not be so alarming as it is generally made. (Most patients would probably get over it at last, even without treatment.) Still it is always a most distressing and occasionally a fatal affection.

No time should be lost, and no means spared to mitigate suffering, even if we could not arrest the process of "local death" and prevent its becoming general. We can generally have the satisfaction of effecting both these objects, and by the same means. The extraordinary pain is a "natural call," an alarm of the whole endangered organism, a true "indication of cure."

The boil theory or metaphor must not lead you to limit the idea of carbuncle to the ordinary dimensions of healthy phlegmon. You need not look out for some less familiar or more learned name, when this species of malignant tumor presents itself of an enormous size, which it often attains with a mushroom rapidity of growth. Dr. Hill saw one on an old lady's back, as large as her head, having swelled out to that extent in the course of two weeks.

Indeed, like many of the *fungi*, these sudden developments seem to thrive on death, to flourish on decayed or decaying vitality. They are true parasites, exhausting the trunk they spring from, killing that they may live, — for they really have a sort of independent vitality. They evidently absorb from the soft parts around them, which wither away, the muscles especially becoming wasted and enfeebled. Emollient applications that would soothe ordinary irritation and inflammation, really seem to nourish these tumors, and stimulate them to more rapid development.

In fact, though we have, for the sake of description, compared these growths to fungi and parasitic plants, we regard them as a result of perverted nutrition, giving rise, by a sort of "equivocal generation," if you please, to a new center of animal vitality,— as a congeries of entozoa feeding on the flesh, — as "organized stomachs," absorbing and digesting, like the sponges, the matter they come in contact with.

Treatment.—*Arnica* is to be used in the early stage of the disease when there is a sense of bruisedness in the part, with some redness and rather dull pain; and this should be followed by *nux vomica* as soon as the symptoms have abated, especially if the patient is in low spirits, and there is torpidity of the liver with rather sallow countenance. This may often be followed by *Silicea*, advantageously, of which one dose has cured carbuncle, with hard swelling, of a viscid consistence, having a badly-colored, dark, purple-red appearance, secreting an acrid, corrosive, fetid, yellowish-green ichor, corroding the cellular tissue and the muscles; faintness, loss of appetite, restless nights; suppression of the pulse, livid countenance. *Arsenicum* is indicated when turning purple, the pain is burning (sometimes as if a *live coal* was on the part) and severe, the patient is in great anguish, and gangrene is threatened; or it is the result of contagion, or has cavities from which lice creep forth.

Dr. S. M. Cate, of Augusta, Me., has furnished us with a report of an interesting case of malignant carbuncle, treated with *Arsenicum* successfully. It was of the most malignant character; in fact, pronounced by allopathic physicians to be *fungus hæmatodes*. The patient was a man aged sixty; locality of the carbuncle, on the back of the neck, size of a tea saucer, oblong in shape, and elevated some three inches; gangrenous in the center, outer parts hard, bluish, and irregular. *Treated* by the saturated alcoholic solution of arsenic applied to the ulcerated surface by a brush wet in water, and five or six drops of the solution put on the brush, and two drops of the solution given internally, three times a day. The symptoms abated immediately, and in six days the sore appeared healthy and healed up rapidly. The *Ars.* was only used twice a day after the sixth day. No medicinal symptoms were noticed.

Mrs. L——, of Cincinnati, aged fifty, treated by one of the authors for a large carbuncle on the back of her neck. The symptoms were those of general prostration of strength, low, feeble pulse, pain in the carbuncle, "*burning*," as if covered with *live coals* of fire. *Arsenicum*, first trituration (decimal), was applied to the surface of the affected part, and the internal use of the 4th. Immediate abatement of the symptoms and rapid recovery to health was the result. Also Mr. R., of Cincinnati, age about fifty-five, treated in the same manner, for a carbuncle of extraordinary size and malignancy. He was very much debilitated, from a recent attack of fever while at the south, from whence he had lately returned. The effect of this remedy was equally speedy and successful. All these cases were treated from four to six years ago, and still remain well. We sometimes have to treat old cases that have been badly, *i. e.*, allopathically treated, and still remain sore and painful. For such, prescribe the remedy according to the symptoms present, as in a recent case. *Lachesis* will be useful when the ulcers are deep and the surrounding surface is livid with dark fluid oozing out of the orifices.

For great nervous prostration, give *Hyosciamus*. A remedy not generally known and not yet "proven," but is doubtless worthy of attention in this disease, is the *Pyrola rotundifolia* (canker letucæ). We have used it successfully in several mild, and *one* very malignant case of carbuncle. The manner of using the plant was to lay the green leaves over the ulcerated surface, and change them as often as they became dry. The good effect would soon be experienced by the pain ceasing, and in a few hours the swelling would begin to subside, the discharge to diminish and become more healthy; in a few days the ulcers would heal, and the patients regain their health.

We formerly used it entirely locally, because we first saw the good effects of its use in that manner, but would now use it internally as well as externally. It is doubtless a specific for this disease in some of its forms, if not in all. But if the carbuncle does not yield *promptly* to carefully-selected remedies, proceed at once to a full and free application of

Caustic potash. Let it not only thoroughly saturate the surface, but pass through the sinuses into the cavities within, until no part of the mass is untouched.

There need not be any fear of increasing the patient's sufferings; on the contrary, after a little smarting for a few moments succeeding the first touches, he becomes perfectly easy. The caustic is here the only effectual anodyne. We have seen a patient who had not been able to sleep for a week before, so pleasantly relieved, that in thirty to forty minutes after the application was begun, she sank into a sound sleep; and afterwards went through a rapid convalescence without a moment's further suffering.

After the application of caustic potash, emollient poultices should be used, changing them frequently and washing off the eschar at every dressing.

The parts destroyed will soon become putrid and slough off.

To correct the *fetor* that attends the gangrene, a dilute wash of pyroligneous acid may sometimes be advantageously employed. After the sloughing of the eschar produced by the caustic, give such specific remedies as are indicated by the symptoms, dressing the sore with wet compresses.

As soon as the diseased portions have sloughed off, a simple dressing is all-sufficient. The Momordica Salve will probably suit. Under it, the parts will readily heal up, provided the patient's strength be supported. To secure this indispensable condition

— The diet should be as nourishing as possible, as soon as the patient's appetite admits of it. A lost appetite should be encouraged and welcomed back, like any other prodigal, but not *forced* or anticipated.

OSTEO-SARCOMA, OR BONE CANCER.

In this disease the bone is enlarged, and its structure altered, from a deposite of flesh-like matter mingling with its substance. The changes thus produced seem to be the result of inflammation, often excited by some mechanical injury, or some long-continued local irritation.

The word has been also applied to tumors in any part that seem to be of a blended osseous and fleshy consistency.

The bone enlarges as the disease progresses, and the internal structure is changed from the proper *cancelli* or hard reticulated tissue to a brownish fleshy mass. As this morbid formation increases, the parieties of the bone are extended and often become very thin, in some places giving way entirely, fungus then filling up the crevice. In other cases (which do not therefore exactly correspond to the definition) the cancelli are only enlarged and their cavities filled with pus. Whenever the swelling opens on the surface, large quantities of pus of a peculiar character are in most cases discharged. "This disease," remarks Mr. Liston, "occurs most frequently in the lower jaw;"—a fact attributed mainly to caries of the teeth, though other exposures of that bone, as to sudden changes of temperature in drinking, may help to account for its greater liability. In other respects, weak and cachectic constitutions are the most liable.

The SYMPTOMS at the beginning are *acute* pain in the affected part, with slight constitutional disturbance.

The part soon begins to swell, becoming hard and elastic, and the pain is more *dull.* At a still later period, acute *lancinating pain* returns. Severe constitutional symptoms now set in, the tumor becomes fluctuating, and in consequence of loose pieces of bone floating in it, *crepitus* can be felt on handling. Eventually the integuments burst, and large fungous growths sprout out with a profuse *bloody discharge.* The patient at this stage is much prostrated, and if not soon relieved by amputation, or the proper medication, can not long survive.

In speaking of the

TREATMENT,

Druitt remarks, page 228–9: — "It is often impossible to distinguish between these two classes" (malignant and non-malignant cases). "The same measures that will cure the curable affections will check the incurable ones." The measures referred to "are repeated leeching, mild mercurial alteratives, sarsaparilla with small doses of iodine and potassium, and change of air and other general tonics." "If these means fail, the only recourse is amputation or extirpation." "But the extirpation of the truly malignant growths should be very early and very complete, partial extirpation being unmeaning and utterly useless cruelty."

Prof. Gibson observes, that "before an osteo-sarcomatous tumor has attained a large size, it may possibly be removed by local and constitutional remedies, without the aid of an operation. Leeches applied to the part itself or its vicinity will be found useful. Blisters also, often repeated and kept open by Savine Cerate, and pressure applied to the part, will prove still more beneficial. As a constitutional remedy, Sir Astley Cooper has extolled the exhibition of the oxymuriate of mercury (corrosive sublimate), combined with the compound decoction of sarsaparilla." "When these remedies fail," continues Prof. Gibson, "the operation will become necessary."

Mr. Liston, after telling what should be done to remove the tumor by medication, if that were possible, concludes thus: — "I must say that I am unacquainted with any remedies capable of performing the above indications. The *knife* only is to be depended upon." Again he says, "all operations on malignant tumors, in their advanced stages, are unwarrantable."

Hastings, in his "Practice of Surgery," after quoting Gibson's language, adds, respecting amputation, "but unfortunately this does not always prove successful, for the disease has reappeared on the stump after the operation." We might continue these quotations, from Old School authority, to a great extent, but we deem it unnecessary, for there is so much unanimity among them on the treatment of this disease, that it would be sheer tautology (though they do not *all* exactly copy each other's words). We have given from English, Scotch, and American standard modern authors, the substance of all that is recommended for this malignant disease; and you can clearly see that it amounts to this: — That if leeches, blisters, mercury, sarsaparilla and low diet, will not *cure* — nothing will! The operation, by amputation or extirpation, is indispensable; but even this, according to the same authority, is often of doubtful utility.

This must be admitted on all hands to be a malignant and difficult disease to manage; but bad as it is, the results of our practice present a very different face to the picture.

We may be called to treat cases so far advanced, — where the constitutional powers are much prostrated, or when some vital organs or large vessels are implicated to such an extent, — that the patient will not live long enough to give the remedies a chance to act. In such a case, we, as well as others, must fail. But if called at the stage of the disease, *when the surgeon is generally consulted*, the chance of success will be very fair, and a failure should be a rare occurrence.

In TREATMENT, if the disease be in a limb, and far advanced, involving the whole surface of the bone, it *may* be necessary to amputate, but even in many such cases we may save the limb as well as the patient. In the early stage of acute inflammation, before pus has formed, use such remedies as are recommended for ostitis (see chap. xi.), with the hope of arresting the inflammatory action and preventing ulceration. But if called too late for this, or for arresting the inflammation, *pus* having formed, the limb continuing to swell, apply an *issue* with caustic potash over the most prominent portion of the tumor, so as to cause an opening into the center of the diseased mass as soon as possible. If it be in the jaw, extract some of the teeth nearest the point of the disease, and through the bottoms of the alveoli, make an orifice to the disease, if it has not already extended to the roots of the teeth, as it does very early. Having thus made an exit for the pus, or if it has opened to the surface spontaneously, wash out the whole cavity freely with strong *soap suds*, and proceed to treat it the same as for any other *cancer* with similar symptoms.

Amputation should not be delayed too long. If the disease

does not yield, and the patient is sinking, operate; if possible, having a healthy joint between the diseased portion and the point of amputation.

CHAPTER XXII.

SCALD HEAD — MAXILLARY ABSCESS — SALIVARY AND LACHRYMAL FISTULAS.

Tinea Capitis — Description — Contagiousness — Ulceration and scabbing — Originates and spreads only among children — Cause? — Plenty of soap the first measure of treatment — Other measures — Bathing and *other* alteratives.

Maxillary Abscess — Cause and consequences — Symptoms — Preventive and early treatment — Mechanical and medicinal — Later measures.

Fistula Parotidea — Cause and progress — Remedial measures, mechanical and medicinal.

Fistula Lachrymalis — Strict and popular definitions — Medicinal treatment in mild cases — Probing often operation enough — A radical cure to be attempted in all cases.

TINEA CAPITIS, OR SCALD HEAD.

This is a disease of the scalp, peculiar to children and young persons. It varies a good deal in its character. Sometimes it appears as a scabby eruption, covering small portions or the whole of the scalp. In some cases a great amount of matter is discharged from the affected parts, in others but little. This discharge may be either thick and purulent, or, as is more frequently the case, a thin and sanious fluid. This matter is often contagious in character, and so irritating, that when it gets about the ears or neck it occasions ulceration. These secondary sores, however, heal spontaneously, showing that the contagious disease belongs exclusively to the scalp, and will not continue long in any other part of the integument. Its diffusion over the scalp, and propagation from child to child show, clearly, that *among children* it is as contagious as the itch. Whatever the cause, we never knew an instance of a grown-up person catching the disease, though adults often *have* it, having retained it from their childhood.

There is often a great *thickening* of the scalp at particular points. At the apex and lower portions of the occiput, in particular, you will often discover callous spots. There will also, in some cases, be considerable *ulceration*. Large and deep cavities will be formed in different points, with raised edges and all the other characteristics of the "indolent ulcer."

In some cases the suppuration or ulceration will be but slight, but the whole scalp will be covered with dry scabs (ptyriasis), which appear at first view, like the thin branny scales of *dandruff;* but when they are combed off, they are seen to be a complete crust, leaving the scalp beneath of a fiery redness, as if recently scalded, and itching and burning from the exposure. It is particularly in this form of the disease that the *hair falls off*, leaving large spots nearly bare, the scalp presenting there an inflamed and shining appearance.

At other times the morbid secretion will be so abundant and the eruption so extensive (impetígo), as to form scabs over the whole head, covering it like a *shell*. And this happens, too, in spite of all exertions to prevent it by the strictest cleanliness, especially if the hair has not before fallen off to a very considerable extent.

The CAUSE of this disease is not well known, further than that, when developed, it becomes contagious. It may be communicated by using the same comb or towel, or by sleeping with one already affected. It is commonly supposed to be most prevalent among poor and ill-fed persons, or such as are living in low, damp and filthy places; but it is not by any means confined to this class. We have seen as many cases in cities among the children of the better-provided classes as among their little fellow *citizens* in rags. It may occur at any age from birth to puberty; but it seldom or never originates in an individual after puberty. Persons who have had it throughout their childhood, may continue to be affected with it up to the meridian of life, if it do not previously *end in consumption*,—as it not unfrequently does, being often connected with a general cachetic condition of the system, which predisposes to pulmonary affections.

It is believed to be owing, in very young children, to a neglect of properly washing them at birth. It is said, also, to have been produced indirectly from scalds and burns, by the action of the irritating secretions on other parts of the head. In some instances there has appeared reason to attribute it to syphilitic virus in the mother.

TREATMENT.

First and foremost let there be no want of *soap and water*. Cleanliness is a principle of treatment that applies to all cases. In anything like a bad case, let your soap-suds be a *lather*, and not only wash the whole head, but *shave* off all the hair. Have the whole scalp bare and smooth, if possible.

Where there is scabbiness with soreness, it will be first necessary to remove the irritation. This can be best done by washing the head twice a day with strong soap-suds — and putting on between times, as a cap, a warm slippery elm poultice, as much of the hair as possible being first removed with scissors. This will soon prepare the parts for the razor. *After* the shaving, *continue* the *soap-suds* night and morning.

The remedies which have been mostly used in this disease are —

Rhus tox., *Arsenicum*, *Baryta carb.*, *Hepar Sulphuris*, *Staphysagria*, *Nitric ac.*, *Dulcamara*, *Oleander*, *Psoricum*, *Calc. carb.*, *Magnes. carb.*, *Natr. mur.*, *Graphites and Phytolacca.*

Rhus tox. is used for the more obstinate cases, where there is much fetid discharge, the hair falls off, with great itching, especially at night, the pus accumulates and forms a thick crust, and there is great trouble in getting rid of lice which accumulate with astonishing rapidity. It may be used with success not unfrequently in the milder forms of the disease.

Arsenicum, when the pus is of an ichorous character, corroding other parts with which it comes in contact, forming itching, burning ulcers. After allaying these symptoms and producing an improvement with *Arsenicum*, if the amendment does not continue, *Rhus tox.* should be given and the cure will generally be soon completed. *Dulcamara*, for scrofulous children where the glands of the neck are affected, the child is pale and the eruption is of a mild form. *Oleander* is indicated in the mild form of this disease where there is a scaly eruption, or where the pimples are like itch vesicles, with great itching and smarting on being scratched, especially in scrofulous persons. *Hepar sulphuris* is most beneficial where the eruption, in mild cases, extends to the neck and face, and affects the eyes; the patient has frequent sweats when asleep. We have known some very bad cases cured by the use of an infusion of the *Scrofularia Marilandica* applied as a wash to the head night and morning, and a small portion of the same taken internally every night.

The *Cornus circinati* is also a valuable remedy, and will often alone be effectual in removing the most obstinate cases. We apply it locally and internally as in the former case, always observing, in either case, to discontinue the remedy as soon as amendment is very evident, or if there is a marked aggravation of the symptoms, which will sometimes occur. In the latter event *the cure is certain.*

We have cured some very obstinate cases where the discharge was abundant and ichorous, with *Phytolacca d.* The tincture was also applied externally, after the washing, before recommended.

Dr. Ganwerky reports an obstinate and ill-looking case of tinea, accompanied with urticaria, which had resisted, for a long time, both allopathic and homeopathic treatment, cured with a single dose of *Psoricum.*

The following report of cases was furnished us by Prof. C. Neidhard, of Philadelphia:

"An aggravated case of tinea was treated by me in the beginning of my homeopathic career. The case in question was a young French lady residing in Philadelphia, who had always consulted Andral, of Paris; Sir Astley Cooper, of London; and the most distinguished physicians of New Orleans, as well as this city, without benefit. The disease might be called an impetigo, large scabs covering the whole head and constantly discharging. The terrible allopathic treatment she underwent, it might be instructive to detail, did time and space permit. I will only mention one remedy employed; it was the horrible pitch skull-cap, by which the whole scab was removed, but of course only for a short time. She was entirely cured under homeopathic treatment, after a long aggravation. Unfortunately very few special indications for the application of remedies can be given by which others may profit. We are too glad to cure our cases, without asking how it was effected. I only know that *Psorine* was the chief remedy in this case. Experience has taught me, that if a remedy acts beneficially in tinea, it will always bring out more of the eruption; if it remains indifferent, it does not suit the case. Judging according to this dogma, *Psorine* undoubtedly had the best effect. I find noted down in my record, the following as the action of *Psorine:*

"'Already, after the fourth powder, the discharge commences to run, spreads behind the ears and becomes very fetid; there also appear pimples in the face, it now itches more through the day, and not, as formerly, at night.' Next to *Psorine*, no remedy had a better effect than *Baryta carb.*

"A second memorable case was a species of tinea, of a squamous nature, on the head, with a peculiar and highly characteristic great redness of the base of the tetter. *Magnes. carb.*, half trit., produced the usual aggravation in such cases in bringing out the tetter to an enormous extent, not only over the whole head, but also over the neck and shoulders. By means of this very aggravation, however, a complete cure was effected. These two cases, as well as my subsequent observation of the water treatment at Græfenburg, have taught me a lesson which I have not forgotten. I am convinced now, that no important and inveterate case of chronic cutaneous disease can ever be radically cured without an apparent aggravation of all the cutaneous symptoms, and this aggravation may not only occur once, but several times, before a complete cure is effected; but, of course, at each renewal in a milder degree. This is, undoubtedly, the cause why so few cutaneous eruptions are radically cured under allopathic treatment.

"*Calc. carb;* this wonderful remedy is employed in diseases of the most diversified character. The cases of tinea to which it is best applicable, are those called by pathologists, Pityriasis, Herpes furfuracious, or dandruff, appearing on the hairy scalp, and are usually very obstinate. In very many cases of this kind, particularly in persons of light complexion, inclined to obesity, I have employed it with eminent success. In order to perform a complete cure, it must, however, be persevered in for a long time, high and low dilutions must be given in alternation. Nearest allied to this remedy in dandruff is *Nat. mur.* I am unable to furnish any special indications for one or the other remedy; all I know, that these two cure oftener cases of this kind. With the internal use of *Nat. mur*, I sometimes combine the external application of salt water.

"My indication for using *Graphites* in tinea capitis, is the seat of the disease behind the ears, with painfulness on the least touch.

"*Oleander* I have used in several cases with great benefit, where the scabs looked very yellow and where the disease was aggravated in winter; hot weather and perspiration also aggravate it; the itching is then intolerable."

As cleanliness of the diseased part is an important consideration in this disease, so also is cleanliness of the whole surface of the patient no less important. The restoration of the healthy function of the *skin*, that all-important eliminating organ of the system, which in all such cases is in an unhealthy condition, is a matter never to be overlooked. Regular baths should be strictly enjoined.

MAXILLARY ABSCESS, OR ULCERATION OF THE ANTRUM.

The ANTRUM HIGHMORIANUM is subject to a disease which is always very distressing, and when of long standing difficult to cure. It rarely occurs in young or very old persons, being generally confined to those of middle age. It may exist for months and years without the sufferer being aware of its nature. For a long time it may pass for mere "tooth-ache;" indeed its most common

— CAUSE is the irritation of the lining membrane of the cavity by *decayed teeth.* The ulcers on the roots of the teeth not unfrequently penetrate into the antrum, thus communicating their irritation or disease to the mucus membrane, and that to the periosteum and bone. *Irritation* also from any other cause, as from a *common cold*, originally affecting the schneiderian membrane, may proceed to inflammation and thence to ulceration; the discharge from which, finding no sufficient outlet into the nose, becomes an additional cause of irritation, until the bone also ulcerates, when the *fetor* becomes almost as great an annoyance to the patient as the pain. It is offensive to everybody about him, particularly at night.

The chief SYMPTOM in the early stage is a severe *pain in the face*, just beneath the prominence of the malar bone, which is constant and unremitting. The neighboring *teeth* not unfrequently become *secondarily affected*, and are extracted without any relief. In other cases, though the teeth may have been the original cause, their roots not entering the antrum itself, or not making a sufficient orifice in it for the matter to flow out, nothing is gained by extracting them, and the patient and surgeon may be still in the dark as to the nature of the affection. If, however, any considerable quantity of matter flow out, there will, of course, be no more doubt. A considerable discharge of offensive *matter* through the *nose*, from the sinus overflowing, is in connection with the seat of the pain, another diagnostic symptom. In some instances the face gradually swells, and becomes very much disfigured. The walls of the antrum may be visibly distended by the accumulating pus. They have been in this way destroyed, opening into the cheek or into the orbit. In connection with the diseased antrum, the inflammation may extend to the frontal sinuses, and purulent collections be formed there also. In all cases of long standing, the chief complaint of the patient is, the fetid effluvium or discharge through the nostrils.

If called to a case of this kind early enough, your OBJECT will be, if possible, to *allay* the *inflammation*. This may often be effected, and *suppuration* with all its inconvenient consequences *prevented*, by a timely use of specific remedies.

If the disease is the result of a sudden cold, whether connected with diseased teeth or not, setting in with chilliness and followed by fever, *Aconite* is the proper remedy, especially if pain in the head is severe, the patient restless, and there is severe drawing or pressing pain behind the malar bone.

Belladonna will be found most serviceable in the acute stage when there is redness of the face and eyes, throbbing pain in the head and affected side of the face, with swelling and a deep flush of the cheek.

When the pains are rending, or tearing and burning, *Arsen.* will be found most useful, especially in the later stage, when suppuration is about to take place, the patient feels weak and faint, from the severity of the pain.

This disease runs its course through the acute stage in a short time, and if resolution is not effected in five or six days, an abscess will most likely form, pus collect in the antrum, and the disease sooner or later extend to the bones.

If pus has formed, let no time be lost in using means to let it off. While it remains it is a source of great mischief, and more or less dangerous. Extract the second or third molar tooth — it may be necessary to take out both. Should the alveolus not communicate with the antrum, with a sufficiently large opening, you may also have to

— *drill a hole* about the size of an ordinary goose-quill. It requires at least that space to let out the pus freely and allow free access for washing out the cavity. The operation may be performed with any common drill, causing little or no pain unless the bone is inflamed.

Inject warm water to remove all pus, once a day at least, and also throw in a low dilution of the specific remedy you are administering.

To prevent the orifice from closing by the growing of the gums or the bone over it, keep in a tènt or canula, removing it several times a day to let off the pus. If the pus is thick and yellow, with little or no pain, *Lycopodium* will be a useful remedy.

If it is thin and ichorous, the parts sensitive to the touch, especially if the bone is diseased, *Assafetida* should be used.

Carbo. veg. is the proper remedy for slow, indolent ulceration, the parts being nearly insensible, the pus fetid and dark colored.

PAROTID OR SALIVARY FISTULA.

Wounds of the face, which sever the parotid or stenonian duct, often cause much difficulty. As the healing process goes on, the duct is closed, and the secretion of the parotid gland is prevented from escaping into the mouth.

It accumulates and forms a *tumor* at or near the original wound, which inflames and sooner or later ulcerates, opening upon the outside of the face.

This *fistulous opening*, out of which pus as well as the saliva secreted by the gland is constantly passing, continues to be sore and painful, and is a source of great annoyance to the patient, both on account of the discharge and the disfigurement of his face.

The proper TREATMENT consists in allaying the irritation and inflammation, and opening a passage for the saliva into the mouth, so that the fistula may be allowed to heal.

Calendula, given internally and applied to the sore by cloth wet in the infusion laid over it, will, in a short time, allay the irritation and bring about a healthy condition.

When the parts become healthy, make an *opening* with a small trochar, or a diamond-pointed steel probe, from the inside of the buccinator muscle, at or near the original point of opening for the duct. In making the orifice, pass the trochar into the open end of the duct at the fistulous opening: or it is better to let it enter the parotid duct a line or two back of the opening, if practicable. Insert a silver or gold *tube* from the mouth into the duct, so as to guide the saliva into the mouth. The tube should be long enough to pass for an inch into the duct, so that it will not be liable to come out into the mouth.

The *Fistula* may then be readily healed, generally requiring only simple dressings. But if it does not heal kindly, resort to the use of *Calendula* as before directed. If this does not effect the healing, the edges may be scarified and brought together. The Canula should be left in the duct until all the parts are sound and healthy, and then removed.

The continual flow of saliva will then prevent any danger of a closure of the duct.

FISTULA LACHRYMALIS.

Any obstruction in the ductus ad nasum causing regurgitation of the lubricating fluid upon the eye, or rather its constant accumulation and consequent *overflow* in the shape of *tears*, is called by this name, although it only strictly applies to the case where there is not only distension of the lachrymal sac, appearing as a tumor at the inner corner of the eye, but where that swelling has occasioned inflammation and *ulceration*, with an opening for the tears *on the face*, instead of into the nose.

In ordinary cases, the stoppage in the duct occasions but slight inconvenience from suffusion of the eye-ball and obscuration of vision.

The inflammation, however, occasionally becomes serious and very painful.

Several modes of TREATMENT are recommended by the allopathic books. That most commonly adopted is an operation and the insertion of a style. But, in the majority of cases, an operation is unnecessary — mere medicinal measures will be quite sufficient.

TREATMENT.

In the early stage of this complaint, while there is inflammatory action in the lower lid and inner canthus, or an abscess at that point, obstructing, for the time, the flow of tears into the duct, the sack being inflamed, *Pulsatilla* should be given.

Calcarea is more suitable for scrofulous persons and in the more advanced stage of the disease. In persons advanced in life, one dose should be given and allowed to act for twenty to thirty days, and if the cure is not complete, some other remedy, as *Sul. or Silic.*, given; and after that has exhausted its action, the *Cal.* may be repeated. In young persons, the *Cal.* may be repeated without any intermediate remedy.

Silicea seems to act more favorably on the left side, and when the eyes are weakened by the regurgitation of tears.

Petroleum is useful when there is more or less inflammation and swelling in the inner canthus, especially of the *right* eye. Dr. Hering says, that there are few instances in which he has failed to cure this disease with internal remedies. That *Petroleum* was the efficacious remedy in a majority of cases, especially where the affection was on the right side — that when he failed with the 30th, lower dilutions were ineffectual. He speaks favorably of the alternation of *Petroleum and Calcarea, Ruta and Staphysagria, Stannum and Pulsatilla.*

We have cured several cases with a single dose each, of *Calcarea.*

In the chronic form of this disease, the subjective symptoms are too obscure to give any exact indication for the proper remedy. In such cases the better plan is to give one remedy as *Cal.*, *Petro.*, *Puls.*, *or Sul.*, and let it act for a few weeks, then repeat or follow by another, according to the effect produced.

It may take several months to cure a case, or it may be cured in a few weeks or days. (For the operation, inserting style, &c., see Part II.)

CHAPTER XXIII.

OPHTHALMIA, — SPECIFIC VARIETIES.

Oculists and surgeons — "Ophthalmia," its species and principles of division — Common Ophthalmia, or simple conjunctivitis, — Catarrhal, Purulent, Gonorrheal and Scrofulous Ophthalmia, described and compared — TREATMENT of each in order — Important and effectual general measures — Difference in the Chronic Stage or Form — *O. Purulenta* — different measures in infants and adults — *O. Scrofularia* — Peculiar and effectual measures in *O. Gonorrhealis*, a curable disease — Importance in all forms of constitutional remedies.

THE eye may be considered as next to the brain itself, the most elevated part of the whole animal organism. It is the agency by which the individual holds most direct communication with the universe. Its structure is the most delicate and diversified of any organ in the body. This complexity of mechanism and variety of constituent tissues, together with its almost constant use or abuse, expose it to a proportionate number of accidents and diseases.

To treat in detail of every morbid derangement of the organs of vision, would require a separate volume, and merely to give a catalogue of them would be useless parade.

Every surgeon, however — that is, every "general practitioner" of medicine, as he is called in England — ought to be competent not only to *treat* all acute disease of this important organ, together with its simpler and more common forms of chronic derangement, but to *distinguish* these, with readiness and accuracy, from the rarer and more complex malformations or disorganizations, which may justify him in referring the case to professed eye-doctors. Although then you may not propose to become professional oculists or exclusively "operative" surgeons, you are still bound to study and discriminate many of the diseases fully treated of only in works devoted to this one organ.

OPHTHALMIA is the generic term for all inflammatory diseases of the eye. This word, like pneumonia, was in general use before the modern device was adopted, of indicating inflammation of a part by its technical name with the artificial termination *-itis.* It seems quite unnecessary to change such *general* and generally understood designations, although *specific* distinctions are well marked in a single word, by such terms as conjunctivitis, sclerotitis, corneitis, iritis and even retinitis.

Inflammation of the eye, however, has other diversities, and requires other classifications, depending on a more important principle than even the anatomical distinction of the part or tissue affected.

As far as nosology or nomenclature is of any importance, these distinct *principles* of classification should be borne in mind. They are independent of and often cross each other. Thus every case of "ophthalmia" *must* in respect of location, imply one or more of the species just mentioned: but, having regard to its cause or character, it *may* be either acute or chronic; either simple inflammation or scrofulous, or rheumatic, &c.; either idiopathic or symptomatic, epidemic or endemic.

SIMPLE CONJUNCTIVITIS or inflammation of the mucous membrane, covering the front of the eye-ball and lining the eye-lids, is, as might be expected from the exposure of the part, by far the most frequent form of "ophthalmia," and that which is generally understood by the word, when no other special form or variety is mentioned. Several varieties of conjunctivitis are, however, of sufficient importance to require distinction.

COMMON OPHTHALMIA,

Or *simple inflammation* of the *membrana conjunctiva*, may be brought on by the introduction of foreign substances between the lids and ball, or *other* modes of external injury, — too strong an impression of light, exposure to cold, &c., &c. In short, the surface of the eye is *peculiarly* liable to all the causes and *predisposing causes* of ordinary inflammation.

The first symptom of the irritation tending to inflammation is an uneasy sensation in the part, a sensation of *itching* or scratching, whether there be any foreign substance actually causing it or not; and not unfrequently the patient will call on some one to look into his eye and remove the supposed offending cause. The next stage is probably more or less *intolerance of light.*

The eye-*ball* soon seems to be swollen, with a diffused redness of the whole visible surface, and a sensation of increased heat. There is also *an increased secretion of tears,* which not unfrequently become *hot and scalding* to the cheeks, on which they fall, from being produced too fast to be all admitted into the puncta lachrymalia.

As the disease continues to *advance,* the *pain* appears to become more *deeply-seated,* darting and burning, sometimes it extends to the forenead. Symptoms of general *fever* may always be detected and are often violent and obvious enough. Costiveness and more or less derangement of the stomach are rarely absent.

In some cases the conjunctiva becomes thickened, presenting a kind of fungous appearance; or there is more or less extravasated fluid of some kind between it and the sclerotic coat, and in rare instances even in front of the cornea. The disease may even spread in the suppurative stage to the extent of separating the cornea from its attachments. This, however, is very rare.

In healthy individuals the inflammation usually *terminates* in *resolution.* It may, however, assume a chronic and obstinate character; but it by no means necessarily follows that it is then so "very difficult to manage," as some distinguished authorities would have us believe

Although exposure to cold was mentioned as one of the ordinary causes of this form of the disease, some peculiarities are presented when it appears epidemic, as

CATARRHAL OPHTHALMIA.

This would appear from the books to be much more frequent in Europe, than among ourselves. It is there a very common accompaniment of influenza.

One of the SYMPTOMS in which this differs from the common form, is at the beginning a *dryness* of the *eye* instead of an unusual secretion of tears. In a short time, however, the pain diminishes, while a copious *flow* of *tears* sets in, which soon changes to a mucous discharge, and then becomes acrid and excoriating. The patient is constantly feverish.

In some cases the whole visible surface of the eye is covered with *pustules* containing a yellowish secretion. This pustular suppuration is one of the circumstances that distinguishes it from

PURULENT OPHTHALMIA. (Egyptian Ophthalmia).

This is considered a very serious disease. One eye is often destroyed by it, occasionally both.

It may attack individuals of all ages.

We have seen it, however, much more frequently in children than in adults. It usually makes its appearance a few days after birth. The cause of this singular fact has been much disputed. Some have attributed it exclusively to gonorrhea, or at least leucorrhea in the mother! We have had cases, however, where the former was certainly not the cause, and when we had every reason to believe that the latter *could* not have been. We are much more inclined to attribute it to the fault of the *nurse* than of the mother. It is more reasonable to regard it as produced by the peculiar but healthy secretions with which the child is always covered at birth; and from which it is not always properly cleansed in the first instance.

The eyes are at first slightly *reddened* and *swollen*. This is soon followed by discharges of *thin matter* rather adhesive in its character, — the lids being frequently glued together by it. When it is very copious, it becomes of a yellowish and sometimes greenish color and very acrid.

The disease extends not only over the whole front of the eyeball, but throughout the conjunctiva membrane lining the lids, which then becomes much thickened and assumes a fungoid appearance. The distended fold of the membrane may project downward and cover the cornea. The cornea itself, more frequently than in simple ophthalmia, becomes involved and sloughs off, destroying the eye.

There is always great *constitutional irritation* attending the *early* stage of the disease, but it generally subsides in a few days, after which the affection becomes *chronic* and continues apparently local.

GONORRHEAL OPHTHALMIA

— is generally regarded as produced by a want of attention to cleanliness in patients having the urethral form of the affection, and allowing some of the matter to get into the eye. This matter is said to have the same reproductive action on any other mucous surface as in the original location. But we are told from high authority, that "there is reason to believe also that the disease is sometimes produced (in the eye) by sympathy or in the way of metastasis, in consequence *of suppressed gonorrhea;*" * that is, be it observed, in consequence of the *cure* of the disease according to the routine course of treatment! "Oh, *medicine!* how many crimes are committed," how many maladies engendered "in thy name!"

The symptoms are much the same in character as those of the last-mentioned form, called especially "*purulent* ophthalmia," but the disease is much more *violent* as well as "virulent." Hence an additional reason for believing that purulent ophthalmia, as it effects new-born children, can not be of gonorrheal origin. When this specific inflammation attacks the eyes of adults — whose systems from their being at the time affected with it elsewhere, may also be supposed in some measure hardened or accustomed to the virus — it often destroys one eye, if not both. How then should the susceptible surface of children's eyes, which can not yet bear the light itself, get off without still worse results than those of "ophthalmia purulenta?"

Of this gonorrhea of the eye, we are told by the author just quoted, that "it unfortunately admits of no relief." A probable reason for that opinion on *his* part, and of a more hopeful one on *ours*, will be given when we come to speak of treatment.

SCROFULOUS OPHTHALMIA

— may be generally distinguished by the constitutional affections and *appearance* of the patient, as well as by the fact of the

* Gibson's Institutes of Surgery, vol. ii, page 810.

eye-disease being peculiarly obstinate under ordinary modes of treatment.

The most peculiar of the local symptoms are irritability and intolerance of light, with little or no pain, however, when the eye is protected from this and other sources of irritation. Occasionally there are some *pustules* or ulcerated spots upon it, which may continue for a long time without any material change.

We shall take up the

TREATMENT

— of the different forms of the disease in the order in which I have mentioned the symptoms. First, then, for

SIMPLE CONJUNCTIVITIS.

In the early stage of conjunctivitis, during the itching or scratching sensation, as from a foreign substance in the eye, or when following this there are great intolerance to light, redness and swelling, injected and inflamed condition of the superficial vessels of the eye, profuse flow of tears, heat, the tears are scalding, the pain darting and burning, with *fever*, *Aconite* should be administered internally and applied, in dilution, to the surface of the eye. Cloths wet in warm, or rather *hot* water, with *Aconite*, should be laid over the eyes, and the light excluded. The heat of the application should be proportioned to the inflammation; highest in the more acute stage, and diminished as the inflammation subsides.

Should there remain, after the acute symptoms have been subdued by *Aconite*, redness of the lids, with a bruised pain when touched, or difficulty of moving the eyes, with *photophobia*, especially towards evening or by candle light, *Hepar sul.* should be used. When the eyes become worse at night, when warm in bed, or worse after slight fatigue, the itching and scratching pains returning, redness of the sclerotica remaining, with morbid sensibility to light, *Mercurius* is the proper remedy. *Belladonna* will be serviceable when there is erysipelatous inflammation of the eyes in the early stage, or later, when in other forms there remains bright redness of the sclerotic coat, the pupils dilated, headache, dizziness and giddiness, pressive pains around the eyes, or pains which penetrate deeply.

In epidemic or CATARRHAL OPHTHALMIA the same tissue is involved as in the common form of this disease. In fact there is but little difference between the two affections, except that the former is generally connected with more or less inflammation of the mucous membranes of the air passages, and always, in the early stage, attended with general *catarrhal fever*.

Aconite is the proper remedy for the early symptoms, which do not differ from those of common conjunctivitis, except that these are more violent. The eye is at first dry, but afterwards, the flow of tears is abundant. The *Aconite* should be used until the fever is subdued.

In the later stage, when there are pustules on the sclerotica, with a free discharge of mucous tears, *Euphrasia* will be appropriate.

Calendula is very valuable in this case, when there is profuse suppuration from the surface of the ball or lids, or both. We use it as a local application as well as internally.

If the eruption on the ball or lids is rather *vesicular* than pustular, *Mercurius* should be administered.

Patients suffering from this disease are always more or less feverish, with chills alternating with fever, the skin dry, the feet and legs cold, and the head hot. Under these circumstances, warm or hot baths, followed by the "wet-sheet pack," will be of great service.

PURULENT OPHTHALMIA.

The incipient stage of this complaint is characterized by many of the symptoms of *Aconite*, especially in adults; and if administered early, it will either remove the disease entirely or so modify it as to render it amenable to *Euphrasia* or *Calcarea*.

The *Aconite* should be given while there is fever during the high inflammatory action, after the acute febrile sypmtoms have subsided, or, as in case of infants, if no fever should be present.

Chamomilla is the proper remedy, especially for children, or when the pains are very severe, the patient is in great anguish, and there is an abundant flow of adhesive mucous and tears. When the pains are excessive and burning, as if coals of fire were in the eyes, the patient in great anguish, great constitutional irritation,

Arsenicum should be administered. When the disease becomes chronic, the constitutional symptoms having subsided, but the purulent discharge continues, the lids swollen and ulcerated, the pain *pressing* or *smarting*, *Causticum* will be found especially applicable. A solution of the remedy should be applied daily to the eyes. If any pustules remain on the ball after the subsiding of the acute stage, *Sepia* will be found most serviceable.

Argentum nitricum is highly spoken of by Dr. Dudgeon, in this form of ophthalmia. He reports one very obstinate case cured in a week by *Argent met.*, six given every night.

For Gonorrheal Ophthalmia, it will be found best to use the remedies that would be most efficacious for gonorrhea located in the urethra.

Pulsatilla is directed by some of the books. *Thuja*, *Cannabis*, and *Argentum nitricum* will be found very efficacious. If the patient is suffering under *syphilitic* taint, *Mer. cor.* or *Cinnabaris*, may be used with advantage.

The introduction of a solution of the *Sesqui-carbonate of potash* by means of a syringe, into the urethra, repeatedly, at such strength as to produce a discharge resembling gonorrhea, was, several years ago, suggested to the authors by Dr. I. W. Prowell, of Lexington, Ky.

It was found that as soon as the "artificial gonorrhea" was produced in the urethra the eye symptoms began to subside, and the proper remedies for gonorrhea in its original character would relieve the eyes, while the artificial disease would also subside in a few days.

We have also used dilute Tr. *Sang. can.* to produce the discharge from the urethra with success.

In the earlier stage of SCROFULOUS OPHTHALMIA, while there is great intolerance of light, pressure and itching, in the eyes, a feeling as if a foreign body or sand were in them, *Sulphur* will be beneficial.

If, however, there is high fever, with severe pain in the eyes and head, *Aconite* is preferable. Or, where the pains are stinging, the lids are partially or wholly paralyzed, coryza, alternate chilliness and fever, *Bell.* is more suitable.

But should the weakness of the eyes continue, with excessive sensibility, little or no pain in a dark room, but the pain severe, smarting and burning, when exposed to light, with excessive lachrymation or preternatural dryness and a rough feeling, *Capsicum* is the most effectual remedy. It should be used both locally and internally. We have employed this remedy at various dilutions, successfully in many cases of this kind. Dr. Dudgeon speaks highly of *Argentum nit.* in this disease. We have used it with excellent effect in several cases. Dr. D—— contends that the cures performed by its local application, as recommended by allopathic authors, are purely homeopathic.

In the treatment of scrofulous ophthalmia, the condition of the general system of the patient must always be taken into account, and the medicines directed with reference to that, as well as for the local symptoms. The *Scrofulous cachexia* will have to be corrected, to a greater or less extent, in many cases before the eye symptoms will yield.

Dr. Boeker reports nine cases of *scrofulous ophthalmia*, with pustulation of the lids and ulceration of the cornea, cured in from six to ten days respectively, by *Mercurius corrosivus*, in solution of half a grain to five scruples of distilled water; two drops given three or four times a day. In some cases he made it twice as strong, and in one case used it locally as well as internally with good effect.

From what we have seen of the action of this article in similar *very bad* cases, we are disposed to consider it one of the best remedies when there is great intolerance to light, pustules on the eye or on the margin of the lids, the lids are swollen and red, and the patient is afflicted with eruptions or glandular swellings.

If the patient has been previously treated with large doses of *Mercury*, *Euphrasia* should be first employed, and followed, if necessary, by the *Mer. cor.*

Arsenicum and Conium in alternation have been successfully used in this disease.

Professor Jas. J. Kitchen, of Philadelphia, in a communication to one of the authors, thus speaks of scrofulous ophthalmia:

"Regarding *Scrofulous Ophthalmia*, there are two remedies, which I have found of great value, and all-sufficient in the cases which have fallen under my notice since practising homeopathy.

They are *Arsenicum and Conium.* In acute cases I give the 3d potence every four hours, in alternation; chronic cases, the 6th; *Ars.* in the morning and *Conium* at night. I have succeeded in every case which I have yet treated."

We will conclude this article with indications for remedies, and report of cases furnished us by Dr. C. Neidhard.

"The following symptoms induce me to use *Sulphur* in preference to any other remedy: Inflammation of conjunctiva and sclerotica, the inflammation sometimes more or less advanced, but always more of a chronic kind, with predominating scrofulous diathesis, sometimes scabs around the eyelids, but particularly a *sensation like sand in the eyes and intolerable itching;* the two last symptoms must always be present, if a beneficial effect is to be derived from *Sulph.*

"Next to *Sulph.* in importance and perhaps even superior to it are, *Acon. and Bellad.* These two remedies are, perhaps, more frequently used in inflammation of the eyes than any others. With me the chief indication for *Acon.* is intense pain; if it does nothing more, it removes that. The following case exhibits a very fair representation of the symptoms which would lead us to select *Bellad.*

"Miss M——, aged twelve, of fair complexion, almost from her birth had been subject to enlargement of the glands of the neck, which suppurated several times whilst under aleopathic treatment, so that they became gradually indurated. She had also frequently suffered from erysipelas of the face, and labored under enlargement of the thyroid gland. All these affections had subsided to a considerable extent during homeopathic treatment of one year. In the spring of 1841, she was attacked with an inflammation of the left eye. The tunica sclerotica of the left eye of a bright red color, with extreme intolerance of light, stinging pains in the eye and head, particularly at night, paralysis of upper eyelid, profuse flow of tears, chills and fever, and bitter taste in the mouth, thirst and want of appetite, coryza on the same side as the affected eye. The symptoms being very striking for *Ballad.*, I accordingly mixed five drops of the tincture in a wineglassfull of water, of which she took a teaspoonful every two hours; at the same time ten drops of the tincture were mixed in a teacupfull of water, with which the eye was frequently bathed. In the space of four days, I had the satisfaction of seeing the inflammation completely removed. The ulcer on the cornea was afterwards cured by repeated doses of *Silic. and Hepar sul.*, in alternation.

"Next in importance, in my estimation, to *Ac. and Bell.*, is *Conium.* The following case will illustrate its action: it occurred in a child aged eight, several months after an unsuccessful vaccination. The inflammation commenced in the left eye and soon involved also the right; intolerance of light and irritability of the eye excessive; she can not bear the least touch on the head; shooting pains penetrating the eyes upwards into the head. Tinct. *Acon.* six drops in half a tumbler of water, every hour a spoonful, soon removed the pains. The intolerance of light, excessive nervous irritability, however, continued. Small doses of *Conium, Sil., Sulph.*, which were most specific in this case, did not prevent the cornea of both eyes from becoming opaque, so that the sight was entirely obliterated. Notwithstanding this apparent unsuccessful issue of the case, the homeopathic treatment was not abandoned by the family, and I was convinced that the homeopathic law would enable me to find a proper homeopathic remedy. As *Con. mac.*, even in small doses, seemed always to exert the best influence, I now gave the strong tincture, four drops in water, three times a day, which dose was gradually increased to eight; at the same time, the eyes were directed to be bathed every two hours with the tincture, mixed with a little water; in four days from the commencement of this treatment, the nebula began to disappear, and the sight was perfectly restored in two weeks.

"I have subsequently used this remedy in several cases with equal beneficial success, sometimes in large, at others, in small doses. It seems to be particularly applicable in inflammation of a bluish-red color, great sensibility of the eye, paralysis of the upper eyelids, and where the patient is of a nervous temperament, with dark complexion, to which, I may add excessive photophobia and specks on the cornea.

"Next in importance in scrofulous ophthalmia, I must mention an important group: *Calc. carb., Hepar. and Graph.*

"The following case was almost cured by *Calc. carb.* Mrs. B——, from Boston, had been under the care of various physicians without receiving any benefit. The symptoms denoting a kind of scrofulous ophthalmia, were the following: Sensation of sand in the eyes; an ulcer is visible in both eyes, which obscures the sight like a veil or mist over the eyes; the pupils are dilated, the eyes are in tears in the morning, with weakness, and are always worse in summer; pain in the left shoulder to the back on sitting much or being fatigued; costiveness, nervous temperament; the eyes feel best in twilight. She also had glandular swellings in her neck in childhood, and dry scabs on the head. After the exhibition of *Calc.*, there appeared a thin, scaly eruption on various parts of the body, with more itching on the right than on the left side. *Calc. c.*, 1st, produced, at first, a violent aggravation, but, afterwards, a great improvement took place in her disease. The lady left the city before the cure was completed.

"The following case will characterize the *Graphites* variety: A little boy, five years of age, had first a cough, which is followed by inflammation of the eye; scabs all around the eyelids, eyes closed in the morning with dry scabs over them and also on the cheek, photophobia, left nostril is obstructed, looks red and tumid at the opening, there is no appetite, and he is very much emaciated. The improvement after *Graphites*, 3d, was every way satisfactory; it removed the whole disease in a few days.

"Several similar cases might be here detailed. My experience with *Graph.* is abundantly corroborated by homeopathic writers. Observations like the following occur frequently throughout homeopathic literature; they point out clearly the cases where *Graph.* would be indicated.

"*Graph.*, says Dr. Knorres, I have found useful in a scrofulous ophthalmia, with ulceration of the cornea and great intolerance of the light. Hartlaub says, *Graph.* opens the gummed up, photophobic eyes of scrofulous children, where there is at the same time an eruption of the face.

"With regard to *Hepar. Sulph.*, Dr. Schroen gives the following indications, to which I have nothing to add: 'In inflammation of the eyes, accompanied by burning pains at the edges of the lids, which are red at the internal surface, photophobia and lachrymation, enormous mucous secretion from the meibomean glands, in consequence, agglutinations of the lids; pustules on the sclerotica and even on the cornea, where some small vessels converge to its periphery. I have frequently employed, with success, *Hep. sul. c.*, though I could not discontinue its use until a considerable lapse of time, for the same symptoms would again return. When the photophobia was excessive, it was necessary to interpose *Bellad.*

"Quite lately, in a case of nebula of the cornea, with ulceration and violent inflammation of the sclerotica, with photophobia after *small-pox*, *Graph.*, next to *Silicea*, contributed more towards its cure than any other remedy. The subject was a young girl, undoubtedly of scrofulous habit.

"A remedy, allied to *Graph.*, and also used in cases of a scrofulous nature, is *Kali. carb.* Both *Graph. and Kali.* have the eyes gummed up in the morning, but *Kali.* has not merely scabs on the lids like *Graph.*, but also violent itching in the eyes, with swelling of the lachrymal duct and flow of tears."

CHAPTER XXIV.

OPHTHALMIA — STRUCTURAL VARIETIES.

Local and structural distinctions — Conjunctivitis and O. TARSI — O. SCLEROTICA — O. CORNEÆ, distinctions and reference — O. IRIDIS, peculiar symptoms and causes — PROCIDENTIA IRIDIS.

THE distinctions in inflammatory disease of the eye, of which we have been speaking, are founded on the character of the diseased action, or that of the patient's constitution. Another principle of division requires consideration. The ordinary cases of inflammation of the eye, — and those, therefore, which are commonly included under the term "ophthalmia," — are such as involve primarily and principally, if not exclusively, the external surface. They are, therefore, more technically described as varieties of *conjunctivitis*.

Other varieties have now to be noticed, distinguished by the particular *part*, or rather the peculiar *tissue* of the eye concerned. These *structural* distinctions and designations sometimes coincide with the *specific* one founded on the character of the disease. Thus, inflammation of the fibrous structures of the eye is like that of such structures elsewhere, rheumatic; while iritis and retinitis may be symptomatic of syphilis.

As a sort of local variety of conjunctivitis, we will first take up what is called

OPHTHALMIA TARSI,

— or, more modernly, *ophthalmitis tarsalis.* This consists in a form of simple inflammation confined to the eyelids, and perhaps originally to the Meibomian Glands. The secretions of these glands, being altered by the disease, become irritating, sometimes very acrid. The *itching* of the eye thus caused, — which is a diagnostic symptom and the principal complaint of the patient, — has occasioned the clumsy name of "PSOROPHTHALMIA."

This perverted secretion of the Meibomian glands is not only acrimonious, but often of a glue-like *adhesiveness*, sealing up the eye when long closed, as in sleep, and causing considerable trouble to *separate* the *lids* again. The force necessary to effect this keeps up the irritation, and increases the chance of the disease running into the chronic form. The *eye-lashes* then not unfrequently drop off, leaving the *edges* of the lids smooth, glossy and red; which, with their baldness, occasions a great disfigurement of the countenance.

The intolerable ITCHING of the eyes, as before remarked, is the first complaint of the patient. He is obliged to be constantly rubbing them, which only aggravates the irritation. The inflammation sometimes extends to the ball of the eye. That of the lids very generally proceeds to *suppuration;* and occasionally there is *ulceration* of the tarsal cartilages.

Closure of the lachrymal duct sometimes occurs, giving rise to what used to be called Epiphora (or mechanical weeping), one form of obstruction which was mentioned under the head of "FISTULA LACHRYMALIS."

THE TREATMENT

— for the acute form of this affection should be that directed for "simple ophthalmia."

As a large portion of these cases are scrofulous, it will be necessary to bear in mind that condition in making our prescriptions.

In the early stage, while there is simply the *itching* and redness with more or less inflammation of the surface of the lid, *Rhus tox.* will generally be sufficient. But in the more advanced stage, *Sulphur* should be the first remedy. If it does not yield to this, and there is an acrid secretion with pimples on the margins, or sties on the lids, *Pulsatilla* will be applicable; or else profuse suppuration, *Mercurius*; or if the pus is adhesive and the edges itch, *Hepar sul.*

If there are ulcers on the lids use *Causticum*. For granulations on the inner surface of the lids, *Capsicum* or *Argentum nit.* will be the best remedies; or if there is a gluey puss discharged, *Hepar* should be used.

The local application of the remedy indicated at the same time it is used internally, will greatly facilitate the cure. We have cured a case with *Hepar sulphuris*, *Pet.* first, applied to the diseased surface with a brush, in a week, which had resisted the efforts of several physicians, with various homeopathic remedies, for a whole year. We have produced similar results by the local application of other remedies in this disease, giving the same internally.

It is worth some trouble to prevent "gluing-up" the eyelids during sleep. For this purpose let the edges of the lids be sufficiently lubricated before going to bed, with some animal oil — lard oil may answer the purpose well enough, and is much better than olive oil, which seems to unite with the secretion and become gluey.

SCLEROTICA OPHTHALMIA.

Inflammation of the second coat of the eye-ball is sometimes popularly and conveniently distinguished as

— *Rheumatic Ophthalmia*, not only from the character of the pain and course of the disease, but from the *fact* that it occurs in persons affected with, or liable to other forms of rheumatism.

In the commencement of the disease, the PAIN is usually in the *temple*, extending downwards *towards* the *eyebrow* of the affected side. When the pain becomes seated within the ball, it is constant, but much more severe of an evening or late at night.

There is, at first, no appearance of disease on the eye. There is no peculiar discharge or irritability, nor any intolerance of light. Soon, however, the *surface* of the eye-ball *seems* to *redden*. The distended blood-vessels are seen, on closer inspection, to run in parallel lines *beneath* the conjunctiva, terminating at the margin of the cornea: they are so numerous as to have the effect of a continuous red surface. The hue, however, is not bright as in conjunctivitis, but rather of a peculiar dark *dusky* dingy shade.

The inflammation *may* become so severe as to extend and involve other coats of the eye.

The most important part of the

TREATMENT,

If *fever* is present, with full, hard, and frequent pulse and thirst, *Aconite* will be useful, and in the commencement of the attack, may arrest it entirely. But, generally, it will have progressed so far before the surgeon is consulted, that this remedy will not be applicable. If there are present *deep*, shooting pains in the head and through the orbit, pains aggravated by moving, pain in the temple and eyebrow, pupils dilated, or sparks before the eyes, *Belladonna* is appropriate. It will frequently be sufficient to complete the cure. *Spigelia* is important in this disease. It should be given when the pains are pressive or shooting, deep-seated in the orbits, a feeling as if the balls are too large, pains violent.

Colocynth will relieve when the pains are burning and extend deep in the head, with spasmodic pains in the side of the head and nose, and great restlessness.

Phytolacca is useful when the pains are of a *neuralgic* character, pressing pain in the upper parts of both eyes; the *left eye* is the seat of the disease.

We once knew a case of violent inflammation of the inner membranes of the eye, and finally amaurosis, produced by the application, in domestic practice, of a roasted poke-root to the back of the neck for headache.

We have used *Calendula* in several cases with admirable success. It is particularly serviceable when the inflammation has arisen from any mechanical injury, or from over-straining the eye as by looking at the sun in an eclipse.

CORNEITIS.

Acute inflammation of the Cornea is unimportant as a distinct species. What is sometimes so called, being strictly speaking, but a variety of *conjunctival* inflammation, over and about the cornea, in which that part of the eye *may* become involved and destroyed, as already mentioned. It occurs chiefly in young persons of a scrofulous constitution, about the age of puberty. Its TREATMENT requires no peculiar directions.

IRITIS, OR IRIDITIS.

Inflammation of the IRIS is accompanied with great sensibility of the eye, and intolerance of light, &c.

The pain is lancinating, extending from the eyebrow to the orbit, and darting in different directions through the ball.

There is *no redness* or change in the outer coat of the eye, though vessels of the second sometimes become affected and enlarged as in *sclerotitis* proper.

On the anterior surface of the iris, red vessels may be discovered; and its swelling, more or less in different parts, causes the *pupil* to appear *contracted* and irregular in shape.

Inflammation of this delicate organ rarely proceeds to ulceration, or even suppuration, but *adhesions* are not unfrequent or unimportant terminations. A deposit of lymph may be thrown out on the surface or rim of the iris, and by obstructing its freedom of action, interfere seriously with vision. Sometimes it is produced in so large a quantity as to fill the anterior chamber of the eye, occasioning immediate obstruction of sight.

The CAUSES of iritis are some of them common to other varieties of ophthalmia. The books enumerate wounds, bruises, sudden exposure to cold, or a strong light, and last, not least important of *predisposing* causes, those inseparables — those Siamese twins, — "syphilis and mercury" — We beg pardon: we ought, of course, to have said, "the *abuse* of mercury!!"

Scrofula, gout and rheumatism, are also mentioned as producing distinct varieties of iritis.

THE TREATMENT

— of iritis is very important, as it is not only a peculiarly acute and painful variety of inflammation, but runs its course very rapidly, and unless arrested or modified, by prompt and effectual measures, will probably occasion irreparable mischief.

The remedies directed for inflammation of other parts of the eye (especially of the sclerotica) are applicable to this affliction.

Aconite may be used, but in the more advanced stage, with pain in the head, *Belladonna* is preferable.

Mercurius cor. is useful when the sight is obstructed by exudations of lymph.

In the chronic stage of iritis, if the pupil is closed, relief is sometimes procured by the application of *Belladonna extract* around the lid; dilatation is produced and the sight restored.

Stramonium will answer the same purpose, or a solution of the latter may be put *into* the eye, while the *Bell.* is smeared on the outside. We have used the two for dilating the pupil preparatory to operations for cataract, and believe they do better than either alone.

Clematis erecta is regarded as a useful remedy in iritis. It is employed when the pain is of a smarting character and the veins are in an injected state.

Ranunculus bulbosus is valuable when, in the early stage, the pupils are fixed, neither dilate nor contract, a sense of pressure in the eyes — pain is burning.

PROCIDENTIA IRIDIS.

This is the name now most generally given to the case, where there is an external *protrusion* of the *iris* through a wound or ulcer in the *cornea* and its coverings.

The *pain* attending this accident is very severe, and the *intolerance of light* peculiar. The least impression of light on the exposed iris is excruciating.

The *pupil* always assumes an unusual *shape* — generally oval.

The form, however, depends on the site and size of the opening in the cornea.

Adhesion is apt to take place between the iris and the parts through which it passes, if it is allowed to remain but a short time exposed; and the protruded part becomes hardened and often ulcerated. Air and light seem sufficient irritants to this delicate part to excite inflammation.

If called soon after the accident has occurred, endeavor to *return the iris*. This can sometimes be easily effected; and when it is done, as it always should be, *immediately*, there will be no further difficulty. Even if some time has elapsed, this *replacement* should be *attempted*. We give this direction on the supposition of a wound. When ulceration of the cornea is the cause, the iris cannot be retained. If the protrusion has been allowed to remain until ulceration or adhesion has occurred, it is too late for mechanical restoration. All the *treatment* is then to *cure the ulcer* as soon as possible.

Calendula, internally and externally, will, in nearly all cases, effect a speedy healing of this.

CHAPTER XXV.

AMAUROSIS AND OPACITIES OF THE CORNEA—STAPHYLOMA AND ULCERS OF THE CORNEA.

AMAUROSIS or Nervous Blindness — Symptoms and Diagnosis — Causes — TREATMENT.

CATARACT, and other opacities, with illustrations.

OPACITIES OF THE CORNEA — Nebula, Albugo and Leucoma defined and treated — Means for generally removing *nebula* without inflammation or division of vessels.

ULCERS OF THE CORNEA, — Described and treated.

"STAPHYLOMA" — Restricted to a variety of opacity, with protrusion of the Cornea — Puncturing the eye — Means for avoiding that operation.

AMAUROSIS.

THE eye may appear sound and perfect so far as we can trace its complex and delicate mechanism; it may reflect the general healthfulness of the body, and seem to us still the mirror of the soul, varying its expression with every shade of thought or feeling, yet all the while be virtually dead — be no better than a glass eye, in respect to the great functions to which all its others are secondary. This *loss of sight* in a seemingly sound organ is distinguished as "nervous blindness." AMAUROSIS, the technical name, may, indeed, be defined *paralysis* of the *optic nerve.*

The early stages of this disease are apt to be neglected. The first SYMPTOM is a sensation of cloudiness, as if vision were obscured by smoke; or it seems to the patient as if threads were drawn across the eye. Sometimes he sees or imagines he sees blue and yellow specks; at others, brilliant spectra intermingled with darker spots. These obstructions or perversions of sight continue to increase, until the patient gradually loses the sense altogether. Not unfrequently, however, he is unconscious of his loss. It may be months after the subsidence of these anomalous appearances in one eye, before the person discovers that he is blind, although the probability is, that in all such cases the blindness was complete the moment he ceased to see the spectra alluded to.

The disease generally progresses with very little *pain*, sometimes none at all. The patient suffers more from anxiety of mind. In the early stages there is commonly, however, a determination of blood to the head.

The pupil is, in most cases, slightly dilated, and does not regularly enlarge and contract like the sound eye with varying degrees of light. The DIAGNOSIS is, however, often difficult. It will sometimes take several trials to find out which is the affected eye. We have found it necessary to blind the sound eye in order to ascertain the sensibility or lack of it in the other, as a completely blind eye will sometimes contract, on the approach of a strong light, from sympathy with its fellow.

The most obvious of assignable CAUSES is any excessive application of the sight, — reading, writing, fine needle-work, &c. Gazing at the sun to watch an eclipse, or at an exhibition of the Drummond light, has been known to produce it. These occasional causes, however, presuppose more general ones. The predisposing cause may be organic diseases of the brain or nerve. The patient is frequently ascertained to have been long afflicted with headache, costiveness, dry skin, &c. Syphilis and mercurialism may be also distinguished among remote causes. Congenital amaurosis may be set down as incurable.

TREATMENT.

The first thing, as common sense would dictate, is to prohibit much exercise of the eye. Reading, needle-work at night, and all straining of the sight, must be forbidden, as well as any particular use or abuse that may seem to have produced or to be aggravating the evil.

Belladonna is an important remedy in amaurosis, especially when the power of vision is nearly or quite extinct, with a sense of pressure in the eyes, occasional throbbing pain in the head, double vision, or the objects appear wholly or partially reversed. Blurs appear before the eyes like a fog or mist, red spots and flashes flit before the vision, a halo appears to surround the candle, the pupil permanently dilated. It is better suited to persons of full plethoric habits, often affected with congestions of the head.

Nux vomica is indicated by contracted pupil, spasmodic motion of the eyes, intolerance to light, intermittent vision, black spots before the eyes, stupefying headache, vertigo and vibrations of light, melancholy mood; particularly useful in cases caused by hard study or fine needle-work.

China is indicated by dilated pupil, insensibility to light or slightly contracted pupil, with the appearance of a white cloud before the eyes, and when the obscuration comes on suddenly; best for persons debilitated by loss of fluids and irritable.

Phosphorus, when the pupils are natural and objects seem to be enveloped in smoke, with black spots appearing before the vision when in a dark room, with luminous vibrations in the light of a candle, the candle appears to be surrounded by a green halo. The patient is gloomy; particularly useful in amaurosis of old persons and onanists.

Ruta graveolens is suitable for contracted pupils with spasmodic action of the lids, involuntary movement of and a sense of weight and pressure in the balls, and motes before the eyes, a *red* halo around the candle. The patient is peevish and irresolute.

Stramonium, when the eyes are staring and glistening, the pupils are dilated, with a sense of weight and tension in the eyes, and specks floating before them, black colors appear grey, there is a red halo around the candle, vertigo and headache. It is best for paralytic cases, and those caused by suppressed menses, hysteria, epilepsy or catalepsy.

China — two doses, at an interval of two weeks — cured a case of incipient amaurosis in a man of fifty years, brought on by excesses and intoxication. The pupils were dilated and scarcely movable, letters appear blurred, back ground of the eye looks smoky.

Nux vom., 12th, one dose, cured a lady of incipient amaurosis. Her sight frequently vanished; black spots like flies before her eyes, mist, constant lachrymation; cannot bear light, feels pressure in them; exerting them produces pain.

Phosphorus, 30, one dose, cured a boy of nine years — was hardly able to see a letter in daylight; all objects are obscured.

Ruta, pure tincture, one drop, cured, in eight days, a man of twenty-nine years. He was unable to read, a mist appeared to be before his eyes.

Sulphur, tr., one drop, cured incipient amaurosis in a woman of forty-five years. Had violent tearing in the forehead, feathery filaments before the eyes. (*Ruckert*, p. 64–5.)

The report of the following cases is furnished by Dr. C. Neidhard.

"The following is the history of a remarkable case of amaurosis attended by me in 1851. Miss M——, aged twenty-three, seamstress, had a white swelling when ten or eleven years old, which was cured, as the saying is, by some external application. A celebrated surgeon of this city, now deceased, gave a great deal of medicine, but only once some medicine as an external application for the amaurosis. For the last four years she has been nearly blind, and for the last three months she was at Willis' Eye Hospital, from whence she was discharged in a greatly aggravated state. The present symptoms, as I noted them down, were the following: — Black specks before the eyes (since homeopathic treatment also white specks), all the time sparks before the eyes, worse in the fore part of the day, better in the evening; the right eye is worse than the left, since she left the Hospital; there is also dimness of sight; she can not read even the largest print, can barely read a little with the left eye; when reading, weight across the eyes; appetite is also worse since she came from the Hospital, sour bitter taste in mouth in the morning; drowsiness and heaviness across the forehead. *Ruta graveolens*, externally and internally, the medicine first prescribed, produced sticking pain like pins on the top of the head, in the organ of benevolence, and fluttering in *left side*, but no improvement of her symptoms. After *Sepia* 30, an eruption like a ringworm appeared on the arm, but it had no effect on the eyes, it only relieved the sour bitter taste in the morning. *Calc. carb.* 3, gave an appetite without any other apparent effect; *Sepia*, again, in the high potence $\frac{1}{500}$, did no more. All these remedies were persevered in at least for one or two weeks each. I mention this particularly, because the subsequent surprising effect of another remedy might be ascribed by some to the reaction of the hospital treatment. Finally, after again reviewing and examining the case in all its bearings, she received internally, *Iodide of Starch* (*Iod. amylum*), from one to three grains daily, with the most beneficial result. It not only removed the white and black specks before the eyes as well as the sparks, but it particularly restored the sight which became nearly as good as ever; she could again read and do everything which she was accustomed to — being well aware that the disease had been brought on chiefly by her straining the eyes in her occupation as a seamstress; I particularly cautioned her to be careful about using them, but the disease has so far not returned.

"Next to *Iodine*, *Causticum* is a remedy which has been of service to me in amaurosis of elderly persons. *Spigelia* is akin to the following group of symptoms: burning, itching in the eyes, sparks before the eyes all day, but particularly at twilight, stiffness in the eyelids, attacks of sudden blindness. Prescribing once *Spigelia* for a headache in a case of diabetes, it produced sudden and entire blindness, which was finally with some difficulty overcome by *Calc. carb. and Bellad.* In the archives of homeopathy, two cases are mentioned in which *Caustic*, given for another disease, caused total blindness; in one case the patient remained blind. In a case of sudden attack of blindness with *double vision*, vertigo and sick headache, I have exhibited *Cicuta virosa* in alternation with *Sulph.*, which was sufficient to cure the disease.

In *Saturnine amaurosis* in a gentleman engaged in the manufacture of white lead, *Plumbum metall.* 3, effected a complete cure. *Symptoms:* like vapor before the eyes, severe costiveness three days or more; no evacuation, appetite good, tongue yellow-coated; evening worse.

"I will also mention in this place that in all swellings and excrescences of the eyelids known in ophthalmic works under the name of *Hordeolum*, *Milleum*, *Verrum*, *Condyloma*, no remedy has been found superior to *Thuja;* this was also the principal remedy used in a scirrhous tumor of the eyes in the case of the Austrian Marshal Radetsky."

CATARACT.

This is, perhaps, the most interesting cause of blindness next to that last treated of. While, however, amaurosis is properly described as "nervous blindness," this as well as corneal affections, to be next considered, may be distinguished as *mechanical* blindness. *That* may be only a functional disease; *these* are necessarily organic. In the former, the proper organ of vision is effected, in the latter some of its media are alone concerned. Hence the obstruction of vision may, in some of these cases, admit of a merely mechanical remedy. This being especially the case in regard to the various forms of cataract, that subject will be fully treated of in Part II.

FIG. 6.

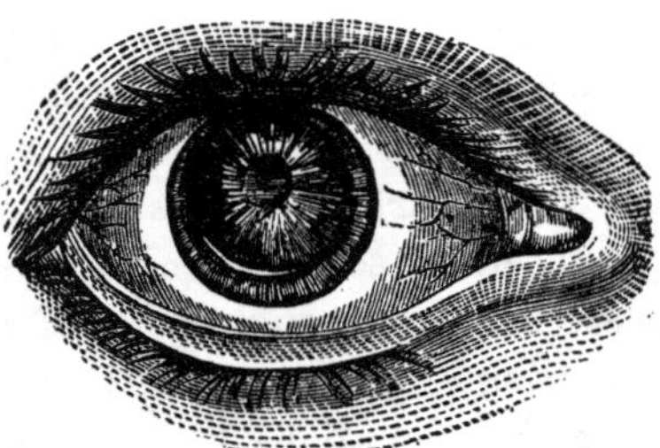

FIG. 7.

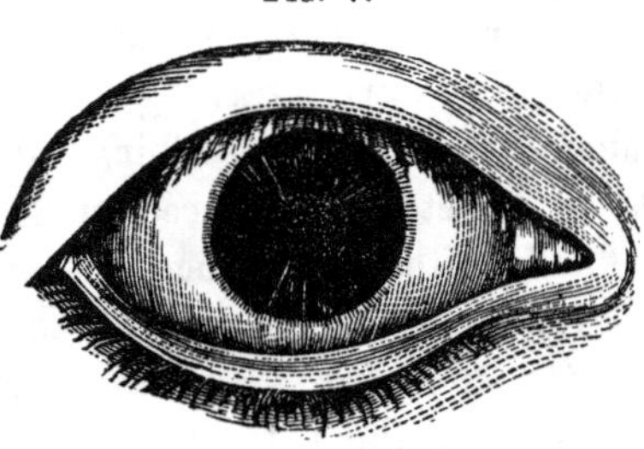

The general distinction between this affection and opacities *of the cornea*, is, that the opacity is here *behind* the pupil, either in the crystaline lens itself, or its covering. Hence by the removal or absorption of these parts, vision may be restored. The general appearance of the three principal forms of cataract is presented in the foregoing cuts: Fig. 6, representing the *hard* LENTICULAR; Fig. 7, the *soft* LENTICULAR CATARACT, and Fig. 8, the *posterior* CAPSULAR.

FIG. 8.

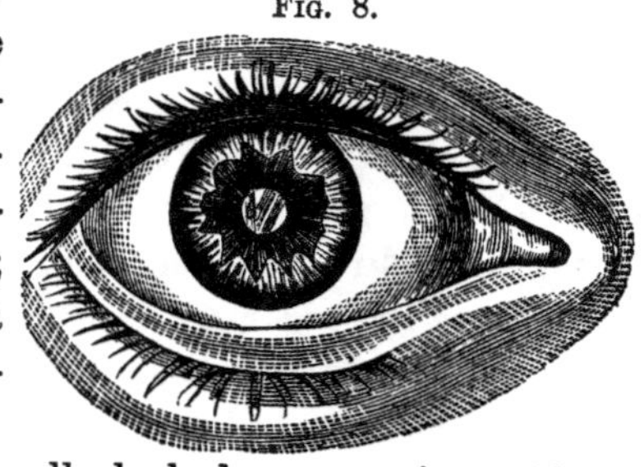

Though this disease is generally looked upon as incurable by any course of medication, and the *knife or needle* is the only remedy supposed to be efficacious in removing the difficulty, *experience* in the use of homeopathic remedies has, in numerous instances, proven that it not only *may* but often is *cured;* especially in the early stages and sometimes even after the lapse of much time, and the disease has become "confirmed." We may yet hope to accomplish much more.

On this subject, Dr. H. V. Mallon, in the British Journal of Homeopathy, writes as follows:

"No medicine or internal treatment has as yet been of any avail in confirmed and ripe cataracts; this was left for better days in medical science, and homeopathy has given us means of cure, which were totally unknown before. I do not mean to say, be it well understood, that homeopathy will entirely supersede surgery, or that we are not to trust this latter means or ever employ it—no; but I wish to draw attention to these three remarks only—that first; In many cases homeopathy will cure, completely cure, 'real cataracts,' even old and ripe ones; second—in many more it will prevent the progress of the cataract on the other eye, when as yet only one is affected; third—that if it does not always succeed in curing, it will always prepare the whole constitution for the surgical operation, prevent inflammatory accidents after it, and secure its success.

"This part of medical treatment has been, to this day, too much neglected, because, to our eyes, this more or less exorganic body seemed not fit for medical treatment, and because we have been accustomed to hear that surgical operation only is of any use.

We have left aside the internal treatment which will often be crowned with far more success than is generally expected. Not the least process in the human body, morbid or natural, can take place without the whole constitution taking part in it. We can not expect that an organ of the body, be it ever so small, can become affected quite independently of the organism, but that it becomes affected in consequence of morbid process existing, though not seen, in the organism itself. I am as far from admitting such confirmed notions as I would be right to admit that the very same organ has no common tie with the rest of the body, and is not one constituent part of it by its nerves, its vessels and all its textures.

"If, therefore, one part of the body is diseased, we must not direct our treatment to it solely, and use what is called a local treatment alone. We must act on the whole constitution in the same way as we would direct our attention to the whole tree when it bears decayed fruit. In this case, and for this very simple reason, it is not only advisable, but necessary, to have an internal, general treatment, and this way of attending to disease will prevent many a failure, and the harm which might ensue from a local treatment. In a case of cataract, therefore, the whole constitution must be acted upon as in all similar diseases. Our Materia Medica has many a remedy against such a state. My intention is not to discuss here the comparative value of each of these, but to make a few remarks on the treatment in general. The remedies reckoned the most important, are *Sulph*, *Silic.*, *Cann.*, *Phos.*, *Calc. and Con.* The antipsorics, of course, must form the basis of the treatment, as the whole constitution must undergo a change from the action of the remedy, which must extend to the primary cause of the disease. This cause is what has been called *psora.* If the psora has been acquired by the patient and the cataract has developed itself after the disappearance, more or less sudden, of the itch, even many years afterwards, the treatment will not only be easy, but sure.

"I have remarked in the few cases which came under my notice, that under the influence of antipsorics, and particularly of *Sulph.*, an eruption was produced, with the intensity of which, the symptoms of the cataract gradually amended. This speaks for the use of antipsorics at once. If there are no accidents which would prevent this mode of treatment, the antipsorics, and at the head of them *Sulph.*, must, therefore, be resorted to, in one or two doses, at intervals of a day, and not repeated till their action is over. Sometimes there are accidental symptoms, which, though not very prominent, will require to be removed by an apsoric before the antipsoric can have any action at all on the constitution; and this is true in other cases, as well as the one under our present notice.

"Should the psora not have been acquired but inherited, the treatment will be longer and more uncertain, particularly if the cataract is already advanced; it is then habitually connected with a bad state of the general health, a long chronic affection, which is to be considered, not as the cause of the cataract, but as its accompaniment only; and the symptoms of the general health keeping pace with them.

"Here the treatment must, at first, be directed to the general health; as long as this is no better, not only will the cataract not be amended, but will make progress, and its cure will be rendered impossible. In regulating the general health of the patient, the cataract will be benefited and its progress retarded. When the health is restored to its normal state, then the eye should alone be attended to, and then only will the disease yield to the treatment. It is not to be understood by that, that no remedial treatment must be used; on the contrary, it will always prepare the constitution, as we have already mentioned.

"According to these views, *Sulph.* is the first remedy to be given; one or two globules of a high potency. Should no improvement follow, another antipsoric to be given in the same way. I do not mention any one in particular, because there is a great danger in prescribing a remedy from a few isolated symptoms. The remedy must be chosen according to the symptoms of the case, and with the greatest care and exactitude, for it is not the size of the dose nor its repetition, nor a succession of remedies, which will be of use in cataract any more than in other chronic cases; it is the right choice of the remedy, of which one single globule will then do much more than many doses of ill-chosen remedies. It is not possible to say that in this or that species of cataract, this or that remedy will cure. The *tout ensemble* of the symptoms must always decide us in the choice of the remedy, and in all cases, no second remedy is to be given before the first has exhausted its action."

The selection of the proper remedy is sometimes a very difficult matter, owing to the fact that the patient appears to be in good health, or at least he does not complain of any pain or unpleasant sensation in the *eye;* the simple fact of *blindness* being the only difficulty. Where, however, there are any symptoms of deranged functions in other parts of the system, or any hereditary dyscrasia taint, or any evidence of suppressed eruptions, the state of the systems must be prescribed for rather than any particular symptoms. When a remedy is selected, its effects should be very closely watched, and if beneficial results are noticed, great care should be exercised not to interfere with its action, by a repetition of the same remedy or the administration of any other, before the first has spent its whole force.

In a case of cataract of ten years' standing, a single dose of *Sulphur* 30, produced a slow but steady improvement in the general health and in the sight for two months, and then the improvement ceased for some ten days, when a repetition of the remedy produced no effect. A dose of *Aurum*, given two weeks after, produced a decided improvement, and the patient was, two months from the time of the exhibition of the *Aurum*, nearly well and constantly improving in health and sight.

The selection may be made from the following remedies, as near as possible, in accordance with the totality of the symptoms: *Sulphur*, *Aurum*, *Conium*, *Phosphorus*, *Causticum*, *Silicea*, *Hyoscyamus*, *Euphrasia*, *Nitric acid*, *Opium*, *Pulsatilla*, *Electro-galvanism and Phytolacca decandria.*

We have produced decidedly beneficial effects by the use of *Phytolacca decandria* in the early stages of cataract. One case was entirely cured in two weeks by drop doses of the third dilution of the tr. daily, and the tincture diluted with water in the proportion of twenty to one, applied to the surface of the eye. Several other cases have been greatly benefited and the progress of the disease apparently arrested in one eye, where the other had for some time been blind.

Phosphorus is said to have cured cases of cataract when the lens was of a green color, sometimes called GLAUCOMA.

Conium is particularly indicated when the opacity arises from a wound or blow upon the eye, or where the blindness is but partial and the patient complains of dazzling light, with black spots or colored bands before the eyes, objects appear red; the ball of the eye looks yellow or pale red.

OPACITIES OF THE CORNEA.

NEBULA, ALBUGO, LEUCOMA.

NEBULA, or "cloudiness," is the result of acute ophthalmia of the conjunctiva, leaving a preternatural deposit which has become permanent, and even organized, between that membrane and the cornea. It may be attended also with an enlargement of the vessels of the conjunctiva where it covers the cornea.

This species of blindness is not complete. It is of course *external* to the cornea itself, and comparatively *superficial.* The opacity may cover the whole of the cornea, yet the patient can distinguish objects as through a vail; and his iris and pupil may be seen through it. At other times the nebula is only scattered, or in distinct *specks*, each of which is furnished with separate vessels. These vessels continue to support (or prevent the absorption of) the deposit, which occasions the difficulty to vision.

ALBUGO in some respects resembles nebula, chiefly differing from it in being *deeper seated.* It is also referable to some preternatural deposit of lymph between the laminæ of the *cornea itself*, to which it gives a *pearly white* appearance.

LEUCOMA differs from the two other varieties of opacity in being more dense, and of a *chalky white* color, although with a shining aspect. It is a transformation of the substance of the cornea itself and an adhesion to the mucous covering. It may result from a small pox pustule or a wound in the part.

TREATMENT OF NEBULA, &C.

The remarks that were made when speaking upon the subject of cataract, are applicable here.

For *specks on the cornea* use, both internally and locally, some of the following remedies: *Belladonna, Sulphur, Hepar, Chelidonium, Conium, Nit. acid and Arsenicum.*

For *opacities* use *Sulphur, Cannabis, Nit. acid, Capsicum and Phytolacca.* With the two latter remedies used locally and internally, we have relieved very obstinate cases, after the other remedies of the books had failed. Dr. Dudgeon reports a case (British Journal of Homeopathy, Vol. II, page 320) of *opacity of the cornea* (*Pannus*), cured by introducing into the eye, matter taken from the eye of a child affected with *purulent ophthalmia.* There was great photophobia, the cornea highly vascular, dull and irregular, with granulations, conjunctiva and sclerotica very vascular, upper lids covered with a mass of fleshy granulations. The inoculation with the matter produced great inflammation and suppuration, but finally terminated in a complete cure.

ULCERS OF THE CORNEA.

These not unfrequently result from the same causes as in other parts of the body, and are more serious, as always endangering vision. They occur not only as the consequences of mechanical injury, or of some variety of ophthalmia, but also of some strong or peculiarly irritating substances thrown into the eye.

The *whole cornea* may be in an ulcerated condition, or the ulcer may be very *small*, appearing on it but as a *speck.* The latter is not always the less dangerous form, as the ulceration is often "burrowing;" and may work its way deep in between the layers of the cornea until it spreads all over the anterior chamber of the eye.

The *edges* of the corneal ulcer are generally elevated and rough; and its *surface* is commonly covered with a brownish pus, similar to that of indolent ulcers in other parts.

Extreme *pain* frequently exists, not only in the ball but the *lids,*—attributable, mainly, to the irritation of the rough and projecting edges of the ulcer.

The principle remedies directed by the authorities for this affection, are *Belladonna, Arsenicum, Calcarea, Euphrasia, Hepar, Lachesis, Mercurius and Sulphur.* Of these, *Calcarea and Euphrasia* have been the most serviceable.

Causticum, though not mentioned in the books as a remedy for ulcers on the cornea, should be placed at the head of the list. Few remedies will compare favorably with it when properly used. It should be applied locally as well as given internally. The local solution should be strong enough to produce slight smarting. The *sesqui-carbonate of potash* is the best for this purpose ; let it be applied either in solution or in form of a powder, with a camel's hair pencil, fixing the ball with a speculum while the application is being made, keeping the eye covered with a poultice of ulmus during the interval. Wash the eye well with warm milk and water at each dressing. As soon as the ulcers assume a healthy appearance, discontinue the caustic applications, but continue the milk and water.

We have had no difficulty in speedily removing the ulcers from the cornea by this course of treatment. If active inflammation should arise, as sometimes occurs, discontinue other remedies and use *Aconite* until the inflammation subsides.

If there is any eruption on the surface of the body or about the face, you should use *Sulphur* for a while before using the *Causticum*.

STAPHYLOMA

is the name given to a disease of the substance of the cornea, resulting in thickening and opacity of its layers, and a considerable protrusion of the anterior surface. This last circumstance gives name to the affection. "Staphyloma" means swelling out *like a grape*. There may be staphyloma of the sclerotic coat also ; but that is less frequent and less important. "Staphyloma Iridis" was spoken of under the more descriptive appellation of "Prolapsus or Procidentia of the Iris." Confining the term to cases in which the cornea is involved, —

"*Complete* Staphyloma" implies that the *whole* of the cornea has become *opaque*.

"*Incomplete* Staphyloma" is when the cornea is still in some degree *transparent*, or at least *translucent*, and vision to a proportionate degree is yet possible.

In advanced stages of the disease, the before enlarged cornea is sometimes absorbed, when both the anterior and posterior chambers of the eye seem to be filled with matter more or less opaque.

The internal and local use of *Arnica* has been successful in the removal of this disease in the earlier stage. The authors treated one bad case with *Calendula*, and in three months all deformity disappeared, and the sight, though not perfect, was so far restored as that he could see to read and write.

In the advanced stage of the disease a restoration of the power of vision is hopeless, as the tissues are too much disorganized. Subdue the inflammation by such means as are directed for ophthalmia.

A case of opacity of the cornea, of three years' standing, resulting from violent inflammation brought on by drinking freely of ice water when quite warm. First, under allopathic treatment, one eye entirely disorganized, could not see objects out of the other. Dr. Hunt applied electro-galvanism. The patient was finally so entirely cured that he was able to resume his trade — that of a carpenter.

CHAPTER XXVI.

AFFECTIONS OF THE EYE, CONTINUED.

HYDROPHTHALMIA — General and partial — Symptoms and progress — Treatment for avoiding paracentesis oculi — That operation a dernier resort, and then but a palliative. — PTERYGIUM — Description and varieties. — ENCANTHIS — Distinction from pterygium — Inconvenience and frequent malignancy — Excision not "the only remedy" — Two cases in proof. — HORDEOLUM.

DROPSY OF THE EYE.

UNCOMPLICATED HYDROPHTHALMIA is a disease of rare occurrence, even in those constitutionally predisposed to serous accumulations in other parts.

The SYMPTOMS are a *gradual* enlargement of the globe of the eye, without, at first, much pain or injury to the sense of vision.

As, however, the accumulation increases, the membranes become very tense, and the eye-ball is visibly *protuberant* from the socket. The *pain* then becomes excessive, and sometimes extends to other parts, giving rise, among other complaints, to violent cephalalgia. At this stage, also, the *sight* is considerably affected. The aqueous humor becomes turbid and opaque. The iris looks as if deeper seated in the eye than natural; and, whenever the eye-ball is moved, appears to be floating and tremulous. Finally, if the morbid fluid is not absorbed or evacuated, irritation and active inflammation set in, and terminate in *suppuration*, to the destruction of the eye.

Partial serous *effusions* sometimes occur between the separate coats, — as between the sclerotic and the choroid, or the choroid and the retina, — but these cases are still less frequent than the accumulation within the chambers. The *vitreous humor* is sometimes absorbed, we are informed, in consequence of the *pressure* from effusion between the choroid and sclerotic coats.

TREATMENT.

Like many other chronic affections, there are so few subjective symptoms that we have to prescribe more from general than local indications.

In the early stage of this complaint, while there is yet some pain and inflammatory symptoms remaining, *Arnica* will prove serviceable; especially if there is soreness and a bruised feeling on moving the eye — the pupil contracted.

Arsenicum is useful when there are burning pains, beating in the head, heat about the eyes, fullness of the face, great weakness and loss of appetite, a sense of prostration.

If it is connected with scrofula or any eruptive disease, *Sulphur* should be given first and then followed, if necessary, by *Ars. or Arn.*

Iodine will be found serviceable when there is much emaciation, with glandular swellings or a tendency to dropsy in other parts, great nervous irritability.

Should the ACCUMULATION *go on* notwithstanding these measures, or should it have been too great, at first, making *immediate relief* indispensable, the surgeon may be obliged to

— PUNCTURE THE EYE. This operation can be performed with a common lancet, if a couching-needle is not at hand. The point may be introduced into the anterior chamber through the cornea; or — where it is less likely to do permanent injury — behind the junction of the cornea with the sclerotic coat, into the posterior chamber, as is usually directed in operating for cataract.

This *tapping* of the eye should be regarded as a mere *palliative;* requiring the same means afterward to obviate reaccumulation, which if used in time, or to a sufficient extent, would have prevented the necessity for resorting to it. It is not a triumph of surgery, but a confession of its inefficiency; and unlike amputation, and some other of its "*handy* work," it is not final, removing for ever the evidence against itself.

PTERYGIUM.

This is a name given to a very common disease, or rather accidental formation, which is not generally of sufficient importance to be accounted morbid. It may, in fact, be nothing but hypertrophy and extension of the Plica Semilunaris. It is a mere membranous reflection of a portion of the conjunctiva, appearing as a triangular patch at the inner canthus, and spreading from the caruncula lachrymalis towards the cornea.

In its early stages, it is *light-colored*, containing few blood vessels. As it is thus but a slight disfigurement, and no inconvenience, it excites but little attention. When inflamed it reddens, and its vessels are then very distinct.

It may *extend*, however, so as to cover more or less of the cornea. Its growth is more rapid when irritated or inflamed. It rarely spreads all over the cornea, commonly ceasing to advance after covering a small segment of it. We have seen several cases where the growth had commenced from each corner of the eye, and gone on to meet the opposite one in the center.

That proceeding from the external canthus is still less serious than the other, and sometimes distinguished as "pinguicula," from its more frequently fatty appearance. Two varieties are mentioned by the writers, the merely *membranous* and the *fleshy*. The variety called PANNUS, is sometimes cancerous.

Pterygium is an abnormal or adventitious growth, and if not inflamed, can not properly be looked upon as a *disease*.

TREATMENT.

If it is inflamed, use such means for removing the inflammation as are directed for ophthalmia.

It sometimes grows suddenly from the surface, having been inflamed by some injury. In such a case, *Arnica or Calendula* will most likely subdue the inflammation, and with the subsidence of that, the pterygium disappears. So favorable a result need not, however, be expected very often.

If, then, there be present no inflammation and the growth has not been removed in whole, or nearly so, by the treatment, the best plan is to *operate — cut it off.* The operation is *simple and safe.* [For the mode of operating, see Part II.]

ENCANTHIS.

This affection of the eye is nearly related to that last described. It is, however, of a more decidedly morbid character, and not unfrequently malignant. Even the "encanthis *benigna*," so called, is a source of great inconvenience. It arises from the same parts as the pterygium; but while that appears as a mere superfluous fold of the mucous membrane, perhaps a little thickened, forming as it were an additional *over*-coat to a part of the eye,

ENCANTHIS is a substantial enlargement or out-growth of the caruncula lachrymalis, and plica semilunaris. It is soft and of a livid hue. As it enlarges it becomes smooth on its surface, which is seen to be numerously supplied with varicose vessels.

Three consequences of this excresence may be distinguished: first, by its size and position it prevents complete closure of the eye, and otherwise impedes the free play of the *lids;* next, both by compression and displacement of the *puncta lachrymalia*, it keeps the eye constantly suffused with *tears;* and, lastly, by these and other modes of irritation, it excites and keeps up a troublesome OPHTHALMIA. Other parts may be so involved as gradually to destroy the whole *eye-ball.*

The MALIGNANT, or, as it used to be called, "inveterate ENCANTHIS," may become very *large*, and perhaps hardened, with lancinating pains, proneness to bleed, and other usual cancerous characteristics.

"The only remedy for this disease," according to prevalent authorities, is *excision* of the caruncula lachrymalis and valvula semilunaris; and we are informed, that even this "frequently fails."

How far we are from being disposed to adopt this view, may be judged from our usual protests against these "necessarily incurable" *judgments*. There is nothing in the nature of the affection in question, or of the parts affected, to render all the resources of the *healing* art unavailing. We can not determine what proportion of cases ought to be cured in a disease of such rare occurrence; but this much we *can* say, — that the *only* four cases that ever fell under our notice *were cured*

TREATMENT.

In the early stage, *Pulsatilla* will be quite sure to remove it. If, however, a high degree of inflammation has arisen before remedies are resorted to, *Aconite* should be used until the acute symptoms have subsided, after which, *Causticum*, applied locally and used internally, will generally complete the cure. *Arsenicum* may, in some cases, be preferable; especially in pale and sickly-looking persons. If the patient be scrofulous, give *Sulphur*, and follow by *Causticum* or *Arsenicum*, if necessary. If pus has formed, give *Hepar* for a day or two, and then puncture; dress with a poultice after puncturing, and wash out the cavity with a weak solution of *Causticum*. *Staphysagria* is recommended as a useful remedy after *Aconite*.

Thuja is worthy of much confidence in this disease, especially in the early stage before the tumor has become much enlarged or indurated. If it assume a *malignant* form and does not yield to remedies apparently indicated by the symptoms in a short time, but continues to increase, the better plan is to *extirpate* the tumor by *Caustic* as soon as possible.

A case of this kind was treated by one of the authors, several years since — an aged gentleman, Mr. D. W——, of Erie county, in this State. The case and the cure were well known, as the disease had been pronounced *cancer* by all who saw it. The tumor, excresence, or whatever it is to be called, was distinctly "encanthis" in respect of its location and origination. It had grown, however, as large as a butternut, — discharged a sanious and corrosive fluid, and was overspread with a net-work of varicose vessels, which poured out their contents on the slightest touch.

The course adopted was the following. The eye was first protected by a slippery elm poultice, wet with vinegar, and the pencil of potassa fusa was freely applied to the cancerous growth, and kept there for several minutes, so as at once to disorganize nearly the whole of it. It was dressed with the simple slippery elm, which was directed to be renewed every three or four hours (a very necessary precaution in all such cases, in order to absorb all the matter as quickly as it is discharged). The sore was further washed in a strong solution of the sesqui-carb., which article, in the powdered state, was also sprinkled occasionally on the face of the slippery elm poultice. After the sloughing of the first eschar, whatever portions of the diseased mass remained were retouched with the caustic, until the whole face of the sore assumed a healthy aspect. It was then regularly dressed as before stated. In the course of a few weeks it all healed up soundly. Eight years have since passed without any recurrence of the disease.

HORDEOLUM,

—which means a "little barley-corn," is the name given to what is called in the vernacular a *sty*, and may be briefly defined as a small *inflamed* tumor on the eyelid. It appears to be simply a modification, from the confined situation, of what would elsewhere become a boil.

The STY, or boil on the eyelid, increases but slowly in size, and although it finally suppurates, shows little or *no* tendency to spontaneous *opening*.

It may remain a long time stationary as a little yellow-topped pimple. If not interfered with it may be eventually absorbed, or changed into a hard indolent tumor, sometimes called grando or chalazion.

Pulsatilla will remove this disease almost invariably in the early stage, before there is much inflammation and fever, but if not used thus early, *Aconite* should be used until the fever subsides. *Puls.* may then be resorted to, or if it becomes chronic and hard, and but slightly painful, except when pressed upon, *Staphysagria* will be beneficial.

If it is quite painful, burning and smarting, *Puls.* having failed, *Arsen.* will be appropriate. When inflamed it should be kept moist and warm by the proper dressings.

CHAPTER XXVII.

AFFECTIONS OF THE MOUTH AND THROAT.

AFFECTIONS OF THE TEETH. — Necessity for studying — Serious disease caused by "bad teeth" — Cases — Crowded Teeth — Caries — TOOTHACHE, neuralgic, rheumatic and from decay — Palliatives and radical cure for the latter — Cleanliness.

EXTRACTION OF TEETH. — Forceps — the dentist's *kit* unnecessary — The new *molar forceps,* with two other pair, all-sufficient — directions for using — hemmorhage — superfine elm *flour.*

EPULIS, or tumor of the gums — neglected beginning and destructive progress — early and later medical treatment — operation. — RANULA, and other tumors or obstructions — incision or abscision.

TONSILLITIS, &c. — Acute inflammation. — CHRONIC ENLARGEMENT — excision — its danger?

CHOKING — symptoms and effects of the accident — pushing *down* or pulling *up* the obstructing substance? — Various means and methods.

AFFECTIONS OF THE TEETH.

WE shall not, at this time, attempt to go into this too much neglected subject, with the minuteness of detail that properly belongs to Dental Surgery. As, however, professed Dentists are not always to be found, except in cities and towns of considerable size, it is absolutely necessary for the *general practitioner of medicine* to understand and practice more or less of *dentistry.* So far as the mechanical part of the business is concerned, with the exception of simple tooth-drawing, we shall leave you to obtain your knowledge from the excellent works on Dental Surgery, which have been published within a few years past. But the *physiology* and *pathology* of the teeth have a much greater claim on your attention. As surgeons, and even as physicians, you are bound to study these subjects. The advantages of a good set of teeth, and of a good *use* of them, in mastication, are little appreciated, and still less are all the *disadvantages* of diseased or decayed teeth.

It must be understood, then, that the local pain and inconvenience of bad teeth are not alone the matters worthy of consideration in this connection; but that, in a great variety of serious affections, the future health, nay, the very life of the patient, may depend entirely on the removal of the decayed teeth. So long as this prolific source of general and local disease remains in the mouth, all your efforts at a removal of other affections will often prove abortive.

Numerous diseases affecting the general system may be traced directly to diseased teeth or gums as their exciting and sustaining CAUSE. Neuralgia, ulceration of the tonsils, tumors or ulcers on the tongue, often becoming malignant, violent and continued headache, with glandular swellings in the throat, proceeding in some cases to ulceration, not unfrequently arise entirely from this source. Serious and intractable disease of the stomach, with general disorder from imperfect digestion, is a still more frequent and less suspected result.

We have been not unfrequently called to patients, during the last five years, who were laboring under chronic diseases of various forms, for which they had been treated by Allopathists, Eclectics and Homeopathists, in turn, for years, but without receiving any material benefit — the ill success owing entirely, we have no doubt, to the failure to recognize and remove the *dental* cause. On examining the mouths of such patients, we have found, in some instances, not more than one or two diseased teeth, but in others, five or six, and perhaps a dozen or more old rotten snags or roots of teeth, which had long since become insensible and ceased to attract attention. Around them was collected a gluey substance, which, if brought in close proximity to the olfactories, would impart the most horridly sickening and putrescent smell imaginable. The gums all around were swollen, inflamed, and more or less ulcerated. Yet of this condition the patients did not complain, nor had any of their medical attendants inquired about it. *Our first prescription* in these cases was "*a dentist*" — utterly refusing to make any other until *all* the diseased teeth and fangs were removed, and the mouth and gums cleansed.

In numerous cases, where the patient and friends had abandoned all hope of recovery, this dental operation, and cleansing of the mouth — the removal of this "Augean Stable" in the highway to the stomach — has been followed by a rapid restoration of general health, without the aid of any other means than perhaps bathing and gentle tonics. We might mention numerous cases.

One young lady of Cincinnati had been for two or three years declining — had been sent from home to consult an eminent stethoscopist and medical professor in relation to her case. He, in connection with his colleagues in the college, after several months' unsuccessful efforts for her relief, pronounced her case one of incurable disease of the heart. She was sent home, with a written request from her medical adviser, that her case be brought before the faculty of another old and celebrated medical college. Their decision in the case confirmed the former diagnosis. Some weeks after this last consultation, one of the authors was requested by the parents of the patient to examine and give an opinion as to the probable *result* — they had no doubt of the correctness of the diagnosis which had been given. In the course of his inquiries, he naturally, in searching for the cause of her bad symptoms, looked into her mouth, when he found, what had been suspected, a number of diseased teeth and decaying fangs, in the condition before described. The services of a dentist were prescribed, and proved most effectual. After removing all the decayed teeth and fragments, the gums soon healed, and, with a little treatment, all symptoms of *heart disease* disappeared, and her health became good.

A gentleman of Cincinnati had been afflicted for a long time with neuralgia and dyspepsia, with numerous other derangements — so that he had been, for months, unable to attend to business, and suffered much, at all times, from severe pains in different parts of his body and head. Though he had many decayed teeth, as they did not ache, he had never suspected that they were doing any harm. His physicians had never intimated anything about injury from his teeth; and when we informed him that they were the cause of all his sufferings, he could not be made to believe it, until we scraped off a portion of the matter from one of them, and induced him to smell and taste it, when the terrible nausea and *vomiting* produced by so small a portion, soon satisfied him. His cure was easily effected by a removal of the foul source of disease.

How any physician, especially a homeopathist, can expect to get the proper effect, or any at all, from minute portions of medicine, while such an amount of filth and *poison* is in the patient's mouth, coming in contact and intermingling with it, we are at a loss to conjecture. The very effluvia from the mouth is enough, in numerous cases, to sicken a well person, and taint the air of the room to an extent far more obnoxious to the effects of homeopathic remedies than any quantity of "perfumery," *camphor or musk*, that we often meet with. What wonder, then, that old cases of "*dyspepsia*," "*general debility*," *&c.*, *&c.*, resist all medication.

To proceed with the different dental diseases, we will first mention

— CROWDED TEETH. The irritation of the gums, caused by the teeth crowding too closely together, will often produce inflammation and ulceration, and if the latter be around the posterior teeth, it not unfrequently produces dangerous inflammation of the tonsils and pharynx. Crowded front teeth will also cause ulceration of the gums, and even the bone itself may not escape. TREATMENT is simple. Extract a tooth from the crowded space — remove the cause, and nature will generally repair the injury. If not, treat the ulcer as in other cases.

CARIOUS TEETH is the term used to denote decay of the body of the teeth, while ULCERATED TEETH is applied to the disease of the fangs or roots. In the case of superficial caries, if the tooth has never, or but seldom ached, and is not now tender, the decayed portion may be removed by the proper dental operations, and the tooth *filled* and saved. But if it is painful and sore, or tender to the touch, by all means extract; for, even if it be cleaned and filled, it will most likely still ache; and if so, it is more than probable that there is disease at the roots, which will do more or less injury to the general health, besides constantly annoying the patient by the local pain, and endangering the jaw

TOOTHACHE. — *Odontalgia.*

The numerous remedies for the common forms of toothache, with their characteristic symptoms, will be found in perusing the homeopathic works. It is therefore unnecessary for us to treat of these forms of *odontalgia*, mostly affecting decaying teeth.

The *rheumatic* form, however, which not only affects the decayed but sound teeth, as well as the jaws, face, head and eyes, is ably treated of in the following excellent article furnished us, among others, by Dr. C. Neidhard, in reply to our inquiries as to the results of his experience.

"*Odontalgia and Cephalalgia Rheumatica.*"

"The symptoms are of the most diversified character; it either affects one or two teeth, or the whole side of the face; sometimes it springs from one side to the other. In severe cases the pain extends to the eyes and ears, often accompanied by swelling of the gums and cheeks. The pain is of a gnawing, aching kind, in some instances an abscess is formed. The cephalic rheumatism generally attacks only one side of the head, shooting along the temporal and occipital muscles, and not unfrequently coryza is present. I have reason to suppose that this affection is confined to this continent, for I find no description of such a toothache as prevailing to any extent in other countries, in the literature of homeopathy; it has the characteristic symptoms of being ameliorated by heat and perspiration and aggravated by cold, particularly draughts of air.

"The remedy on which I principally rely in this complaint, is *Calc. carb.*, from the second to the thirtieth dilution. Rheumatic toothaches and headaches, which had lasted for six months, and even for years, were relieved in a few days, although allopathic, and in some cases homeopathic treatment, had been resorted to in vain. In order to illustrate its action more fully, I will detail some of the cases wherein I have found it useful.

"*Case* 1. For ten days, pain in the malar bone under the eye, the pain is throbbing and worse at night, dark-red, swelling of the gums; the pain shoots also from the lower jaw to the right ear; amelioration from heat and perspiration.

"*Case* 2. Rheumatic pain on the top of head, forehead and arm joints, brought on and increased by draughts of cold air — better in warmth; also pain in bones of face — worse at night.

"*Case* 3. Miss C——. Aching pain in bones of right lower jaw and teeth towards the center; worse in draught of air, with swelling of bones and gums.

"*Case* 4. Mr. J. N——. Dull heavy pain as if in the bones of the right side of the face, moving about from one side to the other in the lower jaw, zygomatic process of temporal bone, cheek bone, and top of head. The patient had suffered excessively for months, and had been attended by a well-known professor of this city distinguished for his enmity to homeopathy. This one had prescribed *Lupuline*, a new hobby, with zinc pills, but with only transient relief. The all-powerful blue pill was then resorted to with like effect, with several more remedies. The pain was extremely violent, without intermission day or night, aggravated by the least draught of air. After receiving the first dose of *Calc. carb.*, he slept for the first time for many nights. *Calc. carb.*, 30, six and and three, given at longer and shorter intervals, entirely cured him: when after the lapse of some months it returned again, it was removed by the same remedy.

"*Case* 5. Martha J——. Similar pain to the last, aggravated by draughts of air, with bluish swelling of gums.

"*Case* 6. Mrs. B——. This case presented swelling of parotid glands with sharp, shooting, drawing, and sometimes beating pain in zygomatic process of temporal bone, sore to touch, aggravated at night, preventing sleep, relieved only by applications of heat; draught of air causes a return of it, gums red and swollen; pain extends to ear and head.

"*Case* 7. In this case the pain came on periodically from ten in the morning to five in the afternoon; it principally affected the bones around the eyes, first one side and then the other; there was also indigestion, hot bread producing pain in the stomach. The conditions, under which the pain was increased or diminished, were the same as in the other cases.

"*Case* 8. Miss C——. In addition to a pain over the eyes similar to the last mentioned, there was sickness at the stomach, acid eructations and vomitings, with pain in region of the liver, and sallow complexion.

"*Case* 9. Henrietta H——. Pain in teeth of left lower jaw, shooting to eyes, ears and head, during the whole summer; aggravated by draughts of air and from eating, gums and cheeks swollen; yellowness of sclerotic coat of the eye.

"Many cases of a similar kind might be here detailed, for they are of almost daily occurrence, but the enumeration of the above will be sufficient to give a general idea of them. In all of them a permanent cure was established in a very few days, even in cases where the disease had lasted for months. I am acquainted with no remedy where the characteristic symptoms are better known, and where a successful issue can be relied on with so much certainty. Upon critically examining and analyzing these cases, we are compelled to acknowledge, that the exact seat of the disease, as well as the nature of the pain, was less essential to the choice of the remedy, in these cases, than the *conditions* under which aggravation took place, namely, the draught of air; and the application of external heat for its amelioration, as highly characteristic. I also consider the sensation of pain as if it were in the bone or periosteum with the swelling of the gums; the pains themselves, as well as their seat, were of the most diversified character; thus we have throbbing, rheumatic aching, dull heavy, sharp shooting, and drawing pains, and the pains also affected various parts of the face, the neighborhood of the eyes, top of the head, lower jaw, zygomatic process of temporal bone, malar bone, etc. The exact nature of the pain seems to me on this account of less importance than the conditions; there is hardly one in five patients who is able to describe the exact nature of the pain from which he suffers. He will, however, have no difficulty in explaining the conditions under which his pain is aggravated or ameliorated."

If a decayed tooth aches, your course is plain — take it out. No well-informed surgeon will ever advise the retention of extensively decayed teeth, however free from pain they may be; or however confident he may be of having a certain remedy for toothache. Nor should country practitioners ever be without the means at hand for their only *safe* and radical cure, — EXTRACTION. The necessary description of instruments and instructions for this *important* part of surgery, we will give in this connection, instead of reserving it for the Operative Part.

Before doing this, however, we would enjoin upon the physician to direct all his patients, whose teeth or gums are unsound or unhealthy, to keep them perfectly *clean.* Direct them to wash the teeth thoroughly with Castile soap and cold water, inside and out, every morning and after each meal. Apply the water with a soft tooth brush, rubbing the teeth and gums briskly. All bits of meat or other food should be removed from between the teeth, by a tooth-pick, immediately after each meal.

EXTRACTION OF TEETH.

The only proper INSTRUMENTS for this often indispensable operation are forceps. Formerly, the *turnkey* was in use, by nearly all, for the back teeth; but as dentistry became generally recognized as a distinct profession, this cruel and clumsy agent was laid aside and intelligent force substituted for mechanical. Dentists have many differently constructed forceps for the different teeth, — at least six or eight pairs. There may be four for the molars, — a special pair for the upper, and another for the lower, on each side, and perhaps even separate ones for the last molars; different ones for the upper and lower incisors; one pair each for the cuspids and bi-cuspids, and several for taking out fangs, — amounting, for a full set, to ten or fourteen pairs of forceps. This formidable array of instruments may do very well for the dentist, though even his efficiency will depend much more on his skill than his tools, but is altogether out of the question with the country practitioner, who must have his tools at hand, being liable to be called on to use them when miles from his office. Dr. Hill seeing and feeling this inconvenience when practicing in the country several years ago (and having before experienced, in his own person, enough of the bruising and mangling of the turnkey), he invented

FIG. 9.

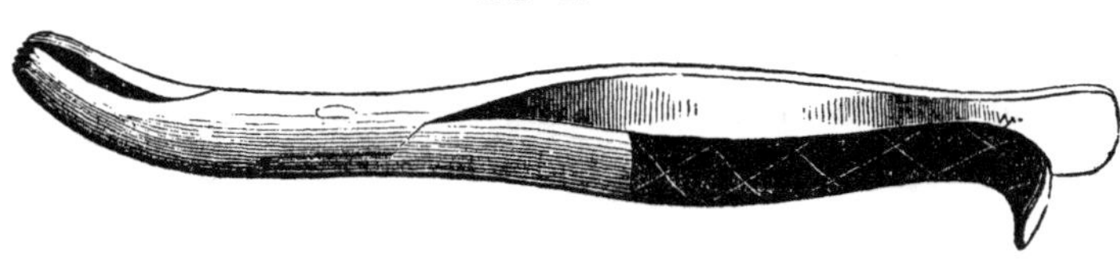

the simple MOLAR FORCEPS (Fig. No. 9). These are a perfect

substitute for all the four, five or six pairs, kept for the same purpose by the dentists. With these *any molar* tooth on either side of either jaw, as well as the bi-cuspids, or any other tooth that is out of the reach of the straight incisor forceps, can be readily ex-

FIG. 10.

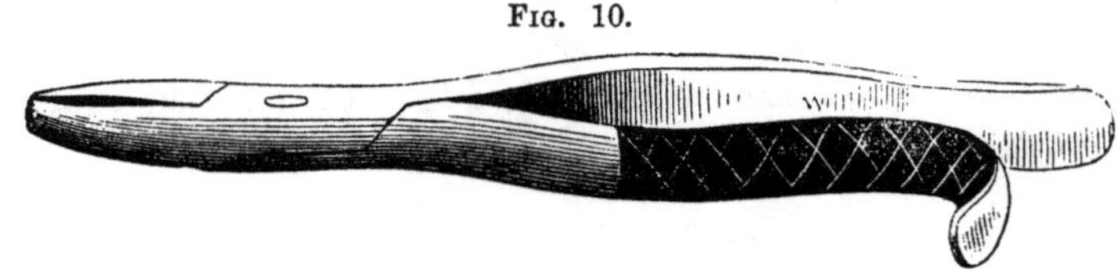

tracted. With these and the common INCISOR FORCEPS (Fig. No. 10), any tooth can be drawn with as much ease, and as little pain to the patient, as with any of the dentist's kit. For the extraction of parts of teeth and fangs, small sharp POINTED CURVED FORCEPS

FIG. 11.

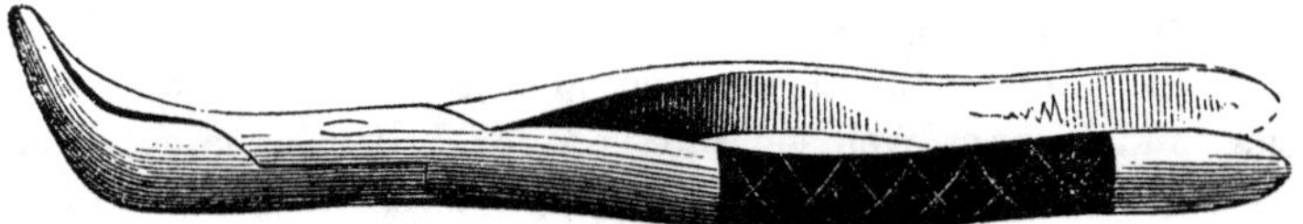

are used (Fig. No. 11). With these three pairs, nearly every tooth or portion of tooth may be extracted.

Before EXTRACTING A TOOTH separate the gums completely from its surface down to the bone, inside and out, as well as between it and the adjoining ones. Then seize the tooth with the forceps, pressing the blades firmly down to the alveolus, and by steady force in the most direct line of the fangs, draw it out. The incisor forceps can be applied to the cuspids in most cases, as well as to the incisors. For the extraction of fangs after detaching the gums, using the fang forceps (Fig. No. 11), press the sharp points as far down at each side of the "snag" as possible, seize and rotate it a little, when it will generally come out easily.

Troublesome *hemorrhage* sometimes, though rarely, follows the extraction of teeth. We have had some very severe cases. The application of common salt to the bleeding surface will usually arrest the flow: even cold water will be sufficient. The surface should be washed out with *Arnicated water* immediately after the tooth is extracted, and if the ruptured vessels are not preternaturally large, it will arrest or prevent hemorrhage. The saturated alcoholic solution of *Phosphorus* arrests hemorrhage from small vessels immediately. Dilute tincture of the *Hamamelis Virginica* (witch hazel), applied to the bleeding gums, arrests hemorrhage "almost instantaneously." But some cases will resist these means, and the blood pours out profusely. We have been able to arrest the hemorrhage, even in the worst cases, by filling the alveoli with *superfine powder* of the Ulmus fulva. (For this purpose it is necessary to have that which is made of the pure *bark*, having not a particle of woody fiber in it.) This forms a coagulum with the blood that completely clogs the mouths of the bleeding vessels, and adheres to the surface with such tenacity as not to be washed off by the flow of blood, or soaked loose by the saliva.

TUBERCLE OF THE GUMS — EPULIS.

This disease occasionally assumes a *malignant* form, — and *extends* rapidly from its original seat to the adjacent parts. If not arrested early it will be very likely to prove fatal.

However trifling *tumors* upon the *gums* may at first appear, to those unacquainted with their occasional malignant termination, the well-informed surgeon will always urge the propriety of early attention to them.

EPULIS generally appears on the gums of the *incisor* teeth, above or below. While the teeth are perfectly sound, and before any appearance of the tumor, they will sometimes be loosened and protruded beyond their fellows. Commonly, however, a small seed-like tumor is seen on the gums, partly between the teeth. This may remain, for several months, nearly stationary, growing so slowly and being so free from pain and irritation as to attract no notice. Finally it looses its hardness, grows more rapidly, becomes very soft, and bleeds on the slightest touch — on its surface becoming accidentally abraded, fungus spreads out with prolific growth.

From this time it *continues* to involve the gums, displacing the teeth, and affecting the glands and other soft parts of the mouth in rapid succession, until the patient is destroyed by the irritation and hemorrhage.

To TREAT this successfully, the proper measures should be adopted early. After it has extended to the lymphatics and the cellular portions of the ethmoid bones, the tongue and palate, success is quite doubtful.

The remedies most useful in this disease, are *Thuja*, *Silicea*, *Phos.*, *Lach.*, *Carbo. veg. and Arsenicum.*

In the early stage of the disease, while there is but little soreness of the gums or tumor, though it may bleed easily, *Thuja* will be quite sure to prove effectual. The tincture should be applied locally. Even in the later stage it has been successful.

Silicea is useful also in the earlier stages, after the gums have become sore and bleed.

Arsenicum, *Phos.*, *Lach. and Carbo. veg.*, are appropriate in the later stage, when it may be looked upon as *cancerous* in its character. It is then to be treated as a soft or fungoid cancer.

RANULA.

This disease consists of a small tumor situated under the tongue, caused by some obstruction to one or more of the Whartonian or Rivinian ducts. The fluid secreted by the sub-maxillary or sublingual glands accumulates at the point of obstruction, forming a tumor which becomes inflamed and painful, and if not opened will ulcerate and prove quite troublesome.

Thuja or Cal. carb. will generally be sufficient to remove the inflammation and discuss the tumor. If, however, notwithstanding these the swelling continues, cut through the surface of the tumor with the points of sharp *scissors*, and take out a small portion of its *substance*. Then wash out the cavity with a solution of *Calcarea carb.*, using the remedy internally once a day for a few days, and if the tumor does not subside, use also *Thuja*.

CHRONIC ENLARGEMENT

of the tonsils frequently occurs after repeated acute attacks, especially in scrofulous persons. This is a source of much inconvenience, if not danger.

The patient is liable to frequent inflammation of the parts — the voice is changed and rendered hoarse — deglutition is obstructed, and respiration often rendered difficult and noisy, especially during sleep. Much deafness is occasionally caused by the enlarged gland obstructing the Eustachian tubes. And, it is said, suffocation has occurred from viscid mucus collecting between them.

Bell. is most used for the acute inflammatory condition; *Hepar sul.* for the suppurative; *Calcarea* for the chronic suppurative stage in scrofulous persons; *Sulphur* in scrofulous persons affected with eruptions; *Ignatia* for delicate females; *Lachesis*, when the throat is much inflamed, with a dark putrescent appearance, *Bell.* having failed to relieve. These may be alternated.

This disease is not unfrequently very obstinate, and it requires a long time to produce any considerable impression upon it. We have employed, with excellent success, the *Arum Triphyllum* and the *Phytolacca*, and in a few cases, the *Stillingia*.*

The *Arum* is indicated more particularly when there is pain, burning or titillation in the throat, with a sense of contraction in the fauces; the throat looks red, there is considerable secretion of saliva and red tongue. The *Phytolacca*, when the soft palate is swollen, the uvula elongated, throat dry and sore, white or yellow mucus about the fauces, especially in the morning.†

Dr. Hartung, in reporting the case of Count Radetsky, drops the remark that he had often cured *swollen and indurated tonsils* with *Thuja occ. and Petroleum*, alternately. Dr. Boenninghausen cured a case of *hypertrophy of the tonsils* with *Staphysagria*, which had resisted several other remedies.

The following is from the pen of Prof. C. Neidhard:

"*Belladonna* is to be exhibited when the swelling of the tonsils is less the predominating, than the extreme scarlet redness and inflammation of them and the surrounding palate and throat; when the glands on the outside of the neck, particularly those on the back of the neck, are also swollen and painful; there is a stiffness on moving the head and neck.

* The *Stillingia Sylvatica* seems to exert a very beneficial influence on this disease. From our knowledge of its pathogenesis by observing the effect of large doses given for syphilis, we were induced to try it in chronic tonsilitis, and we think it bids fair to be a valuable remedy for this disease, especially in scrofulous patients.

† The *Arum Triphyllum* was used in place of *Arum Maculatum*, as the latter was not at hand.

"In similar conditions, but more of a chronic kind, *Calc. c. and Lachesis* are indicated. *Calc. c.*, particularly, when the symptoms are aggravated by a draught of air, and *Lachesis*, when the rigidity of the muscles of the neck is very great.

"In cases characterized by swelling, ulceration of the tonsils and fetid smell from the mouth, with yellow and mucous coating of the tongue, *Merc. Sol. H.*, in the 2d or 3d trit., will seldom be prescribed in vain.

"If the patient complains of a sticking pain in the throat, I have often given, with benefit, *Acid nitric*, generally in the 6th, but also sometimes in a lower dilution.

"If the enlargement of the tonsils and the ulceration was more on the left side, *Lycop.*, 3 to 30, was more to be depended upon than the other remedies.

"But in those very dangerous cases, where the throat is entirely closed by an immense swelling of the tonsils, and where the patient is unable to swallow even a drop of water, gargling the throat with the original tincture of *Bellad.*, mixed in a little water, will perhaps have the most salutary effect.

"In several cases of this kind which fell under my notice, the patients were able to swallow some thin gruel in the space of two hours, after using the *Bellad.* in this form.

"My indication for *Amm. mur.* is a collection of thick, viscid phlegm in the throat, which can not be detached without difficulty.

"If the symptoms of tonsilitis are accompanied by a choking sensation or a feeling of a ball in the throat, I generally prescribe *Ignat. amar.*, and these symptoms at least will always disappear.

"In some cases, where the throat was inflamed, accompanied by a soreness and dryness and swelling of the right tonsil, *Sang. can.* has been very useful to me; in similar cases of a more chronic nature, *Phos. of Lime* may be given.

"Some physicians, even the eminent and successful practitioner, Dr. Gouillou, of Weimar, have counseled the removal of part of the tonsils by the knife, as less dangerous and more sensible, than large homeopathic doses of *Iodine.*

"I am compelled, judging from my own experience, utterly to condemn this practice, having seen, in several cases, symptoms of consumption immediately arise after the excision of these enlarged tonsils. Some of them met with an early death as soon as these outposts of the disease were gone. On the other hand, I am well aware that in prescribing *Iodine* in too large and often repeated doses, we may, it is true, cure the enlarged tonsils, but tubercles will gradually develop themselves in the lungs. The same experience applies to goiter, which may also be cured by large doses of *Iodine*, but if cured too quickly, will often be followed by a very serious cough.

"If the chronic enlargement of the tonsils was accompanied by induration and swelling of the external glands of the neck, *Conium* has, in many cases, removed them. In ordinary cases, particularly in children of stout habit or robust persons generally, *Calc. c.* and *Silicea*, alternating higher and lower dilutions, will be found sufficient. The *Bromide of potash*, also, here deserves to be mentioned in the case of persons of light complexion.

"Profiting by Negrier's observations on *Juglans Regia* in different scrofulous affections, I have of late made use of it in many cases of enlarged tonsils as well as glandular swellings of the neck, and with the most decided success; such cases were particularly benefited in which the glands had a tendency to suppurate, and also where the scrofulous constitution of the patient was fully developed."

FOREIGN BODIES IN THE ŒSOPHAGUS (CHOKING).

A substance lodged in the œsophagus generally stops at the narrowest or most confined place, which is opposite or just above the cricoid cartilage. It is not, however, likely to remain there long, as by the efforts of the patient or others, it is generally pushed further down, and remains at some point above the stomach. It is, however, sometimes raised a little, and sticks fast in the pharynx, opposite the larynx.

The substance may produce so much *irritation* as to cause spasm of the glottis and immediate suffocation. But more generally nothing more than irritation, with difficult or impossible *deglutition* occurs, until a sufficient time has elapsed for inflammation to be induced. The inflammation will soon advance to suppuration or ulceration, and prove very destructive and dangerous to life. Or, if the substance be very large, it may peril life by the direct pressure upon the glottis or trachea. It often happens that a foreign body lodged for a time, at last slips down into the stomach spontaneously, leaving for awhile a tumor behind it, at the point of lodgment.

The TREATMENT for this case is to *extract* the article, if possible; or if it be a substance, the presence of which in the stomach would do no harm, being digestible or soluble, to *push* it down. First, seat the patient, throw the head far back and open the mouth widely; then pass the finger into the pharynx, regardless of the gagging or efforts of the patient to vomit, and as quickly as possible search at every point for the substance. If felt, endeavor to take it away with the *fingers*, by attaching it to the nail. But if you fail in this, immediately introduce *curved forceps* (such as every one should have in a pocket case), along side of the finger, using the finger as a guide. If the object can be seen, of course the forceps alone are sufficient.

If, however, the substance has passed *below the pharynx*, and be proper for the stomach, *push* it down. If it is not, and the patient can still swallow, tickle the fauces with a feather and give mustard. But if he can not swallow, put the oil or extract of *Lobelia* into the mouth, and let him hold it for a few minutes. This will excite vomiting. It may be pushed down with a *Probang*, — a piece of whalebone, with the end rounded and covered with silk to make it smooth. But if this passes by the substance without moving it up or down, attach firmly to the end of the whalebone a piece of very fine sponge, perfectly dry, having its surface lubricated with oil or soap, which will make it still smoother. It must not be so large as to produce suffocation by pressing on the trachea. Pass this down to the substance and press gently upon it. If it moves the substance before it, continue until it enters the stomach, and then carefully withdraw the probang. But if the instrument, with the sponge attached, *passes by* the article, push it on a few inches *further*, and let it *remain* for several minutes. It may even be passed down into the stomach, where, by absorbing fluid, it will become swollen so as to fill up the œsophagus, and when withdrawn, bring up the substance before it. Another plan is to fix threads to the whalebone, with a great number of loops hanging from its end, and along its surface: pass it down beyond the obstruction, and the substance becoming entangled in the loops may be brought up with it.

If it be some substance which would not be digested or dissolved, and too large to pass through the pylorus and be discharged from the bowels, every effort must be made to bring it up. The œsophagus forceps (made for the purpose) must be used, if emetics fail. Or a tube connected with an air-pump, or a common stomach-pump, may be passed down on to the obstructing substance, — when by exhausting the atmosphere above, it would attach to the end of the tube and be withdrawn with it. If the substance fill the passage completely, the œsophagus forceps could not be passed down by, so as to grasp it; and in the attempt to do so, there would be danger of pushing it into the stomach. Hence the resort to the pump is the best plan. One case is named, where a fishhook with a line attached, was fast low down in the œsophagus. A hole was drilled through a bullet, and that let down the throat over the line, when coming in contact with the hook, the latter was disengaged by its weight, and the point then turning up against the leaden ball was prevented from catching hold again, as both were drawn out together.

If the obstruction is in the cervical portion of the œsophagus, and can not be otherwise extracted, it may possibly be removed by the operation of Œsophagotomy.

CHAPTER XXVIII.

BRONCHOCELE AND MAMMARY ABSCESS, — "SWELLED NECK" AND "SWELLED OR BROKEN BREAST."

GOITER or hypertrophy of the THYROID GLAND — where epidemic — persons liable — Relation to scrofula — Progress and Results — Iodine not to be depended on — RADICAL CURE.

INFLAMMATION of the MAMMARY GLAND — Cause, symptoms, and serious consequences — Various stages with appropriate local treatment — Constitutional treatment — Lancing to be generally deferred — Special precautions in puncturing — consequences of their common neglect — contingencies and measures after opening.

BRONCHOCELE OR GOITER.

THIS disease consists in a preternaturally enlarged thyroid gland. It prevails very extensively in Switzerland and other mountainous parts of Europe. It is found in the United States, everywhere, but more frequently in low districts and near the great lakes, where the atmosphere is moist and the soil rich. Individuals of all ages and of both sexes are subject to this disease, but females are by far the most frequently affected with it. It rarely occurs in children before the tenth year, nor is it likely to commence in very old persons. Persons of light fair skin, of relaxed constitutions, light hair, large light eyes and precocious intellects, in short, of the scrofulous habit, are most likely to have goiter. The memory of the child is often very vigorous, and the whole mind in point of development several years ahead of its age. But when goiter appears, a sudden change frequently comes over the mind. Often in bad cases, as the disease progresses, the countenance becomes more pallid, and changes from the brilliant intellectual appearance to a dull unmeaning aspect; the eyes lose their luster and assume a vacant look. Intellectual development seems to be nearly arrested. If it become very large, respiration is more or less obstructed and difficult; the voice changes, and articulation is indistinct.

The intermarriage of persons affected with goiter, is likely to result in the production of the disease in their offspring. Usually the goiter diminishes in cold dry weather, but on the return of warm moist weather it enlarges. In some countries it affects horses, cattle, dogs and sheep.

It begins by a small tumor on one or both sides of the trachea. It may occupy both lobes and the isthmus of the gland, so as to have the appearance of a uniform tumor, or be only on one side, or on both, the isthmus remaining unaffected, dividing the two lobes by a deep fissure. It sometimes extends back on both sides so uniformly as not to have the appearance of a distinct tumor. It is usually slow in its *progress.* In most cases, it is soft and insensible, and may be handled with impunity; in others, it is closely bound down by the muscles, and feels firm and hard. If it becomes inflamed, it is extremely painful, and presents very troublesome symptoms, which are often quite difficult to subdue.

In this country, severe or dangerous cases are very rare. The principal difficulty attending them, in a very large proportion of cases, is the *deformity.* The striking effects upon the mental constitution, before referred to, are, among us, still more rare. Various modes of treatment have been recommended and pursued by allopaths, all of which have had their strong advocates, and most of which have been abandoned, either as useless or too dangerous. IODINE seems, from numerous authorities, to stand higher than any other remedy. It is mostly used in allopathic practice internally, in the form of Iodide of Potassium, and of Iron. It is also applied externally, in the form of an ointment, with lard, or some other convenient vehicle, rubbed on once or twice a day, over the tumor. It is also dissolved in alcohol, and applied as a wash. Extract of *Cicuta* is highly recommended by Prof. Gibson, while he has by no means the same confidence in Iodine that is expressed by others. Of this favorite article he thus speaks: — "The reports of Coindet in favor of this medicine" (Iodine) "were soon fully confirmed by many other continental surgeons; and its reputation rose speedily to the highest pitch; strange as it may seem, however, its decline has been almost as rapid as its rise, being now considered in the estimation of many practitioners, nearly inert, and by others pronounced a most virulent poison. But, from all the statements made on the subject, we have, I think, fairly a right to infer that it is a medicine of great power, calculated, in some cases, to produce a very strong impression on goitrous and other tumors, as many well attested cases decidedly show; and that, on the other hand, it is followed occasionally with tremendous symptoms and even death. Again, it is equally certain that, upon other patients, not the slightest impression has been made by its use, either upon the tumor or upon the constitutions of the individuals who have taken it, sometimes for months together, and in the largest doses. My own experience in its use is very limited, but, judging from this, and from the reports made to me concerning it by my colleagues, in the Philadelphia Hospital, I should feel inclined to doubt its efficacy. Still it is possible we may have been deceived, either by the bad quality of the medicine or by other circumstances. Lastly, it may be stated that Dr. Coindet himself has abandoned the *internal* use of the remedy, and merely employs it in the form of inunction, from which he states that he has derived very beneficial results."

From the foregoing it will be noticed that *Iodine*, while it has been successful in some cases, has in others done injury. From the results of the homeopathic use of this drug in *minute doses*, we are assured that it not only has great power, but it is homeopathic, that is, *specific* to some forms of this disease. Dr. Hugh Cameron, in an able article read before the British Homeopathic Society, remarks, "I shall now in a few words relate the leading features of three cases, which I have selected out of many, because they prove that *Iodine*, administered in infinitesimal doses, will act beneficially in bronchocele when it has been employed in large doses (allopathic) without success; and that this remedy, allopathically prescribed, sometimes increased the disease it was given to cure.

"The first case, a woman aged forty, had the disease from childhood; swelling extended from the sternum to the chin — hard and covered with a net-work of varicose veins. It impeded respiration as well as the circulation, so that she had great fullness of the head, cough, dysnaea, &c.; had been treated with *Mercury*, *Hyd.*, *Potass.*, also *Tincture Iodine*, internally, until it produced giddiness, fainting, palpitation, tremor, pain, and increased fullness and tension in the tumor. For some years she left off all treatment; all the symptoms had greatly increased, when *Iodine* 30 was given and repeated every two days for a week, after which it was repeated at longer intervals for six months, when all symptoms except the swelling disappeared.

"The other two cases were similar, the treatment the same, and with similar success. In the last, however, a young lady, the tumor entirely disappeared."

We have used *Iodine and Spongia*, alternately, with good effect.

Dr. Goullon reports a case of extreme rapid growth and swelling of the *thoroid gland* — a man aged sixty-two — produced by taking large doses of *Kali. iod.* for scrofula. Another of a young girl, four grains of *Kali iod.* produced rapid diminution in a swollen thyroid gland.

Besides *Iodine and Spongia*, or where they fail and the tumor assumes a *diseased* condition, becomes painful, with a swollen and varicose condition of the veins covering its surface, *Carbo. veg. or Lycopodium* should be given. If, however, there are any symptoms of acute inflammation, with redness, increased swelling, with headache and a difficulty of swallowing, use *Belladonna*, repeating the dose every ten or twelve hours, or oftener, as the symptoms require. If there should arise considerable *fever*, *Aconite* is more appropriate. When, however, the fever is of a milder form and there is no redness or sudden increase of swelling, or if suppuration is threatened, *Mercurius* will be beneficial. It should be repeated as often as every four or five hours until the abscess points (if pus has already formed), or the inflammation subsides. *Hepar or Silicea* will aid in forwarding the suppurative action. For the discussion of the enlarged gland, where inflammation has never been present, or after its disappearance, besides *Iodine and Spongia*, *Conium* has been effectual in some cases.

Podophyllum, though it has not been much used by homeopathists, we think will be found equally efficient, in fact far superior, to any of the foregoing remedies. Many years ago, before Homeopathy was known in this country to any considerable extent, Dr. Kilborne, of Columbus, Ohio, was in the habit of prescribing very small portions of this remedy for goitres, and gained quite a notoriety for curing cases which had been treated unsuccessfully with large doses of *Iodine* and other remedies for a long time.

Since becoming homeopathists, we have been using it, and are free to say, that no medicament has acted so promptly and efficiently in our hands as this. We give the 3d or 4th dilution of the tincture, or the same trituration of *Podophyllin*, internally, and apply a dilution of one to fifty of the tincture in alcohol to the tumor. In some cases, however, we have found drop doses of the mother tincture, taken internally, to succeed, when the dilutions failed.

The following remedies may be consulted with advantage: — *Staphysagria, Natrum muriaticum, Causticum, Am. carb., and Thuja.*

MAMMARY ABSCESS.

Although this disease is most commonly met with in lying-in females, it is not exclusively confined to this class of persons. It occurs occasionally among others, and even males are sometimes affected with troublesome mammary swellings. In the case of males, however, this affection rarely, if ever, requires any treatment. It will gradually subside of itself. When abscess forms immediately after delivery, it is usually the result of some mechanical injury, received at that time, or of a sudden cold. It rarely occurs, however, before the lapse of from four to six weeks after parturition.

The first SYMPTOMS are generally slight swelling in some part of the gland, with throbbing pain, which is soon succeeded by a severe chill, and followed by more or less general fever.

In some cases the *chill and fever* will appear before the patient has noticed any affection of the breast. There will be in this case much restlessness and irritability, and, if strict examination be made, a small hard tumor will be found, most generally *far back* towards the base of the gland, which is extremely tender to the touch, though it has not previously occasioned any sensation of pain.

If the inflammation and tumefaction begin on the top of the gland or near the nipple, it will be the first symptom to attract notice. Soon after the occurrence of the chill, the breast enlarges in all directions, and becomes highly inflamed and extremely painful, and so tender as not to bear the slightest touch. The secretion of milk may be entirely suppressed, but generally it continues, though very much altered in its appearance, becoming often injurious and sickening to the child.

Suppuration, if not prevented, will usually take place in about ten days, rarely sooner; but sometimes, if it be allowed to take its course, several weeks elapse before pus is formed, during which time the patient's sufferings are indescribably great.

The matter when formed is not always in one cavity, but may be in distinct cysts. These abscesses are sometimes of the character of sinuous ulcers, having several openings with long pipes winding tortuously into the substance of the breast, from which fungous sometimes sprouts out, and in large masses. This kind of *ulcer* in the breast rarely heals spontaneously. If not arrested, it will sooner or later prove fatal, the constitution of the patient being undermined by the pain, irritation and discharge. Hectic sets in and she soon sinks.

The TREATMENT of these cases, though they are rarely of a malignant or dangerous character, is nevertheless very important, particularly on account of the extreme suffering of the patient.

If called early, before the chill, or soon after, examine the breast critically to ascertain the exact condition of the swelling. If it be still confined to a small compass, we ought by no means to allow it to extend so as to involve other parts in the inflammation. Give *Bryonia*, and repeat the dose every four or six hours, using a low dilution of the same as a wash to the affected part, keeping it constantly wet.*

This remedy will often suffice for cases even where the indura-

* The *extreme tenderness and sensibility* of an inflamed breast will be allayed and the sufferings of the patient greatly palliated (an important consideration in so *distressing* a complaint) in a short time, by having a dish of water, as warm as can be borne, placed below and near the breast, and with a sponge constantly applying the heated fluid to the gland by letting a stream flow gently over it, taking care to keep up the temperature by adding more hot water. The process should be continued for from half an hour to two or three hours if the pain and tenderness are not allayed sooner; it may be repeated at any time, when the extremely painful symptoms return. Whatever medicine is being used at the time, may be put into the water at a low dilution. It will be found that all the remedies indicated in this affection will act more efficiently if applied to the affected part at the same time that they are used internally.

tion is extensive, before any redness appears on the surface, but after the breast swells and the surface becomes red with burning pain, use *Belladonna* in the same manner.

If the inflammation has arisen from any recent injury, *Arnica*, or if from an old one, *Conium* will be appropriate. But if the disease does not soon yield to these remedies, chills will set in, and the patient will be affected with symptoms not unlike a severe paroxysm of ague. If these should occur during the treatment or before its commencement, and the fever be severe, give *Aconite* and *Belladonna* alternately, or *Aconite* internally and apply *Belladonna* to the breast. When the fever subsides, continue the *Belladonna* as long as improvement goes on, but lengthen the intervals of its administration. If, however, some degree of active inflammation should remain after one or two days, the breasts being much indurated, give *Bryonia* in alternation with *Belladonna*, at intervals of six or eight hours.

Should the *induration* continue after the active inflammation has subsided, give *Mercurius solubilis;* to be repeated in one day and afterwards, at longer intervals.

We have employed *Phosphorus* almost to the exclusion of other remedies, not only to facilitate the suppurative process, as recommended by Croserio, but to *prevent* the formation of pus, with more satisfactory results than any other remedy.

Should these remedies have been employed too late to prevent suppuration, and abscess goes on to form, the next object will be to palliate the symptoms and "bring it to a point," with as little pain to the patient and as soon as possible.

Hepar sulphuris, if given early after the symptoms of suppuration have set in, will often so far arrest the suppurative process as to allow but a small part to become involved and very little pus will be formed; besides, it greatly lessens the pain during the process of suppuration and facilitates the "pointing" of the abscess. We may not be consulted until all attempts at *preventing* abscess are fruitless — it may have already formed. *Don't puncture too soon.* It is better here to let the abscess alone, and allow it to open spontaneously, if practicable. Wet compress or an elm poultice should be applied. Flaxseed poultice is very good, as it does not adhere so closely. The elm or flaxseed, wet with scalding milk, and applied quite warm, aids the suppuration. When the matter has collected in considerable quantities, it may be very slow in coming to the surface, and, if its escape is very long delayed, it may do much harm by producing hectic, and, if the lungs are weak, it may seriously affect those organs. If the patient be feeble, scrofulous, or inclined to pulmonary disease, we ought not to wait very long for the matter to make its way to the surface. It is much better, however, in all cases that will admit of delay, to allow it to come so near the surface that nothing but the skin will intervene — and *then open.* But in the cases just particularized this might not occur until fatal injury had been inflicted on the lungs. Examine and ascertain as nearly as possible the seat of the pus, and the point where it approaches nearest the surface. *Puncture* with an abscess lancet at the most depending point at which the pus can be conveniently reached. In puncturing, be *careful in all cases* to make the incision *parallel* with the course of *the lactiferous ducts.* Have the edge of the lancet look towards the point of the nipple. By this means we will avoid severing many, or perhaps any, of the ducts. It will be recollected that the breast or mammary gland is made up of an immense number of little glands, each having a separate duct or tube leading from it, from which the milk secreted by the glandulæ is conducted towards the nipple, from which it escapes by a number of larger ducts. As these little tubes approach the nipple, they run in similar directions, all converging to the same point, the smaller ones uniting — thus lessening their number and increasing their size as they advance. Now, if the lancet be introduced parallel with the tubes, though some may be split, none need be entirely severed, so as to destroy their functions; but if, on the contrary, the lancet be plunged in *across* the ducts — that is, with the flat side towards the nipple, forty or *fifty*, or even *more*, may be cut through, and the cicatrix close them up completely. Thus, the outlet from several hundreds of the still smaller ducts beyond are entirely and forever closed. These glands remaining sound, will secrete milk, as usual, at the next period of pregnancy. There being no way for the milk to escape, it will accumulate along the ducts, between the glands and the obstruction, causing inflammation, abscess, and very generally *ulceration.*

This is the history of thousands of cases operated upon by physicians — or we ought to say *quacks* — whether they are graduates or not — who are too ignorant of anatomy, or too careless in their operations to be trusted with a *cutting instrument.* Let any one enquire into the history, and examine the scars of those unfortunate patients who have been afflicted so strangely with *repeated* abscess and ulceration of the breast, and he will soon become convinced of the truth of our remarks. This kind of surgical disease is moreover particularly liable to take on a malignant character. [See under CANCER, page 226.]

After the escape of the pus, dress the part with the elm poultice as long as there is much discharge, and when it diminishes, with simple cerate. It generally heals kindly. But if it become indolent and heal slowly, give *Phosphorus,* keeping it covered with the cloths or a poultice. It is also very valuable in the ulcerative stage, the ulcers being partly fistulous with fungous growths, the patient being affected with sweats, loss of appetite and much debility, the lungs appearing implicated.

On the disappearance of these hectic symptoms, if the ulcer does not assume a healthy appearance, or if there are sinuous ulcers in the absence of these constitutional symptoms, give *Silicea.* If it inclines to bleed easily when touched, and assumes a dark color with a fetid odor, give *Lachesis. Carbo animalis* may be used with advantage should *Lachesis* have failed to entirely remove these symptoms. The breast should be sustained by a suspensory bandage so as to prevent the pain that would arise from its dependent position.

In some instances, where it has beeen lanced too early, the *wound gapes* open widely, and the substance of the gland turns out like a rose, as large as a coffee-cup. These cases are sometimes called " cancer," and often really become malignant, *if* long *neglected.* In one of the worst cases of the kind we ever saw, the leaves of the Pyrolia rotundifolia (canker-lettuce) were applied in a green state, laid over the sore and changed once in two hours, effecting a perfect cure in the course of two weeks. We have used this article with like success in several similar cases, though none so bad. It deserves to be "proven."

Acid nit. was extremely useful in the case of a female whose two breasts had been removed on account of scirrhus.

Silicea 30; abscess, in the case of a young girl, resulting from violent phlegmon, which came on without any ostensible cause.

Symptoms: pale, livid, emaciated, no appetite, hectic fever and short breath, continual general dry cough. The affected breast was hard and tumid, but pale. Towards the axilla the breast exhibits an opening with callous fistula extending as far as the sternum, the lower half of which is painful and swollen, paralytic pains in the right arm.

Phos. 30; abscess during lactation.

Symptoms: Breast swollen and inflamed; several openings with callous edges suppurating, some parts of the breast remaining hard; suspicious cough, generally dry and frequently accompanied with expectoration of blood, oppressed breathing, circumscribed redness of the cheeks, no appetite, chilliness in the evening, with subsequent heat, especially in the palms of the hands; viscid night sweats.

Phos. 30; abscess in a lying-in female.

Symptoms: Gnawing burning in the thoracic cavity, with short oppressed breathing and dry cough; hectic fever, with coliquative sweats and diarrhea. Breast swollen, hard, dark red, with burning pain and stinging when touched but slightly. Seven ulcers, partly fistulous, partly ulcerated, partly covered with proud flesh, discharging fetid badly-colored copious pus.

Phos. cured a very painful breast, as hard as a stone in many places, but suppurating in others.

Phos. has frequently been curative in inflammation of the mammæ or long suppurations, which continually inflame. (*Ruckert, p.* 309–10.)

CHAPTER XXIX.

HERNIA OR RUPTURE.

DEFINITIONS and distinctions — Inguinal and Femoral Hernia, with illustrations — Irreducible Hernia — the sac and its neck — Omental and Intestinal Hernia — Strangulation, cause and symptoms — mortification and seeming relief — Directions for the Taxis — Original means for effecting reduction — Treatment.

BY the term HERNIA is commonly understood a protrusion of some portion of the intestines or omentum, or both, from the cavity of the abdomen, in the form of a *tumor* found to be suspended in a peculiar *sac* (which is a fold of the peritoneam carried on before the bowel and still enclosing it). The word RUPTURE, which is the popular synonym for hernia, more strictly expresses the *break* or *breach*, or widening of the opening, in the abdominal parietes, through which the viscus or viscera make their escape.

In some cases, as where the accident is caused by a wound dividing the peritoneum, or where the cæcum protrudes from behind that membrane, there will be *no* hernial *sac;* and other viscera than the intestines, as the bladder, ovaries, uterus, &c., may constitute the *tumor.* These rarer cases are still called "hernia." Indeed the most general definition of the word is the protrusion of any viscus from any of the natural cavities. This more extended meaning of the word is always indicated by the name of the particular case. Thus, "hernia ventriculi" is a variety of ventral hernia, in which the stomach, instead of any lower portion of the alimentary tract, is protruded; "hernia vesicalis" involves the urinary bladder; and "hernia cerebri" means a swelling out of the brain and investing membrane at any point where the cranium is deficient, or has been removed. The greater liability of the bowels to this accident than any other parts, arises as well from the great amount and variety of pressure to which they are subject, as the comparative weakness of the parts that cover them in front. The weakest parts are those at which the accident most frequently occurs; and anything that occasions general or local muscular debility, becomes a

— *predisposing* CAUSE: such as dropsy, pregnancy, abscesses, wounds, &c. The *exciting cause* is any sufficient pressure on the viscera, such as *straining* in evacuating the bowels or bladder, or in lifting heavy weights, or some other violent bodily exertion (especially during debility from sickness).

The parts most LIABLE to *be* protruded are, after the omentum, either some of the small intestines, or some part of the arch of the colon. The PLACE where the tumor manifests itself is, in ordinary cases, near the *navel* or the *groin*, running down, in the latter instance, either in front of the thigh or into the scrotum or labia. (See Figures 12 and 13.)

FIG. 12.

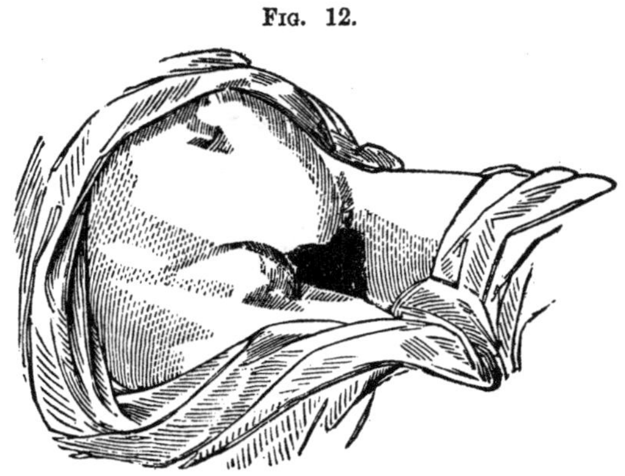

The particular POINTS of protrusion give name to the most frequent cases; and the distinctions are sometimes vitally important. When the rupture is at the navel, the case is sometimes called "Exomphalos," more commonly and correctly "Umbilical Hernia." When at any other point of the abdomen than those we shall now go on more particularly to explain, it is simply "Ventral Hernia." By far the most common points concerned, and most important to be borne in mind, are the *Abdominal Rings* with their intervening *Canal* (for the passage of the spermatic cord), constituting INGUINAL HERNIA (see Figure 12), of which several varieties are to be distinguished; and the *Crural Ring* and *Saphenic* or Lymphatic *Hole*, with the intervening *Femoral Sheath under* or *behind* Poupart's Ligament, giving rise to FEMORAL HERNIA. The amount of protrusion at this part is usually small, and the diagnosis from bubo and other affections of the groin is not always easy. It is more common in women than men.

In INGUINAL HERNIA, the intestine, after passing through the internal Abdominal Ring, may be arrested in the canal, and form a tumor there above Poupart's Ligament: this is "*Incomplete* Inguinal Hernia." "*Complete* Inguinal Hernia" is when the protruded part traverses the abdominal canal and emerges at the External

FIG. 13.*

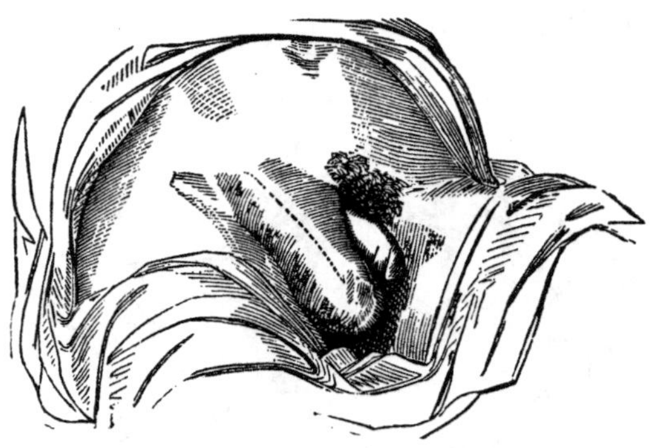

Ring, following the same course that the testicle did in its passage from the abdomen into the scrotum. When the bowels runs on with, or rather, *within* the cord far enough down, it becomes "Scrotal Hernia" (Fig. 13). When a protrusion through the same points occurs in females, the tumor appears in the labia pudendi. This complete Inguinal Hernia is sometimes called the "*Oblique*," in contradistinction to the case in which the bowel forces its way through the space between Poupart's and Gimbernat's Ligaments, leaving the External Ring and the Spermatic Cord on the *outside* of it. This is the "*Direct* or *Ventro-Inguinal* Hernia." This

* This cut represents inguinal hernia when it has not only become complete, but advanced so far as to occupy and distend the tunica vaginalis, then constituting it a case of "scrotal hernia." This, as well as the former illustration, represents the protrusions of a medium size and as they appear in a sitting posture. It will be noticed that the tumor on the thigh (Fig. 12) is much smaller than the pouch of Fig. 13. Its position is also above that of the other, though the other *commences* much higher up in the body. The dotted lines on the tumors indicate the direction of the incisions in operating for strangulation.

protrusion is not often very large, and may extend on towards the scrotum, but is unconnected with the Spermatic Cord or tunica vaginalis.

These distinctions of origin or location are not the only or most important ones to be noticed. Every Hernia is either Reducible or Irreducible, that is, susceptible or not of being put back into its place. The distinction is not the merely relative one depending on the means used for actual reduction. All serious cases would thus be, for awhile, relatively "irreducible;" and when they are neglected, or efficient means are not resorted to in time to prevent such a result, they become absolutely and permanently *irreducible.* This is what is technically meant by the distinction. It is caused by *adhesions* of the sac and contents, or by an enlargement of the tumor from fatty deposit or other growth.

For the sake of beginners, we will observe that this subject of reducibility is not, as it might seem to them, the most important practical question, and is not to be confounded with the subject of *strangulated hernia.* In simply irreducible hernia, the functions of the part go on the same as if they were in their proper place. It is said to be strangulated when (from swelling of the neck of the sac, spasm of the muscular parts around it, distension by flatus or fæces, or from any similar cause) the sanguineous circulation through the part or passage of its proper contents is obstructed,—rendering the death of the part and almost necessarily also that of the patient inevitable, if the case is not speedily relieved. Strangulation occurs most frequently in cases of long-standing rupture; but is by no means to be regarded as a mere variety of "irreducible hernia." It is, of course, irreducible for the time and under the circumstances, and may have been permanently so before the distension or constriction; but many a fatal case of strangulation has been such as admitted of easy reduction, had the patient or the practitioner resorted in time to proper means.

The *neck* of the SAC, of which mention was just made in describing strangulated hernia,—the narrowest part where it immediately protrudes from the abdomen,—necessarily contains a larger amount of the peritoneal membrane crowded and puckered up than the lower expanded part; and becomes thickened and condensed by pressure. Sometimes there are two necks, the sac having enlarged or descended further and drawn out more of the peritoneum, after one part had permanently grown into a neck at the fissure. In Complete or oblique Inguinal Hernia, there are always of necessity two necks, one at the Internal, the other at the External Ring. The body of the *sac* increases in size by distension and growth, as well as further drawing out from the abdomen. Adhesive inflammation, or adhesion without inflammation, soon forms with the surrounding parts, so that when the protruded intestines are replaced, the peritoneal protrusion or *sac* is very rarely returned with them.

It is well for the practitioner to DISTINGUISH between a protrusion of the omentum only, and one of intestine, or of both. The hernial tumor containing OMENTUM only (epiplocele), is insensible and inelastic, feeling to the touch *like dough.* When formed of INTESTINE (enterocele), it is *harder* as well as elastic, and gives *pain* on being pressed. If *both* are included in the sac (entero-epiplocele), you will find one part of it springy and sensitive, while another has the peculiar doughy insensibility.

The protrusion at either of the points mentioned is liable to become "strangulated," i. e. to have the orifice through which it has passed contracted upon it, so as to prevent its return and obstruct its circulation and other natural functions. This is a condition, which, if not relieved, must soon occasion death. Any cause of inflammation or spasmodic irritation, supervening on the simple hernia, may bring about this alarming complication.

The symptoms of STRANGULATED HERNIA are first an irritable condition of the parts, with a hectic flush over their surface, and pain at the point of protrusion and constriction. When inflammation is not itself the cause, it soon follows on strangulation. The pulse becomes hard and quick, and other symptoms of the sympathetic fever set in. There is costiveness, of course, when the alimentary canal is itself obstructed. This symptom occurs also when it is only omental hernia. There may be ineffectual attempts at a discharge per anum. Above the constricted part, the peristaltic movement is inverted. Vomiting early occurs, and continues till the contents not only of the stomach and duodenum, but of all the intestines above the hernia are brought up, the ejections being more or less fæcal. These various symptoms continue more or less severe until

— MORTIFICATION begins, when the patient becomes easy and thinks he is getting *well.* The abdomen sinks; and if examination is made over the protruded parts, *crepitus* may be felt. The vomiting gives place to gulping and ominous hiccough. The apparently flattering changes soon betray themselves by sinking, clammy sweats, rigors, &c. *The hernia subsides* spontaneously, or is easily reduced by the finger. This sometimes precedes any obviously alarming change, and is immediately followed by a *satisfactory stool.*

When this EASY OR NATURAL REDUCTION takes place suddenly in a case of some hours' standing, we may be pretty sure that our patient will die. And here let us warn the young surgeon never to be so inconsiderate as to fall into the error that physicians as well as patients have often done,— mistaking pain for danger, and the ease arising from insensibility, for a ground of hope. The feelings of the patient on his final release from suffering, are well calculated to deceive. What of life is left, when death is begun, often seems all the freer and fuller. The old maxim, "while there is life there is hope," would be truer if it ran, "while there is pain, there is hope."

Still, in rare instances, which are among the wonders of nature, strangulated hernia has been spontaneously recovered from, without either reduction being affected or adhesion taking place; — that is, if it can be called recovery for the protruded parts to slough off and leave an artificial anus.

When called to a RECENT CASE of hernia, if inflammation has *not* yet taken place, we should endeavor by all means, whether there be irritation or not, to "reduce," i. e. to replace, the protruded parts within their natural cavity.

In order to REDUCE with more facility, place the patient on the sound side in a horizontal posture, elevating the hips, however, and flexing the thigh of the affected side upon the abdomen while we draw it down toward the other. By these means we draw off the incumbent mass of intestines, and relax the muscles and integument over the points of protrusion. Although the limb is somewhat in the wav, it is better to maintain this position until the desired object is attained. Then, for what is technically called

— THE TAXIS. Commence pressing up to and within the point of protrusion as much of the tumor as possible with *one fore-finger*, while the other hand supports and gently elevates the whole of the sac. Retain all that is brought up with the first finger, and reach down as far as possible with the middle finger; bringing up and securing with it as before. The fore-finger may then be again brought into requisition, and perhaps the ring-finger also. Continue the operation until all the parts are carefully returned in the inverse order of their emergence, pressing gently all the time with the other hand, so as not to contract the bulk of the sac, and avoid irritating it by too much handling.

We will notice one most efficient MEANS of REDUCTION which appears to have been strangely overlooked; though to us, at least, it has long seemed the most obvious and natural of any that can be devised. We have often easily succeeded in cases where there was considerable irritation, and sometimes even a degree of inflammation, by placing the patient in the position before described, and applying a *large cup* to the abdomen, covering the umbilical region. In one instance the patient had been in terrible pain for several hours, and there was strong evidence of strangulation when Dr. Hill arrived. After regulating the patient's position, and ascertaining the critical state of the case,—it being complete inguinal hernia, with a large tumor too sensitive to allow of the necessary manipulation,—the Dr. looked about for some means of getting the advantage of *traction from within*, as a substitute for pressure from without. The only thing in the room that seemed available, was a half gallon pewter measure. But the *spout* or lip was in the way. He recollected, however, that fire could remedy this obstacle; and seizing the vessel, ran into the kitchen and melted off the projection. Inserting and firing a sufficient amount of cotton, he clapped it on, and instantly had at least a quart of intestines in it,—a considerable proportion of the abdominal contents,—among them, no doubt, part of those that had constituted the *hernia*, for that *was gone*. Instantaneous reduction without external manual assistance, was the happy result.

The internal traction by CUPPING has many advantages over

pushing in by manual taxis, when the latter is not easily affected without much handling. A moment's reflection will satisfy any one that the sudden withdrawal of so large an amount of intestinal mass, must be accompanied with a powerful tendency to what may be called "spontaneous reduction," in comparison with any other artificial means. The force thus brought to bear is precisely in the best possible direction, and is applied to the parts directly concerned, and no others. The difference between this pulling, and the usual pushing in of the knot of intestines, is like the difference between "pulling out" a common bow-knot by the end left for the purpose, and literally untying it by pushing back the loop.

While we are giving our experience, we will relate another original mode of reduction; at which, however, Dr. H. was only an astonished spectator. Occurring while he was quite young, and under peculiar circumstances, it made a strong impression upon his mind, to which, perhaps, he is indirectly indebted for the idea of his own plan. Few things indeed could be more calculated to make a boy think,— and to think of becoming a doctor! An old gentleman living near his father's farm had been subject for a great part of his life to rupture. On several recent occasions it had become strangulated, requiring the aid of a physician. Dr. H.'s father, though not a medical man, was generally called in to assist whenever the old gentleman's "*bu'st* would come down again." On the occasion in question, a doctor had been sent for as usual, but had not arrived, and things were in a worse condition than ever before. Great was the alarm,— and not without reason. Much time had already been lost, during which the patient had been laboring under all the usual violent effects of strangulation. He was now visibly sinking. All the means which the friends and neighbors had ever known or heard of had been already tried without avail. Nothing now was looked for but immediate dissolution. At this juncture, the other persons present were probably as much astonished as Dr H. to see his father, who was a tall, powerful man, seize the patient by the feet, draw them over his shoulders, and spring up from the floor with the sick man hanging at his back,—back to back and head downward. In this style he made several sudden jumps, settling down again very firmly, and, *of course*, heavily on his heels. During this jolting and *traction by inverted gravity*, the strangulation was overcome, the tumor entirely disappearing; and the patient was laid upon his bed again, *cured* by this Brobdignagian operation. The *cupping* plan is certainly an improvement on the *backing*, as far as convenience is concerned, but not probably any more effective than that would prove. In case of *spasmodic* strangulation, the fright of the patient might aid the cure.

Unfortunately, however, we will often not be called in, until it is too late for immediate reduction, dangerous inflammation if not consequent adhesions having occurred in the parts.

Any considerable amount of INFLAMMATION *contra-indicates* other means for immediate *reduction*, but does not by any means authorize an operation. Under the Homeopathic practice the necessity for the knife is often dispensed with.

THE OPERATION for strangulated hernia is sometimes successful and occasionally indispensable, but it should be the *last resort.* Still there is danger in delay; when once determined on, it is to be promptly put in execution. Let all other available means have been attempted before recourse to so dangerous and uncertain a measure; but when it must be done — *do it*, without waiting for the assembling of half a dozen other surgeons, and by delaying lose all chance of success.

Having failed in effecting a reduction by "taxis," inflammation not having already set in, if the tumor is not very sensitive and there is no considerable redness over and around it; the hernia has come on spontaneously from a relaxed condition of the parts, or if it be an old hernia and the strangulation is of a spasmodic character, not depending on any mechanical violence or strain, and there is little or no symptomatic fever, give *Nux. vom.* This should be repeated in two hours if the symptoms do not abate, or if they have been ameliorated, but improvement has ceased. If, however, the patient is not evidently better in an hour and a half, or two hours, after the second dose, you should choose another remedy.

Should there still be no active inflammation, there being redness of the face with hardness and fullness of the abdomen, vomiting of fecal matter or putrid eructations, *Opium* should be given, and may be repeated more frequently than the former remedy. Some recommend a repetition as often as every fifteen minutes. After repeating this remedy three or four times, let the patient rest without any medicine for one, two, or three hours, unless he gets worse. If improvement ceases and is not continued by a repetition of the remedy after the suspension, or if he is not benefited in the first instance, and active inflammation is not present (whether there be fever or not), and if there is pinching pain in the abdomen with a sense of weight and pressure, with burning sensations, the nausea continuing with burning and thirst, give *Alumina*, and repeat the dose in half an hour, if no amelioration takes place sooner; then wait an hour before repeating or changing the remedy, unless symptoms of inflammation arise. When even an amelioration of the symptoms occurs, attempts may be made at a reduction of the hernia, not however by the usual "taxis," as all handling serves to keep up the spasmodic action. But the *cup* may be applied to the abdomen, even if too much tenderness exists in the *sac* to admit of the "*taxis*."

The patient during the whole course of treatment should be kept as much as possible on the back, inclined to the sound side, with the hips and shoulders elevated, and the thighs flexed upon the abdomen, so as to keep the abdominal muscles relaxed, and favor a spontaneous return of the protruded parts, as soon as the spasm is relieved. Should the hernia have been caused by some recent external injury or strain, or if in an old hernia, the strangulation had been caused by a similar accident, *Arnica* should be used, taken internally and applied locally. CALENDULA, however, is important in the early stage of incarcerated hernia arising from violence.

If active and violent inflammation should arise during the treatment or before, either from an injury or from the long continuance of the spasm, with excessive burning pain in the abdomen, nausea, bilious vomiting, abdomen sensitive to the touch, pulse full, hard and frequent, with thirst, give *Aconite*, and in severe cases repeat the dose in one hour, unless amelioration occurs sooner. Should not the patient improve in three or four hours and cold perspiration appear, the pulse becoming irregular and feeble, the vomiting being *acrid*, use *Sulphur*, one dose, and wait two or three hours unless the symptoms change so as to demand some other remedy. If symptoms of *gangrene* appear in the tumor, its surface being moist and purple, give *Lachesis;* or if the surface is dry, the thirst intense and burning, with great prostration of strength, the pulse becoming small and feeble, *Arsenicum.*

While it is generally true that we ought to take into account the known pathology of the case in making our selection, it is equally true that a remedy which will remove certain symptoms produced by unknown causes, may with great propriety be prescribed for similar symptoms, though produced by a known cause, and that, too, a secondary one and quite different from the former. So in the case under consideration, if there are present vomiting, cold perspiration and coldness of the extremities, a cadaverous countenance, great anguish, fear of death and despair, the prominent symptoms of *Veratrum* in cholera, and such as will usually yield to this remedy, we should most assuredly administer it, and may expect favorable results from its action in *hernia,* though the cause may have been a mechanical injury instead of an epidemic.*

* "A few words in regard to strangulated hernia in so far that as an organic cause it gives rise to colicky pains and the relations which our remedy bears to such pains:

"One would suppose that it would be the thing whether the strangulation was congenital, old, recent, or occurred in a rupture produced by external violence, as the cause which produces the pains is always the same. If this were the case, all strangulated *hernia* must yield to the same curative method that had conquered a few cases.

"NUX must then prove curative in all cases, as it has proved of such essential service in some. Still I much doubt if it deserves the name of a specific in those cases; at least, oft-repeated experience must confirm its power. I believe that *Nux* is to be applied with most certainty when the rupture is of recent occurrence and suddenly becomes strangulated, and which could have been cured by *Nux* if the strangulation had not supervened. In a case of this kind, we should attempt the reduction of the hernial protrusion, by means of the taxis; if it is reduced, the pains soon mitigate and all of the symptoms dependent upon it disappear.

"Should, however, we not be able to reduce soon by this method, which is most frequently the case as the constriction of the muscular fibers of the intestines and abdominal ring is increased by the irritation produced by the taxis, and thereby a more powerful resistance is induced, we should, under such circumstances, without useless attempts at reduction, administer *Nux vom.* in the smallest dose. I do not say without reason, in the smallest dose; for where the sensibility of the patient is so much exalted, we should endeavor to avoid every possible exacerbation from the remedy, in order not to bring the life of the patient in still greater

Though some of the authors depreciate all local applications in this disease, and probably so far as relates to their effect in mere spasmodic strangulation, aside from inflammation, they are useless

danger by producing spasmodic complaints. Observations coincide with mine in these cases, that soon after the administration of the remedy the pain ceased, the intestine replaced itself, even if before, this had been impossible with the taxis.

"W——, aged thirty-six years, a stocking weaver, whose frame had been much reduced by care and disease, endeavored to refresh himself by short sleep in the afternoon, for the remaining toils of the day, and despite his miserable nourishment, he always gained sufficient strength, although not without exertion to enable him to pursue his labors. A long time since, I had happily cured him of a chronic hepatic affection, and from that time the man enjoyed at least tolerable health. In the summer I was called to him at night, and on entering his chamber, I found him in bed wringing his hands and exhibiting the following picture of disease:

"Early in the morning the patient had felt as well as usual, had a natural stool as generally, had eaten enough at noon and then taken his usual siesta, from which, however, he was awakened by a griping, stinging pain in the right inguinal region, which, after his arising, continued to increase hourly, and towards evening obliged him to lie down. Notwithstanding, he still hoped that nature would afford him relief, until finally the pains extended over the whole abdomen, which was painfully tense and distended; eructations of wind, vomiting of a greenish, bitter fluid supervened, and he was troubled with restlessness, which he could not overcome. At the same time, he complained much of thirst; the pulse was small, quick, contracted; burning heat over the whole body, with cool, clammy sweats in the face and on the extremities. By external examination of the abdomen, I found in the right inguinal region an elastic swelling, which gave him much pain by pressing upon it, and gave me the idea that hernia existed, although the patient assured me that he had never had a rupture. By more careful examination, it was evident that a hernia which had just arisen existed.

"As twelve hours had elapsed since its first appearance, and the taxis proving of no service, I did not longer delay the application of the proper remedy. On personal experience I could not depend, whether homeopathic remedies were applicable in such cases; I could not upon the experience of other homeopathists. I indeed would not at an earlier period have believed that such a small dose could have proved beneficial in such a case, as according to allopathic rules very large doses of the most violent drastics are frequently given without effect. They had already administered a few enemata of *chamomile* tea without effect, as it had scarcely been possible to give them to the patient. I laid everything aside, gave bread water as drink, and administered *Nux* 24, and waited for its effect. After a quarter of an hour had elapsed eructations and vomiting had ceased, the belly appeared less tense, and the rupture was not so painful to the touch. In about two hours the incarceration was not only overcome, but the rupture had disappeared without ever recurring, as far as I have had opportunity of observing in the individual sense." (*Hartmann's Remedies*, p. 150.)

or even injurious; yet we have in our own experience the most conclusive evidence, that when the part becomes *inflamed*, the frequent application of cloths wet in water, as *hot* as can be endured by the patient (the degree of heat usually being in proportion to the intensity of the inflammation — higher as the inflammation increases), will be a most powerful auxillary to other homeopathic remedies, in restoring a healthy action in the parts. Should the inflammation extend over the abdomen, the hot cloths should be equally extensive.*

* "The Homeopathic Materia Medica possesses already a considerable number of remedies by which the symptoms of incarcerated hernia can be more or less simulated, but only a few of these have been employed up to the present time. In my own practice, I found the greatest assistance from the following:

"*Nux vomica, Acidum Sulphuricum, Lycopodium, Belladonna*, and finally I must mention one or more remedies, which, although it does not appear in the series of symptoms that it is capable of producing, those which accompany the formation and incarceration of a hernia can yet not be dispensed with as an appropriate, intermediate or auxillary remedy in certain forms of incarcerated ruptures, on account of the unlimited influence which it exercises upon the vascular, and chiefly upon the capillary system, and accordingly not only compromises among its symptoms the type of inflammatory fever, but also the type of acute local inflammations; farther, on account of its effects upon the mind which manifest themselves particularly in the form of inconsolable anguish, forebodings of death and great disposition to be frightened — states of mind which we not unfrequently meet with in persons affected with incarcerated hernia; I allude to *Aconitum napellus*.

"The method I have hitherto adopted in the treatment of incarcerated ruptures is as follows:

"Having convinced myself of the existence of an incarceration, I first place the patient in a comfortable reclining posture, the chest and the pelvis somewhat raised in order that the abdominal muscles may be relaxed as much as possible; the lower extremities being at the same time moderately drawn up. The patient having continued in this position for a few minutes, I proceed to the selection of the remedies.

"In reference to the concomitant symptoms, we meet with three forms of incarcerated hernia, which presents materially different marks of distinction.

First Form of Incarceration.

"The rupture has just occurred for the first time, or one that had formerly existed has reappeared, and has suddenly become incarcerated, in which case the rupture is always small, the symptoms appear suddenly and with greater intensity; they consist in a pinching or squeezing and pressive sensation in the region of the rupture; violent dragging pain with periodical tearing, and a sort of spasmodic constriction in the abdomen; nausea, inclination to vomit, and actual vomiting of an acid mucus; obstruction, with frequent inclination for stool; most of these

Two cases are reported in the N. A. Hom. Journal (1851, p. 403), of strangulated hernia cured, one by *Nux and Veratrum* 3d, given every half hour; the protrusion disappeared without taxis.

symptoms are increased by the slightest pressure on the rupture, as also by movement.

"*Nux vomica* corresponds with symptoms of this form of incarceration. I accordingly give ten to fifteen globules of one of the higher potencies every half hour, or every hour. Frequently a remission of the symptoms takes place after the first dose or two; if, at the same time a sensation of movement takes place in the rupture, or if gurgling noise be heard, then a remission of the incarcerating muscular contraction and a speedy replacement without any external treatment may be expected. Should this not be the case, but, on the contrary, the sufferings return again with unabated vigor; or if an oppressive soreness or pain, as if from a wound and a violent burning, prevail in the region of the rupture, and the superincumbent teguments become very sensitive to the slightest touch, or if the heat in the affected parts increase, and thus betokens an increased determination of blood towards these parts; or should the incarceration have been preceded by a fright or some other mental affection, and the patient be in a state of general irritation or excitement, then I usually give one drop of *Aconitum* of the third to the sixth dilution, and an hour afterwards, *Nux vomica* at a lower dilution than in the first instance, and in a liquid form in preference (*Nux vom.* two drops x—xv, Aq., destill. oz. ij), a teaspoonful every half hour to an hour.

Second Form of Incarceration.

"The rupture becomes suddenly incarcerated and is generally small; tearing, dragging pain, both in the rupture itself and in the whole abdomen, predominates; the patient sometimes experiences fugitive stitches in the region of the rupture; the pains undergo periodical remissions — disappearing almost entirely for a time, and then returning with increased violence: the patient feels much exhausted during the remissions; he complains of a general sensation of cold, the abdomen is much distended by flatus; often a continued desire to vomit; the patient eventually vomits an acid-tasting fluid, and, notwithstanding a very urgent inclination for stool, no evacuation takes place.

"In this form of incarceration likewise, *Nux vomica* is an excellent medicine, but *Lycopodium* vies with it in efficacy. I generally administer both these medicines alternately, at intervals of one to two hours. If, however, these symptoms appear in a crural rupture, if they take place in a woman, or has the incarceration in the latter case taken place during or immediately after the appearance of the menses, and if, moreover, the individual is of a mild, yielding disposition, *Lycopodium* is to be preferred. I give this medicine in the middle attenuations (10–15) either in globules or in the liquid form (Tinct. *Lycopodium*, drops x—v. Aq. destill. oz. j), a teaspoonful every half hour, or every hour. If throbbing, burning, and other symptoms indicating *Aconitum* becomes predominant, administer the latter as an intermediate remedy.

The other, *Aconite and Veratrum.* There were present stercoraceous vomiting, great prostration, &c.

Time is a matter of vital importance in this case; therefore, when we have made use of the remedies heretofore directed or any

Third Form of Incarceration.

"The third form of incarcerated hernia (which occurs chiefly in aged persons, and in ruptures of long standing, that have for the most part been kept back by appropriate bandages, or have been continually protruding, and have attained a large size), is that in which the incarceration comes on insidiously and imperceptibly, and betrays itself at first only by a distressing, pinching, and constrictive sensation of the region of the rupture, by uneasiness and fullness in the abdomen, and by periodical sickness and constipation. The rupture is not very painful to the touch, the incarcerated part is also not so tense and hard as in the two preceding forms, but feels more doughy. This incarceration may often exist for days, without any perceptible increase in the concomitant symptoms; gradually, however, twitchings and pinchings, combined with periodical transitory tearing pains, supervene in the abdomen and groin; the sickness then becomes more lasting, a sweetish, saline, or bitter fluid is sometimes eructated, and is not unfrequently followed by vomiting, of a watery fluid, and subsequently of ingesta.

"In this form also two medicines concur; and the one is again *Nux vomica*, which competes with *Acidium sulphuricum* for the rank of priority. If the patient is of a sanguine-choleric temperament, which, however, is but seldom the case, *Nux vomica*, at a low dilution, must be given first; and should the removal of the incarceration not be effected within twelve hours, *Acidium sulphuricum* must be administered. If the incarceration takes place on the left side, and the patient is of a melancholic-phlegmatic temperament, *Acid. sulphuricum* should be employed from the beginning. I have hitherto been in the habit of prescribing in the disorder in question, a drop of the tenth dilution of this medicine to be taken every hour. By means of the foregoing treatment of incarcerated hernia, I say it with heartfelt joy, I have always more readily and more frequently succeeded in attaining the desired result than was the case in my former practice, when I treated my patients in accordance with the principles of the old school.

"If my assistance was sought sufficiently early, it formed a rare exception to the rule when an incarceration of the first and second form was not removed within eight hours, and that of the third form within twenty-four hours. Still more rarely did it happen that homeopathy can not yet renounce the operation as the last resource in the treatment of incarcerated hernia. Whether this will ever be possible, I shall not investigate here; we may, however, presume with every appearance of certainty, that those cases in which the operation is now deemed indispensable, will become more and more scarce, the more closely that the re-provings of medicines yet unknown or untried, will be discovered to approach in similarity individual forms of this disease.

"If the homeopathic medicines do not remove the incarceration within a given space, to be determined by each individual case, but if on the contrary, symptoms of a more troublesome and dangerous character make their appearance; if not only

that may be indicated by the symptoms (bearing in mind that if they do not act promptly, they will not probably be serviceable at all), and the case still remains obstinate, the danger every moment increasing, we must resort to the *operation* or some efficient means for producing *muscular relaxation*, so that the hernia can be reduced without the knife. We prefer to try the latter first. For this purpose we have used, with success, *Lobelia inflata* in doses sufficient to produce a perfect flaccidity of the muscular system. It may be used in the form of the saturated tincture, the etherial oil or liquid extract. Begin the former in half drachm doses, the two latter in one or two drop doses. It should be given in repeated small doses, the minimum dose at first, a little more at the end of a quarter of an hour, double that amount in ten or twelve minutes, and so on, increasing the quantity and diminishing the intervals, until you have brought his system completely under the relaxing influence of the medicine; meanwhile use warm enemas of the same. If we need to bring about still greater relaxation, this may be effected by enemas of *tobacco*, though it is necessary to be cautious in the use of this "poisonous weed," as very little will occasion dangerous symptoms in some patients, while others can take it with impunity and advantage. In *injecting*, use a large syringe with a long pipe, and have the patient retain what is thrown up as long as he possibly can. The relaxing enemas should be repeated once an hour, if not oftener.

When you have brought about complete muscular *relaxation*, have the patient turned in the proper position (if he is not kept

the rupture itself, but also the abdomen and the epigastric region become very sensible to the slightest touch; if the existing pains and the tension of the abdomen becomes more intensely violent; if nausea, the inclination to vomit and the vomiting itself increase and the patient vomits more liquid than he has taken, even during the prevalence of excessive thirst; should traces of bile or of other intestinal contents be discovered in the matter ejected; if high fever, with a hard, full pulse supervene and the patient becomes more and more restless, it is to be presumed that the medicines administered (although no others can be found that correspond better with the form of the disease under treatment) are either not strictly homeopathic to the case or they have been employed in an improper dose, or finally, that the medicine appropriate to this individual case is as yet unproved, and therefore unknown. Under such circumstances I never hesitate for a moment to propose an operation and, if the patient consents, to perform it as soon as possible." (*M. Traub*, *Allg. Hom. Zeit.*, *No.* 12, 31*st.*)

in it all the time) and *endeavor to effect reduction* — as often as you can do so without causing pain. So long, however, as there is much tenderness, attempts at the taxis have little chance of doing good, and may do much harm.

But the application of the large cup to the abdomen, is unattended with any risk of increasing the inflammation. The intestines themselves, it should be remembered, may be quite free from inflammation, though the integuments over the sac are tender to the touch. There is great danger of the peritoneum becoming inflamed, but this is not likely to be more in the natural than in the abnormal situation of that delicate membrane.

The relaxing measure should be *kept up*, even though the patient appear much *prostrated.* They may, however, be carried to an unsafe degree, and your judgment must be exercised in the case according to the symptoms. There is no danger, however, with the articles recommended (except the Tobacco) of any *such permanent* prostration as follows from the use of tartarized antimony.

The enormous doses of *Lobelia* formerly used by the Thomsonians, bringing on the "alarming symptoms" without any danger to the life of the patient, prove that we need be in no great fear of killing our patients, though we may have a *medicinal* disease to treat afterwards. But even the *danger* and the after disease from the use of the *Lobelia,* are by no means to be so much dreaded as the *danger* and *death* of the patient so often following the use of the knife, even in the most skillful hands.

We were consulted in a case in February, 1855, in Cleveland, then under the care of two homeopathic physicians: an Irishman, with strangulated hernia (Scrotal). The tumor was exceedingly large, the patient in extreme agony — all attempts to reduce it by *taxis* had failed, and it was evident that unless relief was afforded soon he must die. Instead of the operation, we advised Tobacco injections, which produced such a state of relaxation as to enable the attending physician to return the protrusion by taxis. Should *twelve hours* elapse without any *favorable* change, recourse should be had to *the operation.* Bear in mind, that with this extreme measure the chances are three to one against the patient. Give him the benefit of it, however, when it is his only chance, or you are sure his danger is greater without it. [For directions how to operate, and the anatomy of the parts concerned, see Part II.]

Chloroform has great power in producing muscular relaxation and overcoming spasmodic contraction.

We once saw, in the *Commercial Hospital* of Cincinnati, a case of dislocated hip, which baffled all the efforts of the attending surgeons, at reduction; their pulley and other extending apparatus breaking in their efforts to make the necessary extension; when chloroform so completely relaxed him, that it not only required no extending force to reduce the dislocation, but the limb had to be held *in situ* until he recovered to consciousness, lest it should fall apart by its own weight.

Radical cure of Hernia.—In the early stage of hernia, soon after the occurrence of the "rupture," by the administration of Homeopathic remedies, a radical cure will generally be effected. The most reliable, especially for hernia in young children, are *Nux. vom., Aurum and Cocculus; Nit. acid and Veratrum* are also sometimes useful. In our experience, *Nux. vom.* is the most reliable, both in children and adults. Dr. Hunt cured one case of long-standing umbilical hernia in a woman, with repeated doses of *Nux.*

Cocculus has been successful in effecting radical cures in children, and the same may be said of *Aurum.*

Nux. and Veratrum alternately have cured hernia in children. RUCKERT reports a number of cases *cured* by *Nux.*, and several more *relieved;* also two cases cured by *Cocculus.*

In any case where the hernial protrusion takes place early, and in fact in all cases, a proper *truss must be applied* to prevent the recurrence of the protrusion, until the cure is complete. For though after reduction, the hernial sac *may* not appear again before we have time to effect a cure, the chances are ten to one that it will, and once this does occur we lose a greater part, if not all, we have gained by the treatment; and still more, the older the case is, the less probability there is of a radical cure by internal medication. The same accident that caused the "rupture" in the beginning, will be more likely to bring it on a second time, when the rupture or distended tissues are still feeble and have but partially recovered from the late injury.

IN RECENT CASES OF RUPTURE in young and healthy persons, a simple *truss* alone will sometimes excite adhesive inflammation, and prevent the necessity for its further use,—the parieties of the abdominal canal or femoral sheath effectually coalescing. But to insure any probability of this desirable result, or for safety against a relapse,

—THE TRUSS should be made to extend from the point of first *emergence* out of the abdominal cavity, to the point of external *protrusion* beneath the integument,—from the Internal to the External Abdominal Ring,—so as to compress the whole Canal or Sheath through which the viscera have passed.

This measure alone cannot be relied on unless applied soon after the accident that caused the original rupture. The patient, moreover, must be kept quiet for several days after the first application of the truss; and whenever it is removed, he should assume the horizontal position, and not be allowed to move until it is securely fixed on again.

In ADULTS, the truss rarely succeeds in effecting the radical cure, even under the most favorable circumstances.

The numerous cases to be met with in every civilized community, sufficiently attest the truth of this last remark. One medical statician has even estimated that *one-eight* of the human family is in the ruptured condition! He must, certainly, have lived among a weak-bellied race. Still, however extravagant may be this estimate, far too many are everywhere suffering or living in fear of death from this common accident; and this, too, where every drug store or apothecary shop is well supplied with trusses of every imaginable form and character, not a few of which claim to be all-sufficient for a complete cure.

We believe it is pretty generally admitted by the most eminent allopathic surgeons of the present day, that the only plan that furnishes any reliable probability of a radical cure, is *an operation with the knife.* But this operation is not even one of the "kill or cure" resources. It *may* kill; and when it does not, may leave the evil operated for as bad as before, or worse. The risk is without anything like an equivalent chance of benefit. Hence, indeed, but few persons are tempted to try in such a lottery of life. The clumsy mechanical resources of the truss has to be still resorted to, without any hope of ever dispensing with such an artificial safeguard.

We have carefully examined all the published reports and have not been able to find the record of any case of Inguinal or femoral hernia, which had existed for years, in an adult, cured by internal remedies; nor even of umbilical (of years' standing in an adult), except the one of Dr. Hunt's. Hernia in children, and *recent* cases in adults, have been *cured.* *Incarcerated* hernia has been *relieved,* — the inflammation subdued and the reduction of the tumor effected, or rendered feasible by the *internal remedies.* But there the record ceases, there the case is left. The truss, with great caution, is the patient's only safeguard. He is doomed to undergo the inconvenience and suffer the fear that necessarily attaches to such a condition, during his whole life; or submit to the dangerous and *uncertain* expedient of an *operation for radical cure,* as recommended and practiced by allopathic surgeons. Such is the condition in which this case is left both by allopathic and homeopathic authorities.

To any one acquainted with the anatomy of the parts concerned in this accident, it is obvious that any mode of treatment, be that medical, mechanical, or surgical, which will effectually *close* the sheath, canal or opening through which the protrusion takes place, will be effectual; and without such a safeguard, such an *adhesion* of the parieties of the canal or orifice to each other, or to their contained parts, so as to effectually prevent future distension, and bar the re-entrance of the intestine, no safety exists or assurance can be given against the return of the accident, at any future period.

It is well known that inflammation excited in these parts, tends to produce adhesions, and if the parieties of the canal or orifice can be kept in contact, and in that situation a moderate degree of inflammation excited, adhesions will take place, effectually closing it. This simple, safe, and efficacious plan for obviationg a dangerous surgical operation, and yet curing Hernia more effectually, was hit upon by that eminently practical surgeon, the late much-lamented *Prof. T. V. Morrow.*

The necessary inflammation was induced by simply using an

irritating plaster.* From observing the effects of that application in a variety of other cases, Dr. Morrow came to the conclusion that it was just the thing wanted, to *insure* the requisite adhesion of any parts of the abdominal parietes involved in hernia. He had long been dissatisfied with the ordinary means resorted to for that purpose. Since his first report of a case so treated and permanently cured [See Medical Reformer, Vol. VI., No. 1, for July, 1846], the plan has been extensively adopted with the most satisfactory success. No failure, so far as we have been able to ascertain, has occurred in a single instance.†

* The plaster he used was made by adding to 1 quart of Tar (to which 4 ounces of Rosin had been added, and boiled to evaporate the water from the tar), 2¼ ounces each, of finely pulverized *Sanguinaria*, *Phytolacca*, *Podophyllum* and *Arum triphyllum*, mixed and stirred together when not quite scalding hot.

† THE PLASTER made use of should be large enough to cover the whole canal or sheath,—say from two to two and a half inches wide and from three to three and a half in length,—and the PAD of the truss should be nearly as large as the plaster.

The PART to which the application is to be made should first be smoohtly *shaved;* the plaster laid on carefully, the pad over it, and a truss brought to press with considerable force, as much as the patient can bear.

The COMPRESSION, however, will have to be gradually lessened as the parts become tender. When the truss is taken off for this purpose, or to re-spread the plaster (which should be done every day), the patient must be made to keep perfectly still in a horizontal posture, with the thigh flexed on the abdomen. After a while the truss will become too painful to be borne; when a large *compress* must be substituted, and carefully kept in place by *bandages* round the body. The patient had then better keep to his bed on his back. When obliged to move at all, he should be directed to apply his hand to the compress, as a further security against accident.

The purulent discharge excited by the plaster, so frequently renewed, will be considerable. If the pain and irritation should at any time be so great as to deprive the patient of *sleep*, or extend downward along the *spermatic cord* to the testicle, remove the irritating applications for a while and substitute an elm poultice. The suppurating process should be *kept up* for from three to four weeks. Probably a shorter time would in most cases suffice; but it is better to err on the safe side. Better let the patient suffer a week too long than run any risk by giving up this essential part of the treatment a single day too soon.

The *surface* may be allowed to heal as soon as the plaster is removed. Dress it first with an emollient poultice, and then with simple cerate.

The TRUSS should be *reapplied*, as soon as it can be borne again, and kept on for eight or ten weeks longer. All applications may then as a general rule, be

UMBILICAL AND VENTRAL HERNIA.

Both these consist in a protrusion of the intestines or omentum through the parieties of the abdomen. When the navel is the point of protrusion, it is *umbilical* hernia, to which *infants* are most subject a short time after birth, from their straining the abdomen in crying, while the bandage around the body securing the umbilical dressings is too loose. It sometimes occurs in *parturient* females, the muscles giving way during their powerful contractions upon the gravid uterus. It may be produced in any individual by any force applied to the abdomen sufficient to rupture the muscles. Hernia may occur at any *other point* along the Linea Alba, or, indeed, at any other part of the abdomen, though it would not be called umbilical, but *ventral.* "Ventral Hernia," then, means an abdominal protrusion at any other point than the Umbilicus, Abdominal Ring, or Femoral Sheath. True Umbilical Hernia is very rare in any others than infants.

The proper TREATMENT is the same in principle, whether for an infant or an adult, and whether the accident occurs at one point or another *above Poupart's Ligament.*

First, for the REDUCTION of it, place the patient upon his back,

discontinued. The pressure, however, should be gradually lessened, before being entirely taken off, and the part frequently bathed in cold water. This CURE will be complete and effectual.

In addition to the means originally devised by Dr. Morrow, we have had reason to believe that advantage resulted in some cases from a few drops of the *oil of eggs,* rubbed on the parts, once or twice a day, after the removal of the irritating plaster. (This oil is obtained by simple pressure, from the heated yolks.) This article which seems to have the effect of promoting adhesion is one of the principal agents relied on in a patent for the cure of Hernia.

The other means relied on in this tolerably successful *secret* treatment, are a pad, truss and plaster. The plaster is an extract obtained by boiling equal parts of the barks of Hemlock, White oak, common break (Pteris aquilina, —probably the rock-break, Pteris atropurpurea), and green osier (Cornus circinata). This is removed once in three or four days, and the surface lubricated with oil of eggs. As the cure progresses, the round leather pad is diminished in size.

One *precaution* is necessary. It is absolutely essential to success, that NO PROTRUSION takes place during the period of treatment. The danger is greatest when the sore is most irritable; and if the patient is not then warned against much straining or motion, all treatment may easily prove a failure. Present restraint is the indispensable condition on which future freedom of action may be *insured.*

with the thighs flexed upon the abdomen and the shoulders a little elevated.

In this position, the protruded portion will generally return spontaneously. If not, it can be easily pushed back by applying the fingers to the tumor. The *taxis* accomplished, apply a TRUSS, under which a *pad* should be placed, made as follows: Take a circular piece of the thick spongy portion of sole leather, of the proper size to cover the opening and extend from one and a half to two inches all round it. Have the pad regularly concave, the center of the depression being about half an inch below the plane of the circumference. Place the patient in the position above described, and bring the parieties of the hole in the muscles in contact, so as completely to close the orifice, by pressing from the sides, while the muscles are in this relaxed condition. The edges being thus kept in contact, apply, directly over the point of protrusion, a layer of raw cotton or soft lint, wet with *Calendula*. This application should be just large and thick enough to fill the excavated surface in the leather, without causing any pressure. Apply the leather pad over it, and secure it by a bandage passed round the body, sufficiently tight to compress the muscles, and keep in contact the parieties of the hole. It is better to fasten the pad to the bandage before it is applied. This should be kept on six or eight days without being removed, unless it produce too much irritation. It should be wet once or twice a day with the medicine, by applying it above and allowing it to soak through the cotton.

In INFANTS, a sufficient amount of adhesive inflammation will generally take place in three or four days to unite the parts; though this dressing should be continued for ten or twelve days, diminishing the strength and pressure gradually. A bandage tight enough to support the muscles, and to prevent distension of the abdomen, should be worn for several months, and the part washed daily with *Calendula*. In an ADULT, it may be necessary to wear the first dressing for a month or more.

When it becomes necessary to remove the *dressings* during the treatment, great care should be taken that no protrusion then occur. The patient should be placed in the same position as when the first applications were made, and the parietes of the abdomen should be firmly held by an assistant, so that no motion will be allowed at the point of protrusion, and the muscles will not be put upon the stretch. The dressings should never be removed when the intestines are full. Great care should be taken to prevent costiveness. If the patient be in poor health aside from this, the proper attentions should be bestowed upon his general system.

CHAPTER XXX.

HYDROCELE, — MEDICAL AND MECHANICAL TREATMENT.

HYDROCELE — causes and varieties — diagnosis — dropsy of the cord — "congenital hydrocele" — Repressive Treatment — Gum-Elastic Bag, &c. — a RADICAL CURE without the operation — Directions for OPERATING and after-treatment — means for avoiding re-accumulation of fluid — Hydatids — Treatment of Dropsy of the Cord — of congenital hydrocele — hydrocele with anasarca — hernia and other complications.

HYDROCELE,

— OR DROPSY OF THE TESTICLE, is quite a common disease. There is sometimes an œdematous condition of the scrotum, with serous effusion throughout its cellular tissue, which may be mistaken for true hydrocele, — as also, on a superficial examination, may scirrhus or any other cause of swelling in the part.

"Hydrocele" is limited to a collection of serum in the tunica vaginalis, a serous membrane enclosing the testicle. It is but an abnormal quantity of the fluid naturally secreted to protect and allow free motion to the part. The immediate *cause* of the disease then, may be either increased secretion or diminished absorption. It may affect persons of all ages, and even exist at birth.

The swelling *begins* at the lower portion of the scrotum, or rather the accumulation naturally sinks and first shows itself there; gradually becoming diffused and extending up towards the abdominal ring. The tumor is finally pyriform in shape, and elastic to the touch, — or it may be described as feeling like a bladder distended with water. It gives no pain on pressure, unless the testicle itself is pressed upon. The skin of the scrotum retains its usual wrinkled state, even though the part may attain an immense magnitude, the serous bag within sometimes containing a pint of fluid. The *fluid* itself is usually crystalline or colorless, occasionally yellowish.

It rarely happens that both sides of the scrotum are effected with this disease at the same time; more on the left than right side.

The *diagnosis* of this disease is sometimes difficult. In order to come to a satisfactory conclusion, you should examine into the history of the case. Recollect that hydrocele proper begins in the form of a tumor at the bottom of the scrotum, and gradually ascends; while *anasarca* of the scrotum is more diffused, pits on pressure and is generally attended with anasarca of other parts or ascites. SCIRRHUS of the testicle presents a uniform enlargement, is also accompanied with pain, and quite heavy, feeling to the patient and the examiner like a ball of lead. In hydrocele, moreover, when recent, before the membrane thickens, the whole mass of the tumor below the substance of the testicle is *transparent* or *translucent*,—as may be ascertained by placing it, when the room is darkened, between your eye and a lighted candle. It may be distinguished from scrotal HERNIA, by observing that in the latter case the tumor commences *above* instead of below, and if the patient *coughs*, the swelling will be enlarged, and a distinct impulse imparted to the finger pressing on it.

The CAUSE of the effusion must be inflammation of the serous membrane itself, but that *may* be occasioned by disease of the testicle, by direct external influences, or by metastasis from other textures of the same order. Most generally the cause can not be ascertained.

When there is enlargement of the testicle in connection with the serous accumulation, the case is called "HYDROSARCOCELE."

HYDATIDS may occupy the tunica vaginalis, and present the appearance of hydrocele, and be mistaken for it. The two diseases not unfrequently coexist, hydatids occupying a part of the cyst, while fluids accumulate in another part. These parasitical growths may adhere either to the serous membrane, the epididymis, or the substance of the testicle. This state of things can only be ascertained by the protruding of the cysts in question out of the wound.

HYDROCELE OF THE SPERMATIC CORD occasionally occurs, sometimes alone, sometimes in connection with effusion in the tunica vaginalis. It occasions an oval tumor near the abdominal ring, or it may be even in the canal above the ring, having so strong a resemblance to INGUINAL HERNIA, as to be easily mistaken for it. It is, however, free from pain, and translucent, and does not go down and disappear, on placing the patient in a recumbent position, as will be the case in hernia, unless it is strangulated, when the nature of the case will be but too evident from other symptoms. Dropsy of the cord is also to be distinguished from VARICOCELE, as will be noticed under that head.

CONGENITAL HYDROCELE has some peculiarities; and cases of the same kind, which occasionally occur in after life, are incorrectly called by the same name. The original connection between the tunica vaginalis and the peritoneum, of which it was a part, continues, and the fluids that collect in the cavity of the *abdomen* descend and accumulate, generally producing dropsy or "hydrocele" of the tunica vaginalis as well as of the cord. This may be distinguished from common hydrocele by placing the patient on his back and raising his hips, when the swelling will entirely recede, but instantly reappear when the erect position is assumed. The other symptoms of hydrocele, as transparency, &c., have to be also considered, as the affection may be mistaken for HERNIA, with which it may also co-exist (the same cause occasioning liability to both).

TREATMENT.

If the *cause* is known, that will often aid us much in the selection of the appropriate remedy. When the disease is the result of an injury, *Arnica* should be used.

This remedy is also applicable when the swelling is of a bluish-red color, large, or when it involves the penis. It is also applicable in congenital cases.

Conium is successful when it arises from a mechanical injury and there is swelling and pain in the testicle.

Rhododendron; especially when the hydrocele effects the left side. Four doses, one every eight days, cured a hydrocele in a boy of eighteen months.

Graphites; in persons subject to erysipelatous affections, eruptions, with constipation; and for dropsical affections of the scrotum and prepuce as well as for hydrocele.

Puls.; in recent cases, or in young children, or when the swelling is of a *bluish-white* color, when the patient has the *Pulsatilla* temperament, or when it is the result of metastasis. It may be sometimes followed by *Digitalis* with advantage.

Digitalis — the *scrotum* looks like a bladder filled with water.

Sulphur is sometimes useful when there is a psoric diathesis.

Besides the foregoing remedies, the following may be consulted: *Mer., China, Aurum, Lyc., Nux v. and Silicea.* The latter especially for scrofulous patients.

Psoricum 30, two doses, one every eight days, removed an accumulation of water in the tunica vaginalis testis; the sequel of repressed inflammation from the pressure of a truss.

Dr. Sterns related a case of hydrocele cured with *Silic.* alone. (*Ger. Cong.*, 1852.)

Dr. Francis Black reports a case of hydrocele of the right side in a man, produced by an injury, which had been twice tapped, the water drawn off and tincture *Iodine* injected, without effecting a cure. The hydrocele reappeared several months after and became very large, causing by its size and weight great discomfort. The cord was also swollen, appearing like hernia descending to the scrotum. It was cured in four weeks by *Graphites* 12 and *Silicea.*

Another case — a child three months old, cured in three weeks with *Graph.* 12.

PRESSURE on the scrotum, as well as suspension of it, will greatly stimulate absorption. Some convenient means of making equable pressure on this part was long wanting. This is supplied by an *India-rubber bag.* The bag should be so small as to require considerable distension to get it on. We have found it convenient to have it previously distended to the requisite size by two or three coils of watch spring, which can be drawn out when it is on. An *improvement* is an elastic open ring at the mouth, which may be conveniently pulled out at any time when it is required to wet the surface with any medicament.

We have succeeded by this new means in *avoiding the operation* and effecting a RADICAL CURE in several severe cases. In slighter forms of the disease, we have often found it suffice.

In some cases of long standing, where the quantity of fluid is large and the tunica vaginalis thickened and insensible, external and constitutional means will not be sufficient. We must then resort to the long-established

OPERATION,

for the purpose of removing the fluid, and preventing its reaccumulation by such means as will substitute *adhesive* for *effusive* inflammation between the folds of the tunica vaginalis.

As this operation is a very simple affair, we give directions how to perform it in this connection. Taking hold of the scrotum from behind, and stretching it tense, make an incision through the integument with a scalpel or bistoury (at any point not too elevated or too near the septum or raphe, between the two sides). Through this cut, introduce the trochar inclosed in a canula, and push them on into the sac in such a direction so as to avoid the testicle.

FIG. 14.

This can be held up out of the way by the left hand, though the contraction of the cord on handling the part (which may be made more effectual by previously applying cold water to the scrotum) will generally draw it out of danger. Withdraw the trochar, and push the canula further on into the sac, and fix it there until all the morbid accumulation has drained off, taking care to allow none of it to pass into the cellular tissue of the scrotum (where it would cause inflammation and perhaps sloughing).

If a trochar is not at hand, all the parts may be cut through with the bistoury, and a catheter or any tube about the size of a goose quill will answer for the canula.

After having drawn off the fluid by means of a canula, inject through it *Arnica tincture*, diluted four to one with water. This is to be left there until it produces considerable smarting or pain; then drawn off and the canula be removed. Take care never to take away the canula until the injection is all withdrawn, or the membranes may contract upon and retain it, producing more mischief than the natural secretion that has been removed. After the removal of the fluid and canula, — insert a TENT (or strip of linen) far enough in to remain, and keep up the inflammation; and prevent the external orifice from closing. Remove it from day to day and apply another, until a sufficient amount of adhesion has occurred.

If too high a grade of *inflammation* should be excited, the tent must be laid aside, and the means to subside it be employed. One of the best local means in such a case is to let the patient sit over the vapor of hot water, after which emollient poultices can be applied until the inflammation has subsided.

This operation for hydrocele is generally effectual. In some chronic cases, however, it may be necessary to employ something more powerful; a solution of the *Sesqui-carbonate of potash* will be good.

Great *care* is to be taken in performing this operation, not to injure the *testicle*, nor allow the lancet or trochar to pass through the opposite fold of the tunica vaginalis, so as to make an opening into the *cellular tissue* on the outside, and cause a diffused inflammation there.

If, after drawing off all the fluid, the tumor does not entirely subside, it is presumptive evidence that it is partly caused by HYDATIDS. If the latter protrude, the nature of the case is sufficiently plain.

If they do not present themselves thus spontaneously, and there is reason to suspect their existence (which cannot be known with absolute certainty beforehand), make a *large opening* and squeeze upon the tumors, when more or less of them will be pushed out, enclosed in their proper membranes or cysts. They may be all dissected away with the knife by laying open the scrotum sufficiently, or clipped off with scissors. This operation is very painful, but generally effectual. Clipping off a considerable portion and letting out their contents may be sufficient. The smaller ones or parts that remain will most likely be obliterated in the progress of the cure, especially if tents are used.

CHAPTER XXXI.

DISEASES OF THE TESTIS, CONTINUED.

HÆMATOCELE — Distinction of symptoms and treatment from Hydrocele.
VARICOCELE — Symptoms and progress — compression, &c.
SARCOCELE — early means or final castration.
FUNGUS TESTIS, Soft Testicle or "Hernia humoralis"— its connection with gonorrhea, and treatment accordingly.
ORCHITIS proper — various causes, symptoms and consequences — treatment.
IRRITABLE TESTES — obscurity and complexity — treatment.
CHRONIC ENLARGEMENT, and other diseases of the testes — causes and dangers — early treatment, or the *radical* cure.

HÆMATOCELE.

THIS is the name given to a swelling of the scrotum, resulting from a collection of blood instead of water in the tunica vaginalis. The extravasation, however, may be in the tunica albuginea (within the vaginalis), or simply an effusion into the cellular membrane of the scrotum.

It may RESULT from blows or other injuries of the scrotum or spermatic cord. A frequent cause is the wounding of some large vessel in operating for hydrocele.

The DIAGNOSIS of hæmatocele from hydrocele depends on its

greater solidity and weight, and being neither transparent nor fluctuating. The history also will frequently determine the nature of the case. The external parts are often thick and black, as in venous infiltration. This may at first occasion suspicion of gangrene; but the color is the only point of resemblance, and the general system is not at all affected.

The TREATMENT should first be directed to arrest any inflammation that may be present by the use of the proper specifics and the external application of warm vapor or water — cold water as used by some, is rather dangerous; as it lessens vitality too much and may hasten gangrene, when there is any tendency to it.

If from contusions or any other mechanical injury, *Arnica*, internally and also as a local application.

Other cases require *Puls. or Zinc, or Nux. v.*, *Rhus.*, and *Sulph.*

If these means fail, the scrotum may be laid open, the coagula evacuated, and the wound allowed to heal by granulation. If after this operation there should be trouble from *fresh* hemorrhage, the bleeding vessel must be found and tied.

Many persons have been very unjustifiably castrated for this disease, the only benefit resulting from the loss of the *sound testicle* being the removal of the blood, which might have been done as just directed.

VARICOCELE.

The disease so called from analogy to the other names of surgical diseases of the parts, is simply a varicose condition of the veins of the spermatic cord. As might be expected from the length and unsupported position of these veins, they are more liable to this relaxed and diseased condition than any others. The left cord is more liable to this state than the right, perhaps from obstruction to the return of its blood at the sigmoid flexure of the colon, as well as from its greater length. The distended part of the cord assumes a cone-shape, with its apex upwards, generally extending from the testicle as a basis up to the abdominal ring. The veins can be separately felt, rolling under the fingers like twisted cords.

There is a constant uneasy sensation in the part, neuralgic

pains not unfrequently extending down into the testicle,—which is often diminished in size, from the proper amount of nutritive fluid being prevented from reaching it.

The swelling sometimes increases so much as to be inconvenient from its mere bûlk, especially if the individual attempts to ride on horseback.

In the TREATMENT of this disease, great care should be taken that the testicle be kept suspended, so as not to pull upon the cord in the least. When the difficulty has arisen from a mechanical injury, *Arnica* is the remedy. If the vessels are at any time unusually swollen and painful, benefit may be derived from a dose or two of *Aconite* with the wet compress; Laurie recommends in most cases to commence with *Pulsatilla* and follow with *Lachesis*, particularly when the vessels present an extremely livid appearance. When severe *burning* pains are present in the tumor, *Arsenicum or Carb. v.* should be exhibited — *Nux. v.* if constipation be present and neither *Pulsatilla* nor *Lachesis* is indicated — this may frequently be followed with advantage by *Sulphur*.

These means frequently succeed in affecting so much relief that the patient suffers no sensible inconvenience. In two instances, one of them a student of medicine, we succeeded in effecting a cure, and by nearly the same means as for the radical cure of hernia. If these fail, resort may be had to the NEEDLES. These are inserted behind the veins so as to cause them, with the help of pressure from a ligature, to close by adhesive inflammation. Great care, however, must be taken that neither the Vas Deferens nor the Spermatic Artery or Nerve be wounded by the needle, or compressed by the ligature,—as any obstruction to the flow of blood through the artery, or the seminal secretion through the duct, would be fatal to the testicle.

SARCOCELE.

This, as the word implies, is a fleshy or flesh-like tumor of the testicle. The most common form is a simple enlargement of the testicle, depending upon chronic orchitis. The tumor is then smooth and almost painless, its weight being the principal source of inconvenience. This termination of inflammation in the part is most common in persons of a scrofulous diathesis, but occurs in others.

Sometimes there is an accumulation of fluid in the tunica vaginalis, at the same time constituting hydro-sarcocele.

Occasionally the tumor is attended with shooting pains, extending to the loins and back, enlarges and becomes knotty and irregular; and if not checked, ulcerates, forming a (*phagedenic*) ulcer with indurated edges, which discharges a very offensive matter; sometimes, however, from the ulcerated surface painful, hemorrhagic fungus shoots out. When not too far advanced to terminate in resolution, we may generally succeed with one or more of the following remedies—*Agar.*,*Aur.*, *Clem.*, *Graph.*, *Lyc.*, *Rhod.*, *Sul.;* but if not, the simplest and safest treatment is castration *at once*, before a malignant character shall have been fully developed and other parts become affected.

THE SOFT SWELLING OF THE TESTICLE, SWELLED TESTICLE, SOFT TESTICLE, OR FUNGUS TESTIS,

—is not an unfrequent affection, which is still called by a sort of *double* misnomer—

"HERNIA HUMORALIS."

This species or result of orchitis is most commonly the consequence of gonorrhea, or rather of its "cure," making its appearance about the time the gonorrheal discharge ceases, or is suppressed. Sometimes it sets in suddenly while the gonorrhea is at its height, a metastasis seeming to occur to one of the testes or both. It may shift again from one to the other.

The only symptom for awhile is the swelling of the testicle, which, however, soon becomes painful. The hardness eventually comes on, which is at first confined to the epididymis; and the pain extends from this part along the course of the cord to the lions. Symptomatic fever generally occurs with nausea and vomiting.

If the disease continues for a long time, a permanent enlargement of the testicle is the consequence; but it frequently subsides in a few days or weeks, at most, leaving no permanent injury. If it occurs during the height of the gonorrheal discharge, it will generally subside on the gonorrhea being re-established.

If there is much fever and inflammation use first a dose or two of *Aconite*, and then the specific remedy, which is generally *Mercurius* or *Pulsatilla*, or *Aurum*, *Clematis*, and *Nitr. ac.* *Puls.* seems to be especially adapted to those cases arising from the suppression of gonorrhea (or when there is a painful drawing and stretching along the spermatic cord to the inflamed testicle, both feeling bruised when touched.) *Merc.*, to a swelling of the testes remaining after gonorrhea. (Hartmann prefers 2d or 3d *Trit. Merc. Sol*).

In all cases preserve as far as possible the horizontal position and use the suspensory bandage — and when much pain and inflammation, the vapor or fomentations of warm water.

Merc. Sol., 5 doses, removed a swelling of the testes remaining after *gonorrhea*. Symptoms —"Testes hard and swollen, the size of a hen's egg, violent drawing pains coming on with a jerk, reaching from the testes to the abdomen and down to the foot; Scrotum, especially the right side, red and shining, tingling in the right testis. Violent chilliness alternating with heat, vertigo and feeling of the whole body as if bruised, tearing pains in the head, especially the right side. Pulse somewhat feverish."

In a case of swelled testicle from the suppression of gonorrhea, which did not yield to the specific remedies alone, the application of cold wet compress over the lumbar region speedily caused a return of the gonorrheal discharge and consequent removal of the swelling.

ORCHITIS,

Or inflammation of the testicle, may arise from other causes than that last considered, and most frequently does,—such as cold, Erysipelas, wounds inflicted during the operation for hydrocele, bruises, and other external injuries. In these cases the symptoms will not at first be so violent as in the case of suppression or metastasis of gonorrhea.

SYMPTOMS.— The pain or irritation will at first appear to be near the bladder, and in the spermatic cord. Very soon the epididymis will swell; and then there will be a general enlargement and thickening, with a painful sensation of the whole testicle, the part feeling exactly as though it were enclosed in a firm compress.

The patient suffers severely from continuous and tearing, stinging pains, which occasionally shoot into the abdomen and groin, and even the hips and loins, and down along the inside of the thighs.

The patient suffers great constitutional IRRITATION. The pulse is hard, full, and quick. The tongue is always furred; skin dry and hot; bowels constipated. If suppuration takes place, there are rigors; and if the process is not soon arrested, the tunica albuginea ulcerates, and the matter is thrown out by fistulous openings, and in most instances fungous growths will appear.

An occasional CONSEQUENCE of this inflammation is absorption of more or less of the substance of the testicle itself, so that it dwindles away to one-quarter or one-eight its usual size.

Arnica externally and internally is the specific remedy, when the disease has arisen from mechanical causes; preceded by a few doses of *Aconite*, if the fever and inflammation should be acute. Next to which we would place *Calendula offic.*, both of which should be given internally, and the diluted tincture applied externally. *Conium* sometimes removes the effects of contusions of glandular organs.

Erysipelatous orchitis generally yields to *Arsenicum;* rheumatic to *Bry.*, *Bel.*, *Rhus. Tox.*, or *Puls.*, *Spongia*, *Staphy* or *Carbo. v.*

Carbo., *Puls.*, *Staph*, especially the latter, are excellent for an aching pain and drawing burning stitches in the testis and spermatic cord.

Clematis; when a swollen and indurated testicle is painful and sensitive, and there is a drawing along the spermatic cord, sometimes accompanied with a crampy, bruised feeling when touched, and drawing and stretching in the lumbar region, thigh, and scrotum.

Spongia, when the pain in the swollen testicle is a crampy, contusive, choking pain, with dull stitches striking suddenly through the part and reaching into the swollen spermatic cord.

Orchitis, when the testicle swells up to the size of a child's head, particularly under the allopathic use of mercury, and nothing but an operation is relied on, frequently yields either to *China*, *Aurum*, or *Sulphur*, *Spongia*, *Iodium*, *positive electricity*, or *Rho-*

dodendron, Chrysanthemum and Mezereum, Merc. Sol. 2d and 3d, are excellent remedies for chronic indurations of the testes.

The vapor or fomentations of hot water and the suspensorium should be used as recommended in the preceding article, and the horizontal position preserved.

Immersing the patient in a warm bath is sometimes of great advantage.

When the acute symptoms have subsided, the disease is apt to become chronic, just as in the case arising from gonorrhea.

If, however, we are called too late to prevent ULCERATION, the safest way is at once *to castrate* — that is, to perform the operation of castration on the affected side. The reason for this is, that the ulceration is not only liable from the peculiar structure and position of the part to become chronic and destructive, but *malignant*, endangering the life of the patient,— or (what some would regard still more seriously), the other testicle.

IRRITABLE TESTES.

After orchitis, when the parts have assumed their natural size and all other visible traces of inflammation have disappeared, a state of irritation continues which is often very inconvenient, and sufficiently important to be treated of as a separate disease. This sequel does not follow proper homeopathic treatment. It may not make its appearance for months after the inflammatory disease has disappeared, and the individual appears to have become, in every respect, healthy. In every case we have met with, the symptoms of spermatorrhea were present, though this is a circumstance which appears to have been overlooked by surgical writers.

The SYMPTOMS are extreme pain in the testicle after coition, tenderness of the whole testicle to the touch, with pain on the slightest motion, extending to the loins and back, and sometimes to the urethra. There is seldom any enlargement of the testes; they may even be dwindled in size. The fixed PAIN is generally located at some particular point, and otherwise of a neuralgic character. The patient is apt to lie on the side opposite to that which is affected.

Nausea and vomiting are often among the concomitant symptoms; and the patient's MIND very soon becomes dejected.

The disease may CONTINUE for a long time, even for several years, perhaps only troubling the patient occasionally, while at other times he is comparatively free from it.

When the testicles have the sensation of being bruised, *Arn.*, *Digit.*, *Argent.*, *Rhod.*, *Coccul.*, *Nat. carb.*, *Acid oxalic.* The last five when both testicles are affected; *Cocculus*, especially when the pain is very severe; when it particularly affects the right testicle, *Dig.*; the left, *Argen.* When the pain is of an aching character, increased by contact and affecting both testicles, *Nit. ac.*, *Thuj.*, *Phos.*, *Scill.*, *Canna.*, *Sulph.* *Caust.*, if felt especially at noon; *Bism.*, if the pain is confined to the right testicle, *Staph.*, if in the left.

The testicles should be constantly supported by suspensorium. It is also important to keep them warm.

CHAPTER XXXII.

FISTULA IN ANO.

Interest taken in this disease? — Definitions and distinctions — Liability of anus to fistula — Causes — Abscesses and treatment — General measures in confirmed fistulas — "*The* operation" exclusively relied on — Its results — Reasons for preferring the ligature to the knife — Directions for applying — and for incomplete cases — Time for cure — Danger in pulmonary complications!

THIS is a disease as common as it is distressing, and in the treatment of which we shall depart very widely from all established authority. We shall therefore endeavor to be quite explicit, and may perhaps appear too minute and particular. This blame we willingly bear — nay, court. The only danger is from the opposite fault.

The author of a recent monograph on this subject, thinks it necessary to inquire why such an affection as that in question, and one so naturally concealed by the sufferer, should be a subject of such general interest, even to non-professional persons.

For every disease, however, there is necessarily a class of persons more deeply interested than even medical men — the sufferers and their friends. This interest is of course more manifest in respect to chronic disease than acute, especially when it is one of great but gradual fatality, and of rare and uncertain cure. It is well, perhaps that the non-professional public are not quite so indifferent about medical matters, as some professional dignitaries would seem desirous of having them. The people generally will find out bye-and-bye, that it is not only their "right," but their *duty* to look into what their physicians and surgeons are doing *with* them, as well as what their lawyers and politicians are doing *for* them, in matters of less consequence, and what their priests and preachers would *have* them *do* in matters of still greater moment. A more intelligent public and more inquisitive patients, are what the profession greatly needs, to make it more industrious in the acquisition of knowledge, and more cautious in reducing it to practice.

"The interest taken in fistula, both by the profession and by the public, can be accounted for," concludes the author alluded to,* "only on the well-ascertained fact, that the disease does not admit of remedy, except from an operation, which was formerly one of great suffering, and even of considerable danger." This curious passage implies not only the absolute necessity, but the *present* safety and matter-of-course *success* of the operation! There are in almost every neighborhood cases which imply something very different from this, and which explain the public interest in the subject by something more than the mere "fact" of an operation. The *real* fact is, that the disease is not only uncured without the operation, but often operated on in vain, and not unfrequently rendered worse than before — or, rather, converted into a new and more distressing surgical disease.

The term "FISTULA" is applied to all *ulcers* that have a long passage and narrow opening, through which the products of ulceration or the contents of natural cavities find exit. It is this latter circumstance, or their opening into some cavity of the body, that

* **Professor Syme, of Edinburgh.**

more strictly distinguishes "fistulas" from other "sinuous ulcers."

Of fistulas generally, it may be observed that they are ulcers of an obstinate character, having no tendency to heal, their sinuses being fortified by callous growths, though almost always exuding a sanious matter, or suppurating unhealthily.

The neighborhood of the *anus* is particularly *liable* to fistula, not only from functional derangement of the rectum, but from laxity of the cellular tissue, causing any abscess or ulcer that forms there to become diffuse, and the mobility of the sphincter preventing the healing process.

"FISTULA IN ANO" is, therefore, understood to imply the result of any abscess about the rectum, which *has opened* either just within or without the anus, or *both* on the external surface and into the bowel. The last condition is necessary to constitute

"Complete Fistula,"—an open communication from the outside of the body into the rectum; one end of the ulcer connecting with the cutaneous surface, the other with the mucous.

The "Incomplete or *blind* Fistula" may connect by its open end either with the skin or the gut, being thus either a "blind *external*" or "blind *internal* fistula."

The SINUS, or fistulous pipe, is very rarely simple or straight. It is commonly not only tortuous in its course (agreeably to the popular usage of the kindred terms, "sinuous and sinuousity"), but branched. Several sinuses may thus exist where there appears only one, or several distinct openings be internally connected, or spring from the same source. This source or origin of the sinus, is always

—An ABSCESS, walled up with hard cartilaginous matter, which is generally continued along the whole course of the sinus or sinuses. The lining of the pipe appears itself a semi-cartilaginous formation, but is to be regarded as a proper mucous membrane, which has the property of continuously secreting the thin yellowish pus, characteristic of fistula.

Notwithstanding this induration, fistulas are always extremely *tender* to the touch, so that it is difficult to probe them, until their morbid irritability has been allayed.

If *neglected*, the local irritation and inconvenience will not long be the worst symptom. Irritation of the lungs is so frequent an accompaniment of this disease, and fatal consumption so often the termination of badly-managed cases, that fistula in ano has ever been looked upon by some as a sort of *alternative* or safety-valve for phthisis pulmonalis!

The most probable CAUSE of the frequency of fistula in this part was before alluded to. Besides the peculiar anatomical structure of the part, and the liability to derangement of its physiological function, external injuries and foreign substances lodged in the rectum have been known to be the remote causes. Habitual *costiveness*, or, rather, inattention to the calls of nature for evacuation, may no doubt give rise to fistula, as it does to stricture of the rectum — the mucous membrane "giving way" to pressure in the former case, instead of being *hardened* to it as in the latter. Ever so little fœcal matter would thus be the commencement of an abscess, which might become a fistula, though the crevice in the rectum should heal, and no fresh irritation occur from that source. Constipation, however, and "torpidity of the liver," are by no means necessary conditions to the formation or continuance of fistula. Erysipelatous inflammation about the anus is still more likely than phlegmonous to degenerate into this kind of ulceration. Long neglected piles may easily become fistulous.

If we have *to treat* a case in the *incipient stage* — which, by the way, will rarely happen, the necessity of early attention being so little known, we can generally arrest the inflammation and prevent the suppuration, by the administration of *Bel.*, *Bry.*, *Phos.*, or the 2d or 3d trit. of *Hepar* or *Calc. phos.* and hot sitz baths frequently repeated. *Calc. phos.* has caused abscesses in the healthy, near the anus, terminating in fistula. Dr. A. Bauer, of Cincinnati, stated to one of the authors, that in proving it upon himself, first an abscess, then a fistulous pipe, was the result which took considerable time to heal up; also that several others, who were engaged in the proving, had symptoms of anal abscess, but did not push it to the same extent that he did. These results would point to it as *the remedy* for the different stages of this disease. We have never employed it except in the suppurative stage, not having been called thus early to a case, since our attention has been directed to it, — when an abscess has formed near the anus, but no fistulous pipes are yet clearly developed — bring it to a head as soon as possible by the frequent administration of *Calc. phos.*, and such other means as are recommended for abscesses (see p. 53–57). And as soon as there is evident *fluctuation* near a convenient part of the surface, puncture. Have an orifice large enough for all the pus that has formed to pass out readily.

Never delay puncturing, for the skin to become attenuated after there is evident fluctuation or *permit* the pus to be pent up until the skin becomes of a livid appearance. Many bad cases of fistula in ano, some with half a dozen fistulous pipes as well as long bills (surgical), are thus manufactured.

As soon as the pus is evacuated, *heal* up the abscess as soon as possible; never "leave the approximation and union of the sides of the cavity to nature," or permit the *orifice* to heal before the abscess fills up. This is easily prevented by the use of a tent.

Keep the patient at rest. Give a dose of the 2d or 3d trit. of *Calc. phos.*, once or twice a day, washing out the abscess daily with a solution of the same or *Aqua calendula*, shield it from the action of the atmosphere, and if the success is such as we have had in a number, the abscess will rapidly heal and the formation of *fistula* be prevented.

Where the suppuration is at all abundant, the *Aqua calendula* should be used as an injection into the abscess and drop doses of the tincture alternated with *Calc. phos.* But we will not often be called on with a view, or in time, to *prevent fistula* — seldom, indeed, in any of its earlier stages.

When an abscess near the rectum is left to open itself spontaneously, it will often be by several orifices, the discharge appearing to come from different points in the surrounding cellular tissue. Some of these openings soon close up, while others, if not prevented by proper measures, will continue to discharge a more and more unhealthy pus, and become indurated and regularly "fistulous." In such a case, give the *Calc. phos.* before recommended and wash out the *opened abscess, and all the sinuses* that can be discovered, with *Aqua calen.*, several times a day, applying a wet compress in the intervals. The "T. bandage" will retain the wet compress in its place. If, however, the parts are not perfectly soft or free from callus, the bandage should not be applied so tightly as to produce any sensible pressure.

This, with the internal treatment and *rest* on the patient's part, will often suffice to cause a very threatening abscess to heal up, instead of becoming a confirmed fistula. But if the case has been longer neglected, and become

— the TRUE FISTULA, with *hardened* pipes, pouring out *sanies* instead of healthy pus, something more will be necessary.

This is the condition in which established "authorities," and all routine practitioners "subject" thereto, consign their patients to the tender mercies of the knife.

"For *the* operation," we shall *not* refer you, as usual, to the Operative Part of the Course; because we would never sanction a measure so often worse than useless, when we can effect the object in view by other means, so much less objectionable, safer, and more certain of success. "The operation," by the way, is simple, and its object rational enough, were there no other means of attaining it, and *were* it oftener secured by that measure. The fistula is connected with the rectum, the sphincter being cut through and kept from uniting again until the ulcer heals up to it from the bottom — that is, sometimes kept open forever after! — the patient losing all control of this important organ, and being subjected for life to an annoyance far more disgusting and distressing than any fistula, and more deprecated by many than death itself.

This "laying open," as it is familiarly called, and of which the books speak as if it were a mere trifle — as to the *mere operator* it no doubt is — this "operation for fistula in ano," is the sum and substance, the beginning and the end, of "regular treatment."

The *success* of this "sole reliance" — to say nothing of its occasionally fatal, and frequently *worse* than fatal consequences just alluded to — may be judged of by the fact that a large majority of the worst cases *we* are called to treat, are those which *have been* operated upon. When not killed or cured, they are, of course, invariably injured by being "laid open." *This* is in private practice. Could the remote as well as immediate results of *hospital* "operations" be "laid open," what a "cutting up" business would *it* not be? Could grave-yards speak (or did their *reg-*

isters record, as they should, the causes of mortality), we verily believe we should find that one-half, if not a far larger proportion, of all who are affected with this variety of fistula, ultimately die, either from the effects of the uncured disease, or of the "surgical cure."

Yet one of our surgical authorities * tells us briefly, that the "treatment of fistula in ano is simple, and *if* the disease be merely local, usually quite effectual!" He is even so well satisfied of this, that he advises us to allow abscesses about the anus to become fistulous! because, forsooth, their cure is then so very "simple and effectual!"

This favorite operation will be found described in every surgical work. Reference can be made to any of them if it is desired to have recourse to so easy and mechanical an expedient. Of all our American writers at least, Gibson alone raises a dissenting voice against the otherwise unanimous opinion; but in doing so, he substitutes no satisfactory course of treatment.

"An opinion very generally prevails," observes Prof. Gibson (Surgery, vol. ii. p. 161), "that every fistula in ano requires an operation. *There can not be a greater mistake.* So far from it, that almost every case, where the patient is tolerably healthy, *might*, I am inclined to think, *be healed*, if attended to in the commencement, and judiciously managed. Nothing will contribute more to this end than absolute rest, simple dressings, moderate diet, and mild laxatives. I have known a fistula protracted and kept open for months, while the patient walked about, and healed in a week by perfect quietude and the horizontal position."

If this be so — if means so simple can lead to a cure in favorable cases, why should not measures a little less "simple," or more powerful, be directed in still more advanced stages; and how mischievous must be the effect of the "generally prevalent opinion," that nothing can be done to prevent or supersede the necessity of "*the operation.*"

If something more specific were used than the Philadelphia professor's "simple dressings," no doubt, with his other stringent conditions (if any patient could be induced to submit to them) of "absolute rest," or "perfect quietude," and the "horizontal posi-

* Miller, Practice of Surgery, p. 289.

tion," many cases *might* be successfully treated, even without recourse to the ligature. That measure, however, is generally indispensable in most all confirmed cases. It does not exact such an absolute *prostration* of the patient, and may be said, with the proper adjuncts, to *insure* success.

The LIGATURE is less objectionable than the *knife*, not only inasmuch as it is less alarming, and, when properly applied, less painful to the patient, and on account of the subsequent treatment being simpler, less confining; but its comparative slowness is itself an advantage. It *gradually* substitutes a healthy for an unhealthy action of the parts, by removing the cause of the latter; and thus not only obviates the liability to relapse, but the greater danger of other diseases occurring on the too sudden drying up of an accustomed drain. This danger is so considerable that it is, in some contingencies, held as a sufficient reason for not curing fistula, and in others, for only venturing on it with the precaution of setting up artificial issues in other parts! With the ligature, moreover, there is no danger of fatal hemorrhage from the hemorrhoidal vessels, or even temporary loss of control over the sphincter, as the division made by the cord usually heals behind it as it goes, if allowed to do so. Another danger obviated is that of inflammation from an extensive wound, in a delicate part and an enfeebled patient.*

* To show what a hobby of *operative* surgery this unfortunate disease has been made, and how authority sustains (by *repeating*) itself, we will subjoin a few quotations. To begin with a popular book of Reference: —

Gardner's recently corrected edition of the well-known Hooper's Medical Dictionary, lays it down, without any qualification, that "the cure is by a surgical operation."

Another American work is quite as positive: "The only effectual treatment is the division of the sinus and the sphincter ani muscle." — (Hastings' Surgery, p. 278 – Philadelphia, 1850 – a compend from Druitt, Gibson, &c.)

"The grand remedy," according to Druitt, in his careful digest of established English practice, p. 253, "is the division of the sphincter ani, so as to prevent the contraction of that muscle for a time [how often, forever!] and cause [how often ?] the fistula to heal from the bottom."

Would it not seem that *medical* surgery had taken a disgust at the part concerned and given it over to *dissection?* One only of our American writers is a little more hesitating or discriminating than the rest. His language (as quoted in the text) is quite a rebuke to the orthodox dictum; but unfortunately it is unaccompanied with any sufficient or satisfactory directions for a better practice than that fostered by the prevalent "mistake."

Dismissing, therefore, all thought of *the* operation, in the

TREATMENT OF CONFIRMED FISTULA,

The first thing is to ascertain as precisely as possible the magnitude, direction and number of sinuses.

The *probing*, however, for this purpose may have to be delayed in consequence of the irritable condition of the parts. In such a case give *Assafetida* when the parts are *very irritable* and the discharge thin and discolored. But if the patient is much prostrated, the matter ichorous, and the pains are somewhat of a

Our German brethren are much more discriminating in their judgments, as well as comprehensive and profound in their inquiries. It may be instructive to show to what an extent these mental and *geographical* differences affect men's opinions. We have consulted the second edition of an elaborate work of established authority in Germany, though of recent date. It consists of three volumes, with a folio accompaniment of splendid plates, all devoted exclusively to *Akiurgy* (that is, knife-surgery), or that *part* of Operative Surgery usually requiring bloody operations. Yet in treating this particular affection, for which *our* authorities resort to the knife alone, the author restricts its use to so few and exceptional cases, that it is equivalent to a proscription of it altogether. A critical history of treatment, *modern* as well as ancient, the whole biography, so to speak, and bibliography of the disease, is given with truly German minuteness and accuracy. The most recent eminent surgeons of England and France are quoted, in corroboration, or for the purpose of justifying a dissent from their conclusions.

Of the four methods of cure — by Ligature, Excision, and Cauterization — the author considers the first two the only ones *not* antiquated. *Liston*, and other of *our* Operative Surgeons, dismiss the subject of ligature as out of date, because formerly associated with the *actual* cautery.

After fully discussing the question between the ligature and the knife, our author gives the former a decided preference: "Verdient die Ligatur im Allgemeinen den Vorzug. — Sie ist mit Ausnahme der S. 261 genannten Fælle ueberall angezeigt."

These excepted cases, in which he allows that incision may be admissible, are either so *very exceptional* as to be out of the question (as, for instance, the possible complication of stone in the bladder, which would certainly indicate the use of the *knife* in a different *direction*), or such as really afford additional reason for the ligature with *our* accompanying means (they being those we should use for "malignant or suspicious" disease, if unconnected with fistula). The only plausible objection to the ligature, is confined to the single circumstance of the *outer* orifice being so far from the anus, that it would be too long in working its way through — a difficulty which we have not experienced, or, which rather resolves itself, in a medical view of the operation, into a positive *advantage*. In these apparent exceptions, moreover, our author premises all the time that the fistulas in question are not old or "hard cases" — "Noch nicht alten Fistela — nicht starker Callositæt der Fis-

burning character, benefit will be derived from the use of *Arsenicum.* If, however, with this irritable condition of the fistula, the lungs seem to be affected, give *Phosphorus* (perhaps, even here, *Calc. phos.*, would be preferable). When it is attended with an Erysipelatous inflammation, *Belladonna* will be beneficial. But if the orifice is surrounded with small pimples and there is a tendency to the development of proud flesh, *Sulphur* should be employed. At the same time make use of hot sitz baths and vapor or fomentations two or three times a day, together with emollient poultices. Keep the patient perfectly quiet. The rectum *must be kept free from fecal matter.* To insure this, if necessary, use *Enemas* twice a day.

After a short time the patient will be able to bear the operation of probing, though it may even then be quite painful. Having thus ascertained the state of the case,

— if the fistula be already "complete," and large and direct enough for the purpose, *arm* a common silver probe with a *ligature.* For this purpose, the best material is saddlers' silk, doubled. Pass

tel" — that is, that they are not bad cases at all, but such as he had before admitted *might* be cured, by proper medical treatment, without even tying, much less cutting.

Lest we be suspected by those to whom this information will be so strange, in their confidence in *partial* authority, and as this valuable work has not yet been translated into English, we will give, not all he says favoring our views, but just one paragraph, in which he lays down formally the cases *for* the knife.

1st Method — *Incision* —

— *indicated* in still *recent cases* (bei noch nicht alten Fisteln), particularly if there be many branches, or the outer orifice be far from the anus, because the ligature would then take too long in working its way through, — where it is desirable to lay open the bowel for the very purpose of exciting stronger and more continuous inflammation — in complication with malignant or suspicious disease of the neighboring parts, which the ligature might render worse, or with foreign bodies, stone in the bladder, for example:

— *contra-indicated* in fistulas, the *inner* opening of which is more than an inch and a half [1½ zoll] above the anus, — where there are many or large hemorrhoidal tumors, — when the fistula has become much hardened with callus, — [bei starker Callositæt der fistel] or when there is great irritability of the rectum, risk (or rather *apprehension* — besorgniss) of a secondary affection or habitual diarrhea." — [Akiurgie von Ernst Blasius, M. et C. D., Prof. der Chir. an der Kœnig. Universitaet zu Halle — III Band, 261 P — Halle, 1841.]

the threaded probe from the external to the internal orifice. When it is through, turn the outer end a little upwards, that the other may be seized by the finger in the rectum, and the string brought down. By separating the nates, the end of the probe and the ligature may be seen; or the rectum may be dilated, and the operation facilitated by the Speculum Ani.

The two ends of the ligature are to be *tied* as firmly as the patient can comfortably bear, and afterwards drawn a little tighter every day. This *tightening* is commonly effected by rolling on or twisting with a piece of wood. A better plan is, before tying, to let the ends of the string pass through a large vial-cork, and over a little wooden roller, fitted to radial grooves cut on the end of the cork. These notches will hold the stick, after turning or twisting, like the fall of a windlass. The surface is thus less irritated, the pressure of the cork being more equable than any "toggle" fixed there.

Fig. 15.

If there are several sinuses, they should all, or the principal ones at least, be treated in the same manner.

While the ligature is on, the parts should be fomented every day, and every sinus thoroughly injected two or three times a day with a dilution of the internal remedy, a strip of patent lint, or a narrow silk ribbon should also be pressed little by little into the pipe behind the ligature, until it is completely filled. This should first be wet in the solution used as an injection, and be permitted to remain from one dressing to another. The degree of pressure it should exert upon the sides of the pipe, is to be determined by the extent of the callus, slight when this is slight, more powerful when it is greater.

As soon as the ligature has *cut* its way completely *through*, foment and poultice, continuing to completely fill whatever fissure may remain with the lint or ribbon tents. Every part will then rapidly heal, the tents causing no impediment to the process, but rather seeming to stimulate to a more healthy and rapid granulation. When the restoration is nearly complete, and but little matter is discharged, the parts feeling soft and natural, the poultice and fomentations may be dispensed with, and some other simple dressing substituted.

There is no danger from this course to the sphincter muscle; the healing process, as was before remarked, following up the ligature, and being generally nearly complete before it comes away. It is sometimes even necessary to prevent this, and keep the fissure open until all callus has been removed; after which it can always be readily healed up.

Should there be other sinuses branching from or leading into the main one, they must not be closed until all callosity at their extremity or along their course has disappeared, and the parts seem natural to the touch and without soreness. Enlarge all such branches by lint or ribbon *tents*, until all appearance of callosity has gone, when the parts may be allowed gradually to heal.

We formerly used the *Sesqui-Carbonate of Potash* in connection with the tents to destroy the callus, but are now satisfied that the simple pressure of the tents upon the sides of the pipe with the internal homeopathic medication is preferable. We should not, however, hesitate to employ the preparation of *Potash* in very old and obstinate callus until it began to dissolve.

If the case be a "*blind internal* fistula," ascertain the point where it approaches nearest the external surface. Open with a pointed probe, and having it thus "complete," proceed as before directed.

If it be a "*blind external* fistula," it need not always be made "complete." By the appropriate medication and the persevering use of the lint or ribbon tents, it may very often be cured without the operation even of the ligature. If, however, it be a very *bad case*, and remain obstinate or get worse, insert the armed or threaded probe clear through the bottom of the sinus, into the rectum; bring the ligature out; and proceed as before directed for "complete fistula." Whenever, on passing the finger into the gut, a hard lump can be discovered at the upper extremity of the sinus, do not delay, but perforate the rectum, and introduce the ligature at once. This laying open of the source of the original sinus is the safer way, inasmuch as the secondary branches, as well as this callus reservoir, can thus be reached, and easily overcome by the process before described, if care is taken to keep open a large orifice by means of the tents.

Recollect that the Elm Poultice (kept on by a "T" bandage) should be used over the affected parts during the whole of the treatment;— the peculiarity of this cure consisting in the callosity being dissolved and carried off by the suppurative process, the fistulous ulcer being made to heal by healthy granulation, and leaving no trace of the morbid formations.

An ordinary case of fistula in ano can be cured in from three to eight weeks, a bad case, especially if the lungs or general health are much affected, will require several months, a much speedier cure would not be desirable in all cases, even were it possible.

The remedies that are recommended by homeopathic authors as having yielded the best results in confirmed fistula, are *Calc.*, *Caust.*, *Puls.*, *Phos.*, *Silic.*, and *Sulph.*, particularly the first and last two above named, though they have given no special indications for their employment. As before stated, judging from the provings of *Calc. Phos.*, by Dr. Bauer and others, and our limited use of this article, we think it will prove *the remedy* in this disease, even in the advanced stages, particularly if *Calc.* or *Phos.* should be indicated and not yield favorable results:

Calc. and Phos. are more particularly adapted to those cases when there seems to be an implication of the lungs. *Calc.* for fistula when the surrounding parts are red, somewhat swollen and hardened.

Phos., where there is much disposition to bleed, edges callus, the pus offensive and badly colored, and much constitutional disturbance, sometimes the fever of the hectic character — *Caust.*, when attended with painful hemorrhoids. *Silic.* when the orifice of the fistula is rather small and surrounded with callus, or when it occurs in cachectic broken down constitutions; discharges sanious yellowish-white ichor, and there is much proud flesh. *Sulph.* when the fistula is surrounded with pimples; throws out proud flesh, rather destitute of sensibility, and discharges a yellowish pus. The attending sympathetic or organic disease of any organ or organs, must be carefully considered in the selection of the appropriate medicine.

It not unfrequently happens that when we are called on to treat a long neglected or mistreated case, the patient is laboring under severe *pulmonary difficulties*, or even already in an advanced stage of consumption. This is the condition in which, according to the books, to cure fistula would be wrong! — the complication which renders even "*the* simple operation" not advisable. The removal of the disgusting local nuisance *by the knife*, has been followed by fatal consequences. The damming up a *crevasse* in the river's bank, without clearing out the natural channel, has been found worse than useless. Therefore, nothing ought to be done! The soul's lease-hold of "the house it lives in" now depends on not venturing to obviate the inconvenience of a smoky chimney.

But be assured that a *proper* cure of the fistula in ano will be the best chance of *preserving* the lungs and the life of the patient. Even where the case is too far gone for a restoration to perfect health — where the object is only to retard the fatal *progress* of consumption, the first step toward it is to restore as far as possible the healthy function of *every other part*, and put an end to every source of *irritation* and *aggravation*.

As to the danger of "drying up a long-established drain," it will be observed that in our mode of "curing up" fistula, instead of at once arresting, we for a long time *increase* the drain from the affected part, changing it, at the same time, from a self-perpetuating sanious and fetid character, to a soothing, self-limiting and sanative suppuration.

When the lungs are not so seriously affected, *their* disease subsides as soon as the free and healthful discharge is excited about the anus. In numerous cases, where the sufferers seemed far gone in consumption, the simple local treatment of fistula was all they required to arrest the pulmonary disease.

A gentleman went from the northern part of the State to Cincinnati, so reduced by apparent consumption, as well as anal fistula, that his friends took their last farewell of him, fully persuaded that he left home but to end his sufferings in death. In four months, he was restored to them in perfect health, as fleshy as he had ever been in his life, and he has since continued to enjoy better health than before his "latter end" was so doubly threatened. His "consumption" was indeed deeply *seated* — fundamentally fixed — but fortunately in the pelvis, instead of the chest.

We might cite many other such cases, but one more must suffice. A gentleman treated by Dr. Hunt, in connection with the late Dr. Morrow, whose lungs appeared affected, had, during the treatment, no less than eight fistulous pipes; he was entirely cured and continued healthy until lost sight of (about three years), nor do we recollect one instance out of the large number treated either by ourselves or the late Dr. Morrow, in which the patient appeared to suffer any inconvenience from *not* having fistula!

CHAPTER XXXIII.

DISEASES OF THE ANUS AND RECTUM, CONTINUED, — PILES, PROLAPSUS, FISSURE AND STRICTURE.

HEMORRHOIDS or *Piles* — Meaning and use of words — Treatment when inflamed — Soothing applications — Hard cases — Ligature preferred to excision — Directions for applying — Case.

PROLAPSUS ANI — Mode of procedure in replacement — Precautions against relapse.

FISSURE OF THE ANUS AND RECTUM — Trouble, danger.

STRICTURE OF THE RECTUM — Causes, constipation and purgatives — Directions for using the *Dilator* — Concomitant and subsequent measures.

PILES OR HEMORRHOIDS.

THESE words are used indiscriminately to express the same affection, — or, rather, several connected affections of the same part; though the prominent idea conveyed by the popular term is that of *tumor*, and by the more learned expression, that of *bleeding*.

SWELLING and BLEEDING *at* the anus are both common affections, very generally occurring in the same individual, and obviously connected, — often as cause and effect, directly or *inversely*. Either symptom may exist, however, without the other. Tumors which do not bleed are distinguished as "*blind* Piles," — such are out of sight within the anus. These internal piles are often of considerable dimensions, because not so liable to burst as the external, which are often called "Bleeding" or "Open Piles."

A person is also said to have piles who is troubled with hemorrhage about the extremity of the rectum, though unconnected with any sensible swelling there, transient or permanent; and tumors or occasional tumefactions occurring there, are spoken of as hemorrhoids, whether they are known to relieve themselves by bleeding or not.

The veins of this part are themselves called *hemorrhoidal*, from their great liability to become engorged and discharge their contents. This liability is occasioned by the anatomical peculiarities as well as the physiological changes of the connected parts. Over distension by costiveness impeding the venous flow, followed as it is by excessive relaxation on the rectum being suddenly evacuated by drastic cathartics, is, no doubt, the most frequent cause. Costiveness may be an *effect* as well as cause of piles, the patient suffering so much from soreness of the rectum that he is disposed to neglect the calls of nature.

The temporary distension or permanent varicose condition of these veins, may be the only tumors in the case; or they may themselves be transformed into real tumors, or their extravasated blood become enclosed in permanent cysts.

These tumors are from the size of a pea to that of a hen's egg, and may be very numerous. When small and few in number, they may exist a long time without serious inconvenience, — and be, of course, neglected. Their becoming painful is often an advantage to the patient. Besides the obvious danger of excessive *hemorrhage* (from which several distinguished men are said to have died), long-neglected piles may excite *inflammation* of the neighboring organs, or by immediate ulceration occasion *fistula* (as was noticed in the last chapter).

In bleeding piles the discharge appears sometimes at regular periodic intervals. Sometimes the sensation resembles that of the passage of wind; but frequently it runs from the patient in a stream, rapidly prostrating him. Generally at first, there are premonitory symptoms, such as some pain in the small of the back and loins, stinging and burning, a sensation of swelling and fullness, with throbbing in the rectum; occasionally, sharp stitches through the pelvis and tenesmus of the anus.

Sometimes the tumors will protrude and become badly inflamed, and it will be necessary to return them before the inflammation can be removed.

In such a case, it is the duty of the surgeon to allay, as soon as possible, the local irritation, that the tumors may be returned, for until that is done, all attempts at relief will be unavailing, the patient will remain in constant pain, and be obliged to keep a recumbent posture.

To allay the irritation for the purpose of returning the protruded tumors, it will be best to evacuate the bowels by repeated enemas of warm water. Frequent lavements of the same, with the application of a warm *ulmus fulva* poultice or some other soothing emollient application, will contribute much to the success. Repeat the enemas, if necessary, to prevent an accumulation of fecal matter in the rectum. In some cases, cold wet compresses answer better, especially when the case is an old long-standing one, and there is rather a chronic soreness than acute inflammation.

During the protrusion of the tumors there will generally be *tenesmus and violent pains* in the *small of the back*, burning in the anus, especially if it be soon after stool, with more or less soreness — symptoms of *Tabacum*, which we have applied to the protruded tumors in form of a poultice in many cases, with the happiest results, allaying the pain and soreness in a few hours. When applied in this manner, it sometimes produces an aggravation of the local affection as well as other pathogenetic symptoms. This should be understood, and when such symptoms appear, the application discontinued. All medicinal symptoms disappear in a short time, and with these a decided amelioration or complete subsidence of the hemorrhoidal inflammation and soreness will generally take place.

This course will succeed in allaying the inflammation so that the tumors can be returned. As soon as this can be done, the warm applications are to be laid aside, and during the general treatment for a removal of the constitutional tendency, *cold sitz baths* should be used daily. The patient should contract a habit of evacuating the bowels *at night*, if possible.

We shall not undertake here to give directions in full for treating common acute cases of "piles," as the directions for the use of such remedies as are relied upon by the profession generally, will be found in all the homeopathic works on practice. We shall only treat, particularly, upon those *old hard* cases which are rarely, if ever, permanently relieved by internal remedies, — such as require the interference of surgery for their *radical cure*.

China should be used for the debility consequent upon a severe attack of bleeding piles.

Nux vom. is a valuable remedy for old cases, where there is an irregularity of the bowels, alternate costiveness and diarrhea.

Podophyllum, 2d trit., is very useful where there is much prolapsus ani, with piles.

Sulphur, where there is burning and itching in the rectum, with pressing-down sensation, especially in scrofulous patients.*

Prof. C. Neidhard, in an article furnished us on this subject says:

"*Nux vomica.* — The indications for *Nux*, are a tendency to constipation of the bowels and a burning, stinging pain with palpitation of the hemorrhoids after the passage of the bowels; they are swelled and may bleed or not.

"*Sulphur* is the constitutional remedy against piles, because its symptoms may be found in all cases of hemorrhoids; it has rending in the rectum, burning, stinging, there can be no doubt that in a great number of cases it will be one of the most important remedies, but we have to investigate whether piles have not some connection with herpes, scrofula, sycosis, syphilis, and choose *Sulph.* or some other remedy accordingly.

"*Acidum, muriat. and nitric.* — These two must be mentioned together, because their action is very similar. I will illustrate their action by a few cases from my practice:

"Miss M—— had, some time ago, an operation performed for, as she thought, the radical cure of her piles, but in a short time they returned again. There was particularly one pile on the verge of the anus, from which she suffered great pain for an hour after the bowels are opened, with sharp stitches. At the same time, she has

* A number of cures have been reported to us effected by the use of the *Buckeye (nut)* Æscalus Glubra, taken in repeated small doses.

a throbbing in the back and a throbbing and aching in the back of the neck; a short time before and during her catamenia. *Calc. c.* gave some relief to the back, but it was only the persevering use of *Nitric acid* which finally cured her. This lady was of dark complexion. Her sister, who was of light complexion, and who was also afflicted with piles, with very similar symptoms, was not benefited at all by *Nitric acid*, but had to take *Muriatic acid* for the cure of her complaint. This led me to investigate the difference between the indication for *Nitric* and *Mur. acid* in piles. To my great satisfaction the above-mentioned fact was also corroborated in other cases, where the symptoms seemed to be very similar in two cases. For many years I have suspected that the symptoms are not everything, that they are only important as disclosing the internal nature of disease and the remedy, but there was generally some great characteristic circumstance, which, if it were only disclosed to us, would be the deciding point for the choice of the remedy. It was Hahnemann who first remarked that *Nitric acid* was more indicated in persons of *dark complexion*, which led me to the natural conclusion that *Mur. acid* might be indicated in those of opposite nature, and I found this supposition corroborated by several facts. A very decided symptom with me for the use of *Nitric* acid is also the *constant weight* and pressure complained of by the patient, *worse on exercise*, sometimes bleeding, and with mucus, *constipation*.

"*Aloes* in the 2d or 3d trit. is a favorite remedy of mine where there is a constant bearing down low in the rectum, with the piles hanging out of the anus like a cluster of grapes; they are also bleeding.

"*Graphites.* — My characteristics for this remedy, are piles accompanied by giddiness, burning, itching in the anus, with discharge of mucus or blood. According to other observers, there is also a sensation of heaviness in the abdomen, chronic constipation with induration in the region of the liver, prolapsus of the rectum.

"In mucous piles, according to my experience, there is no remedy superior to *Antim. crud.*, in the 2d or 3d trit.; the pains are pricking, burning.

"In all piles the palliative aid of cold water can never be dispensed with." *

When the PILES have become hardened, they are nearly insensible unless when inflamed. We have been called on to treat many such chronic cases in which the tumors wore a very malignant appearance, and had already occasioned ulceration to a very considerable extent. The course of treatment which has been successful in every such case, is this:

Place a LIGATURE round the tumor, or round two or three if there are many, passing it through a cork, as recommended in the case of fistula in ano, and tightening it every day, till the strangulated tumors slough off. The patient meantime should constantly keep on an elm poultice, and rest as still as possible, — the bowels being loosened by enemas.

The best *mode* of tying, is to have the patient *strain* down the tumor, over which the silk or linen cord is put as a *loop*, having been *previously* passed through the cork.

After the tumors have come away, the surface should be washed daily with *Aqua calendulæ* until the soreness and tenderness subsides.

The *ligature*, as a means of removing large hemorrhoidal tumors, is far preferable to the *knife*. It is not so alarming to the patient and gives him no pain except on the first application, and for a few moments after each tightening. It avoids all the danger of inflammation, and the still greater danger of hemorrhage. The books are full of instances where patients have sunk under or immediately after the operation.

The disease rarely *returns* after removal by ligature, even though the patient should neglect himself and become costive. But no mode of local treatment — at least none short of this operation by ligature — will effect more than temporary relief, unless proper constitutional remedies are at the same time applied.

We have treated several cases which had been of many years standing, with very large and numerous tumors, all of which had been before subjected to other treatment without anything more

* In highly inflamed piles, according to our experience, warm water or vapor is preferred to cold water.

than temporary relief. In one instance, on placing the patient on his hands and knees, and directing him to strain, a mass of tumors was thrown out on one side of the anus as large as a goose egg, while several smaller ones appeared on the opposite side. In this large mass were several sinuses, from which issued a considerable quantity of thin yellowish matter. The whole tumor was of a dark purple color and extremely tender to the touch. We applied a ligature around the largest one, by means of the cork and loop, as before advised; and although it gave extreme pain, we drew it down with great force and secured it. A large slippery elm poultice was applied (as should be done in all cases to prevent excessive inflammation). The patient soon became easy, and suffered but little pain on subsequent tightening, which was done every day. In a week the ugly mass came away, and all the other tumors disappeared. The patient was entirely cured of a difficulty under which he had been laboring for twenty years. Generally the tumors are smaller and will slough off sooner than this did. The compression of the tumors and cauterization with *Vienna paste* has been recommended by some, but from what we know of cases thus treated we greatly prefer the ligature.

PROLAPSUS ANI

— often exists in connection with piles, especially the variety distinguished as Bleeding Piles. It doubtless often precedes and causes both varieties.

A similar *constitutional* TREATMENT is generally required to that recommended for piles, though it may not often be necessary to carry it out so fully or so long.

When called to a case, if the prolapse be present, the first thing to be done is to *replace* the protruded bowel, so as to prevent any longer exposure to air and other irritating causes. In ordinary cases the patient can do this for himself. The swelling, however, may be so great that immediate replacement is impossible or unsafe. In such an event subject the part to vapor of water. This will generally produce such a softening and diminution, as to render the return of the part quite easy. If not, subject it to a stream or jet of cold water. This will generally cause an immediate return. If this fail, apply *Arnicated* water and cover the surface with wet cloths and keep it warm. After these various means have sufficiently allayed the irritation and substituted a relaxed condition,

— place the patient on his knees, with his hips elevated and head down, and grasp the tumor with a cloth wet in warm water in your hand, gradually compressing and pushing it back with your fingers.

After such an occurrence, the patient should be kept very still for a day or two. If he gets up at all, he should wear a "T" bandage, with a compress on the anus.

For some time to come, the rectum should be every day washed out and invigorated by a cold water injection. The cold water applications should be made daily or oftener.

We have found that lubricating the rectum by an injection of Linseed oil, just before an evacuation of the bowels, may prevent the occurrence of prolapsus, especially when the water irritates, as is sometimes the case.

Either *Nux v.*, *Ign. Merc.*, or *Podophyllum*, will, in nearly all cases, soon relieve.

Nux, when the patient is habitually costive.

Ign., when there is much smarting and burning in the rectum in persons of mild temper.

Podophyl., when the bowels are too loose, affected with diarrhea or dysentery. We look upon this as the best remedy in this disease.

Mercurius for children with enlargement of the abdomen, attended with much tenesmus.

Nit. acid will often be found serviceable, especially with smarting and burning in the anus.

FISSURE OF THE ANUS.

This, as the name implies, is a crack or groove in the rectum, extending up from the orifice, sometimes more than two inches. It is very irritable and tender to the touch, though the edges become thickened and hardened. A sanious fluid is continually exuding.

This affection is as distressing to the patient, as dangerous to health, and not unfrequently as hard to cure as fistula at the same place.

The most reliable remedies for this disease, are *Nit. acid, Ign., Nux v., Phos. and Ars.*

Nit. acid, when there are soreness and smarting in the anus, or pinching, burning and pricking, or itching as from ascarides, with smarting, cramp-like contractions.

Ignatia; sore pains in the anus between stools, swelling of the margin of the anus, painless contractions of the anus. The *fissure bleeds easily;* great tendency to prolapsus ani. This remedy frequently follows *Nit. acid* with advantage.

The best plan is to give the remedy one dose daily for ten or twelve days. If the patient improves, continue the same remedy at longer intervals, if not, use another in the same manner.

Nux v. will be found useful when there is a great tendency to constipation and the anus is extremely sensitive to the touch, so that it is difficult to make an examination.

Phos. will be beneficial in scrofulous persons when there is a purulent discharge from the fissure. It sometimes follows *Nit. ac.* or *Ign.* advantageously.

Ars. is more particularly useful when there is great constriction of the rectum and the constriction extends to the urethra obstructing the passage of urine.

If the anus is at any time much inflamed and very painful, *Nit. acid* or *Ign.* should be given as often as every four or six hours until relief is obtained. The parts may also be subjected to the vapor of water, and a compress of lint wet in hot water should be applied to the anus.

STRICTURE OF THE RECTUM

—is of two kinds, spasmodic and permanent. This is a very troublesome, and often a very serious disease. The permanent stricture comes on gradually, and much harm is often done, as well as valuable time lost, by its being confounded with *constipation.* This is indeed its common but remote cause; and temporary removal of the cause can not undo the lasting effect. The ordinary means resorted to by others than homeopaths and hydropaths, as a remedy for costiveness, are but too likely to insure a return and a continuance of it.

Persons who lead sedentary lives, and neglect the calls of nature, are by far the most liable to stricture. The feces, being habitually retained by a forced action of the sphincter, accumulate in large quantities and distend the greater part of the rectum, while the extremity is firmly contracted. Under these circumstances, the thickening and hardening of the gut is but a protection on the part of nature against the unnatural burden.

In some instances, the rectum becomes diminished in its caliber, by thickening or a deposite into the submucous cellular tissue, to the extent of several inches. Frequently, however, a small callus ring is formed round the bowel, just within the anus, of not more than a quarter or half an inch in width. The difficulty may indeed occur in any other part of the bowel; we have seen it just within the anus in some cases, and in others five or six inches above.

The SYMPTOMS are sometimes difficult to determine, the patient being seldom able to describe his sensations with sufficient exactness; *constipation* is the first indication of the disease. The patient experiences a difficulty in evacuating his bowels, and is obliged to use considerable straining, although the feces appear not to be unnaturally hard. Still the obstruction continues, the passage growing constantly smaller; and the fecal matter at last passes off in a fine stream with some pain, which does not remit as in the spasmodic variety. The swelling being sometimes larger at opposite sides, the discharge takes a thin, flat, tape-like form. This happens after the stricture is well established.

An obstruction may sometimes occur without any thickening in the rectum itself, in consequence of an enlarged prostate gland. When this is the case, the feces will present an indentation or groove on one side only, produced by projection of the gland into the gut.

In cases brought on by sedentary habits, the feces, in the earlier stage of the disease, will pass off in a bulky mass at the first—after a great effort, the latter part of the discharge becoming small and contracted.

For distinction between *permanent stricture* and *cancer of the rectum*, see *Cancer*.

Insert this *dilator* past the stricture, and fasten it in that position by a "T" bandage, requiring the patient to keep it on as long as he can bear it. The bandage should be made of gum elastic, so as to cause a slight but constant upward pressure on the instrument. A short dilator that will pass entirely within the sphincter ani muscle, will be preferable if it can be retained. It need be worn but a short time (ten to fifteen minutes) at each application.

TREATMENT.

In this, as in many other forms of disease, is seen the superiority of homeopathic medication. The spasmodic stricture very promptly yields to *Nux v.*, *Opium*, *Plumbum*, *or Sulph.*

If hemorrhoids are present and aggravate the disease, *Nux*, *or Sulph.*, is generally applicable.

Ignatia, *or Nux Mosch.*, is especially applicable if it occurs in hysterical females. A suppository of tallow at night will frequently be of service, though an enema of cold water, night and morning, answer a much better purpose than either it or the *bougie.*

[Query? The extract of *Belladonna* applied to a rigid os uteri, causes it to dilate — would not it be serviceable in stricture of the rectum?] Warm sitz baths should be used once or twice daily.

In the treatment of permanent stricture, the great remedial means relied on by surgeons, generally, is the *bougie.* This is, however, but rarely necessary with homeopaths. We have agents that are capable of exerting a specific influence on the diseased structure and causing its absorption, and are thus enabled to cure many cases where the *bougie* can not be employed; as in those instances where the stricture is so high up in the rectum that it cannot be reached by the *bougie*, or it is inadmissible from the great irritability of the stricture or the presence of fungous growths.

Nux v., *Plumb.*, *Sepia*, *or Sulph.*, will generally remove the first stage of the disease. When, however, the strictured portion has become inflamed or suppurated, as may be known by the pain being severe, and there is a discharge of blood or pus, much benefit has been derived from a few doses of *Aconite*, followed by repeated doses of *Sulphur*, and when this had ceased to act, the exhibition of *Nat. m.*, *Lach.*, *or Ignatia*, in accordance with the symptoms, should be given.

Ignatia, when there was present a shuddering after each evacuation.

Lachesis, when the pain in the anus was accompanied by a throbbing.

Nux v., especially if in a male or in a person of sedentary habits, addicted to the use of intoxicating beverages, highly seasoned food, or afflicted with hemorrhoids.

Carbo. an. is an excellent remedy in all indurations of mucous membranes.

Enemas are of primary importance in this disease. As a general rule cold water does the best, but from the peculiar irritability of parts in some cases, the cold can not be borne when warm water may be used. They will often overcome stricture which does not yield to the internal remedies, and for which indeed the common practice, the *bougie* or knife, is deemed the only remedy. These should be repeated once, twice, or three times daily, according to the character of the case; less frequently when there is great irritability. Taken on retiring at night and rising in the morning will generally be sufficient. The quantity thrown up should be as large as can be retained, but it should be done with a small pump syringe, through a small pipe, so as to fill the rectum gradually, else the sudden pressure will cause an immediate contraction of the bowels for its expulsion. If there is ulceration of the bowels, the fluid should be warm. *Aqua Calen.* should be used in this case in place of simple water.

The diet of the patient should be strictly attended to. No solid or indigestible substance, such as the hard seeds of grapes, raisins, and other fruits and berries should be allowed. The bran of unbolted flour is often injurious in this disease.

Entirely fluid food, such as milk, soups, &c., is preferable. As an excellent means of obviating costiveness, direct the patient to drink freely of cold water early in the morning, an hour or more before eating, also upon retiring at night.

The following remedies may be consulted with advantage in

this disease — *Sepia*, *Natrum m.*, *Staph.*, *Calc.*, *Cal.*, *Lycop.*, *Ars.*, *Rhus.*, *Hepar*, and *Mezereum*. If, however, the case does not yield to the medication or enemas, and the stricture is within reach and free from ulceration or any malignant appearance, the bougie dilator may be resorted to; one of gum elastic is altogether preferable.

CHAPTER XXXIV.

STRICTURE OF THE URETHRA, URINARY FISTULA, AND DISEASES OF THE PROSTATE GLAND.

STRICTURE OF THE URETHRA — Retention and suppression of Urine — Spasmodic and permanent stricture — Causes and progress — Absorption — Dilatation — Cauterization — Revulsion — Artificial blennorrhea.

FISTULA IN PERINEO — Mechanical cause and condition of cure — Other means and precautions.

ACUTE PROSTITIS — Cause and symptoms — Connection with gonorrhea, or its "cure."

CHRONIC PROSTITIS OR ENLARGEMENT — Causes and liability — Symptoms — Artificial gonorrhea.

STRICTURE OF THE URETHRA.

THIS is a very common and very important subject. The number of men who die from neglect or mal-treatment of this originally simple affection, would surprise the profession as well as the general public, were there, as there *should* be, any means of ascertaining the point and making it a settled matter of fact instead of opinion. "Bills of mortality" are the final test of all medical practice, and should be made use of for its correction and perfection.

RETENTION OF URINE, caused by stricture, gravel or other similar *mechanical* impediments, must not be confounded with SUPPRESSION, which always implies inactivity and disease of the *kidneys*. This fatal affection, however, may be a result of the former. When the retention, or mere "stoppage of water," is complete, occasioning immediate danger or inconvenience, the first measure should be, of course, relief by the catheter. In such a case, the distended bladder can be felt as a tense, round tumor above the pubes; and unless it be relieved of its burden (by relaxation of the spasm, if that be the cause, by the giving way of the urethra behind the point of obstruction, causing fistula in perineo, or by art as directed), it may finally burst into the peritoneum.

The MEMBRANOUS portion of the urethra, between the bulb and the prostate gland, is the PART most liable to be strictured; but the accident or disease may occur at any point between the bladder and the glans penis. The closure of the urethra may be either sudden and temporary, or gradual and permanent; or there may be a constant *partial* stricture, aggravated or made complete by spasmodic action.

In the merely SPASMODIC STRICTURE, there is no diminution of the caliber of the urethra, but a temporary obliteration of it from the sides being pressed together by contraction of the surrounding muscular fibers. The irritation occasioning this may be in the mucous membrane, where it is often caused by gonorrhea. When the urine reaches the irritable spot, or after a small amount has passed it, the irritation is communicated to the muscular tissue, and the closure ensues. The patient has to urinate very frequently, and is generally in a great hurry about it — the stream coming with force and entire freedom for a few seconds, and then *suddenly* stopping. The difficulty may be experienced in coitus as well as in urination; the semen being unable to advance through the urethra, or to return into the ductus ejacalutorius, is driven backward into the bladder, where it remains until that vessel can discharge itself. The irritability of the part will of course be greater at some times than others. A greater or less liability to this sort of inconvenience may continue for many years, without any material change; but, generally, the functional will induce organic disease, — the "spasmodic" will occasion "permanent stricture"— by the thickening of the coats of the urethra, and diminution or obliteration of its channel. Sometimes the morbid irritability continues after the thickening, so that the stream of urine when it passes is both small and interrupted. As the thickening progresses

— in the *Organic* or PERMANENT form of STRICTURE, the patient first notices that the urine does not pass out straight; and then, that the stream diminishes; and at length, when he attempts to force it off more quickly, becomes branched. The channel may continue to diminish until the urine can only pass in drops. That excretion itself changes its appearance, from too long retention, generally becoming yellow; and sooner or later is mingled with pus, showing that the urethra or bladder has ulcerated. The urine may be so thickened that it will coagulate. As the bladder becomes more involved, the patient gradually sinks: frequent rigors come on, with more or less fever. The ulceration may extend along the ureters to the kidneys, or those organs may first become more directly affected by their retained excretions and cease their depurative functions, when the brain soon becomes involved, and coma smooths the way to death. Before this final result, other diseases may be induced, as hernia or piles, from the constant habit of straining.

The most frequent cause of stricture is, as we believe, gonorrhea, or, rather, the fashionable "cure" of that fashionable disease. One distinguished western surgeon is in the habit of accusing, and, as he says, of convicting, all his patients of this charge, however advanced they may be in life, or however respectable their standing in society. His experience, unfortunately, proves rather the prevalence of the sin than the invariability of the penalty. *Post hoc* is not always *propter hoc;* and most strictured men may have had gonorrhea "cured" into them, without proving that it is necessarily *the* sole cause in their cases, much less that there is no other cause. From the analogy of stricture in other parts, we can easily see that whatever occasions frequent irritation, or keeps up a chronic inflammation of the part, is capable of the effect in question. In this case may be mentioned injuries by catheters, the passage of gravel, and even stone in the bladder. The absorption of the special irritant of the part from cantharides, applied for the purpose of vesication, must not be forgotten as a not unfrequent cause.

TREATMENT OF THE SPASMODIC VARIETY.

Always, if possible, ascertain the *cause* and remove it. If it is *gonorrhea,* still active, cure that affection in a *proper* manner.

In cases of *spasmodic stricture* following gonorrhea, we have had the most satisfactory results from *Nux v.* In one case treated by us in Cincinnati, when the patient had been obliged to use a catheter every time of urinating for many years, the urethra closing instantly on the urine passing the irritable point, *Nux v. tr.* in drop doses every night, cured him in ten days. One year after, he had had no return of the stricture. Warm sitz baths were used twice daily, and a cold wet compress kept on the perinæum at night.

Cannabis and *Cantharis* have been most successful in spasmodic stricture arising from other causes, especially in old persons. One case, a man of seventy, where there had been stricture, at times, for several years, and there was present great irritation of the bladder, bloody urine, with an extraordinary quantity, and complete obstruction by spasm of the urethra,—

Cannabis, tr. in drop doses, three times daily, brought perfect relief in three days.

Cantharis is most serviceable when there is burning pain in the urethra, scalding of the urine, and the spasm causes great pain.

Petroselinum is useful, particularly when there is still some gleety discharge with burning and tingling in the urethra. We have used it successfully in some bad cases in the form of an infusion, in doses of a table spoonful three or four times daily.

In cases of spasm from irritation and inflammation brought on by over exertion, stimulating food or drinks after badly treated gonorrhea, we have seen, in numerous instances, immediate relief given by the warm infusion of *Althæa offic.* drank freely. In very bad and dangerous cases, where urination was impossible, and the irritability so great as to forbid the use of a catheter, this remedy taken, as above directed, has allayed the irritation in a short time, so as to allow of *free urination.* The green root is the best for this purpose.

Sulphur is valuable to remove any latent taint in the system that might predispose to a return of the disease.

Carbo an. seems to be better adapted to the *permanent stricture*, when there is a hardness and thickened condition of the mucous membrane of the urethra.

Clematis has also been used with advantage in permanent stricture.

Sang. can. is a valuable remedy in this case, especially when the urethra is very irritable, bleeding when a catheter or bougie is passed.

Petroleum has been used with advantage in some cases.

The following case is reported by Dr. C. Neidhard:

"A merchant of New Orleans had acquired a certain celebrity because, after having been given up by the most celebrated physicians of that city, he had cured himself by taking several tablespoonfuls of the pure quicksilver every day for months in order to cure a lameness of the arm; apparently it had no deleterious effect. He took this prescription from an old and now very scarce work of Dr. Dover, where this practice is recommended. After having taken the *Mercury* for some time, it used to ooze out of his skin, particularly from the legs and genital organs.

"The stricture for which he came to consult me, was caused by several gonorrheas, to which he had been subject at different periods of his life. He had also had syphilis. Dr. Luzenberg, in New Orleans, had given a great deal of *Muriate of Gold* and *Sarsaparilla.*

"His symptoms were the following: occasionally blotches came out on the penis filled with white matter, tingling, burning pain on making water, which is of a reddish color with white sediment; sometimes there is a discharge of a whitish, milk-like color. On sounding his bladder a stricture is discovered six inches from meatus. The concomitant symptoms were: constipation, with occasional discharges of blood per anum, also vomiting of food with bile. The large veins in the groins, slight pain in the kidneys.

"*Tussilago petasites* in alternation with *Carbo. animalis* were exhibited with excellent effect, afterwards *Clematis erecta* completed the cure. With regard to the indications for *Tussilago*, it was my experience in many cases of gonorrhea with similar symptoms. *Carbo. animalis* was prescribed because of all remedies it is one of the best to cure chronic indurations of the mucous membrane from previous inflammation. In the selection of *Clematis erecta* I was guided by the similarity of the symptoms."

It seems to be conceded on all hands, by allopaths and homeopaths, that "old inveterate cases of permanent, cartilaginous strictures" are incurable except by mechanical means.

THIS COMMON MODE of relieving this condition is purely mechanical; the urethra is stretched wider by means of *bougies.* These should be very smooth and well lubricated before being used. The best material for them is gum elastic or gutta percha. It may be necessary to begin with one so small that a common cat-gut fiddle-string will be the most suitable article. Substitute for this a larger one as the parts admit of a change, and that again for others, going gradually from No. 1 to No. 12, or even 16, of the regularly graduated bougies. Let each be kept in and worn constantly or as much of the time as possible, for a day or two before one of the next larger number is inserted.

This DILATATION of the urethra may succeed so far as to remedy the merely mechanical inconvenience for awhile, but it is by no means to be regarded as a cure for the *disease* of stricture. Enlarging the caliber of the urethra does not necessarily rectify the abnormal condition of the mucous membrane.

The stricture may be destroyed by the application of *caustic* directly to the part. The constricted part is generally very small. It may be but like a thread or ligature drawn round the urethra; or it may extend for from half an inch to an inch along its course —rarely more than that. There may be more or less obstruction at several points. The most convenient method of cautérizing any part of the urethra, is to use the modification of Lallemand's *porte-caustique* (Fig. 16). Some nitrate of silver is melted into the

FIG. 16.

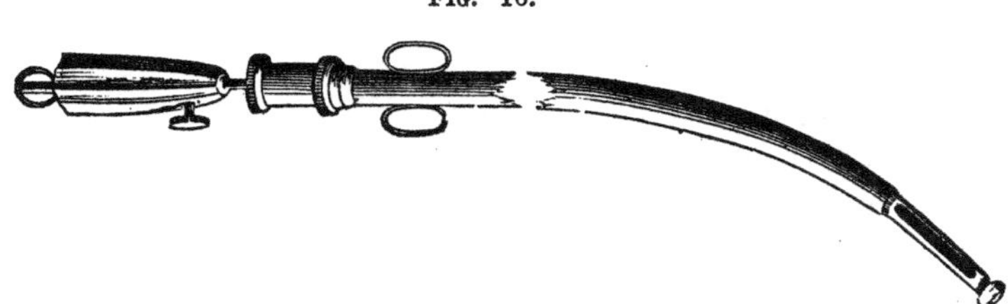

groove at the end of the movable rod, and scraped down smooth and round like the rest of its surface, so that it can be drawn back into the sheath. When the latter is inserted up nearly to the strictured point, the armed rod is pushed out, turned two or three times round, and sheathed again. This instrument can be used with perfect safety, the caustic being so effectually fixed in the notches at the ends of the groove, that it can not fall out, and so covered by the sheath when drawn back, that it can not touch other parts.

But we have had several cases that had undergone the whole course of treatment with this cautery, as well as the bougies, with but slight benefit; and have succeeded with them, as with other cases, by different means.

As it regards cases caused by gonorrhea, our practice may require some defense or explanation. It has been known that such cases were sometimes unexpectedly cured by the re-establishment of gonorrhea in the *natural* way. Taking this hint from nature, and reasoning from the analogy of chronic disease in the mucous membrane of the eye, and the effects of stimulants upon it, to that of the urethra, we determined on a new and peculiar course of treatment. Our plan was, to re-establish a discharge from the parts, resembling, as near as possible, the original gonorrhea; and necessarily accompanied with more or less of acute inflammation, as in that disease. We found the solution of the *Sesqui-carbonate of potash,* injected by means of a syringe through a catheter, answer this purpose effectually. When this lotion is used two or three times a day, it produces considerable irritation of the urethra and a discharge so nearly resembling a gonorrheal one, that it would be mistaken for it by any person unacquainted with the actual exciting cause. The solution should be weak at first, and gradually increased to a saturated one, if the desired effect is not sooner produced.

If the bladder is at the same time involved in the disease, the injections should be carried up into it also; but, in such a case, it is better first to inject warm water into the viscus, that the caustic solution may be more diluted there, than at the original seat of the disease.

This ARTIFICIAL BLENORRHEA may be continued until the proper change is produced in the urethra. This may be known by discontinuing the remedy, at any time, for a few days, and using instead, a simple injection of cold water, with perhaps a little mucilage of slippery elm or gum arabic. Then if, on entering a bougie, any symptoms of stricture be still found, renew the caustic injections, until they are no longer necessary.

The tincture of *Sanguinaria* will produce the same effect as the mild caustic, but is objectionable, inasmuch as it occasions a bloody as well as proper blenorrheal discharge, and, for a time, even aggravates the stricture. A few applications, however, repeated every day or two, if the patient can be induced to submit to it, and followed up by soothing applications, will accomplish the cure more speedily than the caustic solutions.

We have found this mode of treatment equally effectual in cases not caused by gonorrhea.

FISTULA IN PERINEO.

A passage of urine into any part of the perineum is generally a consequence of urethral stricture. It is never a simple opening or artificial urethra. The discharge of so irritating a secretion into parts so lax, occasions extensive ulcers with very offensive suppuration. The case is so plain as to need no special description.

If the cause be stricture, that must be first attended to. After sufficiently dilating the urethra, — or in the first place, if no stricture exist, —

— a *gum-elastic* CATHETER, or, better still, one of *gutta percha* should be placed and *left* in the bladder. When this is constantly worn, as it should be, the patient can move about but little — which is all the better for his chance of successful treatment.

The ulcer thus protected should then be washed with soap and water three times daily for two or three days, until the inflammation consequent upon the irritation of the urine, has subsided. The surface should all the time be covered with an emollient poultice. It will not take long for the inflammation to subside if the part is protected from the urine, well cleansed and shielded by a warm emollient from the air.

This disease is quite different in its character from fistula in ano. It tends to spontaneous recovery, when the irritating cause is removed, whereas the other has no such disposition.

After the subsidence of inflammation, if the sore appears healthy, keep up the simple dressings and let it heal. If, however, it still looks unhealthy and does not incline to heal, apply *Aqua*

Calendulæ and give the dilution internally. Frequently subjecting the parts to the vapor of water, will assist in allaying the irritability and aid the action of the remedies.

If the ulcer remains indolent and indisposed to heal, *Petroleum* internally and applied to the sore, will soon change it to a healthy condition.

It must be borne in mind, that the entire protection of the ulcer from contact with the urine is absolutely essential to success. The patient must observe perfect rest in a recumbent posture as far as practicable. The urine should be frequently voided so as to obviate any danger from accumulation.

DISEASES OF THE PROSTATE GLAND.

ACUTE PROSTATITIS

May be caused by external violence, but is much more frequently a result of gonorrhea.

The SYMPTOMS are a sense of weight and a throbbing pain about the bladder; tenderness of the perineum and a tumefaction of the gland (which last can be best ascertained by examination *per rectum*). There are also frequent attempts to urinate, accompanied with violent pain.

Should the patient be altogether unable to *pass* his *urine*, a small gum elastic catheter may be used; though this is an operation which should be avoided if possible. Warm sitz baths will be of great service in allaying irritation.

If the inflammation is the result of external violence, in the early stage, use *Arnica;* but if later, when there is much swelling and burning or throbbing pain, *Conium* will do better, or these may be advantageously alternated.

If there is present a general feverish condition, *Aconite* may be advantageously used, followed by *Conium*, if the inflammation is not relieved.

The patient should be kept very quiet, and eat but very little; the bowels gently moved by warm enemas.

If gonorrhea be the cause, *Cantharis*, *Puls.*, or *Thuja* will be the best remedies.

If GONORRHEA be present, measures should be taken to "cure" this disease *constitutionally*. Better let it run on and run itself *out*, than merely stop it by astringent injections. No more certain means than these could be devised *for insuring* chronic and permanent disease of the prostate. The virus should be removed from the system, and not locked up in it.

If the gonorrhea has been suppressed, use *Puls.* to restore it. At the same time repeat the hot sitz bath, and apply a wet compress to the affected part.

With the restoration of the gonorrheal discharge, the prostatic inflammation will generally subside. If not, use *Thuja*. If the discharge is bloody and burning, use *Cantharis*.

Should the inflammation have advanced too far for resolution before you are called, the fact will be indicated by rigors and a considerable swelling of the perineum, soon followed by symptoms of acute inflammation of the external *surface*. In such a case, as soon as you are satisfied that

—*matter has formed*, puncture *at once*, lest the abscess extend and burst into the rectum or urethra, when the consequences may be serious and the cure difficult. After the matter has passed off, frequently wash out the abscess with *Calendula;* and if the patient's constitution be good it will soon heal. Gentle compression over the parts will aid the process.

If, however, the abscess open *into the urethra*, which will be known by the sudden discharge of pus through the latter, the urine should be drawn off by catheter and slight compression made on the affected part until it heal. The better way, however, would be even then to puncture through the perineum, and evacuate the abscess, so as not to allow any more matter to pass through the urinary channel. The urethral wound will soon heal, if precautions are taken to prevent the further passage through it of pus or urine. This may be more effectually insured by the patient's constantly wearing the catheter, if he can bear it.

CHRONIC INFLAMMATION of the part in question is seldom the object of medical treatment or observation, except as it results in inconvenience from

ENLARGEMENT OF THE PROSTATE GLAND.

This is a not unfrequent disease, though comparatively little attended to in ordinary practice.

Although when it occurs in *young men*, gonorrhea or its *mistreatment* may have been the original cause, it often comes on in *advanced life*, when there is no ground for such a suspicion.

The *gland* sometimes attains five or ten times its ordinary size. It is also much harder than natural. The middle lobe usually projects into the bladder, and alters the shape and direction of the urethra. It produces but a slight degree of dysuria, but its diagnostic effect is that the bladder is never completely evacuated, and the *urine* rendered *turbid* in consequence.

The first SYMPTOM noticed will probably be a *difficulty* in passing urine, though the desire for it is more urgent and frequent. There is also a sense of *weight* in the perineum, which increases as does the obstruction. Finally the patient is never able completely to evacuate the contents of the bladder. Total *retention of urine* is apt to occur occasionally, especially if the individual is addicted to excesses of any kind. The too long detention of the urine in the bladder may occasion calculous deposites.

The prostatic disease may go on until it extends to the bladder, and all connected parts, producing abscess, ulceration and death.

An additional measure of great efficacy is to establish or re-establish from the mucous membrane of the urethra, a discharge similar to that of gonorrhea. This may be done by

—*filling the urethra* with a strong solution of a mild caustic (*Pot. Sesqui-Carb.*), through a silver catheter passed up to the neck of the bladder and gradually withdrawn, while the injection is being introduced. This is to be repeated two or three times a day until the suppuration is excited, and occasionally afterwards: it is to be kept up for several weeks. Taking care, however, before each caustic injection to nearly fill the bladder with warm water, mucilage of slippery elm, or gum arabic.

This artificial gonorrhea is quite sure to cure the patient when his disease is only the result of "drying up a clap" too suddenly. It is a restoration of the original disease in order to have it really cured. If the prostatic affection proceed from other causes, this urethral drainage, though not so necessary, will still greatly facilitate its removal. The tincture or infusion of Sanguinaria may be used instead of the alkaline solution, but we have found it occasionally too irritating.

CHAPTER XXXV.

SPERMATORRHŒA.

IMPORTANCE of the seminal fluid and of the disease in question — Slight notice of it by medical writers generally — Various and anomalous symptoms — Particularly the nervous and mental — Difficulty and delicacy of various opinions — The physician's confessional. — Causes independent of onanism — Nocturnal and diurnal emissions — Conditions under which emissions take place — Examination of urine — Microscope — Spermatozoa as a means of diagnosis and prognosis — The analagous disease in females — Results, Impotence, Insanity, Catalepsy, &c. — Great prevalence of Spermatorrhœa and its most common cause. — Condition and measures of treatment — Regimen, physical and moral — Affections of the prostate and rectum — Case of ascarides.

UNDER this head, we shall include all affections or symptoms connected with losses of the seminal fluid, — whether they take place in a natural, artificial or involuntary way — that is, by excessive sexual intercourse, by masturbation or by spontaneous emissions.

The semen appears to be pre-eminently a vital fluid, and to have a very close connection with the nervous system; for the most disastrous consequences to that system, and all the functions more directly dependent on it, follow from any immoderate seminal discharges. If this take place in early life, it generally retards the *growth*. It always impairs the *mental faculties* and brings on *premature old age*. It manifests itself in very *serious affections*, presenting strange and anomalous features. Nosologically considered, it is a host in itself. The patient not unfrequently exhibits symptoms so many and multifarious, as to authorize the statement that he is suffering under the whole catalogue of human maladies. To enumerate precise symptoms would be like attempting an exact description of hysteria.

"Spermatorrhœa" is a new word in medical nomenclature. It is mentioned as a disease by few, if any, systematic writers. No standard author, certainly, whose work was published in America, prior to 1848, has noticed the subject in a manner calculated to arrest the attention of the practitioner; or to give him any correct knowledge of the disease or its symptoms. Some "medical authors" have even deprecated the idea of mentioning the subject at all! One work, — an acknowledged text book in many of our colleges, — thus speaks in regard to it: "It is certainly not very consistent with our national character to dilate so freely on a subject, which in a great majority of cases, can only be treated of as the result of the most degrading vice."

Without attempting to give any formal DESCRIPTION of the disease, or to divide it into varieties or stages, we shall name the SYMPTOMS of it as they have presented themselves to our notice. Though this may seem an unsystematic way of proceeding, we hope to enable the practitioner to discriminate the disease, when it shall, as it undoubtedly will, fall into his hands in every day practice.

In some cases the only complaint the patient will make is, that he is suffering under a kind of *continual fever.* He will probably present a hot dry skin, with something of a hectic appearance. Though all the ordinary means of arresting such symptoms may have been tried, he is none the better.

The patient will present *no* evidence of *organic disease.* His lungs are sound; and his liver appears to perform its office tolerably well. On strict inquiry, however, it will be found that he is generally inclined to be *costive,* — has probably been in the habit of taking some kinds of aperient pills. *Dyspeptic* symptoms also are not uncommon, in connection with excessive *languor* and *debility.* The languid or tired feeling is especially manifest, with tremblings of the limbs perhaps, on first rising from bed in the morning.

The SLEEP seems to be irregular and unrefreshing, — Restlessness during the early part of the night, and, in the advanced stages of the disease, profuse sweats before morning. There is also frequent starting in the sleep, from disturbing dreams. The characteristic feature is that the patient almost always *dreams* of sexual intercourse. This is one of the earliest as well as most constant symptoms. When it occurs most frequently, it is apt to be accompanied with painful priapism. A *gleety discharge* from the urethra may also be frequently discovered, especially if the patient examine when at stool or after urinating. This may be more frequent with those who have had gonorrhea, but is *by no means* confined to such.

The patient may confess to being a very nervous subject. He has not only frequent attacks of nervous HEADACHE, but occasional sensations of giddiness, or *vertigo* ringing in the ears, &c., with perhaps a fixed dull pain in the *back* of the head, where a preternatural heat may almost always be discovered. Connected with this will be a stiffness in the muscles of the *neck*, and darting pains through the forehead. Extensive SPINAL IRRITATION is a frequent accompaniment. Some patients will speak of a peculiar aura, like water running over the body, or a sensation resembling the crawling of insects under the skin, especially down the outside of the thighs. Weak *eyes* (as well as weak back), are among the common symptoms. But as might be expected from the direct implication of the nervous system, the MORAL and MENTAL SYMPTOMS are perhaps more to be relied on than any very obvious bodily peculiarities. The disease is well known to be one of the most frequent causes of insanity; and one of its earliest symptoms is incapacity for concentrated *attention*. If the sufferer attempt to pursue any mathematical study, he will fail. He manifests moreover an excessive *want* of *confidence* in his own abilities, even where they do not seem to fail him: he has very often "no mind of his own." He is much afflicted with awful *forebodings*, though he can not tell of what. Some indescribable evil is always about to befall him. In this and several other particulars, the disease very closely resembles *delirium tremens*. It may be confounded with *hypochondria*.

One very frequent and perhaps early symptom (especially in *young females*) is *solitariness*, — a disposition to seclude themselves from society. Although they may be tolerably cheerful when in company, they choose rather to be alone.

The countenance has often a gloomy and worn down expression. The patient's friends frequently notice a great change. Large livid spots under the eyes is a common feature. Sudden flashes of heat may be noticed passing over the patient's face. He is liable also to palpitations. The pulse is very variable, *generally too slow.* Extreme *emaciation*, without any other assignable cause for it, may be set down as another very common symptom. If the evil has gone on for several years, there will be a *peculiar* expression of the countenance — a *general* unhealthy appearance of a character so marked, as to enable an experienced observer to recognize such a case at the first glance, as readily as a banker would a counterfeit bill. In the case of onanists, especially, there is a peculiar *rank odor* emitted from the body, by which they may be readily distinguished. One striking peculiarity of all these patients is, that they can not look a man in the face! Cowardice is constitutional with them.

Whenever we find any considerable number of these more prominent symptoms in the same person, we may *suspect* the nature of the CAUSE. We may encounter difficulty, however, in our attempts to ascertain more. Much delicacy and circumspection are sometimes requisite. By some morbidly sensitive subjects, indirect questions will be *evaded* when their bearing is surmised, and a too abrupt charge *denied.* The best plan then is, after carefully comparing enough of the symptoms to give a moral assurance, and otherwise securing the patient's confidence, to let him understand that we already *know* the nature of the difficulty, and that his life depends on our being allowed to know more — to know, indeed, all about it. At the same time he should appreciate the reciprocal obligations of such professional confidence, which are the same as between lawyer and client. Secrecy on the part of the practitioner is not less a duty than candor on the patient's. The physician's *confessional* should be as sacred as the priest's. All sufferers will not be equally penitents, or ashamed of their weakness. To none, however, can we expect the subject to be a matter of the same *indifference* that it is, and *ought to be*, to us. We are to speak of it only as a disease, a misfortune — except in the case of *continued* masturbation, when we are justified, in the said character of father-confessor, in using all *needful* severity of speech, and withholding all hope of absolution, i. e., of health, except on the condition of effectual repentance, i. e., of entire abandonment of the physiological sin, and implicit submission to whatever *penance* may be enjoined in the way of medicine or regimen.

The original or *predisposing* CAUSE, moreover — and this ought to be always borne in mind — may have been, as the still *exciting* and perpetuating *cause* very generally is, some purely physical disease. Spermatorrhœa *may* be altogether unconnected with onanism, or anything the sufferer *ought* to be made ashamed of. It will, nevertheless, be always attended with many of the same characteristics. In moral judgments, as in legal, the doubt must be given in favor of the accused or suspected. The giving way in our own mind — and much more the giving currency from a mean love of depreciation — to the moral prejudice (i. e., *pre-judgment*), must be often as unjust to the individual concerned, as it is always in itself unjustifiable and *unprofessional.*

Several of these causes, or classes of causes, that may bring on this deplorable state of things, independently of masturbation, we will enumerate: — Ascarides or other accidental sources of irritation in the rectum; piles, fistula, or other diseases about the same part; spinal irritation; irritation or chronic inflammation in the prostate gland; or the same state of things in the urethra itself (often, like the prostatic disease, a consequence of gonorrhea); and mere excess in *lawful* sexual indulgence. Sometimes the difficulty is hereditary.

On closer INQUIRY and EXAMINATION we will often find that "nocturnal pollutions" occur almost regularly. We have treated cases when they happened as often as five times in one night. Many will have the still worse symptom of "diurnal pollution." Soreness and enlargement of the *prostate* may often be detected. The best mode of examining the state of this important organ, is by introducing a finger into the rectum. In attempting to pass a bougie, the *urethra* will probably be found so irritable as to contract irresistibly upon it. The *bladder* may also be very irritable, necessitating a frequent discharge of its contents. The *penis* very generally shrinks up, in its relaxed state, much more than with other men; and in many cases, but not so frequently, the *testicles* have dwindled in size.

The emissions occurring at night will generally wake the

patient, but sometimes they are only known by the stains upon the linen, and the debility and lassitude felt upon the next day. Emissions of semen during the day may be excited by the society of females, impure imaginations, or during stool, or they may follow immediately upon an emission of urine, or the spermatic fluid may pass off mixed with the urine. The latter is the most obscure, insidious, and therefore dangerous form of the disease. Should there be any doubt as to the character of the case, a careful examination of the urine will remove it. Upon collecting the urine in a vessel, it will become slightly turbid, and small globular bodies or flocks of various shapes will be perceived on the bottom of the vessel. Filtering will leave the spermatozoa and other flocks upon the filter; when an examination with the microscope will show the spermatozoa and their condition. The *number*, *activity*, *and size* of the spermatozoa, will show the *extent* of the disease, as well as the *progress* of the recovery.

Where marasmus sets in, the spermatozoa disappear entirely, and nothing is perceived except roundish, little shining bodies, the heads, probably, of the extinct spermatozoa. The prostatic fluid may be distinguished from semen by the absence of the spermatozoa.

The formation of crystals of the oxalate of lime in the urine is a valuable diagnostic in spermatorrhœa.

In FEMALES, this disease — or rather an analogous one brought on by masturbation — displays itself more in nervous symptoms and less in mere debility. "Spermatorrhœa" does not of course strictly apply to their case, or that of boys diseased by irritation of the genital organs before puberty. The injurious effect on their systems is independent of what in adult men appears to be the chief evil — loss of *the* vital or virile fluid. In both these cases, therefore, the ultimate danger to life is less. If the patient, however, is attacked by any common acute disease, it will prove more obstinate than under ordinary circumstances; and the practitioner may be much puzzled to know why his remedies fail of their wonted effect.

The female *onanist* is often "hysterical," adding another difficulty to the diagnosis and treatment of cases so called. We have been frequently called to such persons suffering under some slight and commonly manageable attack, which resisted all usual remedies. Individuals confirmed in the destructive habit, will continue it even when confined to their beds by *other severe* diseases, or perhaps by its very consequences.

Insanity is a more common result to men than women, on account of the greater evil of "spermatorrhœa" proper.

Impotence is most probable; epilepsy and apoplexy are, also, not unfrequent terminations.

CATALEPSY, too, should be enumerated as a result. In fact, we are inclined to believe that a large proportion, if not all cases of this *mysterious* disease, are referable to the source under consideration. Four instances have fallen under our own observation; all of which showed conclusively, to us, that masturbation was their cause.

SPERMATORRHŒA is a malady much more common than many seem to suppose. Married men are by no means to be presumed exempt. Whenever there are sufficient symptoms to indicate its existence, we should not be deterred from pursuing our investigations. When the affection is only slight or occasional, a moderate healthful indulgence of the sexual propensity is often beneficial. Hence marriage itself has often been prescribed as a remedy. Unwonted or excessive stimulus of the parts may, however, aggravate or bring back the disease. Moderation must always be enjoined, if not sometimes *total abstinence* for a time.

ONANISM (which is also to be itself regarded as a *disease*, whether it bring on spermatorrhœa, strictly so called, or not) is most deplorably prevalent. Both sexes, and it might almost be said all ages, are guilty of it or subject to it. It is to be regretted that parents and teachers are so generally ignorant or falsely delicate upon this subject. We are inclined to think, also, that few physicians are fully informed upon it, or act up to their responsibility in taking proper opportunities to inform and caution others about it. Instances are met with of persons who have indulged in the vice, unchecked and scarcely suspecting any evil, from their earliest recollection. The practice often begins long before the age of puberty. One young lady of most respectable character and connections, whom we had to treat for it, informed us that she was subject to leucorrhea when only nine years of age, and to distinct sexual desire before eleven — though her catamenia did not appear *be-*

fore she was twelve! The *prognosis* in all cases where we have the co-operation of the patient is favorable.

TREATMENT.

If the practice of *self*-pollution is ascertained, it must be *abandoned* at once and forever. We must point out inevitable destruction as the consequence of its continuance; and encourage and strengthen the patient's resolution by assurance of ultimate recovery. We must not ourselves be discouraged at having to do this frequently. We have to bear in mind that the patient's memory and resolution are greatly enfeebled; and he will often find himself relapsing before he is aware of it.

Remove all CAUSES that are found to excite the genital organs, whether through the mind or body. All association with the opposite sex is sometimes interdicted; but the policy, as well as propriety, of this may well be questioned. The society of those whom we respect, is the surest means of strengthening self-respect and self-control. Lascivious books, pictures and conversation, are of course to be *denounced*—on medical grounds, which are here one with the moral.

Let the patient take as much EXERCISE as he can in the *open air* (especially in the country). It should, if possible, be of a kind that is profitable as well as pleasant, and such as will engage both mind and body.

The diet must be carefully regulated; all stimulants, tea, coffee, spices, wines, meats, &c., avoided. In one very bad case, after unsatisfactory treatment, with a mixed diet, we found great benefit from the exclusive use of vegetable food; milk, fruits, and farinaceous food should constitute the diet. Supper, if partaken of *at all*, should be eaten *early*, and the bladder and rectum evacuated just before retiring to rest, and the urine frequently voided. The patient should sleep upon a moderately hard bed and rise early in the morning, and think as little as possible about his genital organs or disease. General cold bathing—cold hip baths and injections of cold water—should be daily made use of. Occasional wet-sheet packs should also be employed.

If *nocturnal emissions* are the great evil, direct the sufferer to avoid lying on his back. He often discovers for himself that he rarely escapes when asleep in this posture, and rarely has them in any other. That he may not turn over on his back while asleep, let him fasten something to his body that will prevent it or awaken him on the attempt, such as a hard ball upon the spine attached by a banpage.

If there is any soreness of the *prostate gland* on pressure through the perineum or rectum, it must be removed. Cauterization of the urethra is often resorted to, but in a very large majority of cases does much more harm than good. Some of the worst cases we have had to treat have been made so by previous cauterization. Internal remedies, with soothing and invigorating injections and proper baths, and wet compresses, will be sufficient. The cure may be facilitated in some cases, however, by pressure.

Its efficacy in allaying chronic inflammation of other parts is well known. A pad is applied around the base of the penis so as to bear upon the seminal ducts, "with a silver jugum (yoke), encircling and removing all pressure from the private parts," and secured by a gum elastic strap passing over the body, before and behind, and over each shoulder and buckled in front. According to Dr. Dixon, this is only necessary, in most cases, to be worn during the hours of sleep; and the more active forms of the disease will yield to it alone.

In cases arising from, or aggravated by,

— HEMORRHOIDS, fistula or other affections of the RECTUM (and strict examination should always be made to ascertain whether such an influence is not in operation), such diseases or affections must be removed, before any hope can be entertained of effectually curing the sexual derangement.

If ASCARIDES be the cause, they must be got rid off. The itching about the anus, which is the characteristic effect of this kind of worms, is worse at night, and apt to be aggravated by whatever overheats the body. During the day they will be felt most *hungry* and troublesome about two or three hours after the patient's usual times of eating, particularly after the morning meal, or about nine or ten o'clock.

If the internal use of *Aconite, Ignatia, or Sulphur,* is not sufficient, use injections of oil. or even a solution of *Aloes*, which will soon remove them.

Quite a number of remedies have been recommended for the various forms of this disease, and have been used beneficially with them in connection with hydropathic, dietetic and moral treatment; but they have exerted a conservative rather than a radical influence. They have erected a barrier against the desolation of the swollen stream, but not emptied the clouds; they have girdled the tree, but not plucked it up by the roots. This want of specificness led the authors of the repertory to say, that "For spermatorrhœa properly so called, or emission of semen without erections, there is no remedy which has yet received the sanction of experience." We have one, however, to propose for trial—it is the *Eryngium aquaticum*—which has two remarkable cures reported by Dr. Parks (pharmaceutist, Cin.), to recommend it.

Case 1. A married man injured his testicles by jumping upon a horse; this was followed by a discharge of what was considered semen for fifteen years, during which time he was treated allopathically and homeopathically. Dr. P—— exhibited a number of the usual remedies without permanent benefit. He then gave a half gr. dose three times a day, of the third decimal trituration of the *Eryngium aqua.* In five days the emissions were entirely suppressed, and have not returned to this time (over two years). The emissions were without erections day or night and followed by great lassitude.

Case 2. A married man, not conscious of having sustained any injury, was troubled for eight or ten years with emissions at night with erections. The semen also passed by day with the urine. The loss of semen was followed by great lassitude and depression, continuing from twelve to forty-eight hours. There was also partial impotence. Had been treated allopathically. Dr. P—— gave him *Phos. ac.* for two weeks without material benefit. He then exhibited the *Eryngium* as above, with like excellent and prompt result.

China, Nux. v., Phos., Phos. ac., Sulph., and Electro-magnetism, are our most important remedies.

The efficacy of *China* in removing the disorders induced by a loss of humors is well known to every homeopath. It is particularly indicated where the seminal losses have produced or are causing great sensitiveness of the nervous system, disordered digestion, sleep disturbed by frightful dreams, and physical and mental depression.

Phos. ac.; excessive nocturnal emissions followed by great weakness of the nervous system, the patient feeling chagrined and mortified at his condition. In all cases of spermatorrhœa, there is more or less low spiritedness and distress of mind, as well as the derangement of the digestive apparatus; and the spheres of *China and Phos ac.* are so nearly alike that they are usually recommended to be given in alternation. The distinction we have been accustomed to draw is that in that of *Phos. ac.*, the moral sentiments are more involved. It is not so much the loss of health that afflicts the patient as the idea of the debasing way in which it was lost. Oh! that I had a disease of which I need not be ashamed, he exclaims. In that of *China* he is distressed; in *Phos. ac.*, he is grieved.

Nux. vom.; where the patient has been in the habit of indulging in stimulants, or is of sedentary habits, and constipation or hemorrhoids are present, or previous to the exhibition of *Phosphorus* to diminish the excitability of the nervous system.

Phosphorus; after the excitability of the nervous system has been allayed by *China* or *Nux. v.*, when there is very great nervous prostration or tendency to the development of phthisis.

Aconite, in the form of tincture, one or two drops in a tumbler of water, a teaspoonful every three or four hours, until there is a decided improvement, is recommended by Dr. Hempel for great nervous derangements, sudden starting at the least noise, fitful mood, depression of spirits, apprehensions for the future, dizziness, intense frontal headache, either every forenoon or constantly, dryness of the mouth, coated tongue, distress in the pit of the stomach, vomiting of the ingesta, wakefulness at night, drowsiness in the day time, nightmare, copious and exhausting emissions every night, costiveness.

Electro-magnetism is one of our most efficient remedies in this disease: says Gollmann, "I look upon it as indispensable in the treatment of this affection. I commence the treatment by first inducing with my hand an electro-magnetic current along the back of the patient; after a time I substitute the cylinder in the place of the hand, and lastly resort to the electro-magnetic baths. The passes have to be made along the whole length of the spinal column. Somtimes I apply one pole to the perineum, and the other to the lumbar region. The current has to be induced very methodically. The first application should not last longer than five minutes; afterwards, every application should be increased by one or two minutes, until we gradually prolong it to about fifteen minutes, after which every succeeding application should be decreased and shortened again by one minute. Already, after the first days of the treatment, the patient will perceive an amelioration; his apathy and his indifference to the enjoyments of life will be succeeded by a feeling of ease and physical well being; the seminal losses will either diminish or cease entirely, and all the other morbid phenomena will mend considerably. But even if the improvement should be ever so striking, the treatment should not be discontinued all at once, for their affection is disposed to return; it is therefore advisable to continue the treatment some two or three weeks even after the patient should seem perfectly restored."

Sulphur and Calcarea at long intervals are recommended to eradicate the inclination to the vice of masturbation.

The following remedies may also be consulted:

For seminal emissions without erections, *Trios. per.*, *Bell.*, *Coloc.*, *Nux. v.*

For emissions with amorous dreams, *Arsen.*, *Aurum*, *Argen.*, *China*, *Coloc.*, *Olean.*, *Phos. ac.*, *Staph.*, *Spigel.*, *Samb.*, *Viol. Tri.*

For those without amorous dreams, *Anac.*, *Argen.*, *Bell.*, *Carbo. veg.*, *Cicuta.*, *Bismuth*, *Guac.*, *Merc. sol.*, *Puls.*, *Ruta*, *Verbas.*

For discharge of prostate fluids, *Anac.*, *Calc.*, *Con.*, *Hepar*, *Natr. carb.*, *Nit. ac.*, *Phos. ac.*, *Sep.*, *Silic.*, *and Sulph.*

CHAPTER XXXVI.

VENEREAL DISEASES — GONORRHEA AND SYPHILIS.

GONORRHEA — Symptoms and cause — Relation to Blenorrhea (benigna or common) — Difficulty of forming and stating opinions — Gonorrhea not a merely local disease — Consequences of the common treatment — Ricord's treatment — Homeopathic ditto — Complication — Other modes of treatment and particular specifics. SYPHILIS — Primary, Secondary, Tertiary — Chancres, their varieties — Inoculation — Allopathic use of mercury, a cause of Tertiary Syphilis — Ricord's treatment; Homeopathic ditto — Bubo, inflammatory and indurated — Treatment of Secondary and Tertiary Syphilis.

GONORRHEA.

THE too well-known disease, so called, — or what is now named by some with more etymological propriety, virulent BLENORRHEA,* — may be defined as a specific inflammation, produced by the immediate contact of a virus, the product of the same inflammation, with the mucous membrane of the urethra.

The first symptom is an itching or tingling at the orifice of the urethra; this usually commences from the second to the eighth day after an impure connection, and will probably be first noticed in urinating. It increases in intensity until the patient suffers severe pain, particularly upon urinating. The lips of the urethra become inflamed and swollen, and if the inflammation is not checked, the glans become also involved, and the inflammation extends up higher, successively involving the entire spongy, membranous, and prostatic portion of the urethra, and finally the neck of the bladder. The discharge is at first mucous, but soon becomes thick, purulent, and of a yellowish color. Sometimes it is tinged with blood. In some very severe cases the color of the discharge is greenish, in others the discharge is suppressed, constituting dry gonorrhea. When the inflammation has involved the whole of the spongy portion of the urethra, there is frequent involuntary and spasmodic erection, with a curvature of the penis

* "Gonorrhea" originally meant what we are now obliged to find another word for — *Spermatorrhea.*

downwards. This species of priapism is called *chordee.* When the membranous portion is implicated, there is pain more or less severe in the perineum, with a dragging sensation behind the scrotum during erection, which is not diminished by drawing down the penis. If the inflammation extends to the prostatic portion, the pain in the perineum becomes more intense, preventing the patient sitting down cross-legged, the testes become painful, and urination is attended with scalding, commencing from the posterior portion of the canal, and frequently a twisted or branched stream. In implication of the neck of the bladder there is very frequent and urgent desire to urinate, almost amounting to incontinence.

When the disease is not arrested, it becomes chronic — secondary gonorrhea or gleet,—the pain entirely disappearing, and a muco-purulent discharge alone remaining: sexual intercourse, dissipation, or exposure, will cause a relapse. Authors are generally agreed as to the infectious nature of gleety discharges.

The prepuce occasionally becomes enormously swollen, and phymosis (i. e., inability of drawing the prepuce back over the glans) or paraphymosis (i. e., where the prepuce has been drawn back behind the glans, but in consequence of constriction it cannot be returned) may be the consequence. Either of these greatly aggravates the disease.

The lymphatic glands in the groin may swell, giving rise to *buboes*, though these, it should be remembered, may result from any other irritation.

The constitutional symptoms are in general but slight. In certain states of the system, however, considerable sympathetic fever may be developed.

A first "clap" is generally more severe than subsequent ones.

Its more serious occasional *results* are inflammation of the glans, penis and prepuce, of the testes, prostate gland or bladder.

Acute rheumatism and gout are set down in the books as among the sequelæ of gonorrhea; but we are inclined to refer them, with other unfavorable results, often rather to the treatment than the disease, though it may sometimes excite a dyscrasia giving rise to these and other difficulties. *Orchitis* may result from extension or metastasis. In that case there is often considerable hemorrhage through the urethra.

As to the CAUSE, — although gonorrhea proper never, in all probability, occurs but as the result of infection through an impure coition, — it must never be forgotten that there are many other affections which very closely resemble it, and give rise to a similar discharge, then distinguished as

— BLENORRHEA (or blenorrhea benigna) of the urethra. This may occur from any cause of local irritation or violence, such as the introduction of the catheter. Metastasis of rheumatism and gout may excite the mucous secretion in question. Any cause tending to produce stricture in the part may also have this result. We have known it to result from hemorrhoidal irritation, and disappear of itself when that affection was cured. When mechanical violence is the cause, the mucous inflammation may not show itself for a long time, and thus become the more suspicious.

This PSEUDO-GONORRHEA may be brought on by excess in *venereal indulgence*, where there can be no suspicion of any impurity. Contact with the *menstrual fluid* sometimes occasions urethral inflammation in the male, with most of the other suspicious symptoms. *Leucorrhea* is still more generally believed capable of the same result, — is believed indeed by some speculators to have originally produced, and to be still reproducing, the true gonorrheal virus.

Gonorrhea in females so nearly resembles some forms of *severe leucorrhea*, that it is in many instances extremely difficult, if not impossible, to distinguish them. Simple gonorrhea in them may also be confounded with a discharge accompanying syphilis. The two diseases may coexist and infect any persons exposed, according to their susceptibility.

The DIAGNOSIS, therefore, of this too familiar disease, would often be a very *questionable* matter, but for the ascertainable *fact* of exposure. (The inverse *test*, by inoculating others, — sometimes confiding wives, or still more confiding females, — ought to subject every *man* who tries it to castration, or some other sort of castigation at the hands of his physician.)

The practitioner ought then to be very *reserved* with his *opinions* in these cases; or, rather, he should learn to observe a scrupulous silence as to *causes*, unless where the ends of justice require him to speak, when he should adopt the rule of law which gives every doubt in favor of the accused. It is very seldom that any *good* is to be gained by insisting, even with patients themselves, in tracing these things to *criminal origin*.

The physician's business is not with the *causes*, but with the *consequences*. Though the disease should be found to have affected others, it is still not proof positive that it was of illicit origin. In the case of suspicious leucorrhea, this consideration is important.

Gonorrhea is generally regarded, and too much treated, as a *merely local disease*, sometimes even by homeopathic physicians. But we are satisfied, as the result of considerable observation, that this is no more exclusively a local affection, than rheumatism or gout. It might as well be said, that these are respectively only an inflammation of the small or large joints, — or say that small-pox is a simple disease of the skin, as that gonorrhea is nothing but a diseased condition of the mucous membrane of the part where it shows itself.

Holding this view of the subject, we were always in the habit of prescribing a very different course of treatment from that which is commonly followed, under the idea which we wish to correct. Although the symptomatic fever and other general symptoms may be but slight, and the local symptoms may be easily arrested by a treatment merely local, — the sad results of gonorrhea, years after such "cures" of it, are far too frequent to sanction the opinion that the virus in question can be so readily removed from the system. On the contrary, we have no doubt that it remains ready to develop itself in the same or some worse form whenever any sufficient exciting cause may operate. Thus, on over exercise, it may render the patient much more liable to rheumatism; or, on exposure to malaria, be more certain to bring on an attack of intermittent fever. We have known an instance, when the urethral discharge, with all the primary symptoms of gonorrhea, reappeared during the progress of a bilious intermittent, — and this, ten years after the original infection, and where we were satisfied that there had been no subsequent exposure.

The *reappearance* of the disease after violent over-exertion, is by no means uncommon. Loss of sleep, any thing that causes debility, will readily bring it back, where it has been imperfectly treated or prematurely arrested. Numerous other instances might be adduced of the mischief of an exclusively local treatment. Of all these, however, perhaps *stricture of the urethra* is the worst and most common result of "curing up a clap" by the fashionable astringents.

TREATMENT.

Ricord, the best allopathic authority upon this disease, divides the treatment into what he calls the *abortive and curative.*

The *abortive* consists in the use of strong injections of *Nitrate of silver*, while the disease is confined to the glandular region to destroy the gonorrheal virus and get up an inflammation which shall supersede that arising from the disease. He is not, however, convinced from his experience that this is alone sufficient. Hence he always administers internally *Copaiba and Cubebs.* The *abortive* treatment he does not recommend for *first* gonorrheas, admits it is not always successful, and is sometimes followed by bad consequences. His testimony and admisssions are a sufficient answer to those homeopaths who recommend his abortive as the best homeopathic treatment.

The homeopathic treatment that has given us the most general satisfaction during the inflammatory period, is the use of *Cannabis*, mother tincture, in water. Put five or six drops in a four or six ounce vial, fill with water, and give a tablespoonful three times a day, until there is a subsidence of the pain and decrease of the discharge, which has generally been the case in three or four days; then, leaving the remainder in the vial, fill up again with water and give as before, and so continue till the cure is completed, except when the improvement is progressing rapidly, when the medicine should be given but twice a day. The patient should keep perfectly quiet, live on a *spare* diet, carefully abstaining from all *stimulants*, sleep upon a hard bed, and use as a common drink a weak infusion of *Althea offic.* (the green root is best if it can be obtained). When it is impossible for the patient to remain at rest, the parts should be supported by a suspensory bandage.

If the bowels are disposed to be inactive, cold-water enemas should be employed. If the discharge does not cease with the subsidence of the inflammation, it will be necessary to give a few doses of *Merc.* or *Sulphur* to complete the cure. The former when the discharge is greenish or puriform, the latter when it is serous. They are also particularly useful when the patient has been previously subjected to the allopathic use of *Copaiba and Cubebs.*

When the inflammation has progressed so far as to involve the whole of the spongy portion of the urethra, and chordee is present, *Canth.*, *Merc.*, or *Can.* alone, or in alternation, will control it: where, however, there is much constitutional disturbance, *Acon.* should be given alone or in alternation with *Canth.;* sometimes it may be advantageously followed by *Sulphur.*

Tussilago petastitis, the expressed juice, in teaspoonful doses, is recommended both for acute and chronic gonorrhea.

Hartmann prefers for the inflammatory stage, the mother tincture, three doses a day; while Jahr. recommends three pellets of the 30th dilution, allowing them to act for a week. The general experience of the profession favors the use of the mother tincture.

Petroselinum, *Cinnabaris*, *Copaiba*, *Puls.*, *Thuja*, have been recommended; to which we would add, *Blue ash* (*Fraxinus quadranglata*) *and Phytolac. dec.* — the last especially if there are rheumatic pains in the groin, or generally.

Nux vom. is adapted to gonorrhea with hemorrhoids, or where the patient uses stimulants.

Puls., in connection with a cold wet compress over the lumbar region, when the discharge has been suppressed. Sometimes an injection of a strong solution of the *Sesqui-carb. of potash* into the urethra will aid in re-establishing the gonorrheal discharge.

Dr. C. L. Müller of Leipzig, in his report of the homeopathic dispensary of that place, says "The treatment of gonorrhea was more successful this year than last. This is partly owing to the employment of a new remedy, the *Cochlearia armoracia*, or horse radish. I had a tincture of it prepared, and in many different kinds of gonorrhea found it alone suffice to effect a complete cure, especially where there was some smarting and burning, with difficulty of passing water, and not very copious discharge. It, also, often produced a rapid cure, even in chronic and neglected cases. I can, therefore, recommend this remedy to my colleagues, and shall only observe, that I employed, sometimes, the undiluted tincture, sometimes dilutions up to No. 6."

When Phimosis is present, the penis should be placed in warm water for about half an hour each day, and very weak castile soap-suds frequently injected between the glans and prepuce.

In case of Paraphimosis, use the local bath, as in Phimosis, and a poultice of *Ulmus Fulva*, which will act as an emollient and relaxant, and prevent any difficulty from obstruction of the circulation. Hartmann, and some other authors, recommend the immediate reduction of Paraphimosis by compressing the glans, and at the same time drawing the prepuce back over it, for fear of gangrene. This, he says, is very difficult, and he might have also added very painful. Our experience has taught us it is quite unnecessary. We have treated, and seen under the treatment of others *very* bad cases of paraphimosis and never had any difficulty from *Gangrene.*

For ischuria, *Acon.*, *Canth.*, or *Camph*, and if the case can not be managed without, the catheter may be introduced. If this is held very firmly by the walls of the urethra, it is best to leave it in and run the risk of inflammation and abscess on the outside of the urethra, rather than the danger of being unable to introduce it again. A few doses of *Arnica* should be given after the introduction of the catheter and occasionally repeated, if it is necessary to leave it in the urethra.

For inflammation of the *prostate*, *Acon.*, *Puls.*, or *Thuja* (for this and where there is danger of abscess, see prostitis).

Hemorrhage from the urethra, if from the introduction of a catheter, will yield to *Arnica* internally and as an injection in the form of cold arnicated water. In other cases, *Canth.*, *Canna.*, *Sulph.*, or an infusion of *Millefolium;* cold external applications and compressions are frequently sufficient.

For condylomata, *Thuja*, *Nit. ac.*, *or Cinnabaris.*

For painful swellings of the lymphatic vessels, Hartmann recommends *Calomel*, and if no improvement in sixteen or eighteen hours, *Merc. præcip.*, *Ruber.*

Symptomatic buboes, also urethral chancre, yield to *Merc.* or *Carbo. veg.*

For secondary gonorrhea *Tr. Cantharis*, *Sulph.*, *Merc.*, *Agnus.*,

Caps., *Fer.*, *Nit. ac.*, *Thuja*, *Nat. mur.*, *Sep.*, *Lyc.*, *Hep.*, *Sul.*, *Conium*, *Silic.*, *Psoricum and Syphilin.*

Agnus for a whitish serous gleet, with absence or diminution of the sexual appetite.

Caps., when the discharge is whitish and thick, with scalding at the time of urinating. When the discharge is thin and watery, whether irritating or not, Dr. Owens recommends *Kali hydriodicum.* He states that in four cases it arrested the discharge which was profuse in forty-eight hours. He used the 5th dilution. Hartmann has succeeded in many cases with *Tr. Canthar.*, one drop morning and evening. We have given the same in larger doses and increased until symptoms of strangury, then ceasing all medication; the discharge will then generally disappear with the other symptoms. In other difficult cases he has used an injection of *Acetate of zinc*, ten or fifteen drops in five ounces of water, three times a day. Though a better injection is the diluted *Pyroligneous acid*, which we have found quite a specific; or the tinctures of *San. can.*, *or Macrotys* diluted, or *Merc.*, one grain to the ounce of water. These injections should be used three or four times a day, and the patient should always urinate before using injections.

Hydras. can., in infusion, is a good injection in primary or secondary gonorrhea.

If there are any symptoms of stricture, they are to be treated as recommended for that affection.

SYPHILIS.

LUES VENEREA, "THE POX,"

—THE FRENCH POX, *morbus Gallicus*, *&c.*, were among the older names of the more serious affection, often distinguished as "*the* Venereal Disease."

This terrible scourge of the human race, for several centuries past, seems to be a specific contagion, propagated almost exclusively during the act of venereal intercourse, though capable of being communicated by any mode of contact with a susceptible surface. It is a true inoculation; and may take effect through the cutaneous as well as mucous surfaces. This virus can never be touched with impunity where the cuticle is abraded, or more than usually delicate.

The peculiar ulcer which this virus causes upon the spot where it is deposited is called a chancre. This is the local effect of the virus; its varieties constitute what is denominated a *primary syphilis.*

By the terms *Secondary and Tertiary*, are designated the constitutional manifestations of this virus. The *Secondary* includes the various affections of the skin and mucous membranes. These, Ricord holds, are not capable of being transmitted by inoculation, as are the primary, but may be hereditary. But Sigmund and Waller deny this, and contend that secondary syphilis can be communicated to others. The *Tertiary* symptoms are not inoculable, or hereditarily transmissible, but according to Lugol, engender scrofula. They comprehend tubercles of the sub-cutaneous and sub-mucous cellular tissue; nodes, inflammation of the periosteum, exostosis and caries.

Chancres are most frequently located in the male on the glans, penis and prepuce. In the female, about the labia nymphæ and clitoris, rarely on the os uteri or vagina.

Ricord, Acton, and others contend, that up to the fourth or fifth day, the disease is purely local. This, say they, is proven by the experiments on inoculation, as secondary symptoms never follow chancres when they have been cauterized, prior to the expiration of that period.

The experiments of Ricord are exceedingly valuable, as furnishing us in inoculation with a sure means of diagnosing where we suspect urethral chancre, or in suspicious and important cases. It should never be employed in the gangrenous or serpiginous varieties of chancre, or where the patient can not keep quiet and be temperate, and should always be destroyed on the third or fifth day, by opening the pustule with a lancet and carefully removing the pus, and then filling the cavity with *Vienna paste.* This will form an eschar and finally come off, leaving the parts underneath sound.

When the pus from a chancre is introduced under the epidermis of the same individual, the natural course is thus described by Acton: "During twenty-four hours succeeding the operation, the inoculated point becomes red; in the course of the second and third days, the surrounding parts are slightly swollen and assume a papular appearance, or already traces of a vesicle are seen on the summit; on the third or fourth day, a fluid, which is more or less transparent, is observed beneath the epidermis, and a distinct vesicle becomes apparent, where the papulæ previously existed, and a dark dot is seen in the center, owing to the coagulation of the blood which had escaped through the puncture of the lancet; from the fourth to the fifth day the vesicle assumes a pustular character, and a distinct depression is seen in the center, so that it represents very distinctly at this period the small-pox pustule. The red areola, which has been hitherto gradually augmenting in intensity, now as gradually fades away, and the cellular tissue, which was slightly œdematous, becomes infiltrated with plastic lymph. On the sixth or seventh day the pustule is observed to be wrinkled in consequence of the contents becoming thick, and ultimately a crust takes the place of the pustule. If not interfered with, this crust assumes a conical appearance, increasing always at its base; it may ultimately fall off, or, if removed, leaves an ulcer seated on a slightly œdematous base, in depth, equal to the thickness of the skin; the bottom of the ulcer is covered with a whitish pulpy substance or membrane, which adheres so firmly that it can with difficulty be wiped or washed off. The ulcer is generally circular, and appears as if made with a *punch.* The margin, if viewed by means of a microscope, will be found dentated and covered with a secretion similar to that seen at the bottom of the ulcer. The border is slightly œdematous and raised, and the areola around it of a browner tint than at the previous stages. This œdematous condition of the border occasions a slight eversion of of the edges, and hence the ulcer may assume a somewhat infundibuliform appearance."

The pus from a *chancre* is usually thin, serous, and bloody. Its peculiar characteristic, however, is its power of reproducing this specific ulceration.

The appearance and character of a chancre is modified by the treatment, constitution, habits, and circumstances of the patient. This has accordingly led to a classification, as *gangrenous* or slough ing, *phagedenic*, *serpiginous*, and *indurated* or Hunterian chancre. But in practice we find them more or less blended together.

The first variety is distinguished by its inflammatory type and the strong tendency to destruction of the parts. It is seen in robust plethoric persons.

The *phagedenic* occurs in broken-down cachectic constitutions. The ulcer is usually superficial and tends to burrow. The edges are brownish and undermined; the surface is uneven and granulations are pale or wanting; pus thin and ichorous.

The *serpiginous* variety, not very frequently met with in private practice, heals on one side while destroying the tissue on the other. It has no dark areolæ on their undermined edges, and the base is firm, the secretion being purulent. It will sometimes appear as if it was going to cicatrize rapidly, then again commence the work of destruction. This form, particularly, has hitherto baffled allopathic surgeons.

The *indurated* is called Hunterian, from John Hunter, who first accurately described it. The edges are a little prominent, but the peculiarity is the base, which is hard and does not pass off, imperceptibly diffusing itself into the surrounding parts, but is very circumscribed. Ricord states, that this induration rarely begins before the fifth or sixth day of the existence of the chancre, and is not to be feared if it does not commence before the fifteenth. This form is almost invariably accompanied with enlarged inguinal glands or bubo, which, it is said, never proceed to suppuration.

This variety is under allopathic treatment, *almost always* followed by secondary symptoms. The phagedenic occasionally, and the serpiginous and gangrenous, but rarely.

Hunter held the opinion, that the disease ran its course without any effort of nature to throw it off, and that *Mercury* was *the antidote.* Hence, as soon as a chancre was perceived by his disciples, the patient was *saturated* with this poison, in order to prevent the dire consequences of the disease; since ascertained to be the effects mostly of the remedy. Sir Bransby Cooper says, "Of disease of the bones, which are said to result as a secondary effect of syphilis, I can only remark, that I have for years doubted the truth of the doctrine itself, as I have never known the bones to become diseased unless *Mercury* had been exhibited; and I can hardly bring forward a better proof of this than the fact, that in former times, when such enormous quantities of *Mercury* were given for the cure of syphilitic diseases, the affections of the bones were almost as common as syphilis itself; while now, on the contrary, when the employment of *Mercury* has been so judiciously modified, disease of the osseous system are but of rare occurrence."

Sir Astley Cooper remarks, "I do not think that it is a rare occurrence for the penis to be destroyed by *Mercury;* for a chancre that has remained weeks in a healthy state, shall become irritable, and, by maltreatment, by the injudicious and improper use of *Mercury*, shall slough off and end in the destruction of the penis; this is not a rare case, and is attributed to the venereal disease, but in reality is an effect of the improper use of *Mercury*."

From these admissions, the results of treatment in those countries where no *Mercury* is given for the disease, as well as no treatment, and the experiments in armies and hospitals, it can not be doubted at least, that tertiary symptoms are not in the large majority of cases the result of Syphilis, but of *Mercury*.

In view of these facts, can any Homeopath subscribe to the language of Hartmann in speaking of the treatment of phagedenic chancres? "The organism must be *saturated* with *Mercury* to overcome the dire enemy. Be not afraid of aggravations; away with this foolish bugbear."

Ricord, as was before stated, contends, that chancre, for the first four or five days, is a purely local disease, and if destroyed by caustic, secondary symptoms will never follow. This, he states, has been the invariable result of his experiments, in his large and extensive practice. In the treatment of those cases of longer continuance, he is sparing of the use of the *Mercurial* agents, except when the chancre exhibits signs of induration, when he considers a free use of this mineral indispensable to prevent the occurrence of secondary symptoms. He is free, however, to confess that it is not a certain preventative. In the tertiary form his chief reliance is upon the use of *Iodide of potassium.*

Ricord also holds, that secondary symptoms can occur but once; that there may be relapses, but if once they are cured, the patient is ever after exempt. Also, that the syphilitic diathesis, if once established, can *never be completely eradicated;* remedies will only produce an alleviation and modification of the symptoms.

The *diet* of a patient with chancre should be regulated by the character of the ulcer and his constitution. Where much inflammation is present, it should be very spare, but in phagedenic chancre in debilitated, scrofulous persons (and in such it usually occurs), it should be nutritious. When a chancre is located upon the penis, a suspensory bandage should be employed.

Inasmuch as Ricord declares that the cauterization of a chancre, if without induration within three to five days after its first appearance, will invariably destroy the virus and prevent the development of any secondary symptoms; we would advise the homeopathic surgeon to cauterize chancre if seen within that time and there is no appearance of induration. Remove the pus with lint and fill the ulcer with *Vienna paste.* If it heals without leaving a dark-red or bluish scar, there is no fear of any further difficulty. Usually, however, the surgeon is not called upon until too late for the abortive treatment. The local applications should then be nothing more than lint kept moist with simple water, or a solution of the same remedy used internally. The lint ought to be frequently changed; warm local baths or the vapor of hot water may be advantageously used when much inflammation is present.

The most valuable internal remedies for chancre are, *Aur.*, *Ac. nit.*, *Carb. v.*, *Cinna.*, *Hepar s.*, *Mer. sol.*, *Mer. cor.*, *Silic. and Sul.*

The preparations of *Mercury* were formerly, as was .before stated, regarded by Hunter and his disciples, whether Allopaths or Homeopaths, as the *only* specific for the syphilitic virus, and every *suspected* sore called for the exhibition of the potent remedy. No matter what the character of the chancre, there was but the one remedy.

Ricord, however, has done much to put a stop to this unscientific practice, and to determine the cases proper and improper for its administrations; and in acute phagedena, where Hartmann recommends to saturate the patient, he directs us never, under any circumstances, to give this mineral. He has limited its use almost entirely to the *indurated* chancre.

So also Laurie, in giving his treatment, recommends *Mercurius* for the above; but in the other forms, *Ars.*, *Nit. ac.*, *Sul.*, or some other remedy, is spoken of as more beneficial. And we think, as Homeopaths have a more correct idea of the importance and significancy of induration as a symptom, it will be found that the sphere of *Mercury* in primary syphilis is in indurated chancres. We rejoice in knowing that we can obtain all the beneficial influence of this agent without any fear of the often direful results of its allopathic administration. We also think that *Mercurius cor.* will ultimately be found the best form of the mineral for indurated chancre. Frick, of Hamburgh, produced an ulcer with induration precisely similar to an indurated chancre, by placing some corrosive sublimate between the glans and prepuce. And Laurie speaks of resorting to it successfully in cases where induration was present, when the other preparations had failed. Goullon, of Weimar, particularly recommends it for chancres, but does not, however, particularize the indurated class.

Simple uncomplicated chancres will soon disappear under a few doses of *Mercurius* and water dressings. When, however, inflammation is present, *Acon., or Acon.* and *Sul.*, may be needed; if much irritability is also present, *Ars., Ac. nit., Carb. veg., or Sul.*, will be required. Where there is a tendency to gangrene, *Ars., Carb. v., or Lach.*, will be serviceable. In the case of phagedena the remedy must be selected with special reference to the state of the constitution.

Acton speaks highly of the use of *Iron.* In many of these cases the patients have been subjected to the allopathic use of *Mercury*, which is the real cause of the difficulty. *Ac. nit. and Hepar s.*, will soon produce an improvement.

For the indurated chancre, *Mercurius* is undoubtedly the remedy. Hartmann prefers the *Merc. precip. rub.* Dr. Müller also prefers it. Our own preference for *Mer. cor.* we mentioned before. For the serpiginous variety, Hartmann proposes *Thuja;* benefit may be also derived from *Ars., Carb. v., or Sul.*

Where granulation proceeds slowly, it may be promoted by *Ac. nit., Sil., or Sul.*

Where there is a tendency to the production of condylomata, *Cinna., Thuja, or Nit. ac.*, should be given.

Chancres situated in the urethra require the same treatment as those in other parts.

Gollmann thus speaks of the various remedies for primary syphilis:

"Among the remedies to be employed for the cure of chancre, I mention, particularly, *Acidum nit.;* the specific effect of which has scarcely ever disappointed me. I have found it particularly indicated by the following conditions: chancres of the orifice of the urethra, prepuce, margin of the prepuce; chancres with bloody, fetid, ichorus pus; small chancres without inflamed borders, with flat edges, considerable swelling of the glans and the meatus urinarius, which are of a dark-red color and puffed up; small vesicles in the meatus, on the inner surface and margin of the prepuce, which soon break, suppurate, and form chancres; deep ulcer at the corona glandis, with elevated, lead-colored, extremely sensitive edges; flat little ulcers at the corona glandis, which look clean, but secrete a strong-smelling matter, itching of the prepuce and damp places on its inner surface; burning of the inflamed and swollen prepuce, the inside of which is denuded of the epidermis and covered with small little ulcers, secreting an ichor that has a pungent nauseous odor, and stains the linen like bloody pus; simple flat chancre in the vagina; it is covered with yellow pus and burns and itches; and lastly, inflammation of the vagina and labia majora.

Accordingly, *Acidum nit.* will be found particularly adapted to simple chancre, chancre in the meatus urinarius, and in the vagina.

Arsenicum; Gangrenous ulcers with bloody edges, corrosive pus; ulcers with copious secretion of watery, fetid ichor; painless ulcers with hard edges; lardaceous, stinging, chancrous ulcers, with white places in the middle of the ulcer, gangrenous chancre on the glans and prepuce; sudden gangrene of the penis.

Accordingly, *Arsenicum* will be found adapted to phagedenic gangrenous chancres, and accordingly to the indurated chancre of Hunter.

Argentum nit.; Little ulcers on the prepuce, the tips of which are at first covered with pus, and which gradually spread in extent and become covered with a tallowy or lardacious substance; swelling and knotty hardness of the urethra, inflammation and pains in the urethra, priapism, dysuria, hæmaturia (chancre in the urethra).

Aurum met.; Chancres of the scrotum with fetid, ichorous pus.

Calcarea car.; Chancres of the lower surface of the penis; chancres with burning pain, having the form of rhagades.

Carbo. veg.; Readily bleeding chancres with secretion of ichor.

Causticum; Chancres with acrid, corrosive pus, or watery, greenish secretion, with jerking pain developed out of little blisters, complicated with gout, scurvy, and cutaneous eruptions, disposition to fungous formations (phagedenic chancre).

Hepar sul.; Readily bleeding chancres, with lardaceous edges and feted secretion.

Iodine; Florid chancres with raised edges that are more or less shaggy, watery secretion.

Mercurius Sol.; Red chancres on the prepuce; spreading and deeply-penetrating ulcers on the glans and prepuce; pale-red vesicles on the glans and prepuce, forming small ulcers after breaking; readily bleeding chancres; distressingly painful chancres secreting a quantity of yellowish-white fetid pus; small chancres with a cheesy bottom, inverted red edges; inflamed round chancrous ulcers with swelling of the vagina; chancres with edges resembling raw flesh; not very painful ulcers, sensitive to the contact of linen; vesicles at the forepart and on the sides of the glans, spreading and penetrating more and more; ulcers of the glans and prepuce with cheesy lardaceous bottom and hard edges; a number of small red vesicles at the tip of the glans behind the prepuce, breaking after a fortnight and forming little ulcers which secrete a strong-smelling yellowish-white matter that stains the linen; afterwards the large ulcers bleed and are painful when touched, from which the whole body was sympathetically affected; they were round, thin edges looked raw, and the bottom of the ulcers was covered with a cheesy matter.

Mercurius cor.; Chancres with ichor adhering to the bottom of the ulcer so firmly that it cannot be removed by washing; ulcers with thin pus, leaving stains upon the linen as from melted tallow.

Staphysagria; Smarting vesicles on the inside of the labia majora, painful when touched; chancres with fetid ichor.

Sulphur; Chancres with lardaceous white spots and secretion of fetid ichor; ulcers covered with scurf and looking like itch-sores; chancres on the prepuce, resembling excoriations; superficial chancres, as if the skin were excoriated; red ulcers with lardaceous bottom, here and there lined with a thin matter that can be easily removed; violently itching ulcers, impeding one's walk, torpid ulcers complicated with scrofula, scurvy, gout, and cutaneous eruptions.

Thuja; Vesicles on the glans, erosions on the inner surface of the prepuce, which secrete a humor and suppurate; red spots on the prepuce; granular spots on the outer surface of the prepuce which change to ulcers, become covered with scurf, itch and burn; pustules on the inside of the prepuce, depressed in the center, secreting a humor and suppurating, painful only when touched. Burning pain at the corona glandis; flat, itching ulcers surrounded with redness, with stinging pain, and unclean bottom; whitish chancre with hard edges; chancres with shaggy edges and lardaceous bottom; chancres with sharply circumscribed edges and clean flesh-colored bottom; chancres with thin fetid ichor."

Bubo, or swelling of a lymphatic vessel or gland, is sometimes an attendant of the primary ulcer. Chancres situated around the frenum, meatus of the female, or at the anus, are generally accompanied by bubo. Venereal buboes are of two kinds, inflammatory and indurated. In the first, usually only one gland is enlarged, which rapidly proceeds to suppuration and becomes a chancrous ulcer. In the latter kind, however, several glands are generally enlarged, but manifest no tendency to proceed to suppuration. They do not cause the patient any pain, and do not secrete, as the inflammatory, an inocculable virus. Ricord states that they are an almost invariable attendant of true indurated chancres, and are hence valuable in determining the probability of the appearance of secondary symptoms. And as they frequently, under allopathic treatment, remain enlarged for some time after the chancre has disappeared, they may sometimes in the case of suspicious eruptions decide their character.

Bubo requires in general the same internal treatment as the

primary chancre. *Carbo. v.* is particularly useful in the indurated form; it may sometimes be advantageously followed by *Silic.*

In inflammatory buboes, our aim should be to prevent suppuration; they may require *Bel.* when the inflammation is very severe; or when suppuration is threatened, *Hepar* and *Silic.* Where it is evident from the fluctuations of the gland that pus has formed, it should be evacuated by the lancet; cold applications and hot fomentations are sometimes useful. Compression may also be beneficially employed to aid in preventing suppuration.

Secondary syphilis or the constitutional influence of the syphilitic virus affects the skin or mucous membranes. Syphilitic eruptions are distinguished by their reddish-brown or copper color — the absence of all itching except when they include the axilla, the parts about the anus, &c., when the secretion often causes considerable itching; and their circular form. In syphilitic affections of the throat, the mucous membrane becomes covered with whitened spots as though it had been touched irregularly with caustic, which finally ulcerates. The previous existence of an indurated chancre, or of a chancre with indurated, but not suppurating bubo, will be pretty decisive as to the true nature of the disease.

For secondary symptoms the preparations of *Mercury* have been regarded as most valuable. But in the large majority of cases in which the patient has been under its allopathic administration, an antidote is more needed. Even in some of these cases, however, the protiodide may be used with great advantage.

Though *Aurum*, *Ac. nit.*, *Hepar*, *Iod.*, *Kreosote*, or *Styllin.*, *Syl.*, will generally be required; Dr. Marcy recommends particularly the *Muriate of gold.* Dr. Teste, in a communication to the Societè Gallica, reports some interesting cases, showing that *Kreosote* has a specific influence in syphilis which would not be divined from its pathogenesis. From his report it would seem to be particularly beneficial in the secondary form.

Tertiary syphilis, according to Ricord, can neither be communicated or transmitted. It is then a diathesis which produces scrofula in the offspring. It seldom occurs under six months after the disappearance of the chancre — sometimes years may elapse.

What is often called and treated as tertiary syphilis is, as we believe, in most cases, the effects of the *Mercurial saturation*, which such patients undergo—it is the pathogenetic effects of the remedy and not the virus. Hence, though the provings of *Mercurius* admirably coincide with the symptoms of the patient, it will do no good except as an isopathic remedy. Should tertiary symptoms arise purely from syphilis, *Mercurius* will remove them. They are almost invariably, however, complicated. The aching pains in the bones will then be relieved by *Ac. nit.*, *Aurum*, *Fluoric ac.*, *Lach.*, *Hydrio. pot.*, *Mez.*, *or Phytolac. d.*

For venereal nodes, which usually occur on the tibia or os frontis, and also for caries, necrosis, &c., *see Ostitis*. For venereal whitlow, *Mer.*, *Carb. v. and Silic.*

CHAPTER XXXVII.

ACCIDENTS AND DISEASES OF THE EXTREMITIES.

PARONYCHIA — Locations and varieties — Progress — Treatment — Incision.

CORNS — Kinds of corn, "bunion," &c. — Prevention and precautions — "Corn-curers," — BUNION — a distortion of the joint.

INVERTED TOE-NAIL — Description and effects — Barbarous treatment — A more merciful and successful one.

WHITLOW — FELON.

PARONYCHIA, the more learned name for this very painful affection, indicates its most common location about the ends of the fingers, or "near the nail." It occurs, however, between the joints of the fingers and of the hand. Owing to the peculiar structure of the parts in which or beneath which the inflammation occurs, it is one of the most painful of diseases; the swelling, though often obstructed, is at last great, and the ulceration in which it terminates very destructive.

The SYMPTOMS are very much modified by the location. Four varieties may be noticed.

1st. It may occur in or near the surface, just below the *cuticle*, but about the nail like a common "run-round."

2d. Its seat may be in the cellular or fibrous tissue between the *cutis* and the *sheath* surrounding the tendons; or

3d. *Within the sheath* of the tendons, under the vaginal ligament of the fingers, or, it may be, upon the synovial surface: and

4th. The inflammation may originate within the *periosteum*, between it and the bone. To this last, the appellation of "felon" is restricted by Webster, in accordance with some surgical authorities; but the distinction is too obscure for a *popular* definition. The distinctions are not very clear in many advanced cases.

The *articulating surfaces* may be either primarily or secondarily involved. The latter may also occur in the first variety, which is sometimes distinguished as "onychia." The pain is likely to be greatest or most acute in the *first*, the swelling in the *second* variety: it not unfrequently extends over the whole finger or hand, and beyond, producing, by its irritation, soreness and even swelling of the axillary glands. In the *third* case, the *pain* is the greater, though the swelling is much less, in consequence of the firmness of the vaginal ligament. The progress of the disease is in this situation very slow, and when pus is formed, it is a long time making its way to the surface. The *fourth* variety is still slower in its progress, and less acute in its symptoms, but commonly in its results destructive to the bone itself. In general the deeper the seat of the affection, the greater the danger of and *from* ulceration.

The inflammation, though commencing in only one of the structures mentioned, may involve the whole. While in the *cellular tissue*, near the surface, the pain is severe, and of a throbbing and itching character. The parts are also swollen and red, the redness being diffused. As the disease advances, the swelling determines to some point, generally near the nail. The fluid discharged is commonly sero-purulent.

When *deeper seated*, the throbbing, the heat and the swelling are still greater, and the pain also, after awhile. It is often so intense, so intolerable, as to allow the patient no sleep or rest. It is of a darting character, frequently shooting up the forearm, and even above the elbow. Considerable fever also often attends.

The disease may involve only one bone, or the whole finger;

or it may originate in the palm of the hand. In the latter case the back of the hand may become enormously swollen.

If not properly treated, the inflammation will terminate in *suppuration* in three or four days. In other instances, especially when it is seated upon the bone, within the sheath of the tendons, or under the annular ligament, it may be eight or ten days before any well-marked evidence of suppuration takes place. Extensive sloughing is apt to follow the suppuration. Not only cellular membrane, the sheaths of the tendons, and the tendons themselves may come away, but one or more of the phalangeal bones be lost. When it occurs in the palm of the hand the disease may extend to all the bones, and much impair, if not entirely destroy, the use of the hand forever afterwards. Such serious results by no means always follow; but neither are they of very uncommon occurrence when the disease is neglected or illy treated. The surgeon will meet with instances in his practice, of all degrees of injurious result, from a very slight deformity to a total loss of one or more of the fingers.

The CAUSE may be a bruise or external injury of any kind. Poisons introduced by puncture have been known to produce it. Very often, however, it can be traced to no known source.

The first SYMPTOM complained of is commonly a prickling sensation, as if a thorn or a brier were in the finger. The patient will often attempt to extract the supposed offending cause with a needle or the point of a penknife. This sense of soreness or prickling may continue for several days, without any other painful sensation. This is *the* stage for treatment. After visible swelling and inflammation, it is more difficult to prevent the formation of matter, or to cause the inflammation to subside by resolution.

The remedies which have been most successful in this complaint are, *Alum*, *Hepar*, *Merc.*, *Phytolac.*, *Silicea*, *Sulp.* and *Rhus.*

In the early stage, when the sensation of pricking and burning is present, with slight swelling and redness, especially on the end of the finger, *Alumina* has proved more successful in our hands than any other remedy. We use it internally and apply the clay moistened to the affected surface, renewing or re-moistening from time to time until the symptoms subside.

Phytolacca is more particularly useful when the disease is located in the palm of the hand, the pains being sharp, darting, passing through to the back of the hand, and extending up the arm.

If the pain and swelling should continue, threatening suppuration, *Hepar s. and Silicea*, may be given alternately. These will ameliorate the symptoms, and if pus has already formed, facilitate the pointing of the abscess.

Immersing the affected part in ley, as strong and as hot as can be borne for several hours, will sometimes discuss a felon in the early stage.

When pus has formed and its locality can be distinctly ascertained, the abscess should be *punctured* and the pus let freely off. *Symphytum* is the best remedy in this stage. Let the sore also be covered with cloths wet in dilute tincture of the remedy.

Should the abscess become dark, the pain burning, the pus sanious and ichorous, *Arsen.* is to be used.

Should the purulent discharge be excessive but rather healthy, in appearance, use *Calendula*.

CORNS — CLAVI.

These well-known annoyances are really nothing but a horny thickening of the cuticle, destined, in the first instance, to protect the toes against the unnatural pressure of the shoe or boot. The Latin name *clavus*, is from a supposed resemblance to the head of a nail; the obvious resemblance that gives rise to the vernacular name is much more *palpable*. There are distinctions, however, even in corns.

"*Hard* corns" are the most common, being those formed on the *top* of the toes, by the direct pressure of the leather.

"*Soft* corns" form *between* the toes, in consequence of their pressure on each other. They appear more like irritable warts, having great sensibility; while the hard or proper "corn" is insensible, and only occasions pain by pressure on the surrounding parts.

"BUNION," often considered a variety of this affection, is really a *distortion* of the mentatarsal *joint* of the great toe, forming a broad swelling on the inside of the foot. The cause is generally the same as that of common corns.

When the corn is ripe, or rather completely formed, it has a membrane situated between it and the true skin, so that it may be removed without any abrasion of that surface.

As the first measure in the TREATMENT of corns, oblige the patient to wear boots or shoes large enough to relieve the toes from all pressure, cutting a hole in the leather if need be. Leave them for awhile, without being touched by anything unyielding.

The best of all prescriptions, then, for corns is, "go loose shod." This is a certain preventive, and the indispensable *condition* of cure. Loose boots and shoes, however, will not always be sufficient; and if too loose, so as to rub about, may be as bad as tight ones.

If the parts *around* are inflamed, let them be soaked in warm arnicated water for an hour or more at night, or two or three times a day; and some soothing emollient be applied in the interval. Then, or at first when no preliminary softening is required, *shave off* all the horny substance that can be easily removed; and apply olive oil.

This will soon soften the corn, and if any soreness remains it will soon be relieved by the application of *Arnica*. For bunions use *Silicea.*

We have *removed* corns and warts in numerous instances by the application of *Vienna paste*, and have never yet seen any evidence of the "serious constitutional" effects from it, spoken of in some of the books.

Ant. cr., Phos., Rhus, Bryo., Am. carb., Petr., Acid phos., Sepia., and Sul., are used for corns.

INVERTED TOE-NAIL—ONYXIS.

This is a very distressing disease of the great toe. The NAIL, from some accidental bruise, or the wearing of a tight boot or shoe, or both causes concurring, *curls down* at the sides, and becomes embedded deeply in the flesh. The whole toe *inflames*, swells, and soon suppurates or ulcerates at one or more points about the nail, whence large *fungous* growths frequently shoot out, which are extremely painful and tender to the touch. The patient is unable to wear a shoe or to use the foot. His sufferings are sometimes very great;—so much so, indeed, that he is deprived of sleep; his appetite fails; he becomes feverish and greatly prostrated. We have seen a case where the toe, or rather the fungous mass, together with the swollen toe, was larger than a goose egg, the whole foot and leg being more or less involved. Sinuous openings at several points were discharging unhealthy and excoriating pus. The nail was nearly covered over with the fungus, and the whole toe or tumor (for it had now no appearance of a toe) was so extremely sensitive that a fly lighting upon it would cause pain. These horrid cases were those which had been operated upon (some of them several times) in the usual mode recommended in the books, by cutting through the nail and pulling it off with forceps, or dissecting it out with a knife. In addition to the operation, they had been treated with nitrate of silver, acetate of lead, mercury, &c., &c., but had all the while grown "no better very fast."

Against this barbarous, awkward and *unsuccessful* mode of treating this originally trivial though painful affection, we beg leave to enter a decided protest. The measures generally recommended and practiced are not only unnecessary and cruel, but highly mischievous. On the contrary, the PROPER TREATMENT gives the patient little or no pain, while it is certain to afford permanent relief.

If we are called to one of these bad cases where it is necessary to remove the whole nail, when the toe is in an *inflamed* and painful condition, have the foot elevated and subject the toe to a constant gentle stream of warm water, for from one to two hours each day, and in the intervals cover it with a large elm poultice, kept warm. Continue this course of treatment with the internal use of *Phosphorus*, until all inflammation and soreness have subsided and the parts can be handled with impunity. This will generally take place in three or four days. Then, each time after the part has been bathed for half or three-quarters of an hour, press under the nail with a probe, at whatever point it is the most detached, *pledgets of lint* or cotton wet, as firmly as can be borne. Also, press the pledgets down at the sides, between the nail and the flesh which has risen up and projected over the nail, and fill it up so high that a bandage will press a little on the tents or pledgets. Cover these with a plaster of *Arnica salve* to shield the parts from the air, and apply a *bandage*, moderately tight, over the whole. Then keep it freely wet in *warm water*. Some prefer wetting it in cold water; but we have seen better effects from having it warm.

These *tents* will from time to time pass further and further under the nail, and completely separate the flesh from it. It should be bathed and dressed twice a day all the while.

As *portions* of the nail become *loose*, let them be cut off, until, by thus crowding the tents under at different points, and paring off the nail, we have removed it all.

After the *removing* of the *nail in this manner*, the parts will soon assume the appearance of a healthy ulcer, and readily heal. Nor does the disease, thus cured, *return;* whereas, in many cases — in fact, in most cases — when the nail is violently taken off, the new growth is as bad as the old, and the patient continues to suffer as before.

It will sometimes take several months to effect a cure by the mode recommended, but it is not painful and is certain. This is substantially the mode pursued by Dr. Beach, which has been successful in all cases.

If called in the early stage, when there is but little inflammation, pare off the center of the nail so as to make it shorter than the margins, also cut grooves lengthwise near each margin, nearly through, then press the pledgets of lint, wet in *Aqua calen.*, under the edges so as to elevate them; continuing the bathing with warm water. This course will soon relieve and the nail will generally take such a form as to give no further trouble.

INDEX TO PART I.

PAGE

Amaurosis - 273
Anchylosis - 168
Antrum, ulceration of - 250
Bones, diseases of - 145
" caries of - 146
" necrosis of - 147
" treatment of - 148
Bronchocele - 308
Burns - 98
Cancer - 201
" fungus hæmatodes - 213
" eye - 215
" nose - 217
" lip - 219
" tongue - 223
" breast - 225
" rectum - 230
" penis - 231
" testicle - 233
" uterus - 233
Carbuncle - 237
Cataract - 278
Choking - 305
Cornea, opacities of - 283
" nebula - 283
" ulcer of - 284
Corns - 424
Dropsy of the eye - 286
" " joints - 166
Encanthis - 289
Epulis - 301
Exostosis - 190
Felon - 421
Fistula Lachrymalis - 253
" in ano - 354
" in perineo - 387
Fissure of the anus - 375
Ganglion - 189
Goiter - 308
Gonorrhea - 403
Gums, tubercle on - 301
Hemorrhoids - 368

PAGE
Hematoceie - 347
Hernia - 231
Hernia Humeralis - 350
Hip disease - 169
Hordeolum - 291
Hydrophobia - 70
Hydrocele - 341
Inflammation, general aspects - 1
" practical - 18
" old treatment - 31
" Hom. do. - 38
Inverted toe-nail - 425
Irritable Testes - 353
Lumbago - 162
Mammary Abscess - 312
Maxillary " - 250
Odontalgia - 296
Onixis - 425
Ophthalmia—structural varieties - 255
" common - 256
" conjunctiva - 256—260
" catarrhal - 257
" purulent - 258
" Egyptian - 258
" gonorrheal - 259
" scrofulous - 259—269
" tarsi - 268
Orchitis - 351
Ostea Sarcoma - 242
Parotid Fistula - 252
Piles - 368
Polypus - 192
" of the nose - 193
" of the uterus - 196
Prostate Gland, disease of - 388
Prolapsus ani - 374
Prostitis - 388
Psoas Abscess - 170
Pterygeum - 288
Ranula - 302
Rheumatism - 160
Sarcocele - 349
Scrofula - 151
" constitution - 153
" tumors - 153
" ulcers - 157
Scald Heads - 245
Spermatorrhæa - 391
Stricture of the urethra - 380
" " rectum - 376

PAGE
Staphyloma - 285
Sty - 290
Syphilis - 410
Tetanus - 79
Teeth, affections of - 292
Tinea capitis - 245
Tonsils enlarged - 302
Traumatic Erysipelas - 82
Tumors - 181
" adipose - 182
" fibrous - 184
" cellular - 185
" various - 186
" malignant - 187
" vascular - 187
Tubercle of Gums - 301
Ulcers - 112
" irritable - 113
" indolent - 114
" varicose - 114
" specific - 115
" chronic - 121
Varicocele - 348
Wounds in general - 40
" incised - 43
" punctured - 46
" penetrating - 47
" lacerated - 48
" contused - 51
" gun-shot - 61
" poisoned - 66
" erysipelatous - 82
" of head - 83
" of neck - 93
" of chest - 93
" of abdomen - 95
" of joints - 97
White Swelling - 163
Whitlow - 421

PART II.

OPERATIVE SURGERY.

CHAPTER I.

OF OPERATIVE SURGERY — GENERAL PRELIMINARIES AND MINOR OPERATIONS.

ALTHOUGH external and more or less mechanical treatment is what primarily distinguished Surgery from the general "Practice of Medicine," its more technical and peculiar part, particularly that requiring the use of the knife, is again distinguished from the more *medical*, as "Operative Surgery." Much evil as well as good has arisen from the division.* Physicians have thought themselves privileged to be ignorant of the most necessary resources for external accidents and diseases; and in some countries, they even look down upon the business of the surgeon as a mere *trade*, while that of the physician only is "the profession." While the ordinary run of surgical cases are thus left in the hands of a presumed inferior class — (regularly educated surgeons being still in some parts of Europe obliged by law to reckon *shaving* among their operations, and to keep by them the necessary *implements*, as honorable members of the ancient craft of "barber-chirurgeons") — the more serious cases presumed to require operations, have been transferred to a set of *first class surgeons*, whose business was *only* to operate. Hence, while their art has been advanced to the highest point of excellence, medical surgery, the proper treatment of slighter cases, and the prevention of the necessity for dangerous operations, has been shamefully neglected.

In this country, Surgery stands higher than Medicine in popular estimation, every man who chooses to "doctor" being of course

* This opinion is confirmed by the distinguished German author, quoted in treating of Fistula in Ano. "It is quite an erroneous view, which has long prevailed," says Blasius, "that of regarding the operative surgeon as a mere assistant, who has only to come in and execute the mechanical part of the business, as the physician shall judge it necessary. This view can only lead to mischief." He goes on to show why the operator, as soon as he takes a patient in hand, ought himself to be the physician. "The mere physician does not understand the operation, the local and constitutional reaction it occasions, the special medication or modifications of medical treatment it may require," &c., &c. — [Akiurgie, B. i, s. 5and 6.]

a physician, though he cannot so easily profess to be a surgeon, that requiring more anatomical knowledge than mere amateur doctors can easily attain, and false pretensions to it being more certain to be exposed. Few even of the thousands that yearly graduate in our medical schools, give attention enough to their professors of surgery to practice all its departments. Most of them remain shamefully ignorant of even what is most necessary and indispensable in the emergencies of general practice. As, however, the more serious operations will undoubtedly continue to be generally performed only by those who are specially qualified for them, both by nature and education, some DISTINCTION of *cases* and *practitioners* seems absolutely necessary. That distinction should depend, however, not so much on the difficulty or danger of the operations themselves, as upon the necessity of immediate attention, or the practicability of their being *deferred*. In all serious cases, admitting of sufficient delay and needing special skill, the general practitioner of medicine is justified in calling in the aid of a professed surgeon, or a brother practitioner, who has had better opportunities of getting or *proving* more skill in this department. What a man is known to have done, he will always be thought better able to do than one who has not had the same advantage.

But no man is morally justified in holding himself out to any community as a physician, who is not able and ready to act in all the ordinary emergencies of danger to life or limb. Those operations, then, that like the dressing of wounds, ligating arteries for the arrest of hæmorrhage, adjusting fractures, reducing dislocations, &c., cannot, without greater or less risk, be put off to another time or given over to other hands, should be performed by every medical man at the moment they are needed. For these, then, he should *specially prepare* himself. Other operations, that allow of time for "reading up," or refreshing his memory, he can perhaps afford to be less familiar with; or even, if he prefer, transfer to more ambitious or thorough-going rivals.

Keeping this distinction in view, we shall proceed to give the practitioner the necessary information for *acting for himself* in all cases, enlarging most on those in which he *must* act or be disgraced, — as he ought to be.

It is not every man, or every medical man, that has the QUAL-

IFICATIONS for becoming a GOOD OPERATOR. These we will enumerate, as they stand registered, with true German precision, in the elaborate work of Dr. Blasius. "One may be," as he premises, "an excellent physician, without being cut out for an operator, — may even be well enough acquainted with the principles and technicalities of operative surgery, without being himself able to put them in practice." First, then, "The operator must have had a complete medical education, and have devoted himself more especially and minutely to the study of anatomy." He is moreover to possess a "knowledge of mathematics and physics," and especially their application in "mechanics." 2d. He requires acute senses, (scharfe sinne), particularly that of tact or touch, "good eye-sight, or that which is good for near objects, adroit but steady hands, and general bodily agility." 3d. In respect of "spiritual qualities, he is to be a man of courage and resolution, which, however, must not have degenerated into temerity, but be a union of the highest degree of calmness, circumspection and intrepidity." 4th. To all these natural and acquired endowments, he must add "great practical skill, (fertigheit), to be acquired only by repeated operations in the dissecting room, without which preparation none should venture to operate on the living. Even he who has begun to practice operative surgery, should continue these exercises on the dead, in order to keep himself prepared for the rarer operations." We have given only the texts of this author, omitting his elaborate commentary upon each, lest the student should think it our purpose to deter him from the work, in which it is our business to *encourage* as well as instruct him. Some may think we have already quoted enough to prove that *no* man can ever be a good operator!"*

In order to be prepared for every emergency, the practitioner must have the necessary *means* as well as knowledge. A surgeon altogether without instruments is in almost as absurd a predicament as a physician without medicine. He may and should himself be able to make, or to direct the construction of, such apparatus as can or must be made where they are needed. He must also *possess*, as well as be able to use, such as can only be furnished by a regular manufacturer. His *armamentum chirurgicum* need not,

* Akiurgie, B. i, s. 5 et seq.

indeed, be the formidable and costly array that was once supposed necessary. A good workman requires few tools. In proportion as the art of surgery has been really perfected, its means as well as modes of proceeding have been simplified. Intelligent *principles* have taken the place of empirical rules; and a few instruments, of general availability, have superseded all the ancient cumbersome apparatus. A portable case now contains all that the surgeon needs, instead of a wagon-load, which his armory once amounted to.

The POCKET CASE, indeed, will hold all the practitioner absolutely needs to have always at hand. This should contain abscess lancets, bistouries (straight and curved), scissors, forceps (the simple dissecting, and the dressing or ring forceps), tenacula, probes, (the common eyed and the gun shot), directors, needles (straight and curved), ligatures, lint, adhesive plaster, &c., &c. The varied uses of most of these articles are obvious, to any one who has sense enough to use them at all. A catheter, a portecaustique, or any particular article may be added to this list, as the individual's judgment or occasions may require.

Besides this pocket case, a "surgeon" should always have accessible dental forceps, cupping and scarifying instruments, a tourniquet, sponges, bandages ready rolled, and a good assortment of common splints wrapped ready for use. He will also have to be provided with ether and chloroform, as he knows not at what moment he may be called upon to perform operations when the pain and dread would endanger life. It is not yet generally appreciated how much the *risks* as well as the horrors of operative surgery have been lessened by the discovery of anæsthesia.

Any other instruments or appliances than those usually carried in the pocket case, or just mentioned, are always named, if not described, when giving directions for the particular operations requiring them. Of these instruments, huge folios of plates and descriptions are still being constantly published. These works are for manufacturers and professors, or inventors and improvers interested in particular parts.

The act of "doing up" or adjusting a wound or accessible diseased part is technically called DRESSING, and the appliances, medicinal or mechanical, are the

DRESSINGS.

Of any means used by the operative surgeon, few are of more importance, or require more skill and practice, than the simple roller or BANDAGE. Its usefulness indeed not being confined to this part of surgery, has been repeatedly insisted on, in the first part of this work. The technical varieties of "starched and laced bandages," the "suspensory bandage" (or sling), &c., &c., are all contrivances of obvious significance. When any of them seemed to demand particular explanation, it has been given when directing their use. A French *savant* has shown, with much ingenuity, that the "square bandage" or common pocket or neck *handkerchief*, may be so used as to answer all the purposes of all the many-named varieties and modifications of the roller, used or imagined by all our surgical writers. M. Mayor contends, that besides other advantages to result as he believes from the adoption of his "handkerchief system," great good would ensue from the general knowledge that means so simple were those which the surgeon would apply, and any person, in his absence, *might*—at least provisionally. For the profitable study of reducing things so complex to simple principles, we would recommend our readers to Smith's Minor Surgery (pages 120–180), where a full account of Mayor's method is given.

Some of the other most important *materials* for dressings may be here mentioned. First and foremost, the *water-dressing* should never be slighted for its simplicity. The mere use of water as a *detergent* is not what is here meant, but its continued or repeated application as a refrigerant, emollient and *anodyne*. For the last object warm water is indicated; for the second tepid. Cold water we do not recommend so much as some for directly counteracting inflammation; but as a styptic for the suppression of hemorrhage from small vessels, and as a tonic applied to debilitated parts, its value can scarcely be overrated, even by exclusive hydropaths.

LINT, cotton and flax-tow, are all in use as applications to raw surfaces. The last article is much too coarse, when any thing better can be had. Cotton is now in little esteem, except in case of burns or scalds. One objection to it is, that it is apt to be "fly-blown," and engender "maggots." If used, therefore, it should be perfectly free from specks. Good *lint* can always be made for the occasion, by scraping off with a knife the fine nap of old linen cloth. A supply of the manufactured or "patent lint" saves this trouble. *Charpie* is a sort of lint originally prepared in France, and much used (especially the coarse kind) as outside dressings, and for insertion *into* deep wounds, sinuous ulcers, &c., as an absorbent, compress or medium for applying medicament.

TENTS and PLEDGETS are such masses of charpie or other suitable material, the former of a conical shape, the latter cylindrical. Other modifications of form or size are sometimes nicely distinguished as "rolls, meshes, and pellets." As an inserted absorbent the *sponge tent* is a convenient expedient. It is a piece of sponge that has been saturated in bees-wax, which melts again and runs together, by the heat of the parts, leaving the pores of the sponge free to absorb other matter. Nothing of this kind, however (except where mechanically better for the sake of extraction), is superior to the *slippery elm* powder or *flour*.

TAMPONS are a larger kind of tents, used more especially for the purpose of applying distension or pressure, so as to prevent or suppress hemorrhage. The common puff-ball (Lycoperdon bovista, also the Boletus igniarius) makes a good one.

A COMPRESS is a sort of pad, generally made of folded linen, or other cloth, and used for the purpose of equalizing pressure under the roller, or of bringing it to bear on a particular point. Various shapes and forms of compresses are occasionally mentioned by very precise writers,—"the triangular, the square, the cruciform, the graduated and the pyramidal." Sufficient good sense, at the right time, will recollect or *re-invent* the kind that best suits the case. The *sieve-like* or "cribriform compress" is very useful in allowing the escape of pus, and preventing other dressings from sticking to the wounded part. "The *perforated* compress" or a pad with a central hole in it, is very convenient for applying pressure *around* a sore.

Among the means for keeping divided parts in the requisite proximity, the recently discovered or *invented* article, *collodion*, is by far the most convenient in slight cases, like small cuts or abrasions. It is an artificial cuticle, with the advantage of transparency and considerable tenacity. In the case of longer incised wounds, or other solutions of continuity, where more force is required to bring or keep the parts together, — i. e., to resist muscular contraction, ADHESIVE STRAPS (strips of cloth dipped in the collodion or spread with some gluey preparation, usually "diachylon plaster") should be applied for a considerable distance beyond the parts to be supported. They are apt to occasion more trouble in their removal than application. It is always well and often indispensable to *shave* all the hair off from the surface on which they are to be placed, — which surface must also be perfectly *dry*. To small sores or wounds the arnica plaster is more convenient than the diachylon, as requiring only to be wet instead of warmed, and possessing medicinal virtue.

APPLICATION OF SUTURES.

Divided parts sometimes require to be *sewed* as well as strapped together. This tailoring of human flesh is, however, much less practiced now-a-days than in the older and more mechanical surgery, and fewer *stitches* are found sufficient. In fact, the single stitches now used, are rather varieties of the ligature — a simple *tying* instead of sewing up. Directions need be given for only two of the technical varieties of Suture, — the *twisted* and the *interrupted*. The "Glover's or continued suture," i. e., complete sewing, is now rarely, if ever, employed on the *living* body. The "quilled suture" was a contrivance for dividing and equalizing pressure in long and deep incised wounds, by a quill, or small cylinder of some kind, laid over the edges of the wound and *under* the interrupted suture, the ligatures being tied over it. A skillful use of straps, compresses and the roller, supersedes the necessity for any such means. The "DRY SUTURE" is the least objectionable of any, the needle and thread being only passed through broad bands or bandages of adhesive plaster, placed above and below a deep incision, — the strips of plaster are thus drawn and kept together, and of course the edges of the wound with them. Sutures of any kind are *indispensable* only when it is necessary to restrain the natural mobility of the parts, or prevent permanent muscular contraction.

The TWISTED SUTURE is as often used for the purpose of compression as for mere coaptation. The needle or pin is thrust

FIG. 17.

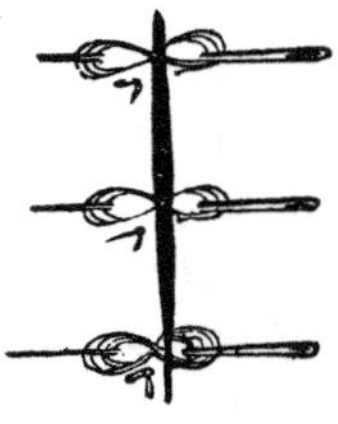

through the lips of the wound, at right angles to its course (or to that of the vein or other part to be compressed), and left there transfixing them. The thread is applied round under the point and head or eye, in successive coils, crossing each other over the middle in the form of a figure 8. It is to be drawn tight enough to bring the divided or desired parts together, and keep them smoothly so; and then tied with a square knot in the center, (fig. 17).

The INTERRUPTED SUTURE is, in reality, like the former, but a substitute for sewing. The needle is only used to introduce the thread or ligature; and each stitch, or rather *tie*, is unconnected with the others. Only one of these may be used: it is seldom that many are needed, when adhesive straps and other means are brought to aid. The curved needle, used for the purpose, should never be pushed so deep as to include more than the skin and a very small portion of cellular tissue beneath. Taking up anything more is avoided by making the puncture, as you *always should*, from the inside *outward*. In this direction it passes through much more readily, and gives less pain. To get the thread in this way through both lips more readily and conveniently, you should have a separate needle at each end. One being passed through from the inner side of each lip, they are both removed, and the thread tied just tight enough to keep the edges together, the ends being turned twice over each other at the first knot, to prevent slipping while the second is being made.

TRAUMATIC HEMORRHAGE

— is an occurrence which ought rarely to be allowed to run on to a fatal or serious extent. *Every person*, let alone surgeons, should understand enough of anatomy and *surgery*, to render at least provisional aid, until the requisite professional means and skill can be obtained. Arterial hemorrhage may be distinguished from venous (which latter seldom requires the same precautions) by its brighter color, greater amount, and, when the parts or vessels are exposed, by its partially interrupted gushes corresponding with the beating of the pulse. All who know that blood comes from the heart, should know whereabouts to put their finger on the main canals or conduits; and when they feel them pulsating, to press down on them toward the nearest bone. If the bleeding is from the upper extremity, it can be stayed by thus pressing upon the brachial artery on the inner side and a little above the middle of the upper-arm. If the injury extends to or above this point, the sub-clavian itself may be controlled by proper care, — pressing it with your thumb, or a large key wrapped in cloth, against the first rib from above and behind the collar-bone. When the alarming bleeding is from the foot, leg, or thigh, the pressure should be made in the hollow of the groin, just below Poupart's ligament. When you want to secure permanent compression, and have not a tourniquet, fasten a handkerchief round the limb, at or near the points indicated, with a hard pad on the course of the artery, upon which sufficient pressure may be made by twisting the handkerchief with a stick. When a main trunk leading to the opened branch cannot be come at, let the divided extremity or wounded part of the artery be compressed with the finger until it can be "taken up." Even this last operation, when it is urgent, ought not to be delayed for want of means. Common needles and thread, at least, are always procurable.

Bleeding from wounds, however, when only the smaller veins, and smallest arteries are concerned, will generally soon cease of itself, or be restrained by simply confining the blood, pressing on the part, or applying cold and other styptics. (See under Wounds.)

THE APPLICATION OF LIGATURES.

By "the ligature," is meant any *string* tied round a vessel or part for purposes of compression. By far the most important of these purposes is the suppression or prevention of hemorrhage. Arteries are also sometimes tied for the purpose of cutting off supplies to morbid growths or hypertrophied parts. Veins sometimes require the ligature, though this is fortunately rare, as its application to them is comparatively a serious operation, from their greater liability to diffuse inflammation. Ligatures for the purpose of strangulation, or the removal of tumors and diseased parts, have been described in speaking of tumors.

LIGATING ARTERIES, or tying up the ends after division, is often the safest as well as readiest way of stopping a flow of blood. They have to be tied, also, along their course, when they are only wounded, and to prevent fatal consequences of disease in other parts. (See under ANEURISM.) The same thing is sometimes done for veins when they are diseased. (See under VARIX.)

In "taking up" an artery, as it is technically called, you seize the extremity with forceps or tenaculum (pulling on it as little as possible, and cutting in, if necessary, to get at it); separate it carefully from any accompanying nerve, though for as little distance as possible from other tissues; pass your ligature round and tie it moderately tight, with *two turns* in your first knot, so that it will not slip while you make the second or "hard knot." The *thread* used should be large enough to allow of firm pressure, without the risk of cutting through the *external* coat of the vessel. The material generally made use of is silk. Animal fibre has some advantage over other substances — at least that of *being softened*, if not also absorbed.

Besides avoiding to include nerves, or to separate too much from the connected cellular tissue, a third invariable rule is not to tie immediately below a large branch. The reason for these precautions is in the nature of the process that follows the ligature. The internal and middle coats of the artery are at once divided by the compression, or very quickly by the consequent inflammation, and their edges adhere, throwing out considerable lymph, in consequence of which there is a swelling of the vessel just above the point. In addition to this, the blood coagulates to the next branch above; so that when the external coat ulcerates, there is a perfect coalescence with the other two and with the neighboring parts, there being no flow or pressure of blood to interfere with the process. The ligature thus "comes away" spontaneously in from five to twenty days, according to the size of the vessel and other circumstances. The stagnant blood and effused fibrin become for awhile very vascular, then gradually less so, whitening and generally changing in from twenty to forty days into a flat fibrous cord. In the case of *veins*, their inner coat is not divided, and the inflammation not becoming adhesive, is more apt to diffuse itself.

Directions for cutting down to and securing PARTICULAR ARTERIES, will be given in connection with other operations or injuries about the particular parts involved.

TORSION of arteries, that is, *twisting* instead of tying the ends, is a practice much used by the French operators and by veterinary surgeons — or horse doctors. It succeeds in the case of small branches, and during operations is quite convenient for the operator. Any other advantage over tying, it would be difficult to establish.

PUNCTURES AND INCISIONS.

To proceed now to cases in which the surgeon is required to cause the loss of blood, instead of stopping it, or that part of operative surgery where the knife is used, "Akiurgy." The simplest and most general occasions for this, are when the *lancet* is needed or supposed to be needed. Indeed the use of this handy little instrument has long been associated with "*bleeding*" for bleeding's sake. Having given our reasons in part for renouncing and denouncing this time *honored* practice, before pointing out the substitutes for it in connection with inflammation, we shall give no particular directions for the operation of *venesection*, much less for that of *arteriotomy*. Every horse-doctor and *good* farmer knows how and where to raise and open a vein. As, however, they do not always, any more than professed or professional bleeders, know how to *stop* the *bleeding*, and treat the *phlebitis*, which their phlebotomy may occasion, you should be always prepared for such accidents. (See under INFLAMMATION.) Sometimes as serious consequences result from the more frequent blunder of not avoiding the course of the nerves, where they cross over the veins opened, or of cutting through the vein, and perhaps into a contiguous artery. This has frequently given rise to a necessity for amputation. (See under TETANUS and ANEURISM.) Veins, however, as well as arteries, are always to be avoided in the *proper*

— USE OF THE LANCET. The most frequent occasion for this, is the *opening* of ABSCESSES. In treating of particular cases, we had occasion to point out where an opening by *caustic issue* was preferable to incision. As a general rule in a chronic abscess, or such as is likely to require much treatment, the potassa pencil is more than a substitute for the "abscess lancet." When it is necessary or desirable to *lance*, it should be done *freely*, — you should really "open" so as to allow an easy escape for all the pus already formed, and *keep open* for the immediate exit of that which may afterwards accumulate, — or till healing by adhesion or granulation be complete. It is proper also in all cases, but especially where the incision is large or deep, to make it in the direction of, or *parallel* with, the muscular fibres of the part, — or with tendons, ducts or blood vessels. Precautions of this kind are sometimes very important. (See MAMMARY ABSCESS.)

All lancing is sometimes called *puncturing;* but generally when the lancet is required at all, much more than its point is brought into use. In opening buboes and other large abscesses the bistoury is often a more available instrument. Mere puncturing is occasionally all that is required, as in certain operations on the eye, and in letting off serum from other parts, in anasarca for instance. But the needle, lancet and bistoury are not the only instruments which the operator should be skilled in the use of, for

DISSECTING

— is sometimes necessary on the *living body*, as well as the dead. In taking out certain tumors and making deep incisions for other purposes, a careful and skillful use of the *scalpel* is indispensable. The mode of proceeding is the same in dissecting for the practical study of anatomy and in practical surgery. "Dissecting," then, should mean the accurate *separating* of parts, with as little cutting as possible. It is well to practice three distinct ways of *holding* and *using* the scalpel: — 1st, between the thumb and two fingers, as a pen in writing (Fig. No. 18), which

FIG. 18.

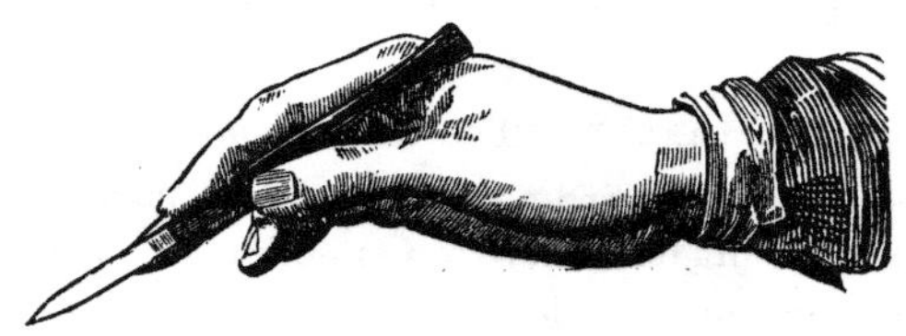

is generally the most proper and convenient position; 2d, when the instrument is held *in* the hand like a common table fork (Fig. No. 19); and 3d, at the points of the thumb and two or more fingers, like the bow of a violin.

The webs of cellular tissue, or more membranous fasciæ, are to be raised and kept *tense*, so that the smallest possible *cut* at the right point may suffice. For holding up these parts, in operating on the living flesh, the *fingers* should be made use of, where practicable, instead of the forceps or tenaculum, as pinching with these is not only likely to give pain, but to injure or kill the parts contused. The fingers should also be made as far as may be, to do the work of the scalpel itself. When the different tissues or layers are *torn*, instead of being cut asunder, the division is more likely to be, in the sense we are now using the word, a true "dissection," and injury of even the smallest nerves and vessels less likely to occur. When small vessels *are torn*, they will not bleed as when they are *cut*.

FIG. 19.

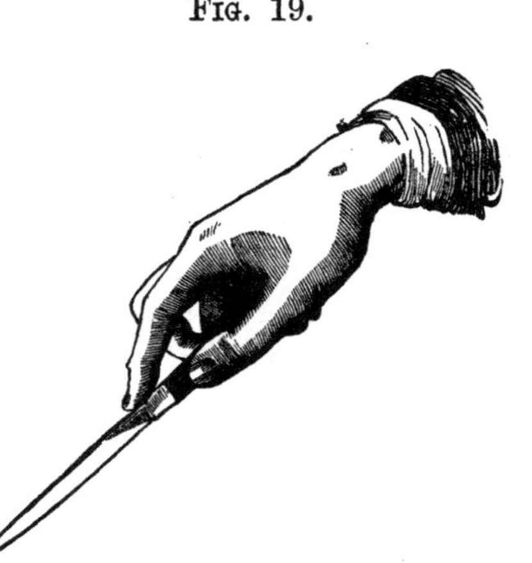

ISSUES, CAUTERIES, INOCULATION, &c.

When it is designed to set up and keep up a suppurative drain from a particular point, the object is sometimes effected by simply opening the integuments with a lancet, and inserting some foreign substance, as a pea, to act as a constant irritant. These *mechanical issues* may prove very mischievous if too near a bony prominence, or where they would interfere with the free play of the muscles or tendons. A somewhat less objectionable means for getting up a suppuration, but still too mechanical, is the *seton*. This was much practiced by the older surgeons. A portion of the integument is pinched up, and a very large needle, called "the seton needle," is run through, leaving behind it a whole skein of silk or other thread. This irritant is pulled a little in one or other direction every day, or as often as is required to keep up the suppuration. These old horse-doctoring practices, with *knife* and *rowel*, are quite unnecessary. They are constant sources of pain and irritation, while acting, if not permanently injurious. Whereas

—the CAUSTIC ISSUE, when any is needed, causes no more pain in the first place, and none at all afterwards, while a constant drain can be much more easily kept up from it; the irritating plaster, spoken of under Hip disease, is far superior to any other species of continued counter irritation, and insures any desirable amount of suppuration. When it is designed to have this plaster act speedily over a larger surface than it would be proper to prepare for it by the caustic, a common fly blister or any of the quicker vesicants (like ammonia or acetic acid) may be previously used. Abscesses may be not only opened, as they often should be, by caustic issues, but encouraged by them to *point* the sooner, while they draw off excessive irritation from within.

The ACTUAL CAUTERY, i. e., literal burning, is a relict of the surgery of barbarous times still occasionally resorted to, though no well-informed surgeon of the present day need ever have recourse to it. It is directed to be performed by means of red or white hot iron. The MOXA is a modification or slower application of this, introduced in recent times from the Chinese "practice of surgery," where we are told it is a prominent operation or charm.

ACUPUNCTURE is another oriental practice, which has been resorted to by allopaths with apparent advantage, in neuralgia and other obstinate affections. It consists simply in thrusting deep into the affected part several needles, giving them a rotary movement. They have been pushed, it is said, into the most vital organs, without injury.

ELECTRO or GALVANO PUNCTURE is when two needles, so inserted, are made the discharging and receiving points of the current, so as to oblige it to pass through a desired part. Various kinds of metals have been used in these *experiments* and with very various success

Vesication is sometimes produced as a means of introducing medical substances or influences into the general system. It is called the *endermic* method of medication. The Homeopathic surgeon will rarely, if ever, have need to resort to these means.

INOCULATION is a mode of artificial or prophylactic poisoning, analogous to endermic medication. It means the insertion of contagious matter for the purpose of exciting the same specific disease that produced it. It has been experimented on and proposed in a great variety of diseases; and was really of great use, and greatly needed, for small-pox, before Jenner discovered a substitute for it in the cow-pox, giving rise to the particular kind of inoculation, hence called

VACCINATION.

This is an operation which every practitioner of medicine ought always to be prepared with the means of performing. The MATTER so called (which, however, should be clear *lymph* taken before the vesicle has reached the suppurating stage, or has any inflamed areola, and from an otherwise healthy patient) should be very carefully preserved from the air, when it is intended for future use. A common and convenient way of keeping it is in bees-wax. The best plan, when convenient, is to have the person to be vaccinated and the person to be vaccinated *from*, both together, and prepare the former for the immediate insertion of the virus before it is taken from the latter. Some vaccinators scrape off the cuticle, others make a good deal of cutting and scarring. These are both unnecessary and cause superfluous irritation. It is sufficient to make a few oblique punctures with the point of the lancet, about the eighth of an inch in length, — if without drawing any blood, all the better. Then wet the point of the instrument in the fresh lymph, to reinsert it for a moment into each puncture. If you have only the scab or dried matter, it may be dissolved in water or slightly moistened, and a minute portion inserted into each orifice, allowing it to remain there for a short time, at least, without disturbance. To avoid irritation, the part had better be loosely bound up, or have court plaster over it after getting dry. A dose of the Homeopathic preparation of sulphur should be given after the maturation of the scab, to remove any psora that may have been communicated by any impurity of the virus.

[For the CATHETERISM or the clearing and enlarging of various accessible canals of the body, which might have been taken up in this connection as a general subject, as well as the EXTRACTION of foreign substances from such canals or cavities, see under the particular heads. Obstruction in the trachea or esophagus, has been treated of as CHOKING, in connection with diseases of the throat; and the extraction of TEETH (which when diseased may well be considered "foreign substances"), in connection with the diseases they give rise to. Other cavities will be considered in connection with operations needed in or near them:—Catheterism of the Eustachian Tube, with diseases of the mouth or ear —of the Urethra, with those of the contiguous parts.]

EXCISION OF TUMORS.

The immediate difficulties or dangers that attend the removal of tumors by the knife, are the hemorrhage that may arise from cutting *blood vessels* and the pain and other disagreeable symptoms that may follow from wounded *nerves*. [For the different kinds of tumors and the cases or stages in which a resort to the knife is most or least advisable, see TUMORS, also CANCER.]

If the tumor be small and near the surface, *one* straight *incision*, through the integuments and cellular substance down to the tumor, is sufficient. The cut should always extend far enough at each side beyond the margin of the tumor, to enable you to dissect it back and distend the lips wide enough. This will allow the tumor to be taken out without straining upon the ends of the wound, which would give severe pain. After laying open the skin,—if it be an ENCYSTED TUMOR, cut freely through the sac, and take out the contained mass with your fingers, the forceps, or a tenaculum which may be hooked into it so that considerable force may be used. If it has no CYST, carefully dissect up the skin and cellular membrane from one side and turn out the tumor, continuing to dissect from the same side as far as you can or until you get it nearly or quite out. If this be not practicable, after passing its center, begin on the other side and complete the dissection. In handling the wound during the operation, take hold of the *skin* with your *fingers*, or direct the assistant to do so, using no forceps to this part if you can possibly hold it without, as the pinching gives much pain. You may seize the *tumor* with forceps if necessary, or hook a tenaculum into it, as it is not very sensitive.

If the tumor be LARGE it may be necessary to make a crucial, elliptical or triangular incision, and dissect up the flaps in different directions before it can be removed. If it ADHERE to tendons or muscles, care should be taken not to wound the tendons or cut away so much of the muscles as to impair their use, unless this be necessary for the removal of *diseased* formations.

If large ARTERIES, *veins*, or *nerves* are involved in the tumor, or lie near it, great caution must be exercised not to injure them; or if arteries are cut during the operation, you should stop proceedings and tie bleeding vessels the first thing, unless the hemorrhage can be restrained by the finger of an assistant or by a compress or tourniquet, as when you are operating on a limb. In this case you may finish the operation before applying ligatures. In operating about the *neck*, special caution and steadiness of hand are required to avoid both nerves and vessels. It is much more dangerous to wound the jugular vein than the carotid artery. The artery may be cut and tied with safety. A wound in the jugular vein, if it admit any air into its cavity (which it is very liable to do), is quite sure to prove fatal. Fatal Inflammation also is much more likely to occur from the tying of large veins than arteries.

When there is no malignant disease connected with the tumor, the skin healthy and the whole mass taken out, after securing the vessels and arresting hemorrhage, cleanse the wound of all clots and extravasated blood and bring the lips together; secure them by adhesive straps or sutures; and dress, as in the case of any other simple wound, so as to promote healing by the first intention.

If the tumor be MALIGNANT or at all *suspicious*, as where the skin closely adheres to it, or is in the least discolored, — or where the vessels over and around it are in a varicose condition, *excise completely* all the discolored skin, together with the tumor. Even *painfulness* or *itching* in the tumor will be a sufficiently suspicious circumstance to demand the same precaution. The best mode of operating in such a case, is to fix a tenaculum, or the three chain hooks of a common dissecting case, to the top of the tumor. Pull firmly upon the tenaculum or hooks, so as to put the skin and cellular tissue violently upon the stretch. Then with a scalpel or bistoury make a circular incision, through the skin, around the base of the tumor large enough to extend at least three-fourths of an inch, if practicable, beyond all trace of the disease or discoloration. Continue to pull on the tumor, and if possible, by moderate force, *pull it off*. But if it adhere too firmly, separate the cellular tissue with the knife. If any arteries are cut (which is less likely to occur in this mode of operating), take them up — apply an elm poultice to the surface, and promote *suppuration* and granulation.

These rules apply of course to all CANCERS OR CANCEROUS TUMORS, where the knife is only used as auxiliary to the cure, by removing a portion or all of the diseased mass at once, instead of doing it by the slower means, — which, however, are afterwards indispensable to a safe treatment. (See CANCER.)

In nearly all cases of large tumors, it will be better to have the patient under the influence of ether or chloroform; and it *may* be very necessary in quite small ones. Even for the operation of the caustic, if the patient's resolution can not be sufficiently roused, there will be far less risk from the anæsthetic agent than from the nervous excitement and shock of fear. The danger to life from the ether, it should be remembered, is little if any, and even the chloroform may by proper precautions be disarmed of all its terrors. The person who administers it should always have *ammonia* ready at hand to use as an antidote, in case the insensibility threaten to be that of death.

ANEURISM.

Aneurism is a diseased state of an artery, inducing dilatation and subsequent rupture. Some suppose rupture of the internal coats, if not also of the external, to be a first or early occurrence. Whether formed by and within, or only from and about the vessel, an enlarging and pulsating "tumor" is the characteristic result. When much of its capsule or sac is not constituted of any of the proper coats of the vessel, but of a cyst produced from the effused lymph surrounding an orifice through which it receives its *deposite* of blood, it is called FALSE ANEURISM. When there is no such covering, the artery only continuing to pour out its blood into the cellular tissue, it constitutes DIFFUSED ANEURISM. When the effusion runs along between the coats of the artery itself, it is sometimes distinguished as a *dissecting aneurism.* The *exciting* CAUSE may be local injury, violent bodily exertion or strong mental emotion. The patient often refers to a strain when "something was felt to give way." There is generally a *predisposing cause* in some form of cachexia, such as syphilis or mercurialism.

The DIAGNOSTIC SYMPTOMS are obvious: — The swelling beats synchronous with the artery, along the *course* of which it occurs, and can be emptied of its contents by simply pressing on the vessel above it. The pulsating is noticed from the first while the swelling is small and soft, thus distinguishing the case from a *tumor* proper, which generally begins hard, and only pulsates while pressing on the artery. The latter is also unaffected by compression on the artery, movement of the part or the patient's change of position.

In its PROGRESS, the coats or boundaries of the aneurism may for a time be strengthened by adhesion with surrounding parts; but these are absorbed as the dilatation proceeds, even bone presenting no obstacle. When it reaches the surface, a mucous canal or internal cavity, it bursts, and fatal hemorrhage is often the consequence. Aneurism may become its own cure by more or less complete coagulation of the blood; by sloughing, in which the artery is included so as to block it up, the same as when small branches are cut through; or by pressure of the effused blood upon the vessel, with a similar result to that of tying it up. This last occurrence is *the* indication of cure; for in

— TREATMENT, *compressing* should be the rule, *ligating* the alternative. Compresses should be applied along the course of the artery, and perhaps to the tumor, in the early stage, but not so firmly as to promote absorption or favor inflammation. Contrivances for these purposes will readily occur to the practitioner. The great difficulty is to prevent their being removed or disturbed by the patient. The *aneurism tourniquet*, lately devised, promises to be an available resource, possessing the peculiar advantage of a lock and key. The surgeon after securing it can put the latter in his pocket. It is better to have the pressure bear most on two points, both above the aneurismal sac, so that one may be a little slackened without allowing free course to the blood. Compression has been at various times the fashion, but again abandoned, apparently from indiscreet and injudicious modes of using it. When the sac is very large, with thin walls and degeneration of the surrounding parts, it manifestly requires caution. As to the mode of applying it, gradual compression seems, in some hands, to have better success, probably from inducing coagulation, than the attempts to at once obliterate.

In many cases and in many parts of the body, however, the LIGATURE is the only resource. There are three principal ways of applying it:—*below* the sac, with the view of inducing coagula,—both *above* and *below*, the sac being then opened,—and that of Hunter, now generally adopted, which consists simply in ligating the vessel at some convenient point between the affected part and the source of circulation. The second method, tying below as well as above, is necessary in varicose aneurism (as after bleeding, when the venesection has been also arteriotomy), when the blood is diffused or ready to burst out and become so, and where there are numerous anastomosing vessels, as in the back of the hand and foot. Tying beyond or below the sac alone, may be proper where it cannot be done above. The greatest triumphs, however, of modern surgery, have been from the simple operation of Hunter. It is contraindicated in *false* aneurism of great extent, in general disease of the arteries or the aneurismal diathesis, and when nature has fairly taken the case into her own hands by the circulation ceasing in and below the part, or by gangrene or caries occurring in its vicinity. Where the neighboring vessels have become thickened and unfit for additional vicarious duty, success will be questionable.

In operating, cut or dissect down at the point chosen with a scalpel or bistoury, and when you have reached the surface of the vessel, work round it with the blunt end of the ANEURISM NEEDLE (see plate, Fig. 20), separating the accompanying nerve or vein from the artery, by *pushing* rather than cutting through the cel-

FIG. 20.

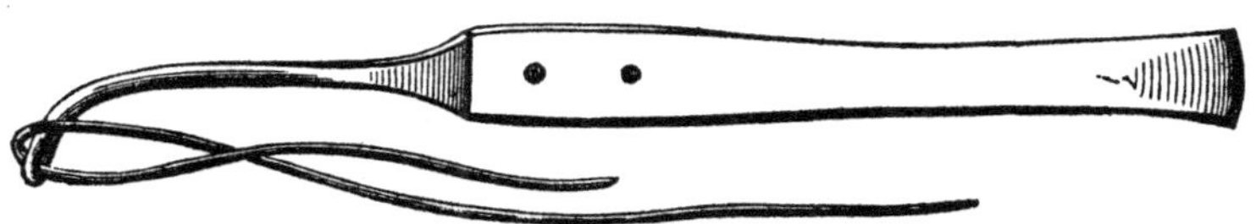

lular substance that connects them, thus avoiding the danger of puncturing such vein or nerve. This is especially necessary where a large vein or nerve is inclosed in the same sheath with the artery, as in the neck or thigh.

It would be difficult to say how far, or how high, this operation may be carried. After the operation, a general expansion of the branches or other arteries supplying the same parts, ensues, and their complete circulation is soon re-established by anastomosis; but, after a time, a few vessels only take on the duty of increased supply, and the rest contract again to their original dimensions. The subclavian has now been frequently tied, and saved life, where nothing else could have done so. Both common carotids have been successfully obliterated; and Sir Astley Cooper even tied the descending aorta with, it was believed, good results, — for a time.

VARICOSE ANEURISM and ANEURISM ALVARIX (results of "venesection" into an *artery*, permanently connecting it to the vein, with the addition, in the former case of a "false aneurism" between them) require, like false aneurism in general, and large diffused aneurism, the double ligature.

NÆVUS, often congenital, appearing as a red shining spot on the skin, and liable to enlarge and bleed profusely, is a similar condition of the small arteries to that of the veins in varix. Large nævi are called "aneurisms by anastomosis." The tumors they occasion are distinguished by their pulsation, their gradual enlargement, and final *frequent* ulceration. [Their treatment was given under the head of VASCULAR TUMORS.]

RECICATRIZATION AND RHINOPLASTICS.

Still another kind of general operation may be mentioned in this place. It belongs to *restorative*, though not at all to medical surgery: unlike most operations, it is constructive instead of destructive. The possibility of restoring lost parts of the body must have been thought of ever since there were sufferers from such losses, particularly when they were such as to occasion positive ugliness. Usefulness itself was secondary to this consideration. Artificial noses were attempted before artificial legs. We are not constituted like some of the articulata, from whose bodies or trunks new limbs will sprout out when the old ones have been amputated. Within restricted limits, lost flesh may be restored by the process of granulation, but the full-formed body seems to lack the principle of completeness or regard for symmetry and appearance. After a burn or scald, the vesicated surface will skin over just as it may happen to have contracted; and the same will take place on any raw surface left by "solution of contiguity," however much flesh may be wanting to complete the form now so defaced. When raw surfaces not originally connected are allowed to remain in contact, they coalesce as readily as parts separated by simple incision in "union by the first intention." This might be supposed to have early suggested a plan for filling up deficiencies; but the difficulty was to know where to get the spare flesh. It really appears that some centuries ago it was procured from other person's bodies, if not the bodies of other animals;—just as before the invention of artificial teeth, the rich ladies in some parts of Europe used to have sound teeth, from the jaws of their poor dependants or neighbors, transferred into their own empty sockets. So, we are informed by history, the Arabs, during the middle ages, and even the Italians on their first introducing this kind of surgery into Europe in the fifteenth century, used to cut off the *nose* of a slave now and then and *engraft* it on to the face of his master or other superior! These are the "Taliacotian operations" (so named from an Italian surgeon Tagliacozzi, who was reputed to practise it), satirized in Hudibras. The exaggerations and even superstitions connected with the matter, occasioned it, as usual, to sink again into undeserved neglect. It was not until within the present century that the plan of making artificial noses was again revived in Europe and America, though it was mentioned by the oldest Greek medical writers, and was in use among the Hindoos. The plan now generally practised of taking the material for the new nose from the forehead, is one of the old Indian methods. The general principle in these transplantings is, that the part removed must be kept for a time in *connection* with both its old and new locations, in order that some circulation may be kept up until the vascular reorganization is complete. (See further in connection with particular localities.)

CICATRICES from wounds, ulcers, and especially burns, sometimes take place in such a way as to occasion much deformity, if not deficiency in the use of the parts. The general cause of this is permanent muscular contraction, as that of the platysma myoides forming "wry-neck." Such a state of things may sometimes be remedied by simple *incision*, dividing the contracted fibres; but more generally the old cicatrix has to be completely *dissected out.* Care must be taken in dressing the new wound, and regulating the position of the parts during healing, that a repetition of the accident do not occur.

CHAPTER II.

DISLOCATION OR LUXATION—GENERAL DIRECTIONS FOR REDUCTION AND TREATMENT.

THIS is a subject which requires the special attention of the general practitioner of medicine. There are few accidents which demand more prompt redress, and in which professional skill or the want of it, is more manifest. It is a department of operative surgery that cannot be safely or conscientiously neglected by any who intend to practice medicine.

By "luxation" or "dislocation," which almost defines itself, is meant the displacement of a bone from the surface of another bone, to which it is naturally articulated. Its distinction from "fracture" is sufficiently obvious in the abstract. When, however, the two accidents occur at the same time, doubt and difficulty may arise. These cases, called compound and complicated, will be taken up separately, after drawing your attention to Simple Dislocation and Simple Fractures.

The readjustment of the separated bones is called the "*reduction.*" If any considerable time has been allowed to elapse, before this is effected, the operation becomes very difficult and sometimes impossible.

The true nature of the difficulty is not always obvious; and the consequence of the medical attendant's failing to ascertain it in time, is that his patient must remain crippled for life.

The student must not rest satisfied with understanding and recollecting the bony frame work of the joints, but study their whole mechanism, including the arrangement of the cartilages and ligaments, and the insertion and action of the muscles. The uses as well as structure of every joint, the play as well as position of every muscle, should be familiar to the mind. The fact of dislocation is as often ascertained by the unnatural position and limited motion of the limb, as from the changed appearance at the joint itself. This is the case, for example, with the shoulder, elbow, and hip. The precise nature of the displacement, if not the fact of any displacement at all, can often be certain only to one who has an exact anatomical knowledge of the parts in all their connections. It is, however, important that the surgeon be familiar with the *external shape* and appearance of the joints, in the living subject as well as their structure and connections from investigations on the dead.

It is sometimes a very difficult matter, even for the most skillful and experienced, to discover the real nature of the case, in consequence of the swelling that is apt to occur. Hence the importance of examination and adjustment as soon as possible after the accident. Too often, however, the surgeon has not an opportunity for this. The direct injury done by the violence, which caused the luxation, or the subsequent irritation from the unnatural position of the parts, has brought on inflammation, which completely prevents any opinion being formed from external appearances. Even the position and movement of the part are sometimes insufficient criteria, as fractures and even sprains may simulate dislocation. In such cases the practitioner should be cautious of giving a positive diagnosis, until he has so far reduced swelling and inflammation as to be able to make the proper examinations.

The SYMPTOMS of dislocation, it must be born in mind, may be a change in the outward *form* of the joint, a greater or less alteration in the *length* of the limb, or in the direction of its *axis*. This last symptom, the altered axis, or *position* of the limb, is chiefly referable to muscular action on the parts in their abnormal position, since the ligaments are generally so extensively lacerated as to retain but little influence. The form of the *head* of the bone has a considerable effect on the direction of the *limb*. Thus, when the head of the thigh bone is thrown up, on the ilium, its easy mobility under the action of the adductor muscles, occasions the knee and foot to turn inwards.

Immediately after a dislocation has taken place, the individual not unfrequently retains the power of *moving* the limb: he is neither so crippled nor *deformed* as to manifest the serious nature of the injury. But in a very short time the muscles become contracted and rigid, and the limb appears permanently deformed.

In some dislocations, the limb being shortened, most of the muscles are *relaxed;* while in others the limb is elongated and the muscles put upon the *stretch*, so much so in some cases, as to cause them to be ruptured. The consequence of such complications is great effusion as well as inflammation. The amount of effused blood will be in proportion to the injury done to the muscles, or to the blood vessels themselves.

Severe *pain* may be occasioned by pressure of the bone on sensitive parts, or its exciting inflammatory susceptibility in parts otherwise insensible. In this way it may even endanger life. Paralysis by pressing on a nerve is not unfrequent. In dislocation of the head of the humerus into the axilla, for example, it may not only impede nervous communication with the arm, but cut off the due supply of blood, and in this manner cause atrophy as well as paralysis. The dislocated clavicle may press on the windpipe or esophagus.

The external *prominence* caused by the *head* of a bone may be transferred to a considerable distance from its accustomed place, and the depression in the latter place becomes a corroborating symptom, as well as the mobility of the new prominence. This displaced prominence may be greater or less than the original one.

The protuberance of the trochanter, for instance, is diminished by the new location of the head of the femur; that of the elbow is greatly enlarged by a backward luxation of the ulna.

If the dislocation has been allowed to remain a considerable time unreduced, there will be more or less *effusion* of adhesive matter into the joints and surrounding tissues. This adhesive effusion, or actual adhesions of the tissues, may cause a sensation of *crepitus* on motion, which may easily be mistaken for *fracture.* But close observation will generally enable the practised ear of the surgeon to distinguish this from the crepitus of loose bone.

The CONSEQUENCES of unreduced luxations, and the *changes* that may supervene in the bone and contiguous parts, are worthy of attention. Sphacelus, as a termination of the inflammation excited, may come on after the reduction as well as for want of it. Its danger to the limb or life of the patient is obvious. But when this danger is escaped or warded off, the principle of adaptation, so observable throughout nature, comes into play. The displaced bone not unfrequently forms a new socket, so that a considerable degree of motion, with the requisite pressure upon it, is regained. The particular result will depend in a great measure upon the length of time since the accident, as well as upon the peculiar structure of the parts where the head is lodged. If it is among muscular matter, the cartilage remains entire and new cartilaginous deposites take place around it, connecting firmly with the neighboring parts. Within this new formation the head of the bone freely moves. If, however, the dislocated head be in contact with another bone, — or there is but a thin muscle between them, which is soon absorbed in consequence of the pressure bringing the bony surfaces in contact, — a remarkable change takes place in the dislocated head. The articular cartilage and the rounded end of the bone are both absorbed, the latter being flattened or hollowed out so as to adapt itself to the contiguous surface, which is also sometimes modified to receive it. Ossific deposits frequently take place around the cavity, forming a deep cup, confining the bone in its new place and allowing it considerable freedom of motion. The muscles become diminished in length in proportion as the limb is shortened.

The CAUSE of dislocation occurring is generally a force exerted on the bone when it is in an oblique direction with respect to its articulating connection, and when the muscles are relaxed and unprepared for resistance. In such circumstances very slight force may be sufficient; though to produce the same result, an immensely greater force would be necessary, were the individual on his guard. When this is the case and the injury has been brought about in spite of resistance, "by main force," extensive laceration as well as luxation occurs. On the contrary, little if any injury is done to the surrounding parts, when the bone has *slipped*, as it were accidentally, out of its place. Such a dislocation may occur from paralysis of one set of muscles, the other retaining their force; or the spasmodic action of the muscles upon either side, may easily effect it, when the antagonistic ones, with the ligaments of the joints, are in a state of relaxation. Ulceration may also be the cause, by detaching the ligaments, as in the Hip Disease.

Dislocations may be connected with *fracture*. This is almost invariably the case when the ankle joint is the one concerned, the fibula rarely escaping fracture. The olecranon process of the ulna is also not unfrequently torn off, when that bone is "put out of joint." Luxations of the head of the humerus are often accompanied with fractures of the scapula. Dislocation of the spine and of the ribs must always, in our opinion, be attended with fracture.

"Compound dislocation" is technically used to imply a dislocation accompanied with laceration of the surface and capsular ligaments, exposing the displaced end of the bone. In such a case, there is generally more or less hemorrhage, with an immediate escape of the synovial fluid. These dislocations are dangerous. Extensive inflammation and suppuration are likely to ensue. The cartilages very soon inflame, suppurate and pass off. The denuded extremity of the bone, even when replaced, only adheres at the joint, and anchylosis is the least unfavorable result. Unless great care is taken immediately after such an accident, to prevent the occurrence of much inflammation, and after resolution to effect early adhesions of the soft parts lacerated, serious evil may be apprehended.

Some joints are more *liable* to compound dislocation than others. The ankle, the wrist and the elbow, are perhaps the joints most frequently subject to this form of accident. It rarely happens with the knee.

PARTIAL DISLOCATIONS may occur. The tibia, for example, may be thrown forwards on the metatarsus, while partially retaining its proper basis. One bone of the elbow may easily be thrown out of place, while the other remains in position.

LIABILITY to dislocation varies in different parts, and also with the age of the individual. Those joints which have the most extensive and varied movements, are the most exposed to this accident—the shoulder more than any other. Very old and very young persons are less liable than others; the former in consequence of the greater fragility of their bones suffering fracture; while in the latter, imperfect ossification allows the separation of their epiphyses from the body of the bones.

The DIAGNOSIS between a *fracture* near a joint and a dislocation of that joint, is sometimes very difficult. In dislocation the bone is not only incapable of its proper motions in the joint, but is generally immovable beyond a certain point or in certain directions, even by the efforts of others. In the case of fracture, on the contrary, there is a loss of control in the direction of motion; but the muscles still act and even move it more freely, while the limb, if it be a limb concerned, can be easily moved by the surgeon. If proper extension and adjustment be made, a *limb* will remain extended, when it has been only dislocated; while in fracture, if it be not immediately secured, it will be drawn back into its former position. In the latter case, moreover, crepitus can generally be heard over the broken ends of bone; whereas no such phenomenon is to be expected in dislocation; nor anything that can be mistaken for it, unless from adhesion or effusion, as already mentioned.

The principal DIFFICULTY the surgeon has to encounter in reduction, is the resistance of the contracted muscles; and this will generally be the greater in proportion to the length of time that has elapsed since the accident occurred. The muscles have a greater contractile force, independent of volition. This is true even of the otherwise voluntary muscles. When a muscle is divided, its separate parts both contract: so in partial paralysis, or loss of voluntary control of motion, the muscle still contracts, and permanently draws the part with which it is connected in a given direction. This sort of contraction will continue an indefinite length of time; for it is not followed by fatigue, as is the case with contraction excited by volition. Moreover, when a muscle has been long thus involuntarily contracted, it becomes incapable of being again extended; the new position is then the natural one; its contraction has become an actual shortening. Thus, when a bone is dislocated, the contraction of a muscle removes it far from the joint, and there it is retained. After it has been long thus relocated, no power short of that which will rupture the muscle is sufficient to replace the bone in its original position. In reduction, then, the surgeon has to overcome this increasing *contraction* or shortening of the muscles. This is generally effected without much force, if *extension* be made soon after the accident (which should always be done, even when complete reduction is not at once effected). If only a few days are allowed to elapse, great difficulty will attend the operation.

An additional difficulty, in cases of long standing, results from *adhesions* of the surrounding parts, by which reduction is often rendered impossible, independently of the contraction of the muscles.

Or, as a third obstacle to reduction, the *socket* from which the bone has been displaced, is more or less occupied with effused matter, so that if sufficient extension can be effected, and the head of the bone brought back to its original position, it cannot re-enter its socket. The matter deposited may even have been ossific, and the original cavity be entirely filled up with solid and resisting substance.

Or, again, a *new socket* may have been formed for the head of the bone, as well as corresponding adhesions or cartilaginous connections. In this way, the head of the bone may be so completely fitted to its new position, that it would be equivalent to a fresh dislocation to remove it, even if you were sure of getting it back to and *into* its original place.

Force alone cannot, then, be depended on in the reduction of dislocations. Constitutional as well as local means must be resorted to, — *physiological*, as well as *mechanical*, principles must be brought to our aid, — especially when any considerable time has elapsed since the accident occurred. In nearly all cases, however, physiological as well as anatomical considerations are involved, and more or less constitutional management is requisite. The surgeon must take into account the natural action of the large muscles, and the direction in which their contraction has a tendency to draw the limb or bone. This, in ordinary cases, and for a long time, is the principle source of difficulty. Every surgeon, therefore, should be well acquainted with the anatomy of the parts, should know individually every considerable muscle connected with the joint, and how much extending and counter-extending force is necessary to overcome its resistance.

The CONSTITUTIONAL MEANS, necessary in some cases to be employed, are such as will immediately bring about a general relaxation of the muscular system. These means are required not only to overcome, what may be called the instinctive resistance of the voluntary muscles, but any spasmodic action that may occur. It is for this reason that blood-letting and antimonial nauseants are generally recommended. But, inasmuch as we have abundant resources, which will produce the desired effect as certainly, and much more safely for the patient, we are not under the necessity of resorting to these objectionable means. The warm bath is a valuable auxiliary; but nauseants, after all, must be chiefly depended on. Antimonial nauseants, however, always objectionable, are here particularly dangerous; for they must be given to a sufficient extent to produce complete relaxation, which cannot be done without excessive prostration and danger of irritation, or even inflammation of the stomach and bowels. In the much decried and much *abused* article *lobelia*, we have a nauseant far superior to tartarized antimony. Not only are its direct effects on the system far better for our purpose, but the most extended experience has proved that it is free from all danger of irritation or too long continued a prostration.

Let the patient then be subjected to a simple warm bath or to a vapor bath, till free perspiration is excited. If not sufficient relaxation, give also the *lobelia*, either in the form of infusion or of an acetous tincture,—give it in small and frequently repeated doses, increasing the quantity until the patient is very much nauseated. If actual vomiting is caused, you can lessen the quantity or increase the interval between the doses, but should not discontinue the operation until complete relaxation is effected. This may be carried indeed to such a point,—and with perfect safety, too,—that the patient's limbs and whole voluntary muscular system will be as flaccid, or nearly as flaccid, as those of a recent corpse. Yet from these and other "alarming symptoms," the subject of them will invariably and spontaneously recover in the course of a few hours. *Tobacco* has been recommended by some surgeons to produce this relaxation; but it is dangerous as well as unnecessary.

When the proper relaxation has been brought about by these internal and external means, the *mechanical operation* of REDUCTION should be at once effected. This consists mainly in what is called extension and counter-extension. The direct extension is usually made by the surgeon's own hand and muscular force. The counter-extension, or fixing of the body so as not to yield to the extending force, may be intrusted to assistants or to properly arranged machinery.

The *extending force* should never be suddenly applied. Begin gently, and gradually increase the strain, until the muscles are wearied or give way. Very great resistance may thus be overcome by a comparatively slight force long continued, and no violence or permanent injury done; whereas the requisite amount of force, if applied all at once, would be sufficient to tear the muscles asunder.

The *counter-extension* requires considerable care, so that when extension is made, the socket into which reduction is to be effected, will remain fixed and unyielding. The requisite force for this purpose is, in many instances, better supplied by mechanical means, the resistance of which is more firm and steady, and more to be depended upon than any amount of manual force. The requisite machinery and the best, when it does not require the loss of too much time to procure it, consists of a set of *pulleys* fixed at some point in the direct line of the intended extension, or Jarvis' adjuster.

The *limb* should if possible be kept in such a position as will of itself produce relaxation of the stronger of the opposing muscles. As a general rule it should be partially flexed.

In some instances the extension should be made directly upon the dislocated bone. In other cases it is better to apply your force to the bone next beyond, as to the fore-arm in dislocations of the shoulder joint. In dislocation of the hip, on the contrary, the extending bandages should be applied above the knee, as their object requires the limb to be bent.

The state of the patient's MIND, independent of conscious volition, exerts much influence over the muscular system, and is a consideration of great practical importance. Resistance to external force is an instinctive or reflex and involuntary act. The adroit surgeon will contrive to *divert* the patient's *attention* as much as possible from the operation. He may, for example, have some piece of good or bad news, some surprising intelligence communicated, or some striking "accident" purposely brought about, at the desirable point of time. The arrival of some long absent friend may be spoken of, or some article let fall with alarming violence. We have succeeded, in otherwise difficult cases, by having an assistant attract the patient's attention by dashing his hand, or something, suddenly through a pane of glass, just at the favorable moment, when everything was ready for effecting the object,— except the patient's mind.

The SUCCESS of your efforts can generally be known by the limb having suddenly regained its original *shape* and capacity for *motion*. The entry of the head of the bone into its proper socket can, besides, be commonly both felt and heard; it "snaps" like a lock when the key is turned. When pulleys are used, however, or when the muscles are very much relaxed, this snapping of the bone into the socket will not be noticed.

After the dislocation has been reduced, the limb should be kept in its original position by bandages and, in some cases, splints also; otherwise a very slight force may throw it out of place again. All the TREATMENT generally necessary, after this, is to keep the bandages over the joint constantly wet with cold water, to which has been added the Tincture of Arnica Montana. We generally add a teaspoonful to each pint of water, and attend to such constitutional symptoms as may arise. As the patient is obliged to keep quiet for a while, his diet should be regulated accordingly.

We have said that this is generally all that is necessary, but we would recommend in all cases of dislocation, for Arnica Mon. and Rhus. Tox. to be given internally, in alternation, once in from three to six hours. We have usually employed the third dilution. The virtues of Arnica in mechanical injuries are so well known, that even others than Homeopaths now frequently use it. There is, however, in dislocations such violence done to the tendons and ligaments as to require the use of the proper specific Rhus Tox. We have found their alternate use to succeed better than when given singly. And in those cases where they have been employed, the patient has not been left with that weakened, lame, irritable condition of the joint; which often, especially in old persons, renders the limb for a long time comparatively useless. But, on the contrary, they have speedily recovered the use of the limb in all its former vigor. All thanks to Homeopathy in developing the specific virtues of remedies.

If the above treatment is faithfully employed, inflammation will not arise from dislocation (at least it has not in our practice). Should it, however, be present when the surgeon is called, or make its appearance at any time, Aconitum should precede the other remedies.

Suppuration about the joint must be carefully guarded against. Hence, as a general rule, emollients are to be avoided. Resolution is here the only safe termination of inflammation. If you would therefore escape ulceration and destruction of the joint, do not allow the lately dislocated part to be moved for some time to come. Too long inaction may indeed occasion some stiffness of the joint; but the danger from this source is little or none compared with the other; and the inconvenience and anxiety of friends may be easily overcome by gradually attempting motion, when the proper time for it has arrived.

As to the exact TIME, after which an attempt should *not* be made to reduce a dislocated bone, *no positive rule* can be laid down. In some instances limbs may be put in place months after the accident. Reduction has been in some rare cases effected even after years of neglect or unsuccessful effort. But as a *general* rule, the lapse of a few weeks will render the success very doubtful. Reduction, in such cases, even when effected, is at the risk of serious injury to the patient. Sir Astley Cooper fixes three months for the shoulder, and eight weeks for the hip, as the periods, after which it will be *too late* to operate,—unless in persons of very relaxed fibre or advanced age. But such rules are subject to many exceptions, however great the experience of the person who makes them. They are at best only probabilities and rules for prognosis. In many instances a much shorter period than he mentions, will make it too late; while in other cases, besides those he excepts, you may succeed after a much longer interval. The degree of approximation toward a new and useful joint, will often be a better criterion than the amount of time elapsed.

Inasmuch as COMPOUND DISLOCATIONS are of much more serious importance than simple ones, the practitioner should well understand the necessity for medical treatment in these cases, aside from the mere mechanical operation of reduction. According to the definition before given, these cases imply that the surrounding soft parts are to a greater or less extent lacerated, with some portions of the dislocated surfaces exposed. The first object, therefore, will be to arrest hemorrhage and remove all foreign substances from the wound. After that the bone should be restored to its natural place and the wound closed as soon as possible. Special care should be taken in this kind of wounds to promote healing by the first intention, bringing the parieties of the wound as nearly as possible into their original position and keeping them there by bandages and compresses. Sutures should never be used.

Some authors recommend us to wrap the wound in lint dipped in blood. But if the bandages applied be first dipped in *cold water*, and afterwards kept wetted, this singular recommendation will be quite unnecessary—a plan by the way, which, besides being so troublesome, is frequently found rather to aggravate or promote than to retard inflammation.

Let the limb be placed in whatever position is easiest, and apply moderate *compression*. The best means for doing this is the Gum Shellac splint [described in speaking of Hip Disease], or Gutta Percha. This should be adjusted to the whole limb,—leaving, however, an open space at the wound, so that it can be properly dressed,—and fixed on by the roller. A more equable pressure can thus be brought to bear than by any other means.

The WOUND itself should be kept constantly covered with lint, over which are laid cloths wet in cold water, mixed with an equal quantity of the Tr. of Calendula Offic., or the Tr. of the apple (Momordica Balsamina), while the same should be given internally in drop doses two or three times a day. Before embracing Homeopathy we employed, in some bad cases, with excellent results, a lotion of equal parts of whiskey and water saturated with salt, with the addition sometimes of about one-sixth part of the Tincture of Camphor; but since, we have had no occasion to use other than Calendula, Momordica Balsamina, Arnica, &c. The Calendula Offic., it would seem from the trials made with it, fills a very important place hitherto unoccupied — that of so controlling the inflammation, so likely to arise from lacerated wounds, as to cause them to heal by the first intention. The Momordica Balsamina we regard as in no respect inferior to the Calendula, and would recommend a trial of it by the profession.

If the dislocation be properly reduced, and the lacerated parts adjusted, the above treatment will almost always bring about adhesion, without suppuration, or even extensive inflammation.

If the BONE be *injured* as well as dislocated, and there be any broken portions in the wound, these must be scrupulously removed, as, if left there, they will become a source of irritation and prevent healing.

POULTICES, as was before remarked, should be avoided, especially in the earlier stage of treatment, as they tend to promote suppuration and counteract the object of speedy adhesion. Yet, when severe inflammation has set in, notwithstanding the precautions mentioned, and suppuration is inevitable, you should use emollients, to bring it about as speedily as possible. Among other advantages, they will then help to ward off the danger of tetanus, which is very apt to occur from severe inflammation about a joint.

If ABSCESSES should form, they should be *opened* as speedily as possible, and no pus be allowed to accumulate about the joint, as it might occasion serious local injury, as well as symptomatic fever. [For treatment, see ABSCESS.]

The patient should have nutritous diet, though only such as is unstimulating. It may even be necessary to give a little ale or wine, when the discharge of large quantities of pus occasions debility.

Attention to the cutaneous function is of great importance. The Alkaline sponge bath should be used every two or three days, and the surface freely sponged with cold water two or three times a day, guarding, however, against a chill by not applying the cold over too much of the body at the same time, or to any part, before reaction is established by the drying, friction and covering of the part last bathed.

Notwithstanding that laceration about the joints, in connection with luxation, is generally looked upon as requiring AMPUTATION, if such a course of management as above directed be resorted to, and proper care and attention given, the limb may generally be saved. Amputation *ought* to be confined to those lacerations, attended with a very extensive crushing of the bones, such as result from being run over by heavy wheels, getting entangled in machinery, and the like. We have employed the term "*very extensive* crushing," since we are persuaded that the surgeon employing Homeopathic medication can save many of those useful limbs now handed over to the tender mercies of the knife. We have had the pleasure, on more than one occasion, of thus exhibiting the superiority of *curative* over *operative* surgery.

The surgeon's attention should not be confined to the palpable injury. He should make strict examination into all other parts of the system. Severe bruises, and even fractures, of other less sensitive parts may have occurred, and the patient not be aware of it, his attention being engrossed by the manifest injury.

We will take this opportunity of mentioning the "*Sweet plan of Reduction,*"—which, although originating with a man supposed to be ignorant of anatomy, is not to be despised by those who think themselves better informed.* There may have been much "humbug" in the practice of professional bone-setters; but the way to put down that and all other humbugs, is to ascertain and

* We were credibly informed that the Sweet family practice upon domestic animals, dislocating their limbs, and then reducing the dislocations.

publish, so that all may distinguish, what little truth and good may be mixed up with the trickery. Unadulterated humbug is seldom long successful.

The "Sweet plan," then, consists in first extending the limb, so as to draw it as much further *out of place* as possible, and then while the patient's attention is adroitly directed to something else, making a sudden *rotary motion*, in the course of which the limb will slip into its place,—though the operator himself may not even know exactly where that place is. This mode very frequently succeeds, when more "scientific" methods have failed;—and the end is of more importance than the means. The plan, however, may be defended on physiological as well as mechanical principles. Whatever may be thought of it, we are happy to acknowledge our indebtedness to it on several occasions. Dr. Hill was sent for in the night to an Irishman, who had fallen through a scuttle on a pile of barrels in the slaughter-house of E. Wilson, on Deer creek, in Cincinnati. He found him suffering much pain from a forward dislocation of the humerus. He immediately pulled the arm as far back and up as he could, causing the head of the bone to protrude more than before under the clavicle, and then with very slight extension, and a violent rotary movement, it snapped into its cavity. In another case, the plan succeeded equally well, where the femur had been dislocated upwards upon the dorsum of the ilium, and remained in that position for fourteen days. The patient was a daughter of Mr. Williams, of Covington.

Dr. Hunt, by the Sweet plan, succeeded, unassisted, in reducing a forward dislocation of the humerus of a stout, athletic man, that had existed for several days. The swelling and inflammation was first partially subdued by the internal administration of Arnica and Rhus. third, in alternation, and the constant application of cloths wet in cold Arnica water. The late professor Morrow likewise successfully applied this rotary principle,—in one case, when the limb had been left unreduced for a much longer time than in either of the above cases.

CHAPTER III.

PARTICULAR DISLOCATIONS—OF THE JAW, CLAVICLE, RIBS, &c.

THE general management of dislocations has been so fully dwelt upon, that in treating of those of particular joints, it will be necessary, for the most part, only to speak of the peculiar attention they may require in a mechanical point of view. Bear in mind, therefore, all through, what has been already said respecting *internal* as well as *local treatment*, so far as it is *medicinal.* We would also again impress upon the mind of the surgeon, the absolute necessity of accurate *anatomical knowledge.* It is impossible to teach surgery and anatomy in the same work, or to teach the former without presuming that the latter is already sufficiently known. In but few cases shall we step aside, to recall to the mind some facts which ought never to be absent.

DISLOCATION OF THE JAW.

This alarming, but not very serious, and even sometimes rather ludicrous, accident, may occur *spontaneously*, while the person is in the act of yawning, or very easily *from a blow* on the chin when the mouth is wide *open.* This you will readily see by recalling to mind the shape and action of the joint.

FIG. 21.

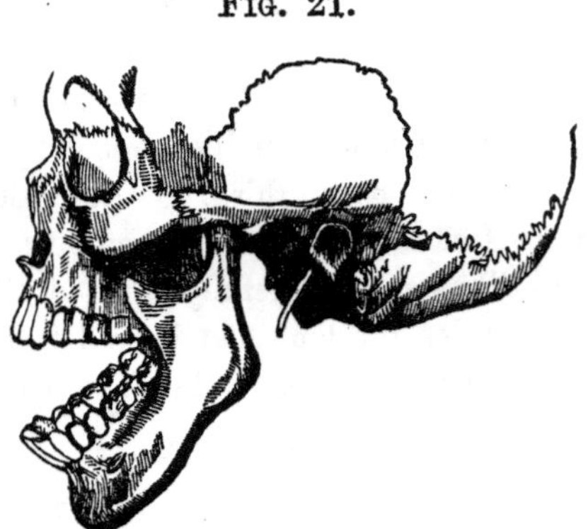

In front of the glenoid cavities, into which the condyles of the lower jaw are articulated, there is an eminence of the temporal bone which in fact forms part of the joint. It is covered with cartilage and synovial membrane, and when the mouth is open the condyle slips forward and rests upon it. When the chin is stretched forward as well as downward, the jaw rises to the summit and is on the verge of dislocation. If in this position it slips further forward, the condyle sinks into the depression anterior to the prominence described, and cannot spontaneously return (as is clearly shown in Fig. 21).

A further reason for the facility of this dislocation is found in the great variety of motion permitted by the joint. Mastication requires the lower jaw to be moved forward and backward, and transversely, in addition to upward and downward as in opening and shutting the mouth. The same muscles assist in several of these movements. The platysma myoides, digastricus and others of the neck, pull it downward. The masseter acts both in the forward, backward, and upward motion. The pterygoid muscles impart the grinding movement, and concur in the protrusion forward.

The SYMPTOMS (Fig. 22) are very obvious. The patient is in a *continuous yawn,* — only a little more so, the teeth of the lower jaw projecting beyond the upper. A very little motion is still possible in either direction, but no effort of the patient, or mere pressure on the chin, can shut the mouth. The posterior part of the cheek is sensibly *protuberant* from pressure of the coronoid process on the buccinator muscles, while behind it, just before and below the opening into the ear, there is a sensible depression. The *saliva* is running out of the mouth, there being an increased secretion from irritation of the glands. The *pain* is sometimes very severe and alarming to the patient and friends, but the accident is rarely, if ever, dangerous.

FIG. 22.

The CAUSES, besides those already noticed, may be any spasmodic action when the mouth is open, or the attempt to bite something too large. It has occurred during the attempt to extract teeth, and in yawning.

The whole TREATMENT consists in doing for the patient what

he cannot do for himself,—"shutting his mouth" for him! The slightest mechanical skill, with any knowledge of the relative position of the parts concerned, will suggest how this is to be effected. The only thing to be feared if the surgeon proceed to do this in the readiest way by manual means, is, that the patient will bite his fingers off for his pains. When the dislocated condyle is raised over the obstacle, it slips back and the mouth closes with great violence.

A very simple and effectual mode of accomplishing the object, is to place two large *corks* or pieces of soft wood, instead of your two thumbs, between the teeth, as far back as possible. Then using these as *fulcrums*, having previously had the head fixed or held by assistants, sieze the jaw and press the *chin* steadily *upward* and backward. A sudden force has sometimes succeeded, but this is not necessary nor desirable.

Other treatment is unimportant. As the accident is liable to recur, bandages or broad ribbons should be tied on, so as to keep the jaw in its place, and for awhile to allow of as little motion as possible.

When only ONE SIDE of the jaw is dislocated,—as happens by violence downward and laterally when the mouth is open,—there is a similar inability to shut the mouth, but it is not kept so widely open; and the lower incisor teeth not only project beyond the upper, but are no longer in a line or parallel with them. The reduction in this case is effected on the same principle of leverage with the jaw itself as in the former: place a cork as far back as possible and raise the chin.

PARTIAL or SUB LUXATION often occurs, the bone slipping from its inter-articular cartilage. It falls back spontaneously with a crack.

DISLOCATION OF THE CLAVICLE.

The collar bone may be separated from its attachments with those of the breast or shoulder, in the former case being pushed forward or backward, and in the latter almost always upward.

At its Sternal Extremity.

The FORWARD protrusion of the end of the clavicle that connects with the sternum is very distinct, the dislocated end rising on the upper part of that bone — (see Fig. 23*). By throwing

FIG. 23. FIG. 24.*

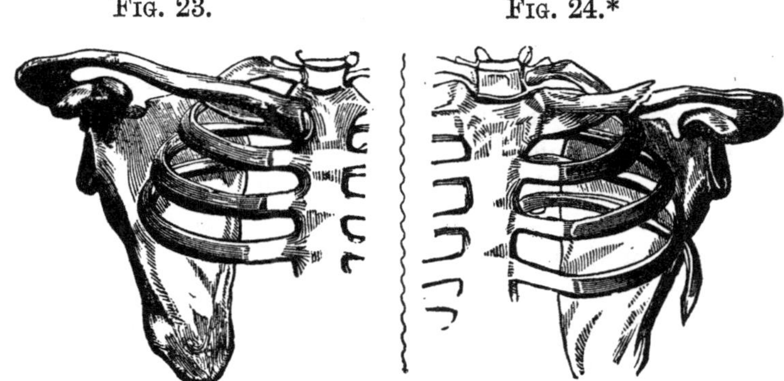

the shoulder back this elevation disappears, but returns again on releasing the shoulder: it descends when the scapular end is raised, and rises toward the neck when that end is depressed. Moving the shoulder, however, gives the patient great pain, and it is with considerable difficulty that he can move it at all. The shoulder looks somewhat flattened, especially if the patient be thin in flesh, — in which case there will be no difficulty in recognizing the nature of the injury at first view. But in very fleshy individuals the *diagnosis* is sometimes attended with considerable uncertainty. The patient complains little except when he attempts to move the shoulder.

The CAUSE of this accident is generally some force applied to the shoulder in such a way as to push the clavicle upwards and backwards, so as to press the other *end* of the clavicle *against* the sternum, but with a tendency to slip forward and *upon* it. It may happen from a fall upon the elbow, when projected from the side and forward.

This dislocation may be but PARTIAL. Some portion of the

* Fig. 24 shows, in contrast, a common form of the *fractured* clavicle.

capsular ligament may not have been ruptured, and the bone thus be prevented from rising entirely above its proper articulating position. Generally, however, when the anterior part of the ligament gives way, the rest also yields, and the dislocation is complete.

The REDUCTION is very simple. If you pull the shoulder backward, the clavicle is drawn down to a level with the sternum, the head falling necessarily into its proper place. The shoulder should be drawn outward also as far as practicable while some downward force is exerted on the clavicle. The arm is to be supported to prevent its weight affecting the direction of the clavicle.

The *keeping* of the bone *in place* is a matter requiring more consideration than the *getting* of it there. For this purpose a particular contrivance is resorted to, called the CLAVICLE BANDAGE, being in effect a sort of "stays" or corsets, buckled round the body and round the shoulders, with a pad or cushion in each axilla. [For illustration and mode of applying, see under *Fracture* of the clavicle.] The arm should be carefully adjusted in a sling, extending from the elbow to the wrist.

[The risk of *deformity* will be noticed after describing the dislocation at the shoulder.]

At the Scapular Extremity.

The clavicle is stated to be much more frequently separated from the SHOULDER than from the sternum, though much greater force would seem to be necessary to produce the result. The CAUSE is almost always a fall upon the shoulder in such a way that the scapula is pressed inwards upon the ribs, and the clavicle separated *upwards*. A very few cases have been recorded of the clavicle getting under the acromion.

SYMPTOMS.—As the scapula is partly supported by the clavicle, when that support is withdrawn it naturally descends. Hence the *shoulder* on the dislocated side is found to be *depressed* when compared with the other, and also contracted or *drawn inwards* towards the sternum. This can be accurately ascertained by *measurement* from the centre of the sternum to the point of the shoulder. On placing the finger upon the spine of the scapula and tracing it along towards the acromion process, the finger is stopped by the *projection* of the clavicle. If the shoulders are drawn back, the point of the clavicle sinks into its proper place, but as in the former case, the deformity reappears on letting go the shoulder. The pressure of the dislocated end of the bone against the integuments occasions a good deal of pain. This, as well as the rupture of the ligaments, which is necessarily considerable, soon brings on inflammation and tumefaction.

In REDUCING, the surgeon stands behind the patient, placing his knee between the shoulders, and drawing them both back until the clavicle sinks into its natural position. Cushions are then placed in each axilla, so as to raise the scapula and keep it from the side; they also serve to protect the arm-pits from irritation by the bandage. The Clavicle Bandage is then applied so as to press upon the clavicle, the scapula and the upper part of the humerus. The clavicle and scapula are thus effectually kept in their proper relative positions. The arm should be not only supported in a sling, as in the former case, but so secured as to keep it all the time pressing slightly upwards and backwards.

SLIGHT DEFORMITY almost always results from these accidents, notwithstanding the utmost skill and care of the surgeon. The adjustment and reunion can very rarely be exact; and the situation of the parts renders the defect manifest. Hence surgeons are always advised to inform the patient and his friends of the great liability, and even probability, of some change from the natural form of the part, — though no serious impediment to motion need be apprehended. We have, however, succeeded in three cases of clavicular accident in so adjusting the parts that not the least deformity could be afterwards discovered.

Two were cases of simple dislocation, the other of compound fracture, where a portion of the bone projected for an inch through the skin. The patient, in the latter case, was a large athletic man, residing in Cincinnati. The accident happened in the spring of 1844. The bone was adjusted and dressed, with the assistance of a student, in the manner hereafter to be described. In the course of a few weeks, the patient went about his business, which was that of a whip-sawyer, without the least difficulty, and it is now impossible to see on which side the accident occurred, except from a slight scar in the skin.

Of the other cases alluded to, one was a dislocation of the sternal extremity of the bone. One subject of it was a young man, — the cause, a fall from his horse. The deformity before the reduction was very great. It is now nearly five years since the occurrence, and no trace of it can be seen or felt.

The remarkably successful results in these cases were owing to some peculiarities in the applications made. In the first instance, a very thick and firm piece of leather was fitted to the part and spread with adhesive plaster. Pretty strong compression was applied over this, so fixing the muscles and integuments as to render them incapable of motion. No disturbance of the parts was permitted, nor were the compresses and bandages removed for eight or ten days. In the second case the Gum Shellac cloth was fitted and spread over the part and shoulder, by which every thing was perfectly secured. And in the third, which was that of a young child, the Gutta Percha was fitted and bound on.

DISLOCATIONS OF THE RIBS AND VERTEBRÆ

— are sometimes spoken of, but these are accidents that can scarcely happen without fracture. "Breaking the neck" or "breaking the back," then, must be really *breaking*, as well as separating the *bones*, of the spinal column. When such a separation really happens, there is seldom any use for a surgeon, — unless to tell exactly what *has been* done. Both these subjects, as also the rare occurrence of partial.

DISLOCATION OF THE PELVIC BONES

— or separation at their symphyses, — will be taken up in connection with Fracture.

CHAPTER IV.

PARTICULAR DISLOCATIONS CONTINUED — THOSE OF THE HEAD OF THE HUMERUS, OR OF THE HUMERUS FROM THE SCAPULA.

THE SHOULDER JOINT.

— from its exposed situation, the great range and variety of motion which it allows of, and the consequent shallownesss of the socket, is more liable to luxation than any other, — perhaps than all others in the body. There are to be clearly distinguished, at least *three* ways or *directions* in which the accident may be brought about. What is sometimes called the *fourth*, is only a partial dislocation.

THE HEAD OF THE HUMERUS on escaping from the glenoid cavity, may be pushed or pulled downwards, forwards, or backwards: — In the first variety, the head of the bone is found in the *axilla*, or resting under the lower side of the inferior costa of the scapula. In the second, it is thrown *forward* upon the pectoral muscles, below the middle of the clavicle, between the coracoid process and the sternum. In the third case, the head is thrown *up* to the higher and *back* part of the inferior costa, or dorsum of the scapula, where the large protuberance can be distinctly felt and seen. "The fourth" or the *partial* dislocation *upwards*, is always attended with a rupture of the capsular ligaments, the head of the bone resting against the outer side of the coracoid process of the scapula. It is difficult to conceive how this should ever happen without a fracture of the acromoin process.

DOWNWARD LUXATION — INTO THE AXILLA.

Among the SYMPTOMS, in this case, — besides the obvious one of the large hard tumor-like protuberance, which can be distinctly

FIG. 25.

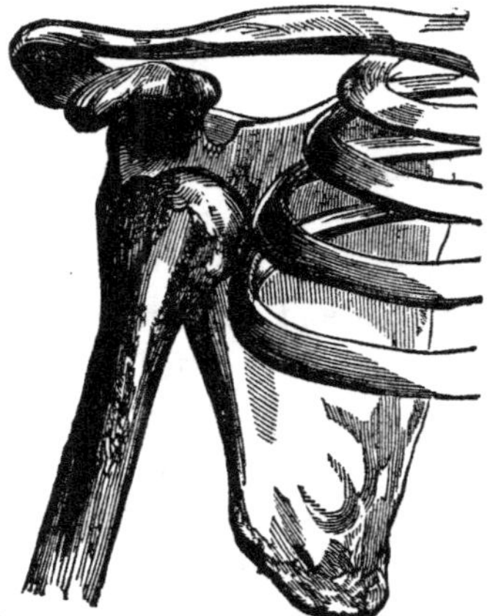

felt in the arm-pit when the arm is raised,— there is a corresponding *hollow* below the acromion process, in consequence of the passing of the head of the humerus out of the glenoid cavity — (see Fig. 25). The natural form of the shoulder is changed, the muscles being flattened, and the arm seemingly elongated. The elbow cannot without great pain be brought to the patient's side, in consequence of pressure of the head of the bone upon the axillary nerves; the patient is inclined to separate his arm from the body and support it with the other hand.

When some time has elapsed, and there is inflammation with much swelling, the bone cannot be readily felt; and to bring its head low enough down for this purpose, the arm should be raised as high as possible. The patient himself can move his arm but little; and even when others raise it for him, the movement is accomplished with difficulty and gives much pain. The patient cannot *rotate* his arm, nor can he raise it to his head, though he can move it directly backwards and forwards with considerable ease. Some patients, however, will have much more motion than others, the spasmodic force of the muscles differing much in different individuals. If the dislocation is of long standing, a *crepitus* can be heard on moving the arm. This results from the effusion of lymph into the joint, and synovial fluid into the cellular tissue; and can be readily distinguished from the *grating* sound of fracture,— which latter continues, while this *crackling* ceases, if the movement is kept up for any length of time.

Among the most definite symptoms should be noticed the *change of axis*. A central line, going lengthwise through the arm, would strike the body lower than in the natural position. In some cases the *fingers* are very much *benumbed* in consequence of the pressure of the bone upon the axillary plexus. If the arm continues out of place, the compression of the nerves and blood vessels may occasion complete paralysis and atrophy of the limb.

All the symptoms stated or alluded to, will not often be necessary to determine the nature of the accident. When, however, much time has been lost, any or all of these signs may be so obscured as to render diagnosis difficult; and it will often be necessary to first reduce the tumefaction before offering a positive opinion. In very young or fleshy persons, the exact state of the case may not be easily ascertained, even immediately after the displacement has occurred.

In REDUCING axillary luxations, the plan generally adopted by the best surgeons of the present day is this — [illustrated by the accompanying cut, Fig. 26]:— the patient is placed in a recumbent position upon the floor or a couch; and the surgeon sitting before him puts his unshod *heel* on the head of the bone in the axilla, and presses it upwards, while he pulls steadily and firmly on the arm, until the head of the bone slips into its place. By this rough-looking management he is generally able to effect his object without assistance. If not, more force may be applied to the arm by means of bandages and straps, which may be lengthened to any extent and placed in the hands of assistants standing behind the principal operator,— he being thus able to direct or deflect the extension, while his heel is still kept firmly pressed against the head of the bone.

FIG. 26.

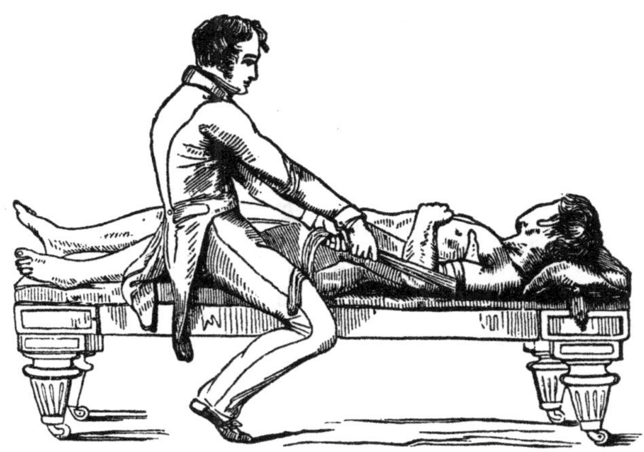

These means are commonly sufficient, and may always be tried in the first instance. If they fail resort must be had to others, by which still

— GREATER FORCE can be brought to bear. Place the patient in a chair (as represented in Fig. 27), and secure the scapula by *counter-extending bandages*, so applied as to let the arm pass through them. These bandages round the shoulder may be made of any strap or girth, buckled or sewed on. They are to be fixed

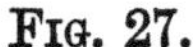

Fig. 27.

behind and somewhat above the patient. The counter-extending apparatus *may* be fixed round the body under the arms, though this does not secure the scapula as when it is closely fixed about the affected shoulder itself.

For the extension, a wetted *roller* should be placed round the arm just above the elbow, so that it cannot slip, with straps or slips of cloth attached. The arm is then to be raised to a right angle with the body, or it would be still better to raise the elbow above the horizontal line with the shoulder, so that the deltoid and spinatus muscles may be more completely relaxed. With the arm in this position, let two or more assistants make extension upon it, a sufficient force being at the same time exerted in the opposite direction upon the scapula bandage. The force must be gradually applied and steadily kept up; for if any jerking occur, alternately relaxing and extending the parts, nothing will be gained but much injury inflicted. When the strain has been kept up for a short time, the surgeon, having his foot resting on the patient's chair or some other convenient support, pushes his *knee* into the *axilla* (see Fig. 28) and presses up the head of the bone, while at the same time he presses down with one hand on the acromion. The reduction may sometimes be much facilitated by making slight rotation upon the arm. In this, as in other cases, it should be remembered that much depends upon the state of the patient's mind. If, while extension is being made, his attention can be diverted from the operation, though but for a moment, much trouble and suffering may be saved.

In cases of very long standing, more force, or a longer continuance of the strain, may be required than could be safely trusted to assistants. The object, it must be borne in mind, is to weary out the contracted muscles; and this would be defeated if the assistants themselves should become weary and let go. Machinery can therefore be used with much advantage [as was represented in both the figures last given, Nos. 26 and 27].

When *pulleys* are made use of, as they may be, both for extension and counter-extension, they must be securely fixed to rings or staples; and the surgeon should begin the extension himself, giving the pulley into the hand of an assistant as soon as he thinks it time to direct the head of the bone.

In RECENT CASES, the arm may frequently be restored to its place *without* any *extension*, or any considerable exertion of force. Seat the patient who has just met with the accident in a chair; spread out the dislocated arm as far as possible from the side; insert your knee into the axilla [in the same manner as represented in Fig. 28, where, however, the pulley and counter-extending bandage are also represented, as they may be used, if necessary], your foot being fixed on a chair for the purpose, and the heel raised, so as to press the knee upward; grasp the humerus just above the elbow with your hand, pressing down at the same time upon the shoulder. If the little knowledge requisite for this simple procedure were generally diffused, a great deal of unnecessary suffering would be prevented, and the usefulness of many an arm restored which is now lost to society. Why should not all intelligent or educated men be surgeons enough for this and other simple operations, that *become difficult* only because people have to wait till professional skill can be called in?

Dr. HILL once succeeded in reducing an arm by this *unassisted means* which had remained some time out of place and resisted other attempts. The parts had become extremely tender, and the contraction and resistance of the muscles were also very great.

Fig. 28.

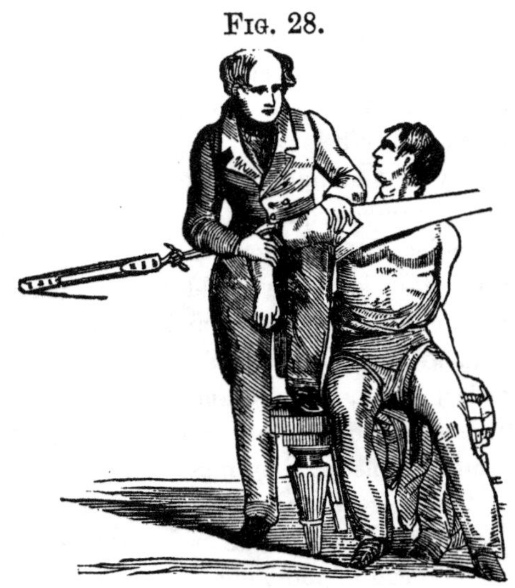

The patient was a drunkard, though sober at the time; and as he obstinately refused to take other medicine for the purpose of bringing about relaxation, — he gave him a pint of whiskey at once, and soon had him "dead drunk."* In that state, he proceeded to the reduction, and soon effected it, without the least difficulty, or the patient giving any sign of pain. On visiting him the next day, he succeeded in a still better operation, — cured him of a worse disease: he persuaded him "to sign the pledge," which he has faithfully kept.

FORWARD LUXATION — UNDER THE CLAVICLE.

The SYMPTOMS of this accident are very distinct. The *head* of the humerus can be plainly felt, and generally seen, upon the pectoral muscle, just below the clavicle. — The point of the *acromoin process* is very distinct, the hollow beneath it being considerable. The coracoid process of the scapula is on the outside of

* This was before the day of ether and chloroform, which may now be used in such a case with many advantages.

the displaced head, — which can be observed to move when the arm is rotated. The *elbow* is thrown further back than in the former case, and still separated from the side. The *arm* is also much shortened, with its axis pointing inward towards the middle of the clavicle. There is great difficulty in moving the arm in any direction, in consequence of the resistance of the muscles, and by the obstruction of the clavicle above, and the coracoid process of the scapula behind. The *pain*, however, is not so great as when the dislocation is in the axilla, pressing upon the nerves.

FIG. 29.

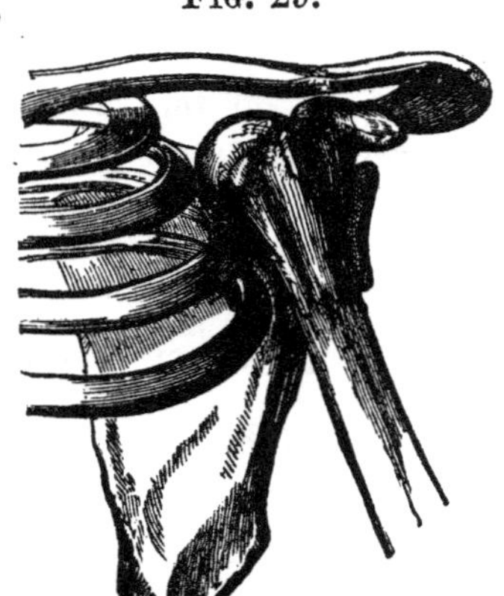

The CAUSE is usually a fall upon the elbow when it is thrown behind the central line of the body, so that the force comes from behind and inwards.

The REDUCTION can generally be effected in a manner similar to that of the former cases. The operator's heel, however (if it is made use of), must here be brought further forward, while the patient's arm is to be drawn obliquely downwards and slightly backwards. But, if much delay has occurred, the case may require steady and continued extension by assistants or suitable mechanical means.

For the *extension* and counter-extension, such bandages and apparatus may be directed as before described. The arm, however, must be so raised as to relax the biceps muscle; and the force applied in a downward and backward direction, instead of horizontal, to prevent the head of the bone being brought against the coracoid process of the scapula. It may be necessary to keep up extension much longer, as the resistance is much greater than in axillary dislocation. When the head of the bone is observed to move, is the time for the surgeon to place his knee or heel against it, and press it backwards into the glenoid cavity. This pressure directly on the head of the humerus can do no good until it has been drawn below the level of the coracoid process.

After the reduction, the arm should be fixed by proper bandages, and hung in a sling, so that no motion be allowed the shoulder joint for some time. Very little force may at first renew the difficulty.

[For *cases* of this variety of dislocation, reduced by the rotary or "Sweet plan," see the conclusion of the Chapter on Dislocation in General.]

BACKWARD LUXATION — UPON THE DORSUM OF THE SCAPULA.

The *projection* of the head of the humerus in this position, can be noticed at *first sight;* and when the elbow is rotated, it is seen to move. It may also be *felt* by applying the finger just below the spine of the scapula. (See plate.) The *motion* of the arm, although not so much affected as in the former case, is greatly impaired. The change in the *axis* of the limb will be obvious.

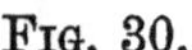

FIG. 30.

This variety of displacement is very rare. But two cases are said to have occurred in thirty-eight years at Guy's Hospital, in the very centre of London.

The REDUCTION is described as being easy. The shoulder is fixed, and gradual extension made directly outwards, the head of the bone being moved slowly forwards into its place. It has been reduced by simply raising the arm, and turning the hand to the back of the head.

PARTIAL DISLOCATIONS

— of the humerus are to be treated on the same principles as the complete. The nature of the injury and the distinct varieties, are not so obvious, but the difficulty of replacement proportionably less. Bandages, to prevent recurrences, are as necessary after partial as complete dislocation.

CHAPTER V.

PARTICULAR DISLOCATIONS CONTINUED — THOSE AT THE ELBOW AND WRIST, AND OF THE THUMB, FINGERS, AND TOES.

OF THE ELBOW JOINT.

Without a minute knowledge of the anatomy and mechanism of this joint, — of the ligaments and tendons connected with it, as well as of the bones and muscles, — no practitioner can be safely trusted in any injury of so complex a part. As the elbow is very much "in the way" of accidents, this is equivalent to saying that every practitioner of medicine ought to know all about it. If he does not, he will often commit serious oversights and blunders, exposing himself to censure and to prosecution for mal-practice, — though this *last* danger is not so great as it ought to be. Hence the frequency of mismanaged or neglected cases.

There may be no less than *five* very distinct species of dislocation at the elbow, besides complications with fracture, &c., to be noticed hereafter. *Both bones* of the fore-arm may be pushed from their attachments with the humerus at the same time, either *backwards* or to one *side*. The *radius* only is susceptible of being displaced *forwards*. The *ulna* may slip *back* over the condyle of the humerus, without the radius; or the radius on its side without the ulna, though this last case is not, properly speaking, a dislocation *of* the elbow joint, but only of a connected bone *at* the joint.

OF BOTH RADIUS AND ULNA BACKWARDS.

This accident, though attended with only a partial loss of *motion*, produces a complete change in the *appearance* of the joint — (as seen in Fig. 31). The posterior projection of the elbow is very prominent. The olecranon process is above the external condyle, instead of being on a level with it, as it should be when the arm is extended. A deep hollow may be felt on each side of it; while in front, under the tendons, the condyles appear like hard tumors. The hand and fore-arm are in a supine position and cannot be entirely turned. Spontaneous rotation of the hand is almost wholly lost.

FIG. 31.

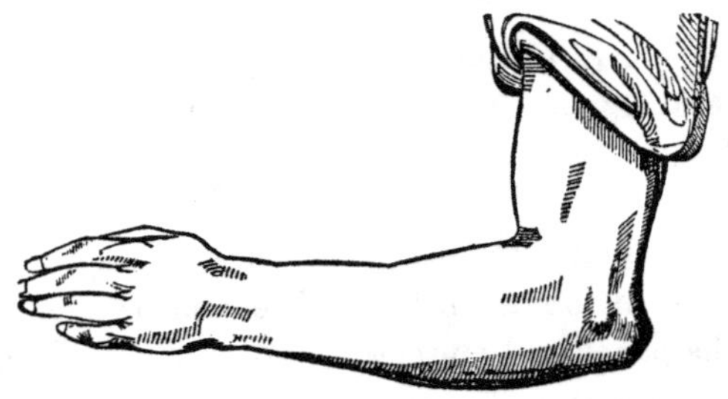

The occurrence is almost always brought about by the individual stretching out his hand to save himself in a *fall*, the pressure coming on it *before* the fore-arm is entirely extended. Thus the whole weight of the body, increased by the height fallen through, is brought to bear on the joint, behind the axis of the humerus.

The REDUCTION is easily effected. The surgeon places his knee on the inner side of the elbow or at "the bend of the arm," pressing most on the dislocated bones so as to keep them from bearing on the end of the humerus, and to separate the coronoid process out of the posterior fossa of the humerus and allow it to pass over the condyles — (a glance at Fig. 32 will give the reason for this direction). Considerable *force* must be used in *bending*

FIG. 32.

the arm while the knee is strongly pressed upon it. This force should be applied slowly and steadily, however, the proper direction being given to the bones as it proceeds. It is frequently desirable to divert the patient's attention, while this flexion and extension are being made.

This dislocation may often be remedied a *long* time *after* its occurrence, in which case you should premise proper applications, such as warm fomentations and emollients, before proceeding to the operation.

After having accomplished the reduction, you should have the joint kept wet with cold water, with Arn., &c., and the arm suspended in a bent* position in a sling. It is still better to put on a splint, which effectually secures the joint. It should not, however, be kept bent too long, — though the danger from this is more to your own reputation than your patient's limb. Dr. Hill once had a case where for fear of reproducing the dislocation, required his patient, a boy of twelve years, to keep his arm in the sling for several weeks. When he took it out the joint was stiff, and he was severely censured for having, as the parents supposed, failed to properly "fix the joint," — though the real fault was in *fixing* it too long. A few days' attempt at motion, with a suitable lotion, restored the proper use of the arm.

LATERAL DISLOCATION OF BOTH BONES.

This mode of displacement, whether *outward* or *inward*, is a modification of the last, the bones being also driven more or less *backwards*.

Fig. 33.

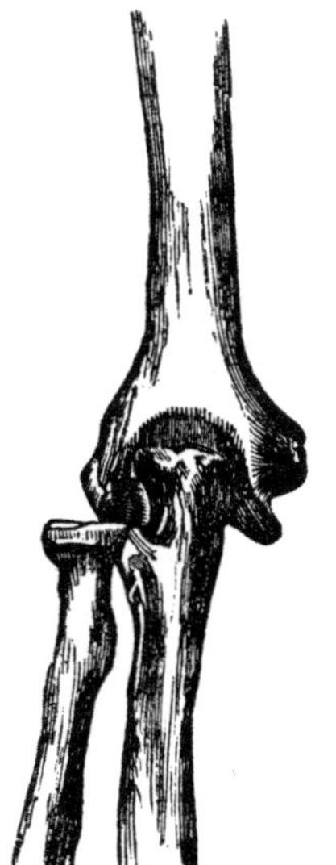

The CAUSE is generally the same as in the last case, the force being directed more to one or the other side.

The SYMPTOMS are still better marked. When the dislocation is *outward* and backward (as in Fig. 33), the projection of the ulna is much greater than when it is only backward. The coronoid process, instead of sinking into the posterior fossa of the humerus, is fixed at the external condyle, and the flat head of the radius forms a projection behind and outside the elbow, with an abrupt cavity above it. Its turning can be distinctly felt on pronating or supinating the hand.

In the *inward* and backward luxation

* See Dislocation in general.

(represented by Fig. 34), the head of the ulna is thrown behind or over the internal condyle, and projects in that direction, while the external condyle is made equally prominent on its side, by the radius leaving its place and occupying that of the ulna, its head resting on the articulating surface or posterior fossa.

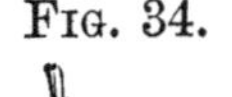

Fig. 34.

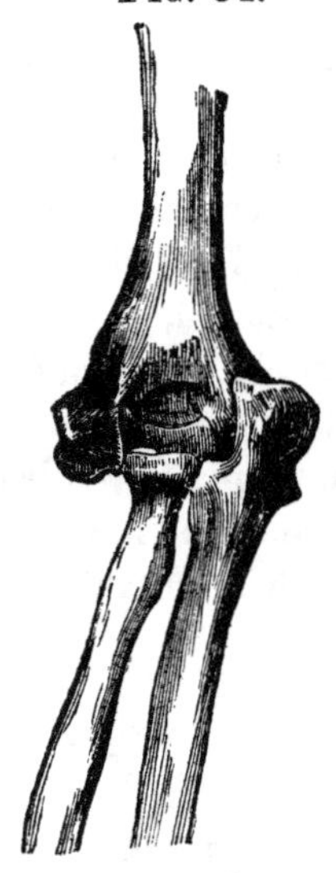

The REDUCTION of these cases is accomplished in the same manner as directed for the simply backward luxation, — to wit: the bending of the arm over the surgeon's knee. Little or no difference of management is required in either case. The operation may even be simpler than the one referred to. There is not the same reason for first separating the bones from the humerus, as when the coronoid process is fixed in its posterior fossa. The tendons of the biceps flexor and the brachialis internus, moreover, being stretched over the end of the humerus, tend to force it back into its natural situation, as soon as the arm is straightened in spite of them. Sir Astley Cooper thus speaks of a case he treated by mere extension — "Finding that the tendons of the biceps and (as I knew) of the brachialis internus, were put upon the stretch, I thought I might make use of them to draw the os humeri backwards, as by the string of a pulley, and I forcibly extended the arm, — when the dislocation was immediately reduced."*

OF THE ULNA BACKWARDS.

The olecranon can be clearly felt behind the humerus. The arm can be neither straightened, nor flexed to more than a right angle. The distinguishing mark of the case is a backward projection of the ulna, together with a twisting inwards of the forearm and hand.

The same mode of REDUCTION may be directed as in the other

* Cooper on Dislocations and Fractures, p. 389.

cases. It is generally more easily accomplished. The *bending* of the arm is here the essential part of the operation, as the fixed radius then acts like a lever to push the humerus back into its place on the ulna.

OF THE RADIUS FORWARDS.

The fore-arm is found more or less bent, but it is suddenly stopped, on attempting to flex it further, *before* it gets to a right angle, the elevated head of the radius bearing against the fore part of the humerus (see Fig. 35). In this place it may be felt

Fig. 35.

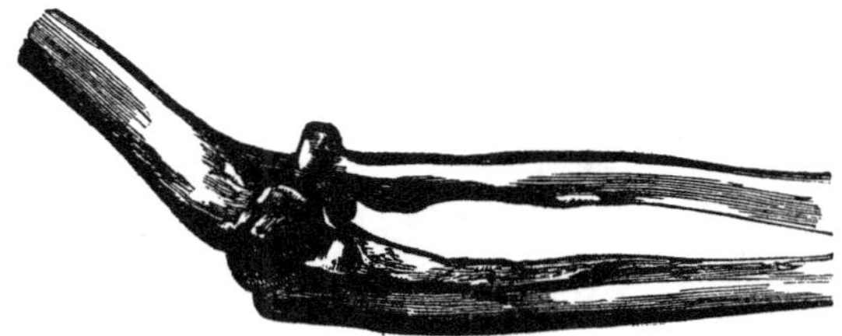

moving, if a finger be pressed into the "bend of the arm" when the hand is rotated. The patient himself is unable to effect this movement to any considerable extent, the hand being kept pronated.

The REDUCTION of this accident would seem to be difficult, if we might judge by the number of unreduced cases, and the neglect were not rather to be attributed to failure of diagnosis, which is still more inexcusable.

Let the surgeon, seizing the patient's hand by one of his, as in "shaking hands," or by the thumb and fore and middle fingers, make steady extension, while his other hand is pressed strongly upon the ulnar side of the head of the radius, pushing it both outwards and downwards. The arm had better be slightly bent, so that the muscles may be relaxed. As the pronator teres tends to draw the bone towards the ulna, force applied between the bones so as to separate them, and at first slightly *raise* the radius, may perhaps aid your operation.

OF THE RADIUS BACKWARDS.

The head of the radius may be both seen and felt behind the external condyle of the humerus (see plate No. 36). The arm is nearly straight and cannot be flexed; the hand pronate and cannot be turned. The surface in front of the joint is relaxed and presents a sudden depression just below the external condyle. If the *front* of the radius be traced from below upwards, the finger will come in contact with the condyle; and if the *side* be traced, the finger will pass over the head on to the olecranon process.

FIG. 36.

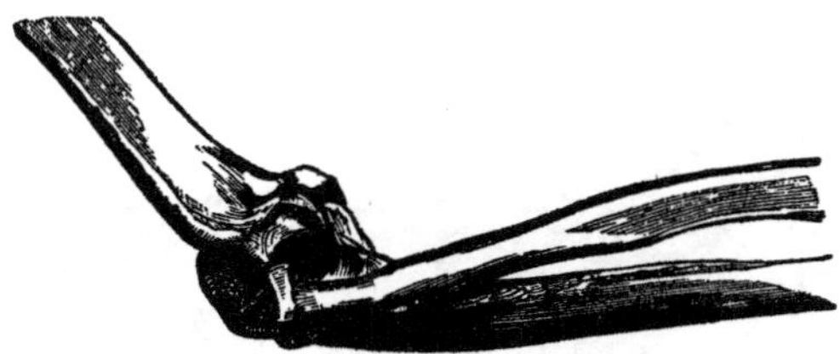

The REDUCTION, if attempted early, is not generally very difficult; but these cases are frequently neglected so long that any attempt to reduce will be fruitless, or result in more injury than benefit to the patient. *Extension* is to be made upon the radius, with counter-extension upon the humerus, while firm pressure is made on the head of the bone until it slips into its place. One assistant can pull upon the hand, while another holds the upper arm, and the surgeon directs the movement of the bone.

LUXATIONS AT THE WRIST, JOINTS OF THE HAND, &c.

THE WRIST JOINT is liable to several displacements. *Both* radius and ulna may be dislocated together, either *forwards* or *backwards*, or each of them may be separately displaced in either direction, — thus making *six varieties* of luxation. First,

OF BOTH BONES FORWARDS: — The projection of the bones of the arm *under* the carpus or forwards, happens from falling upon the *palm* of the hand, the ends of the radius and ulna bearing with great force against the annular ligament, while unprotected by the carpal bones, they being bent backwards. On the contrary, the displacement

— at the BACK OF THE WRIST takes place when a person falls on the *back* of the hand, so that the arm bones may be similarly thrust *over* the carpus, while the carpal bones are thrown forward and upward under the flexor tendons, in front of the fore-arm.

The distinctive SYMPTOMS are indicated in this account of the nature of the accidents. In the former case there will be a manifest protuberance on the *front* of the wrist, with a somewhat similar

FIG. 37.

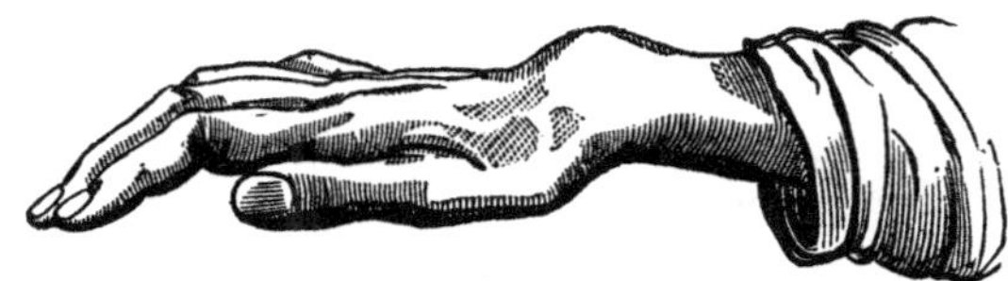

but *smaller* one at the back of the wrist, produced by the carpel bones. The hand is bent back out of the line of the fore-arm. In the latter case, —the luxation *backwards* or to the back of the wrist (represented by Fig. 37), —the symptoms are exactly reversed. There being projections both behind and before in either case, can never occasion their being confounded. The direction of the edges or ends of the projections, as well as of the hand, will immediately show the nature of the case.

Strains of the wrist, produced by falls and other violence, may occasionally simulate dislocation. They may be *distinguished* by the fact of the questionable symptoms coming on gradually, and not showing themselves immediately after the accident, as in actual dislocation. There will also be more flexibility of the hand; nor will the swellings be likely to imitate accurately the separated extremities of the arm and carpal bones.

The REDUCTION is similar in both cases. The surgeon takes hold of the patient's hand in one of his, while the fore-arm is supported by his other hand. An assistant meanwhile holds the arm at the elbow, keeping that joint slightly flexed. As soon as sufficient force is applied in the different directions, the natural action of the muscles throws the bones into their proper place.

As soon as the reduction is effected, compresses should be placed upon the wrist and secured by a roller, the part being kept constantly wet with cold dilution of Arnica water, &c.* The roller should enclose the whole hand, commencing from the end of the fingers and be continued, moderately tight, up to the elbow. A splint should afterwards be added, and the fore-arm suspended in a sling.

These accidents are very *painful* and liable to much swelling, if means are not instituted to prevent it; but uniform and pretty tight bandaging will generally do this, if applied early in connection with the cold water and internal medication. If the parts, nevertheless, become very painful, they should be fomented with warm water, and resort be had to Aconite, Rhus, Ruta, to prevent inflammation.

SEPARATE DISLOCATIONS AT THE WRIST.

Of the Radius alone (the ulna adhering by its ligamentous attachment): — the external or *thumb side* of the hand is twisted backwards and the opposite side inwards or forwards. The extremity of the radius may be felt and generally seen also, forming a prominence in the front of the wrist, its styloid process being removed from its station opposite the trapezium. The same treatment is required for reduction and dressing as in the *complete* dislocation, that is, displacement of both bones together.

The ulna alone is oftener dislocated, or rather detached from the carpus (it forming no part of the wrist *joint*) than the radius alone. The accident is always accompanied with *rupture of the ligament.* The ulna generally projects at the back of the hand. The hand is twisted. The bone may be easily pressed down from where it appears on the back of the wrist, but will not stay in place. When the pressure is taken off, the deformity is renewed, the muscles drawing it up, the ligaments that should keep it down being torn away.

The accident is always to be *ascertained* by the projection of the ulna above a level with the cuneiform bone, and the change in

* See Dislocation in General.

the position of its styloid process, which is thrown out of its proper line with the metacarpal bone of the little finger.

To accomplish the REDUCTION, all that is required to be done is simply to place the ulna down in its proper cavity at the side of the radius, and retain it there by suitable compresses and splints. The latter should extend along the fore-arm in a line with the back of the hand. They should be well padded and then secured by a roller.

OF THE CARPEL AND METACARPEL BONES.

Luxations between these bones are accidents of very rare occurrence. They are easily ascertained when there is no tumefaction, by the bones rising on one side or the other. Any bone so rising can be easily pressed down again and secured, the hand being extended when the pressure is applied. Proper compresses and bandages are then to be kept on until all danger of recurrence has disappeared.

DISLOCATION OF THE FINGERS AND TOES.

FIG. 38.

This accident may be brought about by various causes, — at any of the phalangeal joints, — and in either direction; the smaller bone being pushed over or under the larger, constituting what are distinguished as the *posterior* (Fig. 38) and the *anterior* (Fig. 39) dislocations.

FIG. 39.

The SYMPTOMS need not be described. The nature of the case will be plain at the very first sight. There will sometimes be very great rupture of the ligaments, while at others very slight injury may be done.

In REDUCING a dislocated finger or toe, let the operator place his thumb at one of the divided extremities, and his finger at the other, *then* make extension (as he is represented doing, without the former expedient in the cut, Fig. 40), while the joint is gently flexed; and the parts will very easily regain their proper place, unless

FIG. 40.

considerable time has elapsed since the occurrence of the accident. In such a case, *extension* has to be kept up for some time, and should be perseveringly attempted before the case is abandoned. For this purpose, where much force has to be used and kept up for a long time, a piece of *tape* should be fixed to the finger by the "clove-hitch" (Fig. 41), and the extending force applied to this.

FIG. 41.

Toes are more difficult of adjustment than fingers, owing to their shortness and their joints being less palpable. The dislocation is sometimes brought about by the contraction of the tendons.

DISLOCATION OF THE THUMB.

This is rather a rare occurrence, but deserves separate mention, from the *difficulty* of REDUCTION, occasioned by its strong ligaments and muscles. The deformity and inconvenience resulting from the accident will be a sufficient diagnosis. To reduce it, frequently requires very great extending force. This can be best applied by means of strong tape fixed round the thumb (by the preceding clove-hitch), this being pulled upon while the divided extremity is pushed towards and into its place, in the same manner as directed for a finger or toe, though there is often so much tenderness that the main dependence must be upon the extension by the tape *roller*. During the operation, the thumb is to be flexed or bent towards the palm of the hand, so as to relax the flexor muscles. Care should always be taken to well bandage the thumb with other wet tape, before fixing on that to which the force is to be applied.

CHAPTER VI.

DISLOCATIONS OF THE LOWER EXTREMITIES.

OF THE FEMUR AT THE HIP JOINT.

THIS important JOINT, though well secured by cartilage and

FIG. 42.

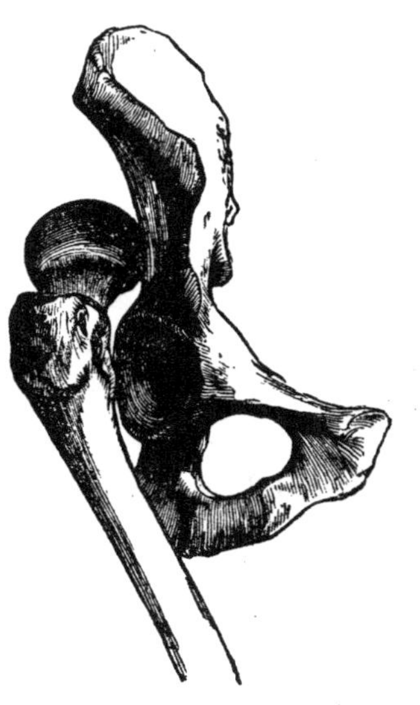

FIG. 43.

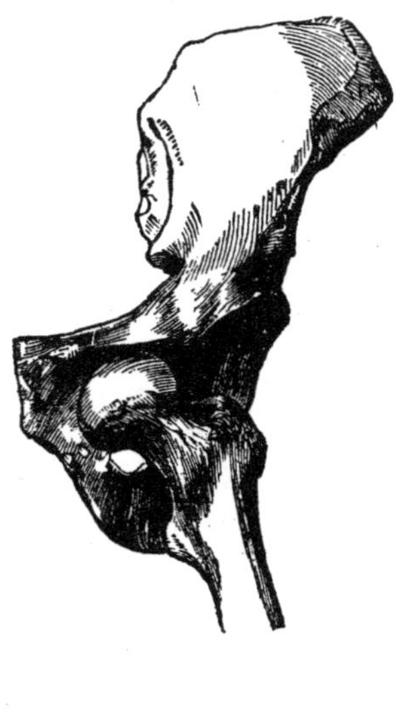

ligament, particularly the cotaloid ligament, which greatly deepens the acetabulum, is subject to too much violence not to be occasionally dislocated. The thigh bone being inserted into it obliquely, requires the more study to understand its mechanism and derangements.

Four distinct dislocations require to be noticed. The head of the femur may be thrown, 1st, *upwards* on the Dorsum of the Ilium (Fig. 42); 2d, *downwards* into the Foramen Ovale (Fig. 43); 3d, *backwards* into the Ischiatic Notch (Fig. 44); 4th, *forwards* and upwards upon the pubes (Fig. 45).

FIG. 44. FIG. 45.

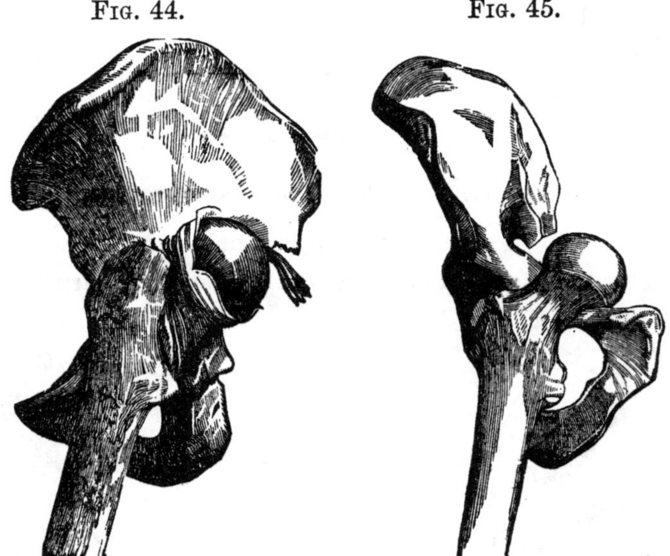

UPWARD DISLOCATION — *on the Dorsum of the Ilium,*

— that where the femur rests on the concave *side* of the pelvis, — is by far the most common, being the necessary result of sufficient violence in an outward and upward direction.

SYMPTOMS. — The limb is from an inch and a half to two inches and a half shorter than its fellow, — from which it cannot be separated, the knee being advanced towards the opposite one, though not reaching it. In plainer language, the knee and foot are both "turned in," the toes resting on the other foot (as seen in the illustrative Fig. 46 — compare also Fig. 42). The thigh can be bent over the opposite one. The round head of the bone can be felt moving upon the ilium, when the knee is rotated, at least if there is not much swelling, or the patient is not very fleshy. The affected "hip" or side of the pelvis is much less evenly rounded than natural, and the trochanter major is nearer the superior *anterior* spinous process of the ilium.

Fracture of the *neck* of the thigh bone, which may be confounded with this accident, rarely occurs except in very *old persons;* and in that case, though the leg is shortened, it can be easily extended, contracting again when the force is withdrawn: the knee also is generally turned *out* instead of *in*.

Fig. 46.

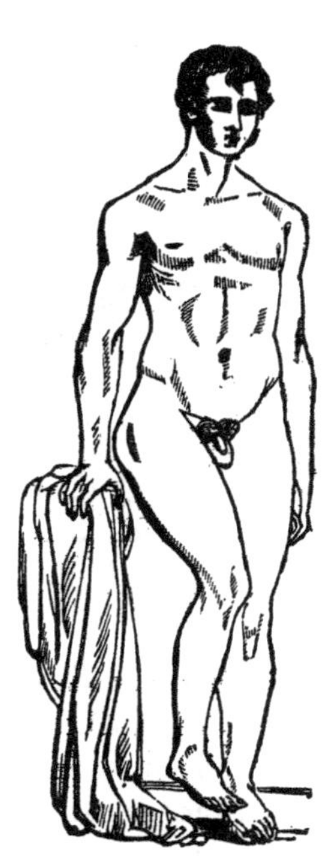

Previous to REDUCTION, it will generally be necessary to produce some *relaxation* of the muscles, in this as in all other dislocations of the hip, and in some cases this must be carried as far as the patient's safety will permit. Repeated doses of some nauseant will effect the object, and as good a one as any is an acetous Tr. of Lobelia, c. p., once in ten minutes. Ether or chloroform may be used. The same or even a stronger preparation of lobelia may be used as an injection. The warm bath may be also resorted to with advantage. The most complete insensibility and relaxation may be produced by the use of ether or chloroform. When the relaxation is deemed sufficient, wrap the patient up, so as not to allow him to get chilly, and proceed to the

— OPERATION, by laying the patient on a table, or placing a board, covered with a quilt or blanket, under him, on the bed. Pass a strong *counter-extending* strap between his legs. A sheet split in two, and folded so as to be about four or five inches wide, will answer the purpose. This should be so placed as to press upwards on the perineum, at the inside of the dislocated limb, passing up before and behind his hip (as represented in the accompanying plate, Fig. 47, and explained by Fig. 42). Fix the two ends of this strap or bandage to some unyielding point, a post, staple in the wall, or the like. Then apply round the leg, just above the knee, a wet bandage. Give it eight or ten turns, fixing by its means your *straps for extension.* These are to be drawn upon by assistants, or what is generally safer and better, to be attached to a pulley, so stationed that the force may bear in the direct line of the limb, with the fastening of the counter-extension. This consideration must be kept in mind when the surgeon or assistant comes to pull on the straps or cord of the pulleys, so that the limb be extended in the direction of its longest axis, and the head of the femur forced directly towards the acetabulum.

FIG. 47.

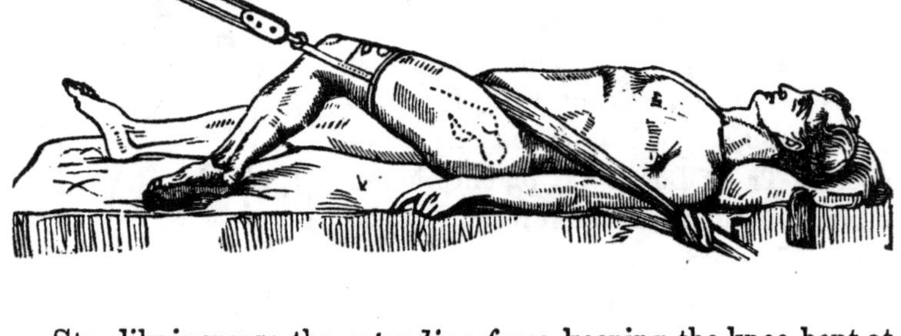

Steadily increase the *extending force*, keeping the knee bent at right angles, until the patient complain, then *hold* for a few moments, without letting back a hair's breadth, until he gets easier. Increase the tension again as far as it can be borne, and so continue, stopping and resuming, until the head of the bone has reached the edge of its socket. At this point, the surgeon intrusting the extension wholly to his assistants, *directs* the movement, rotating the limb a little inwards, and sometimes it is necessary, by means of a towel passing under the upper portion of the thigh, to elevate the head of the bone over the edge of the acetabulum, as it sometimes catches against it. When counter-extension is made by manual force, it can be heard to *snap* as it slips in, but with the more gradual and steady extension of the pulleys this sign is not always to be noticed.

Unless this snapping of the joint is plainly heard, the extending force should not be withdrawn, till the surgeon is fully satisfied that all is right and safe. This he can only be sure of by actual measurement. If reduction has been effected, it will be found that each trochanter major is equi-distant from the superior spinous process, and every other fixed point of its respective side, the length of the limbs being also equal.

To guard against a spontaneous RECURRENCE, apply a compress over the reduced hip, and bandages around the pelvis, so as to prevent all motion as far as possible for several days.

Some *inflammation* and symptomatic *fever* are not unlikely to ensue, when much force has been used and the muscles much bruised or tendons strained. As, in fact, this is always more or less the case, keep the hip and any other injured parts constantly wet with cold dilution of Arnica Tr., and give him Arnica, &c., internally as directed in the general treatment of dislocations. Frequently use the tepid sponge bath. Let him rest perfectly quiet, until all danger is past. Generally, from two to three weeks' confinement will be sufficient. Even then, before he is allowed to use the limb again, passive motion should be practiced several times a day for a few days.

DOWNWARD DISLOCATION — *into the Foramen Ovale.*

In this case, the head of the bone can generally be felt, in thin persons, by examining the inside of the thigh. The trochanter is less prominent than on the sound side. The *leg* is about two inches *longer* than natural. The *body* is *bent* forward from tension of the psoas and iliacus muscles; or, if the patient stand erect, the *knee* will project in advance of its fellow, but is kept wide *apart* from it by the action of the glutei and pyriformis muscles. The *foot* is thus separated from the other, but is neither turned in nor out. Below Poupart's ligament, a *hollow* may be noticed — [compare Figures 48 and 43.]

The REDUCTION is much easier than in upward dislocation. Place the patient on his back, separate the thighs, and fix a girth or folded cloth over the perineum, as directed for counter-

Fig. 48.

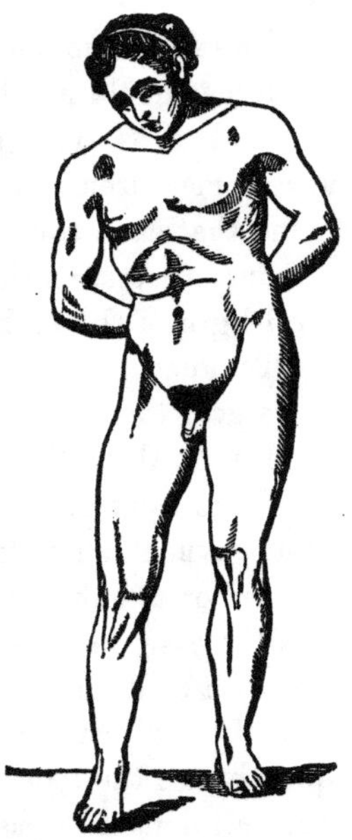

extension in the former case, — so that when the two ends are drawn upon, the force will bear against the inner and posterior surface of the bone — that is, *from* the foramen and *towards* the acetabulum. Pass another strong girth or band transversely around the pelvis, above the acetabulum, the front end passing over the former strap (so as to give to it a more upward direction). This cross or counter-extension is to be made as before from a post, staple, or other fixed point. Force is now to be applied by pulleys (or otherwise) to the first strap; and, as the head of the femur begins to rise, let the surgeon pass his hand under the opposite leg, and, seizing the ankle of the affected one, bring it gently but firmly towards the other. This movement in connection with the pressure at the other end of the limb, will bring it into its proper place.

Fig. 49.

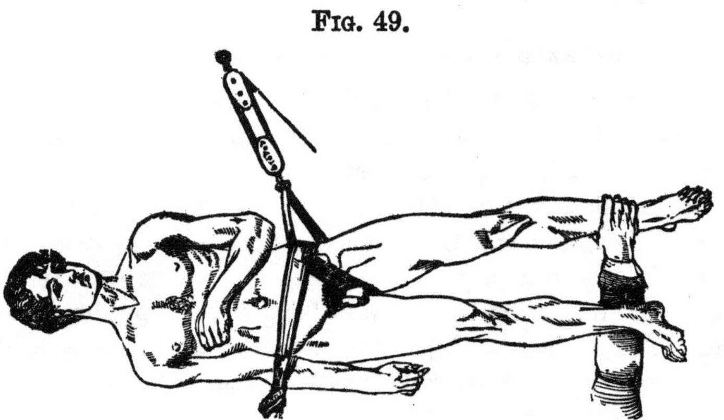

BACKWARD DISLOCATION — *into the Ischiatic Notch.*

In this case, the head of the femur being deeply lodged, can rarely be felt. The position of the *trochanter*, — though it is not turned down, flattening the hip, as in the upward dislocation, — being further back than natural, will indicate the mal-position of the *head* — (Figures 50 and 44). The displacement of the trochanter may be accurately ascertained by measuring, on each side, from the spinous processes of the sacrum. The foot and knee turn inwards, the knee being also a little flexed and advanced forwards, the heel raised, and the ball of the great-toe resting on the base of the other great-toe. The limb is shortened, but not more than from half an inch to an inch. The limb cannot be further flexed or straightened, nor rotated, without much force and pain.

Fig. 50.

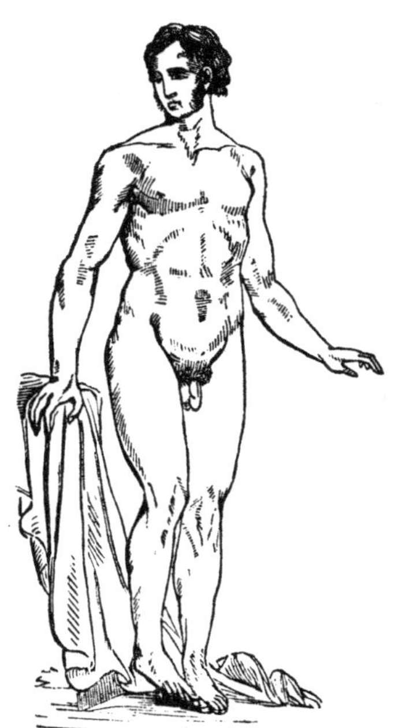

This variety of dislocation is the most *difficult* of all to REDUCE. The patient should be placed upon a table or board, as directed for the first form of dislocation, but on his sound side instead of his back, with the affected thigh drawn over the middle of the other. Use the same means for extension and counter-extension as in that case, with the addition of a towel or strap round the upper part

Fig. 51.

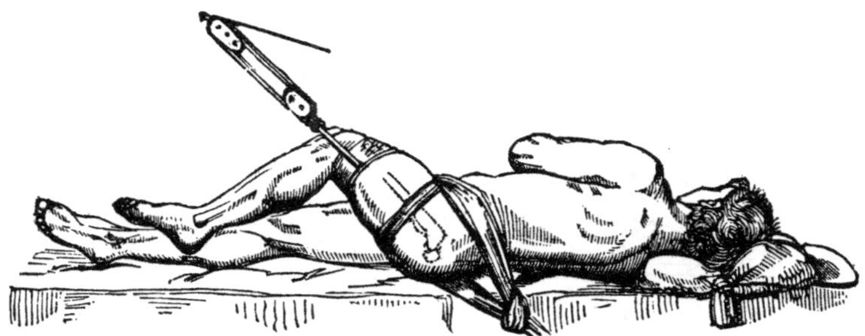

of the thigh (and carried over the shoulders of an assistant), to raise the head, at the very commencement of the operation, out of the notch, or to impart a lifting direction to the extending force. The surgeon should also press the trochanter forwards with his hand.

Fig. 52.

After reduction, secure with bandages, as in other cases.

FORWARD AND UPWARD DISLOCATIONS — *onto the Pubes.*

The head of the bone, in this case, is easily discovered in front and a little above the level of Poupart's Ligament (Figures 52 and 45). This circumstance distinguishes the case from fracture of the cervix, in which accident, as well as here, the *limb* is *shortened* and the foot and knee *everted.* The shortening of the dislocated limb may be from one to one and a half inches. The foot and knee cannot be rotated inwards, but the thigh can be flexed, bringing them forwards. In REDUCING, place the patient on his sound side, and fix the counter-extending force somewhat in front of a line with the body, the point of *extension* being as much behind.

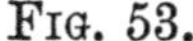

Fig. 53.

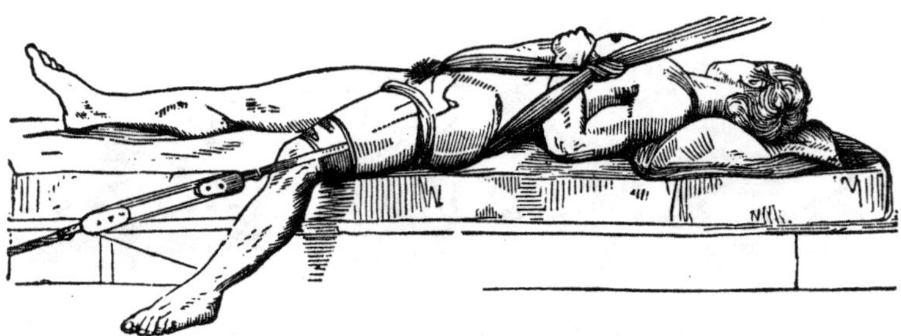

This arrangement of forces will draw the limb *backwards* as well as downwards. Use the *lifting bandage* as the operation proceeds, the assistant pressing down on the pelvis as he raises the head of the bone over the pubes and edge of the acetabulum. When the operation is complete, secure every thing as before directed.

[These dislocations of the hip may, any of them, be occasionally reduced by the rotary plan, mentioned under the head of general directions for reduction. A case where the femer had remained two weeks upon the dorsum of the ilium is there alluded to. Almost every day, during that time, other means had been tried. The object was effected very easily by raising the heel as far as possible towards the abdomen, across the other thigh, and keeping it there for a minute or two; and then, while the patient's attention was directed another way, a sudden circular motion was given to the limb, and the heel brought down again to its natural position, when the bone snapped into its place and all was right.]

DISLOCATIONS AT THE KNEE.

THE PATELLA.

— may be displaced *outwards*, *inwards*, or *upwards*.

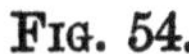

FIG. 54.

Of the LATERAL DISLOCATIONS the *outward* (Fig. 54) is far more common than the inward. In either case, the knee is partially flexed and the joint immovable, the patient complaining of a "sickening" pain in it. In *reducing*, place the patient in a recumbent posture, and raise the limb by the heel, thus taking off the tension of the extensor muscles. Then press *down* the *edge* of the patella most distant from the joint. This will raise the ridge on the posterior *surface* so as to let it pass over the condyle, when it will be naturally drawn to its place by the action of the vasti and rectus muscles.

The UPWARD DISLOCATION, with RUPTURE

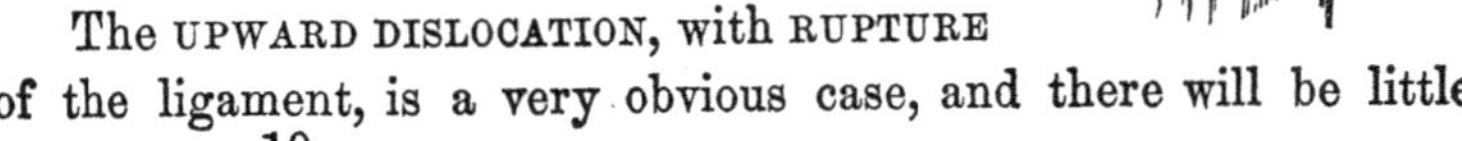

of the ligament, is a very obvious case, and there will be little

10

more difficulty in the *reduction* than in the diagnosis. The difficulty is in keeping it reduced. Special precautions, also, must be taken against inflammation: give Arnica and Rhus, &c., as directed in general treatment of dislocations. But among the best as well as the *handiest* means for *keeping down* both the inflammation and (what is the peculiar object of treatment in the case), *the patella*, at the same time, is the application of a *roller* to the *whole leg* from the toes to the groin. This will restrain vascular excitement, and directly keep the loose parts in proper position, and to a great extent paralyze the muscles of the thigh, that would otherwise be sufficient to overcome all retaining force that could be conveniently applied. The roller should be kept wet with dilute Tr. Arnica.

A very ingenious recent invention for keeping the patella in place, after dislocation or fracture, will be described, with a plate to illustrate, in connection with the subject of FRACTURES.

OF THE TIBIA AT THE KNEE.

This bone may be separated from the femur in four ways, *forwards*, *backwards*, or to *either side*.

The LATERAL displacements are only *partial*, one condyle resting on the head of the bone where the other should be, and that

FIG. 55. FIG. 56.

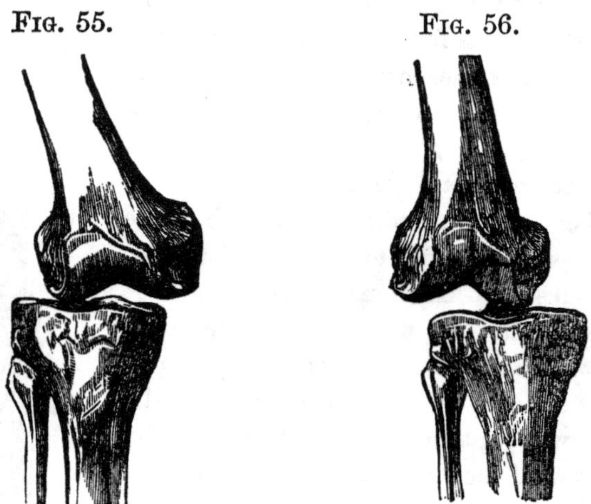

other projecting to one or other side, external, or internal, as the case may be, — a part of the head of the tibia forming another tumor on the opposite side (see Figures 55 and 56).

In the FORWARD dislocation (see Figure 57), the head of the tibia is distinctly seen and felt above the front of the condyles, while these are perceived in the popliteal space. There is such pressure on the nerves and the popliteal artery as to stop the pulsations of the anterior tibial artery, and to cause more or less numbness of the foot.

FIG. 57. FIG. 58.

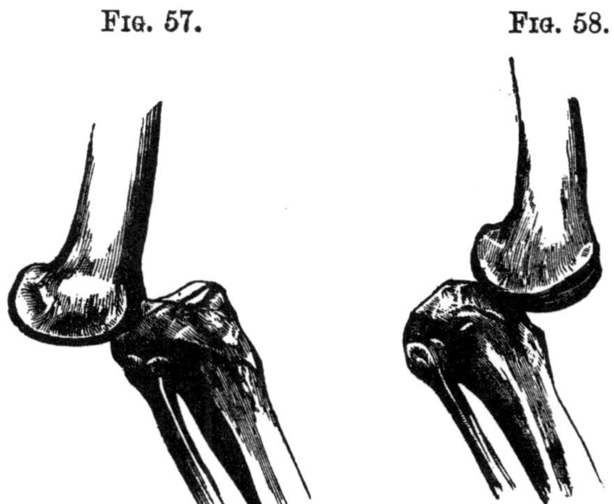

In the BACKWARD luxation (Fig. 58) the limb is slightly bent and sensibly shortened. The condyles project, causing a depression of the ligamentum patellæ; and the *bend* of the limb is, of course, *backward* instead of forward, the *foot* being drawn forwards.

REDUCTION is mainly accomplished in all these cases by simple extension. The pelvis is fixed and the force applied by means of a bandage round the ankle. In most cases the patient can sit in a chair, while you place your own *knee* under *his*. Press also upon the separated head of the bone with your *hands*, while your assistant pulls *suddenly* but forcibly upon the *ankle*. Thus the force of the muscles is counteracted and the limb flexed at the same time. In this manner we have several times succeeded in a few seconds. The success of the manœuvre depends on first raising the heel, as in dislocation of the patella, and then, while the patient's attention is attracted to some other object, quickly extending and flexing the limb *into place.*

OF THE FOOT.

DISLOCATION AT THE ANKLE

— may occur in various directions, *outward*, *inward*, *forward*, and (very rarely) *backward*. There are generally complications.

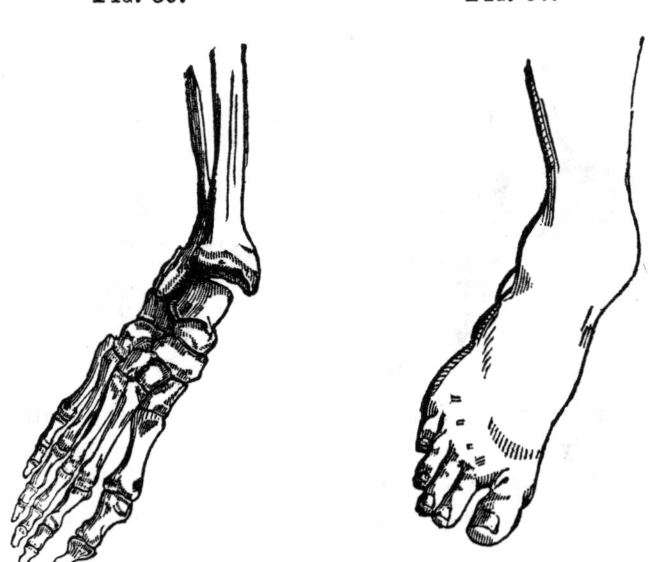

FIG. 59. FIG. 60.

The DISLOCATION INWARDS is the most common. A tumor is caused by the internal malleolus pressing so firmly against the skin as almost to burst through (see Fig. 60). The foot is turned out, but the joint is still movable. The fibula (as here represented — Fig. 59) is almost always *fractured* about three inches above the ankle, where a depression may be felt.

To REDUCE, let an assistant take hold of the foot by the heel and toes, *flexing the leg* to a right angle with the thigh, and — while the thigh is held fast by another assistant just above the knee — make extension at the ankle, the surgeon at the same time pushing the end of the tibia back to its place. There fix it with splints and bandages, and keep it wet with cold dilution of Arnica Tr., to subdue or prevent inflammation.

The OUTWARD dislocation is easily distinguished by corresponding deformity on its side, and other similar symptoms to those of the last case. It is to be *reduced* in a similar manner and *dressed* with great care to avoid excessive inflammation, as the joint is generally much injured. The violence is great: The internal malleolus is frequently, and the astragalus occasionally, fractured.

FIG. 61.

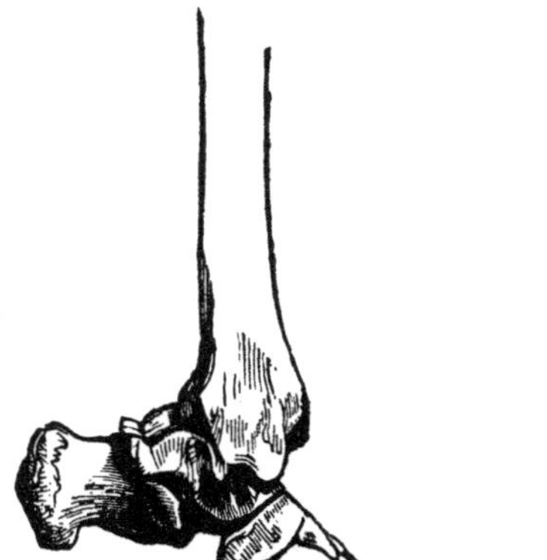

In the dislocation FORWARDS the foot appears shortened and the heel elongated. The toes point downwards, and the foot is immovably fixed in that position, where it is kept by the extremity of the tibia, — which can be felt pressing on the top of the foot or instep, while there is a great depression beneath the Tendo Achillis. *Reduction* and subsequent *Treatment* are the same as in the former cases.

In *all cases* of dislocated ankle, much pain is suffered, and swelling will soon occur. To keep down inflammation, much may be done by *good* and early *bandaging*. A roller should be firmly and (with the aid of compresses) *equably* applied over the whole foot, beginning at the ends of the toes and continuing considerably above the affected joint, even to the knee. Cooling lotions can be applied through the roller.

It should be borne in mind also by the physician, and impressed on the minds of patients, that it may be several weeks or even months, before the foot can be freely used. As soon, however, as the soreness has sufficiently subsided, some *passive* motion should be used to prevent stiffness of the joint. The foot may be regularly flexed and extended several times a day. No weight must be borne upon the foot until thus prepared for it. Where this precaution has been neglected, much inconvenience has often resulted. See remarks on the general directions for the reduction and treatment.

DISLOCATION OF THE TARSUS AND METATARSUS.

When the os calcis, astragalus or other bones of the foot are dislocated, the nature of the case needs no description. *Reduction* can be effected by extension of the foot, in connection with directly pressing the bones into their proper places. They require compresses and bandages to keep them there, and the proper treatment to keep down the inflammation.

DISLOCATION OF THE TOES

—was taken up in connection with that of the FINGERS. The symptoms are very similar in both, and the same principles are applicable for reduction.

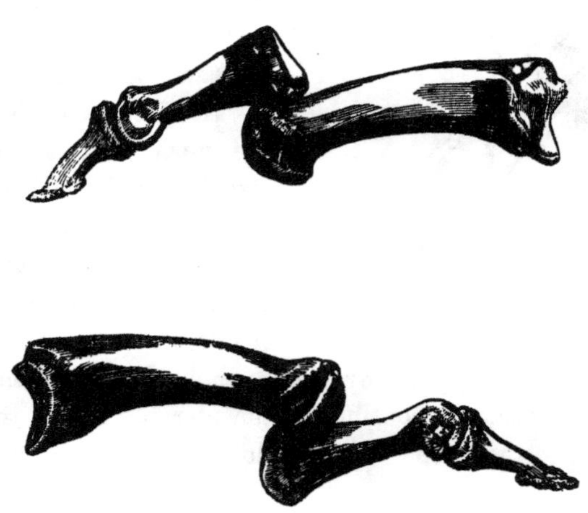

CHAPTER VII.

OF FRACTURE IN GENERAL.

Before entering upon the subject of fractures, we would call attention for a moment to the mechanical means and appliances, — splints, bandages, &c., that will be needed in the treatment of these cases.

There has been a good deal of this sort of apparatus invented, to facilitate the surgeon's object. Some of these inventions, particularly some recent ones, are very convenient. We shall not describe the use of any of them, as they all explain themselves, or have the necessary directions accompanying them. Others still better are no doubt yet to be invented.

Inasmuch, however, as many of them are too expensive for the physician, with a limited surgical practice, to be expected to keep; and as therefore few practitioners, especially in the country, will have access to them when the occasions for using them occur, — we deem it our duty to give such directions respecting splints and all other necessary means, as will enable the country practitioner to furnish himself at the right time with all that is requisite. And we would here remark that, in all cases and all places, the true surgeon will exercise his own ingenuity and judgment, and adapt his mechanical appliances, no less than his medical treatment, to the exigencies of the case before him, regardless of any particular directions or models presented by his teachers or authors. All that the teacher can do, is to communicate such general principles, with such examples by way of illustration, as will prepare the student both to *think* and act aright. With a general knowledge of what is necessary, and a particular knowledge of much that has been done, the practitioner is left free to devise or adopt any plan that may appear to his judgment best, — whether really an improvement on what others have done, or only the best that can be under the circumstances. No lecturer or writer pretends to anticipate all the peculiarities and exigencies of actual practice. Among the illustrations, if we ought not rather say, among the *principles*, with which the student should be familiar, is the proper use of the BANDAGE. Hence some directions on that subject have been given in detail (see chapter on ulcers).

SPLINTS may always be made of thin pine or poplar boards, and then wrapped with cotton cloth when the occasion calls for them, though as manufactured ones are very cheap, the surgeon should always have some on hand of different sorts and sizes, properly covered and ready for use. Still he may not have such as will suit every case. Gutta Percha makes an admirable splint as it can be moulded to any shape desired by being softened in hot water, and very soon becomes hard and firm as board. We would recommend a trial of it.

As a general rule, the simplest apparatus is the most effectual,. — such as the surgeon's own good sense will suggest, at the moment it is wanted.

The violence which CAUSES fracture must be a force applied to some point in the *body* of the bone while its extremities are fixed, or to the *extremities* while the *fixed* point is intermediate. The fixed as well as the moving *force* equally concurs in the effect. Thus the contraction of the muscles acting on the bone often contributes to its fracture, and is sometimes sufficient to produce it without any extraneous force. When what is considered "*the* cause," that is the *moving* force is applied at or near the extremities, the bone generally breaks near the middle; but in other cases at the point on which the force is brought to bear.

LIABILITY to this accident depends much on the age, general health, and constitution of the patient. The imperfectly ossified frame-work of children will often bend rather than break. In old persons, on the other hand, the earthy matter predominates and their bones are quite brittle. Some persons have this brittleness throughout life, and are constantly getting some bone or other broken by accidents that would have no effect on others. In these cases, also, the mending process is often as difficult as the breaking is easy. Some diseased conditions render the bones very brittle, even in young or middle aged persons.

The mode of union between the broken parts is the following. Soon after the accident, coagulable lymph and fibrin, as well as blood, are thrown out by the vessels connected with the parts, and the loose bones become, as it were, slightly glued together, as they may happen to lie in proximity. After a while a "*provisional cartilage*" is formed round the parts, like a capsule, and firmly supports them. This gradually hardens into "the provisional *callus*," — a bone-like ring round the fractured parts, holding them together even more firmly than they were before the accident, — though the proper substance of the bone has not yet become whole again. The ossific process goes on, for from five to twelve months, according to age and constitution, and when it is complete the supporting ring or provisional callus disappears. The provisional union, however, by means of the extraneous deposit, may be regarded as the completion of the reparative process, as far as the surgeon is practically concerned.

The PERIOD, after which it will be *too late* to adjust a fractured bone with the expectation of having it united with the ordinary attentions and appliances, varies much in different cases. It will depend much on the particular *bone* concerned, as well as on the *age* and constitutional habits of the individual patient. The inferior maxillary, for instance, will begin to unite about the *sixth* or *seventh day*, or even earlier in very young subjects, and the provisional union be often completed by the end of *three weeks;* while in very old persons it may be much longer before the process begins, and its progress also will then be much slower. The periods are about the same for the ribs and other bones liberally supplied with arterial blood. In bones but moderately furnished with arteries, and more distant from the source of circulation, as those of the extremities, the *provisional union* may be regarded as commencing, in the earlier period of life, some time between the *eighth* and *tenth day* after the accident, and as being completed in a period of about *five* or *six weeks.* In patients past the meridian of life, the process may be in operation by the twelfth day, but will go on but feebly at first, and is not to be deemed complete or *secure* under from *two* to *four months.*

It may therefore be often "too late" to set or re-set a fractured bone a fortnight after the occurrence of the accident, and in the case of some bones in very young and healthy patients, the lapse of a single week may render any fresh derangement questionable. Simple adjustment and the ordinary dressings will be insufficient in any case that has been neglected till after the period for provisional union to begin.

Hence it is always best, when practicable, to ADJUST a fracture *immediately* after the accident, and to *examine* it again about the *sixth* or *seventh day*, to see that all is right, — after which nothing more is necessary than to keep it so. For this purpose great care must be exercised till after the *tenth* or *twelfth day*, or for *two* or *three weeks*, in old persons. From that time forward there is not so much danger from slight motion.

The *evidence* that this provisional ossification has actually commenced, is an extraordinary sensation of itching and prickling in the part, — which, however, is not necessarily attended with any great or preternatural determination of blood to the part. Any sensible degree of inflammation, it should be remembered, is not essential to the reparative process.

In very young persons, and in some particular bones, the provisional union has commenced in two or three days. In very old persons, and those of feeble and faulty constitutions, it is sometimes a difficult matter to bring about any union. In these cases what is called a FALSE OR UNNATURAL JOINT often occurs. The cause of this, however, is generally the want of proper coaptation.

When *union* does *not* take place after the parts are properly brought together, we are directed to *rub* the fractured *ends* against each other, so as to produce irritation and the supposed necessary inflammation, keeping them afterwards at rest and in contact, that the inflammatory action may become adhesive. If it be a leg or thigh, the part may be supported by strong splints and the patient allowed to walk a little, or rest the weight of his body on it, so as to produce the desired amount of irritation by *pressure*. When the uniting process commences, however, perfect rest of the part must be enjoined. It may even be necessary to cut down and *saw off* the fractured ends that refuse to unite, and bring the *fresh surfaces* into contact.

If, however, you give proper attention to the case in the early stage, no trouble of this kind need be apprehended, — unless in very old and unhealthy persons. Even in these "hard cases," it is probable that the bones would unite, if they were rightly adjusted and kept together, and the patient properly treated and *nourished.* The old and absurd practice of starving patients under the mistaken and most mischievous notion that a reasonable quantity of good palatable food favored the development of inflammation — and that "spare diet," i. e., *starvation* would prevent that "bugbear of the profession," — has done incalculable mischief. The case under consideration is but a single example. This *starving* and *blood-letting,* — this letting out and stopping off *life,* to ward off the *chance* of death, — belong to the same category of ancient absurdities, or one-sided views and exaggerations, still practiced by the great mass of the profession from mere force of habit, — the *vis inertiæ* of mind, — though at the manifest expense of life and limbs.

A FRACTURE is said to be "transverse" when the bone is broken directly across, "longitudinal" when split lengthwise, and "oblique" when in neither of these directions.

CASES of Fracture are DIVIDED into simple and compound, complicated and comminuted.

A SIMPLE FRACTURE is when a bone is broken at one point (or it may even be at more than one place, but —) without extensive laceration of the soft parts, or at all events, without any connected *external* wound.

A COMPOUND FRACTURE implies, — not only a laceration of the soft parts by the fractured ends of bone, or by the instrument with which the force was communicated, so that there must be always more or less "solution of the continuity" of the surrounding parts, but that some portion of the broken bone protrudes *through the integuments.*

A COMPLICATED FRACTURE is distinguished from a "compound" as occurring in connection with the dislocation of a joint, the rupture of some large vessels or ligaments, with a gun-shot wound, or with some condition of the system which impedes the ordinary process of ossification, or renders the ordinary appliances insufficient.

A COMMINUTED FRACTURE is, in more idiomatic phrase, when the bone is "broken to pieces," or very much shattered, — when there are several fractures so near together that the bone is much divided or splintered.

A *simple fracture* is generally attended with but little *danger:* all the others with considerable. The amount of danger depends as much on the age and constitution of the patient as on the nature or *name* of the injury. A simple fracture is more serious in one patient, than the most complicated or comminuted one in another. Any fracture on the person of one whose blood is kept in an inflammatory condition by daily potions of spirituous or malt liquors is attended with danger.

Hence the necessity for AMPUTATION, in any given case, must be decided very much by the discretion or experience of the attending surgeon. Only general rules for aiding his decision, but no precise directions, can be furnished him.

Amputation *may* be requisite if large vessels or nerves are lacerated, tendons ruptured, the bone much shattered, the knee or some other joint irreparably injured; or even if the laceration of the soft parts be so considerable as to lead to extensive mortification and sloughing. The general strength of the patient, as well as the chance or probability of sufficient restorative power, must be considered. Of these and other circumstances, the practitioner must be his own judge at the decisive moment. (See AMPUTATION, Chap. 12.)

If the surgeon is called immediately upon the occurrence of the accident, he should see to the proper removal of the patient to some suitable place for the adjustment of the fracture. This should not be done by the arms of the assistants, but he should be carefully placed upon any convenient litter and thus removed, otherwise a simple fracture may become compound or complicated, and what would have been a case without danger, rendered by injury to nerves, blood-vessels, or by laceration of the soft parts a very dangerous one.

At the same time, the surgeon should consider the circumstances under which the fracture happened, and give, if necessary, the appropriate remedies for the moral symptoms. Thus, if they were of such a character as to frighten the patient, much *opium* should be administered, or if syncope is present, aconite, &c. If it is a case of

SIMPLE FRACTURE,

— the next thing to be attended to is the proper coaptation of the fractured bone, and retaining it in its natural position by the application of splints and bandages. This with an abstemious diet and keeping the limb at rest and wet with cool water would be all that is absolutely necessary for simple fracture upon a healthy person. But very few are truly healthy — many are scrofulous — the vital powers of a host are impaired by the use of spirituous or malt liquors, age, long subjection to the impure air of cities, improper sensual gratification and a multitude of other causes. Many have an irritable temperament in whom the slightest local injury is followed by very great constitutional irritation. Hence even in simple fracture (much more in compound, complicated, or comminuted) there is danger of *irritative* secondary, or symptomatic fever (any fever from a local injury), rising and preventing a favorable termination of the case.

To prevent the rise, or to control it after it has arisen, becomes therefore an important duty of the surgeon.

All classes of allopathists employ the same means to control this, the result of mechanical injury, that they use in other fevers and inflammation, ignorant that any remedy possesses a specific adaptation to *this* form of fever. It would be reasonable to suppose that they who claim to be the "scientifics" and to pay such attention to the causes of disease, would see the inconsistency of such a course of treatment. Blood-letting, topical remedies, purgatives, and sudorifics are the usual means relied upon. Some discard blood-letting and rely upon the others — we, however, reject all, with the exception of topical applications, and employ those remedies that have a specific relation to the *cause*. Our medical treatment is therefore simple, and *efficacious* as simple, because in accordance with God's law. We are thus enabled not only to prevent the rise of much irritative fever, or control it after it has arisen, but to hasten the reunion of the fractured bone which is not attempted to be done by others.

We would therefore recommend in all cases that after carefully adjusting the fracture, splints and bandages should be applied, and occasional doses of *Arnica*, 3d dil., should be given for a day or two, and to facilitate the coaptation of the fractured bone and prevent the rise of irritative fever, the limb should be kept *constantly* wet with cool arnicated water — after which the *arnica* should be alternated with *Symphytum Offic.*, except the fracture implicates the ankle or wrists, when *Ruta* should be alternated instead. Advantage may be derived from occasionally adding the *Tr. of Symphytum* or *Ruta* in place of the *Tr. of Arnica* to the water applied to the limb. This treatment will not only enable you to discharge your patients sooner than those treated by other surgeons, but will enable you to succeed in many cases of fracture which, under other treatment, would result in the formation of a false joint. For the first day or two we prefer to repeat the remedies at intervals of from three to five hours. In those cases where the surgeon is not called until there is a high degree of inflammation, repeated doses of *Aconite*, either alone or in alternation with *Arnica*, should be given until the inflammation is partially subdued, and at the same time the limb should be frequently subjected to the influence of hot vapor from a decoction of arnica flowers, Hops, Hypericum perforatum, or Cynoglossum offic., and in the intervals a fomentation of the same should be applied. But as soon as the *irritative* fever is subdued, treat as first directed. In some cases it is impossible to adjust the fracture before the reduction of the inflammation.

COMPOUND FRACTURES,

— says a distinguished author, "demand all the art of the highest class of surgery, whether relating to their local or to their constitutional management — in compound fractures the present symptoms are severe, and are yet more so in prospect. Local inflammation, extensive suppuration, and possibly gangrene are accompanied by the various forms of severe traumatic fever, assuming the characters of hectic and typhus. In severe cases the constitutional forces are reduced to the lowest ebb, the powers of life are exhausted, and under circumstances of peculiar difficulty the question of amputation is often raised." Such a gloomy picture or so sad a result is not often presented under judicious Homeopathic surgery.

They are to be treated the same as simple ones, so far as regards the "setting" and "fixing" of the divided bones; but the bandages and other apparatus must be so arranged as to enable you to dress the wound, without the risk of subsequent displacement. If called early, adjust the fracture as soon as possible, and bring the edges of the wound together and retain them if possible in complete juxtaposition by strips of adhesive plaster. Keep the wound *constantly* moist and completely shielded from the atmosphere by cloths wet in cold arnicated water. In other respects treat as directed for simple fracture. If the wound heals by the first intention no other treatment is required. But if not treat as for *lacerated wounds.*

If an artery is wounded and the bleeding cannot be arrested by means of cold or styptics, it should be tied before setting the limb.

COMMINUTED FRACTURES

— have to be treated in a similar manner to "compound." If there be *spiculæ* of bone, already separate or loosened, as often happens, remove them with your fingers or forceps, but use no *force.* Unless they come away easily let them remain. If *matter* form and there be no rupture of the surface, puncture and let it off.

When bones are separated from their connections with other bones, as well as broken, — constituting one variety of "COMPLICATED FRACTURE," — or it may be also, a

COMPOUND DISLOCATION,

— in which event as in the simple laceration, strictly so called, — the luxation if it is possible is to be first reduced, and the case then treated as one of "Compound Fracture," — with this difference, that Rhus. Tox. should be occasionally used, and *special care* should be taken to *prevent suppuration.* Use cooling lotions, but *not* emollients. If, however, the inflammation has already gone so far, that suppuration or worse is inevitable, then resort to fomentations and poultices.

SUPPURATION *must be encouraged* as a means of avoiding tetanus and gangrene. The sad consequences of suppuration, described in the books, are by no means inevitable. With the proper local and general treatment, no particular danger to life need be incurred. When the activity of the inflammation has subsided, should the discharge of pus continue profuse, it may be checked and adhesion favored by a few applications of some strong vegetable astringent, such as the Oak-bark, the Geranium, the Rock brake (Pteris atropurpurea), or the Epiphegus virginianus or Marsh rosemary. A wash of some of these articles, with the aid of judicious compression, will soon remove all danger from suppuration. When it is not possible to reduce the dislocation first, which is indeed generally the case, reduce the fracture as though unaccompanied with dislocation; and when the bone is united, attempt the reduction of the dislocation. In five or six weeks union of the fractured bone will probably be so that the dislocation may be reduced. (For other treatment, see WOUNDS and *General Directions for Dislocations.*)

AMPUTATION may have to be resorted to in these cases, though it will be rarely necessary under judicious and efficient medication. When, however, the suppuration is extensive, though the limb as well as life may be saved,

ANCHYLOSIS

— is very apt to follow. This subject might be properly taken up in this place, as it is a result of mechanical injury to a joint, as well as of spontaneous disease. The subject has, however, been anticipated in both these aspects. We mentioned the precautions necessary to be used to prevent this accident, in connection with Scrofulous Diseases of the Joints. Any injury of the joint likely to involve this result will, of course, have to be treated accordingly, bearing in mind the peculiar liabilities and future uses of the part.

The *age*, *habits*, and *general state of health* of the patient with fracture must be carefully considered, in prescribing his diet. If he is robust and of full habit it should be low and unstimulating, but if the vital powers are enfeebled it should be more nutritious. A full supply of pure air is very important — also frequent sponge baths — should the patient be compelled to use the limb before the union of the fractured bones is perfectly firm, the application of a *starched bandage* will afford great support. It should be applied when wet and the limb not moved until it has become dry and firm.

If a fractured bone fails to unite by ossification or callus, and remains loose, a "false joint,"

PSEUDARTHROSIS,

— is formed, the limb being nearly useless. It may occur from a fracture of any of the bones, but is most frequent in the arm and thigh. It may be occasioned by a too early use of the bone, by some fault in the constitution preventing the formation of callus or the deposit of ossific matter, or from a neglect of bringing the fractured ends properly in contact. Whatever may have prevented the union, the result is the same.

The extremities of the bones become smooth and round, and are covered with a kind of ligamentous capsule. In some cases a regular ball and socket joint is formed, so that the ends turn upon each other.

If the patient be old and feeble, little hope of effecting union can be entertained after the lapse of twelve months. In such persons the greatest care should be exercised in keeping the fractured ends in contact, and perfectly free from motion for at least one year after the fracture, unless union takes place sooner. If, however, union is not effected in that time, the patient may be allowed to use the limb. This experiment of using the limb after the lapse of three or four months, or *rubbing* the fragments together for the purpose of promoting callosity, has proved successful.

The *safer* plan in all cases is to keep the parts in juxtaposition by splints and bandages, and give the remedies as before directed *from eight to twelve months*, at least, before any motion is allowed to be made. *Cold bathing* over the whole body, with pure air and nourishing diet, and freedom from mental anxiety, will do much to aid in the cure.

But if you are called to a case *after* the unnatural joint has become established, some more direct measures will be requisite. There are two modes of remedy in use among surgeons. One is, to cut down to the bone, *saw off* the fractured *ends* and place them together firmly, closing the wound and allowing it to heal by the first intention — the limb to be supported by splints, &c., until union is effected. This is successful in some cases, but it is a formidable as well as difficult operation, and has been followed by violent symptoms, and even the death of the patient.

It is said that the *seaton* has been quite successful, though it, like other means, occasionally fails. In performing this operation, the surgeon uses a long seaton needle armed with a skein of silk. The limb is extended by assistants or machinery so as to separate the extremities as much as possible. The surgeon passes the armed needle directly through the limb, from side to side, between the ends of the bones, being careful to avoid large arteries, veins, and nerves. Lint and small compresses are placed over the holes, and the splints and roller applied to support the limb in a proper position. The seaton should be allowed to remain until union is complete. This may take *five* or *six* months, and even in some cases *twelve months.* It is directed to be continued for the latter period, unless union occurs sooner; since cases are recorded in which consolidation of the parts took place after remaining disunited, in spite of the seaton, for a year or more. It might be questioned whether the seaton was of any benefit? The general health of the patient should be attended to: if impaired, every possible means for its perfect restoration should be employed, and all causes calculated to impair it, scrupulously avoided. The accident rarely occurs where there is not some *general* debilitating cause in operation.

CHAPTER VIII.

PARTICULAR FRACTURES OF THE HEAD AND TRUNK.

FRACTURES OF THE CRANIUM

— seldom occur without injury to the brain or its appendages. The danger, therefore, depends not upon the fracture of the bone itself, but the degree of injury to the brain.

The skull-bone may be merely *cracked* in a straight line through one or both plates; or it may be *crushed,* the fractures extending in different directions from a central point. When the outer table only is crushed, it may be depressed into the diploe, or porous space between the two plates.

The SYMPTOMS are generally of easy detection. When the skull is crushed, crepitus can be felt through the skin. There are more or less marks of violence on the surface. If the scalp be torn, as is most frequently the case, the wound should be explored with that best of probes, the *finger*. If much time has elapsed, there will be a considerable tumor, which may prevent the proper examination until it has subsided.

It must not be forgotten that the skull-bone may be bent in without being fractured. If there be evident symptoms of COMPRESSION upon the brain, and these do *not subside* by the use of proper constitutional and local treatment; and it is ascertained, moreever, that the blow upon the head was made by such an instrument as would be likely to produce fracture, without lacerating the surface, — there will be strong reason to suspect its existence. In such a case, if examination through the scalp be not decisive, or be prevented by the swelling, a portion may be removed, sufficient to permit the proper examination, and to trephine, if necessary.

A severe blow on the head, by a fall or otherwise, may occasion fracture of the skull at some other point than that where the foreign force was received. Thus the base of the skull may be fractured, when the top of the head is struck. When the temporal bone is broken in this way, blood will flow out of the ears.

SYMPTOMS of *compression* will always be present soon after infliction of the injury if the bone is depressed, but though an *effect* they are not an *evidence* of depressed bone, as they may result from extravasated blood where there is only a slight fissure without any depression.

SYMPTOMS of *concussion* must be distinguished from those of compression. The former will be present for a short time in nearly all cases of fracture, as well as after other blows on the head, when the bone is uninjured. (See for symptoms and treatment of concussion and compression under WOUNDS OF THE HEAD.)

If there is concussion and there be no symptom of compression, all that is necessary is to DRESS as in any other case, — first removing the hair for some distance round. .Then wash out with warm water, and bring the lips together with adhesive straps and bandaging. Sutures may be necessary, but should be avoided, if possible.

But *if* SYMPTOMS of COMPRESSION come on, or already exist and are not relieved by treatment, it may be necessary to trephine and elevate the depressed bone or remove the extravasated blood. But the symptoms of

— *both* concussion and compression may appear together, and the exact state of the case not be easily ascertained. In such circumstances, the safest plan is to wait, and use means calculated to relieve both states, until they subside or those of compression more clearly develop themselves.

Trephining is always attended, even in the most skillful hands, with much danger to the patient. Hence it should never be done prophylactically, as is recommended by some surgeons, but only in those cases when there is unequivocal evidence of pressure on the brain, which has not yielded to a faithful exhibition of our remedial means, and where we are tolerably certain as to the exact location of that pressure. If you have resolved on using the instrument, place it on such a part of the head as will, if possible, avoid the grooves for the middle meningeal arteries in the parietal and temporal bones, as well as the sutures, and have one edge of the trephine on the sound and one on the fractured bone. (For the mode of proceeding with the *operation*, see TREPHINING.)

FRACTURE OF THE NOSE.

A violent blow upon the nose may not only break in the nasal bones, but the processes of the ethmoidal bone, and do great if not fatal injury by rupturing the membranes of the brain. Commonly, however, a nasal fracture is of trifling importance. It is readily distinguished by the *deformity* resulting, and almost as easily *adjusted* by applying some instrument (as a silver catheter or the smaller end of a gunshot probe) on the *inside* of the nose to push out the depressed bones, while the fingers on the *outside* support and keep them in their place. Treat as for simple fracture.

FRACTURE OF THE LOWER JAW.

This bone may be broken at any part. The accident most commonly occurs near the chin. The case is easily ascertained by the pain and crepitus on moving the bone, by the depression to be felt on tracing along the edge of the jaw with the fingers, — which depression is apt to be greater on one side than on the other, — and is also manifested by irregularity in the line of the teeth.

Fig. 62.

In ADJUSTING, elevate or depress until all the teeth are arranged in their proper place with respect to each other and those of the upper jaw. If, as often happens, the case is complicated with *dislocation* of one of the condyles, that must be first *reduced*, and the fracture then *set*. There is also almost always a good deal of contusion or laceration of the soft parts. For this reason, after the proper dressings, the parts require to be constantly wet with cold arnicated water. (See next illustration.)

Secure the jaw after adjustment, by shutting the mouth closely and *keeping* it shut. Take a piece of stout calf-skin leather, about two and a half inches wide, and long enough to pass nearly or quite from ear to ear and over the chin. Spread upon this some good adhesive plaster, or collodion, and stick it smoothly on. The Gum Shellac cloth or Gutta Percha would do still better than the leather, and need less bandaging over it.

If no *teeth* are wanting in the fore part of the mouth, and there is not sufficient space between them, one or two will have to be *extracted* previously to closing the mouth, in order that there may be a space through which the patient, by means of a tube, may take drink and food in a liquid form. As the patient may not like to lose a front tooth, one of the cuspids or the first of the bicuspids may be chosen.

The BANDAGE for securing the jaw may be of strong muslin or drilling, about two and a half inches wide and two yards long. It is to be split from each end to within six inches of the middle, where a small hole is made for the chin. The two lower ends are brought up over the top of the head, while the upper ones are carried horizontally round to the back of the neck. Several turns should then be made with each pair, some round the head horizontally, just above the superciliary ridge, and others over the crown. They should then be sewed or pinned together, not only at the ends, but wherever they cross. Several other modes are formally described in the books; but just as good or perhaps better plans will readily suggest themselves to the practitioner intent upon the simple object of fixing the bone in its place.

Professor Gibson's plan, represented in the accompanying plate (Fig. 63) is simple and effectual. A compress under each ramus

Fig. 63.

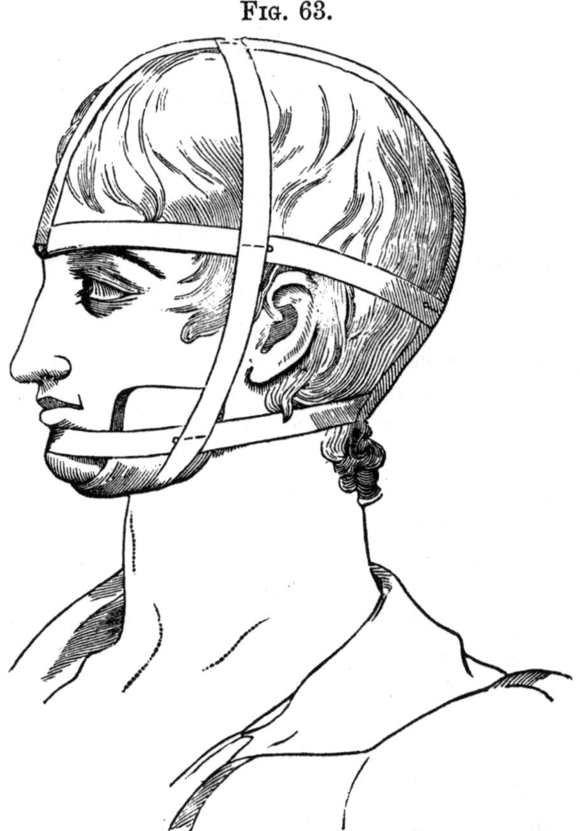

is held by an assistant (to which, however, we much prefer the sticking leather) until secured by the first turns of the roller (one and a half inches in width and four or five yards long). These first vertical turns are repeated over each other several times, and the horizontal ones above the ear over the occiput and forehead next follow; and then several others below the ear and lip. Pins or stitches should be applied wherever the roller changes its direction or the turns cross each other. The median strip over the top of the head, from the neck to the forehead, should be also fastened to each layer as it crosses. Its object is to keep the other turns from slipping.

Dr. Hill was called while engaged in the Eclectic practice in Cincinnati, to a lad who was kicked by a horse in such a way as to occasion three distinct fractures of the inferior maxillary (as represented in Fig. 62), besides other complications. Several of the molars and one of the incisor teeth were knocked out; blood flowed freely from one ear; and there were signs of much cerebral implication. The face and head were very much bruised; the mouth could not be closed; the lower jaw being drawn back as well as down. Each condyle was broken, besides a fracture through the front of the bone. Dr. Hill was called about an hour after the accident, and with the patient's father (Dr. Carter) adjusted the parts, he pressing down and forwards upon the fractured condyles, and then, when the mouth could be closed, arranging the front fracture and the teeth, bringing these on a plane with each other and parallel with those of the upper jaw. This done, an adhesive plaster was placed over the chin, and the whole secured by the *four-tailed bandage* (that first described, before giving Gibson's plan). The parts were kept constantly wet with a preparation, composed of equal parts of common whisky and water, saturated with common salt, to which strong tincture of camphor was added in the proportion of a pint to two quarts of the first mixture; and an active cathartic given on account of the cerebral symptoms. These, with the bleeding from the ear, gradually ceased; the patient continued comfortable; and on the seventh day the dressings were removed for the sake of examination and readjustment. In about a month the cure was complete, leaving scarcely any perceptible deformity, and allowing the complete use of the joints and jaw. He was then unacquainted with the efficacy of Homeopathic remedies in surgery.

FRACTURES OF THE SCAPULA.

These are very rare, except that which separates the acromion process.

When the BODY of the bone is fractured *across*, the parts remain so nearly in place as to cause no deformity. There is pain, however, and crepitus can be perceived on pressing the hand upon it. The TREATMENT in such a case consists in applying bandages around the thorax and over the shoulder, so as to prevent all motion of the parts, keeping their surface wet and cool, placing the hand and fore-arm in a sling and keeping them very quiet.

FRACTURE OF THE ACROMION PROCESS is easily caused by a blow on the point of the shoulder. A *depression* at that point is very manifest, and the natural fullness of the deltoid muscle is wanting. The separated portion of the bone is, with the clavicle, *drawn downwards* and forwards by the sub-clavius and pectoralis major. When the *arm* is pressed *upwards* crepitus may be noticed, but not when it is simply rotated.

To REMEDY this accident, press the head of the humerus up, so as to carry the fragment to its proper place, and fix the arm in that position by the "clavicle bandage,"—*omitting*, however, in this case, to place anything under the arm, as is done in fracture of the clavicle.* The parts must be kept at rest and steadily fixed. (See under FRACTURE OF THE CLAVICLE.)

The NECK of the scapula may be so fractured as to involve only the glenoid cavity and the coracoid process, leaving the acromion entire. This case is apt to be confounded with a dislocation. As the long heads of the biceps and triceps originate from this portion of the scapula, those muscles retain it in contact with the head of the humerus, which is drawn down with it into the axilla, both by the weight of the arm and the contractions of the pectoralis major, latissimus dorsi and subscapularius. The head of the humerus can be felt in the axilla, as when it is luxated. The acromion process is very conspicuous, from a depression beneath. The deltoid is flattened and the arm elongated. Crepitus can be

* Dr. Hill recently had an otherwise extraordinary case brought to him from the country, in which *both* the acromion and end of the clavicle were severed. It was an infant, the damage having been done by the accoucheur in bringing down the arm after "turning."

discovered and the nature of the case readily ascertained, by placing the thumb on the coracoid process and the fingers in the axilla, while the arm is pushed outwards and upwards.

The treatment in this case consists merely of putting the parts properly in apposition, and keeping them there, by the "clavicle bandage" with a wedge-shaped *pad* under the arm, so as to keep arm and shoulder both perfectly fixed and *immovable* until union takes place. (See treatment for SIMPLE FRACTURE.)

FRACTURE OF THE CLAVICLE.

This is a very common accident, and easily distinguished. The "collar bone" usually gives way near the middle with an "oblique fracture" (as in Fig. 64). Passing the finger along the edge of

FIG. 64.

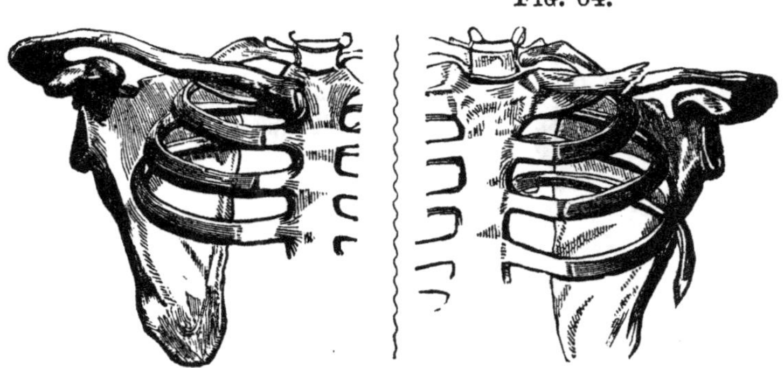

the bone from the sternum, will readily show the point and direction of the split. A considerable tumor often forms at the place. Not unfrequently a spicula of bone will be found protruding through the skin, constituting the case one of "compound fracture." Crepitus occurs in moving the *shoulder*, which is drawn forwards and inwards by the contraction of the pectoral muscles.

In ADJUSTING this case, the surgeon stands behind the patient and puts his knee between the shoulders, drawing them *both* back until the parts of the broken clavicle have necessarily assumed their proper position. The shoulders are to be kept back, and the arms down by suitable apparatus. Before applying the "clavicle bandage," which we will presently describe, we are in the habit of applying a piece of leather tolerably stiff and spread with adhesive plaster, or the Gum Shellac cloth, or Gutta Percha, well fitted to the surface. It should be over two inches wide and extend from the middle or opposite side of the sternum to the point of the shoulder of the affected side. When this is stuck on, it should be covered, first with a compress and then the

— CLAVICLE BANDAGE, which is to be of strong muslin or drilling, about two and a half inches wide, and *almost* unlimited in length. About a yard and a half from the end you intend to begin with, fasten to it a wedge-shaped *pad* (about six inches long, by four or five wide, and three thick at the base). Place the base or thick end of this compress uppermost in the axilla of the injured side. Have the shoulders kept back by an assistant, and bring the short end of the bandage across the back over the sound shoulder, which is to be protected by cotton at every point covered by the roller. Bring the end round in front of the breast to the pad, and there fasten it. Then begin with the other part of the roller. Bring it up over the breast and sound shoulder, and round the back to the axilla of the affected side; and repeat this operation four or five times, stitching the bandage to different points on the pad at every turn. Then bring it across the breast and under the sound shoulder, and obliquely across the back to the top of the affected shoulder; then down in front of this, *under* its axilla, across the back again, and over the sound shoulder; down in front of this and under *its* axilla, — then again over and under each as before, — thus describing "figure 8" with the bandage on the back some six or eight times — (see Figure 65). Cotton pads are to be placed under and in front of the sound shoulder, and on the top of both, to prevent excoriation. Continue the bandage again from the axilla of the sound side across the back and *over* the affected arm, bringing the elbow down to the side as near as may be, while the fore-arm is flexed over the breast, so that the ends of the fingers will reach

FIG. 65.

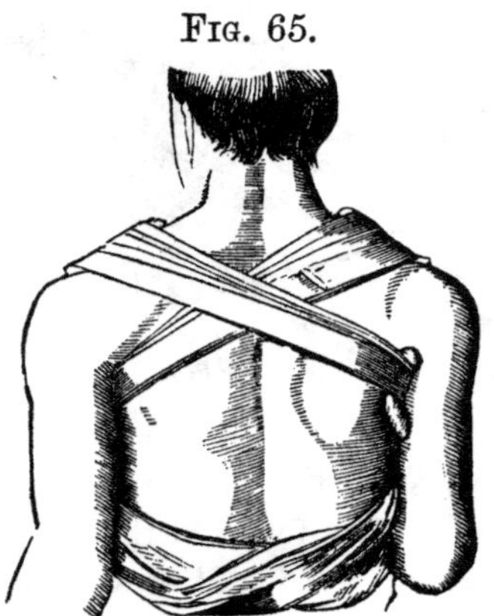

to, or nearly to, the coracoid process of the sound side. Thus make six or eight folds round the body, including the arm in each. Then lay the roller again over the sound shoulder, across the back and round the body, over and below the elbow on the breast, and up in front over the sound shoulder. Make five or six of these oblique turns, and fasten your bandage. Also, stitch the successive folds of the roller, as they overlap each other from the shoulder down below the elbow and up along the fore-arm, so that they may not possibly slip up or down. Next, having covered the affected clavicle with a compress laid over the plaster, confine it with your bandage, brought round from under the sound arm, and obliquely across the breast over the affected clavicle and the shoulder above. Six or eight of these turns complete the operation, so as to keep everything smooth and firm.

Fig. 66.

The modes of applying the bandage laid down in most works, does not seem to us as efficient as this, which we can recommend from experience. It has always fully realized our expectations. Several severe cases, in some of which the fractured clavicle protruded through the skin, were adjusted in the way described; and so perfect was the union that, after the lapse of a year or two, not a trace of the accident could be discovered except a slight scar where the surface was broken through. The surface of the united bones was smooth as on the opposite side.

The *advantage* of applying the bandage in the way recommended, is, that if there be any external wound, it can be dressed, — or the part can be examined, if there be occasion for it, — without so far removing the bandages as to cause any derangement, or indeed allow of the least motion. The *clavicle itself*, though secured by plaster, position, &c., was the *last part bandaged* (which the front view of Figure 66 was intended to represent). This precaution should never be lost sight of. Treat as directed for simple fracture.

Rest for a few days should be enjoined, though with the straight-waistcoat-like protection of the properly adjusted bandage little risk is incurred. Union of bone will take place much quicker at this central part of the body, than in the extremities. Two or three weeks will generally be long enough to keep on the apparatus. Of this, however, the practitioner must judge for himself, in every case guided by the constitutional vigor of every patient.

FRACTURE OF THE STERNUM.

This accident never happens, except from very great force applied directly to the part. It is important on account of the great liability of inflammation extending to the pleura and thoracic viscera. It may always be considered a dangerous case, requiring careful management.

Its SYMPTOMS are a depression at the point of fracture, with pain and crepitus accompanying the movements of respiration. Spread strips of leather, Gutta Percha, or Shellac cloth an inch in width with adhesive plaster. Have the patient take a moderately full inspiration and then hold his breath for a few moments. And while the chest is thus expanded apply the strips spread with adhesive plaster diagonally across the chest from each side crossing each other over the sternum. Next apply a *roller* round the chest, so as to *stop all motion,* causing respiration to be carried on by the *abdominal* instead of the intercostal muscles. Inspiration should be natural while the roller is applied. Keep the patient very quiet. Be very thorough in the application of the cold arnicated lotion to the injured part and in the other treatment as directed for simple fracture.

As an adjuvant the feet should be occasionally immersed in hot water and

Should much inflammation threaten, moderately tight bandages should be occasionally placed around the arms and thighs to prevent an undue determination of the blood to the chest. (See HÆMASTASIS.)

FRACTURE AND DISLOCATION OF THE RIBS.

These cases are spoken of together, because, though fracture of these bones occurs without dislocation, dislocation can rarely, if ever, take place without fracture. It is supposed that simple dislocation may occur at the vertebral extremity, but any force capable of producing it, would be almost certain to break off the transverse process of the vertebra, if not to fracture the rib itself. What is called

"Dislocation of the *cartilage*," from the rib or sternum, is in fact, a rupture or fracture. There is no joint or proper articulation there to be dislocated, and the *symptoms* are simply those of fracture at any other part, except that the extremity of the rib is likely to protrude. It is, however, of rare occurrence.

The fifth, sixth, seventh, or eighth ribs are those most frequently fractured — those below escape by their readily yielding to any force, while the scapula and pectoral muscles protect those above. They are generally broken at or near the angle, viz., three or four inches from the spine, although the blow may have been some distance in front. As this part of the rib is covered with large muscles, it is frequently difficult to detect the injury. Passing your finger along the rib, you will discover the *depression* and *crepitus*. If the rib be torn from the cartilage it will generally project.

When called to a patient whom we suppose has a fractured rib, we should carefully examine to see whether the lungs or pleura have been injured.

The severity of the symptoms and the stethescope will enable us to form our diagnosis.

If it is a case of simple fracture, direct the patient to take a full inspiration, as in fracture of the sternum, and then hold his breath for a short time with the lungs well filled. In this expanded condition of the chest, press the bones or cartilage down to the proper place, and fit on the part a piece of wetted paste-board, or what is better, of Gutta Percha or the Gum Shellac cloth, spread with adhesive plaster. Let it be long enough to extend one-third of the way round the chest, and wide enough to cover one or two ribs on each side of the broken one. It will prevent the displacement of the fractured rib in respiration.

Over this and around the chest a broad bandage should be applied from the arm-pits to the end of the sternum. It is usual to recommend one of flannel, in order that it may not shrink and that all motion of the ribs in respiration may be prevented. We, however, prefer an elastic one, which with the adhesive compress before mentioned will both retain the bones in contact and give an ease in respiration that cannot be enjoyed with the flannel or cotton bandage. Medical treatment same as directed for simple fractures.

UNION will take place, in ordinary cases, in the course of two or three weeks. The bandage may, therefore, in such cases, be dispensed with after that time. The plaster should be kept on a few weeks longer.

If it is compound fracture uncomplicated, treat as if simple, except leaving a hole in the adhesive compress over the wound, so that the cold arnicated or calendula lotion may be applied.

If the intercostal artery is ruptured it may be necessary to tie it. When the pleura is torn, on account of the lungs completely filling the thoracic cavity, they are almost invariably injured. This is indicated by a rush of air with more or less blood at each expiration.

Apply the adhesive compress and the elastic bandage as above. (For treatment, see PUNCTURED AND LACERATED WOUNDS and WOUNDS OF THE CHEST.)

FRACTURE OF THE SPINE

—by which is meant the *Spinal Column*, or fracture of the *body* or *articulating* surface of a vertebra, —is beyond the reach of remedial surgery, since there is always lesion of the spinal chord. The *transverse* processes of the vertebræ may be broken off in connection with fracture or dislocation of the ribs, without any special inconvenience or danger. It is regarded and *treated* altogether as an accident of the ribs. Fracture at most parts "of the spine," then, is very soon fatal, though in some rare instances patients have survived a long time after having the *lumbar* vertebræ broken. Fractures at any higher part cause death in a few days,—above the fourth vertebra of the neck, *instant death.*

PARALYSIS of all the *voluntary* muscles, supplied by nerves proceeding from the spinal column below the point of fracture, is a necessary consequence, even where the organic functions are not immediately affected. Thus, when the lumbar vertebræ or any higher ones are split, the bladder and sphincter ani are paralyzed, and the urine and fæces pass involuntarily.

All that can be done in the way of *treatment* is to counteract inflammation, as in other fractures, and keep the patient as quiet and comfortable as possible so long as he may live. Neither medical or surgical aid is of much avail. As the skin is liable to slough upon pressure, we would recommend the employment of the hydrostatic bed.

FRACTURES OF THE PELVIS.

These are only CAUSED by very great violence, usually crushing in some part of the parietes of the pelvic cavity, and often proving fatal from concomitant injury to the organs within. Such injury may be done at any part of the basin. The acetabulum is among the most dangerous points. Separation or dislocation at the sacro-iliac junction may be also mentioned in this connection.

The SYMPTOMS will, of course, vary somewhat with the part fractured. The principles, however, on which diagnosis and treatment are conducted will be the same. *Crepitus* can generally be *felt* by placing the hand upon the crest of the ilium, on one or other side, while motion is made with the lower extremities or at the spine. Or *auscultation* may be resorted to at the suspected point. The patient can seldom move the hips as he lies in bed, without experiencing great pain. Any movement of the body is likely to cause more or less suffering. Firm contraction of the abdominal muscles generally tends to separate the fractured parts and thus aggravate all the symptoms.

Permanent injury, as well as present suffering, may be produced by moving the patient much for the sake of examination. Therefore, the less the parts are meddled with the better. *Diagnosis* may be aided by learning the kind of accident, and the amount and direction of the force applied.

The first thing to be done, both with a view to EXAMINATION

and TREATMENT, is to place the patient, as gently as possible, in a horizontal position. We are then directed to observe, with as little handling as we can, whether the legs, the spinous processes of the ilia, and other prominent points on each side compare. If there is deformity discovered, making a fracture probable, before going any further with the examination,—

—introduce a *catheter*, to ascertain whether the urethra or bladder be involved in the injury. Should there be bloody urine, or any obstruction to the advance of the instrument, let it remain in the bladder, or as far towards it as it has gone, and proceed at once to

—*apply a roller* round the pelvis in such a manner as to keep all the bones in proper juxtaposition. Then have a *strap* passed *under the nates*, and attached to a pulley suspended over the bed, so that the pelvis may be raised without any muscular effort on the part of the patient.

All possible precautions, topical and general, must be taken against inflammation. (See treatment of FRACTURE.) In addition to the local treatment there recommended, the use of frequent enemas of cold arnicated water may do much good.

If, however, the injury be severe, there is but little hope of saving the patient.

CHAPTER IX.

PARTICULAR FRACTURES, CONTINUED—THOSE OF THE UPPER EXTREMITIES.

OF THE HUMERUS.

THIS bone is generally broken near the middle; it may, however, give way near the condyles, or just under the head, in the part called (in surgery) the neck—(see Figures 68 and 69).

A fracture in any part of the SHAFT of the bone (as in Figure 67) is easily detected. There will be obvious deformity, the parts of the bone being drawn out of a line by the different muscles. The patient feels more or less pain at the fractured point, and is unable to use the limb. By rotating the lower portion of the arm, while the upper is fixed, crepitus can generally be noticed; and the direction and extent of the fracture can easily be ascertained by the touch, on tracing with the finger from the condyles upwards.

Fig. 67.

Fracture of the NECK (Figure 68) is not always easily distinguished from a *dislocation*. It may be borne in mind, however, that it is an accident which seldom occurs, except in old persons. In the fracture, the roundness of the shoulder is not lessened, as when the head of the bone is out of its place. Crepitus will always decide the point. By taking hold of the arm below and rotating, the grating of the fractured portions on each other may be felt, if not heard.

Fracture at or near the CONDYLES (one form of which is also represented in Figure 67 and another in Figure 69) may be mistaken for *luxation* from the fore-arm. The use of the elbow joint will aid in the discrimination. Let the elbow be fixed, and rotation of the hand will seldom be much impeded in mere fracture, even when the condyles are broken off, or have a fissure between them. If the fracture be just *above* the condyles (Fig. 69), as usually happens in the case of children, the arm will be shortened. Crepitus will be decisive.

The TREATMENT, when the *shaft* of the bone is broken, is simple. The proper extension has first to be made, by drawing upon the wrist or elbow the fore-arm being about half bent; and the adjustment then accomplished, by comparing the length and appearance of the limb with its fellow. If it be an *oblique* fracture, great care must be taken not to let the ends of the bones slip by each other, and thus render the arm permanently shorter. The muscles naturally tend to bring about this result.

Have the parts held, when once in proper juxtaposition, by an assistant, while a *roller* is applied, rather loosely, from the elbow to the shoulder. Then place on four *splints* about a quarter of an inch thick, and of a convenient width, so as to cover nearly the whole surface of the arm. Let them be nearly as long as the humerus itself, the inner one being a little the shortest, so as to allow the elbow to be bent. Then continue your roller, bringing it down again over the splints from one end to the other a sufficient number of times to fix them firmly to the arm, and prevent any motion or contraction of the muscles.

Fig. 68.

The fore-arm and hand must be suspended in a *sling* from the neck. It is best to have one of the splints extend from the shoulder to the back of the hand, it being bent to a right angle at the elbow, and secured by the roller being brought down to the hand. This will more effectually protect the arm, by preventing rotation and all other motion of the fore-arm. This splint, and all the others, may be of Gutta Percha or Gum Shellac cloth, two or three thicknesses being stuck together.

Some recommend the roller in the first instance to be carried *from the fingers* up to the shoulder, so as to allow of its being rolled very tight, preventing all motion below, and paralyzing the muscles above. This, however, is not necessary in ordinary cases.

When the *neck* of the humerus is fractured (as in Figure 68), the parts are to be kept in their place, after adjustment, by a wedge-shaped pad in the axilla. The *Gutta Percha* or *Shellac Splint* should then be applied on the outside and over the top of the shoulder and the whole firmly fixed by the clavicle bandage. The Gutta Percha or Gum Shellac cloth is to be spread with adhesive plaster and extend from the neck down near to the elbow, and be wide enough to envelop the whole shoulder and two-thirds of the surface of the arm. Those not yet acquainted with these excellent moldable splints have to trust wholly to their "clavicle bandage."

Fracture just *above the condyles* (Figure 69) can be easily distinguished from dislocation of the radius and ulna backwards, for which it is sometimes mistaken, by extending the arm when all the marks of dislocation are removed, but return on discontinuing the extension, also by crepitus just above the elbow-joint upon rotating the fore-arm upon the humerus. After the proper

FIG. 69.

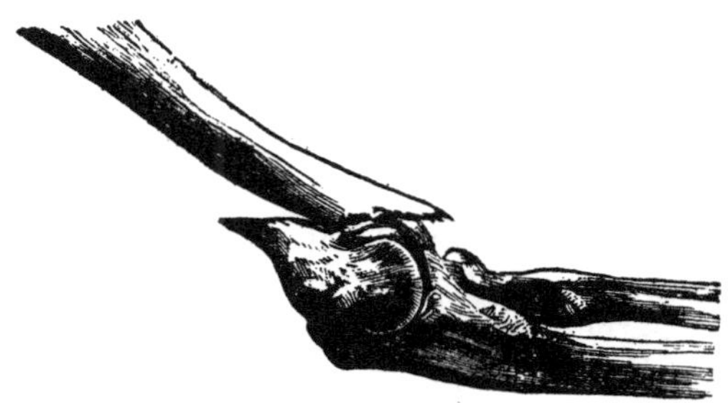

extension and juxtaposition, apply a roller loosely around the arm and fore-arm while bent, and afterwards fix on with it two angular splints, one in front and the other to the back of the arm, reaching nearly from the shoulder to the wrist. Prevent all motion both of the arm and fore-arm, and suspend the latter in a sling. Here again the Gutta Percha or the Shellac cloth makes the best possible splint. Passive motion, for the prevention of anchylosis, may be gently commenced in two weeks, if the patient is young; but if an adult, at the expiration of three.

In true "fracture *of the condyles*" (as in Figure 67), one or the other of the moldable splints should by all means be used. The divided parts are to be pressed together and the splint or cloth cap smoothly stuck on. Let it reach to the wrist. In about eighteen or twenty days remove the first splint, and substitute another, bent about half as much, and take the opportunity of making a little passive motion of the arm backwards and forwards. Keep this on for two or three weeks, and then apply a still straighter one. After this, remove the dressings every two or three days, and move the joint a little. (See treatment of FRACTURES, DISLOCATIONS, and WOUNDS OF THE JOINT.)

"More or less *deformity* is liable to occur in this case, as well as in the preceding, in spite of the best management. This should always be made known to the patient or friends, in order that censure for bad surgery may not be incurred."

So say the best authorities. Our success, however, has been such, in the treatment of those cases that have fallen into our hands, that there has been no deformity or loss of motion. That they were not all mild cases may be learned from the following case of Dr. Hunt's: In July, 1851, a son (æt. 11) of Mr. B. Boffinger, of Cincinnati, fell from a shed, upon his right elbow, which entered the ground for several inches. Dr. Hunt was called, and found the humerus fractured, as in Fig. 69, with the upper part protruding nearly an inch through the skin. There was also a fracture of the internal condyle. Reduction was effected by pressing with the thumb upwards and backwards upon the protruding bone. At the same time, extension was made upon the fore-arm, flexed. A loose bandage being applied from the hand to the shoulder, a strip of Gutta Percha, of the length of the limb, and sufficiently wide to encase the back part of the arm and extend over the condyles, was, after being softened in hot water, fitted to the back part of the limb and permitted to cool.

Another strip of Gutta Percha was fitted over the front part of the arm, and extending down over the fore-arm. After this had become cool and firm, an aperture was made in it over the wound. These splints were then applied and made secure by means of a second roller. By this arrangement, each part was kept in its proper position, and the wound could be dressed without removing the splints and bandages. The medical treatment was the same as that before recommended for fractures, under which there was but little secondary fever; the wound healed with but little suppuration, the bones speedily united, and no permanent anchylosis occurred. At the expiration of a couple of weeks, the splints were taken off, slightly straightened — gentle motion commenced. The patient entirely recovered the use of the arm.

FRACTURES OF THE ULNA PROCESSES.

The Olecranon Process

— is sometimes broken off and drawn up on the back of the arm, leaving a depression between it and the joint (see Fig. 70). If, however, the ligaments be not ruptured, little or no retraction may take place. There is great pain at the part, and the patient is unable to straighten his arm, though he can bend it easily.

Fig. 70.

In treating this accident, the first thing to be done is to place the limb in a straight position, and use means to subdue inflammation and swelling, if any have occurred. After that, bandage the fore-arm pretty tightly from the *ends of the fingers* to the bend of the arm. Then bring down the fractured end of the bone to its proper place and include it in the turns of the roller, which should be continued at this time for some three or four inches further up. Bring back the roller and pass it above and below the joint, in the form of a figure 8, for ten or twelve turns. After that, turn it round the arm again and continue upwards, including all the upper portion of the arm, in order to prevent the contractions of the triceps from again separating the parts.

Place over the bandage, in front of the joint, a strong splint, in order to prevent all flexion, and keep the joint constantly wet with cold water.

After from two to three weeks, passive motion of the joint should be commenced, and continued from day to day, increasing the extent and amount as the patient can bear it.

This is a case in which ossific union does not take place, there being only a ligamentous attachment formed.

The cause of this accident often occasions laceration about the parts, and renders the case one of

"*Compound fracture*," when great care must be taken to prevent dangerous inflammation.

The bandage must, in this case, be so applied as to be removed from the wound in dressing it, without the necessity of removing the splint or the bandage from the arm above. (See treatment of Fractures, Dislocations, and Wounds of the Joint.)

The Coronoid Process

—of the ulna may be separately fractured, though this is

very rare. It occasions a difficulty of bending the elbow, as the action of the brachialis upon the fore-arm is lost. There is also, almost of necessity, a backward dislocation, the coronoid process being nearly all that prevents the triceps extensor drawing the ulna backwards and upwards.

Fig. 71.

All the necessary TREATMENT is to flex the fore-arm and retain it in that position by splints and bandages. (See treatment of FRACTURE.)

This fracture also unites only by ligamentous connection.

FRACTURES OF THE FORE-ARM.

The radius and ulna may both be broken through, or either of them alone (see Figures 71, 72, and 73). These common accidents may be ascertained by *tracing* the bones from the wrist up, until when the finger comes to the divided part a *depression* is felt; by the *crepitus*, on fixing the elbow and rotating the wrist; and by the pain, and more or less loss of motion in the hand.

The only point of TREATMENT that is not obvious, is the precaution of keeping the bones apart, so as to prevent their being drawn into the interosseous space (by the pronator and supinator muscles, and particularly the quadratus, which having a special direct tendency to this result, from its fibres running perpendicularly across the bones, is represented in Fig. 71, near the wrist). The bones thus uniting, would for ever prevent the circular movement of the radius round the ulna, and the full use of the hand. After adjusting the fracture by extension from the wrist, bend the arm at a right angle, having the thumb directly above the little finger, that is, mid-way between pronation and supination. Then apply a roller loosely, and over it two splints, one from the internal condyle to the palm of the hand; another on the outer side, from the external condyle to the back of the wrist. These splints should be convex on the side next the arm, and padded with cotton, or have a cotton compress laid beneath them, between the bones, so as to press into the interosseous space. After this matter is attended to, secure the splints by a roller, extending from the hand to the elbow.

If the *radius alone* is fractured (Fig. 72), it is best to leave

FIG. 72.

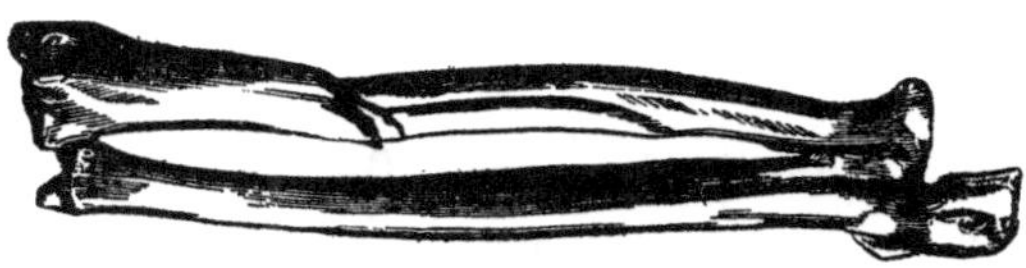

the *hand* loose, so as to let it drop down, and thus exert some force of extension on the bone. But in fracture of *both* bones (Fig. 71), or of the *ulna alone* (Fig. 73), let the splint and band-

FIG. 73.

age extend to the ends of the fingers, keeping the hand and fore-arm in the same line.

After ten or twelve days the splints may, in ordinary cases, be removed, and a starched bandage applied; but care must still be taken that the bones be not forced together. To prevent this, a *compress* had better be put along the interosseous space, at least along the front of the fore-arm. (See treatment of FRACTURES.)

The Lower End of the Radius

— may be fractured at about half an inch, or still less, from the joint. As the hand is *distorted*, it is apt to be mistaken for

FIG. 74.

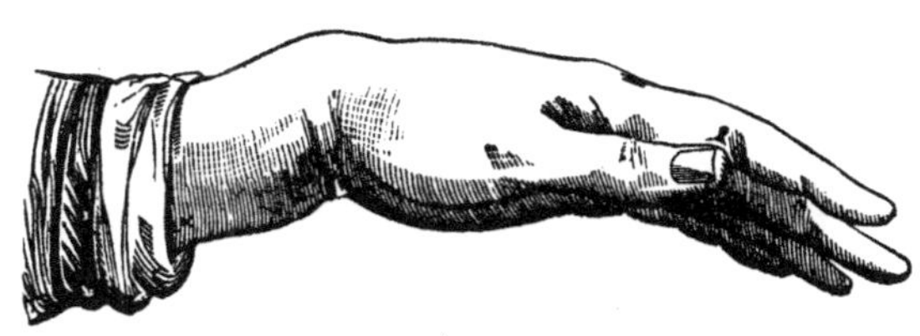

a luxation. If the hand be moved, however, the styloid process of the radius moves with it, which, of course, would not happen if the bone were dislocated.

TREATMENT should be the same as for other fractures of the same bone, except that pads and compresses must be so placed as to aid in keeping the fractured portions together, as well as the two bones apart.

The patient must be forewarned that he will not be able to use the hand to any considerable extent for several months. To prevent anchylosis, however, *passive* motion must begin to be made in three or four weeks.

FRACTURES OF THE WRIST, HAND, AND FINGERS.

The carpal, metacarpal, and finger bones are occasionally broken. The case is an obvious one; and the TREATMENT required is to apply a broad *splint* so cut or molded as to fit the front of the wrist and hand, with the ends slit for the fingers. Splints may be also applied to the back and sides of the fingers. Pad the parts so as to make the pressure equal, and secure the splint with a roller. Should only a finger be broken, it may be set and fixed by four small splints and bandaged with tape; but it will be better and safer to have the whole hand and wrist secured up to the middle of the fore-arm as above directed.

When the carpal or middle metacarpal bones, or the two middle bones of the first phalanx, are the seat of the injury, it is best to have padding in the palm of the hand, quite thick and round, bending the hand and fingers over it, as this will serve to keep the parts properly extended, acting like a ball grasped in the hand.

CHAPTER X.

PARTICULAR FRACTURES CONTINUED — THOSE OF THE LOWER EXTREMITIES.

FRACTURES OF THE THIGH.

THE NECK OF THE FEMUR

— is rarely broken, except in old persons, and oftener in females than males. The fracture generally occurs within the capsular ligament, but may happen outside of it.

The SYMPTOMS by which the accident may be recognized are that the patient cannot stand on the leg, and feels severe pain on moving it. The limb is from one to two inches shorter; the foot and knee are turned out (as seen in Fig. 75), and the heel inclines to rest on the other limb just above and behind the malleolus. On extending or rotating the limp crepitus may be felt or heard. If extension be made and the limb let go, it retracts suddenly.

FIG. 75.

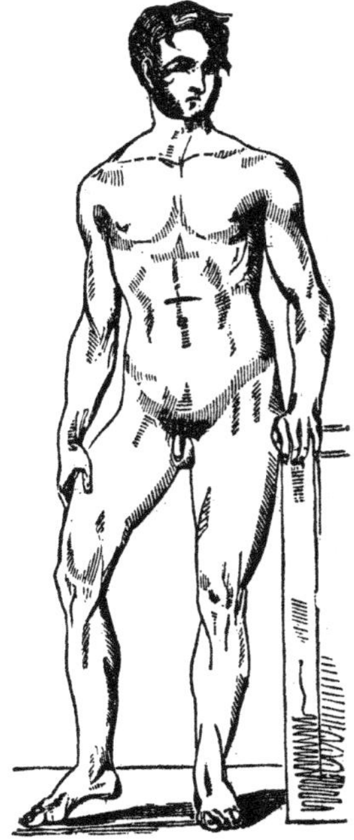

There are *varieties*, however, to be distinguished. When the whole of the bone is not detached, no contraction takes place. In other cases the shortening does not occur for several hours and even days after the accident. In rare instances, also, the foot *turns in* instead of out. "The practical rule," observes Mr. Druitt, "is that when an old person has fallen and is unable to walk, and complains of pain under the hip, this fracture should be carefully looked for, though there may be no apparent shortening or eversion."

A fracture *within the capsular ligament* (Fig. 76) very rarely *unites* by bony connection. Either a strong ligamentous sub-

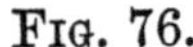
Fig. 76.

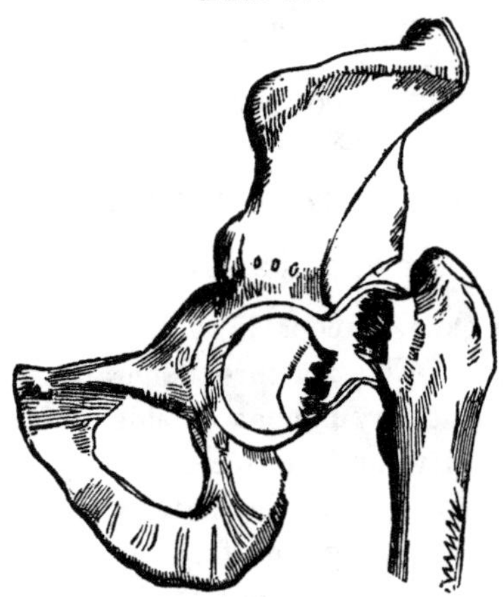

stance has to bind the parts together and serve instead of bone, or there is no *fixed* union at all. In the latter case a sort of "double joint" is formed, the fractured surface of the head becoming hollowed into a socket, and that of the neck rounded so as to play into it. The ligaments of the joint become greatly thickened and strengthened, as is also the case with the obturator externus muscle. The limb in this case is permanently shortened, causing halting in the step.

Treatment.

Sir Astley Cooper, after giving some half dozen different modes of management, thus concludes: —

"Baffled in our various attempts at curing these cases, and finding the life of the patient occasionally sacrificed under the trials made to unite them, I should, if I sustained this accident in my own person, direct that a pillow should be placed under the limb throughout its length; that another should be rolled up under the knee, and that the limb should be thus extended until the inflammation and pain had subsided. I should then daily rise and sit in a high chair, in order to prevent a degree of flexion which would be painful; and, walking with crutches, bear gently on the foot at first, then, gradually more and more, until the ligament became thickened, and the muscles increased in their power. A high-heeled shoe should be next employed, by which the halt would be much diminished. Our hospital patients, treated after this manner, are allowed in a few weeks to walk with crutches; after a time a stick is substituted for the crutches, and in a few months they are able to use the limb without any adventitious support."

"The degree of recovery in these cases is as follows: — If the patient be very corpulent, the aid of crutches will be for a long time required; if less bulky, a stick only will be sufficient; and where the weight of the body is inconsiderable, the person is able to walk without either of these aids, but droops a little at each step on that side, unless a shoe be worn having a sole of equal thickness to the diminished length of the limb. In every case, however, in which there is the smallest doubt whether it be a fracture within, or external to the ligament, it will be proper to treat the case as if it were external, — a fracture which admits of ossific union."

It is stated that Jarvis's patent *Adjusting Machine* has in numerous instances been used with perfect success. We have never tried it in one of these cases, but are inclined to believe it would be superior to any other means yet made use of or proposed. In the absence of this machine, we would recommend straps of Gutta Percha or the Shellac cloth, in addition to the directions quoted above from Sir Astley Cooper. These splints should extend from near the knee up to the thorax, being about four inches wide, and consisting of several thicknesses. After having adjusted the fracture as well as possible, and shaped the gum splint while warm, spread it with adhesive plaster and fix it with bandages on the thigh and body. (See treatment of FRACTURES, DISLOCATIONS, and WOUNDS OF THE JOINT.)

Other modes of treatment can be found described in any of the books. None of them, however, have been attended with any better success than Sir A. Cooper's simple plan, while they often do great harm.

Fracture of the *neck outside* of the *capsular ligament*, differs in some of its symptoms from the former case. It may also occur at any age, while fracture within the capsule rarely, if ever, happens in persons under the age of fifty. Crepitus in the case of external fracture is much more easily distinguished, while the limb itself is not so much shortened or everted. The pain and swelling are greater and often become excessive, with attendant constitutional symptoms. In the intra-capsular fracture, there is but little symptomatic fever after the first few days.

Union by *ossification* will in this case take place in healthy young or middle aged persons, and even in those of a more advanced age whose constitutions are very robust.

The TREATMENT therefore should be such as will keep the parts properly in contact. The length of the limb must be preserved, and the trochanter pressed inwards. Jarvis's apparatus is well adapted to this purpose. We would simply recommend it as the best we have seen, and say nothing about any other means, if it were not too expensive for all practitioners to keep.

Of the *various methods* devised for fulfilling the proper indications, and described in detail by surgical writers, we may remark that no two of them agree in recommending any one as the best. As we consider the two plans of the great — and great because *practical* — English surgeon to be as effectual as any, and better than most, inasmuch as they are simple and cheap, we shall here also take the liberty of repeating his directions in his own language.*

"In the TREATMENT of this injury the principles are to keep the bones in approximation, by pressing the trochanter towards the acetabulum, and to preserve the length of the limb. The foot and ankle of the injured side should be firmly bound with a roller to the foot and ankle of the other leg, and thus the uninjured side will serve as a splint to that which is fractured, giving it a continued support, and keeping it extended to the proper length." (That is, of course, on the presumption that the sound limb itself is *kept* straight, though nothing is said by our author, or others, of preventing *both* limbs being drawn up together.) "A broad leathern strap should also be buckled around the pelvis, including the trochanter major, to press the fractured portions of the bone firmly together; and the best position for the limb is, to keep it in a straight line with the body.

* Sir A. Cooper's Dislocations and Fractures, p. 151 – 2.

"The following plan I have also found successful: The patient being placed on a matress on his back, the thigh is to be brought over a double inclined plane composed of three boards, one below, which is to reach from the tuberosity of the ischium to the patient's heel, and the two others having a joint in the middle by which the knee may be raised or depressed; a few holes should be made in the board, admitting a peg, which prevents any change in the elevation of the limb but that which the surgeon directs; over these a pillow must be thrown to place the patient in as easy a position as possible.

"When the limb has been thus extended, a splint is placed upon the outer side of the thigh to reach above the trochanter major, and to the upper part of this is fixed a strong leathern strap, which buckles around the pelvis, so as to press one portion of the bone upon the other; and the lower part of the splint is fixed with a strap around the knee to prevent its position from being altered. The limb must be kept as steady as possible for many weeks, and the patient may be permitted to rise from his bed, when the attempt does not give him much pain; he is still to retain the strap which I have mentioned round the pelvis; and by this treatment he will ultimately recover with a useful though shortened limb."

The concave Double Inclined splint, recommended by Dr. Beach, will be found, — with he addition of a foot-board which we have taken the liberty of adding (see Fig. 77), — a better

FIG. 77.*

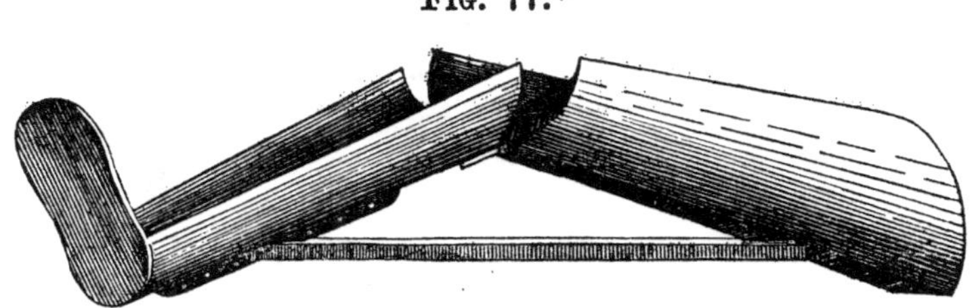

apparatus for fixing the thigh bone than the plain boards of Sir A. Cooper.

* This is simply made of two pieces of soft light wood, such as bass wood, pine or poplar, hollowed out smooth, as a half socket, respectively for the leg and thigh, and joined at the knee with a common butt-hinge. A foot-board is firmly

As these are cases of great importance, and frequently occasion much trouble, we will give another plan, which is simple, and will answer the purpose very well. Mr. Liston, in describing his favorite mode and means of adjustment, thus speaks: — "Whether the fracture is suspected to be within or without the joint, either entirely or partially, the broken surfaces are to be brought in contact and retained immovably in apposition for a time sufficient to admit of union. The limb is put up in apparatus not requiring removal and but little adjustment. This can be effected only in the extended position. Many splints, with foot-boards, straps and screws, are intended for this purpose, some to be attached to the injured limb, others to the sound one; but the apparatus which is most simple and easily to be *procured at all times and in all circumstances*, is at once the best and most efficient. This is a straight wooden board, not so thick as to feel cumbrous, and not so thin as to be pliable or easily broken; in breadth, corresponding to the dimensions of the limb; in length, sufficient to extend from two, three or four inches beyond the heel, to near the axilla; deeply notched at two places at its lower end, and perforated by two holes at the upper. The splint, well padded, is applied to the extended limb, the ankles being protected by proper adjustment of the pads. The apparatus is retained by bandaging (see Fig. 78). A common roller is applied round the

FIG. 78.

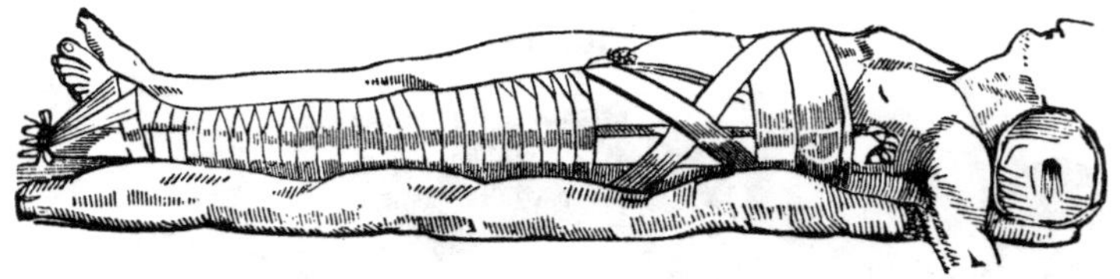

limb, from the toes to near the knee, so as to prevent infiltration, which would otherwise follow pressure above by the rest of the apparatus. The splint is then attached to the rest of the limb

screwed on the lower end. A square stick is fastened by another hinge to the thigh-piece, and has a groove and holes in its lower end to fit over a projection at the back of the leg-piece. In this are several corresponding holes, by which the two are pinned together, thus flexing the limb as little or as much as is desired.

by involving both in a roller from the foot to above the knee; and, in doing this, the bandage, after having been turned round the ankle, should be passed through the notches, so as to be firmly attached to the end of the splint, thereby preventing the foot from shifting. A broad bandage is applied around the pelvis, over the groin and down the thigh, investing all that part of the limb left uncovered by the previous bandaging. A broad band, like a riding belt, is fastened round the pelvis, so as to bind the splint to the trunk, and thereby keep the broken surfaces of the bone in contact. A large handkerchief or shawl is brought under the perineum, and its ends secured through the openings at the top of the board. It is evident that the splint being thus securely fixed, and made as part of the limb, tightening of the perineal band will extend the member and preserve it of its proper length. By care and attention in applying the apparatus, and in adjusting the cushions about the ankle and perineum, there is little or no risk of the skin giving way. The bandages will require to be reapplied once or twice during the cure; and the perineal band should be tightened frequently. The apparatus is retained for six or eight weeks, the time necessary for union varying according to circumstances. After its removal, great care must be taken at first in moving the limb and putting weight upon it: it should be accustomed to its former functions very gradually." (Medical treatment as directed for SIMPLE FRACTURE.)

FRACTURES ABOUT THE TROCHANTERS.

OBLIQUE FRACTURE THROUGH THE TROCHANTER MAJOR.— When this rare accident occurs, the limb is everted and slightly shortened. A fissure can be felt between the shaft of the bone and the trochanter. The TREATMENT of this case does not differ from the last. The limb is to be extended by the proper apparatus, and a strap applied around the hip, with a pad over the trochanter, to keep the fractured portions together. Bony union will readily take place.

The Shaft just below or about THE TROCHANTERS may be broken. This accident will be followed by great pain and deformity, from the psoas and iliacus internus muscles drawing the upper fragment of the bone upwards and forwards to a considerable distance from its proper place. When the separation is at the junction of the *epiphysis* (an occurrence difficult to distinguish), only a ligamentous union will be formed. In ADJUSTING this case, the patient should be placed in a sitting posture, to keep the before-mentioned muscles relaxed. In other respects, the treatment and appliances must be the same as for

FRACTURES OF THE SHAFT OF THE THIGH BONE.

Under this head are included all cases where the femur is broken between the Trochanter Minor and the Condyles. They are easily known. The sufferer generally knows as well what is the matter, if not what to do, as the surgeon. His inability to bear weight upon the limb, the deformity, and the crepitus on extension or rotation, are all obvious signs.

If the fracture be an *oblique* one, the limb will be much shortened by the fractured ends slipping by each other; and even when the bone is broken *transversely*, the parts are apt to be separated and pass each other.

The great point of surgery in your TREATMENT, is to be *sure* to prevent the shortening. For this purpose place the patient in a *sitting* position, so as to relax the psoas and iliacus muscles, and approximate the ends of the bones. Then *extend* the limb until it corresponds exactly with the other, which you ascertain by examining particularly the position of the malleoli and patellæ. After this extension and adjustment, apply a *roller* from the toes upwards to the body.

Three splints must be placed over the first bandage; one from the external condyle to the trochanter, another from the internal condyle to the perineum, and the third from the patella in front of the thigh to the pelvis.

Besides these splints generally directed, another of stout Gum Shellac cloth or Gutta Percha should be applied to the *inferior surface*, from the tuberosity of the ischium to the hollow of the knee. It should be wide enough to cover one-third of the thigh, and perfectly adapted to its surface.

The splints for the front and sides may be made of wood, but are better when formed of the Gutta Percha or the Shellac cloth, which by combining three or four thicknesses, may be as stiff as wood half an inch thick, yet exactly and easily fitted.

All the splints must be firmly fixed with a roller, and then the limb placed on the inclined splint (see Fig. 77), and there fastened by bands or buckles, the foot also being attached to the foot-piece.

The *first* BANDAGE that is rolled from the foot upwards should be so applied to the knee as to allow it to be bent. It is best to have three *separate* strips, one terminating just below the joint, another covering it and there fastened, and a third commencing just above and enclosing the thigh. Thus, if a change in the position of the joint should be required, the bandage may be loosened around it for a moment. At the first bandaging the limb should be partially flexed.

The patient should *not* be permitted to *lie down* for ten or twelve days, as, in that posture, the action of the muscles might disturb the adjustment of the limb in spite of all your dressings. The muscles must not be put upon the stretch before union has taken place. (Medical treatment as directed for SIMPLE FRACTURE.)

FRACTURES ABOUT THE KNEE.

THE CONDYLES OF THE FEMUR

— are oftenest broken in old persons. It is always a serious accident, sometimes a fatal one. It not unfrequently necessitates amputation.

In the TREATMENT much care is required to keep down inflammation, and to prevent irritation of the nervous system, which may easily produce tetanus. *To adjust* the fracture, have the limb straightened, so that the head of the tibia will press upon the condyles, and keep the fractured portions together. Secure by roller and splints. If it be a *compound* fracture, the parts must be so fixed that the wound can be dressed without *unsetting* again, or allowing of any motion. (See treatment for FRACTURES.)

FRACTURE OF THE PATELLA

— is generally *transverse.* The upper part is drawn high up by the rectus femoris. The fissure between the divided portions is very distinct. The patient has not the power of straightening his leg.

Fig. 79.

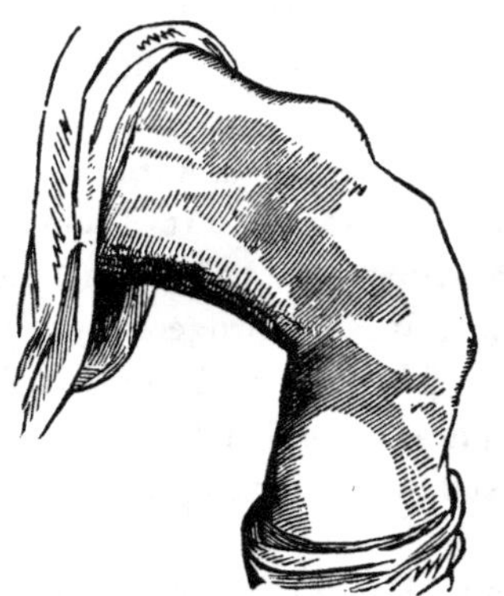

In TREATING this accident, lay the limb perfectly *straight*, and secure it in that position with a *stiff splint* placed on the back of the thigh, extending down the calf of the leg. Apply a roller from the toes to the knee, and affix the splint firmly to the thigh. The divided parts may be brought together in this way: Straps are buckled round below the lower part and above the upper, and drawn together by means of other straps attached to them, and meeting longitudinally at the sides of the knee. Pull the circular straps up and down, until the fractured parts come together, and then secure them firmly. Unless perfect coaptation be preserved, the union will be only ligamentous.

Longitudinal Fracture of the Patella is easily treated. After subduing inflammation, extend the leg, bring the parts together and secure them by bandage, with compresses and paste-board or Gutta Percha splints.

For the difficult object of fixing the patella in its place after dislocation, or keeping its segments together after fracture, an ingenious apparatus has been quite recently invented (represented in Fig. 80). This consists of a ring or case exactly fitting the

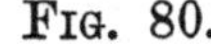

Fig. 80.

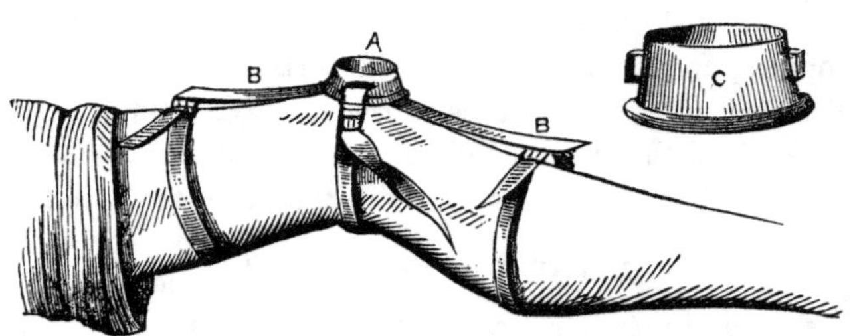

patella, two springs (one up the thigh, the other down the shin), and three straps and buckles. The patella case may be described as a tubular ring or shallow *cylinder* (indicated by letter A in the cut, and shown also on a larger scale at C), very slightly funnel-shaped, about two inches in height, made of heavy tin, with the lower edge rolled outwards, and the inside padded and lined with buckskin. This is exactly fitted over and round the patella, and firmly secured by the strap going twice under the knee, and through the loop or staple on each side. Besides this strap, the curved springs (B B, riveted to the cylinder at opposite points, at right angles to the staples), exert a constant force, tending to press the cylinder down closer, the tendency of the other ends to rise being counteracted by the straps round the leg and thigh. With this apparatus the patient can even walk about without risk of disturbing the fracture or allowing the patella to be displaced. It would be safer, however, in any case, to keep the leg at rest and extended for two or three weeks. For this reason a straight splint should also be fastened under the leg and thigh. After this period, the use of the joint could be gradually resumed, the apparatus in front being still *worn till union is complete.* (Medical treatment as directed for SIMPLE FRACTURE.)

THE HEAD OF THE TIBIA

— may be fractured obliquely, into the joint across the articulating surface. The case is readily distinguished, and the TREATMENT must be the same as directed for fracture at the upper side of the joint through the condyles of the femur. Keep the leg extended by a proper splint, and apply a roller around the parts so as to press the fractured portions together. A pasteboard, Gutta Percha, or Shellac splint will assist much in keeping the parts firmly fixed in their proper position. *Early passive motion* is necessary in this as in the other cases of fracture about the knee joint, to prevent a stiff leg.

FRACTURES BELOW THE KNEE.

FOR A BROKEN LEG

— between the ankle and the knee, — a case too plain to the patient as well as practitioner to need description, — whether the fracture be simple or comminuted, you can generally use with advantage such apparatus as has been recommended for fractures of the neck or shaft of the femur. The most convenient of them for the present purpose will be the double inclined-splints.

The bandage, that is the first thing to be applied in these cases, need not begin over the ends of the toes, nor be so firmly rolled, as was directed for the treatment of ulcers (and there illustrated, Fig. 1). It will be well enough in this case to leave out the toes and heel, and run on with fewer turns and less over-lapping, as is *usually* done in other cases where such looseness is not so safe or effectual. (Figure 81 shows this common bandaging.) This first roller is not to be so tight as to prevent further *extension*, and exact adjustment being made after it is on; for it will be best in most cases, especially

FIG. 81.

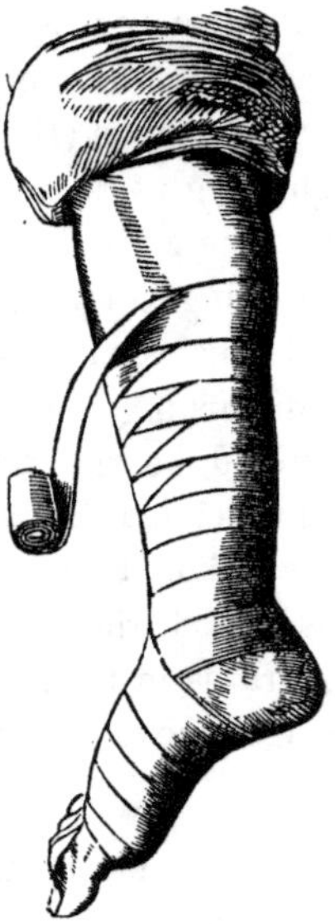

— in OBLIQUE FRACTURES, to place the limb (after provisional rectification with the roller as above) on the inclined-splints, and there extend it so as to compare exactly with the other, and then fix the foot firmly to the board provided for the purpose, by straps that will not stretch or get loose. Remember that the great toe is always to be kept in a line with the inner edge of the patella. After having the bones thus symmetrically adjusted and securely fixed, two or three *splints* should be still applied to the sides and front of the leg, and kept on by a roller, which also includes the large supporting splint or "inclined-plane," fastening the whole firmly together. By this plan you not only make "assurance doubly sure," but can at any time remove the splints, for the purpose of examining or dressing, without the risk of disturbance.

Dr. Hill once, on the spur of the occasion, in a bad case of comminuted fracture, got up the following apparatus, which we shall describe, because, while we believe it as good as any other, it can be readily made wherever there can be found *wood*, with an axe, a hand-saw, an inch or an inch and a half auger, and a jack-knife.

Get two pieces of board, five or six inches wide and half an inch thick (common siding will do), and long enough to reach several inches above the knee and below the foot. Bore a hole near the lower end of each, and also two holes through each at the upper ends. Protect the thigh from the ends of the boards by a roller, to which two pads of cotton cloth are attached. To these pads you fasten your boards by strips of drilling or strong muslin, run through the holes and round the limb. This done, wrap the foot and ankle moderately tight with a roller, and fix, by its means, a strong band to each side of the ankle, and another behind and above the heel. Pass through the lower holes a smooth stick, ten or twelve inches long, and large enough to nearly fill them. Then make extension on the leg by the straps attached to the ankle, or by taking hold of the foot and heel, until the fracture can be properly adjusted, and fix the straps to the cross-piece below, so as to prevent any relaxation. To be certain that the proper extension has been made, you should always measure from some fixed point on the knee or pelvis to the malleolus, and see how the length compares with that of the sound leg. When thus secured in position, roll the leg with the bandage, and apply splints in front, behind and at each side, all fastened on by the bandage. To make this last part of the operation more convenient, the lower ends of the boards may be separated five or six inches further, with but little alteration in the distance of the cross-piece, to which the extending force is fastened, and which may be *turned*, so as to roll up and proportionally to shorten the extending straps, and fixed as long as necessary by a pin, nail, or wedge. This will be safer than to trust to an assistant for holding the foot, until the apparatus can be replaced.

As, however, the patient will get tired of having the limb kept straight, the apparatus may be so contrived as to let him have it bent. There may be circular joints at the knee, which will bend without allowing the distance between the knee and the foot to vary; and a pad may be fixed at the foot, like a sole, extending an inch or more behind the heel, to which the extending straps may be made fast. This contrivance becomes then an equivalent for the inclined-splint, before recommended.

If it is deemed necessary to *keep up* the extending force, a strap may be attached to the foot, and passed over the rounded cross-piece, with a weight attached.

This apparatus, simple as it is, and easily made by any one who can handle the commonest tools, is well adapted to cases of *compound fracture*, where it is necessary to remove the rollers and splints to dress the wound. The danger of *contraction* is entirely *prevented*, while the affected part of the limb can, if necessary, be completely freed from *contact* of splint or bandage.

It is due to the late Dr. Jas. H. Willard, of Brownhelm, Lorain county, Ohio, to state that the apparatus invented and patented by him, is one of the best and most generally available in fractures of the *leg* and *shaft* of the femur. We should be less inclined to make this acknowledgment, if the inventor had taken advantage of his patent right. So far from it, he lent his machine and allowed it to be copied by any one who needed it. This liberality is as honorable as the contrivance is ingenious. It is too complex for verbal description, or perhaps even a common drawing, but could be made, after a model, in a day, by any good joiner or cabinet-maker, with the help of a smith or a few screws, &c., ready made. The frame-work extends the whole length of the limb, and the relative position of each part can be varied to suit any case. The limb is supported on webbing, tightened by a small windlass, which is movable in the frame, as it has also to support the heel. The beam that supports the knee can be raised or lowered, as well as advanced or drawn back on the frame. The whole can with great advantage be first fitted to the sound limb, the injured one then placed on it, and extension there made by bringing the retracted foot down to the foot-board, — previously fixed at the right distance from the knee or tuberosity of the ischium. (See treatment of FRACTURES.)

FRACTURES ABOUT THE ANKLES.

THE FIBULA is not unfrequently broken about three inches above the ankle. This is CAUSED by *twisting* the foot *outwards*, and accompanied with partial or entire dislocation of the ankle. The resulting deformity is considerable: the internal malleolus projects, forming a tumor, and crepitus can be felt, when the foot is moved, just above the *external malleolus*. The dislocation has first to be *reduced*, and the fracture then ADJUSTED, and kept in place by a splint at the back of the leg, and a foot-board, fixing the foot so that the great toe is in a line with the inner edge of the patella. Another splint along the course of the fibula will be necessary, and bandages, as in other cases. Keep both leg and

FIG. 82.* FIG. 83*.

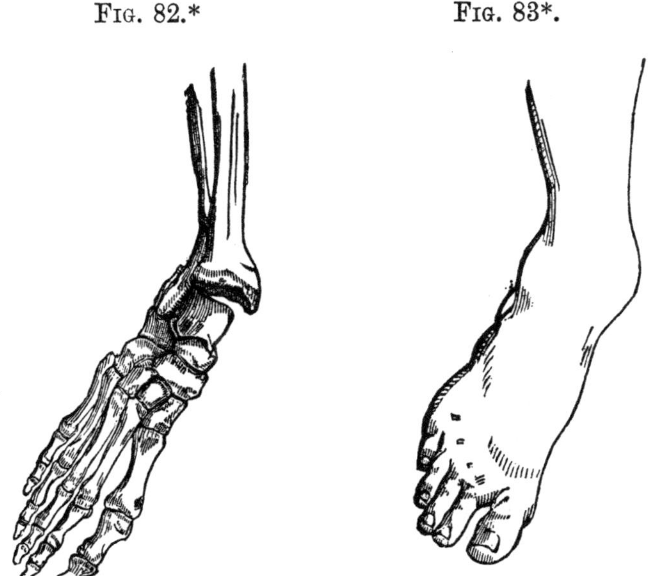

foot quite still, and in the easiest position for the patient, as was stated in the treatment of fractures. Ruta should be used in these injuries about the ankle.

The TIBIA may be fractured near its lower end,—generally obliquely, with the *internal malleolus* broken off (see Fig. 84),—by *twisting* the foot *inwards* with sufficient force. The fracture may be transverse, extending through the fibula. The symptoms, in either case, are the same and obvious:—the foot is seen turned inwards, instead of outwards, as when the fibula *alone* is involved, the external malleolus projecting (as seen in the figure), if not also broken off. The crepitus is to be felt on the inside. The

* Fig. 83 represents the position of the foot and external appearance, Fig. 82 the condition of the bones or surgical anatomy of the case.

treatment is in all respects the same as directed for the former case, except that the one splint is to be applied on the side of the tibia, instead of the fibula (unless the latter be also broken and require another).

Fig. 84.

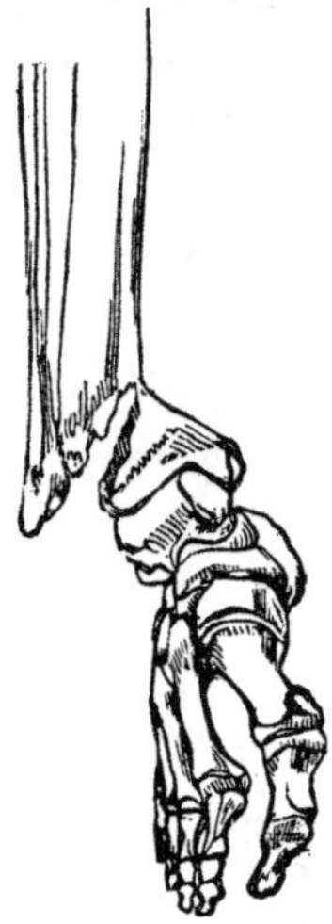

FRACTURES OF THE FOOT

— are in nearly all cases connected with severe contusions, and more or less laceration. Treat them in all respects, aside from the fracture, as you would any other contused or lacerated wound. The bones are to be confined to their proper places with pasteboard, Gutta Percha, or Shellac splints, compresses and bandages. In all cases the foot has to be kept very still, and other precautions used to keep down inflammation.

A faithful application of our remedial means, and a just reliance on the restorative powers of nature, would restore to usefulness many a foot consigned by allopathic surgeons to amputation. We are knowing to several cases, where distinguished old school surgeons have deemed amputation the only safe resort, which have been cured by remedial measures, and a useful foot preserved.

CHAPTER XI.

AMPUTATIONS.

Shall a limb or part of the human body be removed by the knife, and the individual be incapacitated to fulfill many of the duties of life, or to participate in many of its pleasures? nay more, is it necessary to mutilate that the life of the patient may be saved? are questions the surgeon must often decide; and the decision of which should demand great skill in curative surgery, a mature judgment, and the warmest sympathies in behalf of the patient. Yet, do surgeons feel their responsibility? Have they exhausted all curative resources, and given the patient the benefit of every doubt as to the necessity of amputation before they operate?

Does not the eclat and emoluments following an important, successful surgical operation, ministering to their vanity, ambition and self interest, often mislead many a distinguished surgeon? Indeed, do not many of them owe their notoriety, as well as dexterity, to the fact that they have so often found it necessary to resort to amputation? And that it is often a proof of their *ignorance*, is shown by other surgeons (less distinguished in the eyes of the world) curing the very cases they had decided *must* be operated upon. We might instance a number of such. Strange infatuation, that this power to mutilate, which is often the evident result of bad surgery, and always a confession of the poverty of the surgeon's resources, should be considered a proof of great surgical skill. We trust, however, that a brighter day for humanity is dawning, and that it will not be long before *curative* surgery shall have attained its proper position, and that the test of surgical superiority will be the *infrequency* and not the frequency of the necessity for a resort to the knife. And however imperfect this work in other respects, it will not be valueless, if it shall contribute a mite to the furtherance of this desirable object.

Amputation is considered justifiable whenever it is thought the constitution will be unable to stand the shock and continued irritation consequent upon severe mechanical injury; or whenever the disease, upon which any local deterioration is dependant, cannot be removed by medicine. Hence operations are resorted to in gangrene of the extremities,supposed incurable, disorganization of the joints, copious undefinable hemorrhage, necrosis, incurable ulcers and diseases of the skin—in malignant growths—in distortions (operations of expediency), cases of irreducible dislocation, and in severe compound or comminuted fracture. The proper medical treatment that will render amputation, in nearly all of the above cases unnecessary, has been before given. (See GANGRENE, WHITE SWELLING, ULCERS, CANCERS, &c.)

At the time of operating, the patient should be in as good health as possible, and should have become accustomed to the influences to which he will be subjected while convalescent. Hence a patient should not come to the city to be operated upon, in very warm weather, or be operated upon at any time immediately upon his arrival. No sudden changes of diet or such depleting measures as would impair the constitutional vigor should be resorted to as a preventative to inflammation: we have other and better means. The morning is always preferred as the time for operating, as the patient is then refreshed by the night's rest, and in a better condition to stand the shock; there is also time for the surgeon to reach or to secure any arteries in case of secondary hemorrhage, before the hour of repose.

Anaesthetics should be used in all important surgical operations, when we may expect much danger from the shock to the nervous system, occasioned by the pain attending them; except where there is *disease of the heart*, very *great prostration from loss of blood*, or a *tendency to apoplexy*. In these cases, they are *contra-indicated*. The article first known for its anaesthetic powers, is nothing but the common Sulphuric Ether, purified by water, and taken into the lungs instead of the stomach. Chloroform is now, however, generally employed alone or in combination with Ether, to produce anaesthesia.

The best way to administer it is to put it on a handkerchief and hold it near the nostrils, but not so as to prevent some atmospheric air from being breathed with it. It should not be administered soon after eating, as when there is much food in the stomach, sickness and severe vomiting are liable to ensue on recovering from its first effects—a very rare symptom when the stomach is empty.

The regular "AMPUTATING CASE" is very convenient, but by no means indispensable. It contains only four instruments that are not, or ought not to be, in every practitioner's pocket case. These four are the tourniquet, large knife (or knives), saw and bone-forceps. The last article is for nipping off splinters, or dividing small bones, as those of the fingers (for which a particular small saw is also often kept). The knives in use are a large blunt and round-pointed one for circular operations, and two sharp-pointed ones, sometimes called "catlins," of different sizes, for flap operations on different parts. The larger of these, or one of medium size, will answer for all cases, and can be used for the circular operation also. The special "case" should also have a scalpel (for dissecting up the integuments round the bone, &c.), artery forceps and tenaculum, with ligatures, surgeon's needles, lint and adhesive plaster.

It is well enough to have all these things kept *separately* ready and in order for use, but the only essential pre-requisites for the business are the proper knowledge and resolution. A common carving knife well sharpened, or a butcher's knife of the suitable shape, may be handled as scientifically as any. The carpenter's sash saw, if good and properly filed (the teeth set coarsely or wide apart), will go through bone as well as one made especially for the purpose: it *is a surgeon's* instrument when kept and used by one. A substitute for the tourniquet could be contrived by any one who understands the use of it. The bone-forceps are seldom necessary, when the sawing is done as a good *mechanic* would do it — any rough margin of the bone *might*, in case of necessity, be filed off smoothly. These remarks are made, not to encourage any one in setting up as a surgeon without the necessary (or even the best and most convenient) instruments, but to show that these things are of comparatively trifling importance, and do away with the prestige and mystery of all such crafts.

There are *three modes* of amputating. The old and, till lately, most common one is called the *circular operation*. The second, the *flap operation*, which is extensively used in this country. The third is a compound of the two former, consisting of a flap of the integuments, and a circular division of the muscles.

Previous to the introduction of chloroform, the flap operation was preferred on account of the rapidity with which it can be performed and the consequent decrease of pain. But latterly it is objected to that the stumps are not as good, that the vessels are more likely to be injured above the point where the ligatures have been applied, that being cut obliquely, the smaller arteries cannot so readily retract within their sheaths and cease to bleed. Hence there is a greater loss of blood, and a larger number of ligatures are required. It is also thought that the recovery is not so rapid.

AMPUTATION OF THE ARM.

All the preparation absolutely necessary for this operation, is that of the TOURNIQUET (Figures 85 and 86), with a bandage

FIG. 64.*

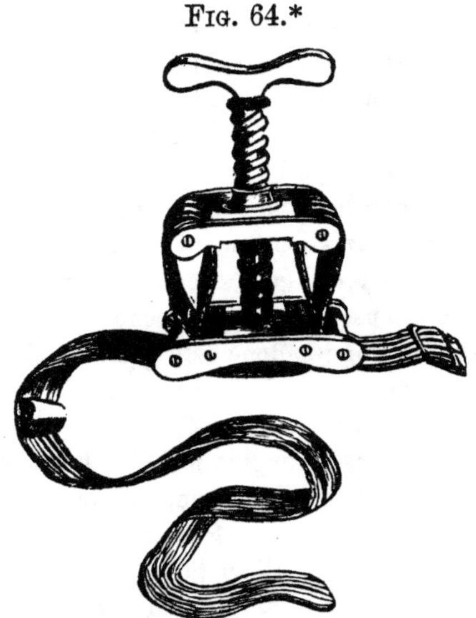

round the fore-arm that it may be held more conveniently. The *pad* of the tourniquet (or the compress under any substitute that may have to be used) should be fixed on the artery as high up as

* Mr. Skey's tourniquet is far superior to the common one as represented in Fig. 85, the description of which we give in his own words:

"It is composed of two semicircles, one of which fits into the other by running in a groove: each half is fixed by a spring catch to the other, and may be enlarged or reduced at will to any size required for the thigh or upper arm. When required for application to the thigh, the circle which is made to open to admit of its application around the limb, is drawn out to its fullest size. In the centre of each semicircle is the pad for pressure and counter-pressure, the former being provided with the ordinary screw. The pads are made small in order to include as little surface in the pressure as is compatible with the safe application of the instrument. When employed for a lesser limb, the arm for example, or the thigh of a child, the circle is lessened to the required size by raising the lateral springs, pressing the outer half or semicircle downwards upon the inner one, by which the larger circle is converted into one of a smaller size, the alteration being obtained by the introduction of two hinges in each half of the instrument."

is necessary to give room for the operation. The *brachial artery* lies near the surface, and may easily be compressed against the humerus at any part of its course. Near the elbow it lies in front of the brachialis anticus, but runs up obliquely towards the axilla, having afterwards, in front of it, the biceps and coraco-brachialis, and, behind it, the triceps with the insertions of the latissimus dorsi and teres major.

The patient is seated in a chair, or laid, in a convenient posture, upon a table or bed. One assistant has hold of the fore-arm to support and steady it, while another grasps the arm with both his hands above the part to be operated on, and pulls back the integuments as tight as possible. If the

CIRCULAR OPERATION

—is the one to be performed, the surgeon, knife in hand, passes his hand under the patient's arm, bringing the knife completely over it towards himself, with the point downwards (see the position of the hands in Fig. 86, representing the commencement of the

Fig. 86.

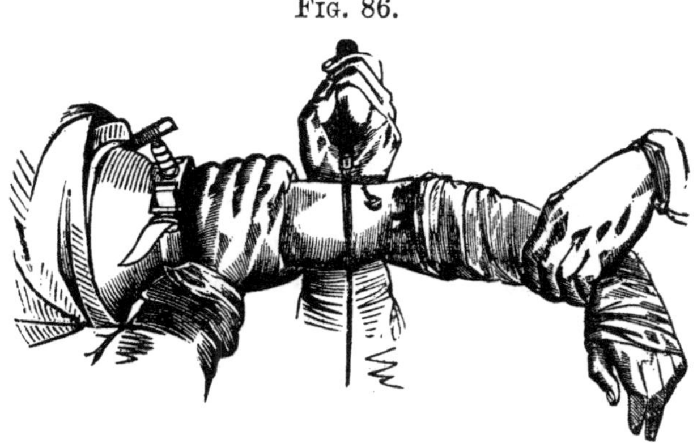

operation on the left arm); and proceeds with his first incision, drawing the blade backwards from hilt to point, completely round the limb, merely cutting through the skin and superficial fasciæ. The instrument is then laid aside or handed to an assistant, and the integument loosened from the muscles beneath by detaching the cellular membrane with scalpel or bistoury. The skin is now forcibly retracted further up, and another incision made, in the same manner as the first, as far up as the skin will permit, dividing all the flesh down to the bone. It is perhaps better to make both incisions somewhat eliptical — or rather twice varied from the circular direction — leaving the muscles longer both before and behind than at the sides.

The next step is to separate the muscles from the bone for an inch or two, with the point of the knife (if a pointed one is used) or a scalpel; and apply a two-tailed retractor (which is made by slitting to its middle a common bandage or strip of muslin, about a yard long and three inches wide). The broader end is to be placed on the under side of the arm, passing the two tails up on each side of the naked bone and crossing them at the top. The flesh is pulled up as far as possible on the bone by an assistant, who retains it there by holding the ends of the retractor. A cut is then to be made all round the bone, close up to the retracted muscles, for the purpose of separating the periosteum. In commencing with the saw, place the heel on the bone where the periosteum has been thus separated, and draw it back so as to have a slight groove for the forward motion. Then saw away steadily, but lightly. Let there be no roughness or hurry in this part of the business. The operator should have hold of the arm above the saw, while an assistant steadies the fore-arm, till the bone is divided and the severed limb quickly put out of sight by the latter. The last few strokes of the saw should be short and gentle, to avoid splintering the bone. Should any splinters nevertheless occur, they are to be carefully removed by the bone-forceps or nippers, and the end of the bone made smooth.

The retractor is now to be removed and the brachial artery taken up and tied. This is done by seizing the end of it with the forceps, and holding it while the ligature is applied. Before that is done, however, the nerve or nerves (according to the part of the arm divided) should be separated from the artery with the fingers or the handle of the scalpel; or the cellular membrane which connects them may be cut off. This separation should go no further than is absolutely necessary to make room for the ligature. Pulling at the artery for this purpose should be gently done, as it is the most painful part of the operation; but it may save the patient many an after pang of the most intense neuralgia, to which he will be forever liable (as well as the immediate risk of tetanus), if the nerve is bound up with the coats of the vessel. Should there be any difficulty in *finding* the artery, in consequence of its retraction after division, the tourniquet is to be loosened a little, when a jet of blood will betray the spout. Seize it immediately and renew the pressure above, till the ligature is applied. Then unscrew the tourniquet, and if there are any *arterial branches* necessary to be secured, the flow of blood through them will determine the fact as well as their location.

As soon as the veins have ceased bleeding, let the stump be cleansed from all coagula, and *dressed* in the following manner. The flesh must be drawn down in mass over the end of the bone, and the edges brought together in a horizontal line across the middle of the stump. There will be no necessity in this case for any sewing. The common adhesive plaster of the shops is sufficient, the straps to be about three-fourths of an inch in width, and long enough to turn over for four or five inches on each side. Place the first across the middle of the seam, taking care to have the edges of the wound exactly adjusted. Another is then fixed on each side of the first, at about a quarter of an inch distance, and more, if necessary, to keep the edges together in the horizontal line. One end of the ligature should be left long enough to hang out between the straps; between which some little space should be allowed for the exit of any matter that may form. Ligatures should always be brought out of the wound in the most direct line from the ligatured artery. Two straps should be laid obliquely across the others, covering and pressing down the corners, so as to make a round, smooth surface. Narrower straps may be applied, if necessary, to close any part of the lips that, having been left free, seem inclined to gape. Lastly, have one strap to go round the arm, binding down the ends of all the others; but not so tightly as in the least to retard the circulation.

Over the straps, the end of the stump should be covered with lint or cotton, kept on by a bandage lightly applied, — but evenly and so as to prevent the adhesive straps from being loosened by any lotions that may be needed, — taking care again, however, not to obstruct the circulation. Let these dressings be kept constantly wet with some cool lotion, as Arnicated water, aqua Calendula or Momordica, as directed for incised wounds. A dose of Aconite should be given, to prevent the rise of inflammation, and repeated if necessary.

If no unfavorable symptoms occur, the first dressing may be left on for four or five days. But if on the second or third day after the operation, there shall be any discharge from the wound, and particularly if of an offensive character; if the dressings be saturated with a bloody or sanious fluid, or the limb be hot and painful or sensitive to the touch, the stump should be dressed.

These symptoms will not usually appear until the third day, except in very hot weather, and the less clearly they are then marked the greater the probability of complete union by the first intention. When the stump is dressed, the strips of plaster should be removed with the greatest gentleness, and not all at once; but commencing from one extremity of the wound, two or three strips may be removed, the edges of the wound being carefully supported and gently sponged, and fresh pieces of plaster applied before the other strips are removed; in this way the wound is supported during the entire dressing, which is very important, since the adhesion is at this time but feeble. We must be careful that in removing the plaster we do not move or pull upon the ligatures, as it might cause secondary hemorrhage.

FOR THE FLAP OPERATION,

— the patient is placed in the same position, and the fore-arm bandaged and held by an assistant, as for the circular method. It is still best to have another assistant to draw back the skin, just as before directed, as this will obviate the accident of having muscle protruding between the skin of the flaps, which frequently occurs when the precaution is neglected. The flaps themselves had better be taken from before and behind than from the sides.

The point of the knife is entered at one side, with the blade held horizontally and passed on, penetrating directly to the bone. It is then turned a little forwards, — the muscles being drawn up in front, — and pushed over the bone, or rather half round it, the point being depressed and emerging from the other side, just opposite to where it entered. By proceeding in this way, the blood-vessels are left behind the knife, to be divided when the second flap is cut. When the blade is fairly through, with the edge looking towards the elbow, it is made to cut downwards and outwards

Fig. 87.

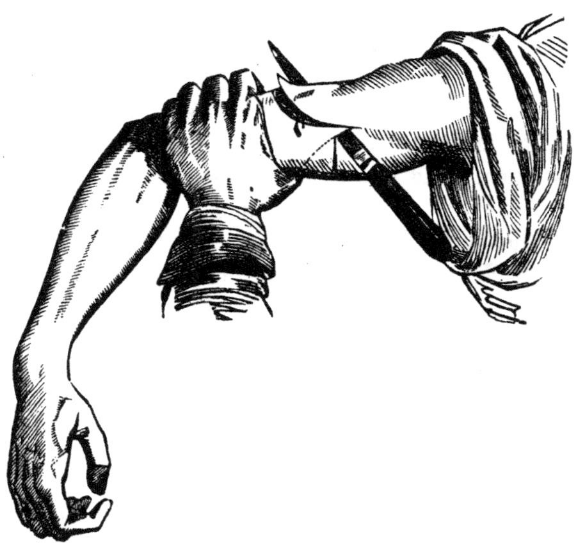

to the surface, making the first or front flap about two and a half or three inches in length. The point is then re-entered in the wound about three quarters of an inch below the former point of entrance, passed on to the bone, round it behind, and out through the former wound a little lower than before.

The edge is then brought downwards and backwards to the surface, making the posterior flap of equal length to the anterior. The flaps are now held firmly back by an assistant, and the edge of the knife made to sweep round the bone, to detach any remaining fibres. It is still better to detach the muscles from the bone, with a scalpel or bistoury, a little further up, and to hold back the flaps with a retractor, as in the circular operation, though it is not here so essential. The periosteum is then to be separated as before, and the bone sawed off as high up as convenient.

The *artery*, — which, in cutting according to the directions above given, will generally be found in the posterior flap, — being secured, and the tourniquet removed, the wound is cleansed, and the edges of the flaps brought exactly together, and secured by adhesive straps. There will be less tendency to gaping of the wound, or protrusion of corners, than in the former operation. If the proper judgment be exercised, the flaps may be made to meet in a line across the middle of the stump. This, however, is far from being the case with many operators. A distinguished surgeon, in three or four successive flap operations, was obliged to *trim* the flaps, in order to make them meet. This had better be done than to leave badly fitting flaps; but it looks very cruel as well as awkward; and every surgeon should have *eye* enough to avoid the necessity for it. It would certainly be better for the Professor alluded to, to take a lesson on *pattern-making* from his tailor, and mark his *cloth* before cutting. Indeed, we would recommend this to beginners, at least: have a piece of paper long enough to go round the limb, and broad enough to become a model of the flaps; fold it twice, and cut off one of the corners nearly circularly from the opposite one, as a center. The paper being unfolded, may be reapplied to the limb, and flaps marked out with a pen, which *must* come equally together.

The directions about the *ligature* and *dressings*, given for the circular operation, apply equally in this case. It is still more necessary that the straps and bandage should keep the larger fleshy mass of the flaps together.

"The third form of operation is commenced by an incision through the integuments only, carried downwards in an arched form, from the point at which it is intended to divide the bone, to the opposite side of the limb. This part of the operation may be performed with a large scalpel. The height of this arch should be fully equal to the semi-diameter of the limb, and when the incision is completed, the flap should be reflected upwards to a line corresponding with its base. A second incision is then to be made through the integuments of the opposite side, similar in form to the first, or the two together may form flaps of unequal size. When sufficiently reflected, the muscles are divided in the same manner as the circular operation.

Other treatment, after amputation, does not differ from that of any other incised wound. The peculiarity of the case, if any, is rather *constitutional* than local. The removal of a considerable part of the limb necessarily *tends* in some degree towards plethora in the smaller system left, supposing the stomach, heart and lungs to produce and elaborate as before. This has been noticed in some cases to occasion a complete and not unfavorable change in the person's constitution. Generally, however, the whole physiological system appears to accommodate itself to the new state of things with surprising facility; though it is long before the individual's mind is so reconciled as to acquire a familiar consciousness of his new bodily condition. He is often caught in the attempt to walk on the leg or strike with the hand — that is in the grave!

CHAPTER XII.

AMPUTATION OF THE FORE-ARM, HAND AND FINGERS.

OF THE FORE-ARM.

THE CIRCULAR AMPUTATION is performed in the same manner as described for the arm above the elbow, except that the *interosseous ligament* must be separately cut with the point of the knife, and that a *three-tailed retractor* has to be used, one strip passing between the two bones. The operation is, in respect to ligating and dressing, the same as in

THE FLAP METHOD,

— of which a plate is given. The patient being in a convenient position, and the brachial artery secured by tourniquet as directed for operating on the arm, the fore-arm is steadily supported by an assistant in a position between pronate and supine, that is, with the thumb upwards; — or the surgeon may so hold the wrist in his left hand while operating with the right; — while the assistant, or another assistant, draws up the integument. Make your posterior or external flap first. Having previously had the integument stretched back as far as possible by an assistant, enter the knife, with the edge towards the hand, at the radial side of the arm. When the point reaches the bone, gently rotate the hand a little inwards, and push the point on close over both bones, taking care not to let it enter between them (a piece of awkwardness that has happened!). As the blade passes over the *ulna*, rotate the radius *outwards* a little, so as to bring the point out further down, under that bone. Then cut downwards and outwards, so that the edge may emerge at about an inch and a half below, and at equal distance from, the points of entrance and emergence. The external flap is now to be raised a little; and the knife entered again at the former point, or a line or two below, and pushed through close in front of the bones, emerging at the same point as before (as represented in Fig. 88). Then bring the edge obliquely downwards, leaving a second flap of similar shape and the same size as the former.

Fig. 88.

Both flaps are then to be drawn a little up, all the textures attached to the bones separated, and the point of the knife passed *between* the bones for the same purpose. The flaps are to be drawn still further up, out of the way of the saw, by the hands of an assistant; or the three-tailed retractor may be used in this case also, though it is not so necessary as in the circular operation. The saw is to be applied, as before directed, but in such a direction as to cut through both bones together, special care being taken, as you get nearly through, not to splinter either of them.

The arteries are then to be separated from the nerves and taken up. The radial, the ulnar and interosseal arteries should be all three tied. The last named may not be easily found without loosening the tourniquet for a moment. After it and the other two are secured, loosen the pressure again, and if any large branches seem to bleed too freely and do not stop on the application of cold water, take up and tie them also in the same manner as the main trunks.

Dress the stump in the same manner as directed for the upper arm.

OF THE FINGERS.

The necessity for removing a finger, or part of it, most commonly arises from its getting crushed in machinery or burnt with gunpowder. The operation is frequently resorted to without necessity. If you use proper means and care in curing the wound, you will very rarely have to amputate. When this cannot be avoided, it should always be an object with you to preserve as much of the finger as possible. The stump of one joint, or even part of a joint, may be of considerable use. Not a joint can be lost from the hand, without injury to its power as well as appearance.

An assistant grasps the wrist, and the surgeon, if about to amputate at a *joint*, and by the *flap* method, seizes the finger (it having been previously wrapped with a bandage, and the others separated from it), and bends the joint at a right angle. A semilunar cut is made on the back of the finger, from side to side, a quarter of an inch below the joint. The joint is opened at its lowest point with a scalpel or bistoury. The knife is passed up to the joint and completely through it, so as to divide the lateral ligaments, — when, of course, the bone is dislocated. The knife is still carried behind it, and as the finger is straightened, made to cut outward and toward the end of the finger, so as to leave a flap on the inner or palmar side long enough to cover the stump (see Fig. 89).

FIG. 89.

The digital arteries may bleed considerably, but can generally be stopped, without a ligature, by cold water. If not, you can close them by twisting with a pair of forceps, though we prefer tying to this torsion. When all bleeding has ceased, the wound is washed clean and the surface of the finger made quite dry, the flap thrown over the end, its edge brought up exactly to where the other side was first cut, and the whole secured with straps. A little lint is then placed over the stump, a bandage applied round the finger and hand, and the hand supported in a sling. The stump generally requires to be kept wet with the usual cool lotion.

It may not always be convenient to cut the flap from the palmar side of the finger, in which case the hand should be reversed and the operation commenced from the palmar side, enough of the integument being left on the back to cover the stump.

In the *circular* amputation an incision is made round the finger, at the distance of a half or three-quarters of an inch below the joint, and the integuments dissected up to it, having previously drawn the skin up as far as it would go. The joint is then separated and the operation completed as before directed.

Amputation BETWEEN THE JOINTS is performed by either method. The difference is not great. The skin should be retracted as far as possible in either case, and the incision made at a proper distance below the point where the bone is to be divided. Another way is, after making the circular cut, to make also a longitudinal one on each side, towards the base of the finger, and then dissecting up sufficient flaps from before and behind to fold over and meet across the center. The bone can be divided by the bone-forceps, or the finger-saw may be used.

Amputation at the BASE of the fingers, or at the *phalangeo-metacarpal* articulation, is effected by making an incision upon the knuckle in an elliptical form around the finger, terminating at the point of commencement. Make it extend down upon the palmar surface of the finger for an inch, or far

FIG. 90.

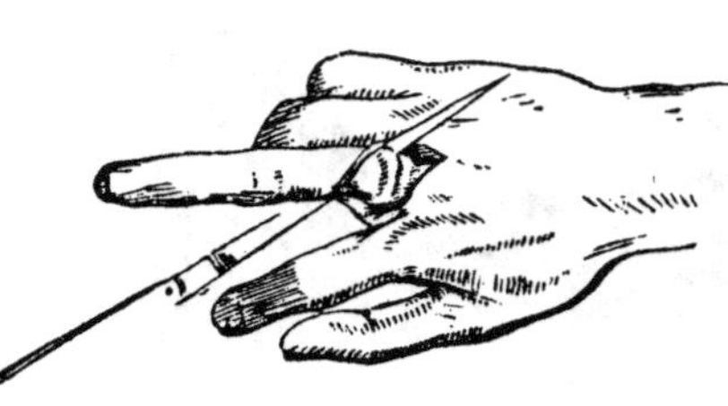

enough to make a flap that will cover the joint. The tendons and ligaments can then be cut through, the bone dislocated and removed by passing the knife through the joint (Fig. 90), and the operation completed as in the case of any of the lower joints.

The METACARPAL BONES are amputated by making an incision through the integuments directly over the bone, commencing above the point where it is necessary to amputate, and carrying the incision down, diverging as you go to one side of the articulation, and then along between the fingers and to the requisite distance on the palmar surface, where it is met by another incision passing by the other side of the articulation. These lines are somewhat curved so as to meet when the bone is taken out. Then divide the tendons and fasciæ at the point of amputation, and lay bare the bone as much as possible for its whole circumference, keeping the knife always in contact with it. After having bared the bone for nearly its whole surface, it should be cut off with Liston's bone-forceps (represented in the act of nipping, Fig. 91), and then completely dissected out.

FIG. 91.

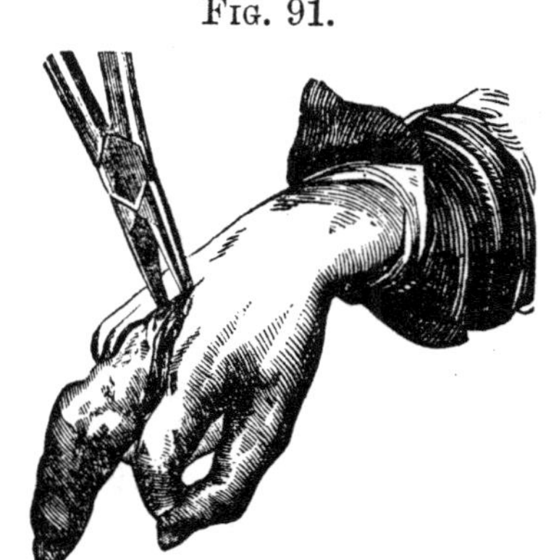

This operation is very severe, and rarely, if ever, necessary. The diseases or accidents for which it is enjoined may be remedied or cured under almost all circumstances. We have never been obliged to perform it, having been hitherto so fortunate as to cure those cases commonly supposed to require amputation.

The arteries must be taken up and tied — the bleeding cannot be otherwise arrested. The lips of the wound are brought together by adhesive straps, lint and bandage applied, the part kept constantly wet, as in other amputations, and the hand supported in a sling. It is best in such cases to keep the fingers forcibly straightened by a splint under the palm of the hand, as they are inclined to cross each other.

THE THUMB

—is amputated between the joints, or at either of the two

Fig. 92.

philangeal joints, in the same manner as the fingers. (See Fig. 92, and directions for Amputation of the Fingers.)

For the *carpo-metacarpal* amputation of the thumb, begin an incision on the back of the hand a little above the upper extremity of the metacarpal bone of the thumb, continuing it down between the thumb and fore-finger. Introduce the point of a narrow bistoury or scalpel at the lower extremity of this incision, passing it up under the metacarpal bone, so as to bring the point out where the first incision began (see Fig. 93), with the edge looking towards the end of the thumb. Then cut outward and downward, so as to make a good flap from the palmar surface to

Fig. 93.

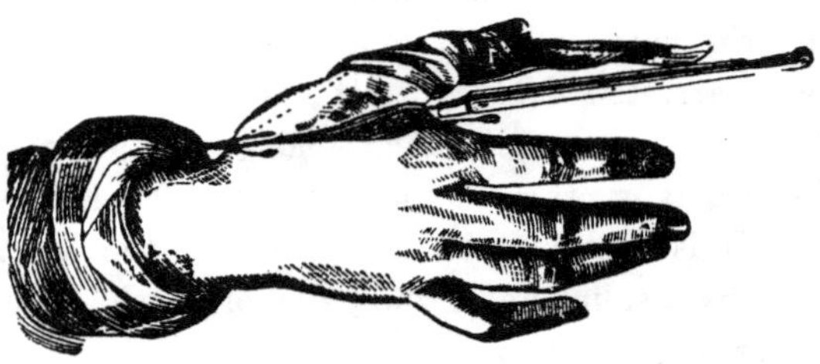

cover the part after the bone is removed. The bone can be readily separated from the trapezium and wholly removed. To arrest the hemorrhage, it will generally be necessary to take up one or more small arteries. Secure the flap in place by adhesive straps, apply your lint and bandage, and support the hand in a sling. (See AMPUTATION OF THE ARM.)

CHAPTER XIII.

AMPUTATIONS OF THE LOWER EXTREMITY.

OF THE THIGH.

ALL necessary arrangements being made, your instruments at hand, and your assistants ready with proper instructions, the patient is placed in a convenient position on his bed, or a table covered with folded blankets. If you conclude not to remove him from his bed, he must be on a mattress, or boards suitably covered. The limb to be operated on should project over the edge of the bed or table, while the other is fastened by bandages to some fixed point, or firmly held by a strong assistant.* After everything else is ready, the patient is rendered insensible by some anæsthetic agent, — if that measure is deemed advisable, — and the operation immediately begins:

— The tourniquet is applied with the pad over the femoral artery, just below Poupart's ligament, and screwed down so as to arrest the circulation at the moment when the surgeon commences his incision. If the *circular* operation is preferred, it is proceeded with in a similar manner to that described for the arm. As, however, the *flap* operation is now more common, we will describe it more minutely.

The operator stands on the outside of the limb to be amputated, if it is the left leg; and on the inside, if the right. He grasps the flesh of the anterior part of the thigh, raising it from the bone; and passes his knife horizontally through it, the point

* This and other precautions will be unnecessary, if the patient is properly under the influence of ether or chloroform.

directed towards the bone till it touches, then inclined over it and down again on the other side as far as possible. After the instrument is through, the edge is brought out, upwards and forwards toward the knee, so as to leave the anterior flap of the required length, according to the thickness of the limb. The knife is now entered again a little below the top of the former incision, passed behind the bone as close to it as possible, and brought out on the other side just below the former point of emergence. The *posterior flap* is then cut (in the direction represented by the dotted line, Fig. 94) a little *longer* than the anterior, as the flexor mus-

Fig. 94.

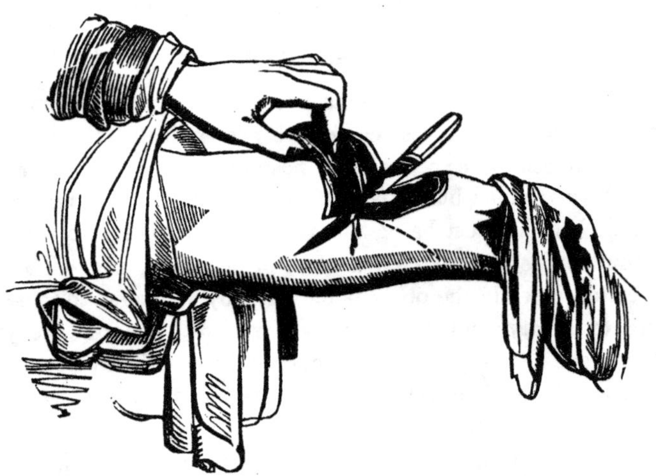

cles are more liable to retract than the anterior,—being larger and stronger, and less firmly attached to the shaft of the bone. The flaps being now drawn back, and held by an assistant, the remaining muscular fibres are severed by a sweep of the knife round the bone; and the bone sawed off close up to the base of the flaps (see Fig. 95), the surgeon steadying the lower portion of the bone with his left hand.

Some surgeons prefer to make the flaps from the inner and outer, instead of the posterior and anterior sides of the bone. This may be done with ease in so fleshy a part; and is perhaps a safeguard against the flaps being so directly separated by muscular contraction.

The femoral *artery* will be found, — when the operation is performed, as here described, — in the posterior flap, unless the op-

FIG. 95.

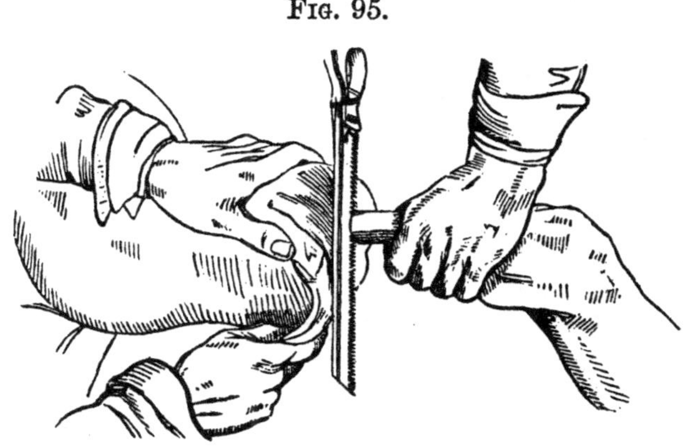

eration is very high up indeed. About the middle of the thigh, it may not be necessary to take up more than the femoral artery. Frequently, however, several branches have to be also secured. To ascertain this and find these branches, loosen the tourniquet for a moment.

It is safer, — and this is the only difference between this operation and that for the arm, — to use *sutures* in securing the flaps. Apply one about the middle of the line of union, and one or two on each side, should they appear necessary. The flaps may gape notwithstanding, and require other means. After adhesive straps have been also applied, with lint and bandage, the stump is to be placed upon a pillow a little elevated, and kept wet with some cold lotion. (See treatment of AMPUTATION OF THE ARM.)

As a precaution against secondary hemorrhage, the tourniquet may be left on the thigh, and tightened as soon as any bleeding is discovered. It is sometimes necessary to re-open the wound and secure any vessels that may have been overlooked, but such necessity should be carefully guarded against.

OF THE LEG.

The rule for deciding where to amputate for injuries below the knee, is different in the case of a rich patient and a poor one.

Amputate, say the authorities, as near the knee as possible, unless your patient be a rich man and able to procure an artificial limb. For the common wooden leg, the knee is the best support, and all the limb left below that joint would not only be useless, but very much in the way, liable to injuries and to suffer from cold. The rule, however, is rather a European than an American one, few patients, in this country, not being able, and not preferring, to procure what is called a cork leg. A medium length of stump below the knee (say six or seven inches from the lower edge of the patella) will be enough to secure a firm socket, and thus be convenient either for using the knee joint, or turning the stump back and resting the weight of the body on it. On such a point the patient's choice should of course be consulted.

The patient being in a convenient position, the femoral artery under the tourniquet, and everything ready, one assistant has hold of the ankle and another of the knee, the latter drawing up the skin while he steadies the limb. The operator (standing as before directed for amputation of the thigh) cuts round the limb, just dividing the skin and cellular tissue down *to* the muscles,—if it is the *circular operation* that is intended,—at least two inches below the point determined on for dividing the bones. (The manner of making this first sweep of the knife is described in Amputation of the Arm.) The integument is now to be dissected up for two inches in front and one inch behind. This being turned up and firmly held by the assistant, the muscles are separated down to the bone by one second circular sweep of the knife, cutting as closely to the retracted skin as possible, and turning the edge a little upward as it passes through the muscles of the calf. A long double-edged *scalpel* or catlin is then passed between the bones, to divide the interosseous ligament and muscles which have not been touched by the circular cut. Every fibre is then to be dissected from the bones for a little distance higher up, and the *three-tailed retractor* applied, one end passing between the two bones and having the wide unslit part below. The muscles being drawn up by the retractor, the bones are sawed off together, as in the case of the fore-arm; any splinters that may (but *ought* not to) be left, removed, and the end smoothed with the bone forceps. In directing the saw, take care to leave the bones of equal length, or, if any difference, to have the fibula the shorter (that it may afterwards be out of the way of blows, &c.—Would not any plan causing adhesion between the two bones of the stump, be a great improvement of the operation?) As soon as the retractor is removed, the anterior and posterior tibial and the peroneal *arteries* will require tying, together, perhaps, with several branches. Secure everything and dress as directed for the fore-arm. The *flap operation* has been thought the best for the leg, as the bones are by it well covered with flesh to protect them from chafing in the socket of an artificial leg, and from blows and cold when turned back on the wooden leg. The surgeon usually commences by entering the catlin behind the bones, cutting forwards and downwards, so as to make a *posterior flap*, three or four inches in

Fig. 96.

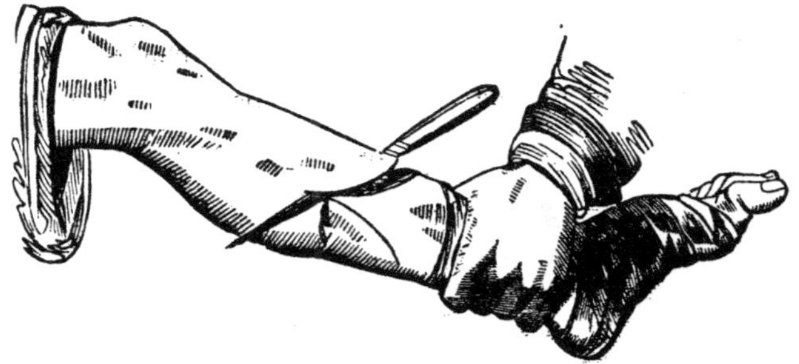

length. For the front flap a semi-lunar *incision* is then made across the limb with the convexity downwards, curving from one end to the other of the base of the first flap. [Mr. Liston prefers making this semi-lunar *incision* first. In the plate, Figure 96, it is represented as already done and the knife ready to cut the second, here, *posterior* flap.] The skin is dissected up a little; both flaps thrown and held back; the textures between and adhering to the bones separated, and the bones sawed off, as before directed. In transfixing the limb, care must be taken not to allow the point of the knife to penetrate between the bones. (For fuller directions and precautions, see operations on the arm.)

When the operation is performed *lower* down towards the ankle, the tendo Achillis will have to be shortened after the flap is made, otherwise it will be left projecting when the integuments contract. More care will have to be used to get the flap of sufficient size at this part, and it will also require to be secured by sutures. A stitch or two, indeed, had better be used, whether the operation be high or low. In other respects the flaps are to be adjusted in a horizontal line, secured by straps, &c., and the wound kept cool as in other cases. (See AMPUTATION OF THE ARM.) The stump should rest on a soft pillow, and be raised above the level of the body.

AMPUTATIONS OF THE FOOT.

Tarso-metatarsal amputation, — or that of all the metatarsal bones together, requires a semicircular incision across the instep, with the convexity forwards, beginning at a point just in front of the articulation of the metatarsal bone of the great toe with the internal cuneiform, and terminating on the outside, at the tuberosity of the metatarsal bone of the little toe. The flap of skin is then to be dissected up and thrown as far back as the tarso-metatarsal articulations; and the point of the bistoury is passed behind the protrusion of the metatarsal bone of the great toe, so as to divide the external ligament which connects it with the cuboides. The dorsal ligaments are then to be cut through in succession and the foot depressed. The other articulations are severed in a similar manner, dividing their ligaments with the point of the knife, taking care that your bistoury is not locked between the bones. The most convenient *order* for taking the joints is, after beginning with the fifth, to separate the third and fourth, then the

FIG. 97.

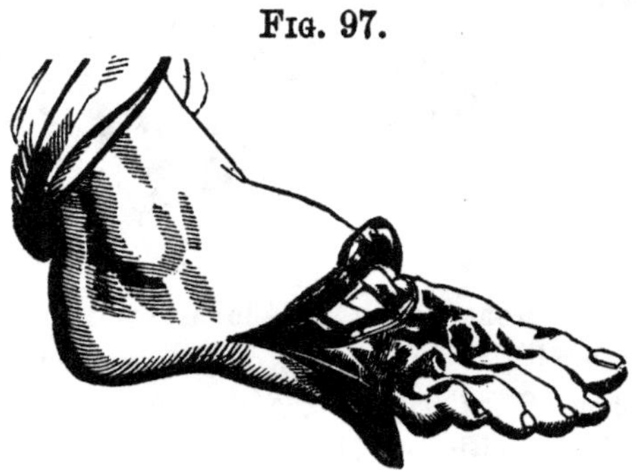

first, and *lastly the second*, — the extremity of the bone being locked between the three cuneiform bones would not be easily dislodged before the others; and it may be sometimes better, for this bone, to use a Hays' saw. When the bones are all disarticulated, the operation is completed by the division of the plantar ligaments, with the point of the knife, and the separation of the extremities of the bones which adhere to their under surface. The blade is then put under the five bones, and carried forwards so as to make a flap from the sole of the foot, sufficient to cover the end of all the tarsal bones (see Fig. 97). The flap should be from an inch to two inches wider on the inner than the outer side. All the arteries being tied, the wound is adjusted and dressed in the usual manner.

PHALANGEO-METATARSAL amputation, or that of all the toes from their junction with the foot, is the most common. A transverse incision is made across the dorsal surface of the metatarsal bones, and the tendons and lateral ligaments of each joint are divided separately in succession. The first phalangeal bones are then dislocated upwards, and the knife passed beneath their metatarsal extremities, cutting out flaps from their inferior or plantar surfaces sufficient to cover the ends of the metatarsal bones. Arteries have to be tied and the flaps secured as usual. The foot must be laid in an easy position on the outer side, so that whatever matter is formed may readily escape. As in the case of single toes and fingers, however, it is better to *divide the bone* than disarticulate, — taking precaution, by means of the bone forceps, not to leave sharp or prominent edges to the bones. This direction for dividing between the joints applies particularly to the *great* and *little toes*, as they both aid very much in walking.

Amputation of separate *toes* is performed precisely as that of the fingers. Occasions oftener occur, however, for removing several at once. Badly managed frost-bites may require this. Hospital Gangrene is another too frequent cause.

CHAPTER XIV.

AMPUTATION AT THE LARGER JOINTS.

THE ARM is removed entire or "excised" from the body at the

SHOULDER JOINT

— in several different ways, by different surgeons; but the one represented in the cut is now the most generally performed, and is as safe and convenient as any. Place the patient in a sitting posture, supported by assistants, who also sustain the arm in a horizontal, or a little above the horizontal position. A transverse incision is made, down to the bone, about four and a half inches below the acromion process. Two other incisions are made, one posterior and the other anterior, commencing high up on the shoulder, and following the margins of the deltoid down to the extremities of the first or transverse incision. The flap is then dissected up from the bone, turned over the shoulder, and held fast by an assistant,—who had better have a dry cloth in his hand, as he may not otherwise be well able to hold the bleeding part. The surgeon next opens the capsule of the joint, and directs the assistant to make a preconcerted lever-like motion, luxating and raising the head of the bone upwards. The axillary artery is then sought for (at the inner margin of the wound), the nerves completely separated from it, the vessel raised, by passing the aneurism needle (see Fig. 20) or blunt end of the probe under it, and tied. This done, the knife is passed between the head of the bone and the

FIG. 96.

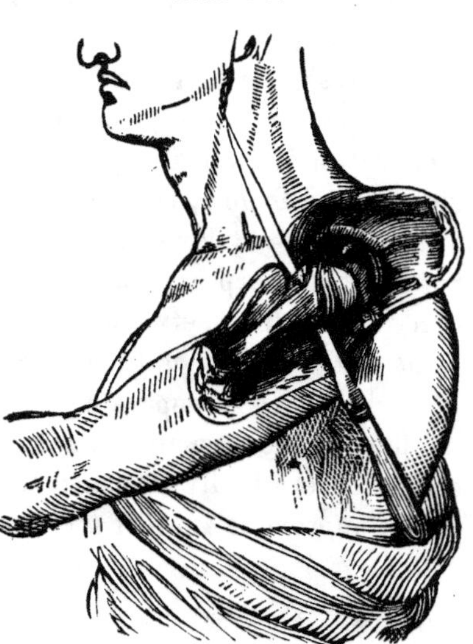

glenoid cavity, with the edge kept close to the bone, and brought outwards and downwards (of course below the ligature), below or beyond the level of the arm-pit (see Fig. 98). All smaller arteries are then tied, cold water applied to stop the venous hemorrhage, and, as soon as that is effected, the deltoid muscles brought down and secured by adhesive straps.

Compression of the *sub-clavian* artery, — which is very necessary, if the axillary artery is cut before being tied, — is a very difficult matter. If, however, circumstances absolutely require the operation to be performed differently, in this respect, from what has been described, the sub-clavian may be commanded by the thumb of a skillful assistant where it passes over the first rib, in the space between that bone and the clavicle. There is no safety in attempting to control it by a key or any mere mechanical compress there; the assistant can feel when he has hold of the artery or when he has lost it.

AT THE HIP JOINT.

This is the most formidable operation in the whole list of amputations, — not only on account of the large extent of surface to be divided, and the large number of nerves and blood-vessels, but the fact that the latter cannot all be secured before cutting. Happily the occasions for a resort to this operation are very rare.

The femoral artery being compressed by the thumb of an as-

Fig. 99.

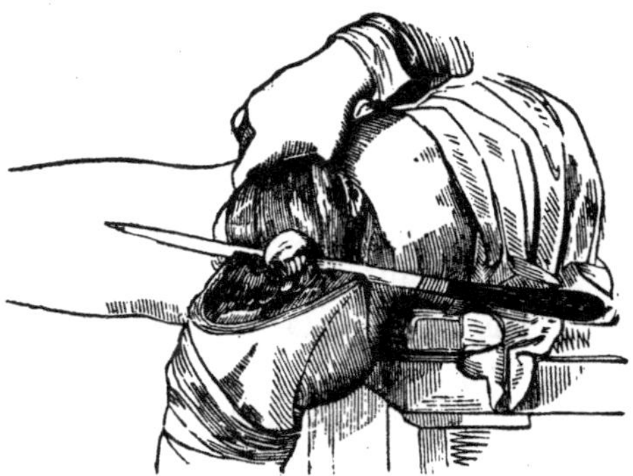

sistant, — the point of the knife is to be entered about half way between the anterior superior spinous process of the ilium and the trochanter major, and then directed through across the front of the articulation, until it emerges on the inside of the thigh. The assistant rotates the limb a little inwards, and the knife cutting downwards is brought out in front, so as to form a suitable anterior flap. The assistant then abducts the thigh and presses it backwards, another holding up the anterior flap, when the capsular ligament is divided in front; and the head of the bone being dislocated by a lever-like motion, the round ligament is severed, and the blade of the knife brought behind the neck of the bone, passing through the posterior part of the capsule (see Fig. 99.) The posterior flap is then formed by cutting downwards, and outwards. The vessels upon the posterior flap are to be tied before any others, as these are large, and bleed most profusely. They must be secured as soon as possible, and those of the front flap also attended to.

Another mode of performing the operation is, to make lateral flaps, by first passing the knife completely through the limb, on the inner side of the joint, and then carrying it forward, so as to form a flap of the adductor muscles. The joint is then cut into, and the ligaments severed, together with the muscles attached to the digital fossa. The surgeon here makes use of a strong curved knife, which is brought downwards and outwards, so as to make the external flap.

The vessels are then to be secured, venous as well as arterial hemorrhage suppressed, and the flaps brought together and secured by sutures, adhesive straps, compress and bandage.

AT THE ELBOW, WRIST, KNEE AND ANKLE

Excision, — as the operation is called, to distinguish it from ordinary amputation, — has been performed at each of these joints; though at all of them (except the wrist) it is liable to so much objection, that it is difficult to imagine cases where it *ought* to be preferred. The rule laid down by Druitt, from the first volume of Guy's Hospital Reports is, that *excision* is "advisable in the shoulder and elbow [?]; — admissible, though of doubtful utility, in the ankle; — inadmissible, except under very peculiar circumstances, in the wrist [?], hip or knee." From this conclusion, we differ, as you will see, in two point

The ELBOW JOINT ought never to be chosen for the point of division on account of disease of the fore-arm, when the smallest portion of the latter, if only an inch, can be preserved. That much of stump, with the use of the joint, will for many purposes be as good as a finger to the patient. Disease of the joint itself would be only an additional reason for cutting above, even if the humerus and integument enough to cover it were sound and preservable. The broad condyles of the humerus, with a thin covering, — a mere skin and bone extremity, — could be no advantage over the round section of bone, well protected, like the natural fingers' ends, with flesh as well as sensitive cutis. Besides, the flap over the uneven end of the bone cannot possibly be secured as smoothly and heal as kindly as in ordinary cases.

When performed, the surgeon passes his knife through the muscles in front of the joint, and cuts downwards and out to the surface, so as to make a flap of them. He then makes a transverse incision behind the joint, through the external lateral ligament; and brings the instrument into the joint, between the head of the radius and the external condyle, to divide the internal and other ligaments. The olecranon process is then sawed through, the head of it being left on the stump. The vessels are secured and the stump dressed as in other cases.

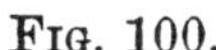
FIG. 100.

AMPUTATING AT THE WRIST may be preferred, because more covering can there be sometimes secured from the thumb and palm than from off the bones above; and because it leaves a stump terminating in two firmly connected ends of bone. After describing the usual mode of operating, we will relate a case where Dr. Hill resorted to this method *not* "under very peculiar" — at least not *favorably* "peculiar circumstances."

For this operation, the brachial artery should be secured as for amputations of the arm above. An assistant supports the fore-arm, and draws back the skin from over and under the wrist. A semi-lunar incision is then made, with the convexity downwards, on the back of the hand; the flap dissected and turned up past the joint, and the joint opened from that side. The ligaments and tendons are freely cut through, and disarticulation effected, the knife being carried through the joint (see plate, Fig. 100), and downwards and forwards on the inside. The palmar flap should be the longer, as it is thicker and better than the other. Arteries have to be secured and everything completed as in other cases.

David Howell had his hand and wrist terribly mangled in the planing machine, at Holmes's factory in Cincinnati. Not only were the carpal, as well as metacarpal and phalangeal bones literally crushed, but the extremities of both radius and ulna severely bruised and divested of much of their covering. Instead of amputating the arm, Dr. Hill merely took away the hand and wrist bones, smoothing off the bruised ends of the radius and ulna, as well as the ragged portions of muscles and tendons hanging to them, but taking care to leave the ligaments connecting the two bones untouched. As there was no flap to be got from the hand, he drew down the skin of the fore-arm by main force, and fastened it over the end of the radius by two sutures and a sufficient number of adhesive straps. To keep it close in place, he put a large cotton wad over the end; and, as a security against contraction, applied a bandage firmly over it and up to the elbow. The stump was kept constantly wet with a solution of common salt, combined with an equal quantity of spirits of camphor (he was then unacquainted with the virtues of Arnica, Calendula, &c.) The healing went on well and rapidly, without ever giving the patient pain after the first two or three hours, almost the whole surface forming adhesion by the first intention. Only two spots, not the size of a five cent piece, required granulation. The limb was entirely well in a few weeks, a smooth and beautiful stump being formed, — which the patient, by an ingenious contrivance of a loop and clasp, was able to use among the machinery almost as efficiently as a good hand.

EXCISION AT THE KNEE would seem, plainly enough, inadmissible, without the experiments relied on in the Hospital Report before quoted. The patient could never walk on the half knee as on the whole one, and would find it very difficult to adjust in any socket for bringing the weight to bear higher up, besides its preventing an artificial knee being substituted. Similar objections apply to

AMPUTATION AT THE ANKLE JOINT. The patient cannot walk on the stump or fix an artificial foot so well as if the leg were divided higher up. The stump is not likely to be so well covered, or to heal so kindly, and the operation itself is more tedious and painful for the patient. Therefore when the whole foot must be lost, amputate *the leg*.

CHAPTER XV.

OTHER OPERATIONS ON THE EXTREMITIES—TENOTOMY, MYOTOMY.

THE ARTERIAL TRUNKS of the extremities have occasionally to be tied for wounds as well as disease. [For cases requiring these to be secured above the limb, see directions for taking up the Axillary and External Iliac Arteries.]

The BRACHIAL ARTERY has occasionally to be tied, or otherwise obliterated, in consequence of a wound in the favorite operation of *bleeding* at the usual point (see treatment for ANEURISM, varicose aneurism, &c). Whether this "false" or *artificial* "aneurism" has followed the occurrence or not, we should, if called to such a case (for the Homeopath, of course, will never have to mend such blunders of his making), adopt efficient means of compression, bandaging in addition the whole arm; or cut down to the artery above and below the wounded part (enlarging the original wound if it is a fresh case, to the extent of two or three inches), and tie it, taking care not to operate on nerve or vein, as the original venesector did on the artery. When to be taken up above this part, the brachial artery is easily found on the inner side, and a little above the middle of the upper arm. Cut down carefully along the border of the biceps, or if going still higher, that of the coraco-brachialis; see that no vein or nerve is included in your ligature, and that there is no higher branch going off to the part affected, and tie.

The RADIAL ARTERY is to be found, — on the upper part of the fore-arm, by cutting on a line from the bend of the elbow to the thumb, and separating the supinator longus and pronator teres, — in the lower part, where it is pressed against the bone in "feeling the pulse" along the margin of the flexor carpi radialis, — and nearer the middle, by making the incision near the ulnar margin of the supinator longus. The ULNAR ARTERY is not so easily reached in its upper part, and it may be better to tie the brachial than cut the thick muscles that lie over it. Above the wrist, however, and for more than half its course you have only to divide the integuments along the outer margin or tendon of the flexor carpi ulnaris, separate this inwards, and pass your needle *from within* to avoid the nerve.

The FEMORAL ARTERY is most conveniently found for ligating just above where it is crossed by the sartorius, the course of the vessel running from the middle of Poupart's ligament to the inner edge of the patella. In cutting, carefully avoid veins and enlarged glands; and after introducing your ligature by passing *the needle* (see Fig. 20) from the inside outwards, close to the coat of the artery, so as to separate it from the great vein and saphenic nerve, ascertain that there are no such branches from above as would render the operation useless — and then tighten and tie. We were called to treat a case where a distinguished surgeon had taken up the femoral artery for aneurism, without arresting the pulsation in the least. The POPLITEAL ARTERY has been occasionally tied, where it lies under the tendon of the semimembranosus.

The ANTERIOR TIBIAL ARTERY is only to be reached, in the upper part of the leg, by a long and deep incision down to the interosseous ligament, the tibialis anticus and the extensor digitorum being separated, — in the lower part, by cutting on the outer side of the tendon of the extensor pollicis. The POSTERIOR TIBIAL ARTERY can be easily secured in the lower part of the leg, but only with so much difficulty in the upper part, that it is perhaps better for any one not a practiced anatomist and operator to go up to the Femoral at once. It is conveniently operated on either just behind the internal malleolus, or for some distance higher up along the inner side of the tendo Achillis. The PERONEAL ARTERY is almost as difficult to meddle with as the *upper* part of the *tibiales.*

Wounds and diseases of the VEINS in the extremities should be treated by *pressure* rather than the ligature, though the latter may be necessary. In these and many other cases the proper application of the *bandage* is one of the most important of

— "surgical operations on the extremities." All other affections or accidents of the extremities, of any frequency or importance, for which operations may be thought of, have, it is believed, been mentioned; and directions given for performing or *avoiding the operation.* Exostosis, or malignant disease in those parts, will require to be treated on the same principles as elsewhere. In affections of the bursæ, ganglia and other tumors, operations may and generally ought to be *prevented* (see ganglion and exostosis). Such an operation as is sometimes called "paracentesis articuli," we give no directions for, as it is at best but a palliative, and its advantage can never compensate for its danger (see treatment for Hydrops Articuli or White Swelling). Of deep puncturing in THECAL ACCUMULATIONS enough was said under Whitlow and Felon. When resorted to with a view of *preventing* tension and suffering, the injury done is often great. The same may be observed of ONYXIS or ONYCHIA as of paronychia. "*The* operation for Inverted Toe-Nail" need only be referred to, for the purpose of calling to your mind the plan for obviating, not only what an established author well characterizes as the "frightfully painful way [of treating] laid down by Cooper and Dupuytren, — that is, by passing the sharp blade of a pair of scissors under the nail, cutting it through, and then tearing away the offending portion with forceps," — but even what he calls "the milder fashion, by cutting through the nail with a pen-knife, just down to the thick layer of cuticle intervening between it and the *quick* (as it is called) and then turning it back." — Druitt's *Modern* Surgery. page 516.

MAL-FORMATIONS of the fingers or toes may often admit of surgical remedy or palliation. The particular case must indicate the kind of operation required. Supernumerary fingers and toes, if really found superfluous, and not rather useful to the possessor (a physician of our acquaintance prizes his "sixth finger" very highly) may be easily removed, as they are not generally attached by regular articulation.

WEB-FINGERS might seem a case requiring only surgery so simple as not to need directions — yet we find some books proposing to make a rhino-plastic or dactylo-plastic operation of it! The difficulty sought to be avoided, is that of reunion after division. A piece of common silk, moistened in olive oil, and kept between the fingers after their separation will effect the object, without ever having a "flap of skin brought from the dorsum of the hand and engrafted between the fingers." The author quoted does not say how the greater deformity resulting from the scar on the back of the hand is to be remedied.

CONTRACTION of the flexors is the most common deformity requiring our aid. In the case of fingers, a mere cut through the skin will often be all the "operation" necessary. The same, with other obvious means, would probably be sufficient for most cases of toes so contracting or overriding each other, — for the inconvenience of which even amputation has been enjoined and submitted to. Recent cases of such "spurious anchylosis," even in the larger joints, may be *made* "transient" by emollients and other obvious medical or mechanical means.

In other cases, however, MYOTOMY or TENOTOMY will have to be the remedy. The most prominent instance for this is the club-foot operation. Similar conditions of the upper extremity or "club-hand" are occasionally met with, not so susceptible of being classified.

CLUB-FOOT. (TALIPES).

There are four varieties of this deformity: —

1st. *Talipes varus* (Fig. 101), which is by far the most common. In this the foot is turned in; the patient walks on the outside of it, the great toe turns inwards and upwards and the heel is elevated. The cause of this deformity is the contraction of the muscles of the calf of the leg and the adductors of the foot.

2d. *Talipes equinus* (Fig. 102). The heel is elevated from half an inch in some cases to four or five inches in others. The patient walks on his toes or the ball of his foot. He may press principally on the side of the little toe, on that of the great toe, or on all of the toes equally with the ball. This is generally caused by the contraction of the *gastronemii* muscles alone, but the flexors of the toes may also be contracted.

3d. *Talipes valgus*. The foot is turned out so that the patient walks on the inner surface, and the external edge is raised from the ground, the sole looking outwards. The heel is also drawn

Fig. 102. Fig. 101.

upwards in this case. The adductor muscles and those of the calf are contracted.

4th. *Talipes calcaneus* (Fig. 103). The toes and foot are elevated, so as to form an acute angle with the leg, while the heel rests upon the ground. Here the *tibialus anticus* and the extensor muscles of the toes are contracted.

Any of these deformities may be caused by disease or accident, but are most frequently congenital.

TREATMENT should be resorted to as early as possible. Whether congenital or accidental, the proper treatment adopted and carried out at the first discovery of the deformity will stand a very great chance of success. But a few years' delay may effect such changes in the bony structure as to render *any* attempt, by operation or other means, abortive.

Fig. 103.

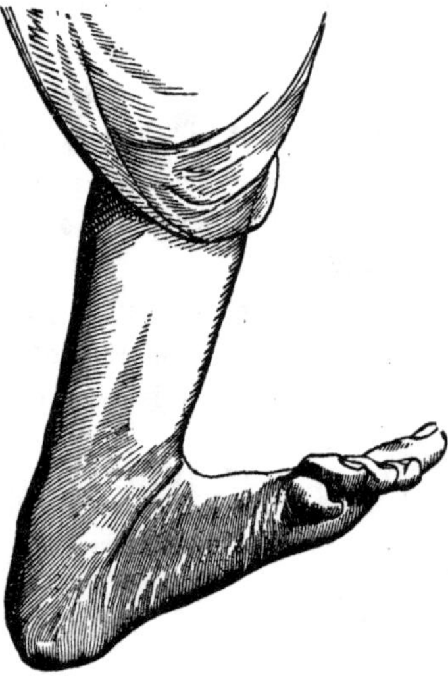

Although in many cases the operation of TENOTOMY may be absolutely requisite, it does not follow that other means might not have succeeded in the same cases, had they been applied early.

The strong probability is, that a large majority of cases occurring under the age of three years *require* no operation, as the proper apparatus early applied will rectify the deformity. The great success of Dr. Chase, of Philadelphia, in these cases proves, at least, that the operation is performed far too often, if, indeed, it is ever necessary in the early stage of the deformity.

We will not attempt to describe all the forms of apparatus necessary for every variety of club-foot. We will simply say that it should consist of a stiff shoe or sole, fixed to a stiff upright shaft, made fast above the knee with a joint at the knee. The shoe is so fixed as to turn easily in the proper direction. The foot is made fast to the sole, to which springs are attached from the upright shaft, in such a manner as to make constant but gentle extension on the contracted muscles, and in a proper direction to rectify the deformity.

Some of these machines made by *Mr. Max. Wocher*, of Cincinnati, are most admirably adapted to the purpose. They can be fitted to any size and shape, so as to cause no pain or excoriation, while the proper force is exerted on the contracted part. All the information he requires respecting the case in order to adapt an instrument to it, is the kind and extent of the deformity, and the length and size of the foot, leg and thigh. We would recommend a trial of this machine or some similar fixture, in all recent cases, before resorting to the

OPERATION.

This is easily performed. It consists simply in a division of the contracted tendon or tendons. In a large majority of cases a *division* of the *tendo Achillis* is all that is requisite. For this purpose the patient is placed on a bed upon his face, or he may sit in a chair with his foot elevated. The skin of the ankle is drawn either backwards or forwards so as to make it tense, and so that when it contracts it will cover the wound. A long narrow bladed knife is used (see Figure 104), which is round and smooth for an inch next the handle. It is passed through the skin flatways between the tendon and the bone, near the anterior surface of the former, from one to two inches above the internal malleolus, and carried through to the skin on the opposite side. The

Fig. 104.

edge is then turned upon the tendon, and while an assistant, or the surgeon, with his left hand, bends the foot in such a manner as to put the contracted muscle firmly on the stretch, he cuts steadily through the tendon. It will separate with a crackling noise.

The space between the divided ends of the tendon will be filled up with coagulable lymph, which eventually becomes firm and serves as a tendon.

The tendon of the *posterior tibial muscle* is most readily divided about two inches behind and above the internal malleolus. The principles of operation are the same. In this case care must be taken not to cut the posterior tibial artery and nerve, which might be wounded if the incision were carried too deeply. The tendon of the *anterior tibial muscle* must be cut where it passes over the ankle joint. The *flexor* of the *great toe* is most conveniently divided on the sole of the foot. It may be seen and felt projecting like a strong cord.

After the operation, the limb should be placed in an easy position, and the patient kept quiet. A strip of adhesive plaster is to be placed over the external wound, and it healed by the first intention. In these operations there will be but a few drops of blood, unless an artery be cut, of which there need be no danger, and cannot be in the first, and last two, cases named. After three or four days, or as soon as the state of the limb will admit, it should be placed in a proper machine for extending the foot and fixing it in its proper situation.

[As the operation for STRABISMUS is similar in principle to this of talipes, and EYE-OPERATIONS form a distinct class, we will now proceed to them, before taking up others on the head and trunk. Myotomy, being a modern operation, has been for a time "all the rage,"—for instances of this, "muscle-cutting gone mad," see Curved Spine, and Flint's Druitt, page 391, with the editor's note, page 329.]

STRABISMUS—SQUINTING.

FIG. 105.

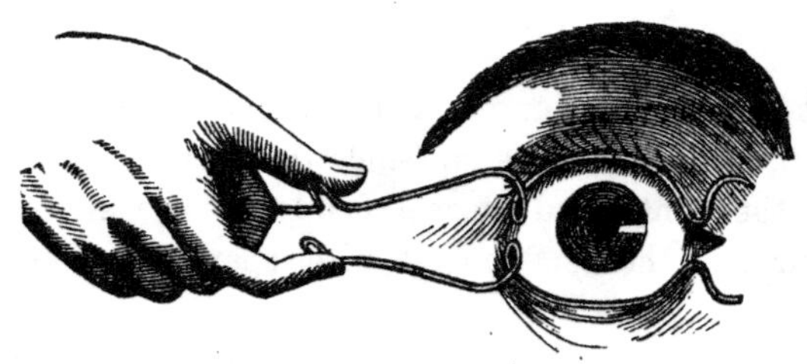

This striking and unsightly peculiarity of the visual organs commonly consists in their axes of motion being no longer parallel, or in their natural relation to each other. Hence the eyes do not act in harmony, and the person seems to be looking two ways at once. If both eyes have changed their natural axes similarly, or received an equal turn to the same side, the patient appears to be looking away from the object before him, or not looking at what he really sees.

Such states of the eye may be *temporary* or *permanent*. In the former case there is a *spasmodic* contraction of some of the muscles of the globe, virtually destroying the function of their antagonist muscles. Such spasms often occurring in connection with the cerebral affections of children, are apt to become habitual, and the occasional *squinting* converted into confirmed *strabismus*. Appropriate treatment for these cerebral affections will be all that is necessary. Mechanical contrivances, such as a patch on the nose or a dark shade over the affected eye, with a small opening for light in the centre, or at the point most likely to counteract the morbid tendency, will be sufficient in some slight cases of strabismus.

The *confirmed* squinting is rather referred to the relative relaxation of the muscles not acting, than to the overpowering contraction of the other, — which is thus allowed to become organic, or a permanent *shortening*. In a large majority of cases, the

Figs. 106. 109. 107. 108.

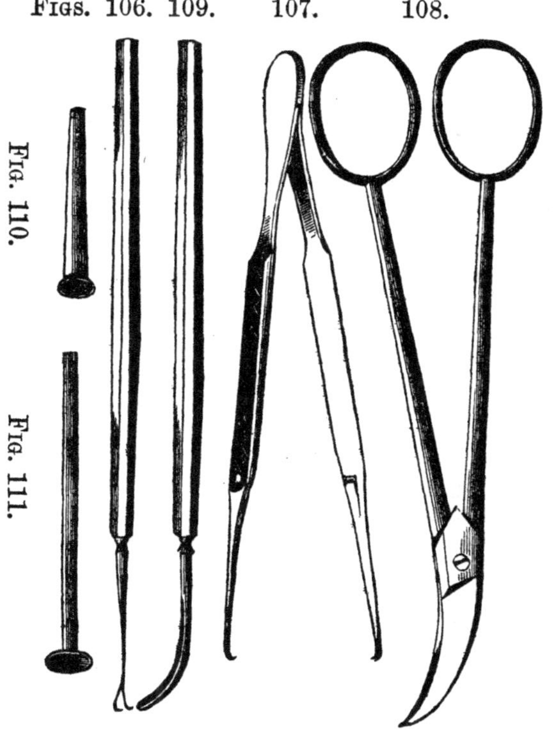

Fig. 110.

Fig. 111.

deficiency of power is in the rectus externus, the internal drawing the eye-ball towards the nose. A current of electricity frequently passed through the relaxed muscle, with the mechanical means before mentioned, will often obviate the necessity of an operation. Strabismus is sometimes also caused by a partial opacity of the cornea; of course, an operation would be useless.

The operation for the relief of this deformity, — or Strabotomy, — consists in dividing the shortened or permanently contracted muscle. This being generally the Internal Rectus, we will describe the process of *its* division. The patient being seated and the eye secured by the speculum or otherwise, the sound eye is to be covered and kept from rolling by gentle but sufficient pressure. The lids and ball of the defective side can be best fixed with the Wirespring Speculum (Fig. 112), shown upon the eye preparatory to the operation in Fig. 105. (See also Note at the beginning of next Chapter.

Fig. 112.

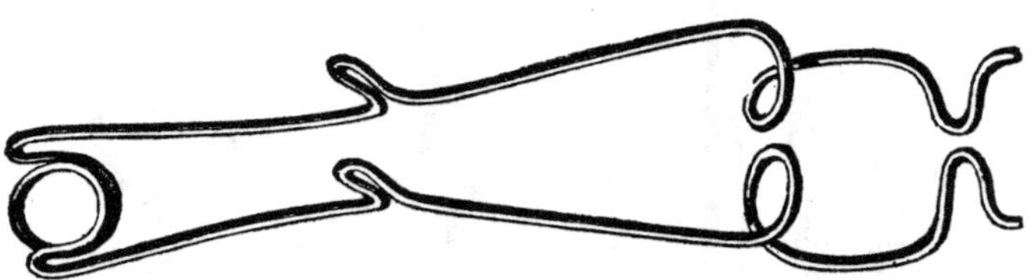

In default of such a means, it is usual to have the upper lid held up by an assistant's fingers, or by a common wire speculum or elevator (Fig. 113), another pair of fingers being required to keep down the under lid (as shown in Fig. 114). These preliminaries adjusted, a double hook (represented separately as Fig. 106) is hitched to the conjunctiva, about half way between the margin of the cornea and the internal canthus, the ball then rolled outward by it, and the handle given to an assistant, by whom it is firmly retained in the same position.

Fig. 113.

The surgeon then raises the conjunctiva with fine hook-forceps (Fig. 107), and cuts perpendicularly into it with curved scissors (Fig. 108), and continues to raise it and divide the cellular tissue until he reaches the muscle, which also he severs with the scissors.

FIG. 114.

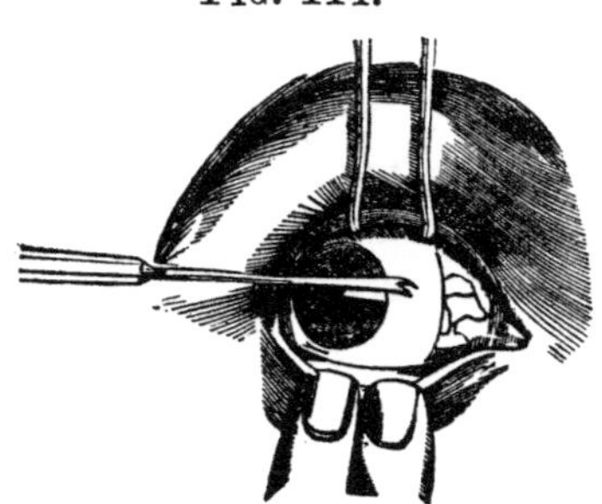

To make sure work, the cellular tissue should be dissected clean from the ball in a perpendicular direction, for at least half an inch. In order to ascertain that the muscle is entirely severed, let the operator introduce under it a blunt hook or director (Fig. 109) as if to raise it up. If any fibres rise over the instrument, divide them.

Then release the eye and let the patient look freely about. If the operation has been complete, he will turn the eye every way, except directly *inwards*. If he can do this also, and the deformity still exists, the operation must be repeated or extended. You must dissect off more of the cellular membrane from the ball, and make sure of severing every muscular fibre. On ascertaining that your object is effected by complete loss of the motion proper to the divided muscle,

— the *eye* is to be *closed* and kept from exposure to air, as well as light, for one or two days. A dose of Aconite should be given, and the eye should also be kept wet with the cold water, though it is very rare that any dangerous inflammation follows the operation.

If it is a *child* that is to be operated on, it should be rolled up bodily, with the arms imprisoned, in a sheet, and laid on its back upon a table, the head and feet being there kept still by two assistants.

As it regards the *result* of the operation, it may be stated as *generally successful*, — though the defect occasionally recurs. The advantage is not always at first very perceptible, — the reciprocal action of the muscles requiring time for re-adjustment. The temporary loss of one muscle will cause the eyeball to project a little more than natural, but not so much as usually to occasion any appreciable deformity. In most cases the ultimate improvement of *sight* or *looks* is very satisfactory.

[For a very interesting dissertation on Strabismus, we would refer the reader to a little volume published by Prof. Hamilton, of Buffalo, in 1845.

CHAPTER XVI.

OTHER OPERATIONS ON OR ABOUT THE EYES.

ALL the qualities of a good operator are peculiarly requisite in OPHTHALMIC SURGERY, particularly his having good eyes and a steady hand. The anatomy and *surgery* of this complex part of the organism must, moreover, have been made a special study; one should have operated on, as well as dissected, thousands of eyes (luckily, hogs eyes will answer the purpose of learning on as well as any).

The OPHTHALMIC CASE should contain at least the following instruments:—The eye-forceps, with interlocking points (Fig. 107); a small spatula and scoop, both of silver; the fine eye-hooks (Fig. 106); Scarpa's curved needle (Fig. 119), and cataract knife (Fig. 122–3); the director or curette (Fig. 109)—to which list we have added the *curved* spring-wire speculum* (see Figs. 112 and 105).

* This instrument we use in all operations upon the eye, where pressure is not inadmissible. Having noticed the difficulties of eye-operations, from the mobility of the ball, and the pain caused the patient by imperfect attempts at fixing it, Dr. Hill, several years ago, had an instrument constructed similar to the one referred to, but with one curve less in it, which answered the principal object effectually, but left the assistant's hand somewhat in the way,—though much less so than the fingers directly on the lid. With the assistance of Mr. Max. Wocher, he had the present instrument constructed about two years ago,—since which time a large number have been manufactured by him and furnished to practitioners from all parts of the country. It perfectly controls the eye, in spite of any efforts voluntary or involuntary, on the part of the patient; and, having a long curved handle, can be not only held firmly, but regulated by the assistant with his hand back at

The *handles* of these instruments should *not* be made round nor of any smooth substance, but purposely roughened and with unequal planes and angles, that the operator may hold them firmly and *feel*, while operating, which way the edge or curve lies. For the latter object, a mark out of some other material is set into the handle of some instruments. It is unnecessary to add that all these articles should be of the best material and workmanship and be kept in the best possible order. Cutting edges should cut loose hair or goldbeater's skin.

The REMOVAL of FOREIGN SUBSTANCES from beneath the lids, or within the coats of the ball, is not always the easiest of operations. The lid can be held back by the elevator (Fig. 113) or the complete speculum (Fig. 112), or everted over a pencil or other convenient article, when the offending substance should if possible be *wiped* away by a camel's hair pencil or moistened sponge. When small, sharp bodies *stick in* the eye, *pressing* them out with the edge of the cataract needle, will often be found more convenient than pulling with forceps. There is danger of increasing the irritation by unskillful attempts at removal. Small smooth substances will soon work down to the canthus or edge of the lids of themselves, by the natural movements of the parts. It has often proved safer when grains of powder or specks of metal have stuck deep in, to leave them there, taking care to keep down inflammation. A capsule has formed round them, and they have continued for life without much injury. Any dissecting out is very dangerous, though some substances will require it — as pieces of percussion caps, which would cause more danger from poisonous corrosion than *need* attend the operation. Small particles of iron or steel may be easily removed by the magnet.

FISTULA LACRYMALIS

— as resulting from affections of the eye itself or the sac or ductus ad nasum, with the minor operations on the parts, was be-

the patient's ear; he can at the same time steady the head. The material is of German silver, in order to be more elastic. The two half circles (seen apart in Fig. 112) are approximated by compressing the handles, so as to enclose the eyeball under the lids, while the forward curves at their ends keep these from falling over it.

fore given. There may, however, be another form of lacrymal fistula or obstruction in the duct of the LACRYMAL GLAND itself, producing dryness instead of suffusion of the eye. This part, however, is rarely the object of surgical or medical attention. When it is, it has to be treated on general principles, with due regard to the susceptibility of contiguous parts. In proceeding to the more common

— OPERATION for Fistula Lacrymalis, place the patient in a sitting posture, and stand behind him. Have a small sharp-pointed scalpel, bistoury, or cataract knife; and holding it perpendicularly to the eye-brows, direct the point to the inferior margin of the internal tendon of the eye-lids (*tendo oculi*), — which can be clearly seen by drawing both lids outwards. In this place and direction, press the point of your instrument directly downwards (as in Fig. 115), until a flow of mucous and tears indicates that it has entered the lacrymal sac. As you then raise it out, make a slight outward cut so as to enlarge the opening. A *probe*, slightly curving forwards and inwards, is then to be introduced and *pushed* through when it meets with obstruction. A few drops of blood from the nostril will show when it has entered that cavity; sometimes there will be quite a stream. Another sign is that, on withdrawing the probe, the patient can blow *wind* out at the eye. The TUBE (see Fig. 110), or Style (Fig. 111), according to preference, is then to be inserted; and the wound healed sooner or later, as the case or operator's judgment indicates.

FIG. 115.

OPERATIONS ON THE LIDS AND CONJUNCTIVA.

Wounds dividing the EYE-LIDS may require sutures (the "interrupted," using very small needles).

When Pulsatilla (our most useful remedy), Borax, Belladonna, Mercurius, Hepar, Euphrasia, are insufficient, EXTRACTION of the

CILLA may be necessary for *trichiasis*, inversion of the lids, or *districhiasis*, the mal-position of the hairs themselves. In the latter case, a touch or two of caustic will often prevent the necessity for repeating the operation.

Entropion or Inversion may be otherwise injurious than from the irritation of the ball by the lashes just referred to, and require for its correction a shortening of the outer fold of the lid, or a lengthening of the inner, and perhaps even a removal of the tarsus. The first object can often be effected by cauterizing the lid on the outside, or by cutting out as large a portion of the skin of the affected lid, opposite the center of the entropion, as will be sufficient, on the approximation of the lips of the wound by means of adhesive plaster or a small suture, to bring the tarsus and ciliac in their natural position; the second, by simply incising the mucous membrane.

Ectropion or Eversion, if it does not yield to Bel., *may* require the *same* treatment as the last case, the complete removal of a part of the lid, or just the *reverse*, a shortening of the mucous fold and a lengthening of the cutaneous. The tarsus may have to be divided or removed as in the former case.

PTOSIS, the elongation or drooping of the lids, may be connected with or induce the former cases, particularly entropion, and be remedied by similar surgery, should Acon. croc. gins., natr. Phell., spig. tart., Viol-od., Viol-tric., Nux v., Petr. or zinc, be exhibited without effect. The opposite fault, or too short eyelids, LAGOPHTHALMOS, may be treated like ectropion, if Rhod. or tabac. does not give relief. Either may be the result of muscular contraction or palsy, and remediable by corresponding means. New eye-lids or parts of lids have been successfully formed from the integument of the temples; and a similar operation, called "rhinorrhaphe," performed for epicanthus, the skin being brought from the back of the nose. In the case of new lids, even cilia have been *planted* by Dieffenbach and others, — rooted and grown into a good hedge or eye-lash. This singular part of the operation is called "Blepharidoplastice."

When the eye-lids grow together, constituting a simple case of ANCHYLOBLEPHARON, they may be much more easily separated than kept separate. The plan we have successfully adopted is to keep the parts constantly lubricated with olive oil, with the other usual precautions for preventing any long closure of the lids for a day or two. SYMBLEPHARON, or adhesion of the lids to the ball, cannot be so easily remedied. The tendency to re-union is obviated with difficulty; and the result of the operation very likely to be unsuccessful, as far as the sight is concerned, from opacity of the thickened membrane. Where a false membrane is the cause of union, the case is more hopeful.

Simple superfluous folds of the conjunctiva may be removed by simple excision.

PTERYGIUM and ENCANTHUS have been taken up in the first part. For their removal, if other treatment is inefficient, raise them with forceps, cut *between* the diseased growth and the membrane beneath with a fine scalpel, and finish the operation with *curved* scissors — or the scissors and forceps alone may be used for the whole operation.

OPERATIONS WITHIN THE GLOBE.

Complete EXTIRPATION OF THE EYE may possibly be required for very bad wounds or malignant disease; though the success of Homeopathy has been such, that these cases ought to be exceedingly rare. (See MALIGNANT DISEASES.) When the knife is used it is usual to first pass a hook into the ball and steady it. The lids being then raised, the ball is separated close to the bone, and the lacrymal gland also removed. The muscles and optic nerve are severed together by a curved knife. If the patient does not intend to wear an artificial eye, we are directed to divide the levator palpebræ, by a transverse incision through the upper lid; and remove a slip of the lid itself, that it may not be too long. We should prefer cutting the muscle off near the lid from within.

PARACENTESIS OCULI, or tapping the eye, often so unnecessarily resorted to, is performed by simple puncture of the cornea or the sclerotica. Sometimes both the vitreous and aqueous humors are evacuated, and even a section of the ball removed with the cataract knife. In these cases the lens and vitreous humor are intentionally removed, leaving room for an artificial or partial glass-eye. In what is called "schlerotic or choroid staphyloma," when there is effusion between the retina and choroid, a cataract-needle is sometimes passed through towards the centre of the vitreous humor. "Staphyloma of the Iris" is connected with that of the cornea and with Prolapsus Iridis.

The formation of an ARTIFICIAL PUPIL (schlerektomy, keratoplastics) is a bold operation, which has been attempted by modern oculists, though hitherto with, for the most part, but questionable or transient success. It is resorted to after staphyloma, onyx, leucoma and other causes of opacity; and for myosis or atresia iridis. In some cases a simple incision is indicated, in others the separation of the iris from its attachments; and in others again the excision of a part. Nothing but *complete* blindness of *both* eyes justifies a resort to the experiment.

By far the most interesting and important operations on the eye-ball, are those for the restoration of sight in the deeper-seated affection called

CATARACT.

This disease of the eye, when well established, is considered by allopathists curable only by an operation. (See Cataract, under DISEASES OF THE EYE.) The blindness (which is rarely complete) results solely from opacity, either in the crystalline lens itself or its capsule, or in both.

FIG. 116.

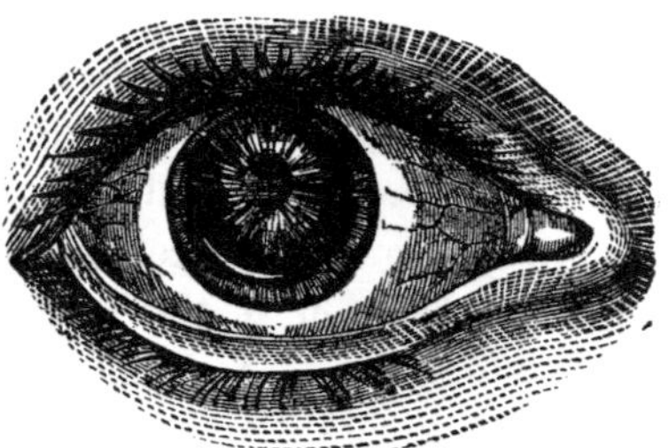

LENTICULAR CATARACT (opacity of the crystalline lens) is divided into the hard and the soft, according to the state of consistency assumed by the morbid change in the part; the various other subdivisions of authors are unimportant. The HARD cataract (Fig. 116) is indicated by a radiated appearance of an amber color in the centre, and gray towards the circumference. A *continuous* gray (Fig. 117), bluish or pure white color, implies a SOFT creamy state of the lens.— "The darker the color, the harder the cataract;—the grayer its appearance, the softer its consistence."—*Liston.*

In simple CAPSULAR CATARACT, when the opacity is in the *anterior* portion of the capsule, there is usually a pearly white *spot* in the centre of the pupil, with a darkening bluish circle around it. The *posterior* capsular opacity (Fig. 118) is easily distinguished, being at some distance behind the Iris, and appearing concave, yellowish and striated.

FIG. 117.

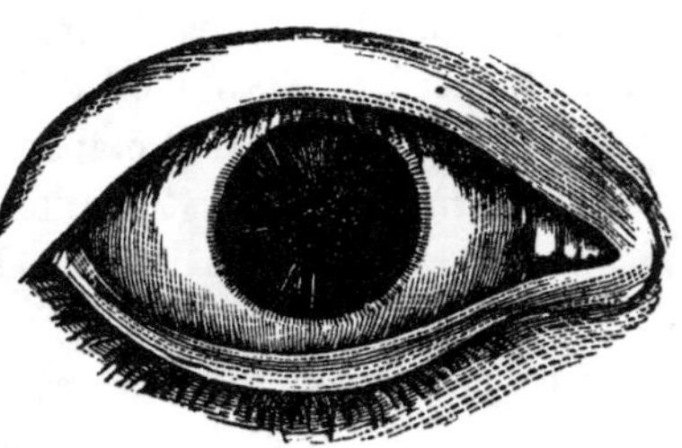

FIG. 118.

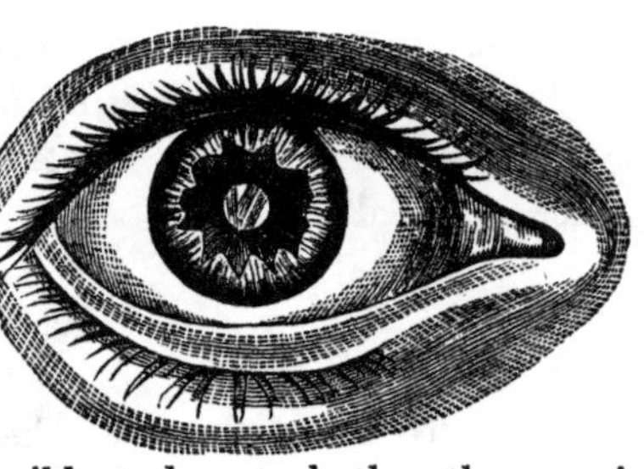

By far the most common cases are those in which both the substance of the lens and its covering are involved, presenting the mingled appearances of both varieties, — the anterior surface not having entirely lost its transparency so as to prevent the interior being seen, — when it is, in fact, impossible to know whether the case is "complete *capsulo-lenticular*," or only "anterio-capsular."

Incipient cataract may be mistaken for glaucoma or amaurosis, but in these the opacity is beyond and behind the pupil, having generally a concave appearance, and the form and sensibility of the iris, as well as the retina, are affected, which is not the case in cataract. On *catoptric* examination, instead of seeing three images of a lighted candle, as in amaurosis and generally also in glaucoma, the second upright and the deep inverted images are both absent or very faint, particularly the last.

While one eye remains sound, it is injudicious to operate. Both eyes should not be operated upon at the same time.

The patient should be in as healthy a condition at the time of operating as possible. Very cold weather is not propitious. The operation is most likely to be successful in congenital cataracts, in those of young persons, and in the hard kind of the aged.

Three *kinds* of OPERATION have been adopted, — Extraction, Absorption and DEPRESSION, or proper —

"COUCHING."

The *patient* should be in every respect as healthy as possible at the time of being operated on. For some weeks previous, at least, he should live temperately, but *not* "starvingly," avoiding all stimulants and stimulating condiments. The *pupil* should be well dilated for one or two days before, by applying to the lids the Extract of Belladonna and to the eye-ball a solution of the Extract of Stramonium (15 gr. to the oz. of water). These should be repeated every three or four hours, or oftener, if necessary. When this important preparation is accomplished,

The patient is seated in a low chair, in a well-lighted room, but not in the sun-shine, nor with the eye in such a position with respect to the window, that the operator will be liable to see images on the cornea. The assistant should stand behind the patient so as to steady his head, and at the same time hold the Speculum Oculi (see Figs. 112 and 105), which not only separates the lids, but securely fixes the ball itself. Usually, the upper lid is held by the fingers of the assistant, or a mere hook-speculum or elevator, and the under lid by those of the surgeon, he having also to prevent the eye from rolling, while his other hand and mind are engaged in the delicate operation. The surgeon had better seat himself on a high chair before the patient, with a foot-stool high enough for him to steady his elbow on his knee while operating. Some, for greater steadiness of the head, prefer the patient to be recumbent; and unless the operator happen to be left-handed, or be ambi-dexter enough for the occasion (as it is desirable that all surgeons should be), he may have to stand behind when a *right* eye is concerned.

The *couching-needle* (the curved one, Scarpa's needle, Fig. 119,

Fig. 119.

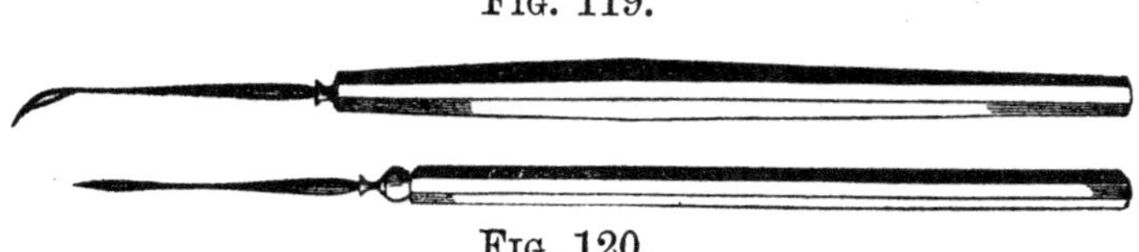

Fig. 120.

is now generally preferred to Hay's, Fig. 120) is to be introduced through the sclerotic coat about two lines from the outer edge of the cornea, and a little below the horizontal axis of the eye (see Fig. 121), for the purpose of avoiding the long ciliary artery. Carry the point on in a slightly-backward direction (which the curved needle will take of itself, if that be used with the point looking backwards) so as not to touch the Iris. When, on looking through the pupil, you can see the point of the needle in front of the lens (Fig. 121), proceed to *detach* the *capsule* from the lens — (the needle has two sharp edges for the purpose). Then push it down out of sight, leaving the lens clear, — if it was only anterior capsular cataract, in which case your operation is complete. But if the *lens itself* or the posterior capsule still appear opaque, move an edge of the needle round its margin so as to separate the lens from the Tunica Hyoloidea; and then placing its flat surface on the top of the lens, push it down (this stage of the operation is the one represented in the accompanying cut, No. 121) below the pupil and a little backwards, so that it may enter the vitreous humor. If it does not move readily, the needle may be thrust into it to *pull* it down. Whether pushed or drawn down, hold it there for a few moments, and then gently raise the needle a little. If the lens follow, press it down, and hold it down again for a longer time. Repeat this process until it no longer returns. Then, and not until then, withdraw your needle, the operation being accomplished. The eye is to be closed and kept constantly wet with cold water, into which a few drops of Arnica Tr. has been poured; Aconite repeated, according to the urgency of the symptoms, to be administered internally, — the patient being also kept in a dark room, and perfectly quiet until all danger of inflammation has subsided. These precautions are required for from two to six weeks, sometimes even for a longer period.

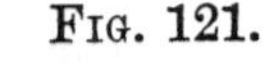
Fig. 121.

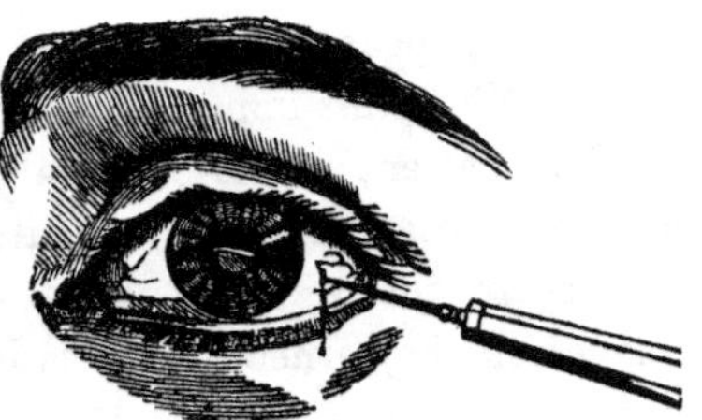

THE OPERATION FOR EXTRACTION

— requires a section of either the upper or lower half of the cornea. The *cornea-knife* used for this purpose has a triangular blade to make one straightforward motion suffice, instead of both a "cut and thrust," and to fill up the section, as it goes, thus preventing the escape of the aqueous humor. For this operation the speculum, so convenient in almost all other eye-operations, cannot be used, as it would compress the globe too much and force out the aqueous humor. Here, therefore, the upper lid must be supported by the Retractor (Fig. 113), and the lower by the fingers of the surgeon (as shown in Fig. 114) — or the fingers of an assistant may be applied to the upper. The operator is advised to touch the cornea once or twice with the flat part of the blade, in order to take off the patient's alarm; and to use his left hand if about to operate on a right eye (unless he prefer to stand behind his patient). He should rest his little finger on the patient's cheek, as if he were writing and the knife a pen. The point enters the transparent cornea, with the edge downwards (see Fig. 122), a little within its outer margin and above its center, and passes straight across, parallel to the iris, emerging at the opposite margin, the wedge-shaped edge advancing in two directions round the cornea, until a complete semi-circular section is made. Some operators prefer to cut upwards (as in Fig. 123), though there is an obvious advantage in having the flap kept naturally in its proper place. The instant the knife is removed, the lids are closed, the operator giving a signal to the assistant. After a brief interval the eye is again

Fig. 122.

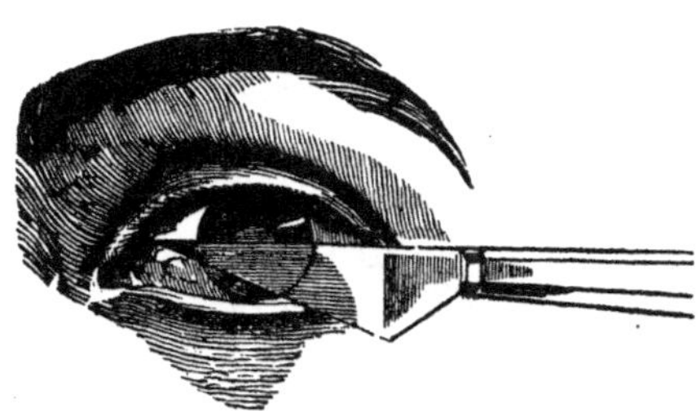

Fig. 123.

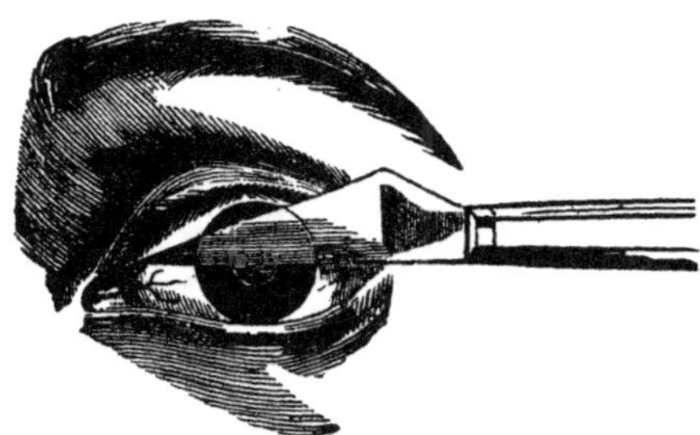

opened, the corneal flap raised (or lowered, as the case may be), the pointed end of the curette or of a needle inserted, and the capsule freely lacerated with it. Very slight pressure may then be applied to the eye-ball, if the lens do not spontaneously pass through the corneal opening. The cornea is then adjusted; but, before being fixed with compress and bandage, it should be opened once more to see that everything is right, and particularly that there is no prolapsus of the iris. Should this accident have occurred, the protrusion may have to be pressed back, or the eye exposed to a strong light, to cause the pupil to contract and draw it back.

THE OPERATION FOR ABSORPTION,

— or SOLUTION, is the easiest method of getting rid of the lens, or opaque coverings, but liable to the objection of having to be repeated, and requiring several weeks for the completion of the cure. It excites little inflammation, and is well adapted for the congenital and other soft cataracts of young persons, but not old, hard cases.

In the *posterior* operation (which is generally preferred) the couching-needle is introduced in the same manner and place as for depression. The capsule is freely broken up by it and the lens cut with it in two or three directions, but not generally dislocated in the first operation. If this is not found sufficient, the lens is broken up into smaller fragments on repeating the operation, which gradually dissolve in the aqueous humor.

In the *anterior* operation, the needle is entered through the cornea about a line anterior to its junction with the sclerotica, and passed forwards through the pupil, breaking up the capsule, if not the lens also. This may do for the first operation, but is liable to cause iritis, even when the pupil is well dilated, as it should be, before the operation.

CONGENITAL CATARACT

— should be early operated on, — when the patients are not more than two or three months old. If neglected for a much longer period, the proper nervous and muscular power of the organ *may* never be gained; and in process of time, though the lens is absorbed, the capsule is thickened to a very unmanageable degree, and will absolutely require extraction or excision. At an early age the method of absorption is sufficient, and easily performed.

CHAPTER XVII.

OTHER OPERATIONS ABOUT THE HEAD AND FACE.

TREPHINING.

THE necessary instruments for this operation are a large and small trephine (or cylindrical saw), a Hay's saw, an elevator and a scalpel. The other instruments which may be required, such as needles, forceps, &c., are found in the common Pocket Case, which every surgeon should always carry with him.

The operation is performed for *fracture* of the skull, with depression, causing COMPRESSION of the BRAIN; — also for compression from extravasation or suppuration, or tumors of the dura mater; and sometimes even for *irritation*, as when disease of the skull causes epilepsy. (For the use and abuse of the operation, see CONCUSSION and COMPRESSION.)

In cases of extravasation or suppuration, the trephine used should be *large*, so as to allow the fluid to escape freely. On the other occasions a *small* one may suffice.

The first thing to be done is to *remove* a sufficient portion of the *scalp*, if that has not been done by the accident. Cut a flap in the shape of the letter D, raising the circular side. If there be any loose pieces of bone, remove them with forceps, completing their separation, where necessary, with Hay's saw. The *pericranium* is next to be separated from the surface of the bone, to which the instrument is to be applied; — or a circular incision for the edge of the instrument will answer the purpose of preventing laceration by the teeth. (To insure this incision being made accurately, we have never seen any thing so good as Gibson's Trephine, with a removable lancet attached.)

Apply the trephine so that the center-pin will rest on a sound portion of the skull. Then press gently and saw through, steadily turning the instrument backwards and forwards, but stopping and removing it frequently to cleanse the teeth with a brush, and to examine the groove, which must be at the same time well cleansed from the saw-dust and blood, by means of a wetted sponge. As soon as the groove is deep enough to steady the instrument, withdraw the center-pin. When you get nearly through the bone, be very cautious, and examine your progress very frequently, lest you cut through the dura mater. As soon as any point of the circle is through the bone, introduce the small end of the elevator, and endeavor gently to raise the whole. When nearly cut through all round, it will break off smoothly and come away with ease. If it should still be very firm, introduce the trephine again and saw a little more, taking care not to let the teeth touch at the point or segment which is already cut through. Continue thus, cautiously, until the elevator can be used without too much violence.

The trephine should not be applied over the course of the middle meningeal *arteries*, nor over a *suture*, if both can be avoided; nor low down on the front portion of the head, unless absolutely necessary. After having removed the extravasated blood or pus, or elevated any depressed portion of the skull, — by "prying" with the elevator as a lever against the opposite firm edge, as a fulcrum, — replace the scalp and secure it by a compress of lint or cotton. The part must be kept wet with cold water or some other cooling lotion, before recommended. (See Wounds of the Head.)

HERNIA AND DROPSY OF THE BRAIN, &c.

Trephining has been resorted to for the removal of circumscribed FUNGUS of the DURA MATER. When a sufficient portion of the cranium is removed, and there still appear nothing to contra-indicate such a proceeding, the fungus is cut out *from* or *with* the portion of the membrane from which it grows, or the ligature is used instead of the knife, though that measure as well as the cautery is *here*, perhaps, really more dangerous than the more favorite surgical means.

"Hernia Cerebri," or PROTRUSION of the BRAIN, has been

treated with a variety of experimental "operations." When the sac of investing membranes becomes strangulated, there is sloughing followed by fungous granulation, which is sooner or later fatal. The "hernia," so called, composed only of coagulated blood, is more speedily fatal. The best treatment is the *preventive* — a natural degree of pressure or protection where any part of the cranium is wanting. Shaving or slicing off the tumor level with the skull has in some cases appeared necessary before the artificial cranium could be borne, and in *some* of these has succeeded. A careful operation to remove the strangulation, enlarging the bony opening if necessary, has enabled some surgeons to replace the brain before it had inflamed or degenerated. When the tumor contains serous accumulations, the greater success has followed simple *puncture*, as in the operation of

PARACENTESIS HYDROCEPHALI. This is one of the questionable operations, which, though resorted to from the earliest records of surgery, has been followed with so little success that it is not generally recommended — even as a last resort. Could it indeed be justified before the brain were seriously injured by the accumulation, there is reason to believe that better results would follow. Other operations and wounds on the parts show that the opening of the brain is not necessarily fatal. The congenital and very advanced cases in which it has generally been tried, were otherwise quite hopeless ones. The same instruments and modes of proceeding are adopted as for serous accumulations in other parts. The place chosen is generally one of the still open fontanelles, avoiding sinuses. One surgeon, who has reported the unexampled result of nineteen operations with but one death, directs the trochar to be plunged in two inches, if necessary, into the ventricles. The water must not be allowed to run out too rapidly, — stopt altogether as soon as any sign of fainting occurs. The cranium must be compressed during and after the flow, to prevent a rush of blood, on the withdrawal of the accustomed pressure on the vessels. The operation has had to be repeated even in successful cases. The wound itself easily heals.

The FRONTAL SINUSES have been opened for the removal of polypi and other products of diseased action. A sawing instrument or very small trephine is recommended for the purpose, in preference to a trochar, or anything that would split the bone. The trochar can be used for opening a second chamber when one is entered. To prevent the fistula which must follow the operation when the connection with the nose is closed up, it has been made a question whether one should endeavor to reopen the original orifice, bore out a new one, or destroy the mucous membrane throughout the sinus by cautery.

The ANTRUM HIGHMORIANUM is sometimes opened for polypi and the presence of foreign substances (as insects), as well as for disease of the part. — (See under "MAXILLARY ABSCESS.") The operation is, in rare cases, required to be performed through other parts than the alveoli, — the mouth or nose, and even through the cheek, just under the prominence of the cheek bones (eminentia malaris). In one case Dr. Hill was obliged to take out half of the palatine process of the upper maxillary with a saw made for the purpose.

EXTIRPATION of the upper JAW, or large parts of it, is a formidable operation, far too frequently resorted to for osteo-sarcoma and other much less serious diseases. — See OSTEO-SARCOMA and CANCER. The origin of the evil in many of these cases is "bad teeth," or bad-medication, particularly mercury. Another result of this much "*abused*" article, is permanent

— ANCHYLOSIS OF THE JAW. — This state, when it results from mere superficial ulceration, has been remedied by dividing the contracted masseter, the knife being used in the mouth.

OPERATIONS CONNECTED WITH THE EAR.

FOREIGN SUBSTANCES in the EAR are more safely removed, when practicable, by syringing, than the use of forceps. Insects should be well deluged with olive oil.

PERFORATION of the external MEATUS, for adhesions or false membranes, may sometimes cause a deafness, supposing no other cause for it. When the operation required is only superficial, it is simple and easy; when deep, very difficult and questionable. In the former case, scissors may be sufficient; in the latter, use a bistoury, sheathed except at the part required to cut. After penetrating half an inch, the operator should cease, at least for a time. When the atresia extends to the tympanum, the case may possibly justify its perforation also.

The TYMPANUM has been perforated when (there being no other cause for deafness) that membrane is itself in an indurated or ossified condition, when the space beyond is blocked up with mucus or otherwise irremovable matter, or when the Eustachian tube is itself irremediably impervious. The wound is not dangerous; indeed it will soon close up, unless prevented by a tube, injections, or a quadrangular perforator. But temporary advantage has generally been the result of the measure. A substitute for the Eustachian tube has been contrived, without cutting the tympanum, by a perforation into the internal ear through the mastoid process, with the insertion of a tube, until the orifice becomes naturally permanent. Appropriate Homeopathic medicine will generally render either expedient unnecessary. And they should in no case be resorted to until after

CATHETERISM OF THE EUSTACHIAN TUBE.—A catheter is sometimes inserted into this necessary appendage to the organ of hearing, to clear or enlarge it for the passage of air, for the purpose of introducing injections of water, air, or vapor into the middle ear, and as a means of diagnosticating some diseases of the ear.

The catheter now generally used is an inflexible silver one, about six inches long, varying from the size of a crow-quill to that of a large goose-quill. The extremity is well rounded, and it should have a curve at about five lines from the further end, which should correspond with the lateral position of the mouth of the Eustachian tube. It will be found most convenient in their repeated introduction to have them graduated with inches.

The orifice of the Eustachian tube is to be found about a quarter of an inch behind the soft palate,—large enough for the insertion of the little finger. The instrument, after being warmed and oiled, is first passed through the nostril of the affected side, with its convexity upwards and its point on the floor of the nose, until the patient inclines to *gag* from its reaching the posterior nares and rounded edge of the soft palate. Then by turning the point further towards the affected side, and a little upwards, it will generally slip into the tube.

Boring the ear for ear-rings is a *surgical* operation that, simple as it is, has been followed by bad consequences. If to be done at all, a needle should be pushed through centrally, avoiding the cartilage, upon a cork — the part having been previously compressed, to lessen its sensibility — and a temporary ring immediately inserted, which, after two or three days, must be moved, to avoid adhesion and insure *cutification.*

Otoplastice. — One of Taliacozzi's operations or directions is for the formation of an entire ear out of the scalp behind. The lower part of the ear has been successfully restored in this way. The Hindoos are said to successfully transplant fresh-cropped ears from other heads!

OTHER OPERATIONS ON OR ABOUT THE NOSE.

Foreign substances in the nostrils, which children are apt to introduce, will sometimes get beyond their reach, and cause some danger and great alarm. A scoop or the polypus forceps will generally enable any one who knows the shape of the cavities, to get them out. A flexible catheter pushed up into the posterior nares by the finger and out at the nose, may often effect the object. Hard sneezing may sometimes aid.

The nostrils are sometimes more or less completely closed, so as to obstruct respiration and injure the speech. When the obstruction is not situated too high, and independent of any malformation of the bones, it may be remedied by obvious means of dilatation or abscision.

A defect, of an opposite character, where the septum between the nostrils is wanting, causing "*flat-nose,*" is *easily* remedied by means of a strip from the upper lip — at least this is one of the easiest of the *plastic* operations, and a part of the regular operation of

— "Rhinoplastics" proper (or *of the Nose* — see Part First, where the general subject is spoken of — the *word* meaning, according to etymology, either plastic operations on the integument generally, or, as it has been of late more commonly used, *nose-moulding,* the type of such operations). As this is a really practical and useful piece of work, we will give fuller directions than for some of the *other* "rhinoplastic" operations. The occasions for it used to be much more frequent when syphilis and mercury were more destructive in their ravages. It was formerly not an uncommon thing in old countries to see men with a flat silver coin stuck in the middle of their face, instead of a nose. The Italian method of taking the material for the new nose from the arm, that being bound up across the patient's face for the purpose, has been almost universally abandoned. Dieffenbach cuts integument from the temples. After these and many other experiments, the ancient plan of cutting from the forehead is found to be the best.

You have first to cut out a *pattern* of the superficies of the desired organ, extended into a plane figure — a triangle with rounded corners at the base — nearly like the "hearts" on common playing-cards, if you do not intend to form a septum at the same time; or more like the "clubs" of the same, if you do. It is better to cut your pattern on a wax-mould of appropriate dimensions. This being laid on the forehead, with its base uppermost, and apex at that of the *late* or future nose, you draw in ink the outlines of your flap. After this preparation, pare off raw and scarify the remaining edges of the old nose. Then cut deep round the marked flap, except just across the apex. Dissect this flap down to the periosteum, holding it with your finger and thumb, and then turn it *round* and *down* into place, moulding it into the proper shape. The connection at the top must not be too narrow or short, but include the fibres of the corrugator muscles; and the bleeding from both surfaces must have ceased before the parts intended to unite are brought together. A few interrupted sutures will be better than adhesive straps or plasters of any kind. A little lint in the nostrils, moistened with sweet oil, will be necessary to keep them open and of the proper size.

The greatest difficulty in this proceeding having been found with the COLUMNA, Mr. Liston introduced the improvement of adding this part from the upper lip, a few weeks after the rest of the operation. He takes a complete strip out of the middle of the lip, for its whole width and thickness. The *skin* and place for attachment being pared, and the frænum severed, the flap (about a quarter of an inch broad) is turned *up* but not *round* or twisted. That additional obstacle to continued circulation is here unnecessary, the mucous membrane becoming cutis and cuticle after sufficient exposure to the air. The twisted suture is here used, both to secure the new septum and to reunite the shortened lip (just as in the common operation for hare-lip). This operation is sometimes required alone, as above alluded to, in cases of lost or low septum, when, as Mr. Liston observes, the appearance of the tumefied lip, as well as of the nose, is improved by the proceeding. "The cicatrix, being in the situation of the natural fossa, is scarcely observable." When the ALÆ alone are wanting, it is recommended to bring them from the forehead, rather than disfigure the face; the long, narrow *sanguiduct* then necessary, is supported for a time by being imbedded in a groove along the surface of the nose.

Granulations will go on rapidly under simple treatment. The temperature of the transplanted part has to be watched and regulated, generally by covering it with flannel, and the application of warm or tepid water. When it has fairly rooted or become connected by anastomosis with the vascular system of its new location, the connection at the top may be cut and that point also moulded into seemly proportions.

HARE LIP — LABIUM LEPORINUM.

This striking deformity consists in a fissure or fissures of the upper lip. When there are two (as in the case represented, Fig. 124), they usually extend downwards and outwards from each nostril. When there is only one, it seldom runs exactly in the middle. The division sometimes extends back through the palate bone, as well as the soft palate. When the teeth project through the severed lip, they add very greatly to the deformity. It is a congenital mal-formation or deficiency, and only to be remedied by

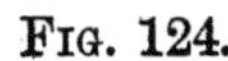
Fig. 124.

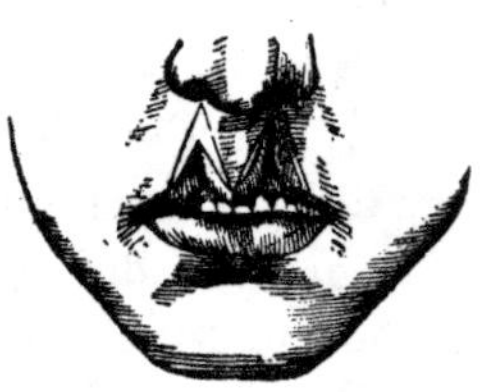

— THE OPERATION. This may be easily performed in a child at any age, though it is preferable to have it two or three years old. If the patient be an adult, let him sit in a low chair and his head be steadied by an assistant. The surgeon, raising the edges of the fissure with his fingers or forceps, places a flat piece of wood between the lip and the gum. In rare cases the lip will be found adherent to the gum, when it will require to be dissected loose. Sponging with cold water will be sufficient to staunch the bleeding. The edges of the fissure are to be pared off from both sides upon the wood with a scalpel or bistoury, so as to leave the sides straight, in the shape of a letter V. When all bleeding has ceased, bring the fresh surfaces together. Be sure that you have the margins even at the lip, and then pass a thin sewing needle through and across the direction of the fissure near its lower extremity. Make it penetrate deep enough to be quite near the inner surface of the lip, where it crosses the fissure. This will keep the inner edges near together, while the outer and all between must be secured by a ligature (or the "twisted suture") over the head and point of the needle in the form of a figure 8. A common waxed thread will be a suitable material, and should be drawn tight enough to bring the wounded edges together, but not so tight as to strangulate the parts and cause sloughing. After the margin is thus secured, introduce two other needles, deep enough to nearly reach the mucous lining of the lip, and apply ligatures as before (see Fig. 125). It is proper to break off the points of the needles with forceps, as they will be in the way. The parts should then be covered with lint, and a bandage applied to retain it, both being kept constantly wet, and treated as ordinary incised wounds. After six days (or four in the case of a child), you can remove the needles and substitute adhesive straps or the collodion. Before attempting to pull them out, take hold of them with the forceps and turn them three our four times round. If anything adheres at the margin of the hole, carefully scrape it off, and see that the surfaces of the needles are smooth. To prevent any rusting, they may be galvanized previous to use; but if a little sweet oil is applied to them before entering, and every time before the lint or bandage is re-wet, there will be no danger of corrosion.

FIG. 125.

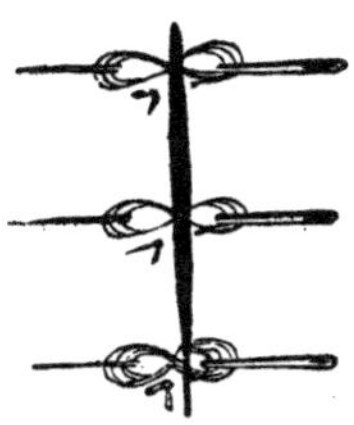

The patient should be confined to a room for several days, and not one allowed to visit him who will be likely to excite him to laugh or cry, and even much talking should be avoided. It is well for security's sake, to pass a long strip of adhesive plaster over the lip, reaching from ear to ear, first pressing the cheeks forward. Such a strap will prevent any tension upon the lip, until it is firmly united and smoothly healed.

Various *modes* of bringing and keeping the divided lip together are recommended by authors, but the foregoing is the plan we have always pursued, and we have been successful in every case. It is simple and convenient, and secures the lip for the time, as well as any other, and much better than most others. The "silver pin" alone, from not bringing the parts together with sufficient force, is very liable to fail. A majority of the cases we have had, had been before operated on in this manner *unsuccessfully*.

If you have a case of the *double* hare-lip, operate on both fissures at the same time, and secure them by the same ligatures and bandage, the intervening portion of lip being transfixed by the needles. If the *teeth* project so as to be in the way, and cannot be pressed back, let them be extracted. Sometimes the *jaw* itself projects too much, in which case *that also* may be trimmed off with the bone forceps, after you have first separated the gum from it.

OTHER OPERATIONS ABOUT OR WITHIN THE MOUTH.

"Cheilo" and "genio-plastice" are Taliacotian operations for the restoration of lost parts of the lips and chin, respectively, the material being procured from any *approximable* part of the neck. *Stomato-plastics* are also sometimes resorted to, in connection with *incisions* for opening or widening of the mouth in congenital, — or other partial cases of

— Atresia oris. Skin already formed has to be brought, we are told, from the cheek, and grafted on to the newly-made or enlarged lip, in consequence of the difficulty of preventing reunion, particularly at the corners. The necessity for any such patch-work may be well doubted: and, fortunately, the necessity for any operation at all is very rare, — the *mouth* is a part least frequently defective in the new-born, or inefficient in the older.

Tongue Tie. — A child is said to be "tongue-tied," when there is a preternatural extension of the *frænum linguæ*, to the tip of the tongue, fixing it firmly to the floor of the mouth. When this malformation is so complete as to prevent the child from sucking, the superabundant frænum should be cut, so as to free the tongue from its attachment. This may be done with blunt scissors, cutting loose about one-eighth of an inch of the *anterior* portion of the membrane. The points of the scissors should be directed *downwards* as near the floor of the mouth as possible, so as to be sure to avoid cutting the lingual artery, which is situated on the inferior surface of the tongue. It is preferable to operate when the child is asleep. Hold the tongue up a little with the fore-finger of one hand and operate under it with the other. But a few drops of blood will flow.

In LANCING the GUMS of teething children, the lancet should be so held and directed as not to injure the sacs of the advancing teeth.

AMPUTATION or EXTIRPATION of the TONGUE, or a part of it, is sometimes resorted to, not only in malignant diseases, but for tumors or hypertrophy, aneurism, &c. The knife and the ligature have had each their advocates in this case. The latter is certainly less immediately dangerous, preventing the necessity for tying the lingual artery, and the risk of other hemorrhage.

For TUMORS of the GUMS, and "gum-boils," for which *knife operations* are too frequently relied on, see under Epulis and Ranula, and in connection with Disease and Extraction of Teeth. For the operation of introducing the style in salivary obstructions, see Parotid Fistula and Fistula Lachrymalis.

The CLEFT or rather DEFICIENT PALATE, — mentioned under Hare lip, as connected with that deformity, and a similar bony deficiency resulting from ulceration, — has been successfully remedied in some instances by a sort of internal "rhino plastic" operation, — notwithstanding the natural indisposition of mucous surfaces to take on adhesive inflammation, and the great difficulty in this case of keeping the parts in quiet apposition. In this operation the new roof is brought from the *walls* of the mouth, or inside of the cheeks, and secured by a sufficient number of interrupted sutures. This difficult operation (called "Staphylorrhaphe," and by one learned author "Uraniskoraphia"!) is only necessary where the palate bones or palatine processes of the superior maxillary, or so great a portion of the soft palate is wanting, as to make it impossible to approximate the edges by simple ligatures, — as is done in the more ordinary

— OPERATION for FISSURE of the PALATE. Some of the same difficulties, however, attend this operation, as the more serious just described. Various plans have been devised for overcoming these, and numerous instruments invented, — some of them so complex as to require several assistants, and make the operation

FIG. 126.

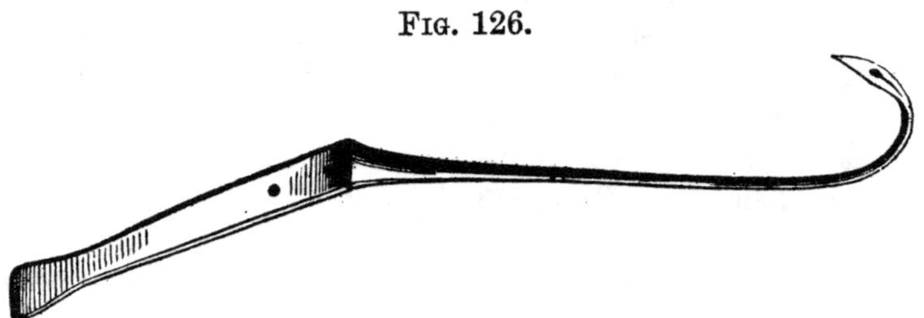

very tedious, thus adding to its uncertainty. Here, as always, the simplest means are the best; and we prefer the *curved needle* (Figure 126), eyed at the point, with a pair of *forceps*, which, like it, has a handle set at an obtuse angle with the blade, so that when either is being used, the hand of the operator may be out of his own light. The patient's head is to be held steadily back by an assistant, and the mouth kept open by wedges far back between the teeth. The edges of the fissure are to be first pared off by curved scissors or bistoury, while firmly held by the forceps. As soon as the bleeding has ceased and all coagula been removed from the wounded surfaces, press the tongue down with a finger and introduce the needle, armed with the ligature, about half an inch from the margin, bringing it out at the fissure. Then seize the ligature with forceps, and withdraw the needle. Thread it again with the same end, and pass it into the fissure, through the opposite margin and out about half an inch on the opposite side, seizing the ligature as before. This operation may be repeated for as many ligatures as the case may require.

TIE them by the aid of the forceps, just tight enough to bring the edges together. There are several other modes of fastening the ligatures in use; and probably the simplest and best of any, is to pass both ends of the thread, after insertion, through a piece of lead, and push this up by the forceps or a canula, till it brings the lips together with sufficient force, and then squeeze or weld it, as it were, together, by stronger forceps. If there is much difficulty in approximating the edges of the wound, make on each side, parallel to the fissure, and beyond the ligatures near the alveoli, a cut of about an inch in length, to take off the tension of the membrane. It is always indispensable for the success of this operation, that the patient be of sufficient age and have proper discretion and self-control, to remain perfectly still, uttering no groan or word. Even for some days afterwards he must not allow himself to make any violent effort of voice, deglutition or respiration, — must avoid sneezing, coughing, and much if not all talking. His diet should be semi-fluid, such that a few small swallows at a time will suffice for both food and drink. Operate immediately after a meal, and let the interval between the future meals be as long as possible. In such a case as *this* even a little "starvation" is justifiable!

OPERATIONS ON THE TONSILS AND UVULA.

Excision of enlarged tonsils (see chronic enlargement of) is performed by means of the instrument represented in Fig. 127. This consists of an angular or rounded blade which can be drawn back, leaving a ring which is to be passed over the part to be re-

Fig. 127.

moved and pressed down around it, so firmly as to make it protrude through as far as desirable. The cutting blade or point is then pushed suddenly forward, a *needle* which protrudes some sixth of an inch beyond the point, transfixing and holding the severed portion to prevent its falling into the throat. This fixing needle or fork is sometimes so arranged that it can be first pushed through the tonsil by a spring and raised, before the blade is advanced. This plan is effectual, so far as its direct object is concerned, but is attended with so much danger from hemorrhage that we do not recommend it. The simpler method with the instrument described is sufficient and devoid of danger. It is well also with it not to cut deep enough to wound any considerable arteries. The little hemorrhage that usually occurs may be readily stopped by cold water, salt, or the dry powder of slippery elm.

EXCISION OR ABSCISION

— of the ELONGATED UVULA can be conveniently performed by the same instrument. It is too simple an operation to need further explanation.

THE STOMACH-PUMP

— is a useful instrument, for the INTRODUCTION of which it may be proper to say a word in this place. When the special instrument is not at hand, the elastic tube belonging to an injecting syringe will answer the purpose very well; and the syringe itself may be used as the pump, — if a large one, one stroke of the piston may suffice. Wetting this tube or the regular one with water will be sufficient lubrication. In introducing it, insert the finger also and press into the pharynx and pass the end down the orifice of the œsophagus; and in withdrawing it, recollect to stop the outer end, so that any liquid in it may not fall back into the stomach.

CHAPTER XVIII.

OPERATIONS ON THE NECK, THORAX AND ABDOMEN.

WRY NECK may be caused by spasmodic or permanent muscular contraction, bad cicatrization, or be connected with disease of the cervical or even lower vertebræ in general spinal curvature. In the first case, when other medical and mechanical means fail, the constricting muscular tendon or fascia is to be ascertained, and divided by "the sub-cutaneous section," no more external wound being made than necessary to admit the instrument. The *snapping* back of the muscle will tell when it has been completely severed; — a compress should be immediately applied to prevent sub-cutaneous hemorrhage.

In all operations about the neck, as in removing tumors, if they are not very superficial, special care is required, on account of the number and variety of nerves and vessels to be avoided. Even the removal of a common parotid tumor may be followed by palsy of the face.

[For knife-operations in the THYROID GLAND, see under *Bronchocele.*]

LIGATING ARTERIES OF THE NECK.

The same general principles apply to the tying of arteries when wounded, as for aneurism or other morbid cause, except that the *wounded* artery should here have a ligature below as well as above the wounded part. When the vessel cannot be reached through the dilated wound, it should generally be cut down to, in the manner now to be directed. First, for the

— COMMON CAROTID, we will mention the particulars of an interesting CASE: — In March, 1848, Mr. Jones, of Washington city, came to Cincinnati to put himself under the care of Prof. R. S. Newton, for osteo-sarcoma of the lower jaw, which had already involved the soft parts with a considerable part of the neck. He had previously consulted several eminent practitioners and professors, without benefit or encouragement. During treatment for the *medical cure*, the facial, the internal maxillary, and the sublingual arteries all sloughed away together. Fortunately, though the accident happened in the night, Dr. Newton was at hand, and *with* his HAND averted the immediate danger from hemorrhage, and continued doing so until six o'clock in the morning. Meanwhile, as it was impossible for him to attend to this and operate at the same time, he sent for aid. As soon as it was light enough, with his assistance and that of Prof. Morrow, who was called, Dr. Hill proceeded to take up the right common carotid. It was necessary, on account of the extension of the disease, to operate about two inches above the clavicle (instead of the spot usually preferred, the middle of a line from the angle of the jaw to the top of the sternum, where the vessel is crossed obliquely by the omo-hyoid muscle); and to be guided wholly by the anatomy of the parts, as from the very great exhaustion of the patient, hardly any pulsation in the artery was perceptible. Another peculiar difficulty experienced, was from the patient's emphatically *hemorrhagic* diathesis. The amount of blood that flowed out from the smallest veins, at the very first incision, would have made an observer suppose we had divided the external jugular. It was the same with every subsequent cut, thus obliging him to stay proceedings until the venous hemorrhage could be averted by styptics. We afterwards ascertained that the patient had been several times in danger of bleeding to death from slight cuts in shaving.) By proceeding very slowly and carefully, however, he got down to the vessel sought for and applied the ligature. All serious hemorrhage immediately ceased; and the patient did not appear to suffer any additional inconvenience from the loss of the artery. Dr. Newton proceeded with his regular treatment.

In the usual place of operating (noticed above), make a superficial incision through the platisma myoides, when the neck is tense, obliquely along the course of the vessel, and along the inner margin of the sterno mastoid for about three inches, and terminating at about an inch above the sternum. The deep fascia and cellular substance are to be divided with the handle of the scalpel, or with your fingers; or, if too firm for this, it may be carefully cut, and the vessel reached just below, or, in some cases, above the omo-hyoideus. Pass the artery needle under the vessel from the inside, bringing it out between the artery and the pneumogastric nerve, the vein being outside of the nerve.

The EXTERNAL CAROTID may require ligating for wounds, when that of its branches will not suffice. It can be tied below the digastricus and ninth pair of nerves, at the level of the hyoid bone; but it would be easier and safer to take up the common carotid.

The ARTERIA INNOMINATA or the RIGHT SUBCLAVIAN (internal to the scalenus muscle) is reached behind the sternal and clavicular origins of the sterno-cleido-mastoideus. A crucial incision is first made along the inner edge and across the origin of this muscle. This, the sterno-hyoid and sterno-thyroid muscles being cut through, the fascia beneath is to be divided *by the finger*, and the ligature inserted from without inwards, taking care to avoid the vena innominata and contiguous large nerves.

The SUBCLAVIAN is much more easily reached and safely tied on either side, *exteriorly to the scalenus.* The first incision, just above and parallel with the clavicle, extends from the sterno-mastoideus to the trapezius. The external jugular is to be carefully avoided. The first long incision had better be made *on* the clavicle, the skin being first drawn down, and all the deepening done without any more cutting. The needle should be passed from below upwards round the artery, — which is found in the angle formed by the edge of the scalenus and the first rib.

The AXILLARY ARTERY may also be reached by incision above the clavicle, extending in an inward curve from near its sternal extremity to the anterior margin of the deltoid muscle, and turning back a flap. It is better, when there is a choice, to cut up to it from the arm-pit, — the first incision being three inches in length near the margin of the latissimus dorsi, between it and that of the pectoralis major.

LARYNGOTOMY AND TRACHEOTOMY.

The former of these is chiefly necessary for the removal of foreign substances. Make an incision through the integuments in the median line from the lower side of the Pomum Adami to the lower margin of the cricoid cartilage. Separate the skin a little with your fingers, and with the handle of your scalpel rupture the cellular membrane between the sterno-hyoid muscles, down to the crico-thyroid membrane. Then pass the point of your scalpel, with a sudden jerk, through the membrane. A quarter of an inch incision will be large enough for the passage of any instrument or the free ingress and egress of air; and this can be enlarged laterally if necessary for the extraction of any foreign substance. Take care that the point of the knife does not pass through and wound the opposite side of the cricoid-cartilage. This operation has to be preferred to the following, in very young children, owing to the shortness of their necks.

TRACHEOTOMY is resorted to in croup and other occurrences preventing respiration through the larynx. The chin and sternum are well separated, and an incision is made in the median line, extending from near the upper end of the sternum to the cricoid cartilage. The cellular tissue at the lower end of the wound is dissected, the operator being very careful to hold aside any veins he may come to. Continuing the incision down to the trachea, the point of the knife is made to enter it at the lowest part exposed, and the edge carried upwards to the desired extent. If the object is to make an entrance and exit for air, a tube is inserted for the purpose, and the rest of the wound closed up. The operation is an easy one, and perfectly safe if the directions are followed — easier on the living than the dead subject. In very fleshy or short-necked subjects, there may be difficulties. Keeping the median line is essential to success. Opening the trachea is almost always to be preferred to the more superficial operation into the larynx.

ŒSOPHAGOTOMY

— has been resorted to as a means of conveying food into the stomach, when the pharynx was impervious. It is sometimes indispensable for the extraction of foreign substances lodged in the throat (see CHOKING). It being ascertained on which side the obstruction adheres or projects, an incision is there made between the trachea and the sterno-cleido-mastoideus. To avoid the recurrent nerve and the thyroid as well as carotid arteries, the dissection should be made chiefly with the fingers, the fascia being cut with the protection of a director. The smallest practicable incision through the œsophagus is to be made — to be dilated if necessary. This operation is only a last resource, and in a large proportion of cases a final or fatal one.

PARACENTESIS THORACIS.

Puncturing of the pleura is a much more serious operation than that of the (diseased) peritoneum. It may be, however, in some cases necessary; and some have even attempted to relieve hydrops pericardi by operation. The most frequent cause for which the operation is justifiably practiced is EMPYEMA, or the accumulation of pus within the pleura. In any doubtful case, a very small trochar or grooved needle is recommended, with a cup to cause the fluid to rise through the narrow tube. The same measure (without the cup ?) is applicable in EMPHYSEMA and PNEUMOTHORAX (when there is air, instead of pus, in the cellular tissue and pleura respectively). In HYDROTHORAX and HÆMATHORAX a resort to the trochar and canula is more questionable. It is certainly contra-indicated where the patient is already too far sunk for the heart and lungs to hopefully resume their functions; where there is a high grade of inflammation or tuberculosis; or where a wound (a fracture of the ribs for instance) is the cause, which by dilatation may be made to supersede the operation, or reaches beyond the inner fold of the pleura and is too deep for it.

For the operation itself some prefer incision with the bistoury to puncturing with the trochar. Make an incision an inch and a half long through the integuments at the upper edge of the sixth rib, a little behind its middle, and carefully separate the intercostal muscles, passing the point of the bistoury on through the pleura costalis. Then introduce the canula, through which the pus or other fluid may pass off. Great care must be taken that air do not pass in through the canula. To avoid this serious danger, an instrument has been recently invented having an air-tight valve, to prevent ingress, while it allows fluids to flow freely out. In the absence of such an instrument, it is well to place the patient upon the diseased side, immediately after the canula is introduced, and to take care to close this before all the morbid fluid is discharged.

PARACENTESIS ABDOMINIS — TAPPING.

OPERATION.—Place the patient in a chair in a sitting posture, pass a bandage made of a sheet, folded about half a yard wide around the abdomen, let it cross behind his back, and put the ends in the hands of two assistants, who must be directed to draw so as to tighten it as you desire, while the fluid escapes. It is well to have this bandage cover the whole abdomen, having a hole in it through which to operate. The surgeon should then make a cut a half or three-fourths of an inch in length (according to the size of the trochar), with a sharp lancet or bistoury, *through the integuments* along the linea alba, two or three inches below the umbilicus. Then introduce a diamond pointed trochar, covered with a canula, and pass it on *into the cavity* (Fig. 128). Withdraw the trochar, leaving the canula in the orifice to conduct off the fluid. The trochar may be pushed in without the previous lancing; or the whole incision may be made with the lancet, and a blunt tube or canula introduced through the opening thus made.

Fig. 128.

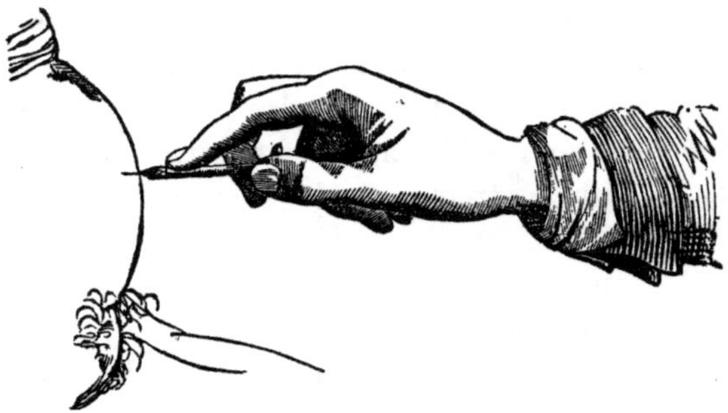

The fluid is received into a proper vessel, while the assistants are directed to draw gradually upon the bandage so as to keep a firm pressure upon the abdomen as the fluid escapes, lest by too suddenly taking off the pressure upon the abdominal vessels, the blood settle down into them from the heart and cause fainting, or even burst the coats of the vessels and cause fatal internal hemorrhage. The fluid being drawn off, the patient is put to bed in a horizontal position, the wound closed with an adhesive strap, and a bandage applied round the abdomen.

If faintness occur during the flow of the fluid in spite of your bandage, you must stop the flow; lay the patient down, and wait a few hours, or perhaps a day or two, before the remaining portion of the fluid is evacuated.

OPERATION FOR STRANGULATED HERNIA.

Though it is presumed that no one will attempt to operate in this case who is not at least a tolerable anatomist, it may be well to enumerate, in order, the textures that will be found over the sac, and that must be cut through before succeeding in the object you will have in view. The symptoms justifying or demanding a resort to this operation, were noticed when treating at length of the disease or accident. (See Hernia, Part I.)

In the most common form of the Oblique Inguinal Hernia

(Fig. 129) we find, immediately under the *skin*, a strong condensed *cellular tissue* derived from the superficial fasciæ of the

Fig. 129.

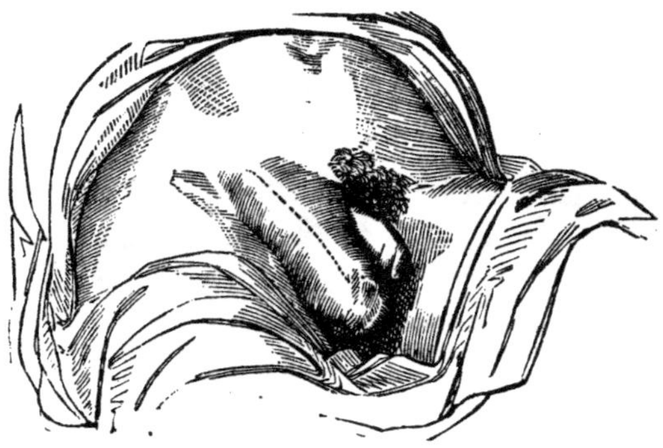

abdomen, in which ramifies the external epigastric *artery*; — next there is the *fascia spermatica*; — then a *tendinous layer* derived from the semi-circular bands, which connect the margins of the external abdominal ring; — lastly, the *cremaster muscle* lies in immediate contact with the sac. The *internal* epigastric *artery*, it should be borne in mind, always lies *internal* to the neck of the sac.

In Complete Inguinal or Scrotal Hernia (Fig. 129), the *Spermatic Cord* lies behind (except the Cremaster muscle, which was mentioned as being found in front of the sac).

Direct or Ventro-Inguinal Hernia has the same covering, except the Cremaster Muscle, there being no connection in this with the Spermatic Cord. In this case both the cord and the epigastric artery lie on the outside of the sac.

The operation is thus performed: — The patient being placed in the position described for the Reduction of Hernia, the parts being shaved and the skin held tense, the surgeon makes an incision through the skin, three or four inches in length, beginning above the neck and running along the course of the tumor (as indicated by the dotted lines in the figures). He then cuts through the successive layers before described, by pinching up a small bit at a time with the forceps, and cutting horizontally through it under their points. This process is repeated until an opening is made to the sac, which can always be distinguished by its bluish appearance. The sac itself is to be opened in the same manner by pinching up a little bit, and cutting through it horizontally. The small director (Fig. 130) is then inserted and an opening

Fig. 130.

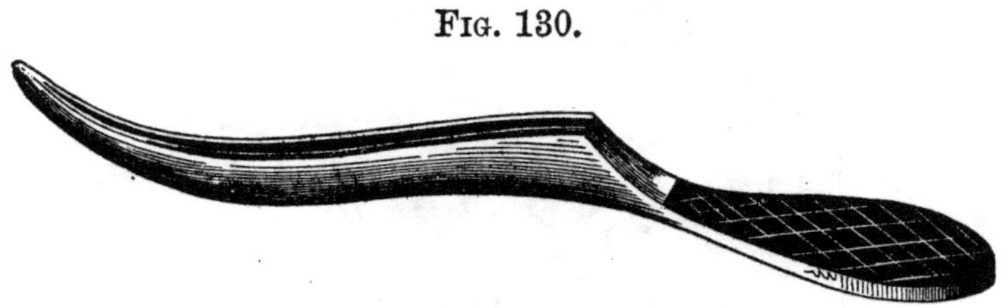

made sufficiently large to admit a finger. The fore-finger of the left hand is introduced (as shown in Fig. 131) and passed up to

Fig. 131.

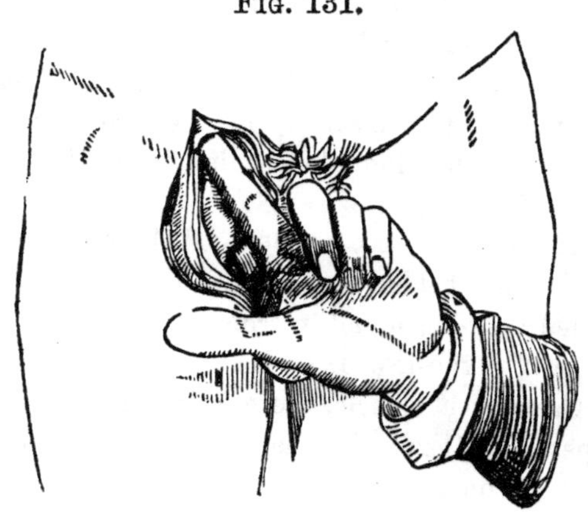

the neck of the sac to search for the stricture, which will generally be found at the internal ring; it may, however, be at the external ring; or there may be a stricture at each. The stricture is to be dilated to admit the finger to enter the abdomen. This is done by what is called a probe-pointed bistoury, — or a similar knife, made for the purpose, not edged quite up to the point, and only for a short space below it (Fig. 132). The blade is passed

FIG. 132.

up *flat-wise* (see Fig. 133) along the finger and pushed on through the stricture. Its edge is then turned upwards, cutting no more than necessary to admit the finger. The CUT must, in all cases, be made DIRECTLY UPWARDS, parallel to the linea alba, whether it be in Direct or Oblique Inguinal Hernia, so as to *avoid* the epigastric artery. If there be no stricture in the neck of the sac, one may be found in the body.

FIG. 133.

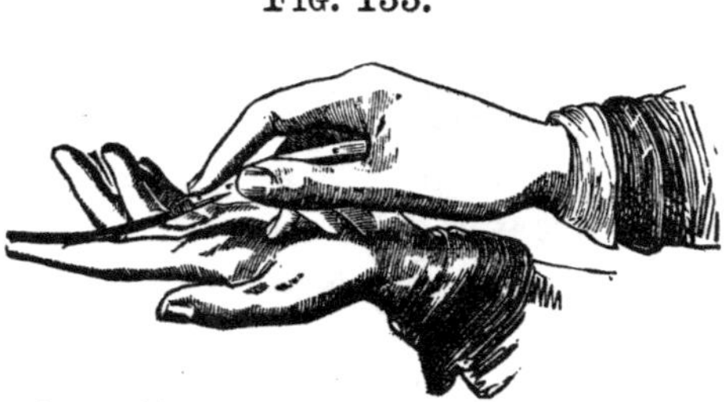

The stricture being thus relieved, and sufficiently dilated with the fingers, strict examination of the parts must be made; for, if firm adhesions have taken place, no attempt should be made at reduction; or if the protrusion has continued so long that fatty deposits around the part have accumulated to too great an extent, the hernia must be allowed to continue. All you can do in such a case, is to let the wound heal, taking precautions against inflammation. When the bowel has mortified, care must be taken not to disturb the adhesions at the neck. The intestine must then be opened, and the mortified part taken out. The only chance is, then, that of an artificial anus.

For FEMORAL or CRURAL HERNIA, the skin is pinched up and divided by a simple incision (as marked out in the case represented in Fig. 134), or, as many prefer, a crucial or angular one, — the safest way of making it being to run a narrow knife through the skin, with its back towards the hernial sac. The superficial fascia of the thigh with its fat, and the fascia propria, must then be divided. Immediately beneath the latter, and contiguous to the sac, may be another layer of fat, liable to be mistaken for omentum. The sac itself is usually very small, seldom containing omentum or serum; and must be cautiously opened, as it embraces the bowel very tightly. The stricture will generally be found at the inner edge of the falciform process. This must be slightly cut, for a line or two only, in an UPWARD and somewhat

FIG. 134.

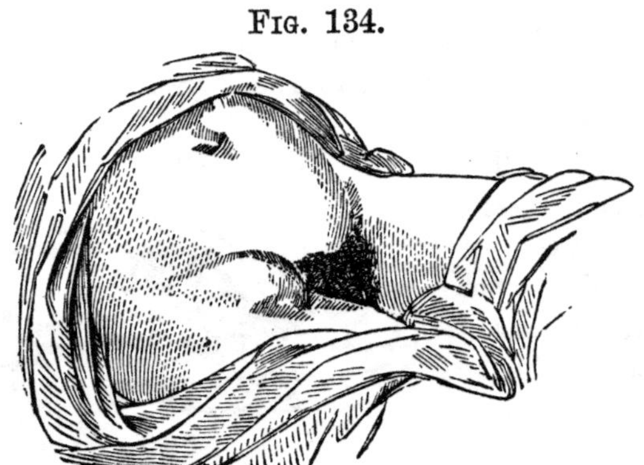

INWARD direction. If carried too far, the incision might penetrate the spermatic cord, or, in females (who are more liable to this form of hernia from greater breadth of pelvis), the round ligament of the womb. If that is not sufficient, a few fibres of Gimbernat's ligament are directed to be severed, although there is great danger of wounding the obturator artery, which often encircles this ligament. When the hernia is freed, reduction is to be effected, as directed in the former case.

FURTHER OPERATIONS ABOUT THE PELVIS.

The ATRESIA ANI of new-born children is often but superficial, or strictly an IMPERFORATE ANUS. Though the integument is closed over it, the end of the rectum can frequently be observed swelling beneath. In such a case a simple incision is to be made into it, and kept open with suitable means. In other cases there is only a narrow adhesion of the walls of the bowel, which may be carefully treated in the same manner. When, after sufficient delay, the rectum cannot be reached, recourse *may* be had to

—the operation for an ARTIFICIAL ANUS. This is sometimes

necessary in adults after closure of the rectum from disease, or its opening into some other cavity of the pelvis. The least inconvenient place for this business, when there is a free choice, is the loins. An incision is made down to the descending colon, where it is uncovered by the peritoneum, just above the left crista of the ilium. The bowel is immediately attached to the lips of the wound by two ligatures, and an incision is then made into it, and the lips of the intestinal wound more closely united with those of the superficial one. In this part the patient ultimately gains control of the new organ, a complete sphincter being formed. In the left groin, where the operation used to be performed, it is much more dangerous, and the result less satisfactory.

About "*the* operations for Fistula in Ano, Hemorrhoids and Prolapsus Ani," enough has been said or implied in giving directions for avoiding them. Nothing but malignant disease would justify a removal of part of the rectum; and then other means than the knife should also be used, if not solely relied on.

The GLUTEAL and SCIATIC ARTERIES may be found for the purpose of ligating in case of wounds, by means of an incision, beginning for the former, an inch, and for the latter, two inches and a half, below the posterior spinous process of the ilium, and cutting towards the trochanter major, severing the gluteus maximus. These incisions have to be both long and deep, and it is often preferable to take up the external or even internal iliac.

The EXTERNAL ILIAC ARTERY is reached by an incision about an inch above Poupart's ligament, and nearly parallel with it, but slightly curved downwards from the ant. post. spinous process of the ilium to the upper angle of the ext. abd. ring. After the obliquous externus has been divided, the other muscles separated from the ligament, and the fascia transversalis as well as cellular connection of the external iliac vein with the artery *torn through*, the needle is passed round the artery, behind the spermatic cord.

The INTERNAL and the COMMON ILIAC, and even the great arterial reservoir, above its first bifurcation, have been ligated. The incision and mode of proceeding is the same for all three. A longitudinal cut of several inches, reaching nearly to Poupart's ligament, is made near the external border of the rectus abdominis, the muscles and transverse fascia beneath, being carefully divided down to the peritoneum, the latter is separated from the iliac fascia; and when the internal iliac is found at the brim of the pelvis, it can be secured; or the finger guided by it to the common iliac, and by that to the AORTA itself, if the intention is to venture so far.

CHAPTER XIX.

LITHOTOMY AND OTHER OPERATIONS ABOUT THE PUBIC REGION.

URINARY DEPOSITS, CALCULOUS DIATHESIS, ETC.

STONE or gravel may accumulate in the kidneys or ureters, as well as in the bladder; or, after escaping from the latter, may be first discovered as an obstruction in the urethra.

In women, calculi of considerable size easily pass the shorter urethra, and that channel may be artificially dilated for the purpose. The male urethra, when dilatation and other means fail, has sometimes to be opened at the membranous portion (the stone being pushed back there if required).

Calculi IN THE KIDNEYS are apt to occasion heat and pain in the loins, hæmaturia and nephritis. If they do not escape into the ureters, they cause atrophy or ulceration of the parts. The *passage* of calculi THROUGH THE URETERS, towards the bladder, is accompanied by very painful and distressing symptoms, coming on and going off *suddenly*, though they may last a day or two. The pain is in the groin and testicles, which are retracted spasmodically, as well as in the loins. Relaxants and diluents are of much avail at these times. *Dr. Bredenoll* cured a case of calculous affection of the kidneys, by a single dose of the triturated calculus, after several homeopathic remedies had been administered in vain. The *isopathic* cure was rapid and permanent.

The SYMPTOMS of STONE IN THE BLADDER are very various, both in kind and intensity. They are chiefly referable to irritation of the neck of the bladder or retention of the urine. They may not be sufficient, or sufficiently noticed, to lead to a discovery of the cause for years after their commencement, and until all means but lithotomy (if not even that operation) are unavailable. There is pain in the glans as well as at the origin of the urethra, particularly after urinating. The stoppage of urine is apt to be sudden, and the patient often discovers that he can succeed in renewing the flow by a change of posture.

In all suspected cases, examination should be made, as we have in art, one simple and

— DECISIVE SYMPTOM. The *sound* — a solid metallic rod, or the "director" used in lithotomy — is introduced, and the patient placed, if necessary, in different postures, and the vesicle searched with it, till the metal and stone are *heard* and felt to come in contact.

OPERATIONS FOR STONE. — Having satisfied yourself from the foregoing symptoms, and from *sounding*, that there is a stone in the bladder, your next step is to decide upon the operation for its removal. Two modes are offered: Crushing with the lithontriptor (called lithontripsy), or cutting in for it with the knife or gorget, called lithotomy. Where circumstances are all favorable for *lithontripsy*, this new method is always to be preferred. Yet there are so many conditions in which this plan is impracticable or improper, that *lithotomy* must be performed in a majority of cases, notwithstanding it has been claimed by some, that the crushing is a complete substitute for the more formidable operation with the knife.

For the use of the lithontriptor, the patient must be an adult, or nearly so, as in younger persons the urethra is too small to admit an instrument strong enough for the purpose. There must be no stricture of the urethra, and no enlargement of the prostate gland, so as to obstruct the passage of the instrument. There must not be much irritability or diminution of the bladder, so that there will be sufficient room to work the instrument. The stone must not be of a large size, nor of the hardest kind, such as that called the mulberry calculus. There must be no adhesion to any portion of the bladder.

The best prospect of success in the use of the *lithontriptor* is when, the urethra and bladder being sound, the prostate in a natural condition, and the patient an adult, the stone is both small and soft. If any of these conditions are wanting, lithotomy is the only resort. Children are, of course, excluded from the list of cases for lithontripsy, by the narrowness of their urethra.

FOR THE OPERATION OF LITHONTRIPSY,

—the patient is placed on a table covered with quilts; the hips are elevated so as to throw the stone back from the mouth of the urethra, and the bladder, if not already full of urine, is to be nearly filled with tepid water, injected through a catheter. The urethra must have been previously dilated by the repeated use of bougies, increasing the size, from time to time, for a week or more, until the *lithontriptor* will enter. This instrument (Fig. 135) is then warmed, oiled, and passed in, closed up, as a common

FIG. 135.*

sound or bougie. When it comes in contact with the stone, the movable half is pushed in so as to open the blades at the joints, and form a sort of firm loop or noose. Rotate this from side to side, and tighten a little occasionally, so as to grasp the stone whenever it gets into the loop. As soon as it is fixed between the blades, as represented in the above drawing, which will be known by your inability to draw the sliding half back, turn gradually upon the arms of the screw, which slowly, but with great force, draws out the slide, and brings the blades together. When the stone gives way, and the instrument closes, re-open it and manœuvre as before to catch any large fragments that may remain;

* Drawn and engraved by G. K. Stillman, from the instrument as manufactured by Max. Wocher, Cincinnati.

continue this until all are finely crushed; then withdraw the instrument, and let the patient turn over, with his face downwards, and evacuate the fluid from the bladder as freely and rapidly as possible: it will carry off with it a large portion of the powdered stone. If the urethra and bladder are not too irritable, inject the bladder full of tepid water immediately, and let it pass off. This may be several times repeated, if the patient can bear it, until all the fragments are washed away. If there be too much irritability in the parts for these injections, you must depend on the natural evacuations.* These, however, may be much aided by a free use, as a common drink, of demulcent diuretics, such as an infusion of Althæa officinalis, or water-melon seed.

A few doses of Arnica should be given to allay the irritation from the use of the instrument.

LITHOTOMY

Before attempting this operation, or even the preceding one, the patient's general health must be as far as possible restored; and all irritation of the urethra, bladder and kidneys allayed. The healthy action of the skin must be promoted. The patient should diet, but not *starve*, for a week or more before the operation. He should be kept quiet and take less than his usual amount of food, free from stimulating condiments. Let him use cold water, but no alcoholic beverage.

Several different modes of operating have been adopted, but the LATERAL OPERATION is now almost universally preferred. It is the mode invariably adopted by one of the best, and doubtless the most successful lithotomist now living (Prof. Dudley, of Lexington, Ky., he having lost only one case in nearly two hundred operations). The bowels having been evacuated by an enema, and the bladder being nearly full of fluid (which should be ensured by tying up the penis for sometime before, or injecting in tepid water through a catheter), the patient is ready for the operation. Place him upon his back, on a table covered by quilts or a mattress. The table should be of such a height as to enable

* We would suggest, as a curative and future preventative, the use of the triturated calculus. See case of Dr. Bredenoll, mentioned in connection with calculi in the kidneys.

the surgeon to work easily while sitting in a chair. Flex the thighs on the abdomen and the legs on the thighs, separate the knees and make him grasp the soles of his feet with his hands. Then fasten the feet and hands together by bandages, first put around the wrists by a noose. Now give him the ether or chloroform until he is insensible to pain, unless you should choose to operate without this advantage for *both*. It is better also at this stage to apply a *bandage* around *each arm* and *thigh*, tightly enough to stop the return of the venous blood as far as practicable, so that a large amount of blood will, for the time, be retained in the limbs, and thus being withdrawn from the general circulation, will greatly lessen the hemorrhage during the operation. The hemorrhage from this operation is not unfrequently dangerous, especially if the pudic artery be cut, as sometimes happens.

Having thus prepared his patient, the surgeon introduces the staff, which is a steel instrument, like the sound, though a little larger, with a groove in its convex surface. An assistant on each side holds the thighs apart, and another holds the patient's head and shoulders firmly. A third holds the scrotum to one side, and supports the staff perpendicularly, drawing it up firmly against the Pubes. A fourth assistant stands by to reach the surgeon his instruments.

The operator before beginning, introduces a finger into the rectum, not only to ascertain that it is empty, but to stimulate it to contraction. The perineum must be previously shaved clean. The knife used has the posterior two-thirds of the edge blunt: it is somewhat longer than the common scalpel. This enters the perineum about midway between the scrotum and anus, on the left side of the raphe, and is brought downwards and outwards, dividing only the skin and superficial fasciæ to about midway between the anus and the tuberosity of the ischium. The section is then deepened *by the finger*, for the purpose of security to the rectum and to blood-vessels. Muscles also should be separated rather than torn. If any portions of the levator ani resist the finger they must be divided by the knife. So also with the transversus perinei, though that muscle is often wanting. The point of the knife has to be applied with great care to any part that resists dilatation. The finger-nail is lodged in the groove of the director, just in front of the prostate and behind the triangular ligament.

Fig. 136.

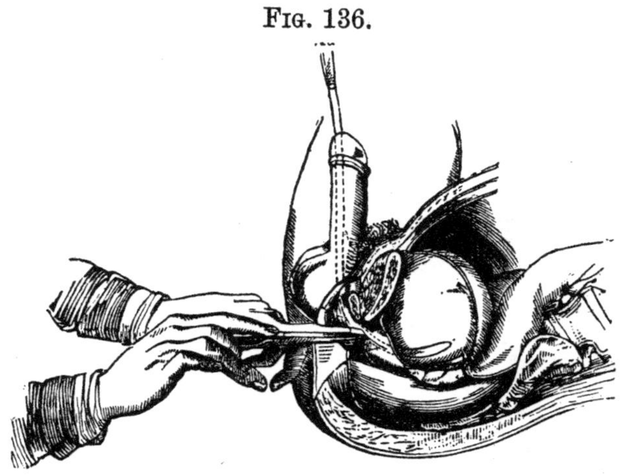

The knife is made to perforate the urethra and enter the groove behind the finger (as shown in Fig. 136), which simultaneously follows it, entering the urethra, which the knife divides far enough for the purpose. The finger moves freely on the dilatable substance of the prostate. The base of that gland is not divided; and the ileo-vesical fascia is left entire, to prevent the danger of urinary infiltration. An incision just large enough for the entrance of the finger can be easily dilated for the exit of ordinary sized calculi. The rule in this "lateral operation" is "a free external wound, and a small internal one." The wider the former, the shallower need be the latter. Care must be taken in withdrawing the knife, not to endanger the pudic artery by bringing it too near the ramus of the ischium.

During the dilatation of the deep wound by the finger, urine escapes; and commonly, the stone or stones descending with it, can now be distinctly felt. The staff is gently withdrawn; and if the stone is found too large to pass through the opening already prepared, a straight probe-pointed bistoury can be passed over the fore-finger still in the wound, dividing the prostatic portion of the urethra on the right side as well as on the left, and then dilating as before. This "bi-lateral" incision can be made in the first place, when the calculus is known before hand to be so large as to require it.

The finger is kept in contact with the stone until it is seized by the forceps (represented by Fig. 137). These should be large

FIG. 137.

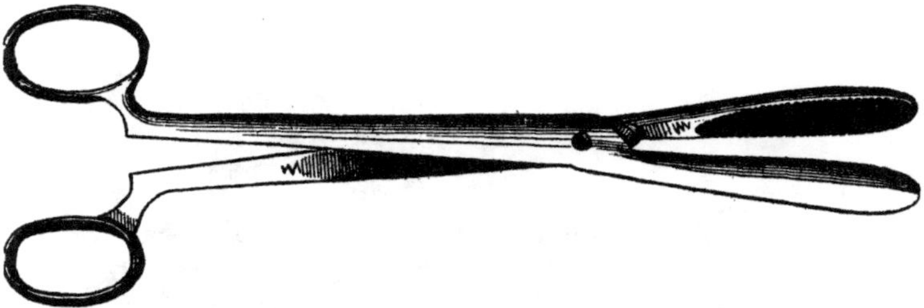

enough in the blades to hold the calculus by as many points as possible, and long enough in the handles to furnish sufficient leverage; while for other obvious reasons, it should be as small as will meet these conditions. To lessen the chance of the stone's slipping, the blades of the instrument may be lined with cotton cloth. If the stone is not immediately clutched, the point of the forceps should be advanced and depressed to the part where it is most likely to be found. The object being seized, it is to be turned round with the forceps, to be certain that no part of the bladder is included, and then elevated and taken out,—the finger being again inserted between the blades of the instrument, to ascertain that the calculus is in the best position, or to put it so if required. Its longest diameter being adjusted in the axis of the instrument, and that in the direction of the axis of the pelvis, obliquely downwards, extractive force is slowly applied, the forceps being at the same time moved to and fro, forwards and backwards, to secure further dilatation. The handles are held together tightly enough to prevent the stones slipping, but not so strongly pressed as to risk its being crushed or broken. The finger must be used to prevent the bladder being pulled out before the stone, and to separate any fibres of the levator ani or other obstacles in the external wound.

In rare cases the stone has been found lodged above the pubes, or in old men in a deep pouch of the bladder behind the prostate, requiring the use of curved forceps. Another difficulty occurs when it is more or less *encysted.* In that case, any projecting part is to be seized, and extraction from the cyst first attempted. This may be aided by the point of the finger or of a probe-pointed bistoury. The complication may require delay for the textures to relax.

In case of the stone being *crushed* by the forceps, — or of a large number of very *small stones,* — the *scoop* will be found a more available means of extraction than the forceps. The stone or fragment having been caught in this, is brought cautiously upwards and steadied in its place as soon as possible by the point of the finger. After the crumbling, or where there is gravel, too minute to be all with certainty scooped out, the bladder is to be syringed out clean, either through the wound or through the urethra, the patient being placed in the sitting posture, for a good stream to run out easily.

The existence or absence of more calculi may be ascertained with considerable certainty by the appearance of the one extracted. If it is found equally rough and uneven all round, it is evidence of never having been in contact with another hard substance. Smoothness of surface, on the contrary, particularly if partial, with a depression or flatness at the part or parts, will indicate the presence of at least another stone. With the "searcher" or the scoop used as a sound, every part of the bladder ought to be explored. Previous to dressing the wound, a tube of sufficient calibre to allow the exit of blood as well as urine, is inserted, and fastened by a "T" bandage. To favor this free escape, the patient is fixed in bed, with the shoulders elevated; and when urine is not passing out freely, the tube should be frequently cleared. The secretion as well as *excretion* of urine should be encouraged, as mnch as possible using as a common drink, an infusion of Althea offic. (green root is best) or water-melon seed.

One object of the tube is to prevent urinary infiltration; and as soon as sufficient plastic exudation appears to have occurred round it for this purpose, or when the urine begins to pass out at the urethra, withdraw the tube and close the wound as soon as possible. The wound heals as in ordinary cases, and generally requires only simple dressings. The first urine that passes through the natural channel causes great pain. If any obstruction or unusual delay occur, the catheter will have to be carefully used.

The chance of *final success* will depend much on the after treatment, though still more, perhaps, on the preparation of the patient for the operation. The success of Prof. Dudley has shown that this elsewhere formidable operation may be rendered a safe one. A repetition is rarely necessary, the removal of one calculus being said to change the diathesis. However this may be, *other* prophylactic measures are proper, and not likely to be neglected by the patient if he knows them. (See note under LITHONTRIPSY.)

Among the casualties which *in hospitals*, and in most hands, make this a too often fatal operation, may be enumerated the dread or *shock* itself (generally to be avoided by the anæsthetic. agents), *hemorrhage* during the operation, and *hectic* from the inflammation and too copious suppuration of the wound. *Cystitis* and consequent peritonitis are generally to be avoided by proper care in the operation. The wound may continue open after the urethra has resumed its functions, constituting a peculiar and mild form of "fistula in perineo," or even fistula *in ano* may be a consequence of inadvertently wounding the rectum.

Urinary infiltration, when it comes on after the operation, may be mistaken for peritoneal inflammation, before the local damage occasioned by it is manifest. When *both* peritonitis and infiltration occur together, it is confessed by some to be a "perplexing" choice between the measures of depletion, supposed indispensable for the one condition, and the requisite support of the patient's strength for the other. "Antiphlogistics" that are *not* debilitating, relieve from all such dilemmas.

OTHER OPERATIONS ABOUT THE PUBES.

PUNCTURE, or paracentesis of the bladder,

— has been resorted to occasionally for the discharge of its contents, where there remains no other means of effecting that object and preserving life. A trochar and canula are pushed into the bladder, as in *tapping* the peritoneum, either just above the front of the pubes or through the fore part of the rectum (in women, of the vagina). By sufficient care a permanent orifice for urine can be made at either point. There is more danger of infiltration and fistula in the rectal or vaginal, than in the suprapubic operation.

CATHETERISM OF THE URETHRA

— for the evacuation of the bladder, is so much more frequently performed than that of any other channel, that the instrument for the purpose is called *the* "catheter." For its use on the *female*, directions are always given in books on Midwifery. The operation on the *male* is sometimes less simple.

It is best to have the patient on his back, with the shoulders somewhat elevated, and the penis held at right angles to the body till the point of the catheter is at the arch of the pubes, and then depressed so as to be parallel with the thighs, when the instrument will slip easily over the triangular ligament and into the bladder. In old men, owing to enlargement of the third lobe of the prostate, the catheter requires to be more elevated than in ordinary cases. The patient should be cautioned not to strain or press upon the abdominal muscles. Any one acquainted with the anatomy of the parts can insert a straight tube as easily as a curved one. When the gum elastic catheter is used, it is generally necessary to have the wire in it to prevent its bending at any obstacle it may meet with.

CAUTERIZATION OF THE URETHRA. — Full directions for this modern operation were given in Part First (see STRICTURE OF THE URETHRA, and a representation of the instrument, Fig. 16).

IMPERFORATE URETHRA.

This is an occasional congenital malformation or imperfection. The remedy is obvious: finish nature's work by pushing in a round trochar, followed by the canula and then by a catheter, and keep the latter in place, till the new orifice becomes water-proof. Connected with this imperfection, and independently of it, there occur what are called,

HYPOSPADIAS AND EPISPADIAS,

— openings of the urethra, in the upper or under surface of the penis. The appearance in most cases is as if the lower part of the urethra were split up and down. When this is the case the parts may be pared or cauterized and made to adhere. Partial deformities of this kind are often borne with through life, the consequence being a scattering stream in urinating, and perhaps an inefficient projection of semen in coitus.

PHIMOSIS AND PARAPHIMOSIS.

These are analogous conditions, both resulting from a constriction of the prepuce, the former before the glans, the latter behind it.

Phimosis may be congenital or acquired — the latter manifesting itself either as an acute or chronic disease. The acute form often occurs from infiltration of the part during gonorrhœa or syphilis. When the contracted edge of the prepuce has slipped over the glans, but is too tight to be returned, forming a kind of ligature behind the corona, from the effects of which the substance of the glans swells still more, — it constitutes *para-phimosis*. If, by compressing the glans and other means, it cannot be got back, the constricting parts may be divided. The other difficulty may require for immediate relief a straight incision, and for permanent comfort or security, more or less of "circumcision."

A director should be used in making the longitudinal incision, and sutures are afterwards necessary to keep together the mucous membrane and the skin that would otherwise contract beyond it. After the operation, a catheter should be kept in the part to protect and *preserve* the urethra.

Directions for the radical cure of HYDROCELE by and *after* the operation, also before and *without* that expedient, were given in the First Part. The same may be observed of VARICOCELE, and some other diseases of the same parts.

AMPUTATION OF THE PENIS.

This is one of the simplest of operations, however terrible it may be thought. Almost the only occasion for it is improperly managed cancer, or other malignant disease (see CANCER OF THE PENIS). When not performed very close up to the pubes, one cut of the knife suffices, it not being necessary even to draw back the skin for a flap, as the corpora cavernosa retract sufficiently as soon as divided. An assistant holds and compresses the stump until the ligatures can be applied; the two dorsal arteries, if not two or three others, have to be tied. Higher up, the operator cuts down to the arteries and ties them before division, — at least the six principal ones.

CASTRATION.

This final operation is thus performed: — The scrotum having been shaved, the surgeon grasps it from behind, and putting the skin upon the stretch, makes an incision from the External Abdominal Ring to the bottom of the scrotum. If the skin is adherent to the testicle, hard, or otherwise in a diseased condition, two elliptical incisions may be made, so as to remove all the morbid part. The cord is next to be dissected out and the artery separated from the other parts and tied. The cremaster muscle and vas deferens should be separated from the artery nearly up to the abdominal ring, in order that their contractions may not carry the artery beyond your reach. The whole cord can then be cut off below the tie, and the testicle and all its covering beneath the scrotum dissected out. The wound must not be closed until all hemorrhage has ceased. It should be closely watched for the first twenty-four hours, as there is a greater liability to secondary hemorrhage than after most operations. In dressing the external wound, two or three sutures should be applied with adhesive straps between them to keep the lips in contact.

These directions apply to one testicle, and have, of course, to be repeated on the other, when the object is complete castration. All ought to know that the removal of one testicle has only the same relation to their peculiar function, which the loss of an eye has to the sense of vision. The principal occasions for the operation have been incidentally pointed out (see ORCHITIS and CANCER OF THE TESTICLE). It is unnecessary to give other modes of operating, as that directed is the one which we in common believe, with nearly all surgeons of the present day, have always found effectual, and which long experience has settled down on as the best. The mode still laid down in some of the books for removal of the testicle, together with the scrotum, need never be practiced, unless the greater part of the scrotum is itself incurably diseased. Some surgeons have occasionally preferred ligature of the spermatic artery, or excision of a part (with ligature) of the vas deferens, to the removal of the testicle. Either operation is followed by atrophy of the part. Castration for any other than remedial purposes need not in the present age of the civilized world be described; such things belong to history rather than surgery

INDEX TO PART II.

	PAGE
Amputations	128
" arm	132
" fore-arm	139
" fingers	131
" thumb	144
" thigh	145
" leg	147
" foot	150
" shoulder joint	152
" hip	153
" elbow	155
" wrist	155
" ankle	157
" penis	215
Aneurism	20
Anchylosis	88
Cauteries	15
Castration	215
Catheterism of the Eustachian Tube	183
" " Urethra	213
Cauterization of the Urethra	213
Cataract, operation for	173
Club foot	160
Dislocations	25
" jaw	40
" clavicle	42
" ribs	46
" vertebræ	46
" pelvis	46
" shoulder	46
" elbow	55
" fore-arm	55
" wrist	60
" meticarpus	63
" fingers	63
" femur	65
" patella	73
" tibia	74
" ankle	76
" tarsus	78
" metatarsus	78
" toes	78

	PAGE
Dissecting	14
Dressings	17
Ear, operations on	182
Eyes, operations on	170
Excision of Tumors	18
Fistula Lacrymalis	169
Fractures	79
" simple	84
" compound	86
" comminuted	87
Fracture of the cranium	90
" " nose	92
" " jaw	92
" " scapula	96
" " clavicle	97
" " sternum	100
" " ribs	101
" " spine	102
" " pelvis	103
" " humerus	104
" " ulna	108
" " fore-arm	110
" " wrist	112
" " hand	112
" " fingers	112
" " femur	113
" " neck of femur	113
" " shaft of "	120
" " condyles of femur	121
" " patella	121
" " head of tibia	123
" " leg	127
" " ankles	128
" " foot	128
Hare lip	186
Hernia	198
Hypospadis and Epispadias	214
Imperforate urethra	213
Incisions	13
Inoculation	15
Issues	15
Laryngotomy	195
Lithontripsy	206
Lithotomy	207
Ligatures	11
Ligating arteries	193
Mouth, operations on	188
Œsophagotomy	196
Operative Surgery	3
Phimosis and Paraphimosis	214

PAGE

Paracenteses Thoracis - - - - - - - - 196
" Abdominis - - - - - - - - - 197
Perforating ear - - - - - - - - - - 182
Pseudarthrosis - - - - - - - - - 89
Punctures - - - - - - - - - - 13
" bladder - - - - - - - - - 212
Recicatrization - - - - - - - - - 23
Rhinoplastics - - - - - - - - - - 184
Strabismus - - - - - - - - - - 164
Sutures - - - - - - - - - - 9
Tenotomy - - - - - - - - - - 157
Tracheotomy - - - - - - - - - - 195
Traumatic hemorrhage - - - - - - - 10
Trepining - - - - - - - - - - 179
Vaccination - - - - - - - - - - 17
Wry neck - - - - - - - - - - 192

www.ingramcontent.com/pod-product-compliance
Lightning Source LLC
LaVergne TN
LVHW021053110826
845150LV00001B/61

9781425567408